LATINO HISTORY DAY BY DAY

LATINO HISTORY DAY BY DAY

A REFERENCE GUIDE TO EVENTS

Caryn E. Neumann and Tammy S. Allen

GREENWOOD

AN IMPRINT OF ABC-CLIO, LLC
Santa Barbara, California • Denver, Colorado • Oxford, England

Library of Congress Cataloging-in-Publication Data

Neumann, Caryn E., 1965–
  Latino history day by day : a reference guide to events / Caryn E. Neumann and Tammy S. Allen.
    pages cm
  Includes bibliographical references and index.
  ISBN 978-0-313-39641-0 (hardcopy: acid-free paper) — ISBN 978-0-313-39642-7 (ebook)
1. Hispanic Americans—History.   2. Hispanic Americans—Biography.   I. Allen, Tammy S.
II. Title.
  E184.S75N47   2013
  973'.0468–dc23   2012047329

ISBN: 978-0-313-39641-0
EISBN: 978-0-313-39642-7

17 16 15 14 13   1 2 3 4 5

This book is also available on the World Wide Web as an eBook.
Visit www.abc-clio.com for details.

Greenwood
An Imprint of ABC-CLIO, LLC

ABC-CLIO, LLC
130 Cremona Drive, P.O. Box 1911
Santa Barbara, California 93116-1911

This book is printed on acid-free paper ∞

Manufactured in the United States of America

Contents

Introduction

This book is a labor of love and discovery. It is a labor of love, because we could highlight the culture that Tammy fell in love with as a young girl in Texas and later as an exchange student in Colombia. And yes, it is a work of discovery, too. For too long the media and education systems in America have promoted stereotypes or limited examples of Latinos. Cinco de Mayo is now celebrated widely and commercially in the United States, but it is truly a Mexican holiday that commemorates the Battle of Puebla when the French marched from Veracruz and were defeated by a small, ill-equipped Mexican army. These authors intend to celebrate the countless contributions that Latinos in the United States have made throughout the past 500 years. And while Latinos certainly have contributed to the fabric of our daily lives and culture in the United States, there has been little written and researched about the subject. This book covers events that took place in the 1500s to events that occurred in this new century. There are entries that cover war, politics, entertainment, the arts, culinary arts, science, sports, business, labor issues, education, and immigration. The Latinos covered in these entries are represented by many nationalities: Spanish, Mexican, Dominican, Puerto Rican, Cuban, Bolivian, Argentine, Chilean, Peruvian, Salvadoran, Nicaraguan, and Costa Rican.

Why write a book about Latino history and culture? The United States is a nation of immigrants, and our story would not be complete if we did not acknowledge or include the scientific discoveries, literature, military service, art, political influence, music, food, and entrepreneurship into our tapestry. This is a culture that has been intertwined with ours since the 1500s. Immigrants dream of opportunity and a better life, and Latinos are no different. They and their children bless us with their talents and contributions. Imagine major league baseball without Ted Williams and Roberto Clemente? What would the space program have been like without the contributions of Ellen Ochoa? Women everywhere would be crushed to not own a pair of Manolo Blahnik shoes (or at least dream of owning a pair). And the program *Sex and the City* certainly would have suffered from not having discussions and fashionable exhibits of Blahnik shoes. Why write a book about Latinos, their history, and their culture? Latino history and culture are broad and profound, and we can certainly learn from others in addition to thinking critically for ourselves when we are confronted by stereotypes or images that others want us to believe.

This book addresses Latino history and culture. Some may question why we aren't covering Hispanic culture. And the answer is that we are doing both. While some people may disagree, the terms Latino and Hispanic are used interchangeably in academia and the media.

The term Hispanic did not appear formally on documents and Hispanics were not counted until the 1970 census during the Nixon administration. This time in history marks the rise and importance of civil rights dialogue, and inclusion in bills and legislation protecting their civil rights was important to Hispanics. The government, therefore, was the first to categorize and impose this term on a group of citizens whose races and nationalities were varied. It is always easier to lump people together rather than deal with them as individuals. The census, however, did not address the issue of ethnicity and race. It is important for all to know that Hispanic/Latino is not a race, but rather an ethnic grouping. Black and white are races. Latino/Hispanic is an ethnicity. Puerto Rican, Cuban, Dominican, and Mexican are nationalities.

So why are there two names to identify one ethnic group? While the government decided to impose a name on a group of people, others did not like to be given an identity by the government. Hispanic is typically the term that you will find on government and official forms, although this changed in the census language in 2000 to Spanish/Hispanic/Latino. Hispanic is also the term that you will hear more on the East Coast. It is the language of the establishment. The term Latino, however, was a term that came from the people. It is typically used in the Midwest, Southwest, and West Coast of the United States. While some prefer this term over Hispanic, it is still a term that has weight and meaning. Some consider it too broad and inclusive of other Latin American countries that are not Spanish-speaking, such as Brazil. I have attended department meetings where there is heated discussion over which countries to include in the Latin American Studies program, and whether the name should be changed to be more inclusive or less inclusive. So, labeling a group of people with a name and an identity is not a good thing. The interesting issue in this debate over Hispanic or Latino is that these are U.S. labels. Outside of the United States, people refer to themselves by their nationalities or nationality of origin. The singer Marc Anthony is not going to travel to London and introduce himself as a Latino or Hispanic. He is going to introduce himself as Cuban. Selena was a Mexican American singer.

In the United States, we like to group and categorize people by race, ethnicity, and class. For almost 30 years, Hispanics were included on the census along with Whites, Blacks, Asians, and Pacific Islanders, which led people to believe for decades that being Latino was a race. Tammy has spent her career explaining to students that being Latino/Hispanic is an ethnicity, not a race. It should also be noted that this ethnic group, the Latinos, are not monolithic, either. They may share some common core values, but they do not share the same history of food, politics, or culture. A Colombian doesn't eat tortillas, but she does eat *arepas,* for example.

In this book, we have used Latino in the title, and we have attempted to be as inclusive as possible in our research and presentation of materials. We mention the birthplaces, nationalities, or origins of the individuals in the entries. And we have presented a wide representation of Latinos and their contributions in addition to the many historical acts that have impacted the lives of Latinos. It is our hope that you enjoy discovering information through the book as much as we did in our journey writing the book.

We would like to express our gratitude to our library colleagues at Miami University Middletown for dealing with all of our book requests. We are happy to have aided the library's circulation numbers. Tammy owes a huge debt of gratitude to her family and support system, Mom and Darlene. Caryn agrees with the 19th-century Scottish historian, Thomas Carlyle, that "Writing is a dreadful labor, yet not so dreadful as Idleness," but she is looking forward to a bit of idleness.

January

January 1

1722

La gaceta de México, the earliest true newspaper in Latin America, appears. Edited by Juan Ignacio María de Castorena, it comes out once a month and features business stories, religious editorials, and social commentaries. Castorena is also notable for his defense of Sor Juana Inés de la Cruz's right to publish her writings.

Book

Castorena y Ursúa, Juan Ignacio María. *Gacetas de Mexico.* Mexico City, Mexico: Secretaría de Educación Pública, 1949–50. A three-volume reproduction of the early Mexican newspapers.

Websites

"La gaceta de México: El Primer Periódico Nacional." A Spanish-language essay about the newspaper and its impact. http://www.ine hrm.gob.mx/Portal/PtMain.php?pagina=exp-gaceta-de-mexico-articulo

Juan Ignacio María de Castorena Ursúa Goyenechea y Villareal. A Spanish-language biography of the journalist along with a painting of him. https://sites.google.com/site/elchauiste/zaca tecanos-ilustres/dn-juan-ignacio-mara-de-ca storena-ursa-goyenechea-y-villarreal

1900

Musician Xavier Cugat is born in Gerona, Spain. His family emigrates to Cuba when he is five, and Cugat is playing the violin in Havana cafes by the time he is eight. After coming to the United States in 1921, he forms a tango orchestra in Los Angeles. Cugat then expands into show tunes and dinner music. His appearances in movies and his work with crooner Bing Crosby make Cugat one of the most popular musicians of the first half of the 20th century.

Books

Cugat, Xavier. *Rumba Is My Life.* New York: Didier, 1948. The musician's biography, written at the midpoint of his life.

Cugat, Xavier. *Xavier Cugat's Latin-American Rhythms for Pianists, Accordionists, Arrangers: A Study of Rhythmic Interpretation of Rumba, Samba, Conga, Tango.* New York: Robbins Music, 1941. Scores of Cugat's best-known works.

Websites

Xavier Cugat. The Internet Movie Database provides a short biography of the musician and a list of the movie soundtracks in which he appeared. http://www.imdb.com/name/nm 0191265/

YouTube: Xavier Cugat. Lists the 30 film clips of the musician playing that are available on the website. http://www.youtube.com/channel/HC3rES9DaUxoA

2003

Democrat Bill Richardson takes office as the 30th governor of New Mexico. Richardson, born to a Mexican mother and a half-Mexican father, spent several years in Mexico as a child. He entered the U.S. House of Representatives in 1982. Known for his peacekeeping abilities, Richardson served on a number of international delegations including one that persuaded Saddam Hussein of Iraq to release two captured Americans. Richardson defined his diplomatic philosophy as make friends, define the goal, brush off any insults, close the deal, and always show respect. On February 13, 1997, he became the U.S. ambassador to the United Nations.

From "Richardson Reflects on His U.N. Days":

> At the United Nations, diplomats who were initially frosty at having a politician—a former Democratic Congressman from New Mexico—thrust on them by Washington seem to have come to appreciate a style that is zany by United Nations standards. [Richardson] is known to have referred to a distinguished diplomat as "what's his name" to wear khakis and blazer into the Security Council. . . . In contrast to Madeleine K. Albright, who was rushed through the corridors of the United Nations with an important-looking phalanx of protective aides when she represented the United States here, Bill Richardson ambles around, joking in English and Spanish with reporters. . . . Mr. Richardson said he has enjoyed everything about United Nations life, including nonstop dinners. "U.N. diplomats and U.N. Secretariat people are quality people, good people," he said. "This perception that the U.N. has a lot of deadbeats is totally false. I've met some of the more talented, intelligent and interesting people here. To achieve our objectives, you have to engage in the social life of the U.N. That's why I spent a lot of time in the Delegates' Lounge. That's why I spent a lot of time at the cafeteria."

(*Source*: Crossette, Barbara. "Richardson Reflects on His U.N. Days." *New York Times*, September 8, 1998, p. A6.)

Books

Rice, Liz. *Bill Richardson: Overcoming Adversity, Sharing the American Dream*. New York: Mason Crest, 2009. A biography of the political leader for children.

Richardson, Bill. *Between Worlds: The Making of an American Life*. New York: Plume, 2007. Richardson's autobiography, which is also available in a Spanish-language version, reflects his extroverted personality.

Websites

Bill Richardson. The politician's personal website includes his biography, news about the Richardson Center for Global Engagement, and his speaking engagements. http://www.billrichardson.com/

Bill Richardson—Project Vote Smart. Provides a biographical summary of Richardson and a listing of key votes that he made, including vetoes as governor. http://www.votesmart.org/candidate/key-votes/26964/bill-richardson

January 2

1947

The people of San Juan, Puerto Rico, elect Felisa Rincón de Gautier, also known as Doña Fela, as their mayor. She is the first woman to serve as mayor of a capital city in the Americas and holds office until 1969. She is notable for developing preschool centers, preserving the history of Old San Juan, and improving public services, especially the public health system.

Books

García Ramis, Magali. *Doña Felisa Rincón de Gautier: Mayor of San Juan*. Morristown, NJ: Modern Curriculum Press, 1995. A biography with a guide to teaching about the mayor's life and two posters.

Gruber, Ruth. *Felisa Rincón de Gautier: The Mayor of San Juan*. New York: Crowell, 1972. The only biography of the famed mayor.

Websites

Felisa Rincón de Gautier. A solid biographical essay of the political leader. http://www.brit

annica.com/EBchecked/topic/503913/Felisa-Rincon-de-Gautier

Museo de Felisa Rincón de Gautier. The residence of the former mayor is now a museum that celebrates her life. http://places.eyetour.com/whatToSee/san-juan/33/museo-felisa-rincon-de-gautier

1969

Christy Turlington, the first Latina to become a supermodel, is born in Walnut Creek, California, to María Elizabeth Parker, a flight attendant from El Salvador, and Dwain Turlington, a pilot for Pan American World Airways. Featured on magazine covers around the world in the 1990s, Turlington also served as the model for Calvin Klein and Maybelline among other brands. In the 21st century, she focused more on philanthropic activities, particularly Every Mother Counts, a campaign to reduce maternal mortality worldwide. She also directed the 2010 documentary *No Woman, No Cry* about maternal mortality in Tanzania, Bangladesh, Guatemala, and the United States.

Books

Borges, Phil. *Women Empowered: Inspiring Change in the Emerging World.* New York: Rizzoli, 2007. Includes a chapter on Turlington's community efforts.

Turlington, Christy. *Living Yoga: Creating a Life Practice.* New York: Hyperion, 2002. Turlington discusses the impact of exercise and meditation upon her life.

Websites

Christy Turlington (CTurlington). The twitter account of the founder of Every Mother Counts focuses on health news. https://twitter.com/CTurlington

Every Mother Counts. The official website of the organization includes information about its mission, leadership, and activities. http://www.everymothercounts.org/

January 3

1862

José Rafael Aragón, the most prolific and perhaps the most talented New Mexican artist of the 19th century, is buried at Santa Cruz de la Cañada Church in New Mexico. A specialist in Catholic religious art, Aragón and his followers produced about one-fifth of all devotional art created in New Mexico between 1750 and 1900. Born in Santa Fe, New Mexico, sometime between 1783 and 1796, Aragón, a painter of *retablos* and altar screens, grew up in a network of artisan woodworker families. He came to operate a guild-like workshop that trained other distinguished *santeros* ("saint makers" who produced art featuring saints) such as José Manuel Benavides (the Santo Niño Santero) and Anastacio Casados.

From Larry Frank, art collector:

[The New Mexicans] were very isolated, lost in this continent, of harsh adversity. They were struggling to endure. Consequently, you have these people with very little outside influence building a kind of linear, abstract, complexly novel art form. It is so charged, so dynamic, that it hardly has any other counterpart in any other folk art.

(*Source:* "Larry Frank, Maverick Collector of New Mexican Art." New Mexico History Museum, Treasures of Devotion Exhibit, http://www.nmhistorymuseum.org/tesoros/VideoPlayers/frank/player3.html)

Books

Carrillo, Charles M., and Thomas J. Steele. *A Century of Retablos: The Janis and Dennis Lyon Collection of New Mexico Retablos.* Phoenix: Phoenix Art Museum and Hudson Mills Press, 2007. With many photographs of the art, this is an accessible book on one of the best private collections of Latino art in New Mexico in the 18th and 19th centuries.

Frank, Larry. *A Land So Remote: Religious Art of New Mexico, 1780–1907.* Two vols. Santa Fe, NM: Red Crane Books, 2001. This is the definitive work on early New Mexican art.

Websites

Colonial Arts: Fine Spanish Colonial Art. This is a gallery website that provides a wealth of information about *retablos,* one of Aragón's specialties. http://www.colonialarts.com/retablos

José Rafael Aragón. The New Mexico History Museum's biography of the artist can be found here along with images of his work. http://www.nmhistorymuseum.org/tesoros/tesoros-lightbox/collection-search-lfc.html

January 4

1992

Arte Público Press, founded by Nicolás Kanellos in 1979 to promote Latino literature, receives a Rockefeller Foundation grant to find, catalogue, research, and publish Hispanic literature, fiction and nonfiction, from before the colonial period to 1960. Without the $2.7 million, the publishing house would not be able to finance the project. It is the oldest and largest nonprofit publisher of Hispanic literature in the United States. Kanellos, of Puerto Rican and Greek heritage, is a University of Houston professor and is often identified as one of the most influential Latinos in the country.

From "In Search of the Latino Writer":

Mr. Kanellos spoke of the repression of Latino writers by the United States literary establishment. He did not assign evil motives, arguing instead that the repression was based upon certain erroneous assumptions: "Hispanics don't read and can't write, so why publish them? No one wants to read about U.S. Hispanics; they are marginal, not even distantly related to the

literary boom taking place in Latin America. Liberals may embrace the great national revolutions in Latin America and their eloquent writers, but similar U.S. Hispanic writers should be deemed 'ethnics,' 'sociological,' 'regional.' " He did not argue the merits of the work; that afternoon, only the politics and sociology and selling of Latino literature interested him and the novelists and the poets whose presentations followed . . .

(*Source:* Shorris, Earl. "In Search of the Latino Writer." *New York Times,* July 15, 1990, p. BR1.)

Books

Kanellos, Nicolás. *Herencia: The Anthology of Hispanic Literature of the United States.* New York: Oxford University Press, 2003. A comprehensive anthology that covers Latino writing from the 16th century to the present.

Kanellos, Nicolás. *Hispanic Immigrant Literature.* Austin: University of Texas Press, 2011. Based on the archive assembled with the Rockefeller Fund money.

Websites

Nicolás Kanellos, Ph.D. Provides the curriculum vitae of the University of Houston professor, with a listing of all the honors that he has received for his contributions to Latino literature. http://www.class.uh.edu/mcl/faculty/kanellos/resume.htm

About Arte Público Press. Official website of the publishing house. http://www.latinoteca.com/arte-publico-press/advisory-board

January 5

1992

Puerto Rico experiences a devastating flood resulting from 20 inches of rain that fell on the island in a 24-hour period. The intensity of the rainfall exceeds all previous records.

The worst flooding struck areas along the Río de La Plata and the Río Grande de Patillas. The damage is estimated at more than $150 million, with 23 lives lost and 167 people hospitalized. About 550 people were forced from their homes, and 4,200 houses were damaged with 78 destroyed.

Books

Steinberg, Ted. *Acts of God: The Unnatural History of Natural Disaster in America.* New York: Oxford University Press, 2006. An environmental historian argues that disasters are created through abuse of the natural world.

Torres-Sierra, Heriberto. *Flood of January 5–6, 1992 in Puerto Rico.* San Juan, PR: U.S. Department of the Interior, U.S. Geological Survey, 1996. The official federal report of the disaster.

Websites

Puerto Rico: Declared Disasters. The Federal Emergency Management Agency lists all federally designated disasters in Puerto Rico. http://www.fema.gov/states/puerto-rico?page=1

Torres-Sierra, Heriberto. *Flood of January 5–6, 1992 in Puerto Rico.* The official federal report of the disaster is available through the U.S. Geological Survey website. http://pubs.usgs.gov/of/1995/0374/report.pdf

January 6

1868

The Comité Revolucionario de Puerto Rico (Revolutionary Committee of Puerto Rico) is formed by Dr. Ramón Emeterio Betances and Segundo Ruiz Belvis while they are in exile in the Dominican Republic. Betances authors several statements attacking the exploitation of the Puerto Ricans by the Spanish colonial system and calling for an immediate uprising. The Grito de Lares rebellion breaks out in September 1868 but collapses in short order.

Books

Betances, Ramón Emeterio. *Betances.* San Juan, PR: Instituto de Cultura Puertorriqueña, 1970. The autobiography of the revolutionary.

Carreras, Carlos N. *Betances: El Antillano Proscrito.* San Juan, PR: Editorial Club de la Prensa, 1961. A biography of the political leader.

Websites

Ramón Emeterio Betances. This Spanish-language site has a short biography of the revolutionary physician. http://www.proyectosalonhogar.com/BiografiasPr/ramon_emeterio_betances.htm

"The Changing of the Guard: Puerto Rico in 1898." The World of 1898: The Spanish-American War offers this essay by Marisabel Brás that covers the Revolutionary Committee of Puerto Rico. http://www.loc.gov/rr/hispanic/1898/bras.html

January 7

1908

Educator Ana G. Méndez is born in Aguada, Puerto Rico. She founded the Ana G. Méndez University System, a private institution that includes the University of Turabo, the University of the East, and the Metropolitan University and serves over 17,000 students.

Websites

Ana G. Méndez University System. The official website for the schools established by the educator includes information about admission and academics. http://www.suagm.edu/

Ana G. Méndez University System—South Florida Campus. The Facebook page for this small campus provides news about the school. https://www.facebook.com/suagmflorida

January 8

1991

The date when Chilean American Isabel Allende began her nonfiction book about the death of her daughter, Paula. Allende begins all of her books on January 8—the day she began her very first novel, 1981's *The House of the Spirits.* Allende, raised and living in Chile, spoke out when her cousin, Salvador Allende, died in a military takeover of the Chilean government in 1973. She fled to Venezuela in 1975 in the face of death threats. She subsequently traveled to the United States in 1988 and met her American husband, William Gordon. Allende became an American citizen in 2003.

From Allende's compilation of interview questions that she has received over the years:

Q. You're famous for your narrative, but are there other writing genres you're interested in exploring as well?

A. I wrote plays in my youth and loved it. I also tried writing children's stories when my kids were small. I told them stories every night, and it was a wonderful training that I have maintained. In 2001, in fact, I wrote *City of the Beasts,* my first novel for kids and young adults. I have written humor for years, and I think that is the most difficult genre of all. I've never tried poetry and I don't think I will.

Q. Do you write in Spanish?

A. I can only write fiction in Spanish, because it is for me a very organic process that I can only do in my native language. Fortunately, I have excellent translators all over the world.

Q. Can you elaborate on the idea of writing fiction—of telling a truth, of telling lies, of uncovering some kind of reality? Can you also talk about how these ideas might work together or against one another?

A. The first lie of fiction is that the author gives some order to the chaos of life: chronological order, or whatever order the author chooses. As a writer, you select some part of a whole. You decide that those things

are important and the rest is not. And you write about those things from your perspective. Life is not that way. Everything happens simultaneously, in a chaotic way, and you don't make choices. You are not the boss; life is the boss. So when you accept as a writer that fiction is lying, then you become free. You can do anything. Then you start walking in circles. The larger the circle, the more truth you can get. The wider the horizon—the more you walk, the more you linger over everything—the better chance you have of finding particles of truth.

Q. Where do you get your inspiration?

A. I am a good listener and a story hunter. Everybody has a story and all stories are interesting if they are told in the right tone. I read newspapers, and small stories buried deep within the paper can inspire a novel.

Q. How does inspiration work?

A. I spend ten, twelve hours a day alone in a room writing. I don't talk to anybody. I don't answer the telephone. I'm just a medium or an instrument of something that is happening beyond me, voices that talk through me. I'm creating a world that is fiction but that doesn't belong to me. I'm not God; I'm just an instrument. And in that long, very patient daily exercise of writing I have discovered a lot about myself and about life. I have learned. I'm not conscious of what I'm writing. It's a strange process—as if by this lying-in-fiction you discover little things that are true about yourself, about life, about people, about how the world works.

Q. Can you talk about the characters?

A. When I develop a character I usually look for a person who can serve as a model. If I have that person in mind, it is easier for me to create characters that are believable. People are complex and complicated—they seldom show all the aspects of their personalities. Characters should be that way too.

I allow the characters to live their own lives in the book. Often I have the feeling that I don't control them. The story goes in unexpected directions and my job is to write it down, not to force it into my previous ideas.

(*Source:* Isabel Allende, http://isabelallende.com/ia/en/interview)

Books

Allende, Isabel. *La Suma de los Días*. Barcelona: Areté, 2007. The author's autobiography.

Levine, Linda Gould. *Isabel Allende*. New York: Twayne, 2002. A biography of Allende that includes an interview with the writer and a selected bibliography.

Website

Isabel Allende. The author's own site, available in English or Spanish, with biographical and bibliographical information, an album of family photographs, and trivia. http://www.isabelallende.com/

2001

Helen Rodriguez-Trias is awarded the Presidential Citizens Medal by President Bill Clinton for her work as a public health leader. Born to Puerto Rican parents, Rodriguez-Trias helped found the Committee to End Sterilization Abuse in 1975 to reduce the number of forced sterilizations carried out on poor women and women from minority groups. In 1987, she began to chair the New York State AIDS Institute and became one of the first experts to publicize the dangers that HIV/AIDS poses to women, children, poor people, and people from ethnic minorities. In 1993, she became the first Latina to serve as president of the American Public Health Association. She died of cancer in 2001.

From an interview with Helen Rodriguez-Trias:

Q. What was my biggest obstacle?

A. A watershed in my life was getting divorced in Puerto Rico—that was my second marriage—and leaving Puerto Rico to become part of the women's movement. In my formation as a professional, there was always a kind of pressure to deny or not use a lot of your personal experience. The science of medicine, to some degree, negates the human, feeling, experiential part of it. But I was now discovering a whole other world out there through my personal experience of a deceptive marriage. That triggered quite a bit of growth in me toward understanding what happens internally to people, what happens in their lives and what they can do or not do. . . . So I went back to New York and I got very involved in reproductive rights. I began to join in the women's movement. At Barnard College there was a conference called the First International Conference on Abortion Rights that was attended by a few thousand women. . . . We organized one of the first consciousness-raising groups of Latino women. . . . A number of incredible things emerged from women talking about their experiences. . . . We shared and we became very bonded. That was the beginning of my identification with women's issues and reproductive health.

Q. Who was my mentor?

A. Dr. Rodriguez-Trias has said she was inspired by "the experience of [my] own mother, my aunts and sisters, who faced so many restraints in their struggle to flower and realize their full potential.

Quite a few people in medical school inspired my work, particularly Dr. José Sifontes, one of my professors. He was one of the pioneers in pediatric tuberculosis. . . . He had a very humble way about him. He was definitely an inspiration because he had a sense that what was happening in the community was something that affected health. He said that tuberculosis was a disease of poverty, of malnutrition, of overcrowding.

Many other people have been great inspirations for me. If you talk about global leadership, I think of Bill Foege. When we were both on the board of APHA, I got to know something about his thinking and how he presented things, his forcefulness."

Q. How has my career evolved over time?

A. Dr. Rodriguez-Trias began her career as a pediatrician in Puerto Rico in the 1960s, but became increasingly concerned with social factors that affected health and access to health care. On moving to New York, she practiced community medicine, supporting grassroots efforts for change in the Puerto Rican community served by Lincoln Hospital in the South Bronx and training medical students to become aware of and involved with the neighborhoods they would serve. Over time, she focused increasingly on policies related to women's reproductive and other health issues, on the health of children, and on the needs of those with HIV and AIDS. Through her leadership in national and international organizations, the impact of her work and advocacy expanded to affect people worldwide, particularly in developing nations.

(*Source:* Helen Rodriguez-Trias, https://www.nlm.nih.gov/changingthefaceofmedicine/physicians/biography_273.html)

Books

The Boston Women's Health Book Collective. *The New Our Bodies, Ourselves: A Book by and for Women.* New York : Simon & Schuster, 1992. Helen Rodriguez-Trias co-wrote the foreword.

Schiff, Karenna Gore. *Lighting the Way: Nine Women Who Changed Modern America.* New York: Miramax Books/Hyperion, 2006. Helen Rodriguez-Trias is one of the women featured in the book.

Websites

Helen Rodriguez-Trias. The National Library of Medicine of the National Institutes of Health provides this biography, part of its Changing the Face of Medicine series, as well as an interview with the physician. https://www.nlm.nih.gov/changingthefaceofmedicine/physicians/biography_273.html

Helen Rodriguez-Trias Social Justice Award. The American Public Health Association offers this award to someone who works to eliminate health disparities. http://www.apha.org/about/awards/trias/

January 9

1941

Singer-songwriter Joan Baez is born in New York City. A folk singer, Baez performed at the historic Woodstock concert in 1969. She has always been especially politically active, moving from helping Latino farmworkers in California to marching in civil rights demonstrations. Baez has had eight gold record albums, one gold single, and six Grammy nominations.

Books

Baez, Joan. *And a Voice to Sing With: A Memoir.* New York: Simon & Schuster, 2009. The singer's extensive recollections of her life.

Fuss, Charles J. *Joan Baez: A Bio-Bibliography.* Westport, CT: Greenwood Press, 1996. A biography and discography of the folk singer.

Website

The Joan Baez Web Pages. The official website for Baez provides her biography, discography, information on her latest release, and her tour schedule. http://www.joanbaez.com/

2006

A group of Latin American countries issue a statement on the problem of undocumented Latino immigrants in the United States following a conference in Mexico City. The Dominican Republic, Mexico, Colombia, and all of the seven Central American countries were responding to the vast numbers of Latin American immigrants coming to the United States for greater economic opportunities. Unauthorized Latino immigrants generally entered from Mexico while about a quarter had entered legally but stayed beyond the terms of their visas. About 60 percent of the immigrants were Mexicans while other large groups came from El Salvador, Guatemala, and Honduras. As the United States debated measures to ensure border security, such as a more secure fence, the countries that formed the major source of immigrants responded to American sovereignty concerns.

From "*Declaración Conjunta de la Reunión de Ministros de Países Mesoamericanos*":

We, the Ministers of Foreign Relations and high officials meeting today. . . . Reaffirm that every migrant, regardless of his migration status, ought to be accorded full protection of his human rights and full observances of the applicable labor laws; and Urge greater cooperation and dialogue toward the goal of reducing and discouraging undocumented migration as well as promoting migration procedures in accord with the internal juridical order of each State and the applicable international human rights law. . .

(*Source:* Holden, Robert H., and Eric Zolov, eds. *Latin America and the United States: A Documentary History.* New York: Oxford University Press, pp. 390–91. Translation by Holden and Zolov.)

Books

Camarota, Steven A. *Immigration from Mexico: Assessing the Impact on the United States.* Washington, D.C.: Center for Immigration Studies, 2001. Useful examination of the costs and value of immigration.

Spickard, Paul. *Almost All Aliens: Immigration, Race, and Colonialism in American History and Identity.* New York: Routledge, 2007. Comprehensive history of immigration in the U.S. from 1600 to the present.

Websites

Country Resources, Migration Information Service. Provides a wealth of data about countries and immigration from these countries to the United States. http://www.migrationinformation.org/Resources/#ca

Guatemalan Americans. Provides a good recent history of Guatemala and Guatemalan immigration to the United States. http://www.everyculture.com/multi/Du-Ha/Guatemalan-Americans.html

January 10

2012

The Tucson, Arizona public schools suspend their Mexican American Studies program after a judge advises that it violates a new state law and the state threatens the school district with the loss of 10 percent of state aid, or $15 million in annual funding. The school board issues a statement that it will revise its social studies core curriculum to increase its coverage of Mexican American history and culture thereby ensuring that all students are exposed to diverse viewpoints. On May 11, 2010, Arizona governor Jan Brewer signed legislation that prohibited the teaching of classes designed for a particular ethnic group. Observers viewed the legislation as targeting Mexican Studies, in the wake of considerable conflict in Arizona over Mexican immigration to the state.

From State of Arizona, House Bill 2281:

Be it enacted by the Legislature of the State of Arizona:

2 Section 1. Title 15, chapter 1, article 1, Arizona Revised Statutes,

3 is amended by adding sections 15–111 and 15–112, to read:

4 15–111. Declaration of policy

The Legislature finds and declares that public school pupils should be taught to treat and value each other as individuals and not be taught to resent or hate other races or classes of people. Prohibited courses and classes

A. A school district or charter school in this state shall not include in its program of instruction any courses or classes that include any of the following:

   1 Promote the overthrow of the United States government.
   2 Promote resentment toward a race or class of people.
   3 Are designed primarily for pupils of a particular ethnic group.
   4 Advocate ethnic solidarity instead of the treatment of pupils as individuals.

B. If the state board of education or the superintendent of public instruction determines that a school district or charter school is in violation of subsection A, the state board of education or the superintendent of public instruction shall notify the school district or charter school that it is in violation of subsection A. If the state board of education or the superintendent of public instruction determines that the school district or charter school has failed to comply with subsection a within sixty days after a notice has been issued pursuant to this subsection, the state board of education or the superintendent of public instruction may direct the department of education to withhold up to ten per cent of the monthly apportionment of state aid that would otherwise be due the school district or charter school. The department of education shall adjust the school district or charter school's apportionment accordingly. When the state board of education or the superintendent of public instruction determines that the school district or charter school is in compliance with subsection a, the department of education shall restore the full amount of state aid payments to the school district or charter school.

C. The department of education shall pay for all expenses of a hearing conducted pursuant to this section.

D. Actions taken under this section are subject to appeal pursuant to title 41, chapter 6, article 10.

E. This section shall not be construed to restrict or prohibit:

   1. Courses or classes for Native American pupils that are required to comply with federal law.
   2. The grouping of pupils according to academic performance, including capability in the English language, that may result in a disparate impact by ethnicity.
   3. Courses or classes that include the history of any ethnic group and that are open to all students, unless the course or class violates subsection A.
   4. Courses or classes that include the discussion of controversial aspects of history.

F. Nothing in this section shall be construed to restrict or prohibit the instruction of the holocaust, any other instance of genocide, or the historical oppression of a particular group of people based on ethnicity, race, or class.

(*Source:* State of Arizona, House of Representatives, Forty-ninth Legislature, Second Regular Session, Bill 2281, 2010, http://www.azleg.gov/leg text/49leg/2r/bills/hb2281s.pdf)

Books

Gutiérrez, David G. *Walls and Mirrors: Mexican Americans, Mexican Immigrants, and the Politics of Ethnicity.* Berkeley: University of California Press, 1995. Explores the ways in which immigration from Mexico has shaped politics in California and Texas.

Rosales, F. Arturo. *Chicano: The History of the Mexican American Civil Rights Movement.* Houston: Arte Público, 1996. The rise of Mexican American studies is one of the most visible outgrowths of the Mexican American Civil Rights Movement, as this book explains.

Websites

Department of Mexican American Studies, University of Arizona. Shows the curriculum and interests of a university-level Mexican American Studies program. http://mas.arizona.edu/

Mexican American Studies Department, Tucson Unified School District. The site of the program at the heart of the controversy. http://www.tusd1.org/contents/depart/mexicanam/index.asp

January 11

1839

Eugenio María de Hostos, a writer and statesman who backed Puerto Rican independence and an end to slavery, is born. Puerto Rico celebrates his birthday as an official holiday on the second Monday of January.

Books

Balseiro, José Agustín. *Eugenio María de Hostos, Hispanic America's Public Servant.* Coral Gables, FL: University of Miami, 1949. More of a pamphlet than a book, this is also the only biography of Hostos in English.

Hostos, Eugenio María de. *Eugenio María de Hostos, Promoter of Pan Americanism: A Collection of Writings and a Bibliography.* Madrid: Imprint Litografía y Encuadernación, [1954?]. A badly dated guide to research about Hostos, but also the only guide in English.

Hostos, Eugenio María de. *Moral Social.* Buenos Aires: Eudeba Editorial Universitaria de Buenos Aires, 1968. A discussion of social ethics in Spanish.

1842

Puerto Rican dramatist, poet, journalist, and historian Salvador Brau is born in Cabo Rojo. Educated in Spain at the University of Barcelona, Brau became the Official Historian of Puerto Rico in 1903. He held the appointment until his death in 1912. He remained politically active throughout his life, first supporting autonomy from Spain, and then advocating for greater Puerto Rican control after the United States took charge of the island.

From Salvador Brau, "The Way We Are" (1883):

The Puerto Rican people have great qualities of character. Some of these are shared by all of Spain's extended family but are very specially ours. Others are so special that one would seek them in vain in any other branch of the Spanish tree in the enormous neighboring continent . . .

In view of our origins it seems strange that the dominant quality of the Puerto Rican character should be independence; but so it is. Whether because of the isolation in which we have lived, or because of the habits of rural life, or out of ignorance of certain social arrangements, the Puerto Rican values his individual liberty very highly and shows no disposition to sacrifice it for conventional labels and formulas . . .

Study the Puerto Rican in any part of the Island and you'll see him eloquent and merry at his gatherings, but circumspect and even withdrawn in public life; very respectful toward authority but avoiding involvement with it to the utmost, even in matters that are important to him. If authority summons him, he responds quickly, but can hardly wait to leave its presence and return to his tiny bit of land and his chores.

In his national duties, he is a model. Is the ancestral soil in danger? At once you'll find him defending it. Is there suffering among his brothers in remote provinces? His purse is open to help them. Does the nation celebrate some glorious anniversary? He joins spontaneously in the general rejoicing.

These are typical characteristics of our people; but at the opposite pole, does some calamity befall him? He asks no one for help. If someone gives it, he accepts; if it is offered, he is wary; if his hopes are dashed, he resigns himself.

(*Source:* Zavala, Iris M., and Rafael Rodriguez, eds. *The Intellectual Roots of Independence: An Anthology of Puerto Rican Political Essays.* New York: Monthly Review Press, 1980, pp. 79–80.)

Books

Brau, Salvador. *Puerto Rico y Su Historia.* NP: Kessinger, 2010. Brau's history of his beloved island, originally published in 1894.

Landrón, Arturo Córdova. *Salvador Brau: Su Vida y su Época.* NP: Coquí, 1968. A biography of the historian.

Websites

Salvador Brau Asencio, Autonomous Municipality of Cabo Rojo. Brau's hometown provides a biography of the man. http://www.ciudad caborojo.net/SalvadorBrau.htm

Salvador Brau, Find a Grave. Provides a photo of Brau's final resting place at Santa María Magdalena de Pazziz Cemetery in San Juan, Puerto Rico. http://www.findagrave.com/cgi-bin/fg.cgi?page=gr&GRid=17695865

1942

Ana Sol Gutiérrez, the first Hispanic to win an elected office in Maryland, is born in El Salvador. Gutiérrez, a Democrat who holds degrees in chemistry and engineering, served as a member of the Board of Education of Montgomery County from 1990 to 1998. In 2003, she won election to the Maryland House of Delegates and continued a focus on education by chairing the Delinquency Prevention and Diversion Services Task Force. A board member of La Raza in the mid-1990s, she is cofounder of Salvadoreans United for Better Education.

Book

Córdova, Carlos B. *The Salvadoran Americans.* Westport, CT: Greenwood, 2005. One of the very few books to look at the lives of these Central American immigrants in the United States.

Websites

Ana Sol Gutiérrez. Project Vote Smart, a nonpartisan voter education program, provides this summary of Gutiérrez's career. http://votesmart.org/candidate/biography/19375#. UGTny648CEY

Maryland House of Delegates: Ana Sol Gutiérrez. Provides a resume and contact information for the legislator. http://www.msa.md.gov/msa/mdmanual/06hse/html/msa13962.html

January 12

1986

Astronaut Franklin Chang-Díaz, a native of Puerto Rico, flies into space as a crew member on the space shuttle, *Columbia*. During the flight, he broadcasts greetings in Spanish to people around the world. Chang-Díaz eventually becomes one of only two astronauts to fly in seven space missions, logging more than 1,600 hours in space and three spacewalks. He is the first Latino to fly in space. After retiring from NASA, he founded the Ad Astra Rocket Company.

From an interview with Franklin Chang-Díaz:

Technology Review: In your talk today, you said that "NASA is a victim of its own success," and that now is the right time for the private sector. Could you expand on this?

Franklin Chang-Díaz: The agency really transformed the world in space with the achievements of the moon landings, but the whole world changed, and NASA didn't change. NASA remained in the glory days of the past, and 40 years have gone by, and NASA is still the same NASA as the 1960s. And I don't mean it in a bad way. It was so wonderful what was done, and people were completely fascinated by it. But a new opportunity has been created because NASA's fascination with its own past in the present has created a gap, a hole, which is perfect for the private sector to move into.

The private sector is going to fill the void in rapid access to low earth orbit, allowing NASA to be NASA, to do what NASA was really meant to do, which is look forward to the frontier. Let the private enterprise build the base camp now that we know how to do it, and NASA can go conquer the summit.

TR: There are a lot of companies building technology for access to low earth orbit, but some still have years of development work and need funding. Can the private sector realistically get it done soon?

FCD: Absolutely. Rockets are not a new invention. Reliable rockets were built in World War II, and they were perfected by NASA in the 50s and 60s, and other countries as well. Also, the technology for rocket propulsion is not rocket science anymore. However, we do need advanced propulsion, which is a completely untapped area of research; very little work has been done, and we need to move into that realm because we are not going to get to Mars on chemical rockets. It is going to be too fragile and too dangerous [of a mission] for chemical rockets. . . .

TR: There are arguments that the private sector needs government money to succeed. How are you handling funding?

FCD: It's always a struggle to continue to get investment, but the way we do it is by meeting our milestones. The one we met [last week] will give us ammunition to seek more private investment. It would also be nice to have government funding. When we created the company, it was an experiment in NASA privatization, and the premise was that we would privatize the project and let the private sector mature the technology to the point where NASA would pick it up again, and that time has arrived. So we are always looking for a contract from NASA that would alleviate our need for private investment.

(*Source:* Sauser, Brittany. "Private Space Technology Powers Up." Massachusetts Institute of Technology's Technology Review, October 5, 2009, http://www.technologyreview.com/news/415570/private-space-technology-powers-up/)

Books

Bizony, Piers. *The Space Shuttle: Celebrating Thirty Years of NASA's First Space Plane.* New York: Zenith, 2011. Includes coverage of the flights made by Chang-Díaz.

Hernández, José M., and Monica Rojas Rubin. *Reaching for the Stars: The Inspiring Story of a Migrant Farmworker Turned Astronaut.* New York: Center Street, 2012. The only full biography of Chang-Díaz.

Websites

Franklin Chang-Díaz, NASA Astronaut. The official NASA biography of the former astronaut. http://www.jsc.nasa.gov/Bios/html bios/chang.html

Franklin Chang-Díaz. The official website of the space scientist includes his biography, space missions, and contact information. http://franklinchangdiaz.com/

January 13

1941

All people born in Puerto Rico on or after this date are citizens of the United States at birth according to the Immigration and Naturalization Act of 1940. The naturalization and citizenship laws were revised to strengthen national defense as World War II loomed on the horizon.

Books

Fahrmeir, Andreas. *Citizenship: The Rise and Fall of a Modern Concept.* New Haven: Yale University Press, 2007. An excellent history of citizenship that argues that formal political citizenship has declined in favor of social citizenship.

Heater, Derek. *A Brief History of Citizenship.* New York: New York University Press, 2004. Easy-to-read account of the requirements of citizenship in the modern world.

Negrón-Muntaner, Frances, and Ramón Grosfoguel, eds. *Puerto Rican Jam: Rethinking Colonialism and Nationalism.* Minneapolis: University of Minnesota Press, 1997. Offers essays that examine the debate over the political status of Puerto Rico and, by extension, the citizenship of Puerto Ricans.

January 14

1894

The Hispanic American Alliance is founded in Arizona by Carlos I. Velasco, Pedro C. Pellón, and Mariano G. Samaniego. It is the first organization founded by Hispanics for Hispanics that spread beyond the borders of the United States. Modeled on the Masons, the group had an official ritual and symbols in the form of a triangle and a circle. Most members were working class poor and the group focused on solving their problems. Over the next few decades, the organization challenged the segregation of Mexican Americans, such as the Winslow, Arizona ordinance that designated one day a week as Mexican swim day at the municipal pool. The alliance dissolved in 1965 because of financial problems and difficulty attracting a new generation of members.

Books

Rosales, F. Arturo. *Chicano!: The History of the Mexican American Civil Rights Movement.* Houston: Arte Público, 1997. An excellent history of the entire Mexican American civil rights movement, albeit one that does not include the Hispanic American Alliance.

Shorris, Earl. *Latinos: A Biography of the People.* New York: W.W. Norton, 1992. A narrative of the history of the Latino experience in the United States.

January 15

1847

Tulio Larrinaga, a founder of the Federal and Unionist parties who tried to obtain U.S. citizenship for Puerto Ricans, is born in Trujillo Alto, Puerto Rico. Larrinaga served as Resident Commissioner beginning in 1904. As such, he continuously addressed the U.S. House of Representatives with calls for Puerto Ricans to control their own government.

Books

Duany, Jorge. *The Puerto Rican Nation on the Move: Identities on the Island and in the United States.* Discusses cultural nationalism among Puerto Ricans.

Negrón-Muntaner, Frances, and Ramón Grosfoguel, eds. *Puerto Rican Jam: Rethinking Colonialism and Nationalism.* Minneapolis: University of Minnesota Press, 1997. Offers essays that examine the debate over the political status of Puerto Rico.

Website

Puerto Rican Nationalism and the Drift toward Statehood. The Council on Hemispheric Affairs provides this excellent summary of the drive for statehood on the island. http://www.coha.org/puerto-rican-nationalism-and-the-drift-towards-statehood/

1865

Chilean-born U.S. Navy seaman Philip Bazaar engages in an assault on Fort Fisher in North Carolina aboard the USS *Santiago de Cuba.* Bazaar and five other sailors carry dispatches during the battle while under heavy Confederate fire. All the men receive the Medal of Honor with Bazaar becoming the first Latino to be so honored. Bazaar entered military service in Massachusetts but the rest of his history has been lost to time.

Books

Gragg, Rod. *Confederate Goliath: The Battle of Fort Fisher.* Baton Rouge: Louisiana State University Press, 1994. The standard account of the battle.

Robinson III, Charles M. *Hurricane of Fire: The Union Assault on Fort Fisher.* Annapolis, MD: Naval Institute Press, 1998. Focuses on the part of the battle that involved Bazaar.

Websites

North Carolina Historic Site: Fort Fisher. The fort, not part of the U.S. National Park Service, is maintained by North Carolina, which provides a history and chronology of the attack. http://www.nchistoricsites.org/fisher/fisher.htm

Congressional Medal of Honor Foundation: Philip Bazaar. A short military profile of the seaman drawn from Department of Defense records. http://www.obregoncmh.org/theforty/PhilipBazaar.html

January 16

1938

Salsa musician Roberto Roena is born in Mayagüez, Puerto Rico. A longtime member of Fania All-Stars, he also leads Roberto Roena y Su Apollo Sound. Roena is a percussionist and plays the bongos on his signature song, "Coro Miyare."

Books

Morales, Ed. *The Latin Beat: The Rhythms and Roots of Latin Music from Bossa Nova to Salsa and beyond.* Cambridge, MA: Da Capo Press, 2003. Covers the Latin influence on American popular music.

Rondón, César Miguel. *The Book of Salsa: A Chronicle of Urban Music from the Caribbean to New York City.* Trans. Frances R. Aparicio with Jackie White. Chapel Hill, NC: University of North Carolina Press, 2008. An exhaustive study of the musical form.

Website

Roberto Roena. This Fania site shows the covers of all of the musician's albums and contains links to listen to some of his music. https://www.fania.com/content/roberto-roena

January 17

1852

One of the first Latina entrepreneurs on the frontier, María Gertrudis Tules Barceló, dies in Santa Fe, New Mexico with a fortune estimated at $10,000 plus several houses. Barceló, born in Sonora, Mexico about 1800, came to the Albuquerque area with her family in the 1820s. She began her career by operating a game of chance in the Ortiz Mountains of New Mexico. Barceló subsequently opened a gambling saloon in Santa Fe that entertained travelers on the Santa Fe Trail and became legendary. A master gambler, she especially excelled at monte and reportedly often took piles of gold from male competitors. She invested her profits in trading ventures and merchandise, profiting even under American occupation. To pay troops quartered in Santa Fe during the Mexican American War, the U.S. Army borrowed funds from Barceló.

Books

Ruiz, Vicki, and Virginia Sánchez Korrol, eds. *Latina Legacies: Identity, Biography, and Community.* New York: Oxford University Press, 2005. Includes an essay by Deena J. González

on the differences between image and reality in Barceló's life story.

Winter, Jonah. *Wild Women of the Wild West.* New York: Holiday House, 2011. A popular account of Barceló's life that illustrates the González essay referenced above.

Website

Gertrudis Barceló. *Encyclopedia Britannica's* Guide to Hispanic Heritage provides a brief history of the merchant. http://www.britannica.com/hispanic_heritage/article-9124916

1914

Héctor Pérez García is born in Llera, Tamaulipas, Mexico, to parents who settle in Texas in 1917 because of the disruptions of the Mexican Revolution. García, a physician and World War II veteran who earned a Bronze Star with six Battle Stars, founded the American GI Forum, an organization of Latino veterans of the U.S. military. He started it after hearing a superintendent of schools boast about his system of segregating Mexican American students from their white counterparts. The forum pushed for the civil and educational rights of Latinos. During the administration of President Lyndon B. Johnson, García became the first Latino to serve on the U.S. Commission on Civil Rights.

Books

Acuña, Rodolfo. *Occupied America: A History of Chicanos.* New York: Harper Collins, 1988. A general history that explains why Mexican Americans needed civil rights organizations.

Allsup, Carl. *The American G.I. Forum: Origins and Evolution.* Austin: Center for Mexican American Studies, The University of Texas at Austin, 1982. The best history of the civil rights group.

Websites

American G.I. Forum. The official website of the organization contains information about chapters and services for veterans. http://www.agifusa.org/

American G. I. Forum of Texas. The Handbook of Texas History Online provides a good history of the first chapter of this venerable organization. http://www.tshaonline.org/handbook/online/articles/voa01

1968

The National Council of La Raza (NCLR, the largest national Hispanic civil rights and advocacy organization in the United States) is founded by 300 people in Crystal City, Texas. Now headquartered in Washington, D.C., NCLR works with nearly 300 affiliated community-based organizations in 41 states, Puerto Rico, and the District of Columbia. As a policy group, it conducts applied research and analyzes the effects of government policies on Latinos. NCLR focuses on five key areas: assets/investments, civil rights/immigration, education, employment and economic status, and health.

From NCLR News Release about Latino Education, September 19, 2012:

NCLR (National Council of La Raza) President and CEO Janet Murguía and U.S. Secretary of Education Arne Duncan hosted a town hall meeting about Latinos and education at the Metropolitan City College in Kansas City, Mo. The town hall is the latest stop on the "Education Drives America" bus tour, a U.S. Department of Education initiative which highlights important educational issues including school reform, student retention, and early childhood education. Today's discussion focused on Latino students, who represent 23 percent of the nation's schoolchildren.

"Latinos are vital to the future success and economic strength of this nation; their contributions to the labor force will help determine how competitive our nation remains in the world,"

said Murguía. "It is fundamental that we ensure their fair shot at a high-quality education which will enable them to meet future challenges and fill future jobs."

Education consistently ranks as a top priority for the nation's Latinos, who are concerned about the quality of their children's education and long-term prospects for success in the labor force. Recent Census numbers show that by 2050, Latinos will represent one-third of the nation's workforce—all the more reason to focus on Latino educational success today.

Latino students continue to lag at the bottom of the achievement gap. Only 63 percent of Latino students are graduating from high school in four years, compared to 78 percent of White students. Studies show that the achievement gap begins early in life—less than half of all Latino four-year-olds attend preschool, which puts them behind their counterparts when entering kindergarten and ultimately places them at risk for poor academic and social outcomes.

"We must lay the foundation for success early in life, and a critical part of that is access to high-quality preschool programs for Latinos," added Murguía. "We also need to raise the bar for our elementary, middle, and high school students—we must set high standards, accurately monitor student learning, and provide effective instruction for all students, including English language learners."

(*Source:* National Council of La Raza. "NCLR President and CEO Janet Murguía and U.S. Secretary of Education Arne Duncan Discuss State of Latino Education at Town Hall in Kansas City." September 19, 2012, http://www.nclr.org/index.php/about_us/news/news_releases/ja

net_murguia_and_secretary_duncan_discuss_
state_of_latino_education_at_town_hall/)

Books

Cordova, Regina, and Emma Carrasco. *Celebración: Recipes and Traditions Celebrating Latino Family Life.* New York: Doubleday, 1996. Part of NCLR's efforts to promote strong Latino families.

Martínez, Deirdre. *Who Speaks for Hispanics? Hispanic Interest Groups in Washington.* Albany, NY: SUNY Press, 2009. Focuses chiefly on the League of United Latin American Citizens and NCLR.

Websites

National Council of La Raza. The official website of the organization has an incredible wealth of fact sheets, policy statements, white papers and other materials relating to the activities of the organization. http://www.nclr.org/

National Council of La Raza. The Facebook site for the organization has over 20,000 "likes" and offers current information about the group's activities. https://www.facebook.com/Nationalcounciloflaraza

January 18

1963

Community leaders from across the Southwest gather in Phoenix on this day to explore why they believe that the American Dream has eluded the 3.5 million Mexican Americans in the region. The leaders, mostly educators, theorize that the continued view of Mexican Americans as foreigners has combined with negative stereotypes of Latinos to lead Mexican American youths to drop out of school. According to statistics quoted at the meeting, Mexican Americans quit school earlier and in greater numbers than any other ethnic group.

From a 2008 University of California at Los Angeles press release about Mexican American education:

Second-, third- and fourth-generation Mexican Americans speak English fluently, and most prefer American music. They are increasingly Protestant, and some may even vote for a Republican candidate.

However, many Mexican Americans in these later generations do not graduate from college, and they continue to live in majority Hispanic neighborhoods. Most marry other Hispanics and think of themselves as "Mexican" or "Mexican American."

Such are the findings from the most comprehensive sociological report ever produced on the integration of Mexican Americans. The UCLA study, released today in a Russell Sage Foundation book titled "Generations of Exclusion: Mexican Americans, Assimilation, and Race," concludes that, unlike the descendants of European immigrants to the United States, Mexican Americans have not fully integrated by the third and fourth generation. The research spans a period of nearly 40 years.

The study's authors, UCLA sociologists Edward E. Telles and Vilma Ortíz, examined various markers of integration among Mexican Americans in Los Angeles and San Antonio, Texas, including educational attainment, economic advancement, English and Spanish proficiency, residential integration, intermarriage, ethnic identity and political involvement.

"The study contains some encouraging findings, but many more are troubling," said Telles, a UCLA professor of sociology. "Linguistically, Mexican Americans are assimilating into mainstream quite well, and by the second generation, nearly all Mexican Americans achieve English proficiency."

"However," said Ortíz, a UCLA associate professor of sociology, "institutional barriers, persistent discrimination, punitive immigration policies and a reliance on cheap Mexican labor in the Southwestern states have made integration more difficult for Mexican Americans."

"Generations of Exclusions" revisits the 1970 book "The Mexican American People," which was the first in-depth sociological study of Mexican Americans and became a benchmark for future research. It found little assimilation among Mexican Americans, even those who had lived in the United States for several generations.

The earlier study had been conducted at UCLA in the mid-1960s by Leo Grebler, Joan Moore, and Ralph Guzmán. In 1992, construction workers retrofitting the UCLA College Library found boxes containing questionnaires from the original study.

Telles and Ortíz pored over the questionnaires and recognized a unique opportunity to examine how the Mexican American experience had evolved in the decades since the first study. The researchers and their team then reinterviewed nearly 700 original respondents and approximately 800 of their children. The vast majority of the original respondents and all the children are U.S. citizens.

(*Source:* Márquez, Letisia. "Mexican American Integration Slow, Education Stalled, Study Finds: UCLA Report Charts Chicano Experience Over Four Decades." March 20, 2008, http://newsroom.ucla.edu/portal/ucla/ucla-study-of-four-generations-46372.aspx)

Books

Altenbaugh, Richard J. *The American People and Their Education: A Social History*. Upper Saddle River, NJ: Pearson, 2003. A study of the American educational system that includes a focus on Latinos.

Macdonald, Victoria-María, ed. *Latino Education in the United States: A Narrated History from 1513–2000*. New York: Palgrave Macmillan, 2004. Illustrates why Latinos have historically had a high dropout rate and includes a history of ASPIRA.

Website

Institute of Behavioral Science, University of Colorado at Boulder. "Trends in Educational Attainment by Sex, Race/Ethnicity, and Nativity in the United States." Includes an examination of Mexican American educational levels. http://www.colorado.edu/ibs/pubs/pop/pop2007–0007.pdf

January 19

1847

Angered by the abusive behavior of American soldiers occupying Taos during the Mexican-American War, Mexicans in the city kill New Mexican governor Charles Bent. A native of Virginia, Bent had worked as a trader on the Santa Fe Trail and, with his partners, established the largest mercantile firm in the Southwest. When Gen. Stephen Kearny bloodlessly conquered New Mexico, he appointed Bent as governor. When most of the army left with Kearny, Bent faced Mexicans who did not support the conquest and Indians who resented Bent's trading practices. The behavior of the remaining U.S. soldiers worsened the situation. A mob murdered Bent's guards, killed and scalped Bent, then dragged his body through the streets. Fifteen other Americans were also killed this evening. The rebellion collapsed within two weeks with the ringleaders executed.

"Come Raise aloft the Red, White, and Blue," a song of the Mexican American War:

TUNE—"*Yankee Ship and Yankee Crew.*"

Come raise aloft the red white and blue,
And march to meet the foe,
Show Mexico's loud boasting crew,
There's death in freemen's blow;
We'll sweep the Gulf, and cross Del Norte,
The Mongiel Spaniard to tame,
We'll shake old Santa Fee's proud forte,
And light up their towns with our flame.
Come raise aloft the red white and blue, &c.

Now on to Texas, boldly go,
And swear by mighty mars,
That down the Mexican's sun shall go,
Beneath our stripes and stars;
The star of Texas brightly glows,
Within each patriot's eye,
And by its light he nobly goes,
To guard her soil or die.
Then raise aloft the red white and blue.

(*Source:* Creator unknown. "Come Raise aloft the Red White and Blue." In *General Taylor's Old Rough and Ready Songster.* New York: Turner and Fisher, 1848, http://lincoln.lib.niu.edu/file.php?file=gt09.html)

Books

Francaviglia, Richard V., and Douglas W. Richmond, eds. *Dueling Eagles: Reinterpreting the U.S.-Mexican War, 1846–1848.* Fort Worth: Texas Christian University Press, 2000. Offers essays that challenge the Anglo-centric view of this war.

Gonzáles-Berry, Erlinda, and David R. Maciel, eds. *The Contested Homeland: A Chicano History of New Mexico.* Albuquerque: University of New Mexico Press, 2010. A history that does not use the standard point of view.

Websites

The Mexican-American War. Northern Illinois University Libraries offers a history of the war along with primary documents. http://dig.lib.niu.edu/mexicanwar/about.html_

The U.S.-Mexican War. PBS provides a graphic-heavy history of the war with a timeline, biographiesofkeyfigures,andalinktoadditional resources. http://www.pbs.org/kera/usmexicanwar/

1979

The United Farm Workers of America is established with César Chávez as its president. The organization has its roots in the National Farm Workers Association (NFWA), which united workers under Chávez, Dolores Huerta, and Gilberto Padilla. The NFWA provided social and legal services, a credit union, a supplies cooperative, a bilingual newspaper, and labor representation.

Books

Del Castillo, Richard Griswold, and Richard A. García. *César Chávez: A Triumph of Spirit.* Norman: University of Oklahoma Press, 1995. The best account of Chávez and his links to the Chicano Movement.

Levy, Jacques E. *César Chávez: Autobiography of La Causa.* New York: W.W. Norton, 1975. Provides an account of Chávez's early years, his initial efforts as an organizer, and his rise to the leadership of Mexican American farmworkers.

Websites

César Chávez: Labor Leader. Enchanted Learning offers a biography of Chávez as well as numerous activities for children that teach about the union leader. http://www.enchantedlearning.com/history/us/hispanicamerican/chavez/

The Story of César Chávez. The United Farm Workers provides a biography of its famed leader. http://www.ufw.org/_page.php?inc=history/07.html&menu=research

2005

Printmaker Carlos Cortéz, an artist who developed the Chicano poster movement, dies. Cortéz helped found the art collective, MARCH (Movimiento Artístico Chicano), in Illinois in 1975. MARCH promotes Chicano and Latino visual arts with an emphasis on the Midwest and Chicago.

Books

Griswold del Castillo, Richard, Teresa McKenna, and Yvonne Yarbro-Bejarano, eds. *Chicano Art: Resistance and Affirmation, 1965–1985.* Los Angeles: Wight Art Gallery, University of California, Los Angeles, 1991. An exhibition catalog with essays on Chicano art.

Jackson, Carlos Francisco. *Chicana and Chicano Art: ProtestArte.* Tucson : University of Arizona Press, 2009. Covers the history and development of Chicana and Chicano visual arts from their beginnings in the 1960s.

Website

About MARCH. The University of Illinois at Chicago sponsors this website, which provides a history of the group and information about the publications of the group. http://tigger.uic.edu/~marczim/lacasa/#a16

January 20

1932

Cuban writer Heberto Padilla is born. Padilla went into exile in the United States during the 1952–1959 dictatorship of Fulgencio Batista. He returned to Cuba in 1959 to become part of the revolution. Chiefly a journalist, he helped create the UNEAC (Union Nacional de Escritores y Artistas de Cuba), Cuba's union for writers and artists. When Padilla returned to Cuba in 1966 after working in Europe for Prensa Latina, he began to clash with revolutionary leaders. For writing a positive review of Cabrera Infante's *Trés Tristes Tigres* after Infante had denounced the revolution, Padilla was labeled as a counterrevolutionary. He was also condemned for producing bourgeois-oriented literature. Padilla and his wife were finally arrested in 1971 in the Padilla Affair, a case that prompted many intellectuals to distance themselves from the Cuban Revolution. Padilla was permitted to fly to the United States in 1980 and he died in 2000 in Alabama, where he taught at Auburn University.

Books

Brown, Wesley, and Amy Ling, eds. *Visions of America: Personal Narratives from the Promised Land.* New York: Persea, 1993. Includes an essay by Pablo Medina on Padilla in exile.

Padilla, Heberto. *Self-Portrait of the Other.* Trans. Alexander Coleman. New York: Farrar, Straus, Giroux, 1990. The poet's autobiography includes his account of going into exile.

Websites

"Cuban Poet Heberto Padilla Dies." Reprints a *Miami Herald* obituary of the poet. http://www.latinamericanstudies.org/cuba/padilla-obituary.htm

Heberto Padilla (1932–2000). Offers a Spanish-language biography of Padilla. http://www.literatura.us/padilla/

January 21

1929

Writer Rolando Hinojosa is born to an Anglo mother and a Mexican father in Mercedes, Texas. Raised in two cultures, their spirit permeates his books. Hinojosa is best known for his *Klail City Death Trip* series which covers the same set of characters from the 1930s to fairly recent times. His first book, *Estampas del Valle y Otras Obras / Sketches of the Valley and Other Works,* won the Quinto Sol literature prize. Hinojosa, a professor at the University of Texas in Austin, has won other prestigious awards, including the Casa de las Américas.

From "Interview with Rolando Hinojosa-Smith: The Writer's Mission":

I was at a conference where a Chicano literary critic said that Rivera,

Anaya, and I represented the old school. Whatever that means. Well, Rudy is best known for Ultima, as he should be, of course, but he's also written short stories and has developed his detective series as well. I doubt the critic has read much of mine, but that's all right, any critic has the right to be wrong at the top of his voice as long as the second amendment to the Constitution gives all of us the right to do so.

He wanted us to get away from our culture and to write fantasy novels; I wonder if he would say the same about Toni Morrison, Alice Walker, and others to stop writing about the Afro-American experience. James Baldwin must be spinning in his grave, to coin a phrase to which the critic is welcomed.

Writers should write what they want to write about; if they are to harken and follow advice from nonwriters, our and all literature is in trouble.

(*Source:* La Bloga. "Interview with Rolando Hinojosa-Smith: The Writer's Mission." http://labloga.blogspot.com/2009/03/inter view-with-rolando-hinojosa-smith.html)

Books

Hinojosa, Rolando. *A Voice of My Own: Essays and Stories.* Houston: Arte Publico, 2011. Discusses many of the challenges of writing, including the decision to write in Spanish or English and writer's block.

Lee, Joyce Glover. *Rolando Hinojosa and the American Dream.* Denton: University of North Texas Press, 1997. Sets Hinojosa's works in the broader context of the American frontier and the American Dream.

Websites

Rolando Hinojosa—Latinoteca. Provides a biography of the writer and a link to a radio interview that he did. http://www.latinoteca. com/code/artePublicoPress/Publications/sh owAuthorDetails?code=167

Rolando Hinojosa-Smith—Department of English, University of Texas at Austin. The professor's academic webpage with a curriculum vitae and contact information. http://www. utexas.edu/cola/depts/english/faculty/rh326

January 22

1848

The Siege of San José del Cabo, part of the Mexican-American War, begins. Mexican militiamen attack a smaller force of American marines and sailors as well as Californio militiamen on Mexico's west coast. The siege ends on February 14 when men from the USS *Cyane* counterattack.

Books

Francaviglia, Richard V., and Douglas W. Richmond, eds. *Dueling Eagles: Reinterpreting the U.S.-Mexican War, 1846–1848.* Fort Worth: Texas Christian University Press, 2000. Offers essays that challenge the Anglo-centric view of this war.

Gonzáles-Berry, Erlinda, and David R. Maciel, eds. *The Contested Homeland: A Chicano History of New Mexico.* Albuquerque: University of New Mexico Press, 2010. A history that does not use the standard point of view.

Websites

The Mexican-American War. Northern Illinois University Libraries offers a history of the war along with primary documents. http://dig.lib. niu.edu/mexicanwar/about.html_

The U.S.-Mexican War. PBS provides a graphic-heavy history of the war with a timeline, biographies of key figures, and a link to additional resources. http://www.pbs.org/kera/ usmexicanwar/

January 23

1929

Angela de Hoyos, the first Mexican American to win international recognition by winning the Bronze Medal of Honor (poetry) from the Centro Studi e Scambi Internazionale in Rome in 1966, is born in Coahuila, Mexico. Her family moved to San Antonio during her childhood. A pioneer of Chicano poetry who was heavily influenced by the activism of the farmworkers, her earlier writings were quite political. She is often cited as one of the first literary fruits of the Chicano movement. In time, her works would be translated into 15 different languages. At the 1994 San Antonio Festival, de Hoyos received a Lifetime Achievement Award and recognition by the Texas Commission on the Arts. She died on September 24, 2009.

Books

De Hoyos, Angela. *Arise, Chicano! And Other Poems*. San Antonio: M&A Editions, 1980. A collection of de Hoyos's poems put out by the publishing house that she owned.

De Hoyos, Angela. *Chicano Poems for the Barrio*. San Antonio: M&A Editions, 1976. A collection of the poet's heavily political works.

Websites

Angela de Hoyos: Voices from the Gaps. This University of Minnesota site provides a biography of the poet, criticism of her work, and a list of her writings. http://voices.cla.umn.edu/artistpages/dehoyosAngela.php

Latino Author Series: Angela de Hoyos. Provides a biography of the poet and a transcript of an interview in which de Hoyos discusses her childhood, the process of writing, and her influences. http://www.neighborhoodlink.com/org/latinoauthors/clubextra/381447566.html

1899

Romualdo Pacheco, the first Latino member of the U.S. House of Representatives with full voting privileges, dies in Oakland, California. (Representatives from territories did not have full voting rights.) He served from 1877 until 1882 as a Republican from California. He is the only Latino to serve as governor of California under U.S. rule, but

only held office briefly in 1875. Born in Santa Barbara, California, in 1831 to a prominent Californio family, he took an oath of loyalty to the United States in 1846 during the Mexican War. Pacheco, a rancher who was especially skilled with a lasso, is also known as the only California governor to rope a grizzly bear. Toward the end of his political career, in 1890, he received an appointment as U.S. Envoy Extraordinary and Minister Plenipotentiary to the Central American States. When the job proved more than what one man could handle, Pacheco became Minister Plenipotentiary to Honduras and Guatemala, a post he held until June 21, 1893.

Books

Genini, Ronald, and Richard Hitchman. *Romualdo Pacheco: A Californio in Two Eras*. San Francisco: Book Club of California, 1985. The only biography of the early California leader.

Melendy, H. Brett, and Benjamin F. Gilbert. *The Governors of California: Peter H. Burnett to Edmund G. Brown*. Georgetown, CA: Talisman Press, 1965. Sets a short biography of Pacheco in the context of his gubernatorial peers.

Websites

Hispanic Americans in Congress: Romualdo Pacheco. The Library of Congress gives a photo and a very detailed biography of this prominent Californio. http://www.loc.gov/rr/hispanic/congress/pacheco.html

The Governors' Gallery: Romualdo Pacheco. The state of California offers short biographies of all governors, including Pacheco. http://www.loc.gov/rr/hispanic/congress/pacheco.html

January 24

1848

John Sutter discovers gold, setting off the California Gold Rush. People rushed to the territory by land and by sea to strike it rich. The largest foreign contingent came from Mexico, many from the state of Sonora, with Chile taking second place with about 7,000 miners. Some of the first men from Latin America who joined the Gold Rush were English and North American merchants, therefore English-speakers, who had married Latin American women. They brought their families to California. Other migrants were experienced in placer mining, the most common type of California mining and the only kind practiced in the early years of the Gold Rush. These miners could point out the most promising gravel formations, identify sites where gold was most apt to be concentrated, and spot boulder formations that might lead to rich gold deposits. They also knew how a gold pan should be manipulated. The Chileans brought a long curving knife, the *corvo,* suited to picking deposits from cracks in rocks, and a winnowing method, the *aventamiento,* that could be used when water was not available.

From the diary of Vicente Pérez Rosales:

I can still see poor Álvarez with the noose around his neck and the attached rope thrown over the branch of a tree, and with his feet tied to the cart which was ready to be driven away. . . . I do not know what he was doing with that group of men headed for the mines; but a shovel was lost, and as there were no other aliens among them but "this descendant of Africans" as the Yankees call the Chileans and Spaniards [Mexicans], they accused him of the theft. Without any further ado, the barbarians became the jury. They were ready to do to Álvarez what they usually do to thieves. . . . Once he recovered he left us, and I never heard of him again.

(*Source:* Beilharz, Edwin A., and Carlos U. López, trans. and eds. *We Were 49ers!: Chilean Accounts of the California Gold Rush.* Pasadena, CA: Ward Ritchie Press, 1976, p. 64.)

Books

Beilharz, Edwin A., and Carlos U. López, trans. and eds. *We Were 49ers!: Chilean Accounts of the California Gold Rush.* Pasadena, California: Ward Ritchie Press, 1976. This is the only account of Chileans in the Gold Rush.

Holliday, J.S. *The World Rushed In: The California Gold Rush Experience.* Norman: University of Oklahoma Press, 2002. Widely acknowledged as the best general history of the Gold Rush.

Websites

"California Gold—Navism and Racism" by Andrea Franzius. Short essay on Mexicans and South Americans in the Gold Rush. http://www.duke.edu/~agf2/history391/nativism.html

Minorities during the Gold Rush. This LearnCalifornia site provides a good essay on Latinos during the Gold Rush as well as a link to an essay on the impact of the Gold Rush. http://www.learncalifornia.org/doc.asp?id=1933

Breaking the Silence—Learning about the Transatlantic Slave Trade. http://www.antislavery.org/breakingthesilence/index.shtml. A UNESCO and Anti-Slavery International supported site that promotes teaching and learning regarding the dangers of slavery and how it can be abolished.

January 25

1971

Puerto Rican actress Miriam Colón is chosen to become a trustee of the American Museum of Natural History, the first Puerto Rican to serve on the board. The founder of the Puerto Rican Traveling Theater (PRTT), Colón may be best known for her portrayal of Mama Montana in the 1983 movie, *Scarface.* A native of Puerto Rico, she had a long history of working off-Broadway because roles for Latinas were hard to find on Broadway. She was also the first Puerto Rican to be accepted into the famed Actor's Studio. Colón began PRTT in 1967 as a way to bring theater to impoverished neighborhoods and to show Puerto Ricans that they came from a culture that was very rich and very old.

Books

Fernández, Mayra. *Miriam Colón, Actor and Theater Founder*. Cleveland: Modern Curriculum Press, 1994. A 26-page children's book.

Seller, Maxine Schwartz, ed. *Women Educators in the United States, 1820–1993: A Bio-Bibliographical Sourcebook*. Westport, CT: Greenwood, 1994. Contains a short essay on Colón by Rosa Luisa Márquez and Barbara Shircliffe.

Websites

Miriam Colón. The Internet Movie Database lists the actor's film and television credits along with a number of photographs of her. http://www.imdb.com/name/nm0173125/

Miriam Colón: Artistic Director and Founder. The official website for the Puerto Rican Traveling Theater gives this biography of Colón. http://www.prtt.org/miriambio.html

January 26

1992

Actor José Ferrer dies of cancer. A Puerto Rican, he was nominated for a Best Supporting Actor Academy Award in 1948 for his performance opposite Ingrid Bergman in *Joan of Arc*. He won a Tony award for his Broadway performance in *Cyrano de Bergerac* and a Best Actor Oscar in 1951 for the film version.

Books

Clooney, Rosemary, and Joan Barthel. *Girl Singer: An Autobiography*. New York: Broadway, 2001. Clooney married Ferrer, had five

children with him, and divorced him for, among other factors, his infidelities.

Lloyd, Jack, and Peter Marshall. *From Cyrano to Magoo: My Years with José Ferrer and Jim Backus*. N.P.: Bear Manor Media, 2011. Lloyd was a long-time friend of Ferrer.

January 27

1987

Actor Martin Sheen, born Ramón Estévez, is arrested with 71 other people at a Nevada Test Site while protesting the 36th anniversary of the first nuclear test. As a young actor seeking jobs over the telephone, Estévez discovered that his Hispanic name won him mostly ethnic roles, so he adopted a stage name. Probably best known for his performance in Francis Ford Coppola's *Apocalypse Now,* Sheen has a long history of supporting social justice causes. He was first arrested in 1986 for protesting against the U.S. Strategic Defense Initiative, more commonly known as Star Wars.

Books

Hargrove, Jim. *Martin Sheen: Actor and Activist*. N.P.: Children's Press, 1991. Part of the People of Distinction series, this book tells the story of Sheen's life to children.

Smith, Emily. *The Martin Sheen Handbook: Everything You Need to Know about Martin Sheen*. N.P.: Tebbo, 2012. A fan's guide to Sheen's life.

Websites

Martin Sheen. This Internet Movie Database site provides a biography, photographs, and a list of acting credits on film and television for Sheen. http://www.imdb.com/name/nm0000640/

Martin Sheen. The official website for Sheen contains information about his activism as well as the television show, "The West Wing," and his other acting performances. http://martinsheen.net/

January 29

1977

Comedian Freddie Prinze dies of a self-inflicted gunshot. Prinze described himself as a "HungaRican" because his father was Hungarian and his mother was Puerto Rican. Best known as a stand-up comic, he had a successful television show, *Chico and the Man,* at the time of his death.

From a comedy performance by Prinze at Mr. Kelly's in Chicago, Illinois, 1974:

> I'm not all Puerto Rican.
>
> I'm half Hungarian: HungaRican.
>
> That was a weird combination to grow up with because I could never figure out how my parents met. A Gypsy and a Puerto Rican.
>
> I asked my mother and she told me that they were on a bus trying to pick each other's pocket . . .
>
> A lot of people think that Puerto Ricans are responsible for cockroaches. I want to clear that up right now! We didn't bring them here. When we got here they were living in the apartments we live in now.
>
> But they're strong. I'm afraid of them. They adapt to any environment. They learned how to talk in my building.
>
> They would threaten me before I went out:
>
> "Freddie! Where are you going? To the grocery store, huh? Don't come back with no roach poison or we lock you out!"
>
> Other things that give people the wrong impression of Puerto Ricans are movies. Like, West Side Story set us back a hundred years—and we were only in the country twenty!
>
> Because if you saw the movie it made people think that all we did was stand in streets whistling and dancing.
>
> They thought we were gay ballet dancers!
>
> And the movie became such a hit that the New York Chamber of Commerce had to keep up the image about Puerto Ricans in New York. So, they hired Gene Kelly and Fred Astaire to choreograph every Puerto Rican wino in Harlem. . . .
>
> The most unbelievable scene in the picture was two A.M., the young lovers, Tony and Maria are out on the fire escape—vowing their love for each other.
>
> And Tony goes: "Maria, I love you."
>
> "Shh! My papa will hear you."
>
> "But I'm whispering."
>
> "Shhh!"
>
> The next thing you know, they sing: "TONIGHT, TONIGHT!"
>
> Her father must have been deaf or have pillows in his ears!
>
> If that had been a black neighborhood at two A.M. in the morning singing, they would have gotten shot!
>
> "What you doing on the fire escape singing, sucker?! People trying to sleep here! Gimme my gun, Mama! You gonna sing all the way to the funeral parlor, baby!"

(*Source:* Santiago, Roberto, ed. *Boricuas: Influential Puerto Rican Writings: An Anthology.* New York: One World, 1995, pp. 184–85.)

Books

Pruetzel, María, and John A. Barbour. *The Freddie Prinze Story: As Told By His Mother.* Kalamazoo, MI: Master's Press, 1978. A biography of the tragic comedian.

Snauffer, Douglas. *The Show Must Go On: How the Deaths of Lead Actors Have Affected Television Series.* Jefferson, NC: McFarland, 2008.

Discusses how "Chico and the Man" continued without Prinze.

January 30

1848

Sam Houston, governor of Texas and one of the men responsible for gaining the independence of Texas from Mexico, declares that "Mexicans are no better than Indians. . . . I see no reason why we should not . . . take their land." His comments are reported in the *New York Herald* on this date. Anglo violence against Tejanos had increased during the Texas War for Independence and continued in the postwar period with many Mexican Americans finding themselves unwanted in their homeland.

"For Texas and For Oregon," circa 1848, a Mexican American War Song:

> TUNE—"Dandy Jim"
>
> Columbia's mighty flag of Mars,
> Has gained two bright and glowing stars,
> But foemen jealous of their light,
> To pluck their glories now unite.
>
> Be ready then to strike the blow,
> 'Gainst Johnny Bull or Mexico,
> Arm for the field both sire and son,
> For Texas and for Oregon.
>
> Each spot bold lads, is all our own,
> 'Twas cultured by our sons alone,
> By freemen's hands that soil was till'd,
> And freemen's hands shall hold it still.
>
> Be ready then to strike the blow, &c.
>
> Our sons upon each spot so free,
> First planted freedom's holy tree,
> They nourished it with blood and toil,
> And have the first right to the soil.
>
> Be ready then to strike the blow, &c.

> Let freedom's pioneers still find,
> That Uncle Sam walks close behind,
> And each spot where their flag's unfurl'd.
> He will defend against the world.
>
> Be ready then to strike, &c.
>
> Let Mexico and Bull unite,
> To rob us of our holy right,
> We'll fire annexation's gun,
> And sweep off ev'ry hostile son.
>
> Be ready then to strike, &c.
>
> Each mountain stream shall like a flood,
> Run purple with the foeman's blood,
> Who from our holy flag would tear,
> The two young stars we've woven there.
>
> Be ready then to strike, &c.

(*Source:* Creator Unknown. "For Texas and For Oregon" in *General Taylor's Old Rough and Ready Songster.* New York: Turner and Fisher, 1848. http://lincoln.lib.niu.edu/file.php?file=gt22.html)

Books

Francaviglia, Richard V., and Douglas W. Richmond, eds. *Dueling Eagles: Reinterpreting the U.S.-Mexican War, 1846–1848.* Fort Worth: Texas Christian University Press, 2000. Offers essays that challenge the Anglo-centric view of this war.

Haley, James L. *Sam Houston.* Norman: University of Oklahoma Press, 2002. A biography of the Texas leader that does not adopt the fawning attitude that most of his other biographies do.

Websites

The Mexican-American War. Northern Illinois University Libraries offers a history of the war along with primary documents. http://dig.lib.niu.edu/mexicanwar/about.html_

The U.S.-Mexican War. PBS provides a graphic-heavy history of the war with a timeline, biographies of key figures, and a link to additional resources. http://www.pbs.org/kera/usmexicanwar/

January 31

2005

Inés Cifuentes, the first woman to earn a doctorate in seismology, resigns as the director of the Carnegie Academy for Science Education. Born to an American mother and an Ecuadorian father in England, Cifuentes earned university degrees in the United States before studying earthquake activity in Guatemala and Nicaragua. Unable to find a job as a seismologist in the United States, she became a science educator in 1994.

Inés Cifuentes writes about how to discuss science with nonscientists, 2010:

> Every day last week at the Ocean Sciences meeting there were talks about education and outreach. And people came, both scientists and science educators. Why? There is a need and desire by scientists to talk about what they do, not just to their colleagues, but to others.
>
> Scientists are using websites, writing blogs, taking photos, shooting video, talking via podcasts—all to bring the ocean (and the tons of data collected) to students, teachers, fishermen, ocean enthusiasts. We are learning that when we talk as we do with our colleagues, we bore people.
>
> We must become storytellers. What does that mean? Instead of relying on giving out information, we have to use emotions, humor, visuals, anything and all to draw people in, hold their attention, and make them learn. Scientists often miss the cool bits that will hook people—a creature no one has seen before, a glider operated by

someone thousands of miles away in a spot humans can't go, drilling through a thousand meters of Antarctic ice to get your instrument where you want it.

> Last Wednesday evening, Randy Olson, a research biologist who has evolved into a filmmaker, ran a workshop where we viewed and gently (mostly) critiqued a series of videos made by scientists at the meeting. They were good, especially those which were made by first-time filmmakers. We should all read his recent book Don't Be Such A Scientist: Talking Substance in an Age of Style. Olson lays out in an easy-to-read style what he has learned as he has transformed himself from an academic scientist to a storyteller who uses film as his medium.
>
> The next decade will bring the vastness of the ocean into our homes as NASA has done with Space. The ocean is essential to life on earth and holds clues to how life began and how it has evolved. The scientists and science educators . . . will have to become the storytellers of the oceans.

(*Source:* Cifuentes, Inés. "Telling (Science) Stories." *GeoSpace: Earth and Space Science*, March 1, 2010, http://blogs.agu.org/geospace/2010/03/01/telling-science-stories/)

Websites

Inés Cifuentes. The National Society of Hispanic Physicists provides this short biography of one of its leading members. http://www.hispanicphysicists.org/recognition/bio%28cifuentes%29.html

Science Hero: Inés Cifuentes. The Society for Advancement of Chicanos and Native Americans in Science (SACNAS) provided this biography for the My Hero Project. http://www.myhero.com/go/hero.asp?hero=Ines_Cifuentes_06

February

February 1

1957

Graphic artist Gilbert Hernández is born to a Mexican-born father and a mother with Texas ancestry dating to the days of Mexican control. Hernández is known for the comic book series *Palomar* and, with his brother Jaime, the *Love and Rockets* series. The artist began to draw in the late 1970s as an outgrowth of his interest in punk rock with his work reflecting a minimalist, Latin American style. He has since become known as one of the most respected creators of American fiction with his female characters separated from those in most graphic novels by being full human beings albeit with the exaggerated breasts typical of the art form.

From a 1988 interview with the Hernández Brothers:

Gilbert: I distinctly remember Fantastic Four #1 sitting on the couch, when Mario [Hernández, the oldest brother] brought it home. I remember the day I picked it up, and Mario said, "This is great, it has monsters in it." We didn't know who drew it or what . . .

Mario: Comics were everywhere. You'd go to the bathroom with comics, you'd eat dinner with comics, it was pretty lax. You could get away with something like that, just be reading all the time.

Gilbert: I imagine our mother let us read comics because she did. It was nostalgic for her, I guess. So, comics were always normal to us, it was an everyday thing. It wasn't until school that we realized that we were abnormal.

Mario: Some kids liked [comics], but we didn't have friends that read comics. The only comic fans we knew on a regular basis were [people we met] at conventions. Up until then we were pretty much comic-book geeks. . . .

Robert Fiore: But punk rock affected your outlook on things other than music.

Gilbert: Yeah, it's hard to explain. I had a bad attitude about everything.

Jaime: Also, it made you realize that you could do what you want.

Gilbert: Yeah, it made me cocky enough to believe that I could do a comic book, and it was good and it was all right, as opposed to being intimidated by the Marvel guys. As lousy as they were, at least they could draw buildings. I couldn't draw buildings unless I made it up, and that intimidated me. And so with punk, I took that musical anarchy to comics. . . .

Gilbert: As soon as I got out of high school, I did comics for myself, vaguely similar to Love & Rockets, but they were just for myself. I used some of the characters from Love & Rockets, that would be Inez and Bang, but I got bored with that, because it didn't seem to be going anywhere. I didn't know what to do with it.

Mario: Even people we asked didn't know what to do with it. There was no place to put it.

Gary Groth: At some point did you have an aspiration to draw them professionally?

Gilbert: No. As a matter of fact, kids in grade school, junior high, and high school said, "You could get a job in comics, you could draw comics, you could work for Disney." But I thought, "What am I going to do there? I don't belong there, there's nothing that I have that they would want." And I've had that attitude all the way up to the first Love & Rockets.

Groth: You never thought of just putting your talent in the service of company characters or whatever?

Gilbert: Maybe in the back of my head I sort of dreamed that, "Maybe I can do Spider-Man one day, but naaah." I do what I do because that's all I can do.

(*Source*: Fiore, Robert et al. "Interview: Los Bros. Hernández," *The Comics Journal*, #126, 1988, http://www.fantagraphics.com/interviews-forums-etc./interview-los-bros.-hernandez-1988.html)

Books

Aldama, Frederick Luis. *Your Brain on Latino Comics: From Gus Arriola to Los Bros Hernández*. Austin: University of Texas Press, 2009.

Includes an interview with Hernández and a separate one with his brother.
Hernández, Gilbert. *Beyond Palomar: A Love and Rockets Book*. Seattle, WA: Fantagraphics Books, 2007. One of Hernández's graphic novels and probably the best known one.

Websites

Artist Bio: The Hernández Brothers. The publisher of the graphic novels of the brothers supplies a biography of them along with covers for all of their work and a link to an interview. http://www.fantagraphics.com/artist-bios/artist-bio-the-hernandez-brothers.html
The Billy Ireland Cartoon Library and Museum. This is one of the few libraries devoted to cartoons and the only museum dedicated to the art form from its beginnings to the present. http://cartoons.osu.edu/

February 2

1848

The treaty ending the Mexican-American War is signed in Guadalupe Hidalgo, a city north of the Mexican capital. Hostilities between Mexico and the United States erupted in 1845 over American annexation of Texas. The war, controversial because many Americans saw it as a grab for territory, began in 1846. Over the next 17 months, almost 17,000 Mexican and U.S. soldiers would die. Upon signing of the Treaty of Guadalupe Hidalgo, the United States acquired more than 500,000 square miles of territory, including present-day Arizona, New Mexico, Nevada, Colorado, and California. Many Mexicans now found themselves living in U.S. territory as Mexico lost one-third of its land.

From "The Treaty of Guadalupe Hidalgo," preamble and first three articles:

> In the name of Almighty God: The United States of America and the United Mexican States, animated by sincere desire to put an end to the calamities of the war which unhappily exists between the two Republics, and

to establish upon a solid basis relations of peace and friendship, which shall confer reciprocal benefits upon the citizens of both, and assure the concord, harmony, and mutual confidence, wherein the two Peoples should live, as good Neighbours have for that purpose appointed their respective plenipotentiaries, that is to say: The President of the United States has appointed Nicholas P Trist, a citizen of the United States, and the President of the Mexican Republic has appointed Don Luis Gonzaga Cuevas, Don Bernardo Couto, and Don Miguel Atristaín, citizens of the said Republic; Who, after a reciprocal communication of their respective full powers, have, under the protection of Almighty God, the author of peace, arranged, agreed upon, and signed the following:

Treaty of Peace, Friendship, Limits, and Settlement between the United States of America and the Mexican Republic.

Article I

There shall be firm and universal peace between the United States of America and the Mexican Republic, and between their respective countries, territories, cities, towns, and people, without exception of places or persons.

Article II

Immediately upon the signature of this treaty, a convention shall be entered into between a commissioner or commissioners appointed by the General-in-chief of the forces of the United States, and such as may be appointed by the Mexican Government, to the end that a provisional suspension of hostilities shall take place, and that, in the places occupied by the said forces, constitutional order may be reestablished, as regards the political, administrative, and judicial branches, so far as this shall be permitted by the circumstances of military occupation.

Article III

Immediately upon the ratification of the present treaty by the Government of the United States, orders shall be transmitted to the commanders of their land and naval forces, requiring the latter (provided this treaty shall then have been ratified by the Government of the Mexican Republic, and the ratifications exchanged) immediately to desist from blockading any Mexican ports and requiring the former (under the same condition) to commence, at the earliest moment practicable, withdrawing all troops of the United States then in the interior of the Mexican Republic, to points that shall be selected by common agreement, at a distance from the seaports not exceeding thirty leagues; and such evacuation of the interior of the Republic shall be completed with the least possible delay; the Mexican Government hereby binding itself to afford every facility in its power for rendering the same convenient to the troops, on their march and in their new positions, and for promoting a good understanding between them and the inhabitants. In like manner orders shall be dispatched to the persons in charge of the custom houses at all ports occupied by the forces of the United States, requiring them (under the same condition) immediately to deliver possession of the same to the persons authorized by the Mexican Government to receive it, together with all bonds and evidences of debt for duties on importations and on exportations, not yet fallen due. Moreover, a faithful and exact account shall be made out, showing the entire amount of all duties on imports and on exports, collected at such custom-houses, or elsewhere in Mexico, by authority of the United States, from and after the day of ratification of this treaty by the Government of the Mexican Republic; and also an account of the cost of collection; and such entire amount, deducting only the cost of collection, shall be delivered to the Mexican Government, at the city of Mexico, within three months after the exchange of ratifications.

The evacuation of the capital of the Mexican Republic by the troops of the United States, in virtue of the above stipulation, shall be completed in one month after the orders there stipulated for shall have been received by the commander of said troops, or sooner if possible . . .

(*Source:* The Library of Congress, Hispanic Reading Room. The Treaty of Guadalupe Hidalgo. http://www. loc.gov/rr/hispanic/ghtreaty/)

Books

Castillo, Richard Griswold del. *The Treaty of Guadalupe Hidalgo.* Norman: University of Oklahoma Press, 1992. Argues that the treaty was interpreted to favor Americans moving westward rather than Mexicans and Indians now living in the United States.

Davenport, John C. *The U.S. –Mexico Border: The Treaty of Guadalupe Hidalgo.* New York: Chelsea House Publications, 2004. Scholarly history of the conflicts along the border.

Websites

Teaching with Documents—The Treaty of Guadalupe Hidalgo. This site for teachers provides an interesting history of the treaty and the early border as well as photos relating to the document. http://www.archives.gov/education/lessons/guadalupe-hidalgo/

Treaty of Guadalupe Hidalgo—Hispanic Reading Room—Library of Congress. Provides the 1847 map used to establish the border as well

as a history of the treaty and links to printed versions of the treaty, including the bilingual Senate one. http://www.loc.gov/rr/hispanic/ghtreaty/

1862

Union Admiral David Farragut famously says "Damn the torpedoes! Full speed ahead!" and becomes a hero for capturing Mobile Bay from the Confederacy during the Civil War. Farragut, the son of a Spanish merchant father who had served in the American Revolution and the War of 1812, became the first person to hold the title of Admiral of the U.S. Navy. He died in 1870. A memorial statue of Farragut, cast in bronze from a propeller of his flagship, USS *Hartford,* is located in Washington, D.C., at 17th and K Street.

Books

Duffy, James P. *Lincoln's Admiral: The Civil War Campaigns of David Farragut.* Edison, NJ: Castle Books, 2006. Farragut provided several critical victories for the Union during the Civil War.

Latham, Jean Lee. *Anchor's Aweigh: The Story of David Glasgow Farragut.* New York: Harper and Row, 1968. A full story of the admiral's life.

Websites

David Farragut. The Civil War Trust provides an excellent biography of Farragut. http://www.civilwar.org/education/history/biographies/david-farragut.html

David Farragut. A detailed biography of the admiral. http://www.nndb.com/people/050/000094765/

February 3

1959

Rocker Ritchie Valens dies at the age of 17 in a plane crash along with the Big Bopper and Buddy Holly, an event memorialized by singer-songwriter Don McLean as the "day the music died." Born Ricardo Valenzuela, he played the guitar with a style and swagger that was still remarked upon 50 years later. Valens was also the solo writer on most of his songs, including "La Bamba," "Donna," and "Come On Let's Go." Valens was memorialized in the 1987 movie, *La Bamba,* and received a star on the Hollywood Walk of Fame in 1989.

Books

Lehmer, Larry. *The Day the Music Died: The Last Tour of Buddy Holly, the Big Bopper, and Ritchie Valens.* New York: Schirmer Trade, 2004. Focuses on one of the most famous events in musical history.

Mendheim, Beverly. *Ritchie Valens: The First Latino Rocker.* Tempe, AZ: Bilingual Press, 1987. One of the better biographies of the doomed musician.

Websites

Ritchie Valens Official Fan Site. That Valens, a man who died long before the invention of the internet, has a fan site speaks of the impact that he made upon his audience. http://www.ritchievalens.com/

YouTube: Ritchie Valens. Links to 26 clips of Valens's performances on YouTube. http://www.youtube.com/artist/ritchie_valens

1962

President John F. Kennedy announces an economic embargo against Cuba. The near-total trade ban takes effect four days later. Kennedy cited the "subversive offensive of Sino-Soviet Communism with which the government of Cuba is publicly aligned." The embargo aimed to topple Cuban leader Fidel Castro but failed. As of 2012, the embargo remained in place despite the fact that many American strategic concerns of the 1960s were no longer relevant, such as curbing Soviet influence and keeping Castro from exporting revolution throughout Latin America. Supporters of the embargo note that other justifications remain including the need to press for greater political

and personal freedoms on Cuba and the confiscation of U.S. property on the island.

Books

Drury, A. Cooper, and Steve Chan, eds. *Sanctions as Economic Statecraft: Theory and Practice.* New York: St. Martin's Press, 2000. Addresses the long-term impact of the Cuban embargo.

Miller, John, and Aaron Kenedi, eds. *Inside Cuba: The History, Culture, and Politics of an Outlaw Nation.* New York: Marlowe, 2003. Shows the influence of U.S. sanctions upon the island nation 90 miles from Florida.

Website

John F. Kennedy Presidential Library. The library contains digital archives that address Kennedy's various struggles with Cuba. http://www.jfklibrary.org/

2005

Alberto Gonzales, the son of Mexican migrant workers, is confirmed by the U.S. Senate to succeed Attorney General John Ashcroft as the nation's top law enforcement officer. A Harvard Law School graduate, he befriended George W. Bush and Bush made him Texas's secretary of state in 1997. Bush then named Gonzales to the Texas Supreme Court. When Bush came to the White House in 2000, Gonzales served as White House counsel. He stepped down from the position of Attorney General in 2007.

From "Embattled Attorney General Resigns":

> Attorney General Alberto R. Gonzales, whose tenure has been marred by controversy and accusations of perjury before Congress, announced his resignation in Washington today, declaring that he had "lived the American dream" by being able to lead the Justice Department.
>
> Mr. Gonzales, who had rebuffed calls for his resignation for months, submitted it to President Bush by telephone on

Friday, a senior administration official said. There had been rumblings over the weekend that Mr. Gonzales's departure was imminent, although the White House sought to quell the rumors.

Mr. Gonzales appeared cheerful and composed when he announced that he was stepping down effective Sept. 17. His very worst days on the job were "better than my father's best days," he said, alluding to his family's hardscrabble past.

"Thank you, and God bless America," Mr. Gonzales said, exiting without responding to questions.

In Waco, President Bush said he had accepted the resignation reluctantly. He praised his old friend as "a man of integrity, decency and principle" and complained of the "months of unfair treatment" that preceded the resignation.

"It's sad," Mr. Bush said, asserting that Mr. Gonzales's name had been "dragged through the mud for political reasons."

Mr. Bush repeatedly stood by Mr. Gonzales, an old friend and colleague from Texas, even as Mr. Gonzales faced increasing scrutiny for his leadership of the Justice Department over issues including his role in the dismissals of nine United States attorneys late last year and whether he testified truthfully about the National Security Agency's surveillance programs.

But Democrats cheered Mr. Gonzales's departure. "Alberto Gonzales was never the right man for this job," said Senator Harry Reid of Nevada, the majority leader. "He lacked independence, he lacked judgment, and he lacked the spine to say 'no' to Karl Rove."

Senator Charles E. Schumer, the New York Democrat who sits on the Judiciary Committee and has been calling for Mr. Gonzales's resignation for months, said this morning: "It has been

a long and difficult struggle, but at last the attorney general has done the right thing and stepped down. For the previous six months, the Justice Department has been virtually nonfunctional, and desperately needs new leadership."

Another Democrat on the Judiciary Committee who has been highly critical of Mr. Gonzales, Senator Russell D. Feingold of Wisconsin, said the next attorney general must be a person whose first loyalty is "to the law, not the president."

(*Source:* Myer, Stephen Lee, and Philip Shen. "Embattled Attorney General Resigns." *New York Times,* August 27, 2007, http://www.nytimes.com/2007/08/27/washington/27cnd-gonzales.html)

Books

Cole, David, ed. *Securing Liberty: Debating Issues of Terrorism and Democratic Values in the post-9/11 United States.* New York: International Debate Education Association, 2011. Includes Gonzales's statement on surveillance of potential terrorists in a discussion of the Constitutional propriety of such actions.

Minutaglio, Bill. *The President's Counselor: The Rise to Power of Alberto Gonzales.* New York: Rayo, 2006. The only biography of Gonzales, a controversial figure in George W. Bush's White House.

Website

Alberto Gonzales Biography. The Academy of Achievement provides an excellent, short biography of Gonzales. http://www.achievement.org/autodoc/page/gon0bio-1

February 4

1513

Antonio de Alaminos, a pilot traveling with Juan Ponce de León's expedition to Florida, discovers the Gulf Stream. His discovery makes Havana, Cuba, into a major port in the Spanish empire and Florida into a strategic site for shipping. The Gulf Stream current runs from the Straits of Florida into the Bahama channel, past the coast of the Carolinas into the open ocean, where it forks northward to Norway and east to the Azores.

Books

Dolan, Sean. *Juan Ponce de León*. New York: Chelsea House, 1995. Good, short biography of the explorer.

Worth, Richard. *Ponce de León and the Age of Spanish Exploration in World History*. Berkeley Heights, NJ: Enslow, 2003. Sets the brutal conquistador in historical context.

Website

Juan Ponce de León: Explorer. Offers a good biography of the explorer with a map of his travels. http://www.enchantedlearning.com/explorers/page/d/deleon.shtml

February 5

1847

The Siege of Pueblo de Taos, the last significant episode in the Mexican-American War, comes to an end. The trouble began with a revolt against American rule in New Mexico in December 1846. Colonel Sterling Price, in command of U.S. forces in the territory, first encountered resistance at Santa Cruz and Embudo before moving to the center of the revolt, Pueblo de Taos. Price laid siege to the town and bombarded its adobe walls with artillery fire before sending the infantry and militia to subdue the rebels. The dead included 150 to 250 rebels (New Mexicans, Pueblos, and Apaches) as well as 7 Americans.

Books

Francaviglia, Richard V., and Douglas W. Richmond, eds. *Dueling Eagles: Reinterpreting the U.S.-Mexican War, 1846–1848*. Fort Worth: Texas Christian University Press, 2000. Offers essays that challenge the Anglo-centric view of this war.

Reilly, Tom. *War with Mexico!: America's Reporters Cover the Battlefront*. Lawrence: University Press of Kansas, 2010. Examines the information given to Americans about the war.

Websites

The Mexican-American War. Northern Illinois University Libraries offers a history of the war along with primary documents. http://dig.lib.niu.edu/mexicanwar/about.html_

The U.S.-Mexican War. PBS provides a graphic-heavy history of the war with a timeline, biographies of key figures, and a link to additional resources. http://www.pbs.org/kera/usmexicanwar/

February 6

1949

Victor Hernández Cruz, arguably the most acclaimed of the Nuyorican poets, is born in Puerto Rico. Unlike some of the other poets, his books have been published by mainstream presses. Cruz, who classifies his work as Afro-Latin, has been a finalist for the Lenore Marshall Poetry Prize and the Griffin Poetry Prize, as well as a recipient of the Guggenheim Fellowship and the National Endowment for the Arts Fellowship. His poems see beauty in the world as it exists, not how it might become.

From an interview with Laverne González:

> My life and work is to clear the smoke—to make things clear—America Vespucci is a strange place with some weird concepts about reality—it is very easy to be confused here. I write from an inner view—realizing that one first understands oneself; because I write about myself from myself I write about people because I am. In words, I try to make the Universe into the whole that it is—there is only one reality—interpreted many different ways. Many people don't know that they are alive. Words are magic and should not be treated lightly.

(*Source:* Kanellos, Nicolás, ed. *Biographical Dictionary of Hispanic Literature in the United States.* Westport, CT: Greenwood Press, 1989, p. 140.)

Books

Algarin, Miguel, and Bob Holman, eds. *Aloud: Voices from the Nuyorican Café.* New York: Holt, 1994. An anthology of 260 poems by 145 poets and the winner of an American Book Award from the Before Columbus Foundation.

Cruz, Victor Hernández. *In the Shadow of Al-Andalús.* New York: Coffee House Press, 2011. A collection of Cruz's poems.

Websites

Center for Puerto Rican Studies, Hunter College. A major source of information about the Puerto Rican experience and a site linked to Nuyorican writers. http://centropr.hunter.cuny.edu/

Nuyorican Poets Café. An important Puerto Rican cultural institution, this is the place where Cruz and other poets have first presented their work to an audience. http://www.nuyorican.org/

1978

The Cruzada Pro Rescate de Vieques (Crusade to Rescue Vieques) sails a small flotilla into military waters to protest the U.S. Navy's restriction on fishing for the duration of a 30-day training exercise. Vieques is sandwiched between the main island of Puerto Rico to its west and the U.S. Virgin Islands to its east. The U.S. military shifted its training exercises, which included target-practice bombings, to Vieques from Culebra in 1971 following years of pressure from Culebra activists. As a result, portions of Vieques were transformed into an environmental nightmare and health hazard. The shores of the island were strewn with the remains of bullet casings, bomb fragments, and other refuse of war. Local residents complained that the target practice devastated their livelihoods, physical health, and emotional well-being. The Navy ended its Vieques training in 2003.

From Rafael Cruz, past president of the Vieques fishing association:

> The struggle began in 1978 because for years Vieques had been mistreated by the Navy. . . . They bombed the most productive fishing areas. Dropped live bombs. Destroyed many fishing traps. . . . The situation in Vieques is that the fishers have families to support. The only factory that has its door opened to whoever wants to work is the sea. If you have a boat you can go fishing. . . . It's the only source of steady employment in Vieques. And here comes the navy saying for thirty days, you can't fish. This is terrible. Because fishers have bills to pay, they have families to support.

(*Source:* McCaffrey, Katherine T. *Military Power and Popular Protest: The U.S. Navy in Vieques, Puerto Rico.* New Brunswick, NJ: Rutgers University Press, 2002, p.76.)

Books

Barreto, Amicar Antonio. *Vieques, the Navy, and Puerto Rican Politics.* Gainesville: University Press of Florida, 2002. Analyzes the political response by Puerto Ricans and U.S. officials to the Vieques controversy.

McCaffrey, Katherine T. *Military Power and Popular Protest: The U.S. Navy in Vieques, Puerto Rico.* New Brunswick, NJ: Rutgers University Press, 2002. Focuses on the grassroots mobilization in opposition to the U.S. Navy.

Websites

History of the Navy in Vieques. Good, anti-training practice site filled with a timeline, news articles, and other sources about the U.S. Navy on Vieques. http://www.vieques-island.com/navy/

Vieques, Puerto Rico Naval Training Range: Background and Issues for Congress. Provides the U.S. Navy's view of the Vieques dispute with a focus on the post-2001 period. http://www.history.navy.mil/library/online/vieques.htm

2012

An undocumented immigrant from Bolivia is sentenced to 20 years in prison by a judge in Virginia for killing a Benedictine nun while driving drunk. The case garnered enormous attention when it became known that the immigrant, Carlos Martinelly-Montano, was twice convicted for drunk driving and federal authorities had twice delayed his deportation hearing. Prince William County sued the federal government to discover when and why Martinelly-Montano had been released from custody. The county then discovered that Martinelly-Montano had had a string of encounters with the police. The final police encounter occurred when his Subaru Outback swerved off the road, hit a guardrail, and then crossed into a northbound lane on August 10, 2010, before plowing head-on into a Toyota driven by Sister Charlotte Lange who was traveling with two other nuns. One of the passengers, Sister Denise Mosier, died at the scene while Lange suffered significant brain damage and Sister Connie Lupton sustained severe injuries.

From "Caught Unawares by an Anti-Immigrant Mood":

> When Mohamed Mejri, a Tunisian immigrant with a limousine business here, first learned that the State Department of Motor Vehicles had refused to issue him a new driver's license, he thought it was a mistake. After all, he had been a licensed driver in Virginia for years. But last fall, the department stopped accepting his federally issued work permit, a document that was his main proof that he was in the country legally, because he does not have a green card. Now, five months later, his business is collapsing, and bill collectors are calling.

Virginia changed its policy in September after an illegal immigrant from Bolivia was charged with hitting and killing a nun while driving drunk in Prince William County. Her death hardened what was already a strong anti-immigrant mood in the state. Virginia's governor, Bob McDonnell, announced that work permits would no longer be accepted as proof of legal residence because they could be held by people who, like the Bolivian immigrant, are in deportation proceedings. The governor said other documents would still be accepted.

> The permit, called the employment authorization document, allows foreign nationals to work in the United States. Asylum seekers, refugees and students are among those who have one. . . . In a letter to a group of lawyers and immigrant advocacy organizations in January, the commissioner of motor vehicles, Richard D. Holcomb, said that in the 11 weeks after the policy was implemented, about 4,000 applicants entered an "elevated review process," a reference to people who used to rely on the employment card. Of those, only 819 did not immediately get a license, the letter said. By early December, more than 60 percent of those people had received a license using other documents, he wrote, and an additional 3 percent were rejected, mostly because they were in deportation proceedings . . .

(*Source:* Tavernise, Sabrina. "Caught Unawares by an Anti-Immigrant Mood," *New York Times,* February 18, 2011, p. A20.)

Books

Ankarlo, Darrell. *Illegals: The Unacceptable Cost of America's Failure to Control Its Borders.* Nashville: Thomas Nelson, 2010. Uses interviews with immigrants, human traffickers, and Border

Patrol agents to look at the high price paid by everyone connected with illegal immigration from Mexico.

Haugen, David M. *Illegal Immigration: Opposing Viewpoints*. Farmington Hills, MI: Greenhaven, 2011. Part of the popular Opposing Viewpoints series, this book provides articles, speeches, and other materials that illustrate the immigration debate.

Websites

"Drunk-Driving Bolivian Gets 20 Years for Killing Nun." This article by R. Cort Kirkwood in *The New American* provides the best explanation of the case. http://www.thenew american.com/usnews/immigration/item/ 2174-drunk-driving-bolivian-gets-20-years-for-killing-nun

"Illegal Alien from Bolivia Kills Nun." This article is found on the website of the Minuteman Project, an anti-immigration group that views undocumented workers as invaders and sees the immigration issue as a border war. http:// www.minutemanproject.com/article.php?id=260

February 7

1917

The Pancho Villa Expedition, the most remembered episode of the Border War, comes to an end. The United States sent an expeditionary force of 4,800 men under Gen. John J. Pershing to capture Villa after the Mexican had attacked the New Mexican town of Columbus, killing 10 civilians and burning the town after stealing supplies and horses. Pershing's men crossed into Mexico in March 1916. The U.S. Army battled the Villistas but failed in its major objectives of capturing Villa and ending the border raids.

Books

Clendenen, Clarence C. *Blood on the Border: The United States Army and the Mexican Irregulars*. New York: MacMillan, 1969. A good account of the clashes between the Mexican and U.S. forces during the Mexican Revolution.

Eisenhower, John S.D. *Intervention: The United States and the Mexican Revolution, 1913–1917*. New York: W. W. Norton & Company, 1993. This is the standard work on the Punitive Expedition.

Websites

Griffith, Joe. "In Pursuit of Pancho Villa." The Historical Society of the Georgia National Guard published this detailed article on the Punitive Expedition. http://www.hsgng.org/ pages/pancho.htm

Yockelson, Mitchell. "The United States Armed Forces and the Mexican Punitive Expedition." The National Archives website includes this article from the Fall 1997 issue of *Prologue* magazine. http://www.archives.gov/publica tions/prologue/1997/fall/mexican-punitive-expedition-1.html

February 8

2012

The U.S. Department of State issues a travel advisory to U.S. citizens considering a trip to Mexico. The government warns that narcotics-related violence has resulted in the deaths of 47,515 people between December 1, 2006 and September 30, 2011, with 12,903 narcotics-related homicides in the first nine months of 2011 alone. Most of the dead were involved in criminal activity but innocent persons have been caught up in the violence. The Department of State reports that the number of U.S. citizens murdered in Mexico increased from 35 in 2007 to 120 in 2011. Some of the dead are Latinos who crossed the border to visit family.

Books

Grayson, George W. *Mexico: Narco-Violence and a Failed State?* N.P.: Transaction, 2009. Looks at the relationship between drug cartels and the Mexican government and Mexican society.

Kan, Paul Rexton, and Barry R. McCaffrey. *Cartels at War: Mexico's Drug-Fueled Violence and the Threat to U.S. National Security*. Dulles, VA: Potomac, 2012. Discusses how Mexican drug violence has made the border into a nexus of national security and public safety concerns.

February 9

1909

Singer and actress Carmen Miranda is born in Portugal. Miranda's family moved to Brazil when she was 10 months old. After gaining fame in her adopted country, Miranda came to Hollywood in 1939. She quickly became one of the most famous Latino musical stars. By 1946, she was reportedly the highest paid entertainer in the United States. Although light-skinned, Miranda built her persona around an exaggerated representation of the black women of northeastern Brazil, the region where the rhythms of the samba originated. In her films, Miranda typically wore absurd costumes with fruit-adorned hats as part of a tropical image. As a result, she has been parodied quite a bit, although the costumes were in the tradition of the lavish American musicals of the era. In Brazil, she was widely criticized for distorting the country's national identity. She succumbed to a heart attack at age 46 in 1955 after a television appearance.

Books

Gil-Montero, Martha. *Brazilian Bombshell: The Biography of Carmen Miranda.* New York: Dutton, 1989. A sympathetic biography of the Brazilian star.

Roberts, John Storm. *The Latin Tinge: The Impact of Latin American Music on the United States.* New York: Oxford University Press, 1979. A survey of musical stars from the 1920s to the 1970s.

Websites

IMDb—Carmen Miranda. Provides a short biography of Miranda, photographs, and a listing of the movies in which she appeared. http://www.imdb.com/name/nm0000544/

"Carmen Miranda: Bananas Is My Business." *Bright Lights Film Journal.* Reviews the 1995 semi-documentary of the same name about Miranda. http://brightlightsfilm.com/16/carmen.php

February 10

2012

Edward R. Roybal, the longest serving Latino in Congress, is born in Albuquerque, New Mexico. Elected to the U.S. House of Representatives from a district that served Los Angeles, the Mexican American Roybal spent 30 years in Congress. A Democrat, he focused on social and economic reform. In 1967, he authored the first bilingual education legislation. In 1976, he helped found the Congressional Hispanic Caucus and later led the group in opposition to sanctions against employers for hiring undocumented workers. Roybal retired in 1993 and died in 2005.

Books

Novas, Himilce. *The Hispanic 100: A Ranking of the Latino Men and Women Who Have Most Influenced American Thought and Culture.* New York: Carol, 1995. Includes a short biographical essay on Roybal. http://www.amazon.com/Mexico-Narco-Violence-George-W-Grayson/dp/1412811511/ref=sr_1_1?ie=UTF8&qid=1348878783&sr=8-1&keywords=mexico+drug+violence

Ralph Nader Congress Project. *Edward Ross Roybal, Democratic Representative from California.* Washington, D.C.: Grossman Publishers, 1972. Profiles Roybal albeit at a time before some of his major political activities.

Website

Hispanic Americans in Congress: Edward R. Roybal. The Library of Congress profiles Roybal and offers a guide to further reading about the politician. http://www.loc.gov/rr/hispanic/congress/roybal.html

February 11

1903

Over 1,200 Mexican and Japanese farmworkers organize the first farmworker union, the Japanese-Mexican Labor Association (JMLA), in Oxnard, California. Soon after, the workers begin a strike against the Western Agricultural Contracting Company for better wages and an end to being forced to buy goods at the company stores. The Oxnard Strike of 1903 ends in a victory for the workers, making the JMLA the first farmworker union to win a strike against the powerful California agricultural industry.

Books

Derks, Scott. *Working Americans, 1880–2003*. Millerton, NY: Grey House, 2003. One of the few general histories of workers in the United States in the early part of the 20th century.

Jourdane, Maurice. *The Struggle for the Health and Legal Protection of Farmworkers*. Houston, TX: Arte Público, 2004. Explores some of the same issues that the early union fought to improve.

February 12

2012

Latin Jazz musicians hold a concert in Los Angeles, on the same night as the Grammy Awards, to protest a decision to eliminate 31 award categories including Latin Jazz, Regional Mexican, Banda, Tejano, and Norteño music. The National Academy of Recording Arts and Sciences, the group behind the Grammy Awards, did not consult the rank-and-file members on the decision.

Books

Fernández, Raúl A. *From Afro-Cuban Rhythms to Latin Jazz*. Berkeley: University of California Press, 2006. The only book-length history of Latin Jazz.

Morales, Ed. *The Latin Beat: The Rhythms and Roots of Latin Music from Bossa Nova to Salsa and Beyond*. Cambridge, MA: Da Capo Press, 2003. Covers the Latin influence on rock music.

February 13

1501

Queen Isabella and King Ferdinand of Spain send the first Spanish governor in the New World, Nicolás de Ovando y Cáceres, to the Caribbean. He sails to Hispaniola with 30 ships and 2,500 settlers, mostly aristocrats and nobles. On April 15, Ovando assumes command of the island. Typical of soldiers of his time, he displays considerable brutality toward the native Taino population, which was expected to provide food for the Spanish and mine gold for them. He also brings the first African slaves to the Americas. Ovando was recalled to Spain in 1509 because of his harsh treatment of the Indians.

Books

Ferguson, Moira. *Jamaica Kincaid: Where the Land Meets the Body*. Charlottesville: University Press of Virginia, 1994. Examines the connection between imperialism and literature, with a particular focus on Ovando.

Lamb, Ursula. *Frey Nicolás de Ovando: Gobernador de las Indias, 1501–1509*. Madrid, Consejo Superior de Investigaciones Científicas, Instituto Gonzalo Fernández de Oviedo, 1956. The only readily-available biography of Ovando is this Spanish-language one.

Websites

Nicolás de Ovando. Encyclopedia Britannica supplies this short biography of the conquistador. http://www.britannica.com/EBchecked/topic/435762/Nicolas-de-Ovando

Nicolás de Ovando. A Spanish language biographical essay. http://www.biografiasyvidas.com/biografia/o/ovando.htm

2001

The U.S. Treasury Department authorizes the release of $96.7 million in frozen Cuban funds to the families of three Miami-based Cuban American pilots who were shot down by Cuban fighter jets on February 24, 1996.

The dead pilots, Armando Alejandre, Carlos Alberto Costa and Mario M. de la Peña, were part of Brothers to the Rescue and were searching for Cuban refugees on rafts to help them. While one pilot had strayed into Cuban air space, the two others were shot down in international territory. The families won a wrongful death lawsuit in 1997 and had sought to access money that had been frozen since 1963. The family of a fourth dead pilot, Pablo Morales, was not part of the suit.

Books

Prellezo, Lily, and José Basulto. *Seagull One: The Amazing True Story of Brothers to the Rescue*. Gainesville: University Press of Florida, 2010. As the title indicates, this account is heavily biased in favor of those opposed to the Cuban regime and supportive of Brothers to the Rescue.

Sweig, Julia E. *Cuba: What Everyone Needs to Know*. New York: Oxford University Press, 2009. Includes a brief discussion of the Brothers to the Rescue episode.

2012

Ramón Saldívar, a scholar of Chicano literature, and Teofilo F. Ruíz, a historian of Spain, receive National Humanities Medals. The medal, awarded since 1997, honors individuals or groups whose work has deepened the nation's understanding of the humanities, broadened engagement with the humanities, or helped preserve and expand Americans' access to important resources in the humanities. Saldívar, who grew up in a working-class, Spanish-speaking household in Brownsville, Texas and is now a Stanford University professor, is honored for exploring the borders of American and Mexican literature. Ruíz, born into a middle-class Cuban family, opposed dictator Fulgencio Batista but also did not like his successor, Fidel Castro. Jailed prior to the Bay of Pigs invasion, Ruíz left Cuba upon his release. Told to pursue teaching at the university level because his accent was too pronounced for the high school classroom, Ruíz is a specialist in medieval and early modern Spain at the University of California, Los Angeles.

Books

Ruíz, Teofilo F. *Spain's Centuries of Crisis, 1300–1474*. Oxford: Wiley-Blackwell, 2011. Shows what was happening in Spain in the decades before it conquered the New World.

Ruíz, Teofilo F. *The Terror of History: On the Uncertainties of Life in Western Civilization*. Princeton, NJ: Princeton University Press. This social history of terror further reinforces that the "good old days" were in reality quite miserable.

Saldívar, Ramón. *Chicano Narrative: The Dialectics of Difference*. Madison, WI: University of Wisconsin Press, 1990. Explores what makes a novel into a Chicano one.

Saldívar, Ramón. *The Borderlands of Culture: Américo Paredes and the Transnational Imaginary*. Durham: Duke University Press, 2006. A study of the famed Mexican American folklorist.

February 14

1912

Arizona achieves statehood as the 48th state in the Union. It is the last of the contiguous states to be admitted to the Union. Probably named after the Spanish word, *arizonac,* which approximated a Native American word for "small spring," Arizona joined the United States following the Mexican-American War.

Books

Officer, James E. *Hispanic Arizona, 1536–1856*. Tucson: University of Arizona Press, 1987. A history of the state from the days of Spanish control to the decade following the U.S. takeover.

Sheridan, Thomas E. *Arizona: A History*. Tucson: University of Arizona Press, 2012. A voluminous history of the state.

Websites

Arizona Capitol Museum. The Arizona Constitution was signed in the Territorial Capitol in Phoenix, which is now this state-run museum on Arizona's history. http://www.azlibrary.gov/museum/

Arizona Memory Project. Contains over 89,000 digital items relating to Arizona history. http://azmemory.azlibrary.gov/cdm/

February 15

1932

Benjamin Cardozo, a scion of a Sephardic Jewish family, becomes the first Latino to be named to the U.S. Supreme Court. Appointed by President Herbert Hoover to fill the vacancy caused by the retirement of Oliver Wendell Holmes, Cardozo had served on the New York Supreme Court. He became known as the most influential liberal judge of his era and is particularly noted for his opinion upholding the Social Security Act.

From the U.S. Supreme Court decision upholding Social Security, 1936:

Mr. Justice Cardozo Delivered the Opinion of the Court

The Social Security Act (Act of August 14, 1935, c. 531, 49 Stat 620, 42 U. S. C., c. 7, (Supp.)) is challenged once again.

This suit is brought by a shareholder of the Edison Electric Illuminating Company of Boston, a Massachusetts corporation, to restrain the corporation from making the payments and deductions called for by the act, which is stated to be void under the Constitution of the United States. The bill tells us that the corporation has decided to obey the statute, that it has reached this decision in the face of the complainant's protests, and that it will make the payments and deductions unless restrained by a decree. The expected consequences are indicated substantially as follows: The deductions from the wages of the employees will produce unrest among them, and will be followed, it is predicted, by demands that wages be increased. If the exactions shall ultimately be held void, the company will have parted with moneys which as a practical matter it will be impossible to recover. Nothing is said in the bill about the promise of indemnity. The prediction is made also that serious consequences will ensue if there is a submission to the excise. The corporation and its shareholders will suffer irreparable loss, and many thousands of dollars will be subtracted from the value of the shares. The prayer is for an injunction and for a declaration that the act is void.

The corporation appeared and answered without raising any issue of fact. Later the United States Commissioner of Internal Revenue and the United States Collector for the District of Massachusetts, petitioners in this court, were allowed to intervene. They moved to strike so much of the bill as has relation to the tax on employees taking the ground that the employer not being subject to tax under those provisions, may not challenge their validity, and that the complainant shareholder, whose rights are no greater than those of his corporation, has even less standing to be heard on such a question. The intervening defendants also filed an answer which restated the point raised in the motion to strike, and maintained the validity of Title VIII in all its parts. The District Court held that the tax upon employees was not properly at issue, and that the tax upon employers was constitutional. It thereupon denied the prayer for an injunction, and dismissed the bill. On appeal to the Circuit Court of Appeals for the First Circuit, the decree was reversed, one judge dissenting. The court held that Title II was void as an invasion of powers reserved by the Tenth Amendment to the states or to the people and that Title II in collapsing carried Title VIII along with it. As an additional reason for invalidating the tax upon employers, the court held that it was not an excise as excises were understood when the Constitution was adopted. Cf. Davis v. Boston & Maine R.R. Co.,—F. (2d)—, decided the same day.

A petition for certiorari followed. It was filed by the intervening defendants, the Commissioner and the Collector, and brought two questions, and two only, to our notice. We were asked to determine: (1) "whether the tax imposed upon employers by Section 804 of the Social Security Act is within the power of Congress under tile Constitution", and (2) "whether the validity of the tax imposed upon employees by Section 801 of the Social Security Act is properly in issue in this case, and if it is, whether that tax is within the power of Congress under the Constitution." The defendant corporation gave notice to the Clerk that it joined in the petition, but it has taken no part in any subsequent proceedings. A writ of certiorari issued.

Congress may spend money in aid of the "general welfare". Constitution, Art. I, section 8; United States v. Butler, 297 U. S. 1, 65; Steward Machine Co. v. Davis, supra. There have been great statesmen in our history who have stood for other views. We will not resurrect the contest. It is now settled by decision. United States v. Butler, supra The conception of the spending power advocated by Hamilton and strongly reinforced by Story has prevailed over that of Madison, which has not been lacking in adherents. Yet difficulties are left when the power is conceded. The line must still be drawn between one welfare and another, between particular and general. Where this shall be placed cannot be known through a formula in advance of the event. There is a middle ground or certainly a penumbra in which discretion is at large. The discretion, however, is not confided to the courts. The discretion belongs to Congress, unless the choice is clearly wrong, a display of arbitrary power is not an exercise of judgment. This is now familiar law. "When such a contention comes here we naturally require a showing that by no reasonable possibility can the challenged legislation fall within the wide range of discretion permitted to the Congress." United States v. Butler, supra, p. 67 Cf. Cincinnati Soap Co. v United States, May 3,1937,—U. S.—; United States v. Realty Co. 163 U. S. 427, 440; Head Money Cases, 112 U. S. 580, 595. Nor is the concept of the general welfare static. Needs that were narrow or parochial a century ago may be interwoven in our day with the well-being of the nation. What is critical or urgent changes with the times.

Congress did not improvise a judgment when it found that the award of old age benefits would be conducive to the general welfare. The President's Committee on Economic Security made an investigation and report, aided by a research staff of Government officers and employees, and by an Advisory Council and seven other advisory groups. Extensive hearings followed before the House Committee on Ways and Means and the Senate Committee on Finance. A great mass of evidence was brought together supporting the policy which finds expression in the act. Among the relevant facts are these: The number of persons in the United States 65 years of age or over is increasing proportionately as well as absolutely. What is even more important the number of such persons unable to take care of themselves is growing at a threatening pace. More and more our population is becoming urban and industrial instead of rural and agricultural. The evidence is impressive that among industrial workers the younger men and women are preferred over the older. In time of retrenchment the older are commonly the first to go, and even if retained, their wages are likely to be lowered. The plight of men and women at so low an age as 40 is hard, almost hopeless, when they are driven to seek for reemployment. Statistics are in the brief. A few illustrations will be chosen from many there collected. In 1930, out of 224 American factories investigated, 71, or almost one third, had fixed maximum hiring age limits; in 4 plants the limit was under 40; in 41 it was under 46. In the other 153 plants there were no fixed limits, but in practice few were hired if they were over 50 years of age. With the loss of savings inevitable in periods of idleness, the fate of workers over 65, when thrown out of work, is little less than desperate. A recent study of the Social Security Board informs us that "one-fifth of the aged in the United States were receiving old age assistance, emergency relief, institutional care, employment under the works program, or some other form of aid from public or private funds; two-fifths to one-half were dependent on friends and relatives, one-eighth had some income from earnings; and possibly one-sixth had some savings or property. Approximately three out of four persons 65 or over were probably dependent wholly or partially on others for support."

The problem is plainly national in area and dimensions. Moreover laws of the separate states cannot deal with it effectively. . . . Whether wisdom or unwisdom resides in the scheme of benefits set forth in Title II, it is not for us to say. The answer to such inquiries must come from Congress, not the courts. . . .

(*Source:* U.S. Supreme Court, No. 910, October Term 1936, *Helvering v. Davis,* http://www.ssa.gov/history/supreme1. html)

Books

Kaufman, Andrew L. *Cardozo.* Cambridge, MA: Harvard University Press, 1998. A monumental study of the justice that is the standard history of Cardozo.

Manz, William H. *Records and Briefs of Landmark Benjamin Cardozo Opinions.* Buffalo, NY: W. S. Hein, 1999. The opinions of one of the most respected Supreme Court justices.

Polenberg, Richard. *The World of Benjamin Cardozo: Personal Values and the Judicial Process.* Cambridge, MA: Harvard University Press, 1997. An excellent biography that, by virtue of its shorter length, is more accessible than the Kaufman study.

Websites

Justice Benjamin N. Cardozo, 1870–1938. The Social Security Agency provides this short history of Cardozo in its Social Security History section. http://www.ssa.gov/history/cardozo.htm

Supreme Court Justices: Benjamin N. Cardozo. Supplies a short biography of the justice http://www.michaelariens.com/ConLaw/justices/cardozo.htm

1968

César Chávez, head of the United Farm Workers, begins a 25-day, water-only fast to protest a potentially violent response to violent attacks on farmworkers. Angry workers thought they could only succeed with violence. Chávez argued that only a nonviolent strategy would keep the movement alive and prosperous. He would repeat the fasts in 1972 and 1988.

Books

Del Castillo, Richard Griswold, and Richard A. Garcia. *César Chávez: A Triumph of Spirit.*

Norman: University of Oklahoma Press, 1995. The best account of Chávez and his links to the Chicano Movement.

Levy, Jacques E. *César Chávez: Autobiography of La Causa*. New York: W. W. Norton, 1975. Provides an account of Chávez's early years, his initial efforts as an organizer, and his rise to the leadership of Mexican American farmworkers.

Websites

César Chávez: Labor Leader. Enchanted Learning offers a biography of Chávez as well as numerous activities for children that teach about the union leader. http://www.enchantedlearning.com/history/us/hispanicamerican/chavez/

The Story of César Chávez. The United Farm Workers provides a biography of its famed leader. http://www.ufw.org/_page.php?inc=history/07.html&menu=research

1970

The crash of a Dominican Airlines DC-9 kills 102 people en route to San Juan, Puerto Rico. Among the dead are the former world boxing lightweight champion Carlos Teo Cruz and most of the members of the Puerto Rican women's volleyball team. The jet experienced failure of both engines shortly after takeoff and fell into the sea near Santo Domingo.

Website

Carlos Teo Cruz. BoxRec provides career statistics and photographs of the Dominican boxer. http://boxrec.com/list_bouts.php?human_id=012684&cat=boxer

1974

Romana A. Banuelos resigns as Treasurer of the United States. The first Latina to hold the largely ceremonial position, she was the highest ranking Hispanic in the Richard Nixon administration. Her signature appeared on all U.S. currency. Prior to taking the federal post, Banuelos headed Romana's Mexican Food Products in Gardenia, California, and cofounded Pan American National Bank in East Los Angeles. Banuelos

and her partners established the bank in 1963 partly in the belief that if Hispanics could increase their financial base, they would have more political influence and be able to improve their standard of living.

Books

Meier, Matt S., et al. *Notable Latino Americans: A Biographical Dictionary*. Westport, CT: Greenwood Press, 1997. Offers a short profile of the banker.

Websites

1963: Romana Acosta Banuelos. The Minority Banking Timeline, part of the Federal Reserve System's Partnership for Progress, offers a short profile of the banker. http://www.fedpartnership.gov/minority-banking-timeline/romana-banuelos.cfm

"From Tortillas to Banks: A Latina's Pursuit of the American Dream." An account of Baneulos's rise on the website of Pan American National Bank. http://egpnews.com/2009/10/from-tortillas-to-banks-a-latina%E2%80%99s-pursuit-of-the-american-dream-is-honored/

February 16

2012

Mexico's President Felipe Calderón calls on U.S. officials to stop gun trafficking across the border to halt vicious drug violence. Speaking in Ciudad Juarez, the border city across from El Paso, Texas, that has become Mexico's murder capital, Calderón said a dramatic increase in violence in Mexico was directly connected with the 2004 expiration of the U.S. assault weapons ban. The violence has badly hurt merchants in Mexican border cities as Americans fear to travel to Mexico.

Books

Grayson, George W. *Mexico: Narco-Violence and a Failed State?* N.P.: Transaction, 2009. Looks at the relationship between drug cartels, the Mexican government, and Mexican society.

Kan, Paul Rexton, and Barry R. McCaffrey. *Cartels at War: Mexico's Drug-Fueled Violence and the Threat to U.S. National Security.* Dulles, VA: Potomac, 2012. Discusses how Mexican drug violence has made the border into a nexus of national security and public safety concerns.

February 17

1914

Julia de Burgos, one of Puerto Rico's greatest poets, is born in Carolina, Puerto Rico. She moved to New York in 1940 but always viewed the city as a cold, inhospitable place. Many of her poems sing of the beauty of Puerto Rico, her love of nature, and her desire for freedom. Burgos died in New York City in 1953.

Books

Agueros, Jack, trans. and comp. *Song of the Simple Truth: The Complete Poems, Julia de Burgos.* Willimantic, CT: Curbstone Press, 1997. The only collection of Burgos's poems in English.

Jiménez de Báez, Yvette. *Julia de Burgos: Vida y Poesía.* San Juan de Puerto Rico: Editorial Coquí, 1966. There is no English language biography of the poet. This study, in Spanish, was originally written as a Master of Arts thesis.

Websites

Julia de Burgos Cultural Arts Center. This Cleveland, Ohio center celebrates Puerto Rican culture. http://www.juliadeburgos.org/

Julia de Burgos. A short biography with photographs of the poet. http://www.elboricua.com/JuliaDeBurgos.html

1929

The League of United Latin American Citizens (LULAC) is created in Corpus Christi, Texas. It is the largest Latino civil rights and advocacy group in the United States. In its early years, LULAC proclaimed its mission to be self-preservation, equal education, and the abolition of illegal segregation as well as racial hatred. In the 1920s, LULAC proved to be politically conservative and worked to improve the image of Mexican Americans among Anglo-Americans. However, members still faced considerable harassment from Anglos who did not want Mexicans to improve their education. Members, who had to be U.S. citizens, sometimes lost their jobs for joining LULAC. Over time, the organization expanded to include Latinos from across the United States. It advocates on behalf of language and cultural rights as well as other civil rights issues.

From LULAC "Aims and Purposes":

> We believe that education is the foundation for the cultural growth and development of this nation and that we are obligated to protect and promote the education of our people in accordance with the best American principles and standards.
>
> We accept that it is not only the privilege but the obligation of every member of this organization to uphold and defend the rights and duties vested in every American Citizen by the letter and the spirit of the law of the land.
>
> As members of a democratic society, we recognize our civic duties and responsibilities and we propose:
>
> That, in the interest of the public welfare, we shall seek in every possible way to uphold the rights guaranteed to every individual by our state and national laws and to seek justice and equality of treatment in accordance with the law of the land.
>
> We shall courageously resist unAmerican tendencies that deprive citizens of these rights in educational institutions, in economic pursuits, and in social and civil activities.

(*Source:* Márquez, Benjamin. *LULAC: The Evolution of a Mexican American Political Organization.* Austin: University of Texas Press, 1993, p. 19.)

Books

Kaplowitz, Craig. *LULAC, Mexican Americans, and National Policy.* College Station, TX: Texas A&M University Press, 2005. Focuses on the years after 1960 as the group connected with the broader societal demand for civil rights for minorities.

Márquez, Benjamin. *LULAC: The Evolution of a Mexican American Political Organization*. Austin: University of Texas Press, 1993, p. 19. A good historical study of the political group, complete with membership information.

Websites

League of United Latin American Citizens—The Handbook of Texas Online. Provides a brief but good history of the organization. http://www.tshaonline.org/handbook/online/articles/wel01

LULAC. The official website of the organization. http://lulac.org/

February 18

1898

Luis Muñoz Marín, the father of modern Puerto Rico, is born in San Juan, Puerto Rico. Muñoz Marín, a poet and journalist, wrote frequently about Puerto Rico's low wages, unemployment, bad living conditions, and inactive government officials in American newspapers and magazines. Beginning in 1926, he edited *La Democracia* in San Juan. In 1932, Muñoz Marín joined the Puerto Rican Senate as a member of the Liberal Party and later helped start the Popular Democratic Party. In 1948, he became Puerto Rico's first democratically elected governor and served until 1965. Muñoz Marín died in 1980, 17 years after receiving the Presidential Medal of Freedom.

Books

Maldonado, A. W. *Luis Muñoz Marín: Puerto Rico's Democratic Revolution*. San Juan: Editorial Universidad de Puerto Rico, 2006. An exhaustive study of the life and times of this modern Puerto Rican leader.

Mann, Peggy. *Luis Muñoz Marín: The Man Who Remade Puerto Rico*. New York: Coward, McCann & Geoghegan, 1976. A short biography of the revered political leader.

Websites

Luis Muñoz Marín. An *Encyclopedia Britannica* essay on the statesman. http://www.britannica.com/EBchecked/topic/397620/Luis-Munoz-Marin

Don Luis Muñoz Marín, the Father of Puerto Rico, 1898–1980. Good biography of the politician that does not attempt a balanced approach to his career and legacy. http://www.elboricua.com/BKLuisMunozMarin.html

1946

The Ninth U.S. District Court of Southern California rules in *Mendez v. Westminster School District* that children of Latin descent cannot be segregated. The decision, several years before the more-famous *Brown* decision, is a major blow against segregation. The case begins when Gonzalo Mendez, William Guzman, Frank Palomino, Thomas Estrada, and Lorenzo Ramirez file a lawsuit on behalf of their children. They argue that it is custom that all children of Mexican or Latin descent are excluded from attending, using, enjoying, and receiving the benefits of certain schools within the Santa Ana district and that these schools are maintained for the exclusive use of people of Anglo-Saxon descent. Mendez and the others argue that this segregation violates the equal protection clause of the Fourteenth Amendment.

From "A Desegregation Landmark":

> In the mid-1940s, Westminster had only two schools—Hoover Elementary and 17th Street Elementary. El Modena, Santa Ana and Garden Grove school districts also mandated separate campuses for Hispanics. Sylvia, Gonzalo Jr. and Jerome Mendez and the other Hispanics attended Hoover, a two-room wooden shack in the middle of the city's Mexican neighborhood. About a mile away stood 17th Street Elementary. A row of palm and pine trees and a lawn lined the school's brick and concrete facade.

"I didn't understand why they wouldn't let my brothers and I in the nice school," said Sylvia Mendez, now 70 and a resident of Fullerton. . . . The U.S. Supreme Court would later cite the 1947 Mendez decision in the 1954 Brown v. Board of Ed. case.

(*Source:* Leal, Fermin. "A Desegregation Landmark." *Orange County Register,* March 21, 2007, http://www.mendezvwestminster.com/)

Books

Martin, Waldo E. *Brown v. Board: A Brief History with Documents.* New York: Bedford/St. Martin's, 1998. Accessible history of the landmark Supreme Court ruling that integrated classrooms.

Strum, Philippa. *Mendez v. Westminster: School Desegregation and Mexican-American Rights.* Lawrence: University Press of Kansas, 2010. Highly readable history of the civil rights case that is often used as a college classroom text.

Websites

Mendez v. Westminster: A Look at Our Latino Heritage. Includes links to the Stanford University Mendez collection, the PBS documentary film on the topic, the trial court decision, and teacher training material. http://www.mendezvwestminster.com/

Mendez v. Westminster. This LearnCalifornia site provides the full text of the decision. http://www.learncalifornia.org/doc.asp?id=1508

1969

Boxer Armando Ramos becomes the first Mexican American to win the world lightweight championship with his knockout of Dominican Carlos Teo Cruz in Los Angeles. Born in California in 1948, "Mando" Ramos fought 10 title fights and was a two-time champion. His victories and charisma set off "mandomania," especially among women. After his boxing career ended in the early 1970s, Ramos founded a nonprofit association, Boxing Against Alcohol and Drugs (BADD). He died on July 6, 2008, the same year that he entered the California Boxing Hall of Fame.

Websites

Mando Ramos. BoxRec provides career statistics for the famed boxer. http://boxrec.com/list_bouts.php?human_id=30295&cat=boxer

Mando Ramos. Entertaining essay on Ramos's career by boxing writer Rick Farris. http://www.cyberboxingzone.com/boxing/wail1100_rick.htm

February 19

1917

The British present the Zimmermann Telegram to the U.S. government, thus prompting the United States to declare war against Germany and enter World War I. German foreign secretary Arthur Zimmermann had sought a military alliance with Mexico. In return for attacking the United States, Mexico was promised the return of the territory it had lost during the Mexican-American War, which was about a third of Mexican land in the form of Texas, New Mexico, and Arizona. The Mexican government declined the offer on the grounds that Mexico lacked the capability to retake the lands. However, by this time, British intelligence officers had captured the telegram and decoded it.

The decoded text of the Zimmermann Telegram, sent by Zimmermann on January 16, 1917:

We intend to begin on the 1st of February unrestricted submarine warfare. We shall endeavor in spite of this to keep the United States of America neutral. In the event of this not succeeding, we make Mexico a proposal of alliance on the following basis: make war together, make peace together, generous financial support and an understanding on our part that Mexico is to reconquer the lost territory in Texas, New Mexico and Arizona. The settlement in detail is left to you. You will inform the President of the above most secretly as soon as the outbreak of war with the United States of America is certain and add the suggestion that he should, on his own initiative, invite Japan to immediate adherence and at the same time mediate between Japan and ourselves. Please call the President's attention to the fact that the ruthless employment of our submarines now offers the prospect of compelling England in a few months to make peace. Signed, Zimmermann.

(*Source:* "The Zimmermann Note," World War I Document Archive, Brigham Young University, http://wwi.lib.byu.edu/index.php/The_Zimmerman_Note)

Books

Friedman, William F. *The Zimmermann Telegram of January 16, 1917 and Its Cryptographic Background*. Laguna Hills, Calif.: Aegean Park Press, 1976. The decoding of the telegram is one of the greatest events in the history of military intelligence.

Tuchman, Barbara. *The Zimmermann Telegram*. London: Folio Society, 2004. This is the standard history of the telegram and an extremely readable account.

Websites

World War I Document Archive. This archive of World War I documents has an international focus and a wealth of material. http://wwi.lib.byu.edu/index.php/Main_Page

WWI Era from a New Mexican Perspective. With maps and primary sources, the City of Albuquerque provides an excellent history of the cross-border conflict between Mexico and the United States as well as a good account of the military actions of New Mexican men. http://www.cabq.gov/parksandrecreation/parks/veterans-memorial-park/documents/WWIEraFromANewMexicanPerspective.pdf

February 20

2012

A federal judge rejects the part of a city ordinance in Fremont, Nebraska, that sought to ban the renting of property to illegal immigrants as discriminatory. Much of the rest of the ordinance is upheld, including provisions that allow the city to check the citizenship status of tenants and require employers to use the federal E-Verify database to ensure that potential employees are legally allowed to work. The legal challenge was filed by the Mexican American Legal Defense and Educational Fund in conjunction with the American Civil Liberties Union.

Books

Bacal, Azril. *Types of Ethnic Identity Responses to Ethnic Discrimination: An Experiential Approach to Mexican American Identity*. Uppsala, Sweden: Goteborgs University, 1994. Discusses how Mexican Americans protest discriminatory behavior directed at Mexican Americans.

Orozco, Cynthia. *No Mexicans, Women, or Dogs Allowed: The Rise of the Mexican American Civil Rights Movement*. Austin: University of Texas Press, 2009. Provides a historical context for this particular protest.

February 21

1862

One of the few Civil War battles fought in New Mexico, the Battle of Valverde resulted in a Confederate victory but not the taking of Fort Craig that the Confederates had sought. When Texas joined the Confederacy, the Union was concerned about the security of New Mexico Territory. Fort Craig guarded the capital of Santa Fe. Brigadier General Henry Sibley of the Confederacy moved his forces to take Santa Fe, held by forces under the command of Col. Edward Canby. Sibley won the battle of Valverde but did not have enough remaining strength to take the fort. The United States lost 202 men while the Confederate had 187 casualties. After the battle, Colonel Canby would blame his defeat on Mexican volunteers in his official report. In reality, several regiments of Latino volunteers fought bravely and with discipline. Canby's version of events became the standard story because of widespread racial prejudice.

From one of Lewis R. Roe's Civil War letters, February 1862:

Upon Col. Canby [Union] assuming command, the forts in Arizona were ordered abandoned, their garrisons concentrating at Fort Fillmore, N.M. on the Rio Grande, 10 miles north of the Texas line and 120 miles south of Fort Craig.

Early in 1862 rumors were afloat that there was a force of Texans [Confederate] variously estimated at from 3,000 to 4,000, marching to invade New Mexico; also that there was a regiment of volunteers from Colorado coming to our assistance. A regiment of New Mexican volunteers, made up of peons and greasers, was also raised. Meanwhile the Texans came on, and encamped opposite Fort Fillmore, N.M. They were encamped there for some time, and a demand was made for the surrender of the fort. . . .

On Feb. 19, 1862, the Texans appeared before Fort Craig, making a show of force, but withdrew on the 20th. They appeared on the opposite side of the river. A portion of our troops were sent across the river on picket. The rebels opened with a few cannon shots, doing no damage. On the morning of the 21st they moved up the river, still on the opposite or eastern side. Leaving a few troops in the fort, Col. Canby put our forces in motion also up the river on the western side. At a wide bottom called "Valverde" we crossed over. The Mexicans did not cross, but

remained on the west bank. The Texans were found posted behind long, low sand ridges. As soon as we came within range, a brisk skirmish fire was kept up for some time. . . .

The recall was sounded, our lines were rearranged with two 12-pound cannons on our right and a battery of four mountain howitzers on our left, commanded by Capt. McRae, Co. F, 7th U.S. was ordered to their support. We lay down behind the pieces while the artillery of both sides kept up a fire for some time. At last the rebels charged us, but were repulsed. Again they came on, this time in far greater numbers. We stood to our posts, the artillerymen standing to their guns as long as possible. We met the Texans at the muzzles of the cannon, but were overpowered by force of numbers.

I heard no orders, no shouting, no yelling. Everybody was busy fighting. We finally gave way, and found that the rest of our force had recrossed the river and were on their way to the fort.

On Feb. 22 the Texans sent in a flag of truce demanding a surrender of the fort. This was refused. They said they would take our fort as they did our battery, with revolvers and bowie knives. But they evidently thought better of it. They moved up the river, capturing Albuquerque, and were on the march for Fort Union, in the northeastern part of the Territory, when they were met by the two regiments of Colorado volunteers.

(*Source:* Wilson, John P., ed. *From Western Deserts to Carolina Swamps: A Civil War Soldier's Journals and Letters Home.* Albuquerque: University of New Mexico Press, 2012, pp. 63–65.)

Books

Taylor, John. *Bloody Valverde: A Civil War Battle on the Rio Grande, February 21, 1862.*

Albuquerque: University of New Mexico Press, 1995. A view of the battle that represents modern thinking about race.

Wilson, John P., ed. *From Western Deserts to Carolina Swamps: A Civil War Soldier's Journals and Letters Home*. Albuquerque: University of New Mexico Press, 2012. Lewis R. Roe's account of serving in New Mexico on the Union side is one of the very, very few surviving accounts from Civil War soldiers in the region.

Websites

Battle of Valverde. The Handbook of Texas Online, sponsored by the Texas State Historical Association, provides a short history of the battle that involved so many Texans. http://www.tshaonline.org/handbook/online/articles/qev01

Valverde. The American Battlefield Protection Program of the National Park Service provides this summary of the battle. http://www.nps.gov/hps/abpp/battles/nm001.htm

2012

The Los Angeles County Board of Supervisors issues a formal apology for the repatriation of more than 1 million U.S. citizens who were forced to relocate to Mexico in the 1930s. During the Great Depression, Mexican workers were seen as taking jobs from Americans. It is estimated that 2 million people of Latino ancestry were persuaded by violence and harassment to move during the mass migration and about 60 percent of those were born in the United States. About 400,000 U.S. citizens and legal residents were pushed to Mexico from California alone.

Books

González, Juan. *Harvest of Empire: A History of Latinos in America*. New York: Penguin, 2000. Written by a journalist, this is an easy-to-read account of Latino migration and influence.

Hernández, Kelly. *Migra!: A History of the U.S. Border Patrol*. Berkeley: University of California Press, 2010. Covers the forced migration of Mexican workers in the 1930s as well as the efforts of Mexican border police to force Chinese immigrants to the American side.

February 22

1819

Spain and the United States sign the Adams-Onís Treaty in which Spain gives up control over Florida after over 300 years of possession. Negotiated by U.S. secretary of state John Quincy Adams and Spanish diplomat Luís de Onís, the treaty gave the United States possession of Florida in exchange for the United States agreeing to pay the claims of Spanish citizens up to $5 million and surrendered claims on parts of Texas west of the Sabine River. The treaty also established a definitive boundary between Spanish-held Mexico and the U.S. territory gained in the Louisiana Purchase. Signed by both Adams and Onís in Washington, D.C., the treaty was not ratified and put into effect until two years later, on February 22, 1821.

From the Adams-Onís Treaty:

The United States of America and His Catholic Majesty desiring to consolidate on a permanent basis the friendship and good correspondence which happily prevails between the two Parties, have determined to settle and terminate all their differences and pretensions by a Treaty, which shall designate with precision the limits of their respective bordering territories in North America. . . .

His Catholic Majesty cedes to the United States, in full property and sovereignty, all the territories which belong to him, situated to the Eastward of the Mississippi, known by the name of East and West Florida. The adjacent Islands dependent on said Provinces, all public lots and squares, vacant Lands, public Edifices, Fortifications, Barracks and other Buildings, which are not private property, Archives and Documents, which relate directly to the property and sovereignty of said Provinces, are included in this Article. The said Archives and Documents shall be left in possession of the Commissaries, or Officers of the United States, duly authorized to receive them. . . .

The Boundary Line between the two Countries, West of the Mississippi, shall begin on the Gulf of Mexico, at the mouth of the River Sabine in the Sea, continuing North, along the Western Bank of that River, to the 32d degree of Latitude; thence by a Line due North to the degree of Latitude, where it strikes the Rio Roxo of Nachitoches, or Red-River, then following the course of the Rio-Roxo Westward to the degree of Longitude, 100 West from London and 23 from Washington, then crossing the said Red-River, and running thence by a Line due North to the River Arkansas, thence, following the Course of the Southern bank of the Arkansas to its source in Latitude, 42. North and thence by that parallel of Latitude to the South-Sea. The whole being as laid down in Melishe's Map of the United States, published at Philadelphia, improved to the first of January 1818. But if the Source of the Arkansas River shall be found to fall North or South of Latitude 42, then the Line shall run from the said Source due South or North, as the case may be, till it meets the said Parallel of Latitude 42, and thence along the said Parallel to the South Sea: all the Islands in the Sabine and the Said Red and Arkansas Rivers, throughout the Course thus described, to belong to the United States; but the use of the Waters and the navigation of the Sabine to the Sea, and of the said Rivers, Roxo and Arkansas, throughout the extent of the said Boundary, on their respective Banks, shall be common to the respective inhabitants of both Nations. The Two High Contracting Parties agree to cede and renounce all their rights, claims and pretensions to the Territories described by the said Line: that is to say.—The United States hereby cede to His Catholic Majesty, and renounce forever, all their rights, claims, and pretensions to the Territories lying West and South of the above described Line; and, in like manner, His Catholic Majesty cedes to the said United States, all his rights, claims, and pretensions to any Territories, East and North of the said Line, and, for himself, his heirs and successors, renounces all claim to the said Territories forever. . . .

The Inhabitants of the Territories which His Catholic Majesty cedes to the United States by this Treaty, shall be incorporated in the Union of the United States, as soon as may be consistent with the principle of the Federal Constitution, and admitted to the enjoyment of all the privileges, rights and immunities of the Citizens of the United States.

(*Source:* Bevans, Charles I., ed. *Treaties and Other International Agreements of the United States of America, 1776–1949.* http://www.tamu.edu/faculty/ccbn/dewitt/adamonis.htm)

1870

Puerto Rican labor leader Santiago Iglesias Pantín is born in La Coruña, Spain. In 1899, he moved to Puerto Rico and became the first labor organizer under U.S. rule for his work with the Partido Obrero Social (Workers' Social Party). Iglesias later became an organizer for the American Federation of Labor for Puerto Rico and Cuba. In 1936, he was elected resident commissioner to represent Puerto Rico in the U.S. Congress. He died in Washington, D.C., in 1939.

Books

Córdova, Gonzalo F. *Resident Commissioner: Santiago Iglesias and His Times*. Río Piedras, PR: Editorial de la Universidad de Puerto Rico, 1993. A massive tome that is the only English-language full biography of Iglesias.

Senior, Clarence. *Santiago Iglesias, Labor Crusader*. Hato Rey, PR: Inter American University Press, 1972. This 98-page biography is a short study of Iglesias's role as a labor leader.

Website

Santiago Iglesias. A profile of the resident commissioner from the Library of Congress. http://www.loc.gov/rr/hispanic/congress/iglesias.html

1964

Tennis player Gigi Fernández is born in San Juan, Puerto Rico. Fernández, a 2010 inductee into the International Tennis Hall of Fame alongside doubles partner Natasha Zvereva, is viewed as one of the greatest doubles players of all time. Fernández and Zvereva amassed 14 Grand Slam titles. Fernández won Olympic gold medals in 1992 and 1996 while being named the top women's player in the world in 1991, 1993, 1994, and 1995.

Books

Iber, Jorge, et al. *Latinos in U.S. Sport: A History of Isolation, Cultural Identity, and Acceptance*. N.P.: Human Kinetics, 2011. Includes challenges that Fernández faced.

Telgen, Diane, and Jim Kamp, eds. *Latinas!: Women of Achievement*. Detroit: Visible Ink Press, 1996. Includes a short biographical essay on Fernández.

Website

Gigi Fernández, Olympic Gold Medalist. The official webpage of the tennis player includes information about her advocacy of youth fitness. http://www.gigifernandez.com/

1968

Corky Gonzales, head of the Crusade for Justice, speaks on the campus of the University of California at Los Angeles (UCLA). He urges Chicanos to reject the Anglo political and social system. At a symposium sponsored by United Mexican American Students and the Associated Students of UCLA later that day, he tells Chicano students to refuse integration with the Anglos, to drop out of politics, and to devote their efforts to teaching other Chicanos how to be proud of their Mexican heritage, their Spanish surnames, and their cultural values.

Books

Gonzales, Rodolfo "Corky." *Message to Aztlán: Selected Writings*. Houston, TX: Arte Público, 2001. One of the leading Chicano activists, Gonzales wrote poems, speeches, and plays in support of Mexican American rights.

Rosales, F. Arturo. *Chicano: The History of the Mexican American Civil Rights Movement*. Houston, TX: Arte Público, 1997. An excellent history of the movement.

Website

A History of Mexican Americans in California: The Chicano Movement. This National Park Service site provides a short, general history of the movement. http://www.cr.nps.gov/history/online_books/5views/5views5e.htm

February 23

1847

The United States wins the Battle of Buena Vista against Mexican general Antonio López de Santa Anna. The American troops were commanded by the future president of the United States, Zachary Taylor.

1936

Francis E. Riggs, police commissioner of Puerto Rico, is shot to death, perhaps in retaliation to the October 1935 killing of Nationalist Party members. Two young Nationalists are accused of his murder and both are soon killed in prison, allegedly while trying to escape. Seven other Nationalist Party members are charged with sedition and attempting to overthrow the U.S. government. The episode is the latest in the dispute over U.S. control of Puerto Rico.

Books

Campos, Pedro Albizu. *La Conciencia Nacional Puertorriqueña*. Ciudad de México, México: Siglo Veintiuno, 1972. The best source on Puerto Rican Nationalist thinking.

Negrón-Muntaner, Frances, and Ramón Grosfoguel, eds. *Puerto Rican Jam: Rethinking Colonialism and Nationalism*. Minneapolis: University of Minnesota Press, 1997. Offers essays that examine the debate over the political status of Puerto Rico.

Website

Puerto Rican Nationalism and the Drift toward Statehood. The Council on Hemispheric Affairs provides this excellent summary of the history of nationalism on the island. http://www.coha.org/puerto-rican-nationalism-and-the-drift-towards-statehood/

February 24

1947

Actor Edward James Olmos is born in East Los Angeles. After rising to fame in the iconic 1980s television show, *Miami Vice,* he received an Oscar nomination for best actor for 1988's *Stand and Deliver*. He has since focused much of his attention on activism, both to advance the image of Latinos in the media, and to improve the quality of life for Latinos. He cofounded the Los Angeles Latino International Film Festival and helped create Latino Literacy Now, both in 1997.

The next year, he founded Latino Public Broadcasting to produce programming for and about Latinos.

Websites

Edward James Olmos. The Internet Movie Database provides photographs and a short profile of the actor as well as a listing of his extensive professional credits in acting, directing, and producing. http://www.imdb.com/name/nm0001579/

Edward James Olmos. The official website for the actor and activist contains news about him and his community efforts. http://www.edwardjamesolmos.com/

February 25

2012

The Casals Festival begins in Puerto Rico. Held at the end of February every year, this classical music festival began in 1956 as a way of changing the image of Puerto Rico and promoting tourism. It is named in honor of famed Spanish cello player and conductor Pablo Casals, who spent the last part of his life in Puerto Rico where his mother had been born.

Books

Blum, David. *Casals and the Art of Interpretation*. New York: Holmes & Meier Publishers, 1977. A solid biography of the famed cellist.

Taper, Bernard. *Cellist in Exile: A Portrait of Pablo Casals*. New York: McGraw-Hill, 1962. Covers the life of the musician in Puerto Rico.

February 26

1978

Golfer Nancy Lopez has her first professional victory at the Bent Tree Classic in Sarasota, Florida. Lopez, of Mexican ancestry, is 21 years old at this time and just turned professional in July 1977. She began playing golf at age 8 in her hometown of Torrance, California, when her father, Domingo, gave her a set of clubs. A year later, she won the California State Golf Championship for her age group. Nevertheless, her local country club refused to allow Mexican Americans on the golf course. Lopez continued to win as she grew up, then left the University of Tulsa to join the professional tour. In 1978, the LPGA named her both Rookie of the Year and Player of the Year. Most of her success came in the 1980s, as she won 25 championships. Lopez enjoyed her last victory in 1997 and retired in 2002. She was inducted into the Ladies Professional Golf Association (LPGA) Hall of Fame in 1987.

From "Nancy's Caddie Knows Who's Boss":

> Almost every round, Nancy Lopez hits a shot that dazzles even her caddie. "I'm impressed," Roscoe Jones will tell her with a smile. So is everybody else. Less than a year after turning pro, 21-year-old Nancy Lopez has won four Ladies Professional Golf Association tournaments this year, two in succession twice. She is the leading money-winner with $81,448 . . . the most dominant young golfer since Jack Nicklaus arrived nearly $3 million ago. . . . With the women's golf tour still struggling for stature, the best thing that could happen to it would be for Nancy Lopez to win almost every week. But with the golf swing perhaps the most elusive thing in sport, that's not going to happen, no matter how good she is. "She's so young, but she plays like a true veteran, it spooks me a little," Jones said. "Her tee ball is very comparable to the longest out here—JoAnne Carner, Jo Ann Washam, Beverly Klass, and Betty Burfeindt—and

with her irons, she's a solid two clubs longer than almost everybody. She can hit a 5-iron 175 yards. . ."

(*Source:* Anderson, Dave. "Nancy's Caddie Knows Who's Boss." *New York Times,* May 27, 1978, p. 13.)

Books

Lopez, Nancy, with Peter Schwed. *The Education of a Woman Golfer.* New York: Simon & Schuster, 1979. Likely rushed into print to capitalize on Lopez's sudden national fame, this is the only autobiography of the star.

Sharp, Ann Wallace. *Nancy Lopez: Golfer.* New York: Lucent, 2008. Superb biography aimed at children that focuses on the challenges that Lopez faced as a Latina.

Websites

Nancy Lopez Golf: Defining the Women's Game. Provides women golfers with tips and shopping options. http://www.nancylopezgolf.com/en/Language.aspx

Nancy Lopez. This is the official LPGA biography of the golfer. http://www.lpga.com/player_results.aspx?id=500

February 27

1853

The Cuban philosopher-priest Félix Varela dies in St. Augustine, Florida. Born in Havana in 1788 and ordained a Catholic priest at the age of 23, Varela publicly called for an end to slavery and support of independence from Spain. Sentenced to death, he fled to the United States. Varela founded the newspaper *El Habanero* in Philadelphia in 1824 to openly militate for Cuban independence. His books on philosophy and education, which had to be smuggled into the island, made him the most popular author in Cuba in the first third of the 19th century.

Books

Amigó Jansen, Gustavo. *La Posición Filosófica del Padre Félix Varela*. Miami: Editorial Cubana, 1991. Discusses the political thought of Varela.

McCadden, Joseph, and Helen McCadden. *Father Varela: Torch Bearer from Cuba*. New York: United States Catholic Historical Society, 1969. The only English-language biography of the political activist.

February 28

1928

Sylvia del Villard Moreno, an Afro–Puerto Rican activist and actress, is born in Santurce, Puerto Rico. In 1968, she founded the Afro-Boricua El Coqui Theater, perhaps the best-regarded proponent of black Puerto Rican culture. Villard died in 1990 in Puerto Rico.

Websites

Sylvia del Villard. The New York Encyclopedia of Famous Puerto Ricans offers a short profile of the actor. http://www.puertorriquenosparalahistoria.exactpages.com/Sylvia%20del%20Villard.htm

Sylvia del Villard. A Spanish-language biography of the performer. http://www.prpop.org/biografias/s_bios/sylvia_del_villard.shtml

February 29

2012

The Puerto Rican Alliance for Awareness releases a video that shows diversity within the Puerto Rican community. The group, founded by Carlos Jiménez Flores and Darlene Vazquetelles, aims to counter negative stereotypes. The video is a response to a television show, *Work It,* in which a character said that he would be a good employee for a pharmaceutical company because, as a Puerto Rican, he was good at selling drugs.

Website

Puerto Rican Alliance for Awareness Releases Much-Anticipated Boricua Video. Covers the controversy. http://www.latinorebels.com/2012/03/05/puerto-rican-alliance-for-awareness-praa-releases-much-anticipated-boricua-video/

March

March 1

1920

Julian Samora, the first Latino to receive a doctorate in sociology, is born in Colorado to parents of Mexican ancestry. He earned his PhD from Washington University in St. Louis in 1953. Samora spent his career trying to bring more Latinos and Latinas into sociology as well as helping to develop an objective basis for understanding the characteristics of minority populations, especially Latinos. A university professor, he spent most of his career at the University of Notre Dame. He died in 1996.

Julian Samora on Mexican American history:

> I have never doubted that our history, our heritage, was important, nor that we had something to contribute to society. But many people have had serious doubts about this, and have hastened to tell us about them. For example, our native language has not always been held in high regard, and even after we have suppressed it or forgotten it and mastered the dominant language we may be told: "But you speak with an accent!" Of course everyone speaks with an accent. But ludicrous as these statements are many of us are persuaded to learn unaccented English by imitating the speech patterns of some of our untarnished leaders, such as Harry Truman, John F. Kennedy, Lyndon Baines Johnson, Jimmy Carter or Henry Kissinger . . .

(*Source:* The Julian Samora Legacy Project, http://samoralegacymedia.org/?page_id=1111)

Books

Samora, Julian. *Mexican-Americans in a Midwest Metropolis: A Study of East Chicago.* Los Angeles: N.P., 1967. Challenges the perception that Mexican American studies have to focus on the southwestern United States.

Samora, Julian, Joe Bernal, and Albert Peña. *Gunpowder Justice: A Reassessment of the Texas Rangers.* Notre Dame, IN: University of Notre Dame Press, 1979. Challenges the popular notion of Texas Rangers as heroic by focusing on their interactions with Mexican Americans.

Website

Julian Samora Legacy Project. The JSLP promotes the work of Samora by advancing Latino Studies through the publication of books and the collection of oral histories, among other activities. http://samoralegacymedia.org/

1954

Three Puerto Rican Nationalists attack the U.S. House of Representatives in a failed attempt to kill American leaders. This is the second violent attack by Puerto Rican Nationalists, with the first occurring on October 30, 1950. Three Congressmen are injured and the attackers, Rafael Cande Miranda, Andres Cordero, and Lolita Lebrón are jailed until 1979. The attackers were followers of Puerto Rican nationalist Pedro Albizu Campos, a Harvard University–trained lawyer who led the Nationalist Party. The Nationalists argue that the United States has no right to claim possession of Puerto Rico.

From "The Political Philosophy of Pedro Albizu Campos: Its Theory and Practice":

> The feudal conception of the law of nations which permitted the conquest by war of one nation by another, and

the holding of the victim as property of the victor, or as a possession should be dead also in the United States. The Kellogg-Briand Treaty, condemning war as an instrument of national policy, is the law in the United States. . . . The law of conquest can no longer be sustained!

(*Source:* Arroryo, Antonio Ma. Stevens, "The Political Philosophy of Pedro Albizu Campos: Its Theory and Practice," Ibero-American Language and Area Center, New York University, 1974, pp. 30–31.)

Books

Campos, Pedro Albizu. *La Conciencia Nacional Puertorriqueña*. Ciudad de México, México: Siglo Veintiuno, 1972. The best source on Puerto Rican Nationalist thinking.
Correa, R. P. Royers. *The Shadow of Don Pedro*. New York: Vantage Press, 1970. Explores Albizu Campos's impact on the debate over Puerto Rican independence.

Websites

Dr. Pedro Albizu Campos. A website biased in favor of Albizu Campos that nevertheless offers a good biography of the man. http://albizu.8m.com/
Albizu: The Documentary. A webpage established to promote a documentary film on the Puerto Rican leader. http://www.whoisalbizu.com/

1961

Operation Pedro Pan begins when the U.S. Children's Bureau signs an agreement with Florida's Department of Public Welfare to provide temporary aid for Cuban refugees, including care and protection of unaccompanied children. The agreement provides for federal funds to cover food, shelter, and clothing as well as transportation costs. This is the first time that the U.S. government has funded foster care of refugee children in the United States. The financing permitted the exodus of Cuban children to continue. Cuban parents sent their children away because they believed that their offspring would have a better life in a democratic country rather than communist Cuba. The indoctrination of children into communism also offended many parents. About 15,000 children, who left Cuba between 1960 and 1962, participated in Pedro Pan. On October 23, 1962, Cuba ended all flights to the United States thereby ending the exodus of children.

Elisa (Elly) Vilano-Chovel immigrated with her sister, Mari, to Buffalo, New York:

The Pedro Pan experience had an enormous impact in my life. I was forced to grow up before my time, estranged from my family, my roots, and my customs and had to become responsible not only for myself but also for my younger sister who could not comprehend what had happened. I am thankful for the opportunity of growing up in this land of freedom because of parents' sacrifice of parting with us. Four decades later families in Cuba continue to be forcefully split by the government's structured control of education away from home and by migration. We were the "sweet hope of our homeland" and missed the chance of living and helping when it was our turn. Nevertheless, I believe that each one of us is part of the solution for a democratic Cuba. I pray that in the future no one will ever again have to choose between freedom and family as our parents did, they are two of our undeniable God-given rights!

(*Source:* Conde, Yvonne M. *Operation Pedro Pan: The Untold Exodus of 14,048 Cuban Children*. New York: Routledge, 1999, p. 213.)

Books

Conde, Yvonne M. *Operation Pedro Pan: The Untold Exodus of 14,048 Cuban Children.* New York: Routledge, 1999, p. 213. Rich with interviews from Pedro Pan alumni and details about the operation.

Dubinsky, Karen. *Babies without Borders: Adoption and Migration across the Americas.* Washington Square, NY: New York University Press, 2010. Scholarly examination of the global politics of child migration with a chapter on Pedro Pan.

Websites

Operation Pedro Pan. The official site of the Miami-based Operation Pedro Pan Group. It provides a good history of the event with a PowerPoint presentation, images, and resources. http://pedropan.org/

Operation Pedro Pan Facebook Group. Provides a link to people who participated in Operation Pedro Pan. http://www.facebook.com/OPPGI

March 2

1917

President Woodrow Wilson signs the Jones-Shafroth Act, giving U.S. citizenship to Puerto Ricans. Additionally, the act replaced the Foraker Act and gave Puerto Ricans the right to elect members of the Senate and the House of Representatives. However, the governor, still appointed by the U.S. president, retained the right to veto any law passed by the legislature. The U.S. Congress also had the right to stop any action taken by the Puerto Rican legislature. The United States maintained control over fiscal and economic matters and exercised authority over mail services, immigration, defense, and other basic governmental matters. The Jones Act, like the Foraker Act, reflected doubt regarding the Puerto Ricans' capability to appropriately manage their own affairs.

From "Citizenship of Porto Ricans":

Secretary [of State Henry] Stimson: When the island was ceded to the United States . . . both on the part of the inhabitants of the island and on the part of the inhabitants of the United States, the relation has been regarded as permanent. The Porto Ricans came to the United States with the utmost loyalty and expressions of good will . . . they have seized upon this particular thing, their desire for citizenship and the fact that we have not given it to them, as the one badge of inferiority which one nation could put upon another. In other words, while it is hard to put a finger on any practical change which the granting of citizenship would make in the relations to this country, sentimentally it is of vital importance in removing what has become a rather deep-seated source of irritation.

(*Source:* U.S. Senate, *Hearing Before the Committee on Pacific Islands and Porto Rico, 62nd Congress, 2nd session, on H. R. 20048,* May 7, 1912, p. 4.)

Books

Ayala, César J., and Rafael Bernabe. *Puerto Rico in the American Century: A History since 1898.* Charlotte: University of North Carolina Press, 2009. Excellent, accessible history of Puerto Rico.

Monge, José Trias. *Puerto Rico: The Trials of the Oldest Colony in the World.* New Haven, CT: Yale University Press, 1999. Provides a good history of Puerto Rico and argues that decolonization should immediately begin.

Websites

Puerto Rico USA Citizenship Foundation. Provides a history of U.S. citizenship for Puerto Ricans with links and other resources. http://www.puertoricousa.com

History of Puerto Rico, 1900–1949. Provides a timeline history of Puerto Rico. http://www.topuertorico.org/history5.shtml

1985

Gus Arriola publishes his last *Gordo* comic strip. Appearing in 220 newspapers since 1941, the strip was the only mass-circulation medium that featured Mexican Americans. Early in the life of the strip, Arriola realized the extent of his influence and began to torpedo stereotypes about Mexicans. His character, Gordo Lopez, was a portly (*gordo* means fat) bean farmer who turned tour guide in the 1960s to introduce readers to Mexican history, folklore, and art. Arriola, born in Florence, Arizona to Mexican-born parents, did not visit Mexico himself until 1961. He taught himself to speak English by reading the Sunday funny pages, the same ones that he would later write. Arriola retired largely because of burnout associated with producing a daily strip virtually single-handedly for almost 44 years.

From a 1998 interview with Arriola:

"Underneath it all," [Arriola] continued, "there was a certain innocence. Gordo wasn't really the ladies' man that he thought he was. So I guess maybe on that level, it didn't really provoke anybody. I never had any complaints. Actually, most of my mail really was very nice. A lot of teachers used to write in to thank me for the cultural and historical material. And language teachers—language teachers loved it."

"Looking back," he went on, "I don't know why there weren't any vicious complaints about it. I never really did get anybody of importance to complain . . . ." "Cats used to send letters to Poosy Gato," Frances [Arriola, wife of Gus] said. "Lots of readers sent us pictures of their cats," Gus added with a gentle chuckle. " There was great interplay between us and the readers, and we just had fun hearing from them. We

were surprised that they would be that moved to write us about something they'd read in the strip. . . . "

"We had some wonderful mail through the years from people who genuinely felt that the Gordo characters were real. And they wrote about them as if they were real. That impressed me more than anything—that we reached people, made them feel what I tried to express. . . . "

"So many people wrote in to say they had gone to Mexico because of reading the strip," Frances said. "They would write to him and say they'd never been interested until they read the strip, and then they wanted to go there."

"And they'd send me cards from Mexico," Arriola said, "saying that they'd gone to a certain village because of some reference in the strip. So the strip created an awareness of Mexico in the general public, and I guess that was my best contribution as far as anything social being achieved. I never got political with it. I shied away from Latin-American political groups. I said, 'Nope—I can't get involved with that.'"

"It's not that I'm not sympathetic," he continued. "It's just that I didn't think my art, or rather my invention in Gordo—I didn't want to use it in that way. I considered myself an entertainer more than a fighter for the cause. I thought I could accomplish the same ends with entertainment. In other words, I could sneak in the back door with a solution rather than to take a stand. Confrontation, taking a hard stand, risk making an enemy of someone. Take a soft stand. Make 'em laugh and sneak in, creating maybe a benevolent attitude rather than a hostile or ignorant one."

(*Source:* Harvey, Robert C., and Gus Arriola. *Accidental Ambassador Gordo: The Comic Strip Art of Gus Arriola.* Jackson: University Press of Mississippi, 2000, p. 233–36.)

Books

Aldama, Frederick Luis. *Your Brain on Latino Comics: From Gus Arriola to Los Bros Hernandez.* Austin: University of Texas Press, 2009. Provides an overview of Latino comics and an interview with Arriola.

Harvey, Robert C., and Gus Arriola. *Accidental Ambassador Gordo: The Comic Strip Art of Gus Arriola.* Jackson: University Press of Mississippi, 2000. Provides a biography of the famed cartoonist as well as numerous strips of *Gordo.*

Websites

Gus Arriola, Cartoonist. The Carmel Art Association provides a biography of one of its members and includes some of his work. http://www.carmelart.org/artists_pages/arriola/arriola.html

Gordo. This website is devoted to Arriola's creation and includes a number of links related to his work. http://www.carmelart.org/artists_pages/arriola/arriola.html

March 3

1851

The U.S. Congress passes the California Land Act, which shifts land and property policies from Spanish to English law. Promoted by California senator William McKendree Gwin as a way to protect Mexican land rights, the legislation had the opposite effect. Only wealthy ranchers—who were typically Anglo-Saxon—could afford to pursue legal claims because of the appeal process enshrined in the law. As a result, legal rights to vast amounts of Mexican-owned land were transferred through various means, both legal and illegal, to Anglo-Americans.

Books

French, Laurence. *Running the Border Gauntlet: The Mexican Migrant Controversy.* Santa Barbara, CA: Praeger, 2010. Addresses controversies over land claims.

Thomas, Lately. *Between Two Empires: The Life Story of California's First Senator, William McKendree Gwin.* Boston: Houghton Mifflin, 1969. A biography of the man behind the California Land Claims Act.

Website

Land Ownership in California and the Transition to a New Government. This National Archives site provides a background to the land claims issue. http://www.archives.gov/pacific/education/curriculum/4th-grade/land-ownership.html

1968

In the largest high school student strike, more than 1,000 students walk out of Abraham Lincoln High School in Los Angeles to protest school conditions. Known as the Los Angeles Blowouts, the strike would pull 10,000 students out of class by week's end.

Books

Macdonald, Victoria-Maria. *Latino Education in the United States: A Narrated History from 1513–2000.* This study, a mix of narrative and primary documents, is the only history of Latino education to cover such a broad span of time.

Rosales, F. Arturo. *Chicano: The History of the Mexican American Civil Rights Movement.* Houston: Arte Publico, 1996. Sets the student strike in historical context.

Websites

These Americans. Provides photos of students and faculty taken at Abraham Lincoln High School in the 1960s. http://www.theseamericans.com/decade/sixties/abraham-lincoln-high-school-los-angeles-1960s/

Timeline: Movimiento from 1960–1985. Lists significant events in the history of the Chicano civil rights movement. http://depts.washington.edu/civilr/mecha_timeline.htm

March 4

1953

Emilio Estefan Jr., a member of the Miami Sound Machine and a music producer, is born in Santiago de Cuba. He fled from the island as a child in the 1960s after Fidel Castro took over. Estefan collected 19 Grammy Awards over the course of his career. He won a Latin Grammy in 2000 as the Producer of the Year for his work with Charlie Zass, Carlos Vives, and Marc Anthony. In 2012, he received the Hispanic Heritage Award from the National Football League. Estefan is married to Gloria Estefan, the lead singer of the 1980s group, the Miami Sound Machine.

Books

Estefan, Emilio, and Quincy Jones. *The Rhythm of Success: How an Immigrant Produced His Own American Dream*. Miami: Celebra Trade, 2011.

N.A. *The Exile Experience: Journey to Freedom*. Miami: The Miami Herald, 2011. Estefan provides this introduction to personal accounts of Cubans who emigrated to the United States.

Websites

Emilio Estefan, Jr. Lists Estefan's professional credits and provides a short biography. http://www.imdb.com/name/nm0261555/

Emilio Estefan Official Site. Reports on Estefan's activities. https://www.facebook.com/EmilioEstefan

March 5

1974

Actress and model Eva Mendes is born to Cuban parents in Miami as the only member of her immediate family to be born in the United States. Raised in Los Angeles, she is best known for the 2001 movie *Training Day* with Denzel Washington. Mendes also served as a model for Revlon cosmetics, one of the few Latinas to have such a modeling job.

Books

Bernardi, Daniel, ed. *The Birth of Whiteness: Race and the Emergence of U.S. Cinema*. New Brunswick: Rutgers University Press, 1996. Explores the impact of whiteness on Hollywood.

Rodríguez, Clara E. *Heroes, Lovers, and Others: The Story of Latinos in Hollywood*. Washington, D.C.: Smithsonian Books, 2004. Covers the history of film from the Silent Era to the Postmodern Era and emphasizes that it is only since the 1980s that Latinos have been portrayed in nonstereotypical ways.

Website

Eva Mendes. Provides a short biography and a listing of her professional credits. http://www.imdb.com/name/nm0578949/

March 6

1836

Mexican forces under Gen. Antonio López de Santa Anna capture the Alamo in San Antonio, Texas. Originally named Misión San Antonio de Valero, the Alamo served as a home to Catholic missionaries and their Native American converts from 1724 to 1793. After the Spanish secularized San Antonio's missions, Spanish cavalry soldiers stationed at the former mission named it the Alamo (the Spanish word for "cottonwood") in honor of their hometown, Alamo de Parras, Coahuila. In December 1835, as the war for independence from Mexico heated up, Ben Milam led Texian and Tejano volunteers against Mexican troops quartered in San Antonio. The victorious volunteers then occupied the Alamo and strengthened its defenses. On February 23, 1836, Santa Anna and his army arrived. About 200 Texians and Tejanos prepared to defend the Alamo together. They held out for 13 days. The known Tejanos who died in the Alamo include: Juan Abamillo, Juan A. Badillo, Carlos Espalier, Gregorio Esparza, Antonio Fuentes, Toribio Losoya, Andrés Nava, José María Guerrero, and Damacio Jimenes.

Letter from William Barrett Travis, commander of the Alamo:

> Commandancy of the Alamo—Bejar, Fby. 24th 1836—To the People of Texas & all Americans in the world—Fellow citizens & compatriots—I am besieged, by a thousand or more of the Mexicans under Santa Anna—I have sustained a continual Bombardment & cannonade for 24 hours & have not lost a man—The enemy has demanded a surrender at discretion, otherwise, the garrison are to be put to the sword, if the fort is taken—I have answered the demand with a cannon shot, & our flag still waves proudly from the walls—I shall never surrender or retreat Then, I call on you in the name of Liberty, of patriotism & everything dear to the American character, to come to our aid.

(*Source:* Texas State Library and Archives, https://www.tsl.state.tx.us/treasures/republic/alamo/travis-02.html)

Books

Matovina, Timothy M. *The Alamo Remembered: Tejano Accounts and Perspectives.* Austin: University of Texas Press, 1995. An anthology of accounts of the Battle of the Alamo by Tejano citizens of San Antonio.

Walker, Paul Robert. *Remember the Alamo: Texians, Tejanos, and Mexicans Tell Their Stories.* Washington, D.C.: National Geographic Children's Books, 2007. Probably the best book on the Alamo for a younger audience, it provides a good summary of the battle, maps, pictures, old photos, and archival drawings.

Websites

The Alamo. The official site for the building that is operated by the Daughters of the Texas Republic. There have been disputes over the portrayal of nonwhites at the Alamo. http://www.thealamo.org/

The Battle of the Alamo. The Texas State Library and Archives Commission provides a wonderful introduction to the battle, several historic images, and copies of significant Alamo documents. https://www.tsl.state.tx.us/treasures/republic/alamo-01.html

March 7

2000

The National Association of Evangelicals (NAE), an umbrella group representing the largest wing of U.S. Protestantism, commits itself at its annual assembly to recognizing minority leadership. The NAE gave a Hispanic affiliate equal billing at the assembly. This inclusion of Latinos is part of the new demographics for evangelicals, with growth in black and Hispanic circles, which tend to combine morally conservative stances with socially liberal policies.

Books

Martínez, Juan Francisco. *Los Protestantes: An Introduction to Latino Protestantism in the United States.* Santa Barbara, CA: Praeger, 2011. Examines the streams of Latino Protestantism and contrasts it with other forms of U.S. Protestantism.

Martínez, Juan Francisco, and Lindy Scott, eds. *Los Evangélicos: Portraits of Latino Protestantism in the United States.* Eugene, OR: Wipf and Stock, 2009. A collection of essays that examine the origins and types of Latino Protestantism.

Website

National Association of Evangelicals. The official website of the organization has sections devoted to public policy, world relief, and church and faith. http://www.nae.net/

March 8

1926

Author and political activist José Luis Gonzalez is born in Santo Domingo, Dominican Republic. The family migrated to Puerto Rico four years later and Gonzalez would become part of the famed "Generation of 1940" that resurrected Puerto Rican literature. Gonzalez graduated from the University of Puerto Rico and then made a brief sojourn to New York City for graduate school, gathering material on Puerto Rican immigrants that would later appear in his writings. In 1948, he became president of the Vanguardia Juvenil Puertorriqueña, a political group that promoted socialism in Puerto Rico. He renounced his U.S. citizenship in 1953 to protest American colonialism and moved to Mexico, where he subsequently obtained Mexican citizenship. The U.S. government retaliated by barring him from re-entering Puerto Rico or the United States until 1971.

Books

González, José Luis. *Antología Personal*. San Juan, PR: La Editorial Universidad de Puerto Rico, 2009. A collection of essays.

González, José Luis. *Puerto Rico: The Four-Storeyed Country and Other Essays*. Trans. Gerald Guiness. Princeton: M. Wiener, 1993. A collection of essays about González's homeland.

Websites

José Luis González. A good biography of the author. http://www.biografiasyvidas.com/biografia/g/gonzalez_jose_luis.htm

José Luis González. Provides a brief biography of the writer along with a listing of his publications. http://www.literatura.us/joseluis/

1942

Ignacio Rodríguez-Iturbe, a civil engineer specializing in water use by ecosystems, is born in Venezuela. In 2002, he won the Stockholm Water Prize, also known as the "Nobel Prize of Water." Rodríguez-Iturbe has been a professor of civil and environmental engineering in the United States since 1987.

Books

Rodríguez-Iturbe, Ignacio, and Amilcare Porporato. *Ecohydrology of Water-Controlled Ecosystems: Soil Moisture and Plant Dynamics*. New York: Cambridge University Press, 2004. Examines water use by plants.

Rodríguez-Iturbe, Ignacio, and Andrea Rinaldo. *Fractal River Basins: Chance and Self-Realization*. Cambridge: Cambridge University Press, 2001. Focuses on river basin drainage.

Websites

Ignacio Rodríguez-Iturbe. His Princeton University webpage contains a curriculum vitae and contact information. http://www.princeton.edu/~irodrigu/

Professor Rodríguez-Iturbe Discusses a New Fish Diversity Model. A 2008 video interview conducted with the engineer. http://www.princeton.edu/main/news/archive/S21/01/07I89/index.xml?section=mm-featured

March 9

1905

The official coat of arms of Puerto Rico is established. The figures on the Commonwealth of Puerto Rico coat of arms copy the ones on the coat that the Spanish Crown granted to Puerto Rico in the early 16th century. As a result, the Puerto Rican coat of arms is the only one in Latin America still in official use since the Spanish conquest.

Books

Abodaher, David J. *Puerto Rico: America's Fifty-First State*. New York: Franklin Watts, 1993. Short history of Puerto Rico that includes the statehood debate.

Fernández, Eugenio Méndez. *Historia Cultural de Puerto Rico, 1493–1968*. San Juan, PR: Ediciones El Cemi, 1971. Provides a cultural history of Puerto Rico.

Websites

Coat of Arms. This site promotes Puerto Rican tourism and includes an excellent history of the coat of arms. http://welcome.topuerto rico.org/reference/escudo.shtml

Puerto Rico—The World Factbook. The Central Intelligence Agency's introduction to Puerto Rico includes statistics. https://www.cia.gov/library/publications/the-world-factbook/geos/rq.html

1915

Poet Francisco Matos Paoli is born in Lares, Puerto Rico. One of the island's most important poets, he published over 20 books and won several major prizes A supporter of Puerto Rican independence, this theme of freedom is reflected in his works. Matos Paoli, secretary of the Partido Nacionalista Puertorriqueña, went to jail in 1950 for inciting people to revolt. Solitary confinement for about 10 months caused him to become mentally ill, a topic that is also found in his poems. Nominated for the Nobel Prize in Literature in 1977, he died in 2000.

Books

Matos Paoli, Francisco. *Song of Madness and Other Poems*. Trans. Frances R. Aparicio. Pittsburgh: Latin American Literary Review Press, 1985. A collection of some of the poet's best known works, including "The Profound Truth."

Silén, Yvan. *Francisco Matos Paoli: O La Angustia de Dios*. San Juan, PR: La Editorial, University

of Puerto Rico, 2009. A critical examination of Matos Paoli's writings.

Websites

Francisco Matos Paoli, poeta. Provides a short biography of the poet. http://www.proyectosalonhogar.com/escritores/FMatosPaoli.htm

Francisco Matos Paoli. A good biography of the poet that captures his personality. http://www.peacehost.net/WhiteStar/Voices/eng-matos.html

1916

Pancho Villa and anywhere from 100 to 500 of his men attack the town of Columbus, New Mexico, and the 13th U.S. Cavalry garrison at Camp Furlong during the Mexican Revolution. Columbus is about three miles from the Mexican border. Villa sought money and supplies to aid his fight against the Mexican government of Venustiano Carranza. He was also angry at the U.S. government for backing Carranza. While the cavalry troopers were initially surprised and unprepared, they organized quickly enough and a firefight raged through Columbus. Much of the town burned to the ground. Ten civilians died along with eight U.S. soldiers and an unknown number of Villa's men. A dozen Villistas were captured with six of them being hanged shortly thereafter and the rest sent to prison to be released to the Mexican government in 1921.

Accounts from participants in the Pancho Villa attack on Columbus, New Mexico:

> Private Johnson, U.S. Cavalry: I asked the boys if there were any prisoners and they answered that nobody took any. I know that I brained one black Mexican with an axe. The boys fought like devils. There were no arms in the hospital tents and the attendants were asleep when attacked. They had to fight with any weapon at hand.

Pablo Lopez, Villista: I had on two crossed belts of cartridges and a bullet hit one of them glancing off. The force of it knocked me down and as I was sitting on the ground, another bullet went through both legs from left to right; still another broke the loading lever on my rifle. I thought it was time to go. A stray horse, also wounded, was standing by and I crawled to it and dragged myself onto it. Having lots of clips for my automatic, I kept emptying my pistol to protect my retreat. My comrades were riding southward too.

(*Source:* Banks, Stephen A. *Doing My Duty: Corporal Elmer Dewey—One National Guard Doughboy's Experiences During the Pancho Villa Punitive Campaign and World War I.* Springfield, VA: Signature Book, 2011, pp. 17–18.)

Books

Anderson, Mark Cronlund. *Pancho Villa's Revolution by Headlines.* Norman: University of Oklahoma Press, 2000. Shows how newspapers in the United States and Mexico covered Villa's exploits.

Quintana, Alejandro. *Pancho Villa: A Biography.* Santa Barbara, CA: Greenwood, 2012. A straightforward account of the Mexican leader's life.

Websites

Francisco "Pancho" Villa. An excellent biography of Villa excerpted from *The Northern Mexico Handbook.* http://www.mexconnect.com/articles/1305-francisco-pancho-villa

Pancho Villa by Jennifer Rosenberg. A short biography of Villa with photographs of him. http://history1900s.about.com/cs/panchovilla/p/panchovilla.htm

March 10

1451

Ferdinand II of Aragón is born at Sos del Rey Católico in Aragón. He married Isabella of Castile in 1469. The two Spanish monarchs shared power as rulers, ultimately uniting Spain in 1479. In 1492, Ferdinand and Isabella commissioned Christopher Columbus to find a sea route to Asia, thereby inadvertently setting the path for Spanish settlement of the New World.

Books

Edwards, John. *Ferdinand and Isabella.* New York: Pearson Longman, 2004. The best biography of the first king and queen of Spain.

Miller, Townsend. *The Castles and the Crown: Spain, 1451–1555.* New York: Capricorn Books, 1964. A biography of Ferdinand and Isabella that also covers their immediate descendants.

Websites

Ferdinand II of Aragón. The Luminarium Encyclopedia provides an excellent short biography of the king. http://www.luminarium.org/encyclopedia/ferdinandaragon.htm

Ferdinand of Aragón. A heavily-illustrated short biography of the king with links to further readings. http://www.heritage-history.com/www/heritage.php?Dir=characters&FileName=ferdinand1s.php

1916

President Woodrow Wilson notifies Mexico's President Venustiano Carranza that he wants to send a military expedition into northern Mexico to find and punish Pancho Villa for his attack on Columbus, New Mexico. Wilson is not confident that the Mexican government has the ability to control or capture Villa. Carranza reluctantly agrees to Wilson's plan but does little to assist the United States for fear of being seen to give up Mexican sovereignty. Wilson chooses Brig. Gen. John Joseph "Black Jack" Pershing to lead the Regular Army troops who make up the "Punitive Expedition." The expedition is the last large-scale cavalry action mounted by the U.S. Army. Pershing's men enter Mexico on March 15. They chase Villa until February 1917. While Pershing captures some of Villa's underlings, he never manages to ensnare the Mexican leader. Meanwhile, the Mexican population is angered by the U.S. invasion with some Mexicans demonstrating against the American forces in their midst. Anti-American demonstrators in Durango City, Mexico, burned the U.S. consulate and dragged the American flag through the streets as one example of anger. Many people on both sides feared that another U.S.-Mexican war was on the horizon.

Sergeant W. H. Harrison of the 13th Cavalry describes the ride into Mexico:

When we went in the sun was burning hot, there was not a breath of air stirring and the dust soon hung over the road like a curtain. It got into our eyes and mouths, and we could hardly breathe. It bothered the horses too. Many of the boys put wet handkerchiefs into their hats to keep the sun from boring into their skulls, and rode along with closed eyes to keep out the dust and glare. Goggles didn't seem to help.

Many of the men were half blinded in a couple of hours. The infantrymen would stumble along with their eyes shut as much as possible. Soon my eyes began to itch around the edges, then they felt as big as camp kettles, and finally everything got dark. I had inhaled a lot of the alkali dust and my throat began to get sore.

During the marches the boys stopped ten minutes every hour to rest. When the word was given they just dropped in their tracks right in the road. Most of them would lie on their backs, covering their faces with their hats. No stops for dinner were made. It was one steady hike from morning until we reached the camping place. The infantry companies were strung out so they would be a day's march apart.

(*Source:* Banks, Stephen A. *Doing My Duty: Corporal Elmer Dewey—One National Guard Doughboy's Experiences during the Pancho Villa Punitive Campaign and World War I.* Springfield, VA: Signature Book, 2011, p. 28.)

Books

Clendenen, Clarence C. *Blood on the Border: The United States Army and the Mexican Irregulars.* New York: MacMillan, 1969. A good account of the clashes between the U.S. and Mexican forces during the Mexican Revolution.

Eisenhower, John S.D. *Intervention: The United States and the Mexican Revolution, 1913—1917.* New York: W. W. Norton & Company, 1993. This is the standard work on the Punitive Expedition.

Websites

Griffith, Joe. "In Pursuit of Pancho Villa." The Historical Society of the Georgia National Guard published this detailed article on the Punitive Expedition. http://www.hsgng.org/pages/pancho.htm

Yockelson, Mitchell. "The United States Armed Forces and the Mexican Punitive Expedition." The National Archives website includes this article from the Fall 1997 issue of *Prologue* magazine. http://www.archives.gov/publications/prologue/1997/fall/mexican-punitive-expedition-1.html

1955

Edwin Janer's theater group, La Farándula Panamericana (Pan-American Showbusiness), produces Spanish playwright José López Rubio's *Celos del Aire* in New York City. The group had begun performing both peninsular works and Latin American plays, all in Spanish, in 1950 as part of a growing Latino theater scene. The theater group, which included the legendary Míriam Colón, disbanded in 1958.

Books

Beezley, William H., and Linda A. Curcio-Nagy, eds. *Latin American Popular Culture since Independence: An Introduction.* New York: Rowman and Littlefield, 2011. Explains the importance of theater to Latin Americans.

Sturman, Janet L. *Spanish Operetta, American Stage*. Champaign, IL: University of Illinois Press, 2000. A history of Spanish lyric theater, including performances by La Farándula Panamericana.

Website

Profile: Frank M. Figueroa. Captures the spirit of the Latino arts community in New York City through a profile of a Puerto Rican radio host. http://www.descarga.com/cgi-bin/db/archives/Profile35?NippdWoF;;278

March 11

1945

Michael A. Mares, the world's primary authority on the natural history of desert rodents, is born in Albuquerque, New Mexico, to parents of Mexican ancestry. In recognition of his work, Mares has had three animals named after him: *Maresomys boliviensis,* a Bolivian rodent; *Tonatia saurophila maresi,* a neotropical bat; and *Lukoschus maresi,* a parasitic mite that lives on neotropical rodents.

Books

Mares, Michael A. *Convergent Evolution among Desert Rodents: A Global Perspective*. Pittsburgh: Carnegia Museum of Natural History, 1980. The book that made Mares into a leader in mammology.

Mares, Michael A. *A Desert Calling: Life in a Forbidding Landscape*. Cambridge, MA: Harvard University Press, 2002. Explains how life exists in a world with little water.

Websites

Inductee Biographies: Michael A. Mares. The Oklahoma Higher Education Heritage Society inducted Mares into its Hall of Fame in 2002. http://www.ohehs.org/hof/michael mares.html

Michael A. Mares. A short summary of the professional interests of the famed mammologist. http://zoology.ou.edu/Mares.htm

March 12

1863

Publisher, poet, and journalist Francisco Gonzálo "Pachín" Marín is born in Arecibo, Puerto Rico. When Spanish authorities suppressed his revolutionary newspaper, *El Postillón,* Marín fled to the Caribbean, Venezuela, and Colombia before landing in New York City. While in the city, he contemplated the life of Latino immigrants and wrote one of his best known works, *New York from Within,* in 1892. In addition to publishing his newspaper, Marín published books and broadsides for the Cuban and Puerto Rican expatriate communities. He died in battle against the Spanish in Cuba in 1897.

From Francisco Gonzálo "Pachín" Marín, *New York from Within: One Aspect of Its Bohemian Life:*

If there is a civilized country capable of astonishing the most indifferent and stoic, the United States, or better yet, New York, is the place.

Its buildings, its portentous architectural works, its elevated railways fantastically crisscrossing through the air, its streets—broad arteries roamed by inexhaustible hordes from all countries of the world—its parks—austerely and aristocratically designed—, its steam engines, its powerful journalistic institutions, its treacherously beautiful women, its wonders, all instill, at first sight, a deep malaise on the foreigner because it occurs to one that these large cities, deafening in their progress, are like the mouth of a horrible monster constantly busy simultaneously swallowing and vomiting human beings;

and it is amidst these great noises and grand centers that our soul finds itself increasingly besieged by that horrendous malady called sadness, and assumes the somber character of isolation and silence.

For the poor in money but rich in ambition, arriving here in the circumstances outlined above, however, New York is a great house of asylum where all who believe, more or less, vigorously, in the virtue and sanctity of work, ultimately find their niche.

Are you very poor? Have you not succeeded yet in finding something on which to invest your talents and energies? Are you feeling the sting of hunger? Are you cold?

Don't distress yourself. Don't despair in any way. Do you see that establishment on the corner whose door continuously opens and closes? Well, it is commonly known here by the name of Lager Beer Hall. . . . Take that table nearby; throw five cents on it; it's a tip in advance; don't go believing anything else. Pay attention now. In the first place, they bring you a big mug of beer, fresh, foamy, poured on smooth glass. Drink it. In this country beer is a necessity; it fortifies and warms limbs numbed by the cold. But . . . don't be a fool! Take care. Let us, before draining the contents of the glass, eat ham, beef, sausage, cheese etc. That stuff you gobble down for starters. At least that's what gastronomy calls it. Well! Good heavens! But principles be gone! You must eat it all. . . . Eat until you've had your fill: I am your host . . .

And after leaving the [Lager Beer Hall], satiated and proud of our find, forgetting the novelistic tortures that made Jean Valjean suffer from such acute hunger, then we recall the real New York, the wise and good New York, hospitable and gay; and we laugh our heads off at the admirers of the Brooklyn Bridge and the Statue of Liberty, of the elevated railway and gigantic buildings, of all the great institutions of this surprising republic, since, never fear, I doubt that there is in this country of inventions and colossal enterprises anything as grand, as portentous, as human as those establishments where for five coppers they feed the hungry and give drink to the thirsty.

(*Source:* Kanellos, Nicolás. *Herencia: The Anthology of Hispanic Literature of the United States.* New York: Oxford University Press, 2002, pp. 342–43.)

Books

Figueroa de Cifredo, Patria. *Pachín Marín, Héroe Y Poeta.* San Juan: Instiuto de Cultura Puertorriqueña, 1967. A biography of the war hero and poet.

Kanellos, Nicolás. *Herencia: The Anthology of Hispanic Literature of the United States.* New York: Oxford University Press, 2002. Provides a short biography of Marín and a long excerpt from *New York from Within: One Aspect of Its Bohemian Life.*

Websites

Francisco Gonzálo Marín. Provides a short biography and two poems by the writer. http://www.proyectosalonhogar.com/BiografiasPr/francisco_gonzalo_marin.htm

Pachín Marín: Poet Puerto Rico Must Not Forget. Provides a biography and a poem. http://desahogoboricua.blogspot.com/2011/03/pachin-marin-un-poeta-boricua-que-no.html

1937

The Nationalist Party of Puerto Rico, a group opposed to U.S. control, holds a march in Ponce to commemorate the abolition of slavery in Puerto Rico and to demand the release of political prisoners. The mayor of Ponce, who had granted permission for the march to take place, revokes his permission an hour before the event under pressure from the Puerto Rican government and the local police. The march proceeds anyway. Police fire on the crowd gathered for the march. By the time the dust settles, 19 people are dead including two police officers and more than 100 are wounded in what becomes known as the Ponce Massacre. More than 10,000 attend the funeral for the demonstrators.

Books

Abodaher, David J. *Puerto Rico: America's Fifty-First State*. New York: Franklin Watts, 1993. A short history of Puerto Rico that includes the statehood debate.

Corretier, Juan Antonio. *Albizu Campos and the Ponce Massacre*. New York: World View, 1965. The march demanded the release of Campos, the most prominent of the political prisoners.

Websites

The Ponce Massacre: Why Is It Important to Remember? Provides a good summary of the incident. http://www.prdream.com/wordpress/2003/03/the-ponce-massacre-why-is-it-important-to-remember/

Remembering Puerto Rico's Ponce Massacre. Democracy Now offers film footage from the 1937 incident as well as a transcript of an interview with political analyst Juan-Manuel Garcia-Passalacqua. http://www.democracynow.org/2007/3/22/remembering_puerto_ricos_ponce_massacre

March 13

1913

Leonor Villegas de Magnón of Laredo, Texas, recruits five other women to cross the border into Mexico to nurse rebel Carrancista soldiers wounded during the Mexican Revolution. The efforts of the women lead to the founding of La Cruz Blanca, a medical relief organization. Villegas de Magnón was born in Nuevo Laredo in 1876. Educated in the United States, she married an American man and settled in Mexico. Meanwhile, her father had moved to Laredo. When he died, the turmoil of the revolution prevented Villegas de Magnón and her family from returning to Mexico after the funeral. Nicknamed La Rebelde, she wrote for a newspaper before becoming involved with nursing revolutionaries. Honored by the Mexican government after the end of hostilities, she died in 1955 in Mexico City. A statue of Villegas de Magnón stands in Nuevo Laredo, Tamaulipas, Mexico.

Books

Lomas, Clara, ed. *The Rebel*. Houston: Arte Público, 1994. Villegas de Magnón's autobiography.

Perales, Monica, and Raúl A. Ramos, eds. *Recovering the Hispanic History of Texas*. Houston: Arte Público, 2010. Contains an essay by Donna M. Kabalen de Bichara on Villegas de Magnón's impact on the Borderlands.

Websites

Leonor Villegas de Magnón. Great Texas Women provides a good biography of the humanitarian. http://www.utexas.edu/gtw/villegas.php

Leonor Villegas de Magnón. The Handbook of Texas Online offers a biography of Villegas de Magnón. http://www.tshaonline.org/handbook/online/articles/fvi19

1967

United Mexican American Students (UMAS) is formed when 250 students representing seven Los Angeles colleges and universities meet. UMAS focuses on the college recruitment of Chicanas/os in the belief that education is critical to advancement of the Chicano community. Over the years, the organization spread throughout the country with some chapters blending with other

Chicano groups such as MEChA (Movimiento Estudiantil Chicano de Aztlán) and others dissolving. By the turn of the century, the group was essentially defunct.

From a Denver Federal Bureau of Investigation report:

> On October 12, 1967, a meeting sponsored by the United Mexican-American Students at California State College at Los Angeles was held and approximately 200 individuals were present. . . . [Rodolfo "Corky"Gonzales] was one of the featured speakers along with REIS LOPEZ TIJERINA. . . . In his speech before the crowd GONZALES stated that the present American middle-class society is sick. GONZALES called for all Mexican Americans to rebel from the present standard way of life. GONZALES stated that the widespread frustration of the Mexican Americans of the Southwest United States will eventually lead to violence. He stated that large-scale violence would be resorted to unless the Federal government changes its ways. He stated that there would be large-scale rebellion unless the government provides basic needs of the Mexican American people.

(*Source*: Vigil, Ernesto B. *The Crusade for Justice: Chicano Militancy and the Government's War on Dissent.* Madison: University of Wisconsin Press, 1999, p. 41.)

Books

Rosales, F. Arturo. *Chicano: The History of the Mexican American Civil Rights Movement.* Houston, TX: Arte Público, 1996. A general history of the movement that spawned the Chicano Park protest.

Shorris, Earl. *Latinos: A Biography of the People.* New York: W.W. Norton, 1992. Sets the Chicano movement in the broader context of Latino history.

Website

United Mexican-American Students. Provides information about the goals of the University of Colorado at Denver chapter which has blended with MEChA. http://www.ucdenver.edu/about/departments/DCODI/EOP/HSEPO/ChaptersOrgs/Pages/MEChA.aspx

1998

The Calle Ocho Festival makes it to the Guinness Book of World Records when 119,986 people form the world's longest conga line. The festival, a one-day event to celebrate Carnaval, takes place each March along Southwest 8th Street in the Little Havana section of Miami.

Books

Bucuvalas, Tina, Peggy A. Bulger, and Stetson Kennedy. *South Florida Folklife.* Jackson: University Press of Mississippi, 1994. Explores social life and customs among Cuban Americans and others.

Menard, Valerie. *The Latino Holiday Book: From Cinco de Mayo to Día de los Muertos—the Celebrations and Traditions of Hispanic-Americans.* New York: Marlowe, 2000. Explains the customs associated with the Calle Ocho festival.

Websites

Calle Ocho. A directory to shops and cultural events that can be found in the community. http://calleocho.com/

Calle Ocho, Little Havana. Describes the sights on the Miami streets and provides a link to more information about the March festival. http://miami.about.com/cs/maps/a/calle_ocho.htm

March 14

2010

Cherie DeCastro of the singing DeCastro Sisters dies in Las Vegas at 87. She was the only member of the group to appear in all of their recordings, television and film appearances, and stage shows. The sisters—Peggy, Cherie, and Babette—were raised in Havana, Cuba, as the daughters of a former Ziegfield Follies showgirl and a wealthy sugar plantation owner. Patterning themselves after the Andrews Sisters, the DeCastros immigrated to Miami in 1942 to pursue a singing career. Cousin Olgita sometimes replaced one of the sisters on stage. Best known for "Teach Me Tonight" in 1954, they performed on most of the major television shows of the 1950s and were inducted in 2000 into the Casino Legends Hall of Fame in Las Vegas.

Books

Austern, Linda Phyllis, and Inna Naroditskaya, eds. *Music of the Sirens*. Bloomington: Indiana University Press, 2006. Sets female singers of the 1950s in historical context.

Dunbar, Julie C. *Women, Music, and Culture: An Introduction*. New York: Routledge, 2011. Explains the cultural impact of women singers like the DeCastro Sisters.

Websites

The DeCastro Sisters. Provides audio clips of several of their songs. http://www.discogs.com/artist/De+Castro+Sisters,+The

DeCastro Sisters Record Label Shots and History. Offers a superb biography of the three sisters and photographs of their records. http://www.colorradio.com/decastro_sisters.htm

March 15

1947

Federico Fabian Peña, the first Latino to serve as Secretary of Transportation, is born in Laredo, Texas and grows up in Brownsville. In 1983, Peña became the first Latino mayor of Denver and he is credited with helping to bring the Colorado Rockies major league baseball team to the city. Appointed by President Bill Clinton to his cabinet in 1992, he left Treasury in 1997 to become secretary of energy.

From Statement of Federico F. Peña, "Nomination of Federico F. Peña to be Secretary of Transportation . . . January 7, 1993":

My goal, if I am confirmed by this body, is a very simple one, but it is also a very challenging one, and that is to make our national transportation system the finest in the world. That means that we have to understand the importance of people getting to work, getting to schools, have to understand the importance of transporting goods to our Nation, and realizing that transportation is at the very essence of rebuilding our national economy.

I fundamentally and strongly believe that an outstanding transportation system will allow our Nation to be globally competitive. That is our challenge, and I look forward to working with you, Mr. Chairman and members of the committee and other Members of Congress, in getting this job done.

The distinguished members of the panel today have told you a bit about my background. I am not going to go into that, only to say this. When you are a mayor of a city, you have got to deal with transportation issues on a daily basis, whether it is building bike paths or transit for people with disabilities or viaducts, or bridges, and yes, airports.

But having done that for 8 years, I think I bring the understanding of locally elected officials and State transportation officials to these problems, and I want to bring that philosophy and that experience to the Department of Transportation to get things done, because I know it is one thing to fund programs, it is something else to see those moneys tied up in the pipeline where projects are not getting done, and I want to make sure that we get that done by bringing my administrative experience to this challenge . . .

I believe I understand some of the issues facing rural America. As a member of the State legislature, we had to deal with statewide transportation planning. Some of the members may not know this, but I am originally from a little town called Brownsville, TX, which is a rural part of Texas, and having grown up in that area I think I understand the issues of the rural parts of our Nation . . .

I think transportation is very important to the quality of life of our country and to Americans. It is more than simply building bridges and bricks and mortar and building new airports. It is how we can improve the quality of life of Americans . . .

Last, but not of least importance, is the question of safety. I think safety has to continue to be a high priority for the transportation sector. We have got to continue to look at efficiency and new technologies in order to ensure that our transportation system is second to none.

(*Source:* "Nomination of Federico F. Peña to be Secretary of Transportation . . . January 7, 1993," http://archive.org/stream/no minationoffede00unit/nominationoffede00 unit_djvu.txt)

Book

Hero, Rodney E. *Latinos and the U.S. Political System: Two-Tiered Pluralism*. Philadelphia: Temple University Press, 1992. Includes a chapter on Peña.

Websites

Federico F. Peña: Next Secretary of Energy. The American Institute of Physics discusses Peña's qualifications for the Energy post. http://www.aip.org/fyi/1997/fyi97.004.htm

Federico F. Peña—Toyota. Provides a biography of Peña, who serves on Toyota's Diversity Advisory Board. http://www.toyota.com/about/diversity/diversity_advisory_board/fe derico_pena.html

1970

Zumba creator Alberto "Beto" Perez is born in Cali, Colombia. Perez created Zumba in Cali when he forgot to take his aerobics music to a class that he was teaching. He improvised by using some salsa and meringue tapes that he had in his backpack. The class loved the new dance-fitness regimen. In 2001, Perez moved to Miami and began to teach Zumba in the United States. Joining with fellow Colombians, Alberto Perlman and Alberto Aghion, Perez formed Zumba Fitness and trademarked the name, Zumba. The men began to sell DVDs and produced an infomercial that introduced the Zumba Fitness Party to a large audience. In 2005, the men opened a Zumba Academy to train instructors. There are now more than 20,000 licensed fitness teachers offering everything from Zumbatronic for kids to Zumba Gold for older adults and Aqua Zumba to anyone who likes the water.

From "Zoom In, Zumba Away":

I recently started doing Zumba, the dance and fitness phenomenon that, in 125 countries, has been whipping some 12 million people into a lather for the last decade, including everyone from Wyclef Jean to the writer Susan Orlean. I can safely say that dance-wise, it's the closest I have ever come to losing my mind. To wit: when I went to an elegant stand-up cocktail party . . . I was moved to enact for a fellow swiller of white wine a bit of Zumba choreography. . . . I was initially drawn to the Z, as I like to call it, because I wanted to be more limber and nimble. Yes, I was also impressed that this combination of Latin dance and cardio workout

can cause you to lose 500 to 1,000 cal-
ories per sweat-soaked hour-long session. . . . I operate at 50 or 60 percent
of the choreography, which is about
average. Certain stuttering Latin beats,
and the fancy footwork they foster,
elude me . . .

(*Source:* Alford, Henry. "Zoom In, Zumba
Away." *New York Times,* January 12, 2012,
pp. E1–E2.)

Books

Drake-Boyt, Elizabeth. *Latin Dance.* Westport,
　　CT: Greenwood Press, 2011. A dance histo-
　　rian examines the cultural significance of Latin
　　dance.
Perez, Beto. *Zumba: Ditch the Workout, Join the
　　Party: The Zumba Weight Loss Program.* Miami:
　　Wellness Central, 2009. This book, with an
　　accompanying DVD, outlines dance steps.

Websites

Zumba.com. The official Zumba website with
　　press clippings and information on finding an
　　instructor. http://www.zumba.com
Zumba Fitness. This YouTube clip, approved
　　by Perez, shows people performing Zumba.
　　http://www.youtube.com/watch?v=Vf0q6q
　　tThF4

March 16

1967

Gilberto Concepción de Gracia, founder
of the Puerto Rican Independence Party in
1946, dies. Born in Vega Alta, he studied
law at the University of Puerto Rico and
George Washington University. Concepción de Gracia specialized in civil and constitutional law, once representing members
of the Puerto Rican Nationalist Party who
were jailed in New York City. When Puerto
Rico gained commonwealth status in 1952,
Concepción de Gracia saw it as just another
name for colonialism. Through a number of

newspaper articles, he continued to push for
independence.

Gilberto Concepción de Gracia on "The
Revolution of 1950":

[The Puerto Rican Independence
Party (PIP)] has accepted and accepts
the electoral struggle in full awareness
of the vices inherent in the system. We
have accepted it knowing that these
vices are aggravating in a colony; the
more so when the ballot box must be
used as a liberating weapon, in conflict
with the representatives of a system that
keeps out people in a state of submission, inferiority, and servitude.

We have accepted it because the
men and women of our party have
total confidence in the intelligence,
civic sense, and courage of our people,
and full faith in their creative capacity.
Furthermore because these men and
women firmly believe that the ballot
box is the fastest and most direct road
to win our independence, and the only
one that can guarantee economic stability for the future Puerto Rican Republic. Having this firm and unshakeable
conviction, the women and men of the
PIP reject the road of armed revolution
and dedicate themselves sedulously, religiously, in body and soul, to building a great party ready and able to win
the elections of 1952 and to make our
country independent.

(*Source:* Zavala, Iris M., and Rafael Rodríguez, eds. *The Intellectual Roots of Independence: An Anthology of Puerto Rican Political
Essays.* New York: Monthly Review Press,
1980, pp. 187–88.)

Book

Ayala, Cesar J., and Rafael Bernabe. *Puerto Rico
　　in the American Century: A History since 1898.*
　　Chapel Hill: University of North Carolina
　　Press, 2007. Covers the dispute over the best

means and whether to pursue Puerto Rican independence.

Websites

Biography of Gilberto Concepción de Gracia. The Puerto Rican Independence Party provides a biography of its founder on its Spanish-language website. http://www.independencia.net/historia/bioGilberto.html

El Coquí: The Mission of Gilberto Concepción de Gracia. A short documentary on Concepción de Gracia's efforts to defend Puerto Rican nationalists in 1936 New York City. http://www.youtube.com/watch?v=d-iclL_KQw8

March 17

1732

Miguel de Quintana, a poet from present-day New Mexico, becomes the first writer in the history of the Southwest to be tried by the Inquisition when formal charges are made against him at the Holy Office in Santa Fe. On May 22, 1734, the Catholic Church office in Mexico City ruled that it did not have enough evidence to prosecute Quintana though it advised that the poet be questioned intensively regarding his claim to be divinely inspired to write. Quintana came to New Mexico in 1694 with Diego de Vargas and worked as a farmer and notary in the village of Santa Cruz de la Cañada. Unusually literate for his time and place, Quintana produced some of the earliest Latino writings.

Books

Lomelí, Francisco A., and Clark A. Colahan, eds. *Defying the Inquisition in Colonial New Mexico: Miguel de Quintana's Life and Writings*. Albuquerque: University of New Mexico Press, 2006. The best source on the poet's life and works.

Shirley, Carl R., and Francisco A. Lomelí, eds. *Chicano Writers*. Detroit: Gale Research, 1992. Includes a chapter on Quintana that identifies him as a forerunner of Chicano literature.

1973

Denver police raid an apartment building on Downing Street owned by the Crusade for Justice (CFJ) as a birthday party for a tenant winds down. The raid is followed by gunfire and an explosion. Luis "Junior" Martinez, a 20-year-old member of the CFJ, died in the confrontation. The police and the CFJ have widely varying accounts of what took place. The Chicano civil rights group, one of the most radical organizations of the era, demands an investigation of the incident by the U.S. Justice Department. Denver police charge that the CFJ had stashed weapons in the building while the mayor refuses to back an investigation. The episode contributed to further bad relations between the CFJ and Denver city officials.

Letter to the editor of the *Rocky Mountain News* by Rodolfo "Corky" Gonzales on May 29, 1974:

In regard to the questions concerning some statements, allegations and charges made by various persons (known or unknown) about myself and the Crusade for Justice to the Rocky Mountain News, I will only say that I refuse to take part in a Roman Circus that can only entertain the News readers and do considerable harm to the Chicano people and community.

I will not be part of a gossip and rumor situation for the benefit of the power structure and those misled individuals who would consider themselves spokesmen or leaders of any segment or the whole of the Chicano movement.

We have taken a position of independence and follow a philosophy of self-determination. We do not claim to have the answers to alleviate all the problems of the Chicano people but we are steadfast in our beliefs that we can provide the solutions and the direction by providing the model through our own efforts, i.e., the establishment of a Learning Center, a day care center, a paper, a source center, a social services division, a leadership development program, an athletic program, a community media committee and economic base. These then are the components that we feel are necessary for the development and education and growth of any progressive group.

We do not claim ownership or control of the Chicano people, but we have assumed the responsibility of educating and influencing the people by our example.

In conclusion, I can only ask that if we are not important in this community and if our actions have no effect, then why are we the subject and interest of so many parties in power, petty politicos and office holders? We can only reason that our effectiveness is measured by the reaction generated.

I'm led to repeat an old adage related to me by my uncle: "The higher you rise, the better target you are for bricks."

We will withstand the bricks, the attempts to destroy us as an organization and the futile efforts to divide us as people. WE SHALL ENDURE.

(*Source:* Gonzales, Rodolfo. *Message to Aztlán: Selected Writings.* Houston: Arte Publico, 2001, p. 243.)

Books

Acuña, Rodolfo. *Occupied America: A History of Chicanos.* New York: Harper Collins, 1988. The standard history of the Chicano movement.

Vigil, Ernesto B. *The Crusade for Justice: Chicano Militancy and the Government's War on Dissent.* Madison: University of Wisconsin Press, 1999. Vigil, a member of Crusade for Justice, was at the Downing Street apartment when the situation with the police began.

Website

Remembering March 17th and the Attack on Crusade for Justice. Chiefly provides a biography of Luis "Junior" Martinez. http://westdenvercopwatch.wordpress.com/2011/03/16/remembering-march-17th-and-the-attack-on-the-crusade-for-justice/

March 18

1988

The movie *Stand and Deliver,* about inspiring East Los Angeles math teacher Jaime Escalante, opens in theaters. Escalante is portrayed by Edward James Olmos, a Mexican American actor who grew up in gang-scarred East Los Angeles before starring in the iconic 1980s television show *Miami Vice.* Olmos is nominated for an Academy Award for his performance. Escalante died at 79 in 2010.

Books

Gradillas, Henry, and Jerry Jesness. *Standing and Delivering: What the Movie Didn't Tell.* Lanham, MD: Rowman and Littlefield, 2010. Discusses what is necessary to create an effective school.

Mathews, Jay. *Escalante: The Best Teacher in America.* New York: Holt, 1988. A biography of the famed math teacher.

Websites

Jaime Escalante: Biography. This A&E television network site offers a short biography of the teacher. http://www.biography.com/people/jaime-escalante-189368

Jaime Escalante on Being a Teacher. A three-minute video clip of Escalante discussing teaching. http://www.youtube.com/watch?v=FFMz8JRg8Y8

March 19

1960

Brazilian jazz singer, composer, and pianist Eliane Elias is born in Sao Paulo. Arriving in New York City in 1981, she soon became the first woman instrumentalist to be featured on the cover of *Downbeat* magazine. All of her more than 20 recordings have reached No. 5 on the *Billboard* charts.

From a *Latin Beat Magazine* interview with Elias in 2011:

Luis Tamargo: You honored the legacy of Brazil's most iconic composer on a couple of heartfelt Blue Note releases—Eliane Elias Plays Jobim (1990) and Eliane Elias Sings Jobim (1998). While listening to these recordings, I realized that the way in which you vocalized Jobim's melodies was similar to the way you would do it on the piano. Is it the same voice, but on a different instrument?

Eliane Elias: Yes and no. What I can do as a pianist is a lot more than what I can do with my voice as an instrument. The type of phrasing, the way it feels, yes, I would do it the same way because that's how I feel the music. But with the voice, I have a smaller range to deal with, so it is different than the way I could do it on the piano, but the general feel is the same.

LT: I wonder if you started singing because you would write certain things that could not be properly phrased by instruments.

EE: Yes. I started doing that on my very first album (Amanda, Passport Jazz, 1984), which I recorded with Randy (Brecker), and then I did some vocals on other subsequent recordings, in which I employed my voice as an instrument, and because I have a certain way of using rhythm and phrasing, and felt that it was the way that I wanted to hear it, the voice took the place of the instrument.

LT: On the CD The Three Americas (Blue Note, 1997), you sought to achieve an organic blend of what Dizzy Gillespie once defined as "Pan-American Music," meaning the fusion of the main musical genres of the Western Hemisphere. By the way, was this the first time that you recorded a tango-style composition?

EE: Yes, that particular tune was called Chorango. It starts as a chorinho, and then becomes a tango. It was an interesting rendition, as it included a violin and a little bit of accordion.

LT: I was quite impressed with your most recent release (Light My Fire, Concord Picante, 2011), as it seems to be more rhythmically diverse and aggressive than some of your prior recordings.

LT: In addition to your marvelous rhythmic section, the CD Light My Fire features some wonderful guests, including the singer-composer from Bahia named Gilberto Gil.

EE: Yes. Gilberto is one of the great composers from Brazil, and it was fantastic to have him on three vocal duets. It was really joyful to bring some elements from the music of Bahia, which I have been including more and more on my records. This is music that has influenced me a lot. I love Bahia!

(*Source:* Tamargo, Luis. "Eliane Elias Speaks: A Dialogue with Brazil's Most Renowned Pianist." *Latin Beat Magazine,* http://elianeelias.com/reviews-articles/interviews/latin-beat-magazine-2011)

Books

Clark, Walter Aaron, ed. *Musics of Latin America.* New York: W.W. Norton, 2012. Covers Brazilian music including bossa nova.

McGowan, Chris, and Ricardo Pessanha. *The Brazilian Sound: Samba, Bossa Nova, and the Popular Music of Brazil.* Philadelphia: Temple University Press, 2009. Includes a chapter on Bahia.

Website

The Official Site of Eliane Elias. Provides news, photographs, and a discography of the singer. Elianeelias.com

March 20

1962

ASPIRA is formed to address the high dropout rate of Puerto Rican students. In 1960, only 13 percent of adult Puerto Ricans had finished high school and over half had less than an eighth grade education. The leaders of ASPIRA, including educator Antonia Pantoja, identified the factors that hampered students from graduating. ASPIRA, whose name is Spanish for "aspire," emphasized the development of leaders and sought to make students aware of their ethnic heritage. In 1968, ASPIRA commissioned Richard Margolis to investigate the conditions of Puerto Rican children in American public schools. The report, titled *The Losers,* showed that schools sabotaged Puerto Rican children's opportunities for equal education.

From Richard J. Margolis, *The Losers: A Report on Puerto Ricans and the Public Schools:*

The observer can but dimly discern the everyday frustrations which many Puerto Rican school children have come to take for granted: their imperfect grasp of English, which often seals both their lips and their minds; their confusion about who they are (what race? what culture?), a confusion compounded by the common ravages of white prejudice; their sense of being lost, or traveling through a foreign country with a heedless guide and an undecipherable map.

(*Source:* Macdonald, Victoria-Maria, ed. *Latino Education in the United States: A Narrated History from 1513–2000.* New York: Palgrave Macmillan, 2004, p. 221.)

Books

Altenbaugh, Richard J. *The American People and Their Education: A Social History.* Upper Saddle River, NJ: Pearson, 2003. A study of the American educational system that includes a focus on Latinos.

Macdonald, Victoria-Maria, ed. *Latino Education in the United States: A Narrated History from 1513–2000.* New York: Palgrave Macmillan, 2004. Illustrates why Latinos have historically had a high dropout rate and includes a history of ASPIRA.

Websites

The Aspira Association: An Investment in Latino Youth. The official webpage of the organization contains information about its programs and history. http://www.aspira.org/

ASPIRA of Illinois. One of the larger state chapters, the Illinois ASPIRA addresses the needs of all family members to make sure that children can succeed in school and proceed to college. http://aspirail.org/

1969

A hundred and fifty Mexican American students stage a walkout at West Side High School in Denver after social science teacher Harry Schaffer allegedly declares in a class discussion: "All Mexicans are stupid because their parents were stupid and their parents' parents were stupid. . . . If you eat Mexican food you'll look like a Mexican." At the time, only one percent of the faculty at the high school were Latino. The students protested the refusal of school administrators to fire Schaffer. The walkout lasted three days during which riots broke out and police battled with protesters. Ultimately, Schaffer was transferred and the school expanded its Mexican American course offerings.

Books

Acuña, Rodolfo. *Occupied America: A History of Chicanos*. New York: Harper Collins, 1988. The standard history of the Chicano movement.

Vigil, Ernesto B. *The Crusade for Justice: Chicano Militancy and the Government's War on Dissent*. Madison: University of Wisconsin Press, 1999. Explains why the students walked out.

Websites

West High, 1969. An account of the walkout by the *Denver Post*. http://www.denverpost.com/news/ci_11968641

West High Chicano Walkout. A short video clip that features a scene on the West High protest from a play titled *A People's History of Colorado*. http://www.youtube.com/watch?v=bHmZVfn0DVA

March 21

1940

Mario Acuña, a scientist at the National Aeronautics and Space Administration (NASA), is born in Argentina. Acuña won the NASA Medal for Exceptional Scientific Achievement for his work on the instruments of the Mars Global Surveyor Mission and numerous space ships. He died in 2009.

Books

Godwin, Robert. *Mars: The NASA Mission Reports*. New York: Collector's Guide, 2000. A collection of the latest results from the Mars Exploration Rovers as well as the Mars Global Surveyor and Mars Odyssey missions.

Gorn, Michael H. *NASA: The Complete Illustrated History*. New York: Merrell, 2005. Portrays some of the projects that Acuña worked on.

Websites

Dr. Mario H. Acuña. Offers an extensive biography of the space scientist. http://www.cielosur.com/videos/mario_acuna.pdf

Mario H. Acuña. The Lunar and Planetary Institute provides an obituary for Acuña. http://www.lpi.usra.edu/features/MarioAcuna/

March 22

1916

Félix Martinez, a newspaper publisher and political leader, dies. In 1890, Martinez began to publish *La Voz de Pueblo* and it became the foremost Spanish-language newspaper in New Mexico. In the 1890s, he also backed the Populist movement through El Partido del Pueblo Unido (The United People's Party). Under his leadership, the group supported a merger between the Populists and the Democrats. In the early

20th century, he became one of the first directors of the Federal Reserve Board, Dallas. He was arguably the most prominent Latino in the United States at the time of his death.

Books

Gonzales-Berry, Erlinda, and David R. Maciel, eds. *The Contested Homeland: A Chicano History of New Mexico*. Albuquerque: University of New Mexico Press, 2010. Includes *La Voz de Pueblo* in the story of Latinos in the Land of Enchantment.

Vigil, Maurilio E. *Los Patrones: Profiles of Hispanic Political Leaders in New Mexico History*. Washington: University Press of America, 1980. Includes a chapter on Martinez.

Website

Félix Martinez. The Handbook of Texas Online offers a solid biography of the publisher. http://www.tshaonline.org/handbook/online/articles/fmadj

2010

A largely Latino crowd estimated to be tens of thousands strong marches in Washington, D.C., to demand immigration reform. The protesters, who came from across the country, converged on the National Mall. Waving American flags and chanting President Barack Obama's campaign slogan "Sí se puede," they called for legislation that would give 12 million immigrants currently residing in the United States illegally a path to citizenship. Like President George W. Bush before him, Obama had promised to reform immigration during his campaign for office but had not acted on the promise. Latinos were among Obama's strongest supporters in 2008.

From "At Washington's Immigration Reform March, A Warning from Latinos":

> [President] Obama had promised during his campaign to make comprehensive immigration reform a priority in his first year—a promise he reiterated

last Thursday to Rep. Luis Gutierrez in exchange for his vote on the health-care reform bill and again on Sunday to the crowd assembled at the Mall via a video address shown on giant screens. . . . "I have always pledged to be your partner as we work to fix our broken immigration system, and that's a commitment that I reaffirm today," he said. . . . But some demonstrators, like Rigoberto Rodriguez, a Chicagoan who voted for Obama and the Democrats in 2008, were disappointed and frustrated by Obama's lack of action on immigration. . . . "If he doesn't keep his word, we're not going to vote. He promised he would reform immigration. If there's not reform, we won't support him," he said. . . . At the rally, Raquel Batista, a Colorado State University student whose parents were migrant farmworkers, says it's hard not to get impatient for change. "It's frustrating that we haven't seen change. We haven't seen what we expected. But I understand that things in the government take time."

(*Source:* Quintanilla, Eloise. "At Washington's Immigration Reform March, A Warning From Latinos." *Christian Science Monitor,* March 22, 2010, n.p., http://www.csmonitor.com/USA/Politics/2010/0322/At-Washington-s-immigration-reform-march-a-warning-from-Latinos)

Books

Newton, Lina. *Illegal, Alien, or Immigrant: The Politics of Immigration Reform*. New York: New York University Press, 2008. Examines the debates over immigration reform beginning with the 1980s.

Spickard, Paul. *Almost All Aliens: Immigration, Race, and Colonialism in American History and Identity*. New York: Routledge, 2007. A comprehensive history of U.S. immigration.

Websites

Center for Immigration Studies. This is the home page for the nonpartisan organization, the only think tank devoted to immigration policy. http://www.cis.org/

Yearbook of Immigration Statistics: 2010. This U.S. Department of Homeland Security page contains immigration statistics that date back to 1820. http://www.dhs.gov/files/statistics/publications/LPR10.shtm

March 23

1913

Sixto Escobar, the first Puerto Rican to win a world boxing championship and, arguably the greatest of all Puerto Rican fighters, is born in Barceloneta. Raised in San Juan, "El Gallito" made his professional boxing debut in 1931 with a knockout of his opponent. Having moved to New York City, he defeated Tony Marino in 1936 to become the world bantamweight champion. Escobar, a man known for his powerful blows, retired in 1940 and served in the military during World War II. He died in Puerto Rico in 1979. In 2002, Escobar was inducted into the International Boxing Hall of Fame with a record of 43 wins, 19 by knockouts, and 22 losses.

Books

Lang, Arne K. *Prizefighting: An American History*. Jefferson, NC: McFarland, 2008. Includes Latinos in the history of the sport.

Liebling, A.J. *The Sweet Science*. New York: North Point Press, 2004. A classic work on the history of boxing by a famed sportswriter.

Websites

Cyber Boxing Zone—Sixto Escobar. Excellent summary of Escobar's career. http://www.cyberboxingzone.com/boxing/escobar.htm

Sixto Escobar. Provides Escobar's boxing record. http://boxrec.com/media/index.php/Sixto_Escobar

1928

The Confederación de Uniones Obreras Mexicanas (Confederation of Mexican Labor Unions) is founded in Los Angeles to address substandard working conditions and poor wages. The union included both agricultural and industrial workers. As a result, its membership tended to fluctuate according to the growing seasons, hovering between 2,000 and 3,000 members at a peak. With the advent of the Great Depression and the deportation of many Mexican Americans, the organization began to collapse. It reconstituted itself as the Confederación de Uniones de Campesinos y Obreros Mexicanos del Estado de California (Confederation of Mexican Peasant and Workers Unions of the State of California), or CUCOM, which had greater success and far more members. The latter organization led a 1936 walkout of celery workers and, a year later, joined the United Cannery, Agricultural, Packing, and Allied Workers of America.

From the constitution of the Confederación de Uniones Obreras Mexicanas:

That the exploited class, the greater part of which is made up of manual labor, is right in establishing a class struggle in order to effect an economic and moral betterment of its conditions, and at last, its complete freedom from capitalistic tyranny.

That in order to be able to oppose the organization each day the more complete and intelligent of the exploiters, the exploited class must organize as such, the base of its organization being the union of resistance, in accord with the rights which the laws of this country concede to native and foreign workers.

That the corporations, possessors of the natural and social wealth, being integral parts of the international association of industry, commerce, and banking, the disinherited class must also integrate by means of its federations and confederations into a single union of all the labor of the world

(*Source:* Gonzales, Sylvia Alicia. *Hispanic American Voluntary Organizations.* Westport, CT: Greenwood Press, 1985, pp. 66–67.)

Books

Acuña, Rodolfo. *Occupied America: A History of Chicanos.* New York: Harper Collins, 1988. Reports on CUCOM but does not acknowledge its link to the earlier group.

Jamieson, Stuart M. *Labor Unionism in American Agriculture.* New York: Arno, 1976. The major reference source on the union.

Websites

Mexican Immigrant Labor History. This PBS site traces the history from 1850 to 1964. http://www.pbs.org/kpbs/theborder/history/timeline/17.html

Review of Zaragosa Vargas's *Labor Rights are Civil Rights: Mexican-American Workers in Twentieth-Century America.* Does not focus on this union but links working class activism to the successes of the Mexican American civil rights movement in the 1960s. http://socialistworker.org/2008/04/04/mexican-americans-jim-crow

March 24

1924

DJ and trombonist Chico Sesma is born in East Los Angeles. He played with numerous big bands in the 1940s. However, Sesma is better known as a major influence on Chicano performers in Southern California. When his musical career slowed in 1949, he was hired as a disc jockey at KOWL; he was someone who could relate to the Mexican American community with a bilingual, Latin music format. Sesma continued as host of the three-hour show for the next 20 years. He made boleros and other variants of Mexican

music cool for Chicano kids growing up in the 1950s and 1960s. In the 1950s, Sesma also began promoting performances by Latino artists. His concerts at the Hollywood Palladium, held from 1959 through 1973, became one of the great musical events for Chicanos in Southern California. The Midniters and Los Lobos have cited Sesma as helping them develop as Mexican American artists.

Books

Morales, Ed. *The Latin Beat: The Rhythms and Roots of Latin Music from Bossa Nova to Salsa and beyond.* Cambridge, MA: Da Capo Press, 2003. Covers the Latin influence on rock music.

Reyes, David, and Tom Waldman. *Land of a Thousand Dances: Chicano rock 'n' roll from Southern California.* Albuquerque: University of New Mexico Press, 2009. Covers the Midniters and other groups that Sesma influenced.

Websites

Chico Sesma and His Orchestra. In this video clip, the musicians play "Cha Cha Bounce." http://www.youtube.com/watch?v=0QlTFNkOODY

Roots of the Eastside Sound—Chico Sesma. Profiles Chico Sesma and his influence in Southern California. http://wwwyoufoundtheastsidesoundcom.blogspot.com/2011/06/roots-of-eastside-sound-chico-sesma.html

1933

William Valentiner, director of the Detroit Institute of Arts, predicts that Diego Rivera's murals, completed today, will rank among the truly great art treasures of America. He turns out to be correct. The *Detroit Industry* fresco cycle, a 27-panel work at the Institute of Arts completed between April 1932 and March 1933, is viewed as the finest example of Mexican mural art in the United States. Rivera regarded it as the best work of his career. Rivera portrayed large-scale industrial production, depicting functional machines with precision to transform them into objects of beauty.

Book

Rivera, Diego, and Gladys March. *My Art, My Life: An Autobiography*. New York: Dover, 1991. The artist's thoughts on his career.

Websites

Diego Rivera: About the Artist. PBS provides a biography of the artist, the subject of one of its *American Masters* television shows. http://www.pbs.org/wnet/americanmasters/episodes/diego-rivera/about-the-artist/64/

Diego Rivera: Paintings, Biography, and Quotes. Probably the best site on the artist as it contains a long biography and many, many images of his works. http://www.diego-rivera.com/

1982

The Sanctuary Movement begins when John Fife, pastor of the Southside United Presbyterian Church in Tucson, Arizona, declares the church a sanctuary for Central American refugees escaping government-sponsored violence in their countries. The First Unitarian Church in Los Angeles, the University Lutheran Chapel in San Francisco, Luther Place Memorial Church in Washington, D.C., and an independent bible church in Long Island, New York, follow suit on the same day. The coordinated action developed into a loose network of more than 75,000 religious people and approximately 250 churches, synagogues, and Quaker meeting houses that declared their places of worship to be sanctuary sites. The members of the Sanctuary Movement acted because of the rapidly rising death toll among civilians in El Salvador and Guatemala as well as the more than 50,000 Salvadoran deportations in 1981. The involvement of the Reagan administration with rightwing groups in the Central American conflicts also prompted the religious people to resist the U.S. government's immigration policy.

The defense offered in court by indicted church workers, March 1985:

The earth itself is to become a sanctuary. This covenant forms us into a people of many nations, cultures, and creeds—a people that the Christians among us sometimes call the church! Protective community with the persecuted is an inalienable requirement of the covenant to hallow the earth. And the intercongregational provisions of sanctuary for Central American refugees is simply the practice of our faith as a covenant people. This means that we cannot agree to ignore any person who asks for our help to escape torture and murder. Many of us, if ordered by the State to do so, might sacrifice a pinch of incense to Caesar, but we cannot sacrifice the lives of Central American refugees. . . . We pray for the strength to love and the courage to remain true to our faith—that the Kingdom may come on earth, in our lives and during our days, and in the lives of all covenant peoples.

(*Source*: Masud-Piloto, Félix Roberto. *With Open Arms: Cuban Migration to the United States*. Totowa, NJ: Rowman & Littlefield, 1988, p. 123.)

Books

Coutin, Susan Bibler. *The Culture of Protest: Religious Activism and the U.S. Sanctuary Movement*. Boulder: Westview Press, 1993. Sets the movement in the context of religious history.

Lorentzen, Robin. *Women in the Sanctuary Movement*. Philadelphia: Temple University Press, 1991. Women have historically performed much of the labor to support a church's mission so it is not a surprise that women aided refugees in the 1980s.

Masud-Piloto, Félix Roberto. *With Open Arms: Cuban Migration to the United States*. Totowa, NJ: Rowman & Littlefield, 1988. Contrasts the U.S. government's response to Cuban immigration with its responses to Haitian and Central American immigration.

March 25

1990

A fire kills 87 people, most of them Honduran and Dominican immigrants, at an illegal club in the East Tremont section of the Bronx. New York City authorities had ordered Happy Land Social Club to be shut down in December as a fire hazard but the order to vacate had apparently either never been received or been ignored by the club's owners. Over 150 firefighters fought the blaze in the small building. Of the 61 men and 26 women who died, most were under age 25. Juan Gonzalez, a Cuban immigrant who had argued with his girlfriend in the club, was charged with setting the blaze while drunk. He received 25 years to life.

From "Analysis of the Happy Land Social Club Fire with Hazard I":

> The New York City Fire Department requested the assistance of the Center for Fire Research (CFR) in understanding the factors which contributed to this high death toll and to develop a strategy that might reduce the risk of a similar occurrence in the many similar clubs operating in the city. . . .
>
> Wall finish throughout the interior of the building was . . . wood paneling. The ceilings were low density fiberboard tiles in the first floor entry and bar, and gypsum board elsewhere. The fiberboard tiles were installed on furring strips under the floor joists and the paneling was on furring strips over plaster. Note the partial sprinkler system on the second floor.
>
> From information reported in the media and observations of the CFR staff during an on-site investigation,

the ignition scenario for this fire was as follows. One dollar's worth (about three quarters of a gallon) of gasoline was poured on the floor of the entryway and ignited. The door from the entryway to the street was believed to be open and the door from the entryway to the bar was believed to be closed. The fire quickly spread to the combustible interior finish within the entry area and, at some point someone opened the door from the bar to the entryway to go out. This opened a path for fire to spread from the entryway into the first floor bar area.

> At some point before or after this interior door was opened, an employee and a patron escaped through the service entrance which was reportedly closed. It is unclear whether these doors were left open or closed and reopened after the fire department arrived. The fire department entered through the front doors and quickly brought the fire under control. Of the seven sprinkler heads on the second floor, four opened, two did not, and one was missing at the time of the site visit but water stain patterns on the ceiling indicated that it had been in place and activated during the fire. Based on damage observations made at the scene, the hollow core door at the base of the front stairway was believed to be closed through most of the fire.
>
> Newspaper accounts indicated that 68 of the 87 victims were recovered from the second floor where they succumbed to toxic smoke. The remainder of the bodies were recovered from the first floor from the rear restroom, each having some burns in addition to smoke inhalation. There were at least three survivors and possibly a few more. . .
>
> While the building had a partial sprinkler system on the second floor,

it played only a minor role in this fire since it was so far removed from the actual fire. If the building had been protected by a complete (operational) sprinkler system, the fire likely would have been extinguished in the entryway. While it is not currently possible to demonstrate this with the models, there are test data for a very similar condition, a gasoline spill in the entryway to an apartment, in which rapid extinguishment was achieved. . . . The FPE-TOOL routine FIRE SIMULATOR indicates that a traditional sprinkler head in the entryway would have activated in about 7 seconds following ignition of the gasoline.

(*Source:* Bukowski, Richard W. "Analysis of the Happy Land Social Club Fire with Hazard I." *Fire and Arson Investigator,* March 1992, http://fire.nist.gov/bfrlpubs/fire92/PDF/f92041.pdf)

Books

Román, Miriam Jiménez, and Juan Flores, eds. *The Afro-Latino Reader: History and Culture in the United States.* Durham, NC: Duke University Press, 2010. A collection of essays including some that discuss the challenges facing Honduran immigrants.

Sagás, Ernesto, and Sintia E. Molina, eds. *Dominican Migration: Transnational Perspectives.* Gainesville: University Press of Florida, 2004. Looks at Dominican immigration to the United States.

Websites

Analysis of the Happy Land Social Club Fire with Hazard I. An official report by Richard W. Bukowski, reprinted from the March 1992 *Fire and Arson Investigator.* http://fire.nist.gov/bfrlpubs/fire92/PDF/f92041.pdf

A River of Tears—Happy Land. This Crime Library report by Mark Gado includes a police diagram of the nightclub along with an excellent summary of the case. http://www.trutv.com/library/crime/notorious_murders/mass/happyland/fuego_3.html

March 26

1948

The American G. I. Forum is created in Corpus Christi, Texas, by 700 Mexican American veterans to improve the conditions for Mexican Americans who had served in the armed forces. It first focused on obtaining G. I. Bill benefits and then moved to address hospital care and Mexican American representation on draft boards. Led by Hector P. García, the organization generally focused its efforts on ending discriminatory practices against veterans but would occasionally support broader efforts to halt discrimination against Latinos.

Books

Acuña, Rodolfo. *Occupied America: A History of Chicanos.* New York: Harper Collins, 1988. A general history that explains why Mexican Americans needed civil rights organizations.

Allsup, Carl. *The American G. I. Forum: Origins and Evolution.* Austin: Center for Mexican American Studies, The University of Texas at Austin, 1982. The best history of the civil rights group.

Websites

American G. I. Forum. The official website of the organization contains information about chapters and services for veterans. http://www.agifusa.org/

American G. I. Forum of Texas. The Handbook of Texas History Online provides a good history of the first chapter of this venerable organization. http://www.tshaonline.org/handbook/online/articles/voa01

1984

Hector P. García becomes the first Mexican American to receive the Presidential Medal of Freedom. President Ronald Reagan honored García for organizing the American G.I. Forum in 1948 to address discrimination against Latino veterans and for other myriad acts of service to the United States.

Books

Acuña, Rodolfo. *Occupied America: A History of Chicanos*. New York: Harper Collins, 1988. Explains why the American G.I. Forum was needed.

Allsup, Carl. *The American G.I. Forum: Origins and Evolution*. Austin: Center for Mexican American Studies, The University of Texas at Austin, 1982. The best history of the civil rights group.

Websites

American G.I. Forum. The official website of the organization contains information about chapters and services for veterans. http://www.agifusa.org/

American G.I. Forum of Texas. The Handbook of Texas History Online provides a good history of the first chapter of this venerable organization. http://www.tshaonline.org/handbook/online/articles/voa01

March 27

1814

Diego Archuleta, the first Latino brigadier general in the United States, is born in Santa Fe, New Mexico. He served in the Mexican National Congress as a delegate from New Mexico in the 1840s. During the Mexican-American War, Archuleta fought against the United States. Upon Mexico's loss, Archuleta took an oath of allegiance to the United States and served in the territorial assembly. With the advent of the Civil War, Archuleta led the New Mexico Volunteer Infantry, which had more Hispanic officers than any other unit in the war. The unit fought in the Battle of Valverde in 1862.

Books

Taylor, John. *Bloody Valverde: A Civil War Battle on the Rio Grande, February 21, 1862*. Albuquerque: University of New Mexico Press, 1995. The best study of this little known battle.

Wilson, John P. *From Western Deserts to Carolina Swamps: A Civil War Soldier's Journals and Letters Home*. Albuquerque: University of New Mexico Press, 2012. The memoir of Lewis Franklin Roe, who fought in the Battle of Valverde.

Websites

American Civil War: Battle of Valverde. Summarizes the Confederate victory in New Mexico Territory. http://militaryhistory.about.com/od/civilwarinthewest/p/battle-of-valverde.htm

Battle Summary: Valverde, NM. The National Park Service provides this synopsis of the battle. http://www.nps.gov/hps/abpp/battles/nm001.htm

1969

The first national Chicano Youth Liberation Conference begins in Denver. Panel discussions over the next three days focus on social revolution and cultural identity according to the conference theme: "Where does the Barrio's Youth, the Student, the Rural Chicano, the Campesino, fit into the Chicano Movement?" Corky Gonzales and the Crusade for Justice, a Chicano group founded in Denver, conduct the general sessions and provide young Mexican Americans with an opportunity to express their views on self-determination. About 1,500 youths attend with participating groups including: United Mexican American Students (UMAS), Mexican American Youth Association (MAYA), the Brown Berets, and the Young Lords. Through his efforts to unite students with the Chicano movement, Gonzales establishes himself as a major Chicano leader.

From an interview by Froben Lozada and Antonio Camejo of the Socialist Workers Party with Corky Gonzales:

I thought about all the young people who are confused and who don't want to identify with these old politicos, those old figureheads. They don't want to identify with the same old answers. They want to get into doing something. I talked to a lot of these young people, and they decided they needed a conference. They wanted to come to Denver. . . . We had to bring the people together. Many youth who graduate from college leave the community and never come back. They don't offer academic leadership in any form. We had to start breaking this down, so that the barrio bato (youth) had a relationship with the student. The student wouldn't go around just carrying the banner of the issues and the problems of the barrio as his cause and yet never relate to it and never be involved in the mud and the dirt and the blood.

(*Source:* Marín, Christine. *A Spokesman of the Mexican American Movement: Rodolfo "Corky" Gonzales and the Fight for Chicano Liberation, 1966–1972.* San Francisco: R & E Research Associates, 1977, p. 12.)

Books

Marín, Christine. *A Spokesman of the Mexican American Movement: Rodolfo "Corky" Gonzales and the Fight for Chicano Liberation, 1966–1972.* San Francisco: R & E Research Associates, 1977. The only biography of the Chicano leader, it contains a wealth of primary sources.

Rosales, F. Arturo. *Chicano!: The History of the Mexican American Civil Rights Movement.* Houston: Arte Publico, 1996. The winner of the Gustavus Myers Outstanding Book Award for its coverage of the movement.

Websites

The Chicano Civil Rights Movement. A timeline of the movement from the Experience Music Project at the Science Fiction Museum and Hall of Fame. http://www.empmuseum. org/documents/education/onlineCourse/Civil_Rights_Timeline.pdf

The Chicano Movement: Brown and Proud. A brief history of the movement by Nadra Kareem Nittle. http://racerelations.about. com/od/historyofracerelations/a/BrownandProudTheChicanoMovement.htm

1990

Televisión Martí begins broadcasting anti-Castro news, entertainment, and sports to Cuba. Its sister station, Radio Martí, began in May 1985. The broadcasts, blocked by the Cuban government, reportedly only reach a small percentage of the Cuban population but remain popular among Cuban Americans strongly opposed to Fidel Castro.

From Nick Miroff, "The Revolution, Televised," 2010:

Over the past two decades, the U.S. government has spent some $500 million to beam news and commentary with an anti-Castro bent into Cuba. But the programming hasn't exactly been a ratings success.

The Cuban government controls all media on the island and views the broadcasts as enemy propaganda, so it jams the signals. The Miami-based stations, Radio and TV Marti, have spent still more money trying to overcome this by transmitting from moving airplanes, but the broadcasts reach less than 1 percent of Cuba's 11 million residents, according to a recent report by the U.S. Government Accountability Office.

Meanwhile, hours and hours of subversive American programming fill Cuba's airwaves each day, attracting millions of viewers on the island with shows like "Desperate Housewives," "Friends" and "Grey's Anatomy." How do they get there? They're broadcast by Cuba's own communist government.

(*Source:* Miroff, Nick. "The Revolution, Televised: You Might Be Surprised What Cubans Are Watching." *GlobalPost,* February 17, 2010, http://www.globalpost.com/dispatch/cuba/100216/tv-radio-marti)

Books

Nordenstreng, Kaarle, and Herbert I. Schiller, eds. *Beyond National Sovereignty: International Communication in the 1990s.* Norwood, NJ: Ablex, 1993. Includes a chapter on televison Martí by Laurien Alexandre.

Walsh, Daniel C. *An Air War with Cuba: The United States Radio Campaign against Castro.* Jefferson, NC: McFarland, 2012. An excellent account of the battle of the airwaves.

Websites

Radio and TV Martí. Summarizes the duties of the Office of Cuba Broadcasting. http://www.bbg.gov/broadcasters/ocb/

Televisión Martí's ID. A clip that shows the identifying images of Televisión Martí. http://www.youtube.com/watch?v=ViwZIHPsCkg

March 28

1750

Francisco de Miranda is born in Caracas, Venezuela. A Venezuelan revolutionary who failed in his efforts to win freedom for his country from Spain, he spent some time in North America. Miranda began his military career in Spain's army and fought for Spain against Great Britain for control of Florida in the 1781 Battle of Pensacola. Spain won the battle and acquired the land. Miranda, who admired the American revolutionaries, returned to North America in 1783 to meet George Washington, Thomas Jefferson, and other notables. He then embarked on his doomed effort to unite the Spanish colonies against Spain. Miranda died in a prison cell in Spain in 1816.

Books

Chávez, Thomas E. *Spain and the Independence of the United States: An Intrinsic Gift.* University of New Mexico Press, 2003. A somewhat dry book that is also the best history of Spanish support of the American Revolution.

Ezell, John S., ed. *The New Democracy in America: Travels of Francisco de Miranda in the United States, 1783–84.* Norman: University of Oklahoma Press, 1963. Miranda's account of his travels through the young country.

Websites

Francisco de Miranda. *Encyclopedia Britannica* provides a superb summary of the life of the Venezuelan revolutionary. http://www.britannica.com/EBchecked/topic/384920/Francisco-de-Miranda

Francisco de Miranda, Precursor of Latin American Independence. Christopher Minster writes this biography of the man often seen as the predecessor of the much more successful revolutionary, Simón Bolívar. http://latinamericanhistory.about.com/od/latinamericaindependence/a/09fmiranda.htm

1775

Juan Bautista de Anza begins seeking colonists for Alta California. Anza had been ordered by the Spanish government to bring a contingent of settlers to Alta California on the trail that he had pioneered. Spain fears that the land will be claimed by Great Britain or Russia if it does not have a strong claim. Anza recruits colonists in the towns of Sonora and Sinaloa. Each family is offered two years of pay, five years of rations, new clothes, weapons, horses, and cattle. Despite the bounty promised, Anza has trouble recruiting because of the dangers of the journey to California. He signs up only the very poor, the ones who have little hope of a better life if they stay in their towns.

From the diary of Juan Bautista de Anza, February 12, 1776:

We set forth, all together now, for the mission of San Gabriel, where we arrived in the middle of the afternoon. Here I learned of the incident that occurred at twelve o'clock the night before. It was that a soldier, one of the old ones of these establishments, who at the time was entrusted with the care of the saddle animals of all the guard and those of the mission, deserted in company with three muleteers of my train and a servant of the sergeant of the expedition. For this purpose they carried off about twenty-five saddle animals, the best of those belonging to both, although the greater part of them belonged to the mission. In this theft were included also two mules belonging to the expedition.

The first that was known of this matter was when one of the muleteers who have remained returned at midnight from the ranch of the soldiers to sleep at his camp and noted some fragments scattered about. Inferring from this that there had been a robbery, he immediately reported to the officer and the commissary , and they went at once to examine the site and the pieces, inquiring for the guard in whose charge they had been. He was not found, but they did find that they had stolen some glass bead, tobacco, and chocolate, which indicated a desertion. A review of all the men being held, it was found that the persons mentioned were lacking, besides two muskets, a saddle, and other things of less importance which they were able to lay their hands on.

In view of all the foregoing, and it not being noticed in the morning that the saddle animals mentioned were lacking, for they were turned out loose in the fields, they sent to where our mounts were being guarded for those necessary to follow the deserters, and Lieutenant Moraga set out after them

with ten soldiers, determined to follow them two days, which is as much as the animals can stand, although they chose the best of them.

I have done all I could to learn whether the disease of desertion has spread to the soldiers, or to persons who have come to settle in these places, but I have not found any one so infected. This seems to be proved by the event itself, for among those who have fled no one from these classes is included. And it is the common opinion that the soldier influenced the other four, for they say he has been under suspicion of desertion ever since he came, and is so desperate and bold that on another occasion he attempted to desert from Baja California on a tule raft . He sailed on it at the will of the wind for a day, but the next day he was wafted back to the very land from which he wished to escape.

(*Source:* Web de Anza, University of Oregon, http://anza.uoregon.edu/Action.la sso?-database=A76&-layout=standard&-op= eq&Date=2/12/1776&-response=format/a 76pg2fmt.html&-maxRecords=10&-nore sultserror=anzaweb/sorry.html&-search)

Books

Bolton, Herbert. *Anza's California Expeditions.* Berkeley: University of California Press, 1930. Although dated, this is an extensive study of Anza's colonizing efforts.

Guerrero, Vladimir. *The Anza Trail and the Settling of California.* Berkeley, CA: Heyday, 2006. Solid history of the Anza Expedition.

Websites

Juan Bautista de Anza Historical Trail. The National Park Service manages this 1,200-mile trail from Nogales, Arizona to San Francisco, California. The website includes a guide that has maps, a historical background, and an audio library of trail sounds. http://www.nps.gov/juba/index.htm

Web de Anza. The University of Oregon provides primary sources and historical background relating to Anza's journey. http://anza.uoregon.edu/

1954

Telemundo, the most popular Spanish-language television network in the United States and the second largest Spanish-language content producer in the world, is founded by Ángel Ramos and launched by WKAQ-TV.

1990

Investigators for the Puerto Rican Senate charge that FBI agents helped conceal the truth about the July 1978 murders of pro-independence radicals Carlos Soto Arrivai and Arnaldo Dario Rosado. The men were slain by police after an undercover officer lured them into attempting to bomb the communication towers on Cerro Maravilla. In the early 1980s an investigation by the Puerto Rican Senate found that the two had surrendered to police officers and minutes later were shot as they kneeled on the ground. In 1988 a former police intelligence agent was found guilty of involvement in the slayings. He and nine other police officers were convicted of perjuring themselves in testimony before grand juries that had investigated the case. The investigators, who include Samuel Dash, former chief counsel to the U.S. Senate Watergate Committee, are looking into whether the Carter Administration was slow in investigating murders to secure the political backing of the island's former governor Carlos Romero Barceló. The governor supported Puerto Rican statehood. The 1988 film, *A Show of Force,* is loosely based on these events. (As of 2012, no one had been charged in the killings.)

Books

Duany, Jorge. *The Puerto Rican Nation on the Move: Identities on the Island and in the United States.* Discusses cultural nationalism among Puerto Ricans.

Negrón-Muntaner, Frances, and Ramón Grosfoguel, eds. *Puerto Rican Jam: Rethinking Colonialism and Nationalism.* Minneapolis: University of Minnesota Press, 1997. Offers essays that examine the debate over the political status of Puerto Rico.

Website

Puerto Rican Nationalism and the Drift toward Statehood. The Council on Hemispheric Affairs provides this excellent summary of the history of nationalism on the island. http://www.coha.org/puerto-rican-nationalism-and-the-drift-towards-statehood/

March 29

1847

The siege of Veracruz, part of the Mexican-American War, ends. Major General Winfield Scott led 10,000 U.S. soldiers against the most heavily fortified city in the Western Hemisphere. The siege began on March 9 when Scott's men went ashore. American forces bombarded Veracruz until Brig. Gen. Juan Morales surrendered his 3,400 men and the city. The United States only lost 13 killed and 54 wounded in the siege. Mexican losses are less clear and were approximately 350 to 400 soldiers killed, as well as 100 to 600 civilians killed. The capture of Veracruz left the route open to Mexico City and the end of the war.

"Uncle Sam and Mexico" (Sung to the tune of "Old Dan Tucker"), circa 1848:

Throughout de land dar is a cry,
And folks all know de reason why,
Shy Mexico's two legged b'ars,
Am 'tacking Uncle Sammy's stars,

Chorus wid drum.—
Den march away,
Den march away—
Den march away, bold sons of freedom,
You're de boys can skin and bleed 'em.

Dey're kicken up gunpowderation,
About de Texas annexation,
Since Mexico makes sich ado,
We'll flog her and annex her too.
Den March away, &c.

Young Texas came ob age quite jam
And den she married Uncle Sam,
She sewed her stars fast to his flag,
An it shall shine dar while dar's a rag.
Den march away, &c.

Dey met us on de Rio Grandy,
We showed 'em Yankee Doodle Dandy,
But when brave Taylor cross de line,
He'll make 'em snort like a steam
    bullgine.
Den march away, &c.

Little Texas when quite in her teens,
Did give 'em a dose of leaden *beans,*
An' now old Sammy is called out,
Dey'll catch salt-petre sour crout.
Den march away, &c.

Since Texas cut off Sant Anna's peg,
We'll *Amputate* Ampudia's leg,
An' so his carcass de air shan't spoil
We'll boil it in his own hot oil.

(*Source:* Traditional. "Uncle Sam and Mexico" in *General Taylor's Old Rough and Ready Songster.* New York: Turner and Fisher, 1848, http://lincoln.lib.niu.edu/file.php?file=gt33.html)

Books

Francaviglia, Richard V., and Douglas W. Richmond, eds. *Dueling Eagles: Reinterpreting the U.S.-Mexican War, 1846–1848.* Fort Worth: Texas Christian University Press, 2000. Offers essays that challenge the Anglo-centric view of this war.

Reilly, Tom. *War with Mexico!: America's Reporters Cover the Battlefront.* Lawrence: University Press of Kansas, 2010. Examines the information given to Americans about the war.

Websites

The Mexican-American War. Northern Illinois University Libraries offers a history of the war along with primary documents. http://dig.lib.niu.edu/mexicanwar/about.html

The U.S.-Mexican War. PBS provides a graphic-heavy history of the war with a timeline, biographies of key figures, and a link to additional resources. http://www.pbs.org/kera/usmexicanwar/

March 31

1927

César Chávez, the organizer of Mexican American farmworkers, is born in Yuma, Arizona, to Librado Chávez and Juana Chávez. His parents operated a grocery and farmed a few acres. With the advent of the Great Depression in 1929, the Chavez family could not pay its debts and lost both the farm and the store. Forced into migrant labor, the family moved to California to weed vegetable gardens and pick fruit. Chávez began to work as an organizer in the 1950s. He founded the group that would become the United Farm Workers in 1962.

From Studs Terkel, "César Chávez":

Oh, I remember having to move out of our house. My father had brought in a team of horses and wagon. We had always lived in that house, and we couldn't understand why we were moving out. When we got to the other house, it was a worse house, a poor house. That must have been around 1934. I was six years old.

It's known as the North Gila Valley, about fifty miles north of Yuma. My dad was being turned out of his small plot of land. He had inherited this from his father, who had homesteaded it. I saw my two, three other uncles also moving out. And for the same reason. The bank had foreclosed on the loan.

If the local bank approved, the Government would guarantee the loan and small farmers like my father would continue in business. It so happened the president of the bank was the guy who most wanted our land. We were surrounded by him: he owned all the land around us. Of course, he wouldn't pass the loan. . . .

We all of us climbed into an old Chevy that my dad had. And then we were in California, and migratory workers. There were five kids—a small family by those standards. It must have been around '36. I was about eight. Well, it was a strange life. We had been poor, but we knew every night there was a bed there, and that this was our room. . . . But that all of a sudden changed. When you're small, you can't figure these things out. You know something's not right and you don't like it, but you don't question it and you don't let that get you down. You sort of just continue to move.

But this had quite an impact on my father. He had been used to owning the land and all of a sudden there was no more land. What I heard . . . what I made out of conversations between my mother and my father—things like, we'll work this season and then we'll get enough money and we'll go and buy a piece of land in Arizona. Things like that. Became like a habit. He never gave up hope that someday he would come back and get a little piece of land.

I can understand very, very well this feeling. These conversations were sort of melancholy. I guess my brothers and my sisters could also see this very sad look on my father's face. [The piece of land he wanted.] It never happened. He stopped talking about that some years ago. The drive for land, it's a very powerful drive.

(*Source:* Terkel, Studs. "César Chávez," in *Hard Times: An Oral History of the Great Depression.* New York: Pantheon, 1970, pp. 58–62.)

Books

Del Castillo, Richard Griswold, and Richard A. García. *César Chávez: A Triumph of Spirit.* Norman: University of Oklahoma Press, 1995. The best account of Chávez and his links to the Chicano Movement.

Levy, Jacques E. *César Chávez: Autobiography of La Causa.* New York: W. W. Norton, 1975. Provides an account of Chávez's early years, his initial efforts as an organizer, and his rise to the leadership of Mexican American farmworkers.

Websites

César Chávez: Labor Leader. Enchanted Learning offers a biography of Chávez as well as numerous activities for children that teach about the union leader. http://www.enchantedlearning.com/history/us/hispanicamerican/chavez/

The Story of César Chávez. The United Farm Workers provides a biography of its famed leader. http://www.ufw.org/_page.php?inc=history/07.html&menu=research

1995

The popular Tejano singer, Selena, is shot and killed by the president of her fan club, Yolanda Saldivar, in Corpus Christi, Texas. Selena Quintanilla-Pérez, born in 1971, was named by *Billboard* magazine as the top Latin musician of the 1990s for the fourteen Top 10 singles that she placed in the Latin Songs chart, including seven No.1 hits. A major force in music, her records have continued to sell well since her tragic death. A 1997 film of her life starred Jennifer Lopez.

Books

Novas, Himilce, and Rosemary Silva. *Remembering Selena: A Tribute in Pictures and Words.* New York: St. Martin's Press, 1995. A short biography of the Tejano star.

Parédez, Deborah. *Selenidad: Selena, Latinos, and the Performance of Memory.* Durham, NC: Duke University Press, 2009. Examines the link between Selena and ethnic identity.

Websites

Selena. A biography of the singer on the website of the A & E television network. http://www.biography.com/people/selena-189149

Selena Quintanilla-Perez. Find a Grave provides a short summary of Selena's life along with details about her burial site in Corpus Christi, Texas. http://www.findagrave.com/cgi-bin/fg.cgi?page=gr&GRid=1460

2007

The U.S. Department of Homeland Security arrests several Argentine and Peruvian immigrants who are wanted for war crimes back in their native countries. The most notorious of the three men who are arrested is Ernesto Guillermo Barreiro of Argentina. During the so-called Dirty War of the late 1970s, he was the chief interrogator at La Perla, a clandestine prison in Cordoba, Argentina's second largest city, where more than 2,000 prisoners were tortured or killed. When a democratic civilian government came to power in Argentina in the mid-1980s, it tried to bring Barreiro to justice. But he defied a court summons to face charges and then quickly helped start a military rebellion that led to passage of an amnesty law that exempted officers below the rank of colonel— he was then a major—from prosecution in connection with human rights abuses on the grounds that they were merely following orders. In 2004, Barreiro fled to the Washington, D.C., area and opened an antiques store. The Argentine Supreme Court overturned the amnesty in 2005. The other two men being held, Telmo Ricardo Hurtado and Juan Manuel Rivera Rondón, are Peruvians. They are accused of having participated in the massacre of 69 peasants in an Andean village in 1985, when President Alan García was trying to suppress the brutal Maoist Shining Path guerrilla movement.

From "Rights Groups Hail Arrests of 3 by U.S. in War Crimes":

> Latin American human rights groups have reacted with satisfaction and muted surprise to the arrest in the United States of three Argentine and Peruvian former military officers accused of human rights abuses who had fled their home countries to avoid prosecution there.
>
> Of the three men detained over the weekend in Virginia, Maryland and Florida and charged with violating immigration laws, the most notorious is Ernesto Guillermo Barreiro of Argentina. . . . "This is big news, and deserves to be celebrated both in Argentina and the United States," said Gaston Chillier, director of the Center for Legal and Social Studies, a leading human rights group in Buenos Aires. "This is someone with a long record not just of crimes against humanity, but also of resistance to efforts to hold him responsible for his actions."
>
> The arrests have put the Bush administration in the unaccustomed position of being praised by human rights groups and news organizations in Latin America. The former officers were detained by a unit of the Homeland Security Department, which is traditionally widely criticized in the region for the way it treats illegal immigrants from Latin America. "This administration has a very poor record as regards international human rights law and the Geneva convention," Jose Miguel Vivanco, the director of Human Rights Watch Americas, said

in a telephone interview from Washington. "However, there is nothing on the record that shows that this administration is interested in protecting individuals responsible for gross violations of human rights, unless they have some link with intelligence agencies." Mr. Vivanco said he was referring to Luis Posada Carriles, a Cuban exile and former C.I.A. asset who is wanted in Cuba and Venezuela on charges that he blew up a Cuban airliner in 1976, killing 73 people. The United States has also declined to extradite Emmanuel Constant, former leader of a right-wing Haitian paramilitary group who has been convicted in absentia there of organizing a 1994 massacre . . .

It is not yet clear how American authorities intend to handle Mr. Barreiro's case. He could either be summarily deported for having lied about his record on his visa application, tried and jailed in the United States in connection with that offense, or extradited to Argentina, normally a time-consuming process. "It would be an irony if an immigration infraction were to delay Barreiro's return," said Horacio Verbitsky, an Argentine author and journalist who has written several books on human rights issues. "The United States could impose no more severe punishment than

to send him back to Argentina, where he faces life imprisonment but will receive due process and the fair trial he denied his victims. . . ."

(*Source:* Rohter, Larry. "Rights Groups Hail Arrests of 3 by U.S. in War Crimes." *New York Times,* April 5, 2007, p. A10.)

Books

Gorriti, Gustavo. *The Shining Path: A History of the Millenarian War in Peru.* First published in Peru in 1990, this account by one of Peru's best-known journalists is acclaimed for its coverage of the early years of the conflict in the 1980s.

Lewis, Paul H. *Guerillas and Generals: The Dirty War in Argentina.* Westport, CT: Praeger, 2001. Well-received account of the conflict between leftist guerillas and the military regime that ruled Argentina between 1976 and 1983.

Websites

Shining Path. This *New York Times* site provides a brief history of the terrorist organization, articles from the newspaper about the group, and a list of web resources chosen by *Times* researchers. http://topics.nytimes.com/top/reference/timestopics/organizations/s/shining_path/index.html

Argentina's Dirty War. Provides a brief history of the conflict. http://www.globalsecurity.org/military/world/war/argentina.htm

April

April 1

1928

Harry Caicedo, who becomes the first Latino chief of the news bureau for a major U.S. daily newspaper in 1958 when he takes that role for the *Miami Herald,* is born to Colombian parents. Caicedo cofounds *Vista,* a weekly English-language magazine aimed at Latinos, in 1975 with Arturo Villar. The magazine had a circulation of 1 million at its peak in the 1980s.

Books

Rodríguez, América. *Making Latino News: Race, Language, Class.* Thousand Oaks, CA: Sage, 1999. Provides a history of Spanish-language newspapers, radio, and television in the United States along with a history of the Latino audience.

Smiley, Nixon, ed. *The Miami Herald Front Pages, 1903–1983.* New York: H.N. Abrams, 1983. Offers a glimpse into the news coverage of the newspaper.

Website

The Miami Herald. This website includes a link to *El Nuevo Herald,* the Spanish-language edition of the newspaper. http://www.miami herald.com/

1977

Mari-Luci Jaramillo is asked to become the U.S. ambassador to Honduras. Jaramillo, an education professor at the University of New Mexico, initially thought the request was a prank by her students. She becomes the first Latino woman to be named an ambassador.

Books

Binns, Jack R. *The United States in Honduras, 1980–1981: An Ambassador's Memoir.* Jefferson, NC: McFarland, 2000. Binns, also a Carter appointee, succeeded Jaramillo in Honduras and his memoir gives another view of the challenges of the job.

Jaramillo, Mari-Luci. *Madam Ambassador: The Shoemaker's Daughter.* Tempe, AZ.: Bilingual Press, 2002. Jaramillo's memoir of her tenure in Honduras.

Website

Honduras Country Profile. This BBC News report provides an objective view of a country with close U.S. ties. http://news.bbc.co.uk/2/hi/americas/country_profiles/1225416.stm

2003

Nils J. Díaz is appointed by President George W. Bush to chair the Nuclear Regulatory Commission (NRC) in Cuba. Díaz earned a doctorate from the University of Florida. He was first appointed to the NRC by President Bill Clinton in 1996. The NRC is the U.S. agency responsible for licensing and regulating all nuclear power plants and other facilities across the country.

Books

Mahaffey, James A. *Nuclear Accidents and Disasters.* New York: Facts on File, 2012. Explains the need for the Nuclear Regulatory Commission through accounts of things that went wrong.

Welsh, Ian. *Mobilizing Modernity: The Nuclear Moment.* New York: Routledge, 2000. Examines attitudes toward nuclear energy in the second half of the 20th century.

Website

U.S. Nuclear Regulatory Commission. This is the official website for the agency. http://www.nrc.gov/

April 2

1513

Juan Ponce de León, the governor of Puerto Rico, arrives in Florida in search of slaves and gold. The first European to set foot in Florida, he lands at Mosquito Inlet on the Atlantic Coast and subsequently sails south around the tip of Florida, perhaps to Charlotte Harbor. Ponce de León names the land Pascua de Florida (Feast of Flowers) because his expedition arrives on Palm Sunday. He then claims Florida for Spain. The governor maps portions of the southern Gulf Coast and then returns to Puerto Rico. Ponce de León is removed from office in 1511 for his extreme brutality toward Native Americans. He dies on an exploring trip in 1521 after Native Americans in Florida shoot him with arrows.

Books

Dolan, Sean. *Juan Ponce de León*. New York: Chelsea House, 1995. Good, short biography of the explorer.

Worth, Richard. *Ponce de León and the Age of Spanish Exploration in World History*. Berkeley Heights, NJ: Enslow, 2003. Sets the brutal conquistador in historical context.

Website

Juan Ponce de León: Explorer. Offers a good biography of the explorer with a map of his travels. http://www.enchantedlearning.com/explorers/page/d/deleon.shtml

1900

Puerto Rico gets its first government under the United States when President William McKinley approves the Organic Act of Porto Rico (amended to "Puerto Rico" in 1932). Popularly known as the Foraker Act for its sponsor, Sen. Joseph Benson Foraker of Ohio, this piece of legislation outlined a colonial government for Puerto Rico. It provided that all the laws of the United States would have the same force and effect in Puerto Rico except for the internal revenue laws. The new island government consisted of a governor and an executive council appointed by the president, a house of representatives with 35 elected members, a judicial system with a Supreme Court, and a nonvoting resident commissioner in Congress. The legislation gave Puerto Rico political stability that would later be essential for attracting business.

From "Foraker Act of 1900":

> Sec. 2. That on and after the passage of this Act the same, tariffs, customs, and duties shall be levied, collected, and paid upon all articles imported into Porto Rico from ports other than those of the United States which are required by law to be collected upon articles imported into the United States from foreign countries: Provided, That on all coffee in the bean or ground imported into Porto Rico there shall be levied and collected a duty of five cents per pound, any law or part of law to the contrary notwithstanding: And provided further, That all Spanish scientific, literary, and artistic works, not subversive of public order in Porto Rico, shall be admitted free of duty into Porto Rico for a period of ten years . . .

(*Source*: Website of Brian Rohan, political science professor, San Diego State University. http://www-rohan.sdsu.edu/dept/polsciwb/brianl/docs/1900ForakerAct.pdf)

Books

Ayala, César J., and Rafael Bernabe. *Puerto Rico in the American Century: A History since 1898*. Chapel Hill: University of North Carolina Press, 2009. Comprehensive and engaging history of the island.

Carrión, Arturo Morales. *Puerto Rico: A Political and Cultural History*. New York: W. W. Norton, 1984. A classic work that focuses on the Puerto Rican search for identity.

Websites

Welcome to Puerto Rico. A good introduction to the geography, culture, and history of the island. http://www.topuertorico.org/

Puerto Rico—The World Factbook. The Central Intelligence Agency's introduction to Puerto Rico includes statistics. https://www.cia.gov/library/publications/the-world-factbook/geos/rq.html

April 3

1971

Las Hermanas forms when 50 women, mostly Mexican American, meet in Houston, Texas, to discuss and pray about the implications of the Chicano movement for the Catholic Church. Between 1971 and 1985, Las Hermanas influenced the policy decisions of major ecclesial bodies such as the National Conference of Catholic Bishops/United States Catholic Conference (NCCB/USCC), the Leadership Conference of Women Religious, and the Secretariat for Hispanic Affairs of the United States Catholic Conference. The group also conducted two notable surveys, on the absence of Latino ministry programs in parishes across the nation and on the exploitation of Mexican nuns as domestics in U.S. rectories and seminaries. The group often worked with PADRES, an organization of Chicano priests. Together, PADRES and Las Hermanas lobbied for the appointment of Chicano bishops, developed the first national Chicano pastoral institute, and contributed to the first formulations of raza theology.

María de Jesús Ybarra, a Chicana nun and member of Las Hermanas, recalled conditions in 1974 as well as some lobbying later that year:

I visited the seminary in Chicago. The [Mexican] sisters were living underground in the basement with no windows [working as domestics]. There was a ramp going up to the kitchen. One sister told me that she had been at the seminary since she was fifteen years old and that she had never gone to Confession in Spanish. She desperately wanted spiritual direction! When the director of the seminary found out I was talking to the young sisters about studying, I was told to leave. . . .

One sister was a daughter of farmworkers. She was working along the route that her parents traveled to pick the fields. She did not allow her parents to stop and visit her because she was ashamed of them. She told me, "I lived in fear for constant years that my order would discover that I was Mexican."

Carmelita asked her order [the Good Shepherds] to borrow a Ford Pinto they had. From San Antonio we drove to Chicago, then New York. We finally ended up in New Orleans. We wanted to see the Hispanic offices, to see what they were doing. We also recruited Hermanas along the way. We had no "official" power. We took notes, talked to the people. Everywhere we stopped it was the same. There were no Spanish Masses, services were held in the church basements or the Spanish-speaking were not allowed to enter the main church . . .

PADRES called a meeting about the appointment of a Chicano archbishop to Santa Fe. . . . Edmundo Rodríguez, Virgilio Elizondo, Carmelita Espinoza, and myself met with some of the bishops. Our strategy was that I would be the soft-spoken sister in secular clothes, and Carmelita would wear a habit but be very radical. They were not expecting it! Carmelita pounded on the desk, "The church is not helping the people . . . it takes too many years to get a priest while the Protestants can get one quicker with good training! The Church is neglecting the Mexicans!"

Well, the bishops . . . named a Chicano archbishop [Roberto Sánchez, the first Latino archbishop in the country] in Santa Fe. It was a joint effort of Las Hermanas and PADRES.

(*Source:* Medina, Lara. *Las Hermanas: Chicana/Latina Religious-Political Activism in the U.S. Catholic Church*. Philadelphia: Temple University Press, 2004, pp. 55, 74–75.)

Books

Henold, Mary J. *Catholic and Feminist: The Surprising History of the American Catholic Feminist Movement*. Chapel Hill: University of North Carolina Press, 2008. This well-written book takes an objective look at Catholic feminism.

Medina, Lara. *Las Hermanas: Chicana/Latina Religious-Political Activism in the U.S. Catholic Church*. Philadelphia: Temple University Press, 2004, pp. 74–75. This engaging book is the only study of the organization.

Websites

Catholic and Feminist: You Got a Problem With That?. Part of the U.S. Catholic website that focuses on conversations with Catholics, this is an essay by a non-Hispanic woman. http://www.uscatholic.org/church/2009/01/catholic-and-feminist-you-got-a-problem-with

The Whole Truth about Catholic Feminism. This review of Donna Steichen's book-length attack on Catholic feminists, on the Living Tradition website, copies Steichen in presenting feminism as a dark cult and a spiritual plague. http://www.rtforum.org/lt/lt53.html

1980

Julian Nava is confirmed by the Senate as the U.S. ambassador to Mexico. Nava, a California State Northridge history professor who was born in Los Angeles to parents who had emigrated from Mexico, is the first Mexican American to serve in this post. He was nearly deported with his family in the 1920s as Mexican Americans were being swept out of East Los Angeles. Appointed by President

Jimmy Carter, he had spent 12 years on the Los Angeles Board of Education. Nava had a somewhat rough term in office as Mexicans faulted him for being loyal to the United States rather than to Mexico or the Mexican American community. Incidentally, Nava served as one of the pallbearers in 1993 for his friend, labor activist César Chávez.

Books

Nava, Julian. *Julian Nava: My Mexican-American Journey*. Houston: Piñata Books/ Arte Público, 2002. Nava's biography addresses his rise from humble beginnings to national prominence.

Nava, Julian. *Mexican-Americans: A Brief Look at Their History*. New York: Anti-Defamation League of B'nai B'rith, 1970. Reprinted in 1980, this work is particularly interesting as it shows Nava's educational activism on behalf of Mexican Americans.

Website

Julian Nava—California Community Colleges, Chancellor's Office. Nava, a graduate of East Los Angeles Community College, is profiled as one of the distinguished alumni of this educational system. http://californiacommunitycolleges.cccco.edu/Newsroom/NotableAlumni/JulianNava.aspx

April 4

1993

Astronaut Ellen Ochoa makes the first of her four flights into space. On this flight, a nine-day mission on the space shuttle Discovery, mission specialist Ochoa uses a robotic arm to capture a satellite and retrieve data on a solar corona to better understand the effect of solar activity upon Earth. Ochoa, who earned a doctorate in electrical engineering from Stanford University, is of Mexican ancestry. She subsequently rose to serve as deputy director of the Johnson Space Center, making her one of the highest achieving women in the space field.

Books

Guzmán, Lila, and Rick Guzmán. *Ellen Ochoa: First Latina Astronaut*. Berkeley Heights, NJ: Enslow, 2006. Published in both English-language and Spanish-language editions, this children's book profiles the astronaut.

Iverson, Teresa. *Ellen Ochoa*. Chicago: Raintree, 2006. While there are no adult biographies of Ochoa, there are good children's books that profile her, including this volume.

Website

Astronaut Bio: Ellen Ochoa. NASA's official bi-ography of Ochoa. http://www.jsc.nasa.gov/Bios/htmlbios/ochoa.html

2004

The Disney movie, *The Alamo,* opens. Much more historically accurate than the 1960 version of the film that starred John Wayne, *The Alamo* sought to present both Latinos and African Americans in a way that acknowledged their contributions. Latinos, particularly Juan Seguin, fought for Texas's independence. The movie, starring Dennis Quaid (Sam Houston), Billy Bob Thornton (David Crockett), and Jasic Patric (James Bowie), proved a box office failure. With a budget of $95 million, it made $22 million in the United States.

From "Disney's 'Alamo' Marketing Mis-cues":

> "The Alamo," by almost any mea-sure, is a difficult movie to market to Latino audiences.
>
> Though the Mexican Army won the Battle of the Alamo, it ultimately lost both the war and Texas, which be-came a bastion of Anglo power in the Southwest and a place where Tejanos, or Texans of Hispanic descent, were relegated to second-class status.
>
> But with Latino moviegoers grow-ing in number and importance in the United States, few marketing experts were surprised when Walt Disney went out of its way to highlight the role of Latinos in its latest version of "The Alamo," with Tejano folk heroes like Juan Seguín figuring prominently.
>
> Disney marketed the film differ-ently to Spanish-speaking audiences, with a distinct print, television and radio campaign. Instead of the slogan, "The Movie Event You'll Never For-get," the Spanish-language ads referred to "The Battle That Divided Mexico," using the view of historians that con-sider the Alamo an episode in a civil war that flared in an area that was once Mexico's northeast.
>
> The history of the Alamo is open to different interpretations, and movie versions throughout the years are testa-ment to the shifting ways in which La-tinos have been portrayed—and more recently courted—by Hollywood.
>
> In D.W. Griffith's "Martyrs of the Alamo" in 1915, and in John Wayne's 1960 version, "The Alamo," Tejanos were pushed to the margins of the story and Mexicans were portrayed as the despotic enemies of a group of cou-rageous, freedom-loving Anglos. The newest version has actors speaking in Spanish and it attempts to balance the dictator Antonio López de Santa Anna, played by the Mexican actor Emilio Echevarría, with noble Tejanos such as Seguín, played by Jordi Molla of Spain.

(*Source:* Romero, Simon. "Disney's 'Alamo' Marketing Miscues." *New York Times,* April 19, 2004, p. 12.)

Books

Matovina, Timothy M. *The Alamo Remembered: Tejano Accounts and Perspectives*. Austin: Uni-versity of Texas Press, 1995. An anthology of accounts of the Battle of the Alamo by Tejano citizens of San Antonio.

Walker, Paul Robert. *Remember the Alamo: Texians, Tejanos, and Mexicans Tell Their Stories.* Washington, D.C.: National Geographic Children's Books, 2007. Probably the best book on the Alamo for a younger audience, it provides a good summary of the battle, maps, pictures, old photos, and archival drawings.

Websites

"The Alamo" (2004)—IMDb. This Internet Movie Database site provides photos of the film, a cast list, and box office information. http://www.imdb.com/title/tt0318974/

The Battle of the Alamo. The Texas State Library and Archives Commission provides a wonderful introduction to the battle, several historic images, and copies of significant Alamo documents. https://www.tsl.state.tx.us/treasures/republic/alamo-01.html

2012

The Pew Hispanic Center, part of the Pew Research Center, releases a study showing that the vast majority of Americans of Spanish heritage do not identify as either Hispanic or Latino. A majority (51%) of those interviewed stated that they most often identify themselves by their family's country of origin with just 24 percent voicing support for a pan-ethnic label. The U.S. government mandated the use of "Hispanic" or "Latino" to identify people of Spanish heritage in 1976. Most of the respondents, 69 percent, see multiple Latino cultures rather than a single culture. Nearly nine in ten Latinos also believe that the ability to speak English is critical to success in the United States. Eight in ten adults speak Spanish and 95 percent believe that it is important for future generations to continue to do so. The study is based on findings from a national bilingual survey of 1,220 Hispanic adults conducted from November 9 to December 7, 2011.

From "When Labels Don't Fit: Hispanics and Their Views of Identity":

- **When it comes to describing their identity, most Hispanics prefer their family's country of origin over pan-ethnic terms.** Half (51%) say that most often they use their family's country of origin to describe their identity. That includes such terms as "Mexican" or "Cuban" or "Dominican," for example. Just one-quarter (24%) say they use the terms "Hispanic" or "Latino" to most often describe their identity. And 21% say they use the term "American" most often.

- **"Hispanic" or "Latino"? Most don't care—but among those who do, "Hispanic" is preferred.** Half (51%) say they have no preference for either term. When a preference is expressed, "Hispanic" is preferred over "Latino" by more than a two-to-one margin—33% versus 14%.

- **Most Hispanics do not see a shared common culture among U.S. Hispanics.** Nearly seven-in-ten (69%) say Hispanics in the U.S. have many different cultures, while 29% say Hispanics in the U.S. share a common culture.

- **Most Hispanics don't see themselves fitting into the standard racial categories used by the U.S. Census Bureau.** When it comes to race, according to the Pew Hispanic survey, half (51%) of Latinos identify their race as "some other race" or volunteer "Hispanic/Latino." Meanwhile, 36% identify their race as white, and 3% say their race is black.

- **Latinos are split on whether they see themselves as a typical American.** Nearly half (47%) say they are a typical American, while another 47% say they are very different from the typical American. Foreign-born Hispanics are less likely than native-born

Hispanics to say they are a typical American—34% versus 66%.

- **The U.S. is seen as better than Latinos' countries of origin in many ways—but not in all ways.** Fully 87% of Latino adults say the opportunity to get ahead is better in the U.S. than in the country of their ancestors; some 72% say the U.S. is better for raising children than their home country; nearly seven-in-ten (69%) say the poor are treated better in the U.S.; and a plurality of 44% say moral values are better here than in their homelands. However, when it comes to the strength of family ties, a plurality (39%) say the home country of their ancestors is better, while 33% say the strength of family ties is better in the U.S.

- **Most Hispanic immigrants say they would migrate to the U.S. again.** Some 79% of Hispanic immigrants say that if they had to do it all over again, they would come to the U.S. When asked why they came to this country, more than half (55%) of immigrant Hispanics say it was for economic reasons, while 24% say it was for family reasons.

(*Source:* Taylor, Paul, et al. "When Labels Don't Fit: Hispanics and Their View of Identity." April 4, 2012, http://www.pewhispanic.org/2012/04/04/when-labels-dont-fit-hispanics-and-their-views-of-identity/)

Books

Gracia, Jorge J.E. *Hispanic/Latino Identity: A Philosophic Perspective.* New York: Wiley-Blackwell, 1999. An introduction to the philosophical, social, and political elements of identity that is heavily used in college classrooms.

Morales, Ed. *Living in Spanglish: The Search for Latino Identity in America.* New York: St. Martin's Press, 2002. Argues that Latinos have resisted homogenization while blending into American culture.

Websites

National Latino Research Center. Based at California State University San Marcos, this research center conducts research that contributes to the knowledge and understanding of the Latino population. http://www.csusm.edu/nlrc/

Pew Hispanic Center. Begun in 2001 as part of the nonpartisan, fact-finding Pew Research Center, the Pew Hispanic Center conducts and commissions studies. http://www.pewhispanic.org/

April 5

2011

The Puerto Rico Tourism Company, founded in 1970 by Gov. Luis A Ferré, becomes the first governmental entity to enter into an agreement with the Environmental Protection Agency to promote green tourism. Puerto Rico attracts about 1 million visitors a year, who create pollution and strain the ecosystem. Under the agreement, Puerto Rico will encourage the hospitality industry to reduce solid waste through such means as reducing packaging and using refillable products, promote water-efficient practices, construct green buildings, and protect vegetation.

Books

Hunter, Colin, and Howard Green. *Tourism and the Environment: A Sustainable Relationship?* New York: Routledge, 1995. Explores whether the tourist industry is truly a green industry.

Shaw, Gareth, and Allan M. Williams. *Critical Issues in Tourism: A Geographical Perspective.* Cambridge, MA: Blackwell, 1994. A scholarly study of social access to tourism, individual consumption of tourism, and the growth of green tourism.

Website

Company Overview of the Puerto Rico Tourism Company. This Bloomberg *Businessweek* site provides information on the leaders and goals of the semigovernmental agency. http://investing.businessweek.com/research/stocks/private/snapshot.asp?privcapId=7743606

April 6

1917

The United States enters World War I. Many Mexican Americans serve in the U.S. armed forces during the war. Others move to the Midwest and Northeast to replace drafted white men in factories, on farms, and on railroads. During the war, European immigration wanes dramatically, eliminating competition for farm work in the West for Latinos as Asians were also disappearing from the fields because of the Chinese Exclusion Act and the Gentlemen's Agreement. By the end of the war, Mexicans dominated farm labor in the Southwest.

Books

Acuña, Rodolfo. *Occupied America: A History of Chicanos*. New York: Pearson Longman, 2007. Discusses the influence of World War I on the formation of a Mexican American identity as well as other effects of the conflict.

Harries, Meirion, and Susie Harries. *The Last Days of Innocence: America at War, 1917–1918*. New York: Vintage, 1997. The best general history of the effects of World War I on the Americans.

Website

WWI Era from a New Mexican Perspective. With maps and primary sources, the City of Albuquerque provides an excellent history of the cross-border conflict between Mexico and the United States as well as a good account of the military actions of New Mexican men. http://www.cabq.gov/parksandrecreation/parks/veterans-memorial-park/documents/WWIEraFromANewMexicanPerspective.pdf

April 7

1922

Conga drummer Ramón "Mongo" Santamaría is born in Havana. A star performer in Cuba who added Afro-Cuban religious influences to jazz music, he came to the United States in 1950. He subsequently added Latin beats to pop and rhythm and blues, including 1963's "Watermelon Man." The song entered the Grammy Hall of Fame in 1998. Santamaría, who played with Tito Puente and many other Latino stars, died in 2003.

Mongo Santamaría on leaving Cuba and playing in the United States:

I spoke with an old mailman, Don Alberto Gómez, who was called "Don" because he was a Cuban patriot who had fought in the Cuban Independence War. He was a very wise man. He told me, "In 20 years you will be as you see me now: carrying mail, no money, and without hope of reaching retirement. So if you are good in music, get out now and leave Cuba. . . ."

Nobody was playing batá. Nobody was playing chekere. And today you see the Puerto Ricans, the Dominicans and everybody play everything because the people became fanatics, and started to learn one way or another. And they play! . . .

You can't learn to play things like guaguancó here [in the United States]. You have to have been where it came from to know that you kill or get killed for women . . . and drums. You have to understand ñañigo, Abakuá. Cándido, Peraza, Patato, Francisco Aguabella.

You can't listen to records and get those feelings.

It was too limited: you were playing in the "barrio" in Manhattan, but outside there was nothing happening. I went with Cal Tjader after Tito Puente and we played for five thousand, ten thousand people, and I saw how the people were crazy about the music. In order to sell records and achieve popularity and to get a name, it was more convenient to play in that way than to play *típico*. If I had wanted to play *típico*, I would have stayed in Cuba! I never got away from my background, but to push the music, to accomplish something big, you have to be in the majority . . .

People don't recognize [salsa] as a Cuban thing that is very old. It did not filter through the Indies, then to Puerto Rico and Cuba, etc. Haven't you ever wondered about the differences between a calypso and a guaguancó? Between samba and guaguancó? It came directly from Africa to these places and stayed there. It did not travel on. There are different areas in Africa. Each area has its own music, religion and language. . . . It's still segmented according to the districts. Whichever type of slave was brought over, that's the kind of music that developed. In Cuba, they came from Yoruba, West Africa, the Congo and Guinea. So the music in Cuba is richer than in the other islands. You find the music in Havana different from the music in Oriente Province.

(*Source*: Gerard, Charley. *Music from Cuba: Mongo Santamaría, Chocolate Armenteros, and Cuban Musicians in the United States*. Westport, CT: Praeger, 2001, pp. 34, 37, 50, 51, 57.)

Books

Dworsky, Alan, and Betsy Sansby. *Conga Drumming: A Beginner's Guide to Playing with Time.* Minneapolis: Dancing Hands Music, 1994. Conga drumming is popular in the United States in part as a result of Santamaría's musical influence.

Gerard, Charley. *Music from Cuba: Mongo Santamaría, Chocolate Armenteros, and Cuban Musicians in the United States.* Westport, CT: Praeger, 2001. Covers Santamaría's life in Cuba and the United States.

Website

Mongo Santamaría. Provides songs, images including album covers, and videos from the musician's career. http://www.last.fm/music/Mongo+Santamaria

1951

Artist Santa C. Barraza is born in Kingsville, Texas, to a working-class Mexican American family. She identifies as a *mestiza,* a Mexica-Tejana. A painter, Barraza has won acclaim for art that sets depictions of family members within the mythic works of the Aztecs, the Mayas, and other Native Americans. The mythic figures and icons, shown in bright greens, reds, blues, browns, and pinks, express a feminist political ideology. She has exhibited her paintings throughout the United States and chairs the Department of Art at Texas A&M University in Kingsville.

From an oral history with Barraza:

You begin to think very male oriented and you begin to think that way, and I guess that's what led me into thinking that—what about the women? And I became exposed to the feminist movement. And I think probably what really led me into thinking more about my identity and my gender is the fact that I did see Peterson and—was it Sutherland's?—exhibition of women artists from 1200 to the 1950's [*Women Artists: recognition and reappraisal from the early middle ages to the twentieth century.* Karen Peters and J.J. Wilson, New York: New York

University Press, 1976]. It came to the University of Texas to the Michener Collection Museum. And I saw the Frida Kahlo paintings and I saw—what is it?—Gonzalez paintings, and I saw Artemisia Gentileschi's paintings, you know, in the style of Caravaggio, and huge, wonderful oil paintings, and I was so enthused.

And at that time I had become part of an art group called Los Quemados [the burned ones] out of Austin and San Antonio, and César Martínez was a member of that. And this was after we were already through with college and we were just doing our art. And then I was working at Steck-Vaughan with my friend Nora, and we became members of—well, I was a member with Amado—Amado Peña was living in Austin. He had gone to Crystal City then he went to Austin. So Amado Peña was there, Carmen Lomas Garza was there, and José Treviño was there in Austin, so we all became— César Martínez, we all became part of his group called Los Quemados, and they broke away from the Con Safo group because they thought it was too conservative, even though I know I've told what's-her-name, [Alicia Gaspar] de Alba [Chicano Art Inside/Outside the Master's House: Cultural Politics and the CARA exhibition. Austin, Texas: University of Texas UP, 1998], when she wrote in her book, that she misquoted us, because she actually interviewed myself and—César Martínez and myself about the Quemados, and she wrote in her book that we wanted to be—that we were not political enough and that that's why we broke away from the Con Safo, which, on the contrary, we didn't think it was political enough, and that's why broke away from them and formed our own group.

Ms. Cordova: Why wasn't it political? What—

Ms. Barraza: The Con Safo? I think at one point—see, I wasn't a member of the Con Safo, but I know Amado Peña was and César Martínez, and also I think José Treviño was a member of that Con Safo group, and they felt that they were accepting a lot of members into the group that weren't really artists, like they accepted Jacinto Quirarte, and he was an art historian. And they were like outraged because they didn't like his book anyway, they didn't like the fact that he didn't include the young Chicanos; he only included like the very conservative established artists that were doing very mainstream art, and they were outraged at that. And so they felt that it was going to be like very European, very conservative art, and they left; they didn't like it. And so they felt that they needed to form a group that was more political, more Chicano, more contemporary, more cutting edge, and so they formed the Quemados because they were burned out with those guys, so they formed the Quemados.

But I was the only female, and Carmen—and then Carmen left Austin, because we were based in Austin. She left Austin and went to—I think she went to Washington and then she went to California. So when she left I was the only female, and so I felt kind of out of place and so I decided, well—at that time I was working at Steck-Vaughan and I told Nora, well, why don't you join the group? And she said, oh, I'm not really an artist; I'm doing more graphic design. But she was a great painter and so I kept talking to her and encouraging her, and finally I talked to Amado and I asked Amado, Amado, how do we get more people involved in the group? And he said, well, have them put a portfolio together and we'll have a meeting and we'll look at their work and then we'll make a decision. So Nora hesitantly did it. She put a portfolio together and showed it to them and they had this little appointment, but of course I wasn't invited, so I wasn't there. So they reviewed her work, and then they told her that they thought she needed more development and she couldn't be part of the group, and she was devastated. And after that happened—and I don't think she remembers it because I talked to her recently about it and she doesn't remember it. But I think that sometimes when things happen to you, you sort of like push it out of your mind, or maybe she just told me that. I don't know.

But anyway, I remember it very vividly because after that incident, I kept telling her that we should form a women's group because the feminist movement was in, and that we should do a Chicana group. And she kept saying no, that she didn't think it was necessary, that we could work on our own, and we would be recognized for what we are. And when that happened to her, she said you know what, let's do it. So then we formed MAS, Mujeres Artistas del Suroeste [1977- mid 1980s].

(*Source:* Oral history interview with Santa Barraza, 2003 Nov. 21–22, Archives of American Art, Smithsonian Institution, http://www.aaa.si.edu/collections/interviews/oral-history-interview-santa-barraza-13254)

Books

Goldman, Shifra M. *Chicana Voices and Visions: A National Exhibit of Women Artists.* Venice, CA: Social and Public Art Resource Center, 1983. An exhibition catalog that includes Barraza's art.

Herrera-Sobek, María. *Santa Barraza, Artist of the Borderlands.* College Station, TX: Texas A&M University, 2001. Provides an autobiography and curriculum vitae as well as numerous photographs of the artist's paintings.

Websites

Cary Cordova interview with Santa C. Barraza, November 21- 22, 2003, Archives of American Art, Kingsville, Texas. http://www.aaa.si.edu/collections/interviews/oral-history-interview-santa-barraza-13254

Santa Barraza, Border Book Festival. Provides an excellent biography of the artist. http://www.borderbookfestival.org/artists/sbarraza.php

April 8

1888

Dennis (Dionisio) Chávez, one of the few Mexican Americans elected to the U.S. Senate, is born in Las Chaves, New Mexico. After earning a law degree from Georgetown University, Chávez entered the U.S. House of Representatives in 1930 and joined the Senate four years later. Chávez firmly backed the New Deal and sought to better relations with Latin America. He became a national figure in 1944 when he introduced a bill prohibiting discrimination in employment on the basis of race, creed, color, national origin, or ancestry. The legislation died but Chávez claimed a notable place in history by laying the groundwork for subsequent civil rights legislation. He remained in office until his 1962 death.

Books

Gould, Lewis L. *The Most Exclusive Club: A History of the Modern United States Senate*. New York: Basic Books, 2005. Excellent general history of this American institution.

Whisenhunt, Donald W. *The Human Tradition in America between the Wars, 1920–1945*. Wilmington, DE: SR Books, 2002. Includes a biographical chapter on Chávez, written by Kevin Allen Leonard.

Website

Dennis Chávez. The U.S. Congress provides this biographical guide to Chávez that is essentially a listing of his professional activities. http://bioguide.congress.gov/scripts/biodisplay.pl?index=c000338

April 9

1910

Mexican labor activist and revolutionary social reformer Sara Estela Ramírez publishes the last of the 22 poems and essays that comprise her known literary work. Ramírez emigrated from Mexico in 1898 to teach in Mexican schools in Laredo, Texas. She soon gained renown for her eloquent speeches and writings in support of workers. After writing for a couple of Mexican immigrant newspapers, Ramírez founded her own newspaper, *La Corregidora,* in 1901. She also founded a literary magazine, *Aurora,* in 1910 shortly before her death.

From a speech read by Ramírez to celebrate the founding of the Society of Workers, circa 1910:

> To call a worker my brother, I need only my heart, and to tell him "Forward!" I need only, like him, a soul swollen with the desire to struggle. . . . Mutualism needs the vigor of struggle and the firmness of conviction to advance in its unionizing effort; it needs to shake away the apathy of the masses, and enchain with links of abnegation the passions that rip apart its innermost being; it needs hearts that say: I am for you, as I want you to be for me; mutualism has need of us workers, the humble, the small gladiators of the idea, it needs for us to salvage from our egotisms something immense, something divine, that can make us a society, that can make us nobly human. . .
>
> The worker is the arm, the heart of the world.
>
> And it is to him, untiring and tenacious struggler, that the future of humanity belongs. May you, beloved workers, integral part of human progress, yet celebrate, uncounted anniversaries,

and with your example may you show societies how to love each other so that they may be mutualists and to unite so that they may be strong.

(*Source:* Kanelos, Nicolás. *Herencia: The Anthology of Hispanic Literature of the United States.* New York: Oxford University Press, 2002, pp. 444–45. Trans. Inés Hernández Tovar.)

Books

Kanelos, Nicolás. *Herencia: The Anthology of Hispanic Literature of the United States.* New York: Oxford University Press, 2002. Includes a short introduction to Ramírez and prints one of her poems.

Tovar, Inés Hernández. "Sara Estela Ramírez: The Early Twentieth Century Texas-Mexican Poet." PhD diss., University of Houston, 1984. There are relatively few sources on Ramírez and this is the most exhaustive.

Websites

Adventures in Feministory: Sara Estela Ramírez. This essay, by Kjerstin Johnson on the *Bitch* magazine site, provides a brief biography of the poet along with some analysis of her writing. http://bitchmagazine.org/post/adventures-in-feministory-sara-estela-ram%C3%ADrez

Sara Estela Ramírez. The Texas State Handbook, sponsored by the Texas State Historical Society, provides a short biography of the poet. http://www.tshaonline.org/handbook/online/articles/fra60

1957

Joseph M. Montoya, a Democrat from New Mexico, is elected to the 85th Congress by special election to fill the unexpired term caused by the death of Antonio M. Fernandez. Montoya moves to the U.S. Senate in 1964, replacing the deceased Dennis Chavez. He is most notable for serving on the Watergate committee that investigated the activities of President Richard Nixon

and his aides. Defeated in a 1976 re-election bid, Montoya died on June 5, 1978.

Books

Gould, Lewis L. *The Most Exclusive Club: A History of the Modern United States Senate.* New York: Basic Books, 2005. Excellent general history of this American institution.

Liebovitch, Louis. *Richard Nixon, Watergate, and the Press: A Historical Retrospective.* Westport, CT: Praeger, 2003. One of the best general histories of the Watergate scandal.

Website

Watergate. Provides a chronological account of Watergate as well as an archive that includes several speeches in audio and video formats by Richard Nixon. http://watergate.info/

1982

Charter air links between Miami and Havana are halted by the U.S. government. Ten days later, the U.S. government announces that U.S. citizens are prohibited from making monetary expenditures incidental to travel in Cuba. The measure is taken as a way of starving Cuba of money.

Books

Haney, Patrick Jude. *The Cuban Embargo: The Domestic Politics of an American Foreign Policy.* Pittsburgh: University of Pittsburgh Press, 2005. Focuses on the responses of presidential administrations, beginning with the Reagan administration, to the Cuban embargo.

Horowitz, Irving Louis. *Searching for the Soul of American Foreign Policy: The Cuban Embargo and the National Interest.* Coral Gables, FL: Institute for Cuban and Cuban-American Studies, 2000. Short study of the reasons for the embargo.

Website

Institute for Cuban and Cuban-American Studies, University of Miami. The institute provides an online database, Cuba Online, of information pertaining to the island as well as publications and lectures relating to Cuba. http://www6.miami.edu/iccas/

April 10

1835

Tiburcio Vásquez, one of the most famous outlaws and a folk hero of the 19th century, is born in Monterey, California. (The feast day of San Tiburcio, his namesake, is August 11, so according to Spanish tradition, Vásquez celebrated his birthday on this saint's day.) Until his capture near Los Angeles in 1874, Vásquez robbed and, on occasion, killed Anglos. For resisting American efforts to make California's Spanish-speaking people into strangers in their own land, Vásquez gained the image of a Robin Hood. However, he was not a hero. He did not share his riches with the poor though many Latinos protected and harbored Vásquez and his band. He gained heroic status because Californios and Mexicans were desperate for anyone who resisted the white society that had marginalized them. He developed into a legend because he was seen as an avenger.

From "The Vásquez Romance," a poem written by Vásquez on the eve of his trial and shortly before his 1875 hanging:

It is in the year 1875, today, the Americans say,
That Tiburcio Vásquez is the leader of all the Mexicans.
The tyrants are saying that he will have to be hanged,
For crimes committed in several counties.
In Los Angeles, it is true, Vásquez lost his head, and the police took him.
No longer will he roam the desert.
For he was ruined by confidence he misplaced,

For with great tyranny a woman betrayed him. . . .
The robberies and damage he has caused to many, he himself has confessed.
But he has never killed anyone, for Vásquez was not an assassin.

(*Source:* Boessenecker, John. *Bandido: The Life and Times of Tiburcio Vásquez*. Norman: University of Oklahoma Press, 2010, p. 350.)

Books

Boessenecker, John. *Bandido: The Life and Times of Tiburcio Vásquez*. Norman: University of Oklahoma Press, 2010. An exceptional biography of Vásquez that places him among the ranks of social bandits.

Secrest, William B. *California Badmen*. Sanger, CA: Quill Driver Books/Word Dancer Press, 2007. Sets Vásquez in the context of others of his ilk.

Websites

Tiburcio Vásquez, Bandit. The University of Southern California Library provides this biography of the bandit hero. http://www.usc.edu/libraries/archives/la/scandals/vasquez.html

"The Haunts and Hideouts of Tiburcio Vásquez." Will Thrall of the Historical Society of Southern California provides this guide to sites associated with Vásquez. http://www.scvhistory.com/scvhistory/vasquez-thrall.htm

1930

Dolores Huerta, cofounder with César Chávez of the United Farm Workers (UFW), is born in Dawson, New Mexico. Huerta grew up as the daughter of a restaurant and hotel owner in the agricultural community of Stockton, California. Often lost in Chávez's shadow, Huerta is a skilled negotiator and lobbyist who directed the UFW grape boycott in the 1960s to protest the treatment of farmworkers. She has also lobbied to end the Bracero Program and to extend government benefits to farmworkers.

She created the Dolores Huerta Foundation in 2002 to help develop community leaders.

Books

Brevard, Lisa Pertillar. *Womansaints: The Saintly Portrayal of Select African-American and Latina Cultural Heroines.* New Orleans: University Press of the South, 2002. Argues that women, including Huerta, are portrayed in a manner that gives them power yet limits them.

García, Mario T., ed. *A Dolores Huerta Reader.* Albuquerque: University of New Mexico Press, 2008. A collection of essays about Huerta combined with interviews that she has given and statements that she has issued.

Website

Dolores Huerta: Biography. Provides photos and a detailed biography of Huerta, including the honors that she has received and the boards that she serves on. http://www.lasculturas.com/aa/bio/bioDoloresHuerta.htm

April 11

1898

President William McKinley, who had been hesitant to involve the United States in the conflict between the Spanish and the Cubans, asks Congress for permission to send troops to Cuba. Congress subsequently declares war on April 25, beginning the Spanish-American War. Categorized as a "splendid little war" for its short duration, the War of 1898 was the first global conflict for the United States and one that spread American influence around the world.

From President McKinley's Request for Congress to Declare War on Spain:

Obedient to that precept of the Constitution which command the President to give from time to time to the Congress information of the state of the Union and to recommend to their consideration such measures as he shall judge necessary and expedient, it becomes my duty to now address your body with regard to the grave crisis that has arisen in the relations of the United States to Spain by reason of the warfare that for more than three years has raged in the neighboring island of Cuba.

I do so because of the intimate connection of the Cuban question with the state of our own Union and the grave relation the course which it is now incumbent upon the nation to adopt must needs bear to the traditional policy of our Government if it is to accord with the precepts laid down by the founders of the Republic and the religiously observed by succeeding Administrations to the present day . . .

The grounds for . . . intervention may be briefly summarized as follows:

First. In the cause of humanity and to put an end to the barbarities, bloodshed, starvation, and horrible miseries now existing there, and which the parties to the conflict are either unable or unwilling to stop or mitigate. It is no answer to say this is all in another country, belonging to another nation, and is therefore none of our business. It is specially our duty, for it is right at our door.

Second. We owe it to our citizens in Cuba to afford them that protection and indemnity for life and property which no government there can or will afford, and to that end to terminate the conditions that deprive them of legal protection.

Third. The right to intervene may be justified by the very serious injury to the commerce, trade, and business of our people and by the wanton destruction of property and devastation of the island.

Fourth, and which is of utmost importance. The present condition of affairs in Cuba is a constant menace to our peace and entails upon this Government an enormous expense . . . and compel us to keep on a semi war footing with a nation with which we are at peace . . .

In view of these facts and of these considerations I ask the Congress to authorize and empower the President to take measures to secure a full and final termination of hostilities between the Government of Spain and the people of Cuba, and to secure in the island the establishment of a stable government, capable of maintaining order and observing its international obligations, insuring peace and tranquility and the security of its citizens as well as our own, and to use the military and naval forces of the United States as may be necessary for these purposes.

(*Source:* Moore, John Bassett. *A Digest of International Law.* Washington, D.C.: Government Printing Office, 1906, vol. 6, pp. 211–23.)

Books

Pérez, Louis A., Jr. *The War of 1898: The United States and Cuba in History and Historiography.* Chapel Hill: University of North Carolina, 1998. An examination of a pivotal conflict in the history of two countries by the foremost scholar of the Cuban past.

Schoonover, Thomas. *Uncle Sam's War of 1898 and the Origins of Globalization.* Lexington: University Press of Kentucky, 2003. Explains why the United States became an overseas imperialist power in the 1890s and shows how it viewed the Caribbean–Central American region.

Websites

The World of 1898: The Spanish-American War. This Library of Congress website provides a history of the war, chronology, bibliography, and links to documents. http://www.loc.gov/rr/hispanic/1898/intro.html

The Spanish-American War Centennial Website. Created to honor the 100th anniversary of the conflict, this site provides guidance on researching a veteran of the war, detailed information about weaponry, and other information useful for re-enactors and Living History groups. http://spanamwar.com/

April 12

1952

Poet Gary Soto, a 1995 finalist for the National Book Award, is born in a Spanish-speaking section of Fresno, California, to Mexican American parents. Soto is the author of many poetry collections, including award nominee *New and Selected Poems.* His works typically focus on the challenges of growing up in Mexican American communities with many of his writings aimed at youths. In 1999, he received the Literature Award from the Hispanic Heritage Foundation.

Books

Soto, Gary. *The Effects of Knut Hamsun on a Fresno Boy: Recollections and Short Essays.* New York: Persea Books, 2000. Biographical works by the poet.

Soto, Gary. *Human Nature: Poems.* North Adams, MA: Tupelo Press, 2010. One of the better-known collections of the poet's work.

Website

Gary Soto. This Poetry Foundation website provides a biography of Soto, a listing of his writings, and an extensive further reading guide. http://www.poetryfoundation.org/bio/gary-soto

1990

Novelist Oscar Hijuelos wins the Pulitzer Prize for fiction for *The Mambo Kings Play Songs of Love,* a tale of two brothers from

Havana who become minor celebrities as musicians in New York City nightclubs. Born to Cuban immigrant parents in New York City in 1951, Hijuelos typically draws on his background when writing. His works address the challenges of being Latino in America.

Books

Hijuelos, Oscar. *The Mambo Kings Play Songs of Love: A Novel.* New York: Hyperion, 2010. The story of two Cuban brothers who form an orchestra in Havana and then come to New York City, this book became a film starring Antonio Banderas and Armand Assante.

Hijuelos, Oscar. *Thoughts without Cigarettes.* New York: Gotham Books, 2011. The autobiography of the writer.

Website

Oscar Hijuelos Biography. This A&E television network website provides a short biography of the writer. http://www.biography.com/people/oscar-hijuelos-188849

2002

Musician Trinidad "Trini" López is inducted in the Las Vegas Casino Legends Hall of Fame. López, who grew up in the barrios of Dallas, has sold over 100 million albums. He is nicknamed "Mr. La Bamba" for his rendition of the song of the same name and is also known for a version of Pete Seeger's "If I Had a Hammer" that stayed in the Top 40 for 48 consecutive weeks beginning in 1963. He had a major influence on American culture in the 1960s.

Books

N. A. *The 1960s: Piano, vocal, guitar.* Milwaukee, WI: Hal Leonard, [2005?]. Contains the score for "the hammer song," also known as "If I Had a Hammer."

Okun, Milton, ed. *Great Songs of Folk Music: Piano, vocal, guitar.* Port Chester, NY: Cherry Lane Music, 2007. Includes the score for López's "Lemon Tree."

Website

Trini López Online. The official website for the musician contains a YouTube link to an interview with him, his memories, and a song list. http://www.trinilopez.com/

April 13

1850

California passes a tax on foreign miners, legislation aimed at pushing nonwhites out of the lucrative mining industry. The Foreign Miners' Tax aimed to discourage immigration by removing an economic incentive for moving to the United States or remaining in the country. The law, primarily directed at forcing Latinos out of the mines, required all persons who were not native-born or who had not become citizens under the Treaty of Guadalupe Hidalgo to pay $20 to take out a license to mine. The law did prove successful in its aim. Mexican miners balked at the exorbitant fee and refused to pay it. ($20 in 1850 is the equivalent of almost $500 in 2012.) When the Mexicans exited the mines, the Chinese remained as the largest nonwhite group of miners. As a result, anti-Chinese sentiment rose throughout the 1850s. The next Foreign Miners' Tax, enacted in 1852, targeted the Asians.

From *Alta California* newspaper:

> [The tax is] decidedly unconstitutional, unjust, impolitic, opposed to every principle of our free institutions. . . . We have said to the world we are free, come and enjoy freedom with us. . . . Knowing this, tens of thousands came to California in the full belief that they would not only meet with gold, but far better, justice and kindness. From Mexico and Peru, and Chile they flocked here, better miners than our own people. They dug, they got gold, and they spent it freely. . . . But the iniquitous law was passed. . . . They

could not stand it. They left by thousands and tens of thousands.

(*Source:* Alta California, "A California Newspaper Deplores the Foreign Miner's Tax," in HERB by ASHP, Item #1809, http://www.herb.ashp.cuny.edu/items/show/1809)

Books

Calderón, Roberto R. *Mexican Coal Mining Labor in Texas and Coahuila, 1880–1930*. College Station: Texas A&M University Press, 2000. Comparative study of Mexican miners in the United States and Mexico.

Holliday, J. S. *Rush for Riches: Gold Fever and the Making of California*. Berkeley: University of California Press, 1999. Well-respected general history of the Gold Rush.

Websites

American Experience—Gold Rush. Basic history of Mexican Americans in the Gold Rush. http://www.pbs.org/wgbh/amex/goldrush/peopleevents/p_mexicans.html

Five Views—An Ethnic Historic Site Survey for California. Provides a good history of Mexican Americans in California in the years after the Mexican-American War. http://www.cr.nps.gov/history/online_books/5views/5views5b.htm

1931

Martha Bernal, the first woman of Mexican ancestry to earn a PhD in clinical psychology in the United States, is born in San Antonio, Texas. Bernal completed her education at a time when few minorities or women pursued doctoral degrees. When she sought a postgraduate position, she was told by universities that they did not hire women. Bernal's experiences with sexism and racism shaped her career as she realized that an absence of women of color in the psychology field translated into an absence of research on minorities. Her research focused on the formation of a Mexican American identity.

Bernal also served as an advocate within the American Psychological Association to improve the status of ethnic minorities. In 1979, she cofounded the National Hispanic Psychological Association. Bernal died in 2002.

Books

Bernal, Martha E., and Phyllis C. Martinelli, eds. *Mexican American Identity*. Encino, CA: Floricanto Press, 2005. Contains an essay by Bernal and her associates on the Mexican American child's understanding of ethnic identity.

Padilla, Amado M., ed. *Hispanic Psychology: Critical Issues in Theory and Research*. Thousand Oaks: Sage, 1995. Includes an essay by Bernal on the adaptation of Mexican American youths in school settings.

Website

Martha Bernal. The American Psychological Association's biography of one of its most respected members. http://www.apadivisions.org/division-35/about/heritage/martha-bernal-biography.aspx

April 14

1921

Ricardo Alegría, an instrumental figure in the development of Puerto Rico's national cultural identity, is born in San Juan, Puerto Rico. Besides pioneering the study of the Taíno (Native American) culture, he is responsible for restoring Old San Juan. Alegría argued that the Taíno did not go extinct since about one-third of Puerto Ricans have Taíno blood. DNA studies later proved him right. Alegría died in 2011.

Books

Alegría, Ricardo E. *Las Primeras Representaciones Gráficas del Indio Americano, 1493–1523*. San Juan: Centro de Estudios Avanzados de Puerto Rico y el Caribe, Instituto de Cultura Puertorriqueña, 1978. Discusses the first images of the Taíno produced in the years immediately following Columbus's arrival in the New World.

Bercht, Fatima, ed. *Taíno: Pre-Columbian Art and Culture from the Caribbean*. New York: El Museo del Barrio and Monacelli Press, 1997. Contains an essay by Alegría that is an introduction to Taíno culture and history.

Website

Ricardo Alegría. The Smithsonian Latino Center provides a short biography and a photo of the famed anthropologist and archaeologist. http://latino.si.edu/virtualgallery/ojos/bios/bios_Alegria.htm

April 15

1991

For the first time, the United States imposes import restrictions on Mayan archaeological artifacts from the Petén region of Guatemala. These restrictions are subsequently extended and then merged into a 1997 ban on pre-Columbian archaeological artifacts from throughout Guatemala. The ban is an effort to preserve pre-Columbian history since the removal of artifacts from their context can make the reconstruction of the past nearly impossible when written records are absent.

Books

Messenger, Phyllis Mauch, ed. *The Ethics of Collecting Cultural Property*. Albuquerque: University of New Mexico Press, 1999. Includes several essays on the battles over pre-Columbian and Mayan art.

Vitelli, Karen D., ed. *Archaeological Ethics*. Walnut Creek, CA: AltaMira Press, 1996. Argues that the looting of artifacts robs people of their history.

Website

Import Restrictions Imposed on Archaeological Artifacts from Guatemala. Part of the *Federal Register*, this Department of the Treasury site provides a justification for and details of the ban on the importation of pre-Columbian culturally significant archaeological artifacts. http://dosfan.lib.uic.edu/usia/E-USIA/education/culprop/gt91fr01.html

April 16

1866

José de Diego, the father of the Puerto Rican independence movement, is born in Aguadilla. After earning a law degree in Spain, he returned to Puerto Rico to argue for its independence from Spain and cofounded the Autonomist Party in 1887. When Spain ceded Puerto Rico to the United States, he sought the right of Puerto Ricans to self-government and founded the Unionist Party in 1904. De Diego also gained a reputation for his romantic poems and combative essays. He died in 1918.

From José de Diego, "Independence" (1916):

It is high time that we lovers and partisans of national independence set down in black and white what needs to be submitted to the next assembly of the Unionist Party.

I withdraw no word of my estimate of our people's readiness to fight and die for their race, honor, and freedom, if fate were one day to demand of us the same sacrifice that all the New World people have made. But no one is so sublimely stupid as to think that we should immediately start gathering in the forest with our machetes. What we have behind us are ideas rather than arms—our faith, our hope, and our right. We have the support of our brothers in Latin America. We have the good traditional instincts of the people of the North against colonial tyrants unworthy to have been born in the land of democracy. All this we have and know we have . . .

Some creatures in our world are born limited in their movements, some in spaces too confined to move at all; later they get wings and roam everywhere, nimble and free. Our ideal of Independence will be born with the limitation of a protectorate, because that limitation is in the environment and necessary to supervise the ideal. Forever? No. Till when? Until the environment and the ideal themselves put an end to it; until wings grow and space extends, in the evolution of means toward the ends of life.

(*Source:* Zavala, Iris M., and Rafael Rodríguez, eds. *The Intellectual Roots of Independence: An Anthology of Puerto Rican Political Essays.* New York: Monthly Review Press, 1980, pp. 134–35.)

Books

Diego, José de. *Obras Completas: Nueva Campañas, el Plebiscito.* San Juan de Puerto Rico: Instituto de Cultura Puertorriqueña, 1973. This book focuses on de Diego's political campaigns.

Diego, José de. *Poemas.* NP: Linkgua, 2012. This is a collection of de Diego's romantic and naturalistic poems.

Websites

José de Diego. *El Boricua,* a magazine for Puerto Ricans, provides a short biography of the writer and politician as well as two of his poems. http://www.elboricua.com/JosedeDiego.html

José de Diego. The Library of Congress provides a brief biography of de Diego with references. http://www.loc.gov/rr/hispanic/1898/diego.html

1978

Federal investigators probing the assassination of the former Chilean ambassador Orlando Letelier in Washington, D.C., in 1976 announce that they believe right-wing Cuban exiles recruited by Chilean agents were behind the murder. Letelier died when a bomb blew up the car that he was riding in on a Washington street. Guillermo Novo, Rolando Ortero, and Orlando Bosch, all Cuban exiles, were named as suspects in the killing. Letelier served in the socialist government of Salvador Allende. A monument to Letelier and the colleague who died with him, Ronni K. Moffitt, stands in Sheridan Circle in Washington, D.C.

Books

Castañeda, Rafael Rodríguez. *El Asesinato de Orlando Letelier.* Mexico: Proceso, 1979. A succinct account of the murder from a non-U.S. perspective.

Freed, Donald, and Fred Simon Landis. *Death in Washington: The Murder of Orlando Letelier.* Westport, CT: Lawrence Hill, 1980. Covers the assassination and its link to Chilean politics.

Website

Letelier-Moffitt Assassination 30 Years Later. The National Security Archive, part of George Washington University, includes accounts of documents that link Chilean dictator Augusto Pinochet to the murders. http://www.gwu.edu/~nsarchiv/NSAEBB/NSAEBB199/index.htm

April 17

1695

Sor Juana Inés de la Cruz dies in Mexico after nursing fellow Hieronymite nuns ill with a plague. A self-taught poet, her poems are among the best representations of the Baroque literary movement. She is also notable for fiercely defending women's right to education and to participate in scholarly debate. Scholars are increasingly recognizing Sor Juana's significance as a theologian, the first woman theologian in the Americas.

She questioned the method and structure of the theology of her era as well as its male-centered suppositions. Sor Juana has become an iconic figure for Latina feminists.

From one of Sor Juana's poems in the 1676 series of *villancicos* celebrating the Assumption of Mary:

To brighten light itself,
to enliven Glory,
to enrich riches,
and crown the crowns;
to make a Heaven of the very Heaven,
to make beauty more lovely,
ennoble nobility,
honor honor itself,
she who is of the Heavens
raises honor, riches, crown,
light, loveliness, nobility,
Heaven, Perfection and Glory.

(*Source:* Gonzalez, Michelle A. *Sor Juana: Beauty and Justice in the Americas.* Maryknoll, NY: Orbis, 2003, p. 62.)

Books

Hind, Emily. *Femmenism and the Mexican Woman Intellectual from Sor Juana to Poniatowska: Boob Lit.* New York: Palgrave Macmillan, 2010. Captures Sor Juana's importance to feminism.
Rappaport, Pamela Kirk, trans. and ed. *Sor Juana Inés de la Cruz: Selected Writings.* New York: Paulist Press, 2005. Wonderful introduction to Sor Juana and one of the few introductory texts in English.

Website

Sor Juana Inés de la Cruz (1648–1695). This Oregon State University website provides a short biography of Sor Juana, an excerpt from her defense of education for women, and a timeline of her life. http://oregonstate.edu/instruct/phl302/philosophers/cruz.html

1961

The Bay of Pigs debacle begins when 1,400 anti-Castro Cubans, trained by the United States, invade the south shore of Cuba. Upon entering the White House in January, President John F. Kennedy discovered a secret CIA plan to remove the communist Fidel Castro from power. According to this plan, exiled Cubans would return in force and inspire Cubans who had remained on the island to rebel against Castro. However, the plan proved too poorly conceived and executed to succeed. The invaders were quickly overwhelmed after landing at the Bay of Pigs and Cuban troops captured more than 1,100 men, many of whom had left families in Florida. Kennedy effectively abandoned the invaders when he refused to provide them with direct military support in the form of air strikes. The United States initially denied any involvement with the invasion. The Bay of Pigs invasion greatly embarrassed the United States and led to questions about Kennedy's competence. Among Latin Americans, the episode brought back memories of Yankee imperialism. The Soviets, likely inspired by Kennedy's blunder and the sense that the United States was now weak, drew even more closely to Cuba. They subsequently placed the missiles in Cuba that set off the Cuban Missile Crisis of 1962. The exiles spent many months in prison with the first group released on December 23, 1962, to a plane taking them to Florida.

From Eduardo Machado's autobiography:

We knew the exiles had landed. We knew that the plan had been set in motion. We even knew the exiles' chances were slim. We also knew there was plenty of U.S. aid on ships mere miles from the Cuban coast, and that if all else failed, the marines could march in to save the day. So on that morning, standing in the street in front of my house, we thought, finally, they're here. It'll all be over soon. But as the parachutes drifted earthward, it was obvious that something was wrong. There were no soldiers touching down in Cojimar. Each parachute carried a crate that cracked open on impact, spilling piles of leaflets through the streets. I stooped down to pick one up. I don't remember if they were in English or Spanish, but we deciphered the message and were stunned by its simplicity: Go out into the streets and overthrow Fidel. What? Obviously we would do that if we had to. But we were supposed to be bolstered by the military might of the U.S.A.! The air force and the marines! The exile army that had trained for two years in South Florida and Guatemala! We were waiting for the Yankees! Then we'd march proudly through the streets and defeat the tyrant! But where were they? . . .

(*Source:* Machado, Eduardo, and Michael Domitrovich. *Tastes Like Cuba: An Exile's Hunger for Home.* New York: Gotham Books, 2007, pp. 48–49.)

Books

Machado, Eduardo, and Michael Domitrovich. *Tastes Like Cuba: An Exile's Hunger for Home.* New York: Gotham Books, 2007. Machado, the son of a family opposed to Fidel Castro, came to the United States as a child in the early 1960s and writes about his experiences as a Cuban immigrant.

Rasenberger, Jim. *The Brilliant Disaster: JFK, Castro, and America's Doomed Invasion of Cuba's Bay of Pigs.* New York: Scribner, 2011. Extensive account of the failure based upon declassified CIA documents.

Websites

The Bay of Pigs—John F. Kennedy Presidential Library and Museum. Good history of the episode with links to archival material and Kennedy's speech on the topic. http://www.jfklibrary.org/JFK/JFK-in-History/The-Bay-of-Pigs.aspx

Invasion at Bay of Pigs. J. A. Sierra's site is a popular account of the invasion with a good list of references. http://www.historyofcuba.com/history/baypigs/pigs.htm

1966

A high explosive placed under a car at the Miami home of Antonio Prio Socarras, a former Cuban government minister of finance, rips apart two cars and shatters windows while leaving a foot-deep crater in a driveway. Prio held power in the 1950 government of his brother, Carlos, who governed before Fulgencio Batista took over.

Books

Alexander, Robert J., ed. *Presidents of Central America, Mexico, Cuba, and Hispaniola: Conversations and Correspondence.* Westport, CT: Praeger, 1995. Covers the administration of Cuba's Carlos Prio Socarras.

Grandin, Greg, and Gilbert M. Joseph, eds. *A Century of Revolution: Insurgent and Counterinsurgency Violence during Latin America's Long Cold War.* Durham, NC: Duke University Press, 2010. Sets Cuban terrorism in the context of the Cold War.

Website

Amy Zalman, "History of Cuba—State Sponsor of Terrorism." Argues that Cuba has little connection with state-sponsored terrorism and provides links to related articles on about.com. http://terrorism.about.com/od/cuba/a/Cuba.htm

1976

César Andreu Iglesias, a Puerto Rican labor leader and journalist, dies in San Juan. A communist who suffered persecution for his political views, he was one of the cofounders of the General Confederation of Workers. He supported the Puerto Rican independence movement through novels and other writings.

Books

Andreu Iglesias, César. *The Vanquished: A Novel.* Chapel Hill: University of North Carolina Press,

2002. Probably the author's best-known work and somewhat autobiographical, it is a novel about hope in the midst of political defeat.

Sánchez-Boudy, José. *Las Novelas de César Andreu Iglesias y la Problemática Puertorriqueña Actual*. Barcelona, Spain: Bosch and Casa Editorial, 1968. Discusses Andreu's writings in the context of Puerto Rican politics.

Website

The Vanquished. The University of North Carolina Press reprints the afterword, a superb biographical essay by Arcadio Díaz-Quiñones, to its edition of Andreu's well-regarded book. http://uncpress.unc.edu/browse/page/128

April 18

2005

PepsiCo announces that it is introducing some of its Mexican brands to the United States as part of an effort to woo the country's fast-growing Latino population. The company began selling Mirinda, an orange-flavored drink, in cities with large Hispanic communities last year and plans to add apple-flavored Manzanita Sol later this year. The two products are PepsiCo's best-selling drinks in Mexico after its flagship cola. Retailers in heavily Latino areas had been pushing for the products.

Books

Benitez, Cristina. *Latinization: How Latino Culture is Transforming the U.S.* Ithaca, NY: Paramount Marketing, 2007. Addresses changes in food consumption among other topics.

Korzenny, Felipe, and Betty Ann Korzenny. *Hispanic Marketing: Connecting with the New Latino Consumer*. New York: Routledge, 2012. In light of demographic trends, the Latino consumer has gained the attention of marketers.

April 19

1949

Baseball player Saturnino Orestes Armas "Minnie" Minoso, nicknamed the Cuban Comet, breaks the color line for Latino ballplayers in Major League Baseball when he plays his first game for the Cleveland Indians. His first full season comes in 1951 with the Chicago White Sox. Minoso, a native of La Habana and a seven-time All Star, retires with a career .389 on-base percentage.

Books

Bjarkman, Peter C. *A History of Cuban Baseball, 1864–2006*. Jefferson, NC: McFarland, 2007. Minoso developed into a standout player in Cuba, as did many other players in the U.S. Major Leagues.

Minoso, Minnie, and Herb Fagen. *Just Call Me Minnie: My Six Decades in Baseball*. Champaign, IL: Sagamore, 1994. Minoso's autobiography.

Website

Minnie Minoso Statistics and History. Provides career statistics for Minoso and ranks him against other players. http://www.baseball-reference.com/players/m/minosmi01.shtml

1980

The Mariel boatlift begins with Cubans leaving from the port of Mariel, located about 28 miles west of Havana. On this day, the Cuban government announces that Cuban Americans could travel to Cuba to pick up refugees and it contacts Cuban Americans directly to encourage them to make the journey. Cuban Americans immediately begin to sail for their relatives with any vessel that appears capable of making the voyage. Thousands of fishing boats, yachts, and other small craft depart from Key West and Miami for Mariel. The vessels typically load up with more refugees than the boats can safely carry. The first refugees arrive on April 21. By the time the boatlift comes to an end, over 125,000 Cubans have made the journey to the United States. Only 27 people perished at sea, chiefly because of the search and rescue efforts of the U.S. Coast Guard. Only two percent or 2,746 Cubans were criminals under U.S. law. However, reports that criminals and the mentally ill were among those thousands arriving daily fed a public backlash.

From U.S. government statements:

U.S. State Department, April 23, 1980: Those boat owners and captains who are taking people out of Cuba and trying to land them in the United States are playing into the hands of the Cuban authorities. . . . While we are deeply sympathetic with those in this country who want to expedite the departure from Cuba of those who are seeking freedom from Castro's regime, we cannot condone this procedure. The transportation of undocumented persons to this country is contrary to U.S. law and policy. It is a felony to bring to the United States any alien not duly admitted by an immigration officer and is punishable by penalties of up to five years in prison, fines of $2,000, and the forfeiture of the vessel.

U.S. Coast Guard, May 14, 1980: All U.S. citizens in Cuban Ports and enroute Cuba are advised to return to the U.S. at this time. The U.S. will arrange alternative transportation for Cuban citizens desiring to emigrate through an organized sea lift that will ensure safe and orderly transportation. Vessels not under charter or hire by the U.S. government are subject to heavy fines and possible seizure if they transport Cuban citizens in violation of U.S. Immigration Laws. All U.S. boats in Mariel and those enroute Cuba are advised to return to the U.S. without delay.

Rear Admiral Benedict L. Stabile to the Cuban Border Guard, May 17, 1980: This marine tragedy [sinking of the *Olo Yumi*, a 35-foot pleasure craft overloaded with 52 people and containing life jackets for only half the passengers] happened because too many persons were put on board the small boat. The Coast Guard again urges the Border Guard to prevent future disasters by not allowing boats departing Mariel to go overloaded. To permit boats to go to sea in an unsafe condition is inconsistent with our mutual concern for safety at sea.

(*Source:* Larzelere, Alex. *Castro's Ploy—America's Dilemma: The 1980 Cuban Boatlift*. Washington, D.C.: National Defense University Press, 1988, pp. 138–39, 143–44, 171.)

Books

Engstrom, David W. *Presidential Decision Making Adrift: The Carter Administration and the Mariel Boatlift*. Lanham, MD: Rowman and Littlefield, 1997. Explores the response of President Jimmy Carter to the boatlift crisis.

Larzelere, Alex. *Castro's Ploy—America's Dilemma: The 1980 Cuban Boatlift*. Washington, D.C.: National Defense University Press, 1988. Well-researched and exhaustive history of the boatlift.

Websites

Cuban Information Archives. Provides photographs of the Mariel boatlift. http://cuban-exile.com/doc_326–350/doc0332.html

U.S. Coast Guard Operations during the 1980 Cuban Exodus. This essay by Benedict L. Stabile and Robert L. Scheina looks at the boatlift from the Coast Guard's perspective. http://www.uscg.mil/history/articles/USCG_Mariel_History_1980.asp

1999

Security guard David Sanes Rodríguez is killed in Vieques when pilots from the USS *John F. Kennedy* fly off course during war games and drop two 500-pound Mark 82 bombs in a civilian area. Sanes's death further inflames Puerto Ricans who are angry about the economic and environmental destruction caused by the U.S. Navy's target practice in Vieques, home of the Atlantic Fleet Weapons Training Facility.

Books

Barreto, Amílcar Antonio. *Vieques, the Navy, and Puerto Rican Politics*. Gainesville: University Press of Florida, 2002. Examines the conflict between the needs of the U.S. Navy for a training site and the desire of the people of Vieques to live without the turmoil caused by the Navy.

McCaffrey, Katherine T. *Military Power and Popular Protest: The U.S. Navy in Vieques, Puerto Rico*. New Brunswick, NJ: Rutgers University Press, 2002. Covers the protests by residents of Vieques against the naval facility in their midst.

Website

History of the Navy in Vieques. Takes a stance against the Navy in Vieques while reprinting news articles and other primary sources relating to the dispute. http://www.vieques-island.com/navy/

April 20

1923

Musician Tito Puente, "King of the Mambo," is born in New York City to Puerto Rican parents. An arranger, composer, and singer, Puente rose to fame in the 1950s. He helped popularize Afro-Cuban and Caribbean music among a mainstream audience. Puente won the first of his five Grammy Awards in 1979. He died in 2000.

Tito Puente speaks to *Fania*:

Q. You've been in the business for over 50 years. What was the happiest time of all to be making music?

A. In the '50s you had to work hard, because the competition was so good. Plus, you had to look good and put make-up on. Usually, the pretty boys were the worst musicians

and the ugly ones were really good, like Charlie Parker and Thelonius Monk. The geniuses.

Q. In all your records, the swing is always there. Is it possible to learn how to swing?

A. It's a God given gift. Many people study music, all of them have the same books, but some excel more than others. Like my friend Giovanni Hidalgo. He plays five congas with a talent that's just out of this world. I've always surrounded myself with excellent percussionists, which is not to my advantage because they play better than me.

(*Source:* Interview with Tito Puente, *Fania,* posted September 2011, http://www.fania.com/content/interview-tito-puente)

Books

Conzo, Joe, with David A. Pérez. *Mambo Diablo: My Journey with Tito Puente*. Milwaukee, WI: Backbeat Books, 2012. Biography of Puente by a man who played with him.

Payne, Jim. *Tito Puente: King of Latin Music*. Milwaukee, WI: H. Leonard, 2006. Provides a biography and discography of Puente.

Websites

Tito Puente. This site, operated by the A&E television network, provides a biography of Puente. http://www.biography.com/people/tito-puente-40846

Tito Puente—"El Cumbanchero." This 1965 television clip shows Puente in his performing heyday. http://www.youtube.com/watch?v=v6fhsmVyNaw

April 21

1836

The Battle of San Jacinto is fought, giving Texas independence from Mexico. During the amazingly brief battle, Sam Houston's men shout "Remember the Alamo!" and Mexican resistance collapses. Mexico loses 630 killed and 730 taken prisoner while

Texas loses only 9 men in one of the most lopsided victories in history. Mexico's Antonio López de Santa Anna is captured the day after the battle and soon signs the agreement ending the war between Texas and Mexico. On May 14, 1836, Texas and Mexico signed the Treaty of Velasco ending the fighting although both sides remained hostile. Santa Anna would return to battle in the Mexican-American War in the next decade.

From William S. Taylor's recollections of the battle:

When the Mexicans commenced retreating from their breastworks at San Jacinto . . . Santa Anna, General Cos, and other officers of note among them hastened to join the forces at the old Fort Bend on the Brazos, under Filisola. Santa Anna and all his cavalry but four attempted their retreat by way of Vince's Bridge, not knowing that this bridge had been destroyed by Deaf Smith, on the morning of that day. About the time this retreat of the Mexicans was commenced, Captain Karnes called for all those having loaded guns to follow him in the pursuit . . .

The distance of Vince's Bridge from the battleground was about four miles, over a very wet muddy plain, and, for perhaps a quarter of a mile, knee deep to our horses in mud and water. . . . While pursuing the Mexicans on the road to Vince's Bridge, we overtook numbers, their horses being too tired to enable them to escape; and as we overtook them, we felt compelled to kill them, and did so, though on their knees crying for quarter, and saying, "Me no Alamo—me no la Bahia," meaning that they were not in either of those horrible massacres. As there were but some fifteen or eighteen of us, and some sixty of the Mexicans we were pursuing, besides Santa Anna, Cos, and several other officers, we saw it was impossible for us to take prisoners, and

we had but little disposition to do so, knowing that they had slaughtered so many of Fannin's men in cold blood; after they had surrendered as prisoners of war, under solemn treaty stipulations that they should be sent safely to New Orleans. . . .

When within 300 or 400 yards of the bridge, we discovered Vince's black stallion, with a fine-looking officer on him, dressed in uniform. Captain Karnes, supposing it was Santa Anna himself, (as it was rumored that he was riding Vince's horse,) made for him. When he came up to him, on the bank of the bayou, the officer dismounted, and Karnes asked him if he was Santa Anna. He replied that he was, supposing that quarter would be given to Santa Anna. Whereupon Captain Karnes struck at him with his sword, hitting him a glancing blow on the head, as he stood on the bank of the bayou. When he discovered that no quarter would be showed to him, he jumped into the bayou, saying at the same time that he was not Santa Anna. Whereupon some pistols were discharged at him, killing him in the bayou. We then continued our pursuit up and down the bayou, killing all we overtook, till we had killed all we could find.

(*Source:* Dimmick, Gregg J. *Sea of Mud: The Retreat of the Mexican Army after San Jacinto: An Archeological Investigation.* Austin: Texas State Historical Association, 2004, pp. 9–11.)

Books

Dimmick, Gregg J. *Sea of Mud: The Retreat of the Mexican Army after San Jacinto: An Archeological Investigation.* Austin: Texas State Historical Association, 2004. Dimmick tells the story of the collapse of the Mexican Army, an event which ended the Texas Revolution.

Moore, Stephen L. *Eighteen Minutes: The Battle of San Jacinto and the Texas Independence*

Campaign. Dallas: Republic of Texas Press, 2004. Provides a good history of one of the shortest and most significant battles in Latino history.

Website

The Battle of San Jacinto. The Texas State Library and Archives Commission provides a superb summary of the battle, several historic images, and copies of significant related documents. https://www.tsl.state.tx.us/treasures/republic/san-jacinto.html

April 22

1451

Isabella I of Castile is born. She joined with her husband, Ferdinand, to expel Jews and Muslims from Spain or force their conversion to Catholicism, to unite Spain, and, perhaps most significantly, to sponsor Columbus's four voyages to the Americas. Although Columbus was not the first explorer to visit the New World, he is remembered because he sent excellent records of his voyages to Isabella and Ferdinand's government in Spain. Previous explorers, with no obligation to report to bureaucrats, did not leave very good records.

1929

Writer Guillermo Cabrera Infante is born in Gibara, Cuba. Cabrera Infante went to jail in 1952 and had to quit journalism school for publishing a short story that offended the Batista government. After his release, he continued to be censored and several of his friends were killed or imprisoned by Batista. In 1959, he traveled with Fidel Castro to the United States, Canada, and South America. Three years later, Castro sent Cabrera Infante to Brussels as a cultural attaché. While overseas, Cabrera Infante won major literature awards. Returning to Cuba, he did not like Castro's dictatorial turn and publicly denounced Castro in 1968. Though a resident of London, he was a frequent lecturer

in the United States and taught at a number of American schools. The Cuban Embassy protested one of his readings in Washington, D.C., in 1981. The 1997 winner of the Premio Cervantes de Literatura, he achieved international status as a fiction writer. Cabrera Infante died in 2005.

From "The Translator Within: A Conversation with Guillermo Cabrera Infante":

> I have a compulsion to tell all. Just ask me about something and I will tell you instantly what I know. You don't have to invent the ways of making me talk. I'll always do the talking. In fact, I'm very close to Mr. Memory in Hitchcock's *The Thirty-nine Steps*. I tell the truth in spite of myself—even if it will cost me dearly . . .

> I am always rewriting. I don't have a problem with the blank page at all. I just write whatever I imagine or concoct. And then comes *the* problem—which is rewriting. And not only in books like *Tres tristes tigres* or *La Habana para un Infante difunto*. Even with articles in Spanish or English that I write now in London, I can rewrite them forever. I actually lose money on those articles. Because they should take me only one afternoon but sometimes they take more than a week. But that's only because for me in English, in Spanish, in French, words are not solitary.

> One word gives in turn the possibility of not merely two but three more words that are there because the first word suggested them. This doesn't only happen in translation. It happens in all I write. . . .

> I wanted to be as famous as [Ernest Hemingway] was. It's not a question of being influenced by his style. Or his characters. But rather by his way of life, if you will. Influenced by his living style. Though of course, with the passing of time I believe that he did something that writers do a lot. He spent so much time in futile endeavors that

it's baffling. I mean, that ritual of going every day at 11 o'clock in the morning down to Cojimar, onto his boat and into the ocean and the Gulf Stream to try and fish the biggest fish possible was sheer lunacy. Having nothing to do with real living, it had everything to do with fantasy. I went once in his boat into the ocean across the Gulf Stream—and it was hideously boring. . . . He came to the Havana driving a Mercury convertible, went to the Floridita or the Zaragozana to eat and to drink. That was certainly appetizing, but the rest of his life was not appealing but appalling. And that's something writers do a lot: wasting time. Faulkner believed he was a Southern gentleman who should ride after the fox every Saturday . . .

(*Source:* Levine, Suzanne Jill. "The Translator Within: A Conversation with Guillermo Cabrera Infante." In *Guillermo Cabrera Infante: Assays, Essays, and Other Arts,* edited by Ardis L. Nelson, pp. 135–38. New York: Twayne, 1999.)

Books

Feal, Rosemary Geisdorfer. *Novel Lives: The Fictional Autobiographies of Guillermo Cabrera Infante and Mario Vargas Llosa.* Chapel Hill: North Carolina Studies in the Romance Languages and Literatures, 1986. Scholarly study of *La Habana Para Un Infante Difunto.*

Nelson, Ardis L., ed. *Guillermo Cabrera Infante: Assays, Essays, and Other Arts.* New York: Twayne, 1999. Chiefly a collection of scholarly essays about Cabrera Infante's writings.

Websites

Guillermo Cabrera Infante, Encyclopedia Britannica. This biography, in an exceptionally well-regarded publication, is an excellent introduction to the writer. http://www.britannica.com/EBchecked/topic/87729/Guillermo-Cabrera-Infante

Interview: Guillermo Cabrera Infante: The Art of Fiction, Paris Review. This 1982 interview focuses on his literary works. http://www.theparisreview.org/interviews/3079/the-art-of-fiction-no-75-guillermo-cabrera-infante

1970

Chicano residents of Barrio Logan in San Diego begin to occupy the Coronado Bridge underpass. The Logan Heights neighborhood, heavily Mexican American, had been disrupted in the 1950s when the City of San Diego changed the zoning from residential to industrial, allowing auto junkyards to move in. The construction of the I-5 highway further disrupted the community as did the building of the bridge. In 1969, the state of California gave San Diego land in Barrio Logan to construct a park but the city moved slowly. When bulldozers finally appeared, they were there to construct a California Highway Patrol station. Angry residents, feeling betrayed by the city, protested for 12 days with the activists demanding that San Diego immediately begin construction of a long-promised community park in the location. During the occupation, many community members begin building the park themselves with shovels, pickaxes, hoes, and rakes. Chicano Park, with 7.4 acres, results from negotiations with the city.

Statement by an anonymous San Diego State student, April 1970:

The word culture is used. To you [Mexican] culture means Taco Bell and the funny Mexican with the funny songs. We gave you our culture of a thousand years. What have you given us? A social system that makes us beggars and police who make us afraid. We've got the land and we are going to work it. We are going to get that park. We no longer talk about asking. We have the park.

(*Source:* http://www.chicanoparksandiego.com/history/page1.html)

Books

Rosales, F. Arturo. *Chicano: The History of the Mexican American Civil Rights Movement.* Houston, TX: Arte Público, 1996. A general history of the movement that spawned the Chicano Park protest.

Shorris, Earl. *Latinos: A Biography of the People.* New York: W.W. Norton, 1992. Sets the Chicano movement in the broader context of Latino history.

Websites

Chicano Park. The Chicano Park Steering Committee offers a history of the park, a look at its murals, and information on activities relating to the preservation of the park's history and vitality. http://chicano-park.org/

History of Chicano Park. Tied to the Chicano Park Documentation Project, this site provides information on the art, culture, and history of the park. It offers the most detailed history of the park. http://www.chicanoparksandiego.com/

1993

César Chávez dies in his sleep in San Luis, Arizona. A week later, on April 29, a crowd estimated to be 35,000 strong stands in 90 degree heat in Delano, California, to form a funeral procession for the leader of United Farm Workers. State flags flew at half mast, by order of the governor, as tributes came for Chávez from Pope John Paul and President Bill Clinton.

From Peter Matthiessen, "César Chávez":

In recent years, beset by the unremitting prejudice of California's Republican administrations, which were elected with the strong support of agribusiness, the embittered Chávez embarked upon a table-grape and lettuce boycott against nonunion growers, protesting the use of dangerous pesticides, which threaten the health not only of farmworkers but of the public. The new boycott never took hold. What was lacking seemed to be the fervor of those exhilarating marchers under union flags, the fasts, the singing, and the chanting—*"Viva la huelga!"*—that put the fear of God in the rich farm owners of California. These brilliant tactics remained tied in the public perception to La Causa, a labor and civil rights movement with religious overtones which rose to prominence in the feverish tumult of the sixties; as a mature A.F.L.—C.I.O. union, the U.F.W. lost much of its symbolic power. Membership has now declined to about one-fifth of its peak of a hundred thousand.

With the funeral march over, the highway empty, and all the banners put away, César Chávez's friends and perhaps his foes are wondering what will become of the U.F.W. A well-trained new leadership (his son-in-law has been named to succeed him, and four of his eight children work for the union) may bring fresh energy and insight. But what the union will miss is Chávez's spiritual fire. A man so unswayed by money, a man who (despite many death threats) refused to let his bodyguards go armed, and who offered his entire life to the service of others, was not to be judged by the same standards of some self-serving labor leader or politician. Self-sacrifice lay at the very heart of the devotion he inspired, and gave dignity and hope not only to the farmworkers but to every one of the Chicano people, who saw for themselves what one brave man, indifferent to his own health and welfare, could accomplish . . .

During the vigil at the open casket on the day before the funeral, an old man lifted a child up to show him the small, gray-haired man who lay inside. "I'm going to tell you about this man someday," he said.

(*Source:* Peter Matthiessen. "César Chávez." *New Yorker,* May 17, 1993, p. 82.)

Books

Del Castillo, Richard Griswold, and Richard A. García. *César Chávez: A Triumph of Spirit.* Norman: University of Oklahoma Press, 1995. The best account of Chávez and his links to the Chicano Movement.

Levy, Jacques E. *César Chávez: Autobiography of La Causa.* New York: W. W. Norton, 1975. Provides an account of Chávez's early years, his initial efforts as an organizer, and his rise to the leadership of Mexican American farmworkers.

Websites

César Chávez: Labor Leader. Enchanted Learning offers a biography of Chávez as well as numerous activities for children that teach about the union leader. http://www.enchantedlearning.com/history/us/hispanicamerican/chavez/

The Story of César Chávez. The United Farm Workers provides a biography of its famed leader. http://www.ufw.org/_page.php?inc=history/07.html&menu=research

April 23

1966

Graphic artist Javier Hernández is born. His comic book character, El Muerto, became the subject of an award-winning film of the same name in 2007. Hernández's work generally contains Latino themes, such as his Dead Dinosaurio, a figure brought to life by an Aztec boy to fight against the European conquest of Mexico. Once viewed as a disposable type of low art, cartoons have begun in the 21st century to gain considerable recognition as an art form worthy of respect.

Books

Aldama, Frederick Luis. *Your Brain on Latino Comics: From Gus Arriola to Los Bros Hernández.* Austin: University of Texas Press, 2009. An overview of Latino comics combined with interviews with the cartoonists.

Van Lente, Fred, and Ryan Dunlavey. *The Comic Book History of Comics.* San Diego: IDW, 2012. General history of the art form.

Website

Javzilla. Javier Hernández's blog focuses on his work as a cartoonist, publisher of comic books, and comic art instructor. http://javiersblog.blogspot.com/

April 24

1898

Ernesto Antonini, a cofounder of the Partido Popular Democrático de Puerto Rico (Popular Democratic Party of Puerto Rico) in 1938, is born. He served as a member of Puerto Rico's House of Representatives, heading the branch from 1945 until his 1963 death.

Books

Farr, Kenneth R. *Personalism and Party Politics: Institutionalization of the Popular Democratic Party of Puerto Rico.* Hato Rey, PR: Inter American University Press, 1973. A history of the organization that Antonini helped create.

Pierce Flores, Lisa. *The History of Puerto Rico.* Santa Barbara, CA: Greenwood, 2010. Good, brief account of Puerto Rico's past.

Website

Partido Popular Democrático. The official site for the political party. http://www.ppdpr.net/

April 25

1854

The editor of the Afro-Cuban newspaper *El Mulato,* Carlos de Colins attacks other Cuban exiles for supporting efforts to annex Cuba to the United States. Based in New York City, de Colins started his newspaper in 1854 to unite the Cuban revolutionary movement with the movement to abolish slavery. He saw annexation as a threat that would result in Cuban cultural annihilation but he chiefly feared that Cuban blacks and mulattos would be forever enslaved.

Books

Lazo, Rodrigo. *Writing to Cuba: Filibustering and Cuban Exiles in the United States*. Chapel Hill: University of North Carolina Press, 2005. Contains a chapter on *El Mulato*.

Villafaña, Frank. *Expansionism: Its Effects on Cuba's Independence*. New Brunswick, NJ: Transaction, 2012. Sets the history of U.S. attempts to acquire Cuba in the context of American expansion.

Website

History of Cuba: Spanish-Cuban-American War. J. A. Sierra's website provides context for the War of 1898 that left Cuba under American control. http://www.historyofcuba.com/history/scaw/scaw1.htm

2001

Puerto Rico's Governor Sila Calderón approves legislation that prohibits activities that produce noise of 190 decibels or greater along the island's shores. The law is an effort to block the U.S. Navy from conducting bombing exercises at its Vieques Island range. Based on the law, Puerto Rico's attorney general files a complaint, seeking the restraining order against the Navy.

Books

Barreto, Amílcar Antonio. *Vieques, the Navy, and Puerto Rican Politics*. Gainesville: University Press of Florida, 2002. Examines the conflict between the need of the U.S. Navy for a training site and the desire of the people of Vieques to live without the turmoil caused by the Navy.

McCaffrey, Katherine T. *Military Power and Popular Protest: The U.S. Navy in Vieques, Puerto Rico*. New Brunswick, NJ: Rutgers University Press, 2002. Covers the protests by residents of Vieques against the naval facility in their midst.

Website

History of the Navy in Vieques. Takes a stance against the Navy in Vieques while reprinting news articles and other primary sources relating to the dispute. http://www.vieques-island.com/navy/

April 26

1966

At a press conference in Los Angeles, Mexican American leaders promise militant action on a national scale until the federal government takes immediate steps to provide Mexican Americans with equal educational and employment opportunities. The leaders are Albert Peña, president of the Political Association of Spanish-Speaking Organizations; Augustine Flores, national president of the American G.I. Forum; Miguel Montes, president of the Latin American Civic Association; Bert Corona, vice-president of the Mexican-American Political Association; and Rodolfo "Corky" Gonzales, founder of the Crusade for Justice.

Books

Gonzales, Rodolfo "Corky." *Message to Aztlán: Selected Writings*. Houston, TX: Arte Público, 2001. One of the leading Chicano activists, Gonzales wrote poems, speeches, and plays in support of Mexican American rights.

Rosales, F. Arturo. *Chicano: The History of the Mexican American Civil Rights Movement*. Houston, TX: Arte Público, 1997. An excellent history of the movement.

Website

A History of Mexican Americans in California: The Chicano Movement. This National Park Service site provides a short, general history of the movement. http://www.cr.nps.gov/history/online_books/5views/5views5e.htm

April 27

2010

The U.S. Army Reserve's 307th Dental Company from Vallejo, California, returned from Mateare, Nicaragua, after providing dental services for over 1,200 Nicaraguans. Many of the soldiers were Latinos who used their Spanish language skills to help the Nicaraguans. The mission was conducted in conjunction with Beyond the Horizon, a humanitarian and civic assistance project focused on providing medical and engineering support to Central Americans. The soldiers performed over 3,200 dental procedures, ranging from cleanings and fillings to extractions and root canals. Many patients also received dentures.

Books

Baldwin, Maria T. *Amnesty International and U.S. Foreign Policy: Human Rights Campaigns in Guatemala, the United States, and China*. El Paso, TX: LFB Scholarly Publishing, 2009. Explains why the United States needs to improve its image in Guatemala.

Glick, Edward. *Peaceful Conflict: The Non-Military Use of the Military*. Harrisburg, PA: Stackpole, 1967. Explains the importance of employing troops in civic actions.

Website

Miles, Donna. "Beyond the Horizons Strengthens Bonds in Guatemala, Honduras." This Department of Defense website explains the importance of the Beyond the Horizons program to military training and national defense. http://www.defense.gov/news/news article.aspx?id=116918

April 28

1977

The first national Chicano arts festival, Canto al Pueblo, is held in Milwaukee, Wisconsin, from April 28 to May 9. Organized by Arnold Vento, Reimundo "Tigre" Pérez, and Ricardo Sánchez, the festival includes art exhibitions, art happenings, musical performances, and literary readings.

Books

Griswold del Castillo, Richard, Teresa McKenna, and Yvonne Yarbro-Bejarano, eds. *Chicano Art: Resistance and Affirmation, 1965–1985*. Los Angeles: Wight Art Gallery, University of California at Los Angeles, 1991. Addresses the push for acknowledgement of Chicano contributions to art.

Jackson, Carlos Francisco. *Chicana and Chicano Art: ProtestArte*. Tucson: University of Arizona Press, 2009. Focuses on the efforts to gain recognition for Mexican American art during the Chicano movement.

Website

Chicano Art. This forum explores the contemporary Chicano/a aesthetic vision and its link with Mesoamerican roots. http://www.chicanoart.org/

1981

Actress and entrepreneur Jessica Alba is born to a Mexican American father. By taking the lead role in 2000 in *Dark Angel,* Alba became one of the few Latinas to star in a prime-time television show. Alba, a mother of two, was named one of the most creative people in the country by Fast Company magazine in 2012 for cofounding The Honest Company with Christopher Gavigan. The company creates and sells eco-friendly baby care products and household cleaners. Alba has focused particularly on disposable diapers as holding the greatest potential for innovation. The Honest Company's diapers create absorbency using a mix of wheat, corn, and wood-fluff; the company claims that its diapers are 35 percent more absorbent than conventional diapers. The effort addresses the social responsibilities of business, one of the main issues facing businesses in the late 20th and early 21st centuries.

Books

Boons, Frank. *Creating Ecological Value: An Evolutionary Approach to Business Strategies and the Natural Environment*. Northampton, MA: Edward Elgar, 2009. Examines the trend among businesses to consider their impact upon the environment.

Korzenny, Felipe, and Betty Ann Korzenny. *Hispanic Marketing: Connecting with the New Latino Consumer*. New York: Routledge, 2012. Addresses the importance of sustainability to increasing numbers of Latino consumers.

Website

The Honest Company. Official website for the consumer products company. https://www.honest.com/

April 29

2010

The U.S. House of Representatives votes in favor of the Puerto Rican Democracy Act HR2499, a bill to allow Puerto Ricans to vote on statehood, independence, or a continuance of the status quo. Opposition to the statehood bill comes from conservatives concerned about its cost and supporters of English-only laws who fear that Puerto Rican statehood could turn the United States into an officially bilingual nation. Supporters of statehood argue that Puerto Ricans presently have second-class status. The U.S. Senate does not support the bill but it is likely to be introduced again.

From "The Puerto Rican Democracy Act":

111th Congress 2d Session
H. R. 2499

An Act

To provide for a federally sanctioned self-determination process for the people of Puerto Rico.

Section 1. Short Title

This Act may be cited as the "Puerto Rico Democracy Act of 2010".

Sec. 2. Federally Sanctioned Process for Puerto Rico's Self-Determination

(a) First Plebiscite– The Government of Puerto Rico is authorized to conduct a plebiscite in Puerto Rico. The 2 options set forth on the ballot shall be preceded by the following statement: "Instructions: Mark one of the following 2 options:

- "(1) Puerto Rico should continue to have its present form of political status. If you agree, mark here XX.

- "(2) Puerto Rico should have a different political status. If you agree, mark here XX."

(b) Procedure if Majority in First Plebiscite Favors Option 1– If a majority of the ballots in the plebiscite are cast in favor of Option 1, the Government of Puerto Rico is authorized to conduct additional plebiscites under subsection (a) at intervals of every 8 years from the date that the results of the prior plebiscite are certified under section 3(d).

(c) Procedure if Majority in First Plebiscite Favors Option 2– If a majority of the ballots in a plebiscite conducted pursuant to subsection (a) or (b) are cast in favor of Option 2, the Government of Puerto Rico is authorized to conduct a plebiscite on the following 4 options:

- (1) Independence: Puerto Rico should become fully independent from the United States. If you agree, mark here XX.

- (2) Sovereignty in Association with the United States: Puerto Rico and the United States should form a political association between sovereign nations that will not be subject to the Territorial Clause of the United States Constitution. If you agree, mark here XX.

- (3) Statehood: Puerto Rico should be admitted as a State of the Union. If you agree, mark here XX.

- (4) Commonwealth: Puerto Rico should continue to have its present form of political status. If you agree, mark here XX.

Sec. 3. Applicable Laws and Other Requirements

(a) Applicable Laws– All Federal laws applicable to the election of the Resident Commissioner shall, as appropriate and consistent with this Act, also apply to any plebiscites held pursuant to this Act. Any reference in such Federal laws to elections shall be considered, as appropriate, to be a reference to the plebiscites, unless it would frustrate the purposes of this Act.

(b) Rules and Regulations– The Puerto Rico State Elections Commission shall issue all rules and regulations necessary to carry out the plebiscites under this Act.

(c) Eligibility To Vote– Each of the following shall be eligible to vote in any plebiscite held under this Act:

  (1) All eligible voters under the electoral laws in effect in Puerto Rico at the time the plebiscite is held.

  (2) All United States citizens born in Puerto Rico who comply, to the satisfaction of the Puerto Rico State Elections Commission, with all Commission requirements (other than the residency requirement) applicable to eligibility to vote in a general election in Puerto Rico. Persons eligible to vote under this subsection shall, upon timely request submitted to the Commission in compliance with any terms imposed by the Electoral Law of Puerto Rico, be entitled to receive an absentee ballot for the plebiscite.

(d) Certification of Plebiscite Results– The Puerto Rico State Elections Commission shall certify the results of any plebiscite held under this Act to the President of the United States and to the Members of the Senate and House of Representatives of the United States.

(e) English Language Requirements– The Puerto Rico State Elections Commission shall—

  (1) ensure that all ballots used for any plebiscite held under this Act include the full content of the ballot printed in English;

  (2) inform persons voting in any plebiscite held under this Act that, if Puerto Rico retains its current political status or is admitted as a State of the United States, the official language requirements of the Federal Government shall apply to Puerto Rico in the same manner and to the same extent as throughout the United States; and

  (3) inform persons voting in any plebiscite held under this Act that, if Puerto Rico retains its current political status or is admitted as a State of the United States, it is the Sense of Congress that it is in the best interest of the United States for the teaching of English to be promoted in Puerto Rico as the language of opportunity and empowerment in the United States in order to

enable students in public schools to achieve English language proficiency.

(f) Plebiscite Costs– All costs associated with any plebiscite held under this Act (including the printing, distribution, transportation, collection, and counting of all ballots) shall be paid for by the Commonwealth of Puerto Rico.

Passed the House of Representatives April 29, 2010.

(*Source:* Benitez, Franky. "The Puerto Rican Democracy Act Passed April 29, 2010." http://juliorvarela.com/2011/02/22/the-puerto-rican-democracy-act-h-r-bill-2499-passed-april-29–2010/)

Books

Abodaher, David J. *Puerto Rico: America's Fifty-First State.* New York: Franklin Watts, 1993. Short history of Puerto Rico that includes the statehood debate.

Melendez, Edgardo. *Puerto Rico's Statehood Movement.* Westport, CT: Greenwood Press, 1988. An examination of the movement since its 19th century beginnings by a political scientist.

Websites

Statehood for Puerto Rico. Provides a history of the statehood movement, albeit on a site that is not very polished. http://www.nopuertoricostatehood.com/

United States Council for Puerto Rico Statehood. This organization supports self-determination for Puerto Ricans and the site contains statements from political leaders, including U.S. presidents, on statehood. http://www.prstatehood.com/home/index.asp

1979

The movie, *El Super,* premieres in New York. The movie is representative of new images of Latinos, an outgrowth of the social movements of the 1960s and 1970s. In the movie, Raymundo Hildalgo-Gato stars as a former Havana bus driver who can only get a job as a superintendent in a large tenement on New York's Upper West Side because he refuses to learn English. The film, which also features Zully Montero and Elizabeth Peña, is about the disorientation of exiles who serve as living metaphors for the human condition. It is based on Ivan Acosta's play of the same name that was originally produced by the Cuban Cultural Center in New York in 1977. *El Super* is the first film directed by Leon Ichaso and Orlando Jiménez-Leal.

Books

Bernardi, Daniel, ed. *The Birth of Whiteness: Race and the Emergence of U.S. Cinema.* New Brunswick: Rutgers University Press, 1996. Explores the impact of whiteness on Hollywood.

Rodríguez, Clara E. *Heroes, Lovers, and Others: The Story of Latinos in Hollywood.* Washington, D.C.: Smithsonian Books, 2004. Covers the history of film from the Silent Era to the Postmodern Era and emphasizes that it is only since the 1980s that Latinos have been portrayed in nonstereotypic ways.

Website

Latino Film Fund. The fund promotes the production of and appreciation for Latino-themed movies. http://latinofilmfund.org/

April 30

1598

Juan de Oñate, the last conquistador, formally declared that New Mexico belonged to Spain. Born in Zacatecas, Mexico, in 1530 to a wealthy mine owner of Basque descent, Oñate spent the first half of his life fighting Native Americans and searching for silver. On September 21, 1595, he received a contract from King Philip II of Spain to settle New Mexico. Although the Spanish hoped to spread Catholicism, most colonists enlisted with Oñate's expedition to get rich by finding a new silver strike. When riches were not found, Oñate resorted to harsh measures to control his men. He was also known for being especially brutal to the Acoma Indians, who revolted against the Spanish colonizers. All of the troubles in New Mexico prompted the Spanish to temporarily abandon the fledgling colony. Oñate remained to found the town of Santa Fe. However, Spanish law finally caught up with the conquistador and he was banished for using excessive force against the Indians and his own men. Oñate spent his last years trying to clear his name before dying in Spain in 1626.

Books

Kessell, John L. *Pueblos, Spaniards, and the Kingdom of New Mexico.* Norman: University of Oklahoma Press, 2010. Explores the fraught relationship between the Pueblo Indians and the Spanish in 17th-century New Mexico.

Simmons, Marc. *The Last Conquistador: Juan de Oñate and the Settling of the Far Southwest.* Norman: University of Oklahoma Press, 1991. This is the standard and most recent biography of the founder of New Mexico.

Websites

Juan de Oñate. This site, part of the Texas State Historical Association's *The Handbook of Texas Online,* provides a detailed biography of the Mexican leader. http://www.tshaonline.org/handbook/online/articles/fon02

Juan de Oñate, Pioneer of New Mexico. Examines the current attitudes toward Oñate. http://www.cantos.org/consult/Onate.html

1997

Día: Children's Day/ Book Day is begun by Pat Mora, a celebrated Mexican American author of poetry and children's books. The celebration is based on the Mexican celebration of April 30th as the Day of the Child. Mora sought to link the celebration of children with the concept of literacy. Latino faculty and staff at the University of Arizona then backed the idea as did Reforma: the National Association to Promote Library and Information Services to Latinos and the Spanish-Speaking.

In subsequent years, the celebration spread around the United States.

From "Día History":

> The goals of this observance from its inception have included a daily commitment to:
>
> 1. honor children and childhood,
> 2. promote literacy, the importance of linking all children to books, languages and cultures,
> 3. honor home languages and cultures, and thus promoting bilingual and multilingual literacy in this multicultural nation, and global understanding through reading,
> 4. involve parents as valued members of the literacy team,
> 5. promote library collection development that reflects our plurality.

(*Source:* Pat Mora: "Día History." http://www.patmora.com/dia/dia_history.htm)

Books

Mora, Pat. *Zing: Seven Creativity Practices for Educators and Students.* Thousand Oaks, CA: Corwin, 2010. Each essay encourages teachers to get in touch with their own creativity and then spread that creativity to students.

Reyes, María de la Luz, and John J. Halcon, eds. *The Best for Our Children: Critical Perspectives on Literacy for Latino Students.* New York: Teachers College Press, 2000.

Websites

The Latino Family Literacy Project. The organization provides staff development training to educators seeking to foster the involvement of Latino parents in a family reading routine that helps children build strong English-language skills. http://latinoliteracy.com/

Pat Mora: "Día History." Provides the best history of the event, from the perspective of its founder. http://www.patmora.com/dia/dia_history.htm

May

May 1

1782

Pedro Allande y Saavedra, commander of the Royal Presidio of Tucson (Arizona) is wounded in an attack by Apache Indians. Despite the severity of his wound, he continued to direct the defense of the presidio and reportedly held off 600 warriors with only 20 Spanish soldiers. His efforts saved the young settlement from total destruction and preserved the northernmost outpost of the Spanish in Arizona. His campaign against the Apaches likely prompted them to accept a peace settlement in 1786 of free rations and a permanent settlement that anticipated the U.S. Indian policy of the 19th century. Allande received a new assignment in 1786 because his superiors recognized that the troops under his command had suffered from his violent disposition, aggravated by overexertion and a disabling wound.

From the Statement of Pedro Allande y Saavedra to the King of Spain, circa 1786:

Since the day [Allande] was appointed captain of this Tucson presidio, February 19, 1777, he has spared no effort to make it a success. He supervised the building of the walls and the houses of adobe in the two settlements here. He has been the very first in this area to insist on frequent practice maneuvers for troops, training them in marksmanship and drilling them both on horseback and afoot. He surrounded the presidio with a palisade of rough logs, since it lacked a fortified gate and wall, and erected four baluartes [bastions] for the guards. He constructed its magazine and guardhouse and built a fine church at his own expense . . .

On May 1, 1782, 600 Apaches tried to wipe out the two settlements at Tucson and massacre the entire population. He valiantly defended the presidio with only twenty troops. . . . The Apaches were able to commandeer many houses outside the fort. From these they were able to conduct both their offensive and defensive operations. They used them as hospitals and carried their dead and wounded into them. Despite our sentries and the impenetrable outer palisade, the Indians were able to effect considerable damage with their first assault, mortally wounding a retired soldier, another soldier, and a settler. They cut into the right leg of the present petitioner in a number of places, though he was able to kill two of them with his own hand, even after he was wounded. Using another soldier as a crutch, he continued his rounds of the stockade and sentry bastions to direct gunfire so devastating that the enemy was forced to retire with great losses. . . . Though the present petitioner was on the verge of collapse, since a nerve was severed in one of his wounds, he refused medical attention until the complete victory was won and the honor of Your Majesty was vindicated. He received a commendation of valor from our commandant general, the Caballero de Croix, who promised to bring this to the attention of Your Majesty . . .

In summary, all of the Apache attacks on this presidio have been repulsed with heavy losses to the enemy. Lines of countless Apache heads have crowned the palisade. The petitioner has endured untold fatigues in his campaigns. Then there were the cold nights without a campfire, which has always been his policy so as more surely to surprise and punish the enemies of Your Majesty. Often the water was bad and the intense heat of the climate here has caused him continuous pains in his stomach, at times convincing him that the end of his life must be near. The wounds in his right leg have many times swollen and burst, prompting the sympathetic officers of his campaigns to urge him to turn back. He has never once done so.

For these many reasons, the present petitioner prostrates himself at the feet of Your Majesty and begs for assignment as governor of Puebla or some other position in a regiment of cavalry or dragoons where he can continue his illustrious career with less stress on himself and his family.

(*Source:* McCarty, Kieran. *Desert Documentary: The Spanish Years, 1767–1821.* Tucson: Arizona Historical Society, 1976, http://www.library.arizona.edu/exhibits/desertdoc/memoir.htm)

Books

Kessell, John L. *Spain in the Southwest: A Narrative History of Colonial New Mexico, Arizona, Texas, and California.* Norman: University of Oklahoma Press, 2002. Very readable and extensive account of the Spanish invasion.

Naylor, Thomas, and Charles W. Polzer, eds. *The Presidio and Militia on the Northern Frontier of New Spain: A Documentary History.* Tucson: University of Arizona Press, 1986. Illuminates the defensive difficulties of the Spanish on the frontier.

Website

McCarty, Kieran. *Desert Documentary: The Spanish Years, 1767–1821.* Reproduced by the University of Arizona Library, this book reprints documents relating to the Spanish in Arizona in the colonial period. http://www.library.arizona.edu/exhibits/desertdoc/memoir.htm

1900

Charles H. Allen is inaugurated in San Juan as the first governor of Puerto Rico under the Foraker Act. Under the legislation, the U.S. president appointed the governor and members of the Executive Council, who served as the upper house. Americans held the top positions because the whites believed that the Puerto Ricans were not yet capable of self-government. Few of these Americans spoke Spanish or had substantial understanding of Puerto Rico. Federal appointments ended in 1947.

Books

Abodaher, David J. *Puerto Rico: America's Fifty-First State.* New York: Franklin Watts, 1993. A short history of Puerto Rico that includes the statehood debate.

Cabán, Pedro A. *Constructing a Colonial People: Puerto Rico and the United States, 1898–1932.* Boulder, CO: Westview Press, 1999. Covers the Foraker Act.

Website

Foraker Act (Organic Act) of 1900. This Library of Congress site on the Spanish-American War sets the Foraker Act in historical context while providing a short summary of its provisions. http://www.loc.gov/rr/hispanic/1898/foraker.html

2006

The Great American Boycott, or *El Gran Paro Estadounidense,* is held to protest the treatment of illegal immigrants and to demand immigration reform. May 1 is chosen because it is International Workers Day.

From "Lou Dobbs Tonight: The Great American Boycott" on CNN, May 1, 2006:

Dobbs: Good evening, everybody.

Hundreds of thousands of illegal aliens and their supporters today

Casey Wian, Cnn Correspondent:

failed in their attempt to shut down most of our cities to support amnesty for all illegal aliens. The protesters boycotted work, school and shops and held protest and demonstrations. But what the illegal alien lobby called the "Great American Boycott" did not materialize. It certainly did not paralyze most of our cities, as those organizers had hoped.

Today's demonstrations took place in more than 50 cities from coast to coast. The size of the demonstrations varied from a few hundred people to several hundred thousand. . . .

Lou, the so-called "Great American Boycott" has been everything it was advertised to be and everything it was not.

(Begin Videotape) Wian (voice over):

They marched and shouted, waving Mexican and American flags, dancing in the streets. They skipped school and work and shut down businesses.

Unidentified Female:

The money is not the big deal. The big deal is to help the people to get their papers.

Wian:

All because Congress voted to secure the nation's border and toughen criminal penalties against illegal immigration.

Unidentified Female:

I think it's important that we do a boycott today to show that we are important, that we have rights.

Wian:

In California, home to more than two million illegal aliens, amnesty advocates continued to recast the national debate as an attack on all immigrants.

Maria Elena Durazo, President, L.A. Federation of Labor:

The essential reason why there is an outrage by the immigrant community in Los Angeles and throughout the country is because immigrants work hard every day in every industry that you can think of.

Wian:

The second most powerful man in California politics even declared illegal aliens have a right to U.S. citizenship.

Fabian Nunez, Speaker, Calif. State Assembly:

What's most important here is the immigrants, their rights to the legalization and their rights to citizenship.

Wian:

The goal was to cripple the U.S. economy. At the Los Angeles produce market, deliveries continued, though more slowly. Truck traffic is light at the Port of Long Beach, normally the nation's busiest. Many shippers unloaded over the weekend to avoid boycott-related delays. Los Angeles International Airport reports no impact on its operations.

Unidentified Female: But thousands of southern California schoolchildren stayed home, costing school districts tens of millions of dollars in state funds. I stayed out of school, but it's for a good cause. Us Mexicans, we need to have some rights.

Wian: The vast majority of southern Californians not participating in the May Day boycott enjoyed a smooth commute to work on uncrowded freeways and buses. There were minor inconveniences, including interruptions of newspaper deliveries, catering and janitorial services.

Border security activists fought back. Some, including Tucson's Border Patrol Union, planned major purchases of big-ticket items for May 1st. Plenty of marchers also defied the boycott, spending money for T-shirts, flags and food. . . .

(*Source:* "Lou Dobbs Tonight: The Great American Boycott." CNN, May 1, 2006, http://transcripts.cnn.com/TRANSCRIPTS/0605/01/ldt.01.html)

Books

Haugen, David, and Susan Musser, eds. *Illegal Immigration: Opposing Viewpoints*. Farmington Hills, MI: Greenhaven Press, 2011. Contains essays that debate such topics as whether illegal immigration threatens or improves the American economy and whether it harms or helps border communities.

LeMay, Michael C. *Illegal Immigration: A Reference Handbook*. Santa Barbara, CA: ABC-CLIO, 2007. Provides a background history, a chronology, documents and data, and biographies of major figures in the immigration debate.

Newton, Lina. *Illegal, Alien, or Immigrant: The Politics of Immigration Reform*. New York: New York University Press, 2008. Examines the debates over immigration reform beginning with the 1980s.

Websites

Center for Immigration Studies. This is the home page for the nonpartisan organization, the only think tank devoted to immigration policy. http://www.cis.org/

Yearbook of Immigration Statistics: 2010. This U.S. Department of Homeland Security page contains immigration statistics dated back to 1820. http://www.dhs.gov/files/statistics/publications/LPR10.shtm

May 2

2011

An audit of the Mexican American Studies program in the Tucson school district is released by Cambium Learning. The audit was conducted in 2011 at the request of Arizona's Superintendent of Public Instruction, John Huppenthal. While Cambium recommended that the program be continued, Huppenthal ordered that it be shut and the state later threatened the district with loss of funding if it continued to offer the classes.

From "Curriculum Audit of the Mexican American Studies Department":

High School Course Texts and Reading Lists Table 20: American Government/Social Justice Education Project 1, 2—Texts and Reading Lists

- *Rethinking Columbus: The Next 500 Years* (1998), by B. Bigelow and B. Peterson

- *The Latino Condition: A Critical Reader* (1998), by R. Delgado and J. Stefancic
- *Critical Race Theory: An Introduction* (2001), by R. Delgado and J. Stefancic
- *Pedagogy of the Oppressed* (2000), by P. Freire
- *United States Government: Democracy in Action* (2007), by R. C. Remy
- *Dictionary of Latino Civil Rights History* (2006), by F. A. Rosales
- *Declarations of Independence: Cross-Examining American Ideology* (1990), by H. Zinn

American History/Mexican American Perspectives, 1, 2—Texts and Reading Lists

- *Occupied America: A History of Chicanos* (2004), by R. Acuna
- *The Anaya Reader* (1995), by R. Anaya
- *The American Vision* (2008), by J. Appleby et al.
- *Rethinking Columbus: The Next 500 Years* (1998), by B. Bigelow and B. Peterson
- *Drink Cultura: Chicanismo* (1992), by J. A. Burciaga
- *Message to Aztlán: Selected Writings* (1997), by C. Jiménez
- *De Colores Means All of Us: Latina Views Multi-Colored Century* (1998), by E. S. Martínez
- *500 Años Del Pueblo Chicano/500 Years of Chicano History in Pictures* (1990), by E. S. Martínez
- *Codex Tamuanchan: On Becoming Human* (1998), by R. Rodriguez
- *The X in La Raza II* (1996), by R. Rodriguez
- *Dictionary of Latino Civil Rights History* (2006), by F. A. Rosales

- *A People's History of the United States: 1492 to Present* (2003), by H. Zinn

(*Source:* Curriculum Audit of the Mexicazn American Studies Department, Tucson Unified School District, May 2, 2011, pp. 116–17, http://www.tucsonweekly.com/images/blogimages/2011/06/16/1308282079-az_masd_audit_final_1_.pdf)

Books

Gutiérrez, David G. *Walls and Mirrors: Mexican Americans, Mexican Immigrants, and the Politics of Ethnicity.* Berkeley: University of California Press, 1995. Explores the ways in which immigration from Mexico has shaped politics in California and Texas.

Rosales, F. Arturo. *Chicano: The History of the Mexican American Civil Rights Movement.* Houston: Arte Público, 1996. The rise of Mexican American studies is one of the most visible outgrowths of the Mexican American Civil Rights Movement, as this book explains.

Websites

Department of Mexican American Studies, University of Arizona. Shows the curriculum and interests of a university-level Mexican American Studies program. http://mas.arizona.edu/

Mexican American Studies Department, Tucson Unified School District. The site of the program at the heart of the controversy. http://www.tusd1.org/contents/depart/mexicanam/index.asp

May 3

1916

Henry B. González is born as Enrique Barbosa González in San Antonio, Texas. Elected to the 87th Congress by special election on November 4, 1961, to fill the vacancy caused by the resignation of Paul J. Kilday, he was a Democrat who represented the San Antonio area. He gained some fame in 1986 when, at the age of 70, he punched a man in the face for calling him a "communist" at a popular

San Antonio restaurant. González served on the House committees on Missing Persons in Southeast Asia, Small Business, and Assassinations. He chaired the House committee on Banking and Currency. González served until 1998, when he was replaced by his son, Charlie. He died on November 28, 2000.

Books

Auerbach, Robert D. *Deception and Abuse at the Fed: Henry B. González Battles Alan Greenspan's Bank.* Austin: University of Texas Press, 2008. As chair of the House Banking Committee, Gonzalez was one of the most powerful figures in Washington, D.C., and one of the few who challenged Greenspan's management of the financial system.

Rodriguez, Eugene Jr. *Henry B. González: A Political Profile.* New York: Arno Press, 1976. A picture of the politician at the peak of his power.

Websites

González, Henry Barbosa. The Handbook of Texas Online provides an excellent short biography of the politician. http://www.tsha online.org/handbook/online/articles/fgo76

González, Henry Barbosa. The official congressional synopsis of González's political career. http://bioguide.congress.gov/scripts/biodis play.pl?index=g000272

May 4

1855

American filibuster William Walker, the "Grey-Eyed Man of Destiny," leaves San Francisco with a force of about 60 men to conquer Nicaragua during a civil war in the country. One faction, from the city of Léon, invited Walker to assist them since he had earlier attempted a takeover of Mexico. Walker imposed the laws of Louisiana on the part of Mexico that he controlled, thus reestablishing slavery. His actions are viewed as an effort to expand slavery. Once in Nicaragua,

Walker developed a force of 100 Americans and 200 Nicaraguans and then quickly took control of the country. The most famous filibuster of the antebellum era, Walker badly damaged diplomatic relations between the United States and its Latin American neighbors although President Franklin Pierce did recognize Walker's presidency of Nicaragua in 1856. He ruled Nicaragua, reestablishing slavery in the country until a coalition of Central American armies joined by a private army created by U.S. business leader Cornelious Vanderbilt defeated him in 1857. Walker returned to the United States but was captured by the British while attempting to return to Nicaragua. The British turned Walker over to Honduras, which executed Walker by firing squad in 1860, largely because he was seen by the entire region as a threat to peace and security.

Letter from Máximo Jerez, general of Nicaragua Forces to Commodore Paulding of the United States Naval Forces, March 29, 1858:

> Sir: I did not receive until the 27th instant your esteemed favor, dated at Havana on the 16th of January last, in which you are pleased to request of me, in writing, the message which, in the name of his excellency the President of this republic, I delivered to you when I visited you on board of the Wabash in the Bay of San Juan, in the beginning of January last.
>
> The intelligence of the capture of William Walker and the adventurers who accompanied him, effected at Punta de Castilla by the American forces under your command, was received by the government of this republic and by all the people of Nicaragua with much satisfaction, because the act was a signal rebuke of an aggression so bold and unjust on the rights and territory of Nicaragua. I had the honor of being the organ of the sentiments of the government of Nicaragua

on the occasion referred to. I knew how to appreciate at their just value the noble motives which actuated you, and in its name I gave you the thanks due to those motives.

I avail myself of this occasion, commodore, to renew to you the assurance of the distinguished respect and esteem to which you are entitled and to subscribe myself your most obedient servant.

(*Source:* Nicaragua Filibuster: William Walker [May 8, 1824–Sept. 12, 1860]. http://www.latinamericanstudies.org/filibusters/Paulding-Walker-1857.pdf)

Books

Carr, Albert Z. *The World and William Walker.* Westport, CT: Greenwood Press, 1975. Sets Walker amidst the filibustering craze of the antebellum era.

Rosengarten, Frederic Jr. *Freebooters Must Die!: The Life and Death of William Walker, the Most Notorious Filibuster of the Nineteenth Century.* Wayne, PA: Haverford House, 1976. An entertaining biography of one of the most colorful men of the 19th century.

Websites

Nicaragua Filibuster: William Walker (May 8, 1824–Sept. 12, 1860). Supplies photographs, a map of Walker's trip to Nicaragua, and a guide to further reading. http://www.latinamericanstudies.org/william-walker.htm

William Walker. The Virtual Museum of San Francisco offers a reprint of Fanny Juda's 1919 essay on the infamous Filibuster, first published in *The Grizzly Bear.* http://www.sfmuseum.org/hist1/walker.html

May 5

1862

The battle commemorated in Cinco de Mayo celebrations, the Battle of Puebla, takes place in Mexico between nationalists led by Benito Juárez and French forces. Cinco de Mayo celebrates Mexican independence from foreign occupation but it is strictly an American holiday. Mexico does not celebrate it. The commemoration of Cinco de Mayo began in California shortly after the battle; it was started by expatriate Mexicans who wanted to celebrate a victory by democratic forces while honoring their heritage.

From a speech delivered by Rafael H. González, head of the Mexican Patriots Club in Virginia City, Nevada on May 5, 1865, just after the end of the U.S. Civil War:

Liberty, whose first dawn begins to appear on the horizon of my country, after the smoke which had obscured it in Richmond has been put out, will make us free and independent. Now that holy and formidable struggle of the United States has ended; and today the complications into which the intruder Maximilian will enter, will show him, very soon, the road he ought to follow. . . . Just as there is no rose without a thorn . . . there is nothing begun for the good of humanity that has not been conquered with blood. . . . Without this war of giants that we have witnessed in the United States, the postulant wound of slavery would not have been healed.

(*Source:* Hayes-Bautista, David E. *El Cinco de Mayo: An American Tradition.* Berkeley: University of California Press, 2012, p. 174.)

Books

Hayes-Bautista, David E. *El Cinco de Mayo: An American Tradition.* Berkeley: University of California Press, 2012. This is the only scholarly history of this American holiday.

Hoyt-Goldsmith, Diana. *Cinco de Mayo: Celebrating the Traditions of Mexico.* New York: Holiday House, 2008. A children's book that covers traditional ways of celebrating Cinco de Mayo, which, contrary to the title is a Mexican American holiday and not a Mexican one.

1981

Carolina Herrera, a Venezuela-born socialite, has her first showing of evening clothes. Herrera opened her fashion house earlier this year. In the 1970s, she became known for appearances at Studio 54 and other Manhattan hotspots but by the 1980s she wanted to do something different with her life. Herrera's womenswear collection becomes enormously successful and is still in existence in the second decade of the 21st century. The label's clients include Renée Zellweger, Nicole Kidman, Caroline Kennedy Schlossberg, Ivanka Trump, and Meryl Streep.

Books

Kotur, Alexandra. *Carolina Herrera: Portrait of a Fashion Icon*. New York: Assouline, 2004. An illustrated biography of the fashion queen.

Riehecky, Janet. *Carolina Herrera: International Fashion Designer*. Chicago: Children's Press, 1991. A children's biography that emphasizes Herrera's career.

Websites

Carolina Herrera—Designer Fashion Label. Provides information about fashion shows featuring the label, clients who wear the label, and where to buy the label. http://nymag.com/fashion/fashionshows/designers/bios/carolinaherrera/

Carolina Herrera. The official website for the designer and her label. http://www.carolinaherrera.com/

1991

Riots break out in the ethnically diverse Washington, D.C., neighborhood of Mount Pleasant after a rookie African American police officer, Angela Jewel, shoots a 30-year-old Latino. Daniel Enrique Gómez, an immigrant from El Salvador, advanced on Jewel while wielding a knife, as officer Grisel del Valle later testified. Gómez admitted being drunk, which is why the officers were attempting to arrest him, but denied holding a knife. The community had heard that Gómez was shot while his hands were handcuffed behind his back. The three days of rioting were the worst episodes of violence since Martin Luther King Jr. died in 1968. By the end of it, 230 people had been arrested and 50 wounded, many of them police officers, with 81 buses and police cars vandalized as well as three dozen businesses damaged. A subsequent investigation by the U.S. Civil Rights Commission found a pattern of abuse of Latinos by the police. The ultimate effect of the riot was to give more recognition to Latinos in the District of Columbia.

From "Woes of D.C. Hispanics Exposed":

Street disturbances in Washington this week have highlighted the plight of the city's underprivileged Hispanic community. Unemployment is rampant. Housing is overcrowded. And relations with a black-dominated city police force, with whom the Latino population often cannot communicate, are strained to the breaking point. "There's an underlying cry for help here from a community of people who have been neglected," says Elaine Grant, director of the Wilson Center, a social services agency for Washington's Latin immigrants. . . . Washington's Latinos say the police harass them, are brutal during arrests, and do not respond as quickly to 911 calls as they do when whites or blacks call.

Only 140 of the 4,900 members of the Washington, D.C., police force are Hispanic, according to a department spokesman. Among the top several dozen officers, none speaks Spanish. Washington's 1990 census recorded a Hispanic population of 32,000, but

Ms. Grant of the Wilson Center and other activists in Hispanic affairs put the figure at between 80,000 and 120,000 people—documented and undocumented—or at least 10 percent of the city's population. Most are from Central America, and from El Salvador in particular. According to Grant, half are either unemployed or underemployed. Some employers treat them badly, believing that they will not risk deportation by raising a fuss.

The fact that Hispanics have now vented their rage so publicly is all the more noteworthy, given their usual desire to lay low. Such street violence is unusual for Salvadorans, according to Tony Mendez, a local Hispanic leader. But he also points out that some of those wreaking havoc in Mt. Pleasant Sunday night were setting police cars on fire in a sophisticated manner, taking flares from the cars' trunks, lighting them, and putting them in the gas tanks. Some of the rioters, he said, had served in the Salvadoran military and some had been guerrillas.

Washington's new mayor, Sharon Pratt Dixon, acknowledges that the Latinos have a point. "I think their concerns are legitimate," Mayor Dixon said. "We do need to be more responsive." Since the disturbances began Sunday night, Dixon has held meetings with leaders from the Hispanic community and promised to appoint a commission to study the community's problems.

(*Source:* Feldmann, Linda. "Woes of D.C. Hispanics Exposed." *Christian Science Monitor,* May 9, 1991, p.7.)

Books

Gilje, Paul A. *Rioting in America.* Bloomington: Indiana University Press, 1996. A history of rioting since colonial times but with no particular focus on Latinos.

Gottesman, Ronald, ed. *Violence in America: An Encyclopedia.* New York: Charles Scribner's, 1999. Covers all aspects of violence, including riots.

Websites

Mt. Pleasant 20 Years after the Riot—The Kojo Nnamdi Show. Provides photographs of the riot and links to related sites. http://thekojonnamdishow.org/shows/2011-05-05/mt-pleasant-20-years-after-riot

The 20th Anniversary of Mt. Pleasant Salvadorian Riots—YouTube. Provides television news coverage of the anniversary of the riots with clips of the rioting.

May 6

2012

American and Mexican military forces simultaneously conduct a coordinated disaster response exercise in southern Texas and in the Mexican states of Nuevo León, Tamaulipas, and San Luis Potosí. It is the first time that the two nations have cooperated in a disaster drill. A U.S. Army spokesperson explains that natural disasters do not recognize borders and therefore cooperation is necessary to minimize the suffering of people. The soldiers and sailors plan medical evacuations, establish communications, set up search-and-rescue missions, and arrange to clear routes.

Books

Auf der Heide, Erik. *Disaster Response: Principles of Preparation and Coordination.* St. Louis: Mosby, 1989. Explains the steps necessary to minimize human suffering in the event of a disaster.

Enarson, Elaine, and Betty Hearn Morrow, eds. *The Gendered Terrain of Disaster: Through Women's Eyes.* Westport, CT: Praeger, 1998. Disaster response typically assumes that all people have one gender—male.

May 7

1991

Linda Alvarado became the first Hispanic to own a major league baseball franchise when she joined a group that bought the Colorado Rockies. Alvarado, who saw Sandy Koufax pitch on her first date with her future husband, owns a construction company and fast-food restaurants. Her ownership percentage of the team is small. She was subsequently named as the recipient of the Sara Lee Corporation's Frontrunner Award (1993) and the Revlon Business Woman of the Year Award (1996). She was also named one of *Hispanic* magazine's 100 most influential Hispanics in America in 1996.

Books

Dater, Adrian. *100 Things Rockies Fans Should Know and Do Before They Die.* New York: Triumph Books, 2009. A fun guide to the history of the club.

DeMarco, Tony. *Tales from the Colorado Rockies.* N.P.: Sports Publishing, 2008. Looks at the rise of the first Major League Baseball team in the Rocky Mountain time zone with stories about its players, managers, and front-office personnel.

2011

The first Latino Comics Expo is held in San Francisco at the Cartoon Art Museum to celebrate the contributions of Latinos to this art form. Since the days of Gus Arriola in the 1960s, Latino cartoonists have developed a great range and a growing audience for their art form.

Books

Aldama, Frederick Luis. *Your Brain on Latino Comics: From Gus Arriola to Los Bros Hernández.* Austin: University of Texas Press, 2009. Includes an interview with Hernández and a separate one with his brother.

Hernández, Gilbert. *Beyond Palomar: A Love and Rockets Book.* Seattle, WA: Fantagraphics Books, 2007. A graphic novel from one of the most popular Latino cartoonists.

Websites

Artist Bio: The Hernández Brothers. The publisher of the graphic novels of the brothers supplies a biography of them along with covers for all of their work and a link to an interview. http://www.fantagraphics.com/artist-bios/artist-bio-the-hernandez-brothers.html

The Billy Ireland Cartoon Library and Museum. This is one of the few libraries devoted to cartoons and the only museum dedicated to the art form from its beginnings to the present. http://cartoons.osu.edu/

May 8

1942

Jockey Ángel Cordero Jr. is born in Santurce, Puerto Rico. Cordero, the son of a famous Puerto Rican rider, rode his first winning horse in 1960. In 1982, he became the first jockey ever to earn more than $9 million in purses in a season. By the time he retired in 1992, Cordero won 7,076 victories in 38,684 races with over $164 million in earnings. He is a three-time winner of the famed Kentucky Derby. Cordero entered the Racing Hall of Fame in 1988.

From "Angel Cordero: Jockey the Fans Love to Hate":

> Every jockey is occasionally booed and screamed at for a losing ride on a favorite, but Cordero becomes the public's focus of almost every race he rides in. It doesn't matter if his horse is 3-1 or 20-1 on the morning line, Cordero's presence is rarely irrelevant. In New York, he is one of the fundamentals of handicapping: through bettors consider speed, class, form, pace, track condition, post position, appearance,

weight—and Cordero. . . . "They call me every gutter word and say they want to kill me, but then they bet my horse even when he's not the best horse," Cordero says . . . "It's because of who I am and the way that I ride and act," he says. "I'm flamboyant so the public singles me out, like Reggie Jackson or Ali."

(*Source:* From Crist, Steven. "Ángel Cordero: Jockey the Fans Love to Hate." *New York Times,* December 12, 1982, p. S1.)

Books

Gruender, Scott A. *Jockey: The Rider's Life in American Thoroughbred Racing.* Jefferson, NC: McFarland and Company, 2006. Argues that although jockeys are often viewed as second-rate athletes, chiefly because of their small size, these self-employed, independent contractors are exceptionally tough individuals.

Haskins, Steve. *Tales from the Triple Crown.* Lexington, KY: Eclipse Press, 2008. Includes a chapter on Cordero's Kentucky Derby win aboard Spend a Buck.

Websites

Latino Sports Legends—Ángel Cordero, Jr. http://www.latinosportslegends.com/bios/Cordero_Angel-bio.htm Provides a short biography of Cordero.

National Museum of Racing and Hall of Fame—Angel Cordero, Jr. http://www.racingmuseum.org/hall-of-fame/horse-jockeys-view.asp?varID=20 Focuses on Cordero's career, including significant mounts and major races won.

2002

Chefs across the country remove Chilean sea bass, also known as toothfish, from their restaurants because the fish has become too popular, threatening future supplies. The Antarctica Project launched the "Take a Pass on Chilean Sea Bass" campaign in partnership with the Washington-based nonprofit organization, the National Environmental Trust. First commercially sold in the United States by Chileans, the fish now comes primarily from fishermen of many nationalities frequenting the waters around Antarctica.

Books

Clover, Charles. *The End of the Line: How Overfishing Is Changing the World and What We Eat.* New York: New Press, 2006. Discusses the consequences of consuming fish without any thought for the future.

Knecht, G. Bruce. *Hooked: Pirates, Poaching and the Perfect Fish.* Emmaus, PA: Rodale, 2006. A history of the poaching of the Patagonia toothfish, otherwise known as the Chilean sea bass, which includes documentation on how the fish became popular throughout the world.

May 9

1871

In only the fifth major league game ever played, Fordham University graduate Esteban Bellán, a native of Cuba, is the Troy (New York) Haymakers' third baseman in their National Association debut. Bellán, who came to New York City in 1865 to study at Fordham, remains with the club for another year before joining the New York Mutuals for a handful of games in 1873. He is representative of a number of Cubans who learned to play baseball in the United States. Spain, concerned with baseball's association with subversives, banned baseball-playing in Cuba in 1869, briefly rescinded the ban, then banned it again in 1873. The Spanish thought that the game was more than a North American import and that it possibly served as paramilitary exercise preparing Cubans for battle against the Spanish. Bellán returned to Cuba to play baseball and to become one of the founders of the famed Almendares baseball club.

Books

Antón, Alex, and Roger E. Hernández. *Cubans in America: A Vibrant History of a People in Exile.* New York: Kensington, 2003. Includes coverage of Cubans playing baseball in the United States.

Echevarría, González. *Pride of Havana: The History of Cuban Baseball.* New York: Oxford University Press, 1999. The only history of Cuban baseball that includes its early years.

Website

Cuban Baseball: Esteban Bellán. Fordham University offers this biography of one of its most famous baseball-playing alumni. http://www.library.fordham.edu/cubanbaseball/e_bellan.html

1928

Tennis player Richard "Pancho" Gonzáles is born. He grew up in Los Angeles. Ranked as the best player in the world for eight years beginning in 1954, Gonzáles possessed an especially feared serve. In 1968, he was inducted into the International Tennis Hall of Fame.

Books

Gonzáles, Pancho, and Cy Rice. *Man with a Racket: The Autobiography of Pancho Gonzáles.* New York: Barnes, 1959. The autobiography of the tennis star.

Heldman, Gladys, ed. *Tennis by Pancho Gonzáles and Dick Hawk.* New York: Cornerstone, 1967. Gonzáles offers tips on how to play the game that he dominated.

Websites

Ricardo "Pancho" Gonzáles. Latin Sports Legends provides this biography of the tennis player. http://www.latinosportslegends.com/pancho_gonzales_bio.htm

Richard Pancho Gonzáles. Journalist Bud Collins provides this superb short biography of Gonzáles for the ATP World Tour. http://www.atpworldtour.com/Tennis/Players/Go/R/Richard-Pancho-A-Gonzales.aspx

1933

Diego Rivera is fired for painting a controversial portrait of Russian communist leader Vladimir Lenin in one panel of his mural for the RCA Building in Rockefeller Center. The Rockefellers, including family patriarch John D., may have been the wealthiest people in the United States at this time, with their money derived from the oil industry. In short, they greatly appreciated capitalism. Rivera, perhaps the greatest Mexican painter of the 20th century, was a lifelong Marxist who enjoyed painting murals because they were more accessible to ordinary people than elite galleries and art museums. Rivera later created a nearly identical mural in the Palace of Fine Arts in Mexico City.

From a *New York Times,* May 10, 1933, report on the incident:

> Halted as he was at work last night on his scaffold in the Great Hall of the seventy-story RCA Building in Rockefeller Center, Diego Rivera, the celebrated mural painter whose communistic leanings have frequently enveloped him in controversy, was informed that the fresco on which he was engaged, and which he had regarded as his masterpiece, was no longer acceptable to the Rockefeller family.
>
> Turning sadly with a few of his assistants and devoted friends to his "shack" on the mezzanine of the building, Señor Rivera found that his telephone had been cut off. He also found awaiting him a letter from Todd, Robertson & Todd, enclosing a check for $14,000, completing payment in full of the $21,000 he had been promised for three murals.
>
> The letter expressed regret that Señor Rivera had been unable to come to some compromise on the paintings and said that the check was to be regarded as terminating his employment,

although none of the three panels for which he had been contracted had been finished.

A crowd of about 100 art students and other admirers of the painting previously had been ushered from the hall by representatives of Todd, Robertson & Todd, the managing agents on behalf of John D. Rockefeller, Jr., and mounted and foot police were on duty outside the building to prevent any demonstration when Señor Rivera was called away from his work.

No demonstration materialized immediately, but about 10 o'clock, two hours later, between 75 and 100 men and women sympathizers of the artist paraded in front of the building, shouting "Save Rivera's art," and "We want Rivera." They carried banners on which similar sentiments were emblazoned.

With an air of resignation rather than bitterness, Señor Rivera described in his broken English his design for the mural which, covering a space sixty-three feet long and seventeen feet high, was to have depicted "human intelligence in control of the forces of nature." A sketch of it had been shown to the Rockefeller family and approved by them, Señor Rivera said.

The entire scheme for the mural decoration of the Great Hall was worked out by Señor Rivera, with the approval of the RCA art commission. His panel, the only one in color, was to have occupied the central position, and was to have been flanked by Brangwyn's chiaroscuro on the left, and Sert's on the right. Señor Rivera intended to portray the emancipation of mankind through technology.

But when the actual painting began, objection was raised, he said, to a figure of Lenin joining the hands of a soldier, a worker, and a Negro,

which was to have topped the painting. In the background were crowds of unemployed.

Señor Rivera said that he had been told that Mr. Rockefeller and his advisors did not find the mural as "highly imaginative" as they had expected it to be, and that its effect was unpleasant. They also objected to the brilliant colors in the background, he said.

(*Source:* Frank, Patrick, ed. *Readings in Latin American Modern Art*. New Haven: Yale University Press, 2004, pp. 36–37.)

Books

De Larrea, Irene Herner. *Diego Rivera: Paradise Lost at Rockefeller Center*. Mexico: Edicupes, 1987. Focuses on the 1933 controversy.

Rivera, Diego, and Gladys March. *My Art, My Life: An Autobiography*. New York: Dover, 1991. The artist's thoughts on his career.

Websites

Diego Rivera: About the Artist. PBS provides a biography of the artist, the subject of one of its *American Masters* television shows. http://www.pbs.org/wnet/americanmasters/episodes/diego-rivera/about-the-artist/64/

Diego Rivera: Paintings, Biography, and Quotes. Probably the best site on the artist as it contains a long biography and many, many images of his works. http://www.diego-rivera.com/

1979

Actress and political activist Rosario Dawson is born in New York City to parents of Afro-Cuban and Puerto Rican heritage. Dawson has appeared in *Kids* (1995), *Men in Black II* (2002), and *Sin City* (2005) as well as portraying Dolores Huerta in *Chavez* (2012). In 2004, she joined with Maria Teresa Kumar to found Voto Latino. The New York City–based organization aims to increase voter registration among Latinos. Dawson has been recognized by both *Newsweek* and the

Hispanic Heritage Foundation for her efforts to galvanize Latino voters.

Websites

Rosario Dawson. The Internet Movie Database provides Dawson's acting credits. http://www.imdb.com/name/nm0206257/

Voto Latino. Supplies election information including information about registering to vote. http://www.votolatino.org/

May 10

1948

Sandra María Esteves, one of the first women to stand out among New York Puerto Rican poets writing in English, is born in the Bronx, New York. Very aware of the invisibility of English-writing Latinas in the 1970s, she read her poems wherever she could. Esteves won a New York State Creative Artists Public Service Fellowship for Poetry in 1980.

Books

Dick, Bruce Allen. *A Poet's Truth: Conversations with Latino/Latina Poets.* Tucson: University of Arizona Press, 2003. Includes an interview with Esteves.

Esteves, Sandra Maria. *Bluestown Mockingbird Mambo.* Houston: Arte Público, 1990. A collection of the poet's works.

May 11

1846

President James K. Polk tells Congress that Mexican troops have crossed the boundary with the United States and shed American blood upon American soil. Two days later, Congress declares war on Mexico. Historians view the United States as the aggressor as did many Americans in the 1840s.

From the memoirs of Ulysses S. Grant:

Generally the officers of the army were indifferent whether the annexation [of Texas] was consummated or not; but not so all of them. For myself, I was bitterly opposed to the measure, and to this day regard the war [with Mexico] which resulted as one of the most unjust ever waged by a stronger against a weaker nation. It was an instance of a republic following the bad example of European monarchies, in not considering justice in their desire to acquire additional territory.

Texas was originally a state belonging to the republic of Mexico. It extended from the Sabine River on the east to the Rio Grande on the west, and from the Gulf of Mexico on the south and east to the territory of the United States and New Mexico—another Mexican state at that time—on the north and west. An empire in territory, it had but a very sparse population, until settled by Americans who had received authority from Mexico to colonize. These colonists paid very little attention to the supreme government, and introduced slavery into the state almost from the start, though the constitution of Mexico did not, nor does it now, sanction that institution. . . . The occupation, separation and annexation were, from the inception of the movement to its final consummation, a conspiracy to acquire territory out of which slave states might be formed for the American Union.

Even if the annexation itself could be justified, the manner in which the subsequent war was forced upon Mexico cannot. The fact is, annexationists wanted more territory than they could possibly lay any claim to, as part of the new acquisition. Texas, as an independent State, never exercised jurisdiction over the territory between the Nueces River and the Rio Grande. Mexico never recognized the independence of Texas, and maintained that, even if independent, the State had no claim south of the Nueces. I am aware that a treaty, made by the Texans with Santa Anna while he was under duress, ceded all the territory between the Nueces and the Rio Grande; but he was a prisoner of war when the treaty was made, and his life was in jeopardy. He knew, too, that he deserved execution at the hands of the Texans, if they should ever capture him. The Texans, if they had taken his life, would have only followed the example set by Santa Anna himself a few years before, when he executed the entire garrison of the Alamo and the villagers of Goliad.

(*Source:* U.S. Grant, "Causes of the Mexican War," http://www.sewanee.edu/faculty/willis/Civil_War/documents/Grant.html)

Books

Francaviglia, Richard V., and Douglas W. Richmond, eds. *Dueling Eagles: Reinterpreting the U.S.-Mexican War, 1846–1848*. Fort Worth: Texas Christian University Press, 2000. Offers essays that challenge the Anglo-centric view of this war.

Reilly, Tom. *War with Mexico!: America's Reporters Cover the Battlefront*. Lawrence: University Press of Kansas, 2010. Examines the information given to Americans about the war.

Websites

The Mexican-American War. Northern Illinois University Libraries offers a history of the war along with primary documents. http://dig.lib.niu.edu/mexicanwar/about.html

The U.S.-Mexican War. PBS provides a graphic-heavy history of the war with a timeline, biographies of key figures, and a link to additional resources. http://www.pbs.org/kera/usmexicanwar/

May 12

1924

Poet Claribel Alegría is born in Estelí, Nicaragua. Though primarily known as a poet, the prolific Alegría has published in a range of genres, sometimes in collaboration with her husband and principal translator, Darwin J. Flakoll. Alegría published her first poems in 1941. After moving to New Orleans to attend high school, Alegría graduated from George Washington University with a bachelor's degree in philosophy and letters in 1948. Later that same year, she published her first book of poetry, *Anillo de silencio,* in Mexico. Alegría has often spoken in interviews of the writer's role as the voice of the voiceless, of poetry as a weapon against repression, oppression, exploitation, and injustice. Alegría's novel of the 1932 massacre known as the Matanza, *Ashes of Izalco,* was a finalist in 1964 in the Biblioteca Breve contest, sponsored by the Spanish publishing house Seix Barral. In 1978 she won Cuba's prestigious Casa de las Américas Prize for her volume of poetry, *Sobrevivo*. In 2006, Alegría capped her career with the Neustadt International Prize for Literature. Perhaps most important, Alegría brought Central American literature, especially women's writing, to the attention of the American reader, and with it she brought a concern for the political situation in El Salvador and Nicaragua in particular. Her works have been translated into more than 10 languages.

From "This is a Night of Shadows":

This is a night of shadows
of sword-memories
solitude overwhelms me
No one awaits my arrival
with a kiss
and a rum
and a thousand questions.

(*Source:* Alegría, Claribel. *Sorrow: A Bilingual Poetry Edition*. Trans. Carolyn Forché.

Willimantic, CT: Curbstone Press, 1999, p. 5.)

Books

Beverly, John, and Marc Zimmerman. *Literature and Politics in the Central American Revolutions*. Austin: University of Texas Press, 1990. Traces the development of popular revolutionary poetry and testimonial narrative as reactions to historical events in Nicaragua and El Salvador, and the importance of women poets such as Alegría.

Boschetto-Sandoval, Sandra M., and Marcia Phillips McGowan. *Claribel Alegría and Central American Literature: Critical Essays*. Athens: Ohio University Center for European Studies, 1994. An excellent collection of essays on Alegría's major works and themes that includes an interview with the poet and a chronology of her life and works as well as a bibliography of her publications and publications about her work.

Websites

Claribel Alegría. A superb biography of the poet with links to her poems from the Academy of American Poets. http://www.poets.org/poet.php/prmPID/275

Claribel Alegría: Voices from the Gaps. Excellent biography and critical analysis of Alegría with a listing of her works and writings about her. http://voices.cla.umn.edu/artistpages/alegria Claribel.php

1931

Mathematician Manuel Berriozál is born to a German mother and Mexican father in San Antonio, Texas. In 1979, he helped create the San Antonio Pre-freshman Engineering Program (PREP) for middle school and high school students despite a comment from a member of the Texas Education Coordinating Board that the funds would be wasted since "the Mexican American community is not where engineers come from." PREP has since been duplicated in 30 other Texas communities and 8 other states.

Book

Macdonald, Victoria-Maria. *Latino Education in the United States: A Narrated History from 1513–2000*. This study, a mix of narrative and primary documents, is the only history of Latino education to cover such a broad span of time.

1968

Thousands of people join the Poor People's March in Washington, D.C., to call for better treatment of the poor. Martin Luther King Jr. planned the march and organizers decided to proceed with the event after his death as a tribute to him. Many Latinos from around the country participated in the campaign, including César Chávez and Dolores Huerta.

Books

Fager, Charles. *Uncertain Resurrection: The Poor People's Washington Campaign*. Grand Rapids, Eerdmans, 1969. Fager published this book a year after the march, which gives it the flavor of the era but also prevents it from being objectively historical.

McKnight, Gerald D. *The Last Crusade: Martin Luther King, Jr., the FBI, and the Poor People's Campaign*. Boulder, CO: Westview Press, 1998. The only recent history of this particular event in the story of the 1960s civil rights movement.

May 13

1947

Operation Bootstrap begins as a way to shift the Puerto Rican economy from dependence on low-paying agricultural jobs to dependence on high-paying industrial jobs. On this date, the Puerto Rican legislature approved Act No. 184 granting tax exemption on income, property, excise, and municipal taxes to new industries for a period of 10 years with an additional 3 years of partial exemption. Puerto Rico became the only part of the United States where industry could operate with a 100 percent tax exemption. Operation Bootstrap ended in 1996 when Congress terminated the tax exemption. By that time the program had wildly succeeded, and yet it did not live up to expectations in terms of solving all of Puerto Rico's employment issues. Operation Bootstrap transformed Puerto Rico from an agrarian economy to an urban, industrial economy with a 10-fold increase in per capita Gross National Product between 1950 and 1980. Population growth, however, exceeded job growth.

From "Self-Help for Puerto Ricans":

> In carrying out her famous "Operation Bootstrap" Puerto Rico has been a pioneer in a number of ways. The Operation's social and economic programs have not only been sensationally successful but they provided examples that underdeveloped nations and colonies through the world are now studying. One of the unique features of the work being done . . . is the Migration Division of the Puerto Rican Department of Labor. Puerto Ricans believe that this is the first time in history that the government of an area from which people are migrating has come to the aid both of the migrants and the communities to which they are going.

(*Source:* From n.a., "Self-Help for Puerto Ricans." *The New York Times,* September 9, 1958, p. 34.)

Books

Maldonado, A. W. *Teodoro Moscoso and Puerto Rico's Operation Bootstrap.* Gainesville: University Press of Florida, 1997. The best study of the program and its leader.

Pérez, Gina M. *The Near Northwest Side Story: Migration, Displacement, and Puerto Rican Families.* Berkeley: University of California Press, 2004. Looks at the failures of Operation Bootstrap and the role of the government in migration.

Websites

Operation Bootstrap. Detailed history of the program from Lehman College in New York City. http://lcw.lehman.edu/lehman/depts/latinampuertorican/latinoweb/PuertoRico/Bootstrap.htm

Operation Bootstrap, Puerto Rico Encyclopedia. Good history of the program. http://www.enciclopediapr.org/ing/article.cfm?ref=06102003

May 14

1719

Jean-Baptiste Le Moyne de Bienville, the governor of French Louisiana, captures Pensacola from the Spanish during the War of the Quadruple Alliance. The Presidio Santa María de Galve, founded in 1698, had guarded the town. The presidio consisted of a wooden fort, named San Carlos de Austria, as well as a church and village outside the fort. Expensive to maintain, the presidio helped Spain hold Florida. However, Spanish royal officials were either unable or unwilling to correct the acute manpower and supply shortages that led to the presidio's demise.

The Viceroy of New Spain, Fernando de Alencastre Noroña y Silva, the Duque de Linares, 1714:

> In order to maintain the presidio de Santa María de Galve in the situation that it is now found in, more than one hundred thousand pesos are necessary each year . . . This expense is supported only by the Royal Estate since there are no other revenues which pertain to it and can be applied for these purposes. The requests of the Governor of that Plaza are so continuous because of

its isolation by land from places from which it could be aided, [and because] the uselessness and infertility of its terrain and the inclemency of its weather with its great variation are such that those who live there are continually suffering serious illnesses.

(*Source:* Bense, Judith A. *Presidio Santa María de Galve: A Struggle for Survival in Colonial Spanish Pensacola.* Gainesville: University Press of Florida, 2003, pp. 51–52.)

Books

Bense, Judith A. *Presidio Santa María de Galve: A Struggle for Survival in Colonial Spanish Pensacola.* Gainesville: University Press of Florida, 2003. Examines the impact of the war on Spanish control of Florida.

Marley, David F. *Wars of the Americas: A Chronology of Armed Conflict in the New World, 1492 to the Present.* Santa Barbara, CA: ABC-CLIO, 1998. Contains an essay on the War of the Quadruple Alliance that sets it in historical context.

Website

Presidio de Santa María de Galve. The Department of Anthropology and Archaeology at the University of West Florida provides a short history and a map of the old military installation. http://uwf.edu/anthropology/research/colonial/santamaria/

1876

Puerto Rican writer and political activist Luis Lloréns Torres is born in Juana Díaz. He studied in Barcelona and Granada before returning to Puerto Rico to start a career as a lawyer. He also wrote poems. Among the first modernist writers, Lloréns Torres cofounded the *Revista de las Antillas* in 1913.

Books

Caraballo-Abréu, Daisy. *La Prosa de Luis Lloréns Torres.* Río Piedras, PR: Editorial de la Universidad de Puerto Rico, 1986. Reprints many of the essays written by the activist.

Ortíz García, Nilda S. *Vida y Obra de Luis Lloréns Torres.* San Juan de Puerto Rico: Instituto de Cultura Puertorriqueña, 1977. A biography of the activist; he does not have an English-language biography.

Website

Luis Lloréns Torres. A short biography with photographs. http://www.elboricua.com/LuisLlorensTorres.html

1930

Miguel A. Ondetti is born in Buenos Aires, Argentina. As a senior research chemist for the Squibb Corporation in New Jersey, Ondetti discovers a class of drugs known as ACE (angiotensin-converting enzymes) that are effective in the treatment of high blood pressure. Ondetti received the Perkin Medal, the highest award given for innovation in the chemical industry in the United States. He died in 2004.

Website

Miguel A. Ondetti. The Chemical Heritage Foundation supplies a biography and resume of the chemist along with his oral history. http://www.chemheritage.org/discover/collections/oral-histories/details/ondetti-miguel-a.aspx

1936

Carlos García, a mechanical engineer who helped test spacecraft materials for the National Aeronautics and Space Administration (NASA), is born to parents of Mexican ancestry in Las Vegas, New Mexico. García also worked as a program analyst in the development of the Space Nuclear Auxiliary Power program, a system for using nuclear power as a source of energy in satellites and space probes.

Book

Bizony, Piers. *The Space Shuttle: Celebrating Thirty Years of NASA's First Space Plane.* Minneapolis: Zenith Press, 2011. Provides a history of the major space exploration effort of the last decades of the 20th century and the first decade of the 21st century.

2004

Héctor Barreto, founder and past president of the United States Hispanic Chamber of Commerce (USHCC), dies. Born in Mexico City, Barreto moved to Missouri in 1958. After working a series of jobs, he opened a series of businesses, including a restaurant and a construction firm. In the 1970s, he began to work to increase opportunities for Hispanic entrepreneurs and cofounded USHCC in 1979. He advised both the Reagan and George H. W. Bush administrations on economic policy, advocating closer ties with Mexico.

Website

United States Hispanic Chamber of Commerce. The organization aims to promote Hispanic businesses and foster sustainable prosperity. https://www.ushcc.com/index.cfm?

May 15

1911

Virologist Jordi Casals-Ariet is born in Girona, Spain. He came to the United States in 1936 as a medical researcher. Casals-Ariet developed a system for classifying viruses that has become the basis of essentially all modern viral taxonomy. He also identified the Lassa virus in 1969, after this new and deadly disease appeared in Nigeria. He was almost killed by the Lassa virus which he contracted in his lab at Yale University, but was saved after doctors transfused him with blood from a nurse who had survived the disease.

Book

Oldstone, Michael B. A. *Viruses, Plagues, and History: Past, Present, and Future.* New York: Oxford University Press, 2010. Covers the Lassa virus.

Website

Jordi Casals-Ariet. The U.S. National Library of Medicine provides this biography of the famed virologist. http://www.ncbi.nlm.nih.gov/pmc/articles/PMC390228/

1991

Brothers to the Rescue, a Miami-based group of Cuban American pilots led by José Basulto, begins to search for raft people in the Florida Straits who are fleeing Cuba. The pilots, strongly opposed to the regime of Fidel Castro, eventually venture close to Cuban air space in 1996, and four of them are killed in February when Cuban forces shoot down their planes.

From a speech by Brothers to the Rescue leader José Basulto on March 2, 1996:

> Before we set out today, let us remember our four fallen brothers who gave their lives for freedom, justice and Cuba this last Saturday, February 24, 1996. Mario de la Peña, Carlos Costa, Armando Alejandre and Pablo Morales will live in our hearts and minds. We ask Our Lady of Charity, patron mother of Cuba, to have mercy on us, who will have to learn to live without them. May She instill in us the gentleness and sense of justice of Mario, the dedication and humility of Pablo, the courage of Armando and the strength of character and discipline of Carlos, and the love of all four for Cuba. We ask this in the name of our Lord Jesus Christ.
>
> Having said this, I would like to thank you all for being here today. I would specially like to thank the families of the four fallen young men for their courage, faith and love. I also wish to thank my wife, children and grandchildren for the love and support they have provided in this most difficult moment. To the people of the United States and the international community

we extend our gratitude for your solidarity. We also thank the press for their objective coverage of this tragedy.

We wish to clearly state before we set out for this flight to honor the memory of Pablo, Armando, Mario and Carlos, we wish to clearly state to our people inside and outside the island that THIS IS OUR STRUGGLE. The struggle of all Cubans for a free and democratic homeland. This is OUR STRUGGLE, and all Cubans are responsible for this.

We reaffirm an essential concept: The destiny of Cuba is the responsibility of all Cubans, no matter where he or she may be. We must stand together as a single people and a single nation.

And it is because of this, because we bear a sacred responsibility for Cuba's fate, that today we state these basic tenets which we as free Cubans have decided to pursue:

1. The brutal killing of our four young brothers over international waters was a direct result of the growing resistance to the Castro regime within Cuba and this regime's increasing inability to deal with it. The dictatorship sought to punish Brothers to the Rescue for its continued support for the Cuban resistance and specifically for the Cuban Council inside Cuba. The February 24 killings marked the culmination of a wave of repression by the dictatorship directed against the internal opposition that resulted in hundreds of arrests throughout Cuba. The martyrdom of these young men marks the beginning of a new alliance of all Cubans inside and outside the island in pursuit of freedom for our country.

(*Source:* The Brothers to the Rescue Archives, Florida International University, http://www2.fiu.edu/~fcf/struggle.html)

Books

Prellezo, Lily, and José Basulto. *Seagull One: The Amazing True Story of Brothers to the Rescue.* Gainesville: University Press of Florida, 2010.

Soderlund, Walter C. *Mass Media and Foreign Policy: Post–Cold War Crises in the Caribbean.* Westport, CT: Praeger, 2003. Includes an essay on the "shoot-down" of Brothers to the Rescue planes by Cuban forces in 1996.

2006

President George W. Bush sends about 5,000 National Guard members to support the Border Patrol along a 2,000 mile stretch of the U.S.-Mexico border. The plan is opposed by Vicente Fox, the president of Mexico, on the grounds that a more comprehensive solution to illegal immigration is needed.

Books

Hernández, Kelly Lytle. *Migra!: A History of the U.S. Border Patrol.* Berkeley: University of California Press, 2010. Covers the conflict between Mexico and the United States over border control in the only substantive book devoted to the Border Patrol.

Maril, Robert Lee. *Patrolling Chaos: The U.S. Border Patrol in Deep South Texas.* Lubbock: Texas Tech University Press, 2006. Addresses one of the busiest borders of the United States and one with a considerable history of violence.

2006

María Elena Durazo becomes head of the Los Angeles County Federation of Labor, AFL-CIO. The position makes her one of the most powerful labor leaders in the country. Durazo became the first woman to head a major union in Los Angeles in 1989 when she took over the hotel workers union, UNITE-HERE Local 11, a union with 70 percent Latino membership.

Books

Dubofsky, Melvyn, and Foster Rhea Dulles. *Labor in America: A History.* Wheeling, IL: Harlan Davidson, 2010. A survey of labor history by two of the best known scholars in the field.

Josephson, Matthew. *Union House, Union Bar: The History of the Hotel and Restaurant Employees and Bartenders International Union, AFL-CIO.* New York: Random House, 1956. A substantial history of the group that Durazo would later lead, though the age of the book weakens its value.

May 16

1824

Mexican folk hero Juan Nepomuceno Cortina is born into a wealthy family in Tamaulipas, México. Cortina grew up on land around Brownsville, Texas, that was part of a large land grant held by his mother. During the Mexican-American War, he fought on the Mexican side. After the war he was accused of cattle rustling, but his political connections among the Mexican population prevented the cases from proceeding beyond a grand jury indictment. Cortina objected to the Texans who were using the legal system to abusively acquire land from Mexican Americans. He shot several white officials in Brownsville and became an idol to poor Mexicans. He started the Cortina Wars and then served on the Union side during the Civil War. Cortina died in 1894.

Books

Baum, Bruce, and Duchess Harris, eds. *Racially Writing the Republic: Racists, Race Rebels, and Transformations of American Identity.* Durham: Duke University Press, 2009. Includes a chapter on Cortina.

Goldfinch, Charles W., and José T. Canales. *Juan N. Cortina: Two Interpretations.* New York: Arno Press, 1974. The Anglo-Americans saw Cortina as a bandit while the Mexican Americans saw him as an avenger.

Thompson, Jerry. *Cortina: Defending the Mexican Name in Texas.* College Station: Texas A&M University Press, 2007. A scholarly biography of an entertaining figure from Texas's past.

Website

Juan Nepomuceno Cortina. The Handbook of Texas Online provides a biography of Cortina and a guide to further reading. http://www.tshaonline.org/handbook/online/articles/fco73

1894

Home economist and cookbook author Fabiola Cabeza de Vaca Gilbert is born in La Liendra, New Mexico, to a family of considerable wealth. She attended New Mexico Normal University (now New Mexico Highlands University) where she earned a teaching degree in 1921. Eight years later, she completed a bachelor's degree from New Mexico State University and took a job with the New Mexico State Extension Service. Gilbert observed the cooking and household practices of people in northern New Mexico and then blended the best practices with the newest research on nutrition. In 1939, Gilbert published *Hispanic Cookery,* which eventually sold more than 100,000 copies. Ten years later, Gilbert published *The Good Life: New Mexico Traditions and Food,* which remained in print into the 21st century. Her 1953 book, *We Fed Them Cactus,* is a historical account of the settlement of the Southwest. Gilbert retired in 1959 and died on October 14, 1991, in Albuquerque.

From *The Good Life: New Mexico Traditions and Food:*

The snow had been falling all morning but it had not kept Doña Paula from cleaning out her adobe oven. Back and forth she went from her kitchen to the patio, wearing a heavy wool dress to keep out the cold. The blue handkerchief tied around her head was bright and gay in the snowy air. From the back porch she picked up an armful of dry wood. In less than fifteen minutes she had a fire burning in the outdoor oven. When the fire crackled and popped and flames leaped to the top of the oven, she went into the house to make the loaves of bread that would go in as soon as the oven was hot enough. . .

While the *bizcochitos* (anise-flavored sugar cookies) baked, Doña Paula prepared the filling for the *empanaditas* (fried turnovers). A bowl full of meat, cooked dried apples, a large pinch of salt, cinnamon, clove, ground coriander seed, a touch of ginger, two cups of thick molasses and two handfuls of raisins made the filling. This would cook while she made the dough. . . . As soon as darkness settled in the village, the children with snap sacks started after *aguinaldos,* Christmas gifts. At each door they stopped and sang, "Let us pray, Let us pray/ Angels from heaven are we/Asking for gifts in His name/Please do not turn us away." After the hymn was sung, the door opened and the children received gifts of food. How proud Doña Paula was of her gifts of *molletes* [sweet rolls], *bizcochitos,* and *empanaditas* for the children. She made enough for them and for the Christmas eve repast.

There was so much to be done before Midnight Mass. The lime hominy had been cooking all day and it was all ready but for the seasoning. Doña Paula who was a proud cook had to have everything well seasoned. From a string of chile in her store room she took three pods; she removed the stems and seeds and washed the pods. She took the lid off the kettle, added the chile, oregano, salt, garlic, and onion. Now she could get ready for Mass. The *tamales* which she had made the day before were frozen on the back porch and they could cook while they were at church.

She looked out of her bedroom window. The *hogueras* [bonfires] were already lighted outside the church so she must hurry or she would miss being with her friends by the bonfires. After the mass, everyone went to the manger to kiss the Infant Jesus' feet. Each one brought a gift for Him—a penny, a nickel, or a dime. Outside the church everyone was merry, wishing his friends happiness. The one making the wish first, earned a gift from the one to whom it was made. Then they went home to a hot morning breakfast of *pozole, tamales, empanaditas,* and *carne con chile.*

(*Source:* Gilbert, Fabiola Cabeza de Vaca. *The Good Life: New Mexico Traditions and Food.* Santa Fe, New Mexico: The Museum of New Mexico Press, 1982, pp. 28–29.)

Books

Gilbert, Fabiola Cabeza de Vaca. *The Good Life: New Mexico Traditions and Food.* Santa Fe, New Mexico: The Museum of New Mexico Press, 1982. Reports on the food traditions that the author grew up with and experienced in northern New Mexico and provides 80 recipes for New Mexican dishes.

Gilbert, Fabiola Cabeza de Vaca. *We Fed Them Cactus.* Albuquerque: University of New Mexico Press, 1994. A memoir of growing up as part of an old Latino ranching family in the years prior to New Mexico's statehood.

Websites

New Mexico Genealogical Society. Rich site that provides information on the history of New Mexico as well as help researching family trees. www.nmgs.org

New Mexico Office of the State Historian. Superb site that divides the state's history into story, place, people, and time apart from providing links to research centers. http://www.newmexicohistory.org/home_html.php

May 17

1954

The U.S. Supreme Court rules in *Brown v. Board of Education* that public schools cannot discriminate along racial lines. While the decision addressed the complaints of the black plaintiffs, it also applied to people of Hispanic descent. Latino children had suffered for years from unequal treatment in schools. In particular, discrimination in Texas stemmed from historic conflict between Anglo-American settlers and Mexican landowners in the early 1800s. While the Mexican-American War resolved landownership disputes, tensions remained well into the 20th century. Chief Justice Earl Warren had won a 9–0 decision from his fellow justices but at the cost of not establishing a timetable for integration. As a result, segregation and its related issues persisted into the 1970s. Discrimination in the rural areas, in particular, lasted far longer than in the metropolitan areas with segregation in farm districts lasting into the 1970s.

Gregoria Ortega, a Victoryknoll nun who taught among Chicanos in Abilene, Texas, in the 1970s recalled:

> [The Anglo-Americans of Abilene] had a real hatred for Mexicans and Catholics. Mexicans had been lynched there. . . . [Chicano students] had many complaints. . . . Being hit just for being Mexican; teachers leaving the room with gavachos [slang for an Anglo-American] in charge and never choosing a Mexican student; being the only ones suspended for fights that Anglos were also involved in; having only one Chicano teacher in the whole school.

(*Source:* Medina, Lara. *Las Hermanas: Chicana/Latina Religious-Political Activism in the U.S. Catholic Church.* Philadelphia: Temple University Press, 2004, pp. 48–49.)

Books

Patterson, James T. *Brown v. Board of Education: A Civil Rights Milestone and Its Troubled Legacy.* New York: Oxford University Press, 2004. The decision was supposed to improve the quality of education afforded to minority students but it has had mixed results.

Whitman, Mark. *Brown v. Board of Education: A Documentary History.* Princeton: Markus Wiener Publishers, 2004. Provides a wealth of documents relating to the landmark decision but not much analysis.

Websites

Brown v. Board of Education. The National Center for Public Policy Research's Constitution and the Courts Archives has made the full Supreme Court decision available. http://www.nationalcenter.org/brown.html

Brown v. Board of Education National Historic Site. The school at the center of the Supreme Court decision is now a National Park Service site. http://www.nps.gov/brvb/index.htm

1939

Antonio Paoli, one of opera's greatest tenors and a native of Puerto Rico, is awarded a pension by the Puerto Rico legislature as his health is in decline. By this time, Paoli had not performed in 20 years but from the 1880s to the start of World War I, he was the most renowned tenor in the world. He became the first Puerto Rican to make a sound recording in 1907 and the first person in the world to record an entire opera when he performed Leoncavallo's *I Pagliacci.* Paoli succumbed to cancer on August 24, 1946, at the age of 75.

Websites

Antonio Paoli. The History of the Tenor website offers a painting and a biography of the "king of tenors." http://historyofthetenor.com/page.php?28

Antonio Paoli. In this audio clip from a 78 rpm record, Paoli sings "Esultate," followed by "Ora e per sempre addio" from Giuseppe

Verdi's opera, *Otello*. http://www.youtube.com/watch?v=61KJant-bi0

1945

Ann Aurelia López, the first Latina to earn a doctorate in environmental science, is born in San Bernadino, California. Her father is a Mexican American. López earns a PhD in 2002 at the University of California at Santa Cruz. Her research focuses on the working conditions of migrant farmworkers.

Book

López, Ann Aurelia. *The Farmworkers' Journey.* Berkeley: University of California Press, 2007. Looks at historical farming practices in Mexico and agribusiness in California, two systems that involve migrant farmworkers.

May 18

1846

U.S. troops occupy Matamoros during the Mexican-American War. Mexican troops under Gen. Mariano Arista crossed the Rio Grande in late April and engaged with Americans under the overall command of Gen. Zachary Taylor. On May 7, Americans and Mexicans engaged in an artillery duel, the first major battle of the war, near Palo Alto. Following their victories at Palo Alto and Resaca de la Palma, American forces marched into Matamoros and began a bloodless occupation. Mexican forces had withdrawn to the relative safety of Monterey, about a 100 miles to the south.

Books

Francaviglia, Richard V., and Douglas W. Richmond, eds. *Dueling Eagles: Reinterpreting the U.S.-Mexican War, 1846–1848.* Fort Worth: Texas Christian University Press, 2000. Offers essays that challenge the Anglo-centric view of this war.

Reilly, Tom. *War with Mexico!: America's Reporters Cover the Battlefront.* Lawrence: University Press of Kansas, 2010. Examines the information given to Americans about the war.

Websites

The Mexican-American War. Northern Illinois University Libraries offers a history of the war along with primary documents. http://dig.lib.niu.edu/mexicanwar/about.html

The U.S.-Mexican War. PBS provides a graphic-heavy history of the war with a timeline, biographies of key figures, and a link to additional resources. http://www.pbs.org/kera/usmexicanwar/

May 19

2006

A "March on Washington" is held to protest the treatment of illegal immigrants. In the past three months, hundreds of thousands of illegal aliens and their supporters have held protests in 39 states and organized boycotts of work, school, and businesses in hopes of pressuring Congress into crafting legislation that would create a path to citizenship. The protests have attracted hundreds of thousands of marchers. There are an estimated 11–12 million undocumented immigrants.

From "Legal Immigrants Fear Backlash from Another March":

> Carlos Castro of Woodbridge, Va., said he does not support the planned May 19 "March on Washington" because, he says, such protests are not helping the immigrant community. "It's putting undue pressure on our legislators and I think it's going to work the opposite way," said Mr. Castro, 51, a prominent business owner who came to the United States in 1980 from El Salvador. "Instead of sympathy and help, we're going to start creating some

antagonism and friction that is unnecessary at this time."

Mr. Castro and other legal immigrants, as well as U.S.-born Hispanics, said the rallies are brewing a negative image that creates a backlash against foreign-born or ethnic-looking persons. Others said illegal aliens are mocking the laws they broke when they entered the United States and are flaunting the defiance in the faces of Americans and those who had to endure the long legal process to enter the country and pursue citizenship.

Al Rodriguez, a man of Mexican descent who was born in Arizona, called the rallies "a slap in the face." "[The boycott] was very positive for us who are against illegal aliens and very negative for those who are for amnesty," the retired Army colonel said. "They come here and work illegally and then they turn around and bite the hand that's giving them a job and paying them by boycotting. . . . Pro-illegal groups are trying to say just because we're American Hispanics, we're with them. They're idiots if they think that." His son Daniel, a retired Army civilian employee, said he sees the illegal alien protesters as "blackmailers." "They don't have rights," said Daniel Rodriguez, 56, of Fairfax. "I think the simple solution is if they want to be here, they should apply for visas and come here legally. . . ."

Daniel Cortez, an activist whose uncle started a radio station that later became Univision, said he will attend the rally to promote assimilation and downplay the "reconquista" attitudes of some younger illegal aliens, who seek to take back the land and desecrate the American flag. "We have to recognize that America has abused our immigrants [and] I want these legislators to atone for their violations of the past," said Mr. Cortez, 54. "But at the same time I'm going to tell my own people that you've got to learn English . . . and promote assimilation, the American flag and wanting to become American citizens."

(*Source:* Summers, Keyonna. "Legal Immigrants Fear Backlash from Another March." *The Washington Times,* May 9, 2006, p. B01.)

Books

Euchner, Charles. *Nobody Turn Me Around: A People's History of the 1963 March on Washington.* Boston: Beacon Press, 2011. While Martin Luther King Jr. did not lead the first March on Washington, his 1963 event is arguably the most famous and the reason why subsequent groups have headed to the National Mall.

Haugen, David M. *Illegal Immigration: Opposing Viewpoints.* Farmington Hills, MI: Greenhaven, 2011. Part of the popular Opposing Viewpoints series, this book provides articles, speeches, and other materials that illustrate the immigration debate.

Websites

"Illegal Immigrants Rally in Chicago." This article, written by conservative pundit Michelle Malkin and placed on her website, includes quotes from bloggers and marchers. http://michellemalkin.com/2006/03/10/illegal-aliens-protest-in-chicago/

"Rallies across U.S. Call for Illegal Immigrant Rights." This CNN Politics site offers an article on the 2006 marches in support of better treatment of illegal immigrants. http://articles.cnn.com/2006-04-10/politics/immigration_1_jaime-contreras-national-capital-immigration-coalition-illegal-immigrant-rights?_s=PM:POLITICS

1895

Cuban independence leader José Martí is killed in battle in Cuba at Dos Ríos. He went into exile briefly in the United States while organizing the resistance against Spain.

A Cuban national hero, Martí was a prolific writer who also gave many speeches in opposition to Spanish rule in Cuba. Nicknamed the "Apostle of Cuban Independence," his death mobilized Cubans to pick up arms against the Spanish in a revolt that would eventually lead to American involvement in Cuba.

Books

Montero, Oscar. *José Martí: An Introduction.* New York: Palgrave Macmillan, 2004. One of the few scholarly studies of Martí available in English.

Pérez, Louis A. Jr. *José Martí in the United States: The Florida Experience.* Tempe, AZ: ASU Center for Latin American Studies, Arizona State University, 1995. A biography of the Cuban leader by the dean of Cuban history.

May 20

1915

Teatro Carmen opens in Tucson, Arizona, with a performance of *Cerebro y Corazón* by the Mexican playwright Teresa Farias de Isassi. It is one of the first theaters dedicated to performing plays entirely in Spanish. It is named for its founder, Carmen Soto Vásquez. The adobe theater, still standing, became an Elks Lodge in 1937 before reverting to a theater later in the century. The site is now a historic landmark.

Website

Borderlands Theater. This theater troupe used Teatro Carmen in the 1990s for its performances, an experience related in an account on this site. http://www.borderlandstheater. org/about/borderlands-history/

1985

Radio Martí, an anti-Castro station named after Cuban patriot, José Martí, begins broadcasting to Cuba. The Cuban government immediately jams the signal. It also suspends an immigration agreement that provided for the return to Cuba of nearly 3,000 Cubans with histories of crime or mental illness in exchange for the United States accepting up to 20,000 Cuban immigrants annually. The United States had also agreed to accept about 3,000 Cuban political prisoners. Radio Martí broadcasts news, entertainment, and sports for about 14-1/2 hours each day from studios in Washington, D.C., and a 50,000-watt transmitter in the Florida Keys. It is a branch of the Voice of America and received approval from Congress in 1983. Ronald Reagan pushed for Radio Martí at the instigation of Jorge Mas Canosa, a Cuban American political leader strongly opposed to Fidel Castro.

From "Cubans Tuning out Radio Martí's 1950s Sound":

Few Cubans want to admit they listen to Radio Martí, the new broadcasting service to Cuba. Fewer still want to discuss it. But those Cubans who will talk about the broadcast—besides Government officials who have strongly criticized it—are not giving it rave reviews. The response is the same from many foreign diplomats and other non-Cubans here who have been studying the broadcasts. Some listeners call it Radio Reagan or the Deceiver. They say it is old-fashioned and out-of-step with modern Cuban society. Many also call it disappointingly dull, but less stridently propagandistic than they had expected. "But it's like something out of the 1950s: the music, the programs," said a woman in her late 30s who manages an office and who said she was not a particularly strong supporter of the Cuban Government. . . . "It's so funny listening to their soap operas after living in revolutionary Cuba for the last 26 years," she said. "They sound so silly." Richard H. Araujo, the acting program director of Radio Martí, said in a telephone interview from Washington that he suspected the criticism was "Cuban Government propaganda to try to discredit" the station.

(*Source:* Treaster, Joseph B. "Cubans Tuning out Radio Martí's 1950s Sound." *New York Times,* June 4, 1985, p. A2.)

Books

Skoug, Kenneth N. Jr. *The United States and Cuba under Reagan and Shultz: A Foreign Service Officer Reports.* Westport, CT: Praeger, 1996. Includes a chapter on Radio Martí.

Walsh, Daniel C. *An Air War with Cuba: The United States Radio Campaign against Castro.* Jefferson, NC: McFarland, 2011. Provides a history of American propaganda broadcasting in Cuba.

Websites

Broadcasting Board of Governors—Radio and TV Martí. Official website for the stations. http://www.bbg.gov/broadcasters/ocb/

The Jorge Mas Canosa Freedom Fund. Provides Mas Canosa's biography. http://www.jorgemascanosa.org/pages/Biography.htm

May 21

1542

Spanish conquistador Hernando de Soto dies near the convergence of the Arkansas and Mississippi rivers. Made governor of Cuba and *adelantado* of Florida by the king of Spain, De Soto set off to search for gold with 700 men. The group landed at Tampa Bay, proceeded into present-day South Carolina, crossed the Appalachian Mountains, and moved into Mississippi before finally reaching the Pánuco, Mexico. It is one of the most extraordinary marches in history. The battles along the way weakened Native American tribes, who were also exposed to European diseases.

Books

Clayton, Lawrence A., Vernon James Knight Jr., and Edward C. Moore, eds. *The De Soto Chronicles: The Expedition of Hernando de Soto to North America in 1539–1543.* Tuscaloosa: University of Alabama Press, 1993.

Duncan, David Ewing. *Hernando de Soto: A Savage Quest in the Americas.* New York: Crown Publishers, 1995. A more balanced account of Soto, this book takes into account his brutal treatment of Native Americans, which was often dismissed in the past.

Website

Hernando de Soto. Enchanted Learning has designed this site for K-12 users with a short biography of de Soto and a map of his explorations. http://www.enchantedlearning.com/explorers/page/d/desoto.shtml

1916

Lydia Mendoza, "*La Alondra de la Frontera* (The Lark of the Border)," is born in San Antonio, Texas. Also dubbed the "First Lady of Tejano Music," Mendoza began playing the mandolin with her mother and father in the city in the late 1920s as part of the family group, Cuarteto Carta Blanca. In the early 1930s, she caught the attention of a promoter and began to appear on radio. Mendoza recorded on the Blue Bird label starting in 1934, accompanying herself on the 12-string bajo sexton. Her most popular song, "Mal Hombre," became a nationwide hit. Mendoza subsequently recorded for all of the major Mexican American record labels. In 1999, she received the National Medal of Arts for her contributions to music. Mendoza, slowed by a stroke, died in 2007.

Book

Strachwitz, Chris, and James Nicolopulos, comp. *Lydia Mendoza: A Family Autobiography.* Houston: Arte Público, 1993. A good biography but not an objective one.

May 22

1903

Cubans reluctantly approve the Platt Amendment to their new Constitution. An instrument of American imperialism, it sharply restricted the independence of the new government. It mandated that Cuba could not form a treaty with a third party, that it had to balance its budget, and that it acknowledged the right of the United States to intervene in Cuba for the preservation of Cuban independence and the maintenance of a government that could protect life, property, and individual liberty. Lastly, the amendment gave the United States a lease for a naval station at Guantanamo Bay, a base that remains in operation.

Books

Pérez, Louis A. *Cuba under the Platt Amendment, 1902–1934*. Pittsburgh: University of Pittsburgh Press, 1991. A superb study by one of the most respected historians of the Cuban past.

Williams, Mark Eric. *Understanding U.S.–Latin American Relations: Theory and History*. New York: Routledge, 2012. Discusses the impact of the Platt Amendment.

1930

Artist Marisol Escobar, known professionally as Marisol, is born in Paris into a wealthy Venezuelan family. Marisol settled in Los Angeles with her father, after the early death of her mother, during World War II. A protégé of Willem de Kooning, she began to exhibit at galleries in the late 1950s with sculptures that were described as a mix of pop art, dada, and folk art. She often used found objects and her works were known for a mysterious, macabre quality. Most of Marisol's exhibitions were held in the 1960s and 1970s when she was known as a rival of Andy Warhol.

Books

Congdon, Kristin G., and Kara Kelley Hallmark. *Artists from Latin American Cultures: A Biographical Dictionary*. Westport, CT: Greenwood Press, 2002. Includes an essay on Marisol.

Whiting, Cécile. *A Taste for Pop: Pop Art, Gender, and Consumer Culture*. New York: Cambridge University Press, 1997. Includes several essays on Marisol's performance of gender in her art.

2010

Dominican American novelist Junot Díaz is named as the first Latino to sit on the 20-member Pulitzer Prize board of jurors. Díaz won a Pulitzer in 2008 for *The Brief Wondrous Life of Oscar Wao*.

Books

Díaz, Junot. *The Brief Wondrous Life of Oscar Wao*. New York: Riverhead Books, 2008. The acclaimed novel by the Dominican American author.

Díaz, Junot. *This Is How You Lose Her*. New York: Riverhead Books, 2012. Follows the life of a Dominican American man and his relationships with women.

May 23

1954

Jaime Fernández-Baca, a nuclear physicist, is born in Lima, Peru. A resident of the United States since the late 1970s, he heads the U.S.-Japan Neutron Scattering Program and is a senior researcher at the Oak Ridge National Laboratory in Oak Ridge, Tennessee.

Books

Johnson, Leland. *Oak Ridge National Laboratory: The First Fifty Years*. Knoxville: University of Tennessee Press, 1994. Recounts the history of a place that has played a major role in developing nuclear technologies.

Mahaffey, James A. *Atomic Awakening: A New Look at the History and Future of Nuclear Power.* New York: Pegasus Books, 2009. A solid history of a form of power that is both promising and terrifying.

May 24

1870

Naturalist Ynés Mexía is born in Washington, D.C., to a Mexican diplomatic family. She collected more than 150,000 samples of plant material, including 500 that were previously unknown. Mexía's collection is scattered around the world, including the Field Museum of Natural History in Chicago, Gray Herbarium of Harvard University, and various European botanical gardens.

Books

McLoone, Margo. *Women Explorers in North and South America: Nellie Cashman, Violet Cressy-Marcks, Ynes Mexia, Mary Blair Niles, and Annie Peck.* Mankato, MN: Capstone Press, 1997. A short biographical essay in a book that is more of a long pamphlet.

Tinling, Marion. *Women into the Unknown: A Sourcebook on Women Explorers and Travelers.* New York: Greenwood Press, 1989. Includes an essay on Mexia's collecting in South America.

1997

Astronaut Carlos Noriega returns safely after logging a total of 221 hours and 20 minutes in space, traveling 3.6 million miles in 144 orbits of the Earth on the space shuttle *Atlantis.* Born in Peru, Noriega served in the U.S. Marine Corps before joining NASA in 1994. He returned to space in 2000 on the *Endeavor* before retiring in 2005.

Book

Bizony, Piers. *The Space Shuttle: Celebrating Thirty Years of NASA's First Space Plane.* New York: Zenith, 2011. Includes coverage of the flights made by Noriega.

Website

Carlos I. Noriega, NASA Astronaut. The official NASA biography of the former astronaut. http://www.jsc.nasa.gov/Bios/htmlbios/noriega.html

May 25

1944

Artist Humberto Calzada is born in Havana. He has lived in the United States since 1960 and is best known for his paintings of the architecture of Cuba. His work is notable for a dreamlike realism and the use of universal symbols.

Books

Bosch, Lynette M. F. *Cuban-American Art in Miami: Exile, Identity, and the Neo-Baroque.* Burlington, VT: Lund Humphries, 2004. Sets Calzada's art in the context of the exile experience.

Fuentes, Ileana, et al. *Humberto Calzada.* Coral Gables, FL: Lowe Art Museum, University of Miami, 2006. An exhibition catalog that includes essays by art historians about the artist's work.

Website

Humberto Calzada. A short profile with photographs of the artist. http://www.insulaverde.com/English—AboutArtist/aboutmain.html

May 26

1924

The Immigration Act of 1924, also known as the Johnson-Reed Act, is enacted. Created to preserve the predominantly Northern European racial mix of the United States, the legislation was expressly anti-immigrant. The law limited the number of immigrants to 165,000 annually. It discriminated against immigrants from southern and eastern Europe and barred Asians completely. However, it did not limit Mexicans or other Latino immigrants. Farmers needed Mexican labor to pick crops and many U.S. businesses wanted the financial benefits from Pan-American trade.

From remarks in opposition to the Immigration Act of 1924:

U.S. Representative Martin Mdden (R-Illinois), chair of the House Appropriations Committee [and an immigrant from England]:	The bill opens the doors for perhaps the worst element that comes into the United States—the Mexican *peon*. . . . [It] opens the door wide and unrestricted to the most undesirable people who come under the flag.
Senator Matthew M. Neeley (D-West Virginia):	On the basis of merit, Mexico is the last country we should grant a special favor or extend a peculiar privilege. . . . The immigrants from many of the countries of Europe have more in common with us than the Mexicanos have.

(*Source:* Acuña, Rodolfo F. *U.S. Latino Issues.* Westport, CT: Greenwood Press, 2003, p. 74.)

Books

Acuña, Rodolfo F. *U.S. Latino Issues.* Westport, CT: Greenwood Press, 2003. Sets the dispute over the Immigration Act in the context of other controversies in Latino history.

Spickard, Paul. *Almost All Aliens: Immigration, Race, and Colonialism in American History and Identity.* New York: Routledge, 2007. A narrative of American history that focuses on the challenges posed by race and ethnicity.

Websites

Immigration Act of 1924—History of Foreign Relations. This U.S. Department of State, Office of the Historian site provides a brief history of the legislation. http://history.state.gov/milestones/1921–1936/ImmigrationAct

Comprehensive Immigration Law (1924). Provides the text of the law with the country-by-country quotas. http://www.civics-online.org/library/formatted/texts/immigration1924.htm

May 27

2011

To recognize the many contributions that Cuban immigrants brought to Key West, parade-goers dress in Cuban attire and conga from the shores of the Atlantic Ocean to the Gulf of Mexico. Key West is only 90 miles from Cuba and has long had close ties with the island.

Books

McIver, Stuart B. *Hemingway's Key West.* Sarasota, FL: Pineapple Press, 2002. Ernest Hemingway, the novelist, spent much of his life shuttling between Key West and Cuba.

Ronning, C. Neale. *José Martí and the Émigré Colony in Key West: Leadership and State Formation.* New York: Praeger, 1990. Martí, the great Cuban patriot, spent several years in exile while amassing support for a revolt against Spanish rule in Cuba.

May 28

2000

Juan Pablo Montoya becomes the first Colombian to win the Indianapolis 500. A race car champion in Colombia, Montoya won the CART (Championship Auto Racing Teams) Rookie of the Year in 1999. He began racing on the Formula One circuit in 2001.

Website

Juan Pablo Montoya. The official website of the driver includes the results of his races. http://www.jpmontoya.com/2012/

May 29

1968

Members of the Crusade for Justice, a Chicano group, stage a protest against the government's lack of adequate poverty programs for Mexican Americans by taking over the basement of the Hawthorne School in Washington, D.C.

Books

Acuña, Rodolfo. *Occupied America: A History of Chicanos.* New York: Harper Collins, 1988. The standard history of the Chicano movement.

Vigil, Ernesto B. *The Crusade for Justice: Chicano Militancy and the Government's War on Dissent.* Madison: University of Wisconsin Press, 1999. Vigil was a member of Crusade for Justice.

2012

Dolores Huerta receives the Medal of Freedom from President Barack Obama at a ceremony in the White House. A cofounder of the United Farm Workers, Huerta is also credited with influencing Obama's work as a community organizer. The medal is awarded to individuals who make a meritorious contribution to the national interests of the United States, to world peace, or to other significant endeavors.

From an interview with Dolores Huerta by *Teaching to Change LA,* 2003:

TCLA: What role do you play in the community?

DH: My role in the community is to get involved with issues, especially issues that pertain to immigrants, women, labor, and the environment.

TCLA: Where did you attend high school and what were the conditions like?

DH: I went to Stockton High School in Stockton, California and that school was pretty racist, as some high schools still are today. We had a big division between a lot of the rich kids from the north side and the poor kids from the south side and east side. There was a lot of discrimination: most of the Latino kids that I graduated grammar school with dropped out of high school. So, it was a struggle to get through high school because of the racism in the school. But I did graduate because it would've never occurred to me to even think about dropping out. My parents both had a high school education.

TCLA: Did your elementary school value students whose families spoke languages other than English?

DH: In grammar school, all of us came from different backgrounds—Mexican, Japanese, Filipino, Italian, Greek. The teachers were very hard on students. We had four hours of English everyday—penmanship, writing, grammar, reading—and a couple of hours of math everyday. . . .

TCLA: What should be done to achieve equality in our current school system?

DH: To achieve equality in our schools, I think teachers need to be given the resources that they need in order to be able to teach. My daughter is a teacher and she doesn't have what she needs. The kids are struggling right now in the sense that they are not *ta*ught in a language that they could learn. While they might learn English, they're losing out on everything else.

TCLA: What would you recommend to students and parents who want to make changes in their schools?

DH: Number one, we have to start with the money. A lot of these school boards get money and it never comes down to students. And we need to support the whole "education not incarceration" movement, so that the money goes to schools, not jails. Students must get involved, send letters to the legislature and the governor. And parents need to get involved and see what's happening in their children's schools. They need to support them and make them understand. Like I used to tell my kids when they went to racist schools, "You don't have to live with these teachers forever. You're just there for a little while. Learn what they have to teach you and realize that something is wrong with them, not you." The main thing is to hang in there, you know. I mean a big part of winning is staying in there and not giving up.

(*Source:* García, Mario T. *A Dolores Huerta Reader*. Albuquerque: University of New Mexico Press, 2008, pp. 291–93.)

Books

Brevard, Lisa. *Womansaints: The Saintly Portrayal of Select African-American and Latina Cultural Heroines*. New Orleans: University Press of the South, 2002. Includes a discussion of Huerta, who is often described in media accounts as "saintly."

García, Mario T. *A Dolores Huerta Reader*. Albuquerque: University of New Mexico Press, 2008. Contains a number of essays about Huerta's work with farmworkers and several interviews with the longtime activist.

Website

Dolores Huerta: Biography. Provides photos and a detailed biography of Huerta, including the honors that she has received and the boards that she serves on. http://www.lasculturas.com/aa/bio/bioDoloresHuerta.htm

May 30

1932

Composer and accordion player Pauline Oliveros is born in Houston, Texas. When Oliveros began composing in the 1950s, few women composers existed. Sex-based discrimination bedeviled her career and prompted Oliveros to design compositions that acted as feminist statements about artistic freedom and self-expression. Her *To Valerie Solanas and Marilyn Monroe in Recognition of Their Despair* (1970) is one of the earliest attempts to relate music to feminism. Her mother, Edith Oliveros Gutiérrez, also gained fame as a composer.

Books

Mockus, Martha. *Sounding Out: Pauline Oliveros and Lesbian Musicality*. New York: Routledge, 2008. Examines how Oliveros's sexual orientation has shaped her work.

Von Gunden, Heidi. *The Music of Pauline Oliveros*. Metuchen, NJ: Scarecrow Press, 1983. The only full biography of Oliveros.

2009

Nine-year-old Brisenia Flores and her father, Raul, are shot and killed in their home in Arivaca, Arizona. Flores's mother is wounded. Shawna Forde, the leader of the home invasion robbery, is sentenced to death in 2011. Forde, an opponent of illegal immigration with a history of run-ins with the police, led the vigilante group, Minutemen American Defense. The Flores case attracted the attention of a number of Latino groups partly because it raised fears of violence by rogue militias.

Book

Marrero, Pilar. *Killing the American Dream: How Anti-Immigration Extremists are Destroying the Nation.* New York: Palgrave Macmillan, 2012. Includes a discussion of the Flores murders.

May 31

1943

The Zoot Suit Riots begin when a fight breaks out between white U.S. Navy sailors on leave and Latino youths in Los Angeles. One sailor is badly hurt. The next night, 200 Navy sailors cruise Los Angeles by taxi looking for Latino teenagers and young men. They beat up many Mexicans, mostly those wearing zoot suits. (A zoot suit contains extra fabric and is typically worn with double-soled shoes, making it provocative when people are conserving materials in support of the war effort.) Over the next two nights, sailors are joined by marines and other servicemen in the continuing riot. A group of musicians leaving a recording studio are attacked as are black motorists and street workers. A black defense worker has his eyes gouged out with a knife. The rioters stop short of entering Los Angeles's African American district because a violent defense has been organized. They return to Mexican neighborhoods. No police or military authorities intervene. The worst violence occurs on June 7 when soldiers, sailors, and marines from as far away as San Diego travel to Los Angeles to seek out Mexican youths. They are joined by civilians. Approximately 5,000 whites gather in downtown LA. They

stop streetcars to look for zoot-suiters and search bars, stores, and movie theaters. The police stand by and watch groups of sailors beat Mexican Americans. They do arrest zoot-suiters though, including some found lying on the pavement with injuries. Only nine servicemen are arrested versus hundreds of Mexican Americans. By June 9, however, the violence had mostly ceased. The federal government had pushed military officials to declare Los Angeles off-limits to all military personnel while the Los Angeles City Council passed a resolution banning the wearing of zoot suits in public.

From "Zoot Suits Become Issue on Coast":

The zoot suit with the reet pleat, the drape shape, and the stuff cuff has been the object of much amusement and considerable derision from Harlem to the Pacific during the last two or three years. Psychiatrists may have their own ideas about it, but, according to the reasoning of many newcomers to the armed services, especially hundreds of young sailors in [Los Angeles], the zoot suit has become the symbol these last ten days of a fester on the body politic which should be removed by Navy vigilantes, if police will not or cannot do the job. Adventures of the Navy boys in trying to accomplish their purpose have been watched with such interest in all quarters—bringing cheers from some and causing concern to others—that newspapers were snatched up eagerly on downtown street corners. . . . The "zooters," investigators report, are products of slum districts, are boys of 16 to 20 years who are not intellectually inclined as a rule, who enjoy notoriety and who are not amenable to parental discipline. There is insistence on every side that the problem presented by their scraps with the Navy is not intrinsically one of race; that it is merely unfortunate, that the wearers of the zoot suits are chiefly Americans of Mexican descent, along with some Negroes.

(*Source:* Davies, Lawrence E. "Zoot Suits Become Issue on Coast." *New York Times,* June 13, 1943, p. E10.)

Books

Alvarez, Luis. *The Power of the Zoot: Youth Culture and Resistance during World War II.* Berkeley: University of California, 2009.

Peiss, Kathy. *Zoot Suit: The Enigmatic Career of an Extreme Style.* Philadelphia: University of Pennsylvania Press, 2011. A cultural history of "the drape."

Websites

American Experience: *Zoot Suit Riots.* The website for the PBS documentary of the same name. http://www.pbs.org/wgbh/am ex/zoot/

The Zoot Suit and Style Warfare by Stuart Cosgrove. Reprints a *History Workshop Journal* article from 1984 on the riots.

June

June 1

1903

One of the earliest and most important strikes by copper miners begins when workers, mostly Mexican and Mexican American, walk out of the Clifton, Morenci, and Metcalf mines in Arizona. Although the territorial legislature had reduced the work day from 10 to 8 hours and prohibited mines from cutting wages, mining officials reduced wages. Several thousand miners walked off the job in protest. The strike failed because many Anglo workers refused to join Mexican laborers in striking and because a major flood struck Clifton on June 9 creating chaos.

Books

Dubofsky, Melvyn, and Foster Rhea Dulles. *Labor in America: A History.* Wheeling, IL: Harlan Davidson, 2010. A survey of labor history by two of the best known scholars in the field.

Young, Otis E., Jr. *Western Mining: An Informal Account of Precious-Metals Prospecting, Placering, Lode Mining, and Milling on the American Frontier from Spanish Times to 1893.* Norman: University of Oklahoma Press, 1970. Mining did not change much in Arizona between 1893 and 1903, the time of strike.

June 2

1998

Californians approved a mandate for English-only instruction in the public schools by a margin of 61 to 39 percent. Proposition 227 came in response to fears that national unity would be damaged by encouraging the use of Spanish. The movement against bilingual education has a long history. In the United States, bilingual education was not uncommon in the 18th and 19th centuries. Linguistic diversity was acknowledged and tolerated, if not always encouraged. In California, both English and Spanish schools existed. In the late 19th century, the movement for the Common School, or public school, and compulsory education gained momentum as large numbers of poorly-educated immigrants arrived on American shores. The influx of these immigrants, who were predominantly Catholics from southern and eastern Europe, created a strong xenophobic reaction among the native-born, who were chiefly Protestants of northern and western European stock. City and town leaders became increasingly worried about changes in their communities resulting from a swelling among the ranks of the children of the foreign-born. Mandatory education served as a means to ensure that the children of immigrants were assimilated. State legislatures began to pass laws regulating the language of public school instruction. California, among others, passed an English-only instruction law. In 1923, in *Meyer v. Nebraska,* the Supreme Court stopped the English-only trend by ruling that a Nebraska state law prohibiting the teaching of a foreign language to elementary students was unconstitutional. Following this decision, the strict English-only instruction laws were generally either repealed or ignored. However, the Court had also declared in *Meyer v. Nebraska* that the United States is an English-speaking country and schools could require the use of English. At the millennium, English-only legislation made a comeback.

From "Proposition 227," Articles 1 and 2:

Proposed Law

SECTION 1. Chapter 3 (commencing with Section 300) is added to Part 1 of the Education Code, to read:

Chapter 3. English Language Education for Immigrant Children

Article 1. Findings and Declarations

300. The People of California find and declare as follows:

(a) Whereas, The English language is the national public language of the United States of America and of the State of California, is spoken by the vast majority of California residents, and is also the leading world language for science, technology, and international business, thereby being the language of economic opportunity; and

(b) Whereas, Immigrant parents are eager to have their children acquire a good knowledge of English, thereby allowing them to fully participate in the American Dream of economic and social advancement; and

(c) Whereas, The government and the public schools of California have a moral obligation and a constitutional duty to provide all of California's children, regardless of their ethnicity or national origins, with the skills necessary to become productive members of our society, and of these skills, literacy in the English language is among the most important; and

(d) Whereas, The public schools of California currently do a poor job of educating immigrant children, wasting financial resources on costly experimental language programs whose failure over the past two decades is demonstrated by the current high drop-out rates and low English literacy levels of many immigrant children; and

(e) Whereas, Young immigrant children can easily acquire full fluency in a new language, such as English, if they are heavily exposed to that language in the classroom at an early age.

(f) Therefore, It is resolved that: all children in California public schools shall be taught English as rapidly and effectively as possible.

Article 2. English Language Education

305. Subject to the exceptions provided in Article 3 (commencing with Section 310), all children in California public schools shall be taught English by being taught in English. In particular, this shall require that all children be placed in English language classrooms. Children who are English learners shall be educated through sheltered English immersion during a temporary transition period not normally intended to exceed one year. Local schools shall be permitted to place in the same classroom English learners of different ages but whose degree of English proficiency is similar. Local schools shall be encouraged to mix together in the same classroom English learners from different native-language groups but with the same degree of English fluency. Once English learners have acquired a good working knowledge of English, they shall be transferred to English language mainstream classrooms. As much as possible, current supplemental funding for English learners shall be maintained, subject to possible modification under Article 8 (commencing with Section 335) below.

306. The definitions of the terms used in this article and in Article 3 (commencing with Section 310) are as follows:

(a) "English learner" means a child who does not speak English or whose native language is not English and who is not currently able to perform ordinary classroom work in English, also known as a Limited English Proficiency or LEP child.

(b) "English language classroom" means a classroom in which the language of instruction used by the teaching personnel is overwhelmingly the English language, and in which such teaching personnel possess a good knowledge of the English language.

(c) "English language mainstream classroom" means a classroom in which the pupils either are native English language speakers or already have acquired reasonable fluency in English.

(d) "Sheltered English immersion" or "structured English immersion" means an English language acquisition process for young children in which nearly all classroom instruction is in English but with the curriculum and presentation designed for children who are learning the language.

(e) "Bilingual education/native language instruction" means a language acquisition process for pupils in which much or all instruction, textbooks, and teaching materials are in the child's native language.

(*Source:* California Secretary of State, Primary 98—Proposition 227 English Language in the Public Schools Initiative Statute, 1998, http://primary98.sos.ca.gov/VoterGuide/Propositions/227text.htm)

Books

Gonzalez, Roseann Duenas, and Ildiko Melis, eds. *Language Ideologies: Critical Perspectives on the Official English Movement*. New York: Routledge, 2000. Focuses on the impact of the English Only movement on education.

Tse, Lucy. *Why Don't They Learn English: Separating Fact from Fallacy in the U.S. Language Debate*. New York: Teachers College Press, 2001. Shows how incorrect assumptions about language influence policy debate in the United States.

Websites

English Only. This PBS site explores the history of English-only initiatives, tracing the debate back to anti-German language efforts in the late 18th century. http://www.pbs.org/speak/seatosea/officialamerican/englishonly/

U.S. English. The official site of the U.S. English Foundation, which is dedicated to promoting English as a common language. The foundation promotes legislation making English the only language of the United States. http://www.us-english.org/

2003

Narciso Rodríguez, the son of Cuban immigrants, wins the Womenswear Designer of the Year award from the Council of Fashion Designers of America. Rodríguez launched his own label in 1997 after working on womenswear for Donna Karan and Calvin Klein. He first drew considerable public attention when he designed the wedding dress for Carolyn Bessette when she married John F. Kennedy Jr. His clients include a number of well-known women, such as actresses Sarah Jessica Parker, Claire Danes, and Salma Hayek. Rodríguez became the first American to win the Womenswear Designer of the Year award twice after winning initially in 2002.

From "A Phoenix Rises to Take His Influence Global":

"What I'm trying to capture with the look is something more sensual, more feminine," Mr. Rodriguez said. "For me, designing is such a personal thing. It's really emotional—that's part of my Latin upbringing." His first signature collection . . . plays with sparkling knee-length bias sheaths in gossamer layers of chiffon. These are clothes that models like Naomi Campbell or Kate Moss might wear. What inspired Mr. Rodriguez's move from the sharp corners of minimalism toward the soft swishes of romanticism was, he said, fashion's growing tendency to forget the intended subject of design. "Clothes seemed to be about ego, not about women being beautiful," he said. His concepts begin with men's wear fabrics, which are then dressed in traditional women's guises with bias cutting, pleating, and drapes.

(*Source:* White, Constance C.R. "A Phoenix Rises to Take His Influence Global." *New York Times,* December 30, 1997, p. B7.)

Books

Mendes, Valerie, and Amy de la Haye. *Fashion since 1900.* London: Thames and Hudson, 2010. Provides a history of the fashion industry with a focus on fashion in its socioeconomic, political, and cultural context.

Rodriguez, Narciso, and Betsy Berne. *Narciso Rodriguez.* New York: Rizzoli, 2008. Contains sketches and photographs of Rodríguez's work as well as notes about his designing process.

Websites

Council of Fashion Designers of America. This is the website for the trade group that has twice honored Rodríguez. http://www.cfda.com/category/about/

Narciso Rodríguez. The designer's website emphasizes a gallery. http://www.narcisorodriguez.com/

June 3

2001

Actor Anthony Quinn dies. A man who started his career playing a variety of ethnic villains, Quinn came from Mexican ancestry. In 1952, he won a Best Actor Oscar for *Viva Zapata!*. He was probably best known for playing the lead, on film and on Broadway, in *Zorba the Greek*.

Books

Marill, Alvin H. *The Films of Anthony Quinn.* Secaucus, NJ: Citadel Press, 1975. Analyzes much of Quinn's work in his heyday.

Quinn, Anthony, with Daniel Paisner. *One Man Tango.* New York: HarperCollins, 1995. Quinn's autobiography.

Website

Anthony Quinn. The Internet Movie Database offers photographs of the actor along with a short biography and his acting credits. http://www.imdb.com/name/nm0000063/

2003

The European Space Agency (ESA) launches its Mars Express mission with help from Adriana C. Ocampo. Born in Barranquilla, Colombia, Ocampo settled in Pasadena, California, as a child in 1970. She joined NASA as a planetary geologist in 1983 and worked on projects for the *Mars Observer*. She left NASA to join the ESA in 2002. In 1992, she won the Woman of the Year in Science award from the Comisión Femenil, a Los Angeles-based organization that promotes the advancement of Latinas.

Books

Duxbury, Thomas C., John D. Callahan, and Adriana C. Ocampo. *Phobos: Close Encounter Imaging from the Viking Orbiters.* Washington, D.C.: National Aeronautics and Space Administration, Scientific and Technical Information Branch, 1984. Illustrates Ocampo's work.

Guidici, Cynthia. *Adriana Ocampo.* Chicago, IL: Raintree, 2006. A children's biography of the scientist.

Hopping, Lorraine Jean. *Space Rocks: The Story of Planetary Geologist Adriana Ocampo.* New York: Franklin Watts, 2005. An adult biography, albeit a short one, of Ocampo.

June 4

1944

Artist César A. Martínez is born in Laredo, Texas. Through prints, drawings, and paintings, Martínez interprets motifs well known to Chicano artists, such as pre-

Columbian stamp designs and the Our Lady of Guadalupe. He is particularly known for original visual answers to questions of identity and the nature of Chicano art, history, and culture. His work is also characterized by symmetrically balanced compositions. Critics have noted this style represents a willingness to use the most direct visual route to his audience rather than elaborate formulations. Martínez's most famous pieces are from his *Bato Series*. He resides in San Antonio.

From "An Interview with César A. Martínez":

I think that the [art] is, of course, very Chicano—consciously. This is about culture and identifiable images. But I think that our own people tend to look at work like this as a cultural artifact, as opposed to art. They couldn't care less about the background. They go for the character. You might think that painting a figure is difficult. Well it is, but the background is a thing in itself, and it has to work. . . .

[There] has been a progression from when I first started producing work as a professional in the early 1970s to the present. I have continually added themes—general themes, ideas, series of work which have names . . . the very first pieces that I ever exhibited in major exhibitions were those early woodcuts.

They were very individual ideas that I went through great pains to express effectively. Later, my ideas began to come together and I started thinking in terms of series of works. Just about everything has always been there in my mind gestating.

Sometimes it takes years for an idea to become cohesive enough, and for me to find a format on it. I think the South Texas [Series] took probably over ten years to actually get going. . . . The themes suggest themselves. If I feel there's a visual possibility in a theme, then I start thinking about it—it's always in my mind. . . .

Art history is very important to me and I have a very good working knowledge of art history as it pertains to me. Sometimes I have an idea and then at some point I'll be going through some of my art books. I'll see some work of art by some other artist and that might trigger an idea of how to approach a subject. Art history for me is like a Sears and Roebuck catalogue. Sometimes the very subject suggests a way.

Some things are best expressed through drawing. In other series, painting becomes more important. In other series, mixed media. . . .

I have never been a good sketcher or organized sketcher. Probably the best ideas originate as doodles. Then the sketches become more formal, and I start narrowing in, but sometimes I'll just be doodling.

Even though I have never claimed to be a political artist, to me culture has always been an underpinning and the thing that unites us, regardless of different political ideologies. Since I have been a professional artist, cultural references have been an interesting tool to use and have had to do with those things that resulted from the Chicano movement. Art was certainly a supportive arm of the movement. I think there is much more metaphoric material that goes beyond the specific putting it on a universal plane.

(*Source:* Quirarte, Jacinto, and Carey Clements Rote. *César A. Martínez: A Retrospective.* San Antonio, TX: The Marion Koogler McNay Art Museum, 1999, pp. 29–31, 36.)

Books

Goldman, Shifra M. *Dimensions of the Americas: Art and Social Change in Latin America and the*

United States. Chicago: University of Chicago Press, 1994. Solid study of the political side of Latino art.

Quirarte, Jacinto, and Carey Clements Rote. *César A. Martínez: A Retrospective*. San Antonio, TX: The Marion Koogler McNay Art Museum, 1999. Excellent introduction to the artist that reproduces much of his art and includes a chronology as well as a listing of exhibitions of his work.

Websites

Chicana and Chicano Space, A Thematic Inquiry-Based Art Education Resource: Questions and Answers about César A. Martínez. A critical examination of some of the artist's work plus a biography of the man by the Hispanic Research Center of Arizona State University. http://mati.eas.asu.edu/ChicanArte/html_pages/MartinezIssOutl.html

The Chicano Collection: César A. Martínez. Cheech Marin's site provides a short but good biography of the artist. http://www.thechicanocollection.net/artists/cm/index.html

June 5

1967

Reies López Tijerina, leader of the Allianza Federal de Mercedes, takes control of a courthouse in Tierra Amarilla, New Mexico, to protest violations of civil rights and land possession. The incident quickly enters the mythology of the radical left. He is acquitted of kidnapping in December.

Books

Gardner, Richard. *Grito! Reies Tijerina and the New Mexico Land Grant War of 1967*. New York: Harper and Row, 1971. Gardner includes photos in his account of Tijerina's attempt to reclaim the land once owned by Mexicans.

Tijerina, Reies. *They Called Me "King Tiger": My Struggle for Land and Our Rights*. Houston, TX: Arte Público, 2000. Tijerina's autobiog-

raphy, written after he had essentially gone into retirement.

1991

Sidney Gutiérrez, a Mexican American, flies into space as the pilot of the space shuttle *Columbia*. He lands the spacecraft successfully on June 14 at Edwards Air Force Base in California. Gutiérrez joined the astronaut corps in 1984. He flew one more mission before spending the rest of his NASA career in a support capacity.

Book

Bizony, Piers. *The Space Shuttle: Celebrating Thirty Years of NASA's First Space Plane*. New York: Zenith, 2011. Includes coverage of the flights made by Noriega.

Website

Astronaut Bio: Sidney Gutiérrez. The official NASA biography of the former astronaut.

June 6

1961

Thrash metal vocalist and bassist Tom Araya is born as Tomás Enrique Araya Díaz in Viña del Mar, Chile. Best known for playing with the American band Slayer, Araya used his earnings as a respiratory therapist to finance the band's first album in 1983. *Hit Parade* magazine named him as one of the greatest metal singers. Thrash metal, an especially aggressive variety of hard rock, came into prominence in the early 1980s with Slayer as one of its founding bands.

Books

Dome, Malcolm. *Thrash Metal*. N.P.: Omnibus, 1990. Includes coverage of Slayer among the bands profiled.

Sharpe-Young, Garry. *Thrash Metal*. N.P.: Zonda, 2007. Provides a history, photographs, and discography for Slayer.

June 7

1980

In response to reports that Fidel Castro is emptying out his prisons through the Mariel Boatlift, President Jimmy Carter orders the Justice Department to deport Cubans who had committed serious crimes in Cuba.

Books

Engstrom, David W. *Presidential Decision Making Adrift: The Carter Administration and the Mariel Boatlift*. Lanham, MD: Rowman and Littlefield, 1997. Explores the response of President Jimmy Carter to the boatlift crisis.

Larzelere, Alex. *Castro's Ploy–America's Dilemma: The 1980 Cuban Boatlift*. Washington, D.C.: National Defense University Press, 1988. Well-researched and exhaustive history of the boatlift.

Websites

Cuban Information Archives. Provides photographs of the Mariel boatlift. http://cuban-exile.com/doc_326–350/doc0332.html

U.S. Coast Guard Operations during the 1980 Cuban Exodus. This essay by Benedict L. Stabile and Robert L. Scheina looks at the boatlift from the Coast Guard's perspective. http://www.uscg.mil/history/articles/USCG_Mariel_History_1980.asp

June 8

1938

Arthur Alfonso Schomburg, founder of the New York Public Library's Schomburg Center for Research in Black Culture, dies in Harlem. Born in Puerto Rico, Schomburg viewed himself as an *afroborinqueño,* or black Puerto Rican. He collected literature and art from the African diaspora because, "The American Negro must rebuild his past in order to make his future." Schomburg, as a collector, was part of the Harlem Renaissance of the 1920s.

Books

Schomburg, Arthur A. *Racial Integrity: A Plea for the Establishment of a Chair of Negro History in Our Schools and Colleges . . . July 1913*. Baltimore: Black Classic Press, 1979.

Sinnette, Elinor Des Verney. *Arthur Alfonso Schomburg: Black Bibliophile and Collector: A Biography*. New York: New York Public Library, 1989. An account of the man who founded one of the most popular research centers on African American life.

Websites

The Life and Contributions of Arthur Schomburg. This African American history site profiles the scholar as a part of the Harlem Renaissance. http://afamstud.intrasun.tcnj.edu/harlemrenaissance/tevingt2/schomburgbio.htm

The Schomburg Center for Research in Black Culture. A branch of the New York Public Library, the center collects, preserves, and provides access to materials documenting black life while promoting the study and interpretation of the history and culture of peoples of African descent. http://www.nypl.org/locations/schomburg

June 9

1967

President Lyndon B. Johnson establishes the Inter-Agency Committee on Mexican-American Affairs to seek solutions to Mexican American problems and to assure that federal programs are reaching the Spanish-speaking with the assistance that they need.

Book

Bornet, Vaughn Davis. *The Presidency of Lyndon B. Johnson.* Lawrence, KS: University Press of Kansas, 1983. A scholarly account of LBJ's days in the White House from 1964 to January 1969.

June 10

1954

Operation Wetback begins rounding up undocumented workers. Targeting targeted illegal Mexican immigrants in Arizona, California, and Texas, this U.S. government program was conducted with the cooperation of the Mexican government. It succeeded in forcibly repatriating thousands of undocumented immigrants from the Southwest and it persuaded many others to return home before being captured. Led by Commissioner of Immigration Joseph M. Swing, Operation Wetback only targeted workers. The government did not seek to punish those employers who hired undocumented workers. When the raids began, many undocumented Mexican workers refused to report to work. Some hid in their hotel rooms or other places of residence until the raids stopped mid-September, 1954. Of the 1 million Mexicans deported, many were shipped out of the country with their American-born, U.S.-citizen children.

From "'Wetback' Tide Slowed: Border Patrol Drive in West Gains, Commissioner Says":

> Joseph M. Swing, the Immigration Commissioner, said today the flow of illegal Mexican "wetbacks" across the Rio Grande was "drying up" as a result of a new crackdown by the Border Patrol . . . on June 17 the patrol was apprehending "wetbacks" at the rate of 2,000 a day, while the daily average now was below 1,000. They are replaced by legal Mexican workers "so there has been no interruption in harvesting or other necessary agricultural operations."

(*Source:* From n.a., *New York Times,* June 28, 1954, p. 39.)

Books

García, Juan Ramón. *Operation Wetback: The Mass Deportation of Mexican Undocumented Workers in 1954.* Westport, CT: Greenwood Press, 1980. The only book focused entirely on Operation Wetback.

Kirsten, Peter N. *Anglo over Bracero: A History of the Mexican Workers in the United States from Roosevelt to Nixon.* San Francisco: R and E Research Associates, 1977. The only history of Mexican laborers.

Websites

Operation Wetback. A short history of the program in a website devoted to the history of the Mexican-U.S. border. http://www.pbs.org/kpbs/theborder/history/timeline/20.html

Operation Wetback—The Handbook of Texas Online. Superb history of the program on a site owned by the Texas State Historical Association. http://www.tshaonline.org/handbook/online/articles/pqo01

1998

The World Cup tournament, a series of soccer matches that takes place every four years between teams representing countries, begins today. Baseball, football, and basketball remain the most popular sports in the United States, but soccer has been gaining fans rapidly since the 1990s. The growth of the Latino community has been credited with expanding support for soccer. It has long been the most popular sport in the rest of the world.

From "For a Month, Soccer Is Life":

> At least once a year, Juan Ospina finds himself driving 24 hours nonstop just to watch a soccer match. He sometimes takes off from work to head to one of the Queens bars that broadcast games from South America. And in case there was any doubt of his devotion, he has been known to shave the name of his native

country, Colombia, onto the back of his head and paint the colors of the Colombian flag across his face. "I think the people at work think I'm a little crazy," said Mr. Ospina, a translator at Queens County Family Court. "But soccer is in the blood of most Latin American countries, and people will go to extremes for their teams."

Nowhere is that more apparent than in neighborhoods along Roosevelt Avenue, a bustling spine of immigrant Queens. Under the rumbling el, dozens of restaurants and sports bars that cater to Latin Americans have been advertising for weeks that they will broadcast the 64 World Cup games on "pantallas gigantes," huge-screen television sets. . . . The police in northern Queens have plotted strategy for handling soccer revelers after each game involving a Latin American country. . . . The disturbances in parts of Queens in 1994 certainly never approached the soccer rioting that has become familiar in Europe and Latin America. But thousands of soccer fans rushed onto Roosevelt Avenue, stopping traffic and shutting the thoroughfare with impromptu soccer games and raucous rejoicing.

(*Source:* Toy, Vivian S. "For a Month, Soccer Is Life: In Queens, World Cup Opens Frenzy of Fútbol and Pride." *New York Times,* p. B1.)

Books

Goldblatt, David. *The Ball Is Round: A Global History of Soccer.* New York: Riverhead, 2008. This 1000-page book is a comprehensive account of soccer's development and the politics that often swirls around the game.

Kuper, Simon, and Stefan Szymanski. *Soccernomics: Why England Loses, Why Spain, Germany and Brazil Win, Why the U.S., Japan, Australia and Even Iraq Are Destined to Become the Kings of the World's Most Popular Sport.* New York: Nation Books, 2012. A newspaper columnist and an economist examine soccer.

Websites

Previous FIFA World Cups. The governing body of the World Cup provides a listing of winners, photos, highlights, statistics, recipients of awards, and matches leading to the Cup. http://www.fifa.com/worldcup/archive/index.html

Soccer Net. This ESPN site provides current news about the sport. http://soccernet.espn.go.com/?cc = 5901

June 11

1937

Stella Quintanilla and Carmen Cortez, representing Houston's Club Chapultepec, write a "Letter from Chapultepec" in which they enumerate the concerns facing the Tejano community. They write, "The Mexican people find it impossible to rent or buy in any decent section of town and are forced to live in dirty crowded conditions in houses out of which Americans have moved." The FBI began investigating Quintanilla as a result of the letter, which was sent to Leona B. Hendrix of Kansas City, who may have been a leader of the National Business and Professional Women's Council.

Books

González, Juan. *Harvest of Empire: A History of Latinos in America.* New York: Penguin, 2000. González, a journalist, covers the efforts of Mexican Americans to get decent housing.

Shorris, Earl. *Latinos: A Biography of the People.* New York: W. W. Norton, 1992. Captures the struggles of Latinos through the years by relating a range of stories.

1942

Sociologist Maxine Baca Zinn is born in Santa Fe, New Mexico, to a family of Mexican ancestry. She is notable for her efforts to integrate the experiences of Latinas and other women of color into the study and practice of sociology. In 2000, she won the Jesse Barnard Career Award from the American Sociological Association, a group that now has an award named after Zinn.

Book

Zinn, Maxine Baca, D. Stanley Eitzen, and Barbara Wells. *Diversity in Families*. Boston: Allyn & Bacon, 2011. One of several sociology textbooks co-authored by Zinn.

Website

Maxine Baca Zinn. The Michigan State University Department of Sociology's official profile of the emeritus professor. http://sociology. msu.edu/faculty/profile/baca-zinn-maxine/

June 12

1901

Gregorio Cortez, a Mexican American farmworker, kills Sheriff W. T. Morris in Karnes County in central Texas in an exchange of gunfire that also left Cortez's brother, Romaldo, seriously wounded. Morris, a former Texas Ranger, had come to the farm where the brothers, both migrants from the border region, were sharecropping to look for horse thieves. Morris and his deputy did not have a good command of Spanish and the Cortezes did not speak English well. Morris accused the Cortezes of being horse thieves and drew his gun. Likely fearing that they were about to be killed, Romaldo Cortez charged Morris who then shot him. Gregorio shot Morris with a gun that he had hidden behind his back. Morris's deputy fled the scene with Cortez expecting that he would soon be lynched by Anglo-Texans. Gregorio left Romaldo with family members and headed to the Mexican border. Along the way, he evaded numerous posses, through skillful riding and help from local Mexican Americans. He also killed a second sheriff. When Cortez learned that his wife and children had been imprisoned and that the authorities were carrying out reprisals against those who had helped him, he turned himself in at Laredo, Texas. Mexican Americans still had some political control in Laredo. Nonetheless, Cortez was returned to Karnes County where, under constant threat of lynching, he was tried and convicted. The governor of Texas eventually pardoned him in 1913. Cortez's ride captured the imagination of Mexican Americans who were frustrated by decades of Anglo domination. He became the subject of many songs, or *corridos*. Cortez died in 1916.

From "El Corrido de Gregorio Cortez":

In the country of El Carmen
A great misfortune befell;
The Major Sheriff is dead;
Who killed him no one can tell.
At two in the afternoon,
In half an hour or less,
They knew that the man who killed him
Had been Gregorio Cortez.
And in the country of Kiansis
They cornered him after all;
Though they were more than three hundred
He leaped out of their corral.
Then the Major Sheriff said,
As if he was going to cry,
"Cortez, hand over your weapons;
We want to take you alive."
They let loose the bloodhound dogs;
They followed him from afar.
But trying to catch Cortez
Was like following a star.
All the rangers of the county
Were flying, they rode so hard;
What they wanted was to get
The thousand-dollar reward.
Then said Gregorio Cortez,
And his voice was like a bell,
"You will never get my weapons

Till you put me in a cell."
Then said Gregorio Cortez,
With his pistol in his hand,
"Ah, so many mounted Rangers
Just to take one Mexican!"

(*Source:* Limón, José E. *Mexican Ballads, Chicano Poems: History and Influence in Mexican-American Social Poetry.* Berkeley: University of California Press, 1992, p. 64.)

Books

De Leon, Arnoldo. *They Called Them Greasers: Anglo Attitudes Towards Mexicans in Texas, 1821–1900.* Austin: University of Texas Press, 1983. Sets the context for Cortez's actions in Texas and explains why Mexican Americans turned him into a folk hero.

Limón, José E. *Mexican Ballads, Chicano Poems: History and Influence in Mexican-American Social Poetry.* Berkeley: University of California Press, 1992. Examines the politics surrounding Latino songs.

Websites

El Corrido de Gregorio Cortez. This entry, part of the Texas State Historical Society's Handbook of Texas Online, provides a history of the song including its controversial revival by historian Américo Paredes in 1958.

Gregorio Cortez. Features a brief history of *corridos* and conflicts between the Texas Ranger and the Mexican Americans. http://www.laits.utexas.edu/jaime/jnicolopulos/cwp3/icg/cortez/index.html

1916

Raul Castro, governor of Arizona from 1975 to 1977, is born in the historic mining camp of Cananea, Sonora, Mexico, to a copper miner. His family came to Arizona in 1926. A Democrat, Castro served as ambassador to El Salvador and Colombia during President Lyndon Johnson's administration and left the governorship to become ambassador to Argentina for President Jimmy Carter.

From *State Out of the Union:*

"They just don't understand the border or our history," Castro said. At the age of 95, Castro had experienced nearly a century of his state's history. After he retired from his legal practice in Phoenix, Castro and his wife left affluent Paradise Valley and purchased a historic home on Nogales' hillside border neighborhood. "I've lived along this border all of my life. I even spent time in San Diego and Tijuana. I worked in Mexico in Agua Prieta. I used to walk across the border. I'd go to Juarez, El Paso. . . ."

Castro grew up in Douglas, where a smelter treated the ore from Bisbee's copper mines. His father ensured Castro's international and border-crossing upbringing; he would read aloud from Spanish-language newspapers from Mexico and Texas in the parlor room. He died, though, when Castro was 10, leaving behind his wife and 10 children in the hardscrabble mining region. Castro's mother became a partera, or midwife. His brothers found work in the mines or smelter. Notably studious, Castro was the first child in the family to finish high school, and he earned a football scholarship to the Arizona State Teachers College in Flagstaff.

This was no free ride. Over the next decade, Castro went through a series of achievements and setbacks from racial discrimination that would have derailed most people. As a child, he had walked four miles to school while Anglo children in the same area were picked up by a school bus. During his school breaks, Castro earned half the salary of his Anglo counterparts at the smelter.

Despite a number of honors, Castro couldn't find a teaching job after he graduated from the college in the 1930s. Not that his problem was a secret: "The community would never hire a Mexican American," he told me in his Nogales living room. Forced to hit the road as a migrant worker and bantamweight boxer, Castro roved across the country at the height of the Great Depression.

When his younger brother turned down a chance to attend college, citing the futility of the job market, Castro returned home and found a job across the border at the U.S. consulate in Agua Prieta. With impeccable bilingual skills, Castro was hired to handle the protective services for Americans in Mexico. He spent the next five years carving out an impressive niche in borderland diplomacy. His work didn't go unnoticed. His main supervisor praised Castro's level of diplomatic skills and then suggested he look elsewhere for work: No Mexican-born alien would ever have a future in the American Foreign Service.

The experience both devastated and challenged Castro; he headed to Tucson to pursue a law degree at the University of Arizona. . . . Active in the Red Cross, the YMCA and other civic groups—"I joined everything I could join, including the Tuberculosis Association"—Castro was the first Mexican-American in Arizona to be elected county attorney. Within a few years, he ran and won another historic election as a Superior Court judge.

(*Source:* Biggers, Jeff. *State Out of the Union: Arizona and the Final Showdown over the American Dream.* New York: Nation Books, 2012.)

Book

Biggers, Jeff. *State Out of the Union: Arizona and the Final Showdown over the American Dream.* New York: Nation Books, 2012. Biggers interviewed Castro, a Mexican immigrant, to portray the conflicts in Arizona over Latino immigration.

Website

González, Daniel. "Agents Stir Outcry by Detaining Former Arizona Governor Raul Castro, 96." *The Republic,* July 4, 2012. The Border Patrol stopped and interrogated the former governor in 100 degree heat because he exuded some radiation from a pacemaker check, thereby making news throughout the country. http://www.azcentral.com/news/articles/2012/07/03/20120703agents-stir-outcry-by-detaining-former-arizona-governor-castro.html

1965

The Puerto Rican Family Institute is founded in New York City with financing provided by New York City's Council Against Poverty. It was part of President Lyndon Johnson's War on Poverty. Social worker Agustin Gonzalez led the Institute's Program to Preserve the Integration of the Puerto Rican Migrant Family. Gonzalez, who migrated to New York in 1952 from Puerto Rico, had observed that the city was not meeting the needs of poor families, especially those within minority groups.

Books

Bauman, Robert. *Race and the War on Poverty: From Watts to East L.A.* Norman: University of Oklahoma Press, 2008. Explores efforts by the administration of Lyndon B. Johnson to break the cycle of poverty.

Orleck, Annelise, and Lisa Gayle Hazirjian, eds. *The War on Poverty: A New Grassroots History, 1964–1980.* Athens: University of Georgia Press, 2011. A collection of essays documenting the massive federal effort to raise the quality of life in the United States without regard to race or ethnicity.

June 13

1899

Puerto Rican essayist and literary critic Antonio S. Pedreira is born in San Juan.

Founder and co-editor of the journal, *Indice,* and director of Hispanic Studies at the University of Puerto Rico, Pedreira became a major influence on Puerto Rican literature. He feared that the island was losing its cultural identity. His 1934 book on the meaning of being Puerto Rican, *Insularismo,* is one of the most influential books written on the island nation. He died in San Juan in 1939.

Books

Pedreira, Antonio S. *Aristas, Ensayos.* Río Piedras, PR: Edil, 1969. A collection of the essayist's writings.

Pedreira, Antonio S. *Insularismo: Ensayos de Interpretación Puertorriqueña.* San Juan, PR: Editorial Plaza Mayor, 2001. Essays that examine what it means to be Puerto Rican in the first half of the 20th century.

1903

Consuelo "Chelo" González Amezcua, the first female Mexican American painter to gain fame, is born in Mexico. Raised in Del Rio, Texas, she was self-taught. Offered a scholarship to Mexico City's San Carlos Academy, she had to refuse it because of the need to help support her family in the wake of her father's death. Known especially for her intricate ink drawings which she called "filigree art." Amezcua became a well-known artist late in life, exhibiting her work in galleries and museums in the United States and Mexico beginning in the late 1960s. She died in 1975.

Book

Meier, Matt S. *Notable Latino Americans: A Biographical Dictionary.* Westport, CT: Greenwood Press, 1997. Contains an essay on the artist.

Websites

Chelo González Amezcua Papers, 1934–1976. The artist's papers are housed at the Nettie Lee Benson Latin American Collection at the University of Texas in Austin. http://www. lib.utexas.edu/taro/utlac/00237/lac-00237. html

Consuelo "Chelo" González Amezcua. The Anthony Petullo Collection of Self-Taught and Outsider Art supplies this excellent biographical essay on Amezcua. http://www.lib. utexas.edu/taro/utlac/00237/lac-00237.html

1911

Nobel Prize winner Luis Walter Alvarez is born in San Francisco to a family with Cuban roots. A physicist, he developed the bubble chamber to detect radiation. One of the most notable physicists of the 20th century, he spent his career on the faculty of the University of California at Berkeley. Besides winning the Nobel Prize in 1968 for his contributions to elementary particle physics, he held over 40 patents.

Book

Alvarez, Luis W. *Alvarez: Adventures of a Physicist.* New York: Basic Books, 1987. Engaging memoir.

Website

Luis Alvarez. The Nobel Prize Committee supplies this biography of a 1968 winner. http:// www.nobelprize.org/nobel_prizes/physics/la ureates/1968/alvarez-bio.html

2006

Sculptor Luis Alfonso Jiménez Jr. dies in an accident at his studio in Hondo, New Mexico. Known for representing the Chicano experience, many of the works of the El Paso–born artist reference the flow of human beings across the U.S.-Mexico border.

From an interview of Luis Jiménez conducted December 15–17, 1985:

Peter Bermingham: Luis, we were talking about your early years in this country. You were

Luis Jiménez:

born in El Paso 45 years ago, and you were telling me about your parents who. . . . Part of your roots are in Mexico and part in Texas. Could you tell me, summarize that again for me, just briefly?

Okay. I was born in El Paso, Texas. I was delivered by a Japanese doctor right before Pearl Harbor, and he split right after that. [laughs] _____ no bearing to the art world. It was always interesting _____. Both sides of my family came from Mexico during the twenties when there was an awful lot of upheaval in Mexico, and you had a mass immigration into the United States. On my father's side, his mother—my grandmother—was a bookkeeper in Mexico and actually was a career woman. She didn't have my dad until she was 40 years old. . . . So that's where she had gotten her education at a time when women were not educated in Mexico. And so I also come from

this long family of what is really a minority within a minority, which are Mexican Protestants. . . . And so, my dad came to the United States when he was nine. He was actually not legal in the United States until right after I was born, which is another thing that's sort of not really too relevant in a way; I mean, it's certainly nothing I was aware of as a kid. But it was a fact. On my mother's side of the family, they left when Villa came to the north, as my mother put it—her dad was the mayor of the little town in Chihuahua called Meoki, and of course they were the targets for the Villa forces. And the other part of it—and of course, you know, Villa was never very popular around the house for that reason, but. . . .

I was first beginning to try to work my ideas out in metal, because that was what I, I had learned that the shop also was metal. I, you never did, you know, people say,

"Well, you learned the fiberglass in the shop." I didn't learn any fiberglass in the shop. I've learned fiberglass on my own. There was, the shop was geared toward metal technology, and that was what I knew how to do, as well as casting, because I built the foundry in Austin along with three other students, and we were doing our own castings. So it was all metal. Plus there was that whole macho trip out of the, you know, early sixties of, you know, every sculptor, you know, is a David Smith-type guy. . . .

(*Source:* An interview of Luis Jiménez conducted December 15–17, 1985, by Peter Bermingham, in Tucson, Arizona, for the Archives of American Art. http://www.aaa.si.edu/collections/interviews/oral-history-interview-luis-jimenez-13554)

Books

Anaya, Rudolfo et al. *Man on Fire: Luis Jiménez*. Albuquerque, NM: The Albuquerque Museum, 1994. An exhibition catalogue in English and Spanish with essays about the sculptor's art.

Huerta, Benito, ed. *Luis Jiménez: Working-Class Heroes: Images from the Popular Culture*. Kansas City, MO: ExhibitsUSA, Mid-America Arts Alliance, 1997. An exhibition catalogue for a traveling exhibit of the artist's work.

Websites

Luis Jiménez Online. The Art Cyclopedia provides this collection of links relating to the late sculptor. http://www.artcyclopedia.com/artists/jimenez_luis.html

Oral History Interview with Luis Jiménez, 1985 December 15–17. An interview of Luis Jiménez conducted December 15–17, 1985, by Peter Bermingham, in Tucson, Arizona, for the Archives of American Art. http://www.aaa.si.edu/collections/interviews/oral-history-interview-luis-jimenez-13554

June 14

2011

President Barack Obama becomes the first sitting U.S. president to visit Puerto Rico since John F. Kennedy made an official visit half a century earlier in 1961. Puerto Ricans make up the largest Latino community in the United States after Mexican Americans with more of them living on the mainland than on the island. Obama's stop of several hours is reported to be a bid for votes in the 2012 election. Despite the possible political motives of the trip, Puerto Rico has a tradition of erecting a statue of any U.S. president who visits and therefore Obama's likeness will appear next to that of Kennedy.

Books

Barreto, Matt A. *Ethnic Cues: The Role of Shared Ethnicity in Latino Political Participation*. Ann Arbor: University of Michigan Press, 2010. Discusses whether ethnic affiliation will trump political affiliation.

DeSipio, Louis. *Counting on the Latino Vote: Latinos as a New Electorate*. Charlottesville: University Press of Virginia, 1996. Covers the potential voting power of Latinos and the barriers keeping them from the polls.

Website

President Barack H. Obama. An official biography of the president from the White

House. http://www.whitehouse.gov/admin
istration/president-obama

June 15

1955

Chilean American poet Marjorie Agostín is
born in Bethesda, Maryland. She published
her first book in the United States, *Conchalí,*
in 1980. It dealt with her longing for Chilean
culture and her severing of ties with a Chilean culture that oppressed women.

Book

Stavans, Ilan. *The Scroll and the Cross: 1,000
    Years of Jewish-Hispanic Literature.* New York:
    Routledge, 2003. Contains an essay by Agostín.

June 16

1945

Private Felix Longoria is killed in action in
the Philippines, beginning a dispute over
the burial of his remains. Longoria, a Mexican American resident of Three Rivers,
Texas, and a truck driver, joined the U.S.
Army in 1944. The 26-year-old Longoria
remarked to a friend that everyone else was
going to war and that he might as well go
too. About six months after being sent to the
Philippines, Longoria volunteered to join a
patrol that was trying to dislodge Japanese
snipers. He was killed by small arms fire
from the enemy. Six months after his death,
Longoria's mother received the medals that
he had earned: a Bronze Service Star, a Purple Heart, a Good Conduct Medal, and a
Combat Infantryman's Badge. Longoria's
body remained in the Philippines until January 1949. The Army informed Longoria's
widow that it had exhumed his remains
and was sending them to Texas. Beatrice
Moreno Longoria wanted to bury her husband in his hometown of Three Rivers.

The local funeral home, Manon Rice Funeral Home, refused to conduct a funeral
for Private Longoria because whites would
not like it if Latinos used the chapel and
the business would be damaged. Beatrice
Longoria, who had no other suitable place
in Three Rivers to conduct a service, decided that a war hero deserved better treatment. She noted that her husband was good
enough to die for South Texas and the rest
of his country but not good enough to use
his hometown's only funeral chapel. The
American G.I. Forum backed Longoria
by organizing a protest that reached the U.S.
senator from Texas, Lyndon B. Johnson.
Senator Johnson arranged for Longoria to
be buried in Arlington National Cemetery
with full military honors. President Truman sent a telegram in support of Longoria.
Newspapers soon picked up the story and
it became a major scandal, even damaging
diplomatic relations with Mexico. Publicity
generated by the event brought new members into the ranks of the American G.I.
Forum. The organization would eventually
become a major force in the fight for the
rights of veterans and Mexican Americans.

From a telegram sent by U.S. senator
Lyndon B. Johnson to Beatrice Moreno
Longoria's representative, Dr. Hector Pérez
García, on January 11, 1949:

> I deeply regret that the prejudice of
> some individuals extends even beyond
> this life. I have no authority over civilian funeral homes. Nor does the federal government. I have today made
> arrangements to have Felix Longoria buried with full military honors in
> Arlington National Cemetery here in
> Washington, where the honored dead
> of our nation's wars rest.

(*Source:* Carroll, Patrick. *Felix Longoria's
Wake: Bereavement, Racism, and the Rise of
Mexican American Activism.* Austin: University of Texas Press, 2003, p. 66.)

Books

Allsup, Carl. *The American G.I. Forum: Origins and Evolution.* Austin: University of Texas Center for Mexican American Studies, 1982. Solid history of the civil rights organization.

Carroll, Patrick. *Felix Longoria's Wake: Bereavement, Racism, and the Rise of Mexican American Activism.* Austin: University of Texas Press, 2003. This is the best study of the case and its impact.

Websites

Felix Z. Longoria, Private, U.S. Army. This website, by Michael Robert Patterson, provides information about the men and women interred in Arlington National Cemetery. The information on Longoria includes newspaper articles and material on his widow. http://www.arlingtoncemetery.net/longoria.htm

Felix Longoria Affair. The Handbook of Texas Online, sponsored by the Texas State Historical Association, provides a solid history of the cause célèbre. http://www.tshaonline.org/handbook/online/articles/vef01

1951

Roberto Durán, one of the greatest boxers of all time, is born in El Chorrillo, Panama. Nicknamed "Manos de Piedra" (Hands of Stone), he was named by the Associated Press as the best lightweight boxer of the 20th century. Durán won the World Boxing Association championship in 1972 in a bout at Madison Square Garden in New York City. In a November 1980 bout with Sugar Ray Leonard, Durán quit playing, reportedly saying "No más" (No more). Durán continued to box, with most of his bouts held in the United States, but the episode badly damaged his reputation. Durán appeared in the 1979 movie *Rocky II* and had minor roles in American television shows in the 1980s. He finally retired in January 2002, following a car accident.

From a September 2006 interview with Roberto Duran by ESPN.com:

ESPN.com: If you could have one chance to do one of your fights over again, which fight would it be and why?

Duran: There would be four. Vinnie Pazienza, [Hector] Camacho, Leonard and [Thomas] Hearns.

If I could, I would fight that first Leonard fight again.

ESPN.com: The first Leonard fight? Why?

Duran: Because I would beat him more convincingly [Duran won by unanimous decision in June 1980]. [As for] The second one, I didn't have enough time to train. [Leonard won by an eighth-round TKO]

ESPN.com: Your car accident five years ago: How has that changed your perspective on life?

Duran: I really feel that if it wasn't for the accident, I'd still be fighting. I would have handled some of these fighters. I would have made sure that the doctors would have declared me physically sound; and after that, I would have trained.

ESPN.com: Even at 55, you'd still be fighting?

Duran: I would have been stronger and faster.

ESPN.com: If ["The Contender" host] Sugar Ray Leonard asked you to make an appearance on the show, would you consider it?

Duran: I would do a guest appearance. Yes, we're good friends. We get along very well now. I consider him my friend now, after all these years.

ESPN.com: If there were such a thing as one commissioner of boxing, and that person was empowered to rule the sport and you were that person, what would you change to improve boxing?

Duran: I would take out the old referees, the ones that have been refereeing all of these championship fights, and recycle them with some new blood. Some of the old refs have favoritism toward some of the fighters that are currently fighting. There should be a changing of the guard with the refs, the same way there are with fighters.

(*Source:* "Even at 55, Roberto Duran Packs a Wallop." ESPN.Com, September 27, 2006, http://sports.espn.go.com/sports/boxing/news/story?id = 2604943)

Book

Kimball, George. *Four Kings: Leonard, Hagler, Hearns, Duran and the Last Great Era of Boxing.* London: Mainstream, 2008. Provides a biography of Durán and sets him in the context of the boxing world of the 1980s.

Websites

The Official Website of Roberto Durán. Excellent site that includes a biography, career statistics, a photo gallery, and quotes. http://www.cmgww.com/sports/duran/

Roberto Durán. BoxRec provides career statistics for the boxer as well as his opponents. http://boxrec.com/list_bouts.php?human_id = 80&cat = boxer

June 17

1833

Painter Francisco Oller y Cestero is born in Bayamón, Puerto Rico. He became the only Latin American artist to participate in the development of impressionism when he moved to Paris in 1858. Oller returned to Puerto Rico in 1865 and gained renown as one of the first artists to focus on the Puerto Rican landscape and the customs of ordinary people. In 1872, he became the first Puerto Rican to be named painter to the royal court of Spain. Oller died in 1917.

Books

Delgado Mercado, Osiris. *Francisco Oller y Cestero (1833–1917): Pintor de Puerto Rico.* San Juan, Puerto Rico: Centro de Estudios Superiores de Puerto Rico y El Caribe, 1983. A biography of the famed painter.

Oller y Cestero, Francisco. *Francisco Oller, un Realista del Impresionismo: Exposición Organizada por el Museo de Arte de Ponce en Conmemoración del Sesquicentario del Natalicio del Pintor Puertorriqueño Francisco Oller (1833–1917).* Ponce, PR: Museo de Arte de Ponce, 1983. A catalogue of an exhibit of the painter's works held on the 150th anniversary of his birth.

1872

Manuel Marius García, the first Mexican American to graduate from the University of Texas, is born in Camargo, Tamaulipas, Mexico. He grew up near Rio Grande City in Texas. He graduated from the University of Texas in 1894 with a Bachelor of Arts degree in classics. He worked as a teacher and principal before moving to Laredo to work in the family bank.

Website

Manuel Marius García. The Handbook of Texas Online, presented by the Texas State Historical Association, supplies this biography of García. http://www.tshaonline.org/handbook/online/articles/fga84

1953

Jane L. Delgado is born in Cuba. The family migrates to the United States in 1955. Delgado is the president of the Washington,

D.C.–based National Alliance for Hispanic Health and Human Services Organization, the largest agency in the United States to focus exclusively on health issues faced by Latinos and Latinas.

Website

National Alliance for Hispanic Health and Human Services Organization. The official website of the organization includes a blog by Delgado. http://www.hispanic health.org/

June 18

2012

The James Beard Foundation announces that it will make restaurants and chefs in Puerto Rico eligible for the culinary industry's most prestigious honors. Beginning with the 2013 James Beard Awards, chefs in Puerto Rico will be eligible for the "Best Chef South" award. Puerto Rico's restaurants will also qualify for awards in national categories such as Outstanding Chef, Outstanding Restaurant/Restaurateur and Service, as well as for the America's Classic award, an honor bestowed annually on five restaurants.

Books

Cabanillas, Berta, and Carmen Ginorio. *Puerto-Rican Dishes*. Rio Piedras, PR: Editorial Universitaria, Universidad de Puerto Rico, 1956. Supplies recipes for traditional Puerto Rican dishes.

Sterling, Emma Duprey de. *Cocina Artesanal Puertorriqueña*. San Juan, PR: La Editorial de la Universidad de Puerto Rico, 2004. A cookbook of more elaborate dishes from Puerto Rico.

Website

James Beard Foundation. The official website for the organization includes recipes and award information. http://www.jamesbeard.org/

June 19

2012

The American Civil Liberties Union (ACLU) releases a report charging the Puerto Rico Police Department (PRPD) with permitting a culture of abuse. Titled "Island of Impunity: Puerto Rico's Outlaw Police Force," the report alleges that use of excessive or lethal force is routine and civil and human rights violations rampant. The PRPD, with 17,000 officers, is the second-largest police department in the United States. There are 4.6 police officers per 1,000 residents, more than twice the national average.

Books

Berg, Bruce L. *Policing in Modern Society*. Boston, MA: Butterworth Heinemann, 1999. Addresses all the requirements of modern policing.

Mladek, Klaus, ed. *Police Forces: A Cultural History of an Institution*. New York: Palgrave Macmillan, 2007. Essays discuss the history of this complicated profession.

Website

Island of Impunity: Puerto Rico's Outlaw Police Force. The ACLU provides the entire report online. *http://www.aclu.org/human-rights/ island-impunity-puerto-ricos-outlaw-police-force*

June 20

1919

A fire at the Teatro Yagüez theater in Mayaguez, Puerto Rico, kills dozens of people, perhaps as many as 150. Opened as an opera house, the theater was showing a silent movie at the time of the fire. The architect, Sabàs Honoré, rebuilt the theater after the fire and it remains a historic site.

Books

Maines, Rachel. *Asbestos and Fire: Technological Trade-Offs and the Body at Risk*. New Brunswick, NJ: Rutgers University Press, 2005.

Provides an excellent study of the threat of fire in the United States in the 19th and 20th centuries.

Rhodes, Gary D. *The Perils of Moviegoing in America, 1896–1950.* New York: Continuum, 2012. During the first 50 years of cinema-going, fires in theaters were surprisingly common.

June 21

1875

The newspaper *San Antonio Express* states that Mexicans are being killed "promiscuously" on Texas highways because Gov. Richard Coke had advised Texans to resolve border troubles by killing Mexicans.

Books

González, Juan. *Harvest of Empire: A History of Latinos in America.* New York: Penguin, 2000. González, a journalist, covers the efforts of Mexican Americans to get decent housing.

Shorris, Earl. *Latinos: A Biography of the People.* New York: W. W. Norton, 1992. Speaks of the struggles of Latinos through the years by relating a range of stories.

1938

Printmaker Malaquías Montoya is born in Albuquerque, New Mexico, and raised in San Joaquin Valley in California. His entire family, seven children and two parents, worked as farm laborers. Montoya graduated from the University of California, Berkeley, in 1969 but his three oldest siblings never went beyond the seventh grade. Montoya cofounded the Mexican American Liberation Art Front (MALAF) in the San Francisco Bay Area in 1968. The short-lived collective was one of the first examples of artists working together to promote Chicano art.

An artist's statement by Malaquías Montoya:

Through our images we are the creators of culture and it is our responsibil-

ity that they are of our times. My work depicts honesty and promotes an attitude towards existing reality; a confrontational attitude, one of change rather than adaptability—images of our time and for our contemporaries.

I am much more articulate and able to express myself more eloquently through my art. It is with this voice that I attempt to communicate, especially to that silent and often ignored populace of Chicano, Mexican and Central American working class, along with other disenfranchised people of the world. This form allows me to awaken consciousness, to reveal reality and to actively work to transform it. What better function for art at this time? A voice for the voiceless.

(*Source:* Malaquías Montoya's official website. http://www.malaquiasmontoya.com/)

Books

Jackson, Carlos Francisco. *Chicana and Chicano Art: ProtestArte.* Tucson: University of Arizona Press, 2009. Covers the history of MALAF.

Pohl, Frances. *Framing America: A Social History of American Art.* New York: Thames & Hudson, 2002. Covers the general history of art from the time of the Spanish conquest.

Romo, Terecita. *Malaquias Montoya.* Los Angeles: Chicano Studies Research Center, 2011. The only biography of the influential Chicano artist.

Website

Malaquías Montoya. The official website for the artist includes a statement from the artist apart from his biography and exhibitions. http://www.malaquiasmontoya.com/

June 23

1935

Maurice A. Ferré, the first U.S. mayor born in Puerto Rico, served six terms as leader of Miami from 1973 to 1985. His election was a sign of the increasing power of Latinos in Miami. Unlike Ferré, however, most Latinos in Florida hailed from Cuba. During his tenure, Miami emerged as a major city in the Americas.

Books

Muir, Helen. *Miami, U.S.A.* Gainesville: University Press of Florida, 2000. Covers the history of Miami during the Ferre years.

Nijman, Jan. *Miami: Mistress of the Americas*. Philadelphia: University of Pennsylvania Press, 2011. Discusses how Miami progressed from a sleepy backwater for vacationing Northerners to a major city with a very strong Latino flavor.

June 24

1703

Fray Antonio de San Buenaventura witnesses the marriage of an Indian man, Nicolás, from the Jarame tribe, with Isabel, a member of the Sana tribe. Witnesses included two Spanish soldiers and two men from the pueblo of San Juan Bautista. The marriage took place at San Antonio de Valero Mission, which is now the Alamo in present-day San Antonio, Texas. From the early days of contact, the Catholic Church supported the idea of intermarriage between Spanish soldiers and colonists and native women. Besides marrying Spanish Mexican men, Indian women at Spanish missions also wed other Native Americans.

Books

Chipman, Donald E., and Harriett Denise Joseph. *Spanish Texas, 1519–1821*. Austin: University of Texas Press, 2010. A general history of the region that includes relations between the Spanish and the Native Americans.

Woods, James M. *A History of the Catholic Church in the American South, 1513–1900*. Gainesville: University Press of Florida, 2011. A general history of Catholicism that includes Texas.

1928

Chemist Juana "Jennie" Luisa Vivó Acrivos is born in Havana, Cuba. The author of more than 100 papers, she spent her career in academia at Stanford University and San Jose State University.

Website

Juana "Jennie" Vivó Acrivos. Provides the chemist's curriculum vitae and photograph. http://works.bepress.com/juana_acrivos/cv.pdf

June 25

1991

The 29-minute documentary, *Plena Is Work, Plena Is Song,* is broadcast on PBS. Created by Susan Zeig and Pedro Rivera, it is a tribute to Puerto Rican working class culture and its African roots. The title reflects the important role played by *plena,* a percussion-heavy musical form akin to the blues, to communicate resistance to oppression both in Puerto Rico and on the U.S. mainland. The filmmakers feature *pleneros,* singers of *plenas,* on sugar plantations and docks in Puerto Rico as well in the barrios of New York City. The roots of this Latino musical form apparently go back to the early 20th century when it grew out of *bomba* music in southern Puerto Rico among poor farmers and artisans. By the late 1920s, RCA had developed the first *plena* recording artist, Canario (Manuel Jimenez). By midcentury, new *pleneros* like Mon Rivera and Rafael Cortijo sought to elevate the status of the music by moving it from the streets into concert halls. However, the music still addressed all the concerns of the working class, from unrequited love to mechanization and unsafe factory conditions. During the 1960s *plena* lost much of its audience, but the music still holds a place in the hearts of Puerto Ricans.

"Plena de Amor" by the group Plena Libre, translated by Tammy S. Allen

Vengo a contarle una historia,	I come to tell you a story,
vengo a dejar mis memorias	I come to share my memories
Todo el mundo lo sabía,	Everybody knows it
lo que mi mente traía.	what is on my mind.
Un sentimiento de amor,	A feeling of love
que ahora cambia por dolor,	that now changes because of pain,
que ahora cambia	
siempre por dolor	that now changes always because of pain.
Sucede que hace unos días,	A few days ago
ese amor se derrumbó	this love failed
Esa negrita te digo	That girl I'm telling you still doesn't know
que todavía no sabe	that she took my love away
Que mi amor se lo llevó	
Y ahora quedo yo con mi dolor	Now I am left with my pain
Dentro de mi corazón.	trapped inside my heart.
Y ahora quedo yo con mi dolor	Now I am left with my pain
Dentro de mi corazón.	trapped inside my heart.
Sucede que hace unos días,	A few days ago
ese amor se derrumbó	this love failed
Esa negrita tan linda te digo	That girl I'm telling you still doesn't know
que todavía no sabe	that she took my love away
Que mi amor se lo llevó.	
Ay ahora quedo yo	Now I am left forever with my pain
Siempre con mi dolor	trapped inside my heart
Dentro de mi corazón	Now I am left with my pain
Y ahora quedo yo con mi dolor	trapped inside my heart
Dentro de mi corazón.	
CORO:	CHORUS:
Tengo una pena	I have sorrow
tengo un dolor	I have pain
Y eso me pasa por creer	This happened to me because I believed in
en el amor, en el amor	love, in love.
(Repeat 2 times)	
Juraste amarme 500 años	You swore that you would love me for 500 years
Y ahora creo que todo	And now I know that it was all a lie
fue para mi n engaño.	
Coro	Chorus

Y en esta gran pena	And I feel this great sorrow because
Que siento yo	you played with our love
Tu la causaste por jugar	with our love
Con nuestro amor,	
Con nuestro amor	
Te di mi vida y mi corazón	I gave you my life and my heart
Y tú me pegaste con el desprecio	And you gave me disrespect and
engaño, de tu amor	your love's deceit
de tu amor, de tu amor, tu traición	Your love's deceit and betrayal.

(*Source:* "Plena De Amor." Plena Libre, Radio UOL, http://www.radio.uol.com.br/#/letras-e-musicas/plena-libre/plena-de-amor/1220269)

Books

Abrash, Barbara. *Mediating History: The MAP Guide to Independent Video*. New York: New York University, 1992. The Media Alternatives Project (MAP) provides a good introduction to small films by Puerto Rican and Chicano filmmakers.

Glasser, Ruth. *My Music Is My Flag: Puerto Rican Musicians and Their New York Communities, 1917–1940*. Berkeley: University of California Press, 1997. Looks at the social history of Puerto Rican music.

Websites

Plena: Music of Puerto Rico. Superb introduction to the history and style of the music. http://www.musicofpuertorico.com/index.php/genre/plena/

Smithsonian Folkways—*Bomba* and *Plena*. Provides a wonderful introduction to the music and includes audio links. http://www.folkways.si.edu/explore_folkways/bomba_plena.aspx

mainstream hit movie about doomed Latino singer Ritchie Valens. He is a founding member of the California Arts Council and a recipient of the Presidential Medal of the Arts.

Books

Broyles-González, Yolanda. *El Teatro Campesino: Theater in the Chicano Movement*. Austin: University of Texas Press, 1994. A history of the performing arts aspect of the civil rights movement.

Harding, James M., and Cindy Rosenthal. *Restaging the Sixties: Radical Theaters and Their Legacies*. Ann Arbor: University of Michigan Press, 2007. Includes two chapters on the legacy of El Teatro Campesino.

Website

The Official Site of El Teatro Campesino. Provides information about Valdez and the theater as well as information on its current schedule. http://www.elteatrocampesino.com/

June 26

1940

Luís Valdez, the father of Chicano theater, is born in Delano, California, to migrant farmworker parents. In 1965, he founded El Teatro Campesino, a farmworkers' theater troupe, in Delano. The troupe was the spark that created the Chicano theater movement. Valdez also wrote and directed *La Bamba* (1987), a

June 27

1776

Lieutenant Josef Joachín Moraga of Spain and his troops occupy the port of San Francisco and then begin the construction of a presidio and mission. Moraga had joined the expedition led by Juan Bautista de Anza to colonize Alta California for Spain. Anza brought 240 men, women, and children from Sonora,

Mexico to California. Anza surveyed the San Francisco area with Moraga and then left his lieutenant in charge while he returned to Mexico. Moraga is the one who took the settlers into San Francisco. Moraga served as the first commander of the Presidio of San Francisco. He died there in 1782.

From a letter by Josef Joachín Moraga to Viceroy Antonio Bucareli y Ursua, March 20, 1777:

There appeared before us a herd of elk to the number of eleven, of which we got three without leaving our road. This merciful act of the infinite providence of the Most High is noteworthy, for the soldiers were by now tired out by the difficulties of the road and weak on account of the customary fare, consisting only of maize and frijoles, on which they were being fed, a reason why the women with continuous sighs were now making known their great dissatisfaction. But this refreshment of meat appearing before us, and we being able with such ease to take advantage of it, the soldiers not only were revived with such a plenty of food, but they were also delighted with the prospect of the abundance of these animals which the country promised. And it is certain, most Excellent Sir, that these elk are of such size and have such savory flesh that neither in quantity nor in quality need they envy the best beef. Their height, which I measured, is seven palms. The length of the body is two varas and a half, and the horns are seven palms long, so that seen with such a crown of antlers they present a very agreeable picture. I noticed that [above] each eye they have a hole resembling the eye itself. This day at one in the afternoon we camped on the Arroyo de las Llagas de Nuestro Padre de San Francisco, having experienced that it was so hot that the families suffered

great discomfort, a thing which caused us surprise in view of the experience which we have had of the coldness of this climate. . . .

On the 27th at half past six in the morning I set out with the soldiers from the site of San Matheo, and at half past eleven, without any incident, we camped at the port of San Francisco and the Laguna de los Dolores. This very day I gave orders to the sergeant to set the soldiers at cutting trees for the building of their houses, an occupation which they continued daily. . . .

Although I have lacked artisans, I have not on that account omitted the greatest care that the buildings should be erected in the best and surest way permitted by such a scarcity of these artisans. . . . The place where the fort is situated, although it is not the most level in its entire extent, yet it is one of those most protected from the strong wind which prevails here and one of those nearest to the [harbor]. No arroyo runs close to it, but with a well which I had opened on a slope very close to the presidio, I discovered a spring sufficient for all necessities and which would be superabundant even though there were a larger number of families. Firewood is abundant and close by, and not far away there is a lake suitable for washing the clothing.

(*Source:* Web de Anza, University of Oregon, http://anza.uoregon.edu/moraga.html)

Books

Eldredge, Zoeth Skinner. *The Beginnings of San Francisco.* New York: John C. Rankin, 1912. The best source of information in print on Moraga and his men.

Guerrero, Vladimir. *The Anza Trail and the Settling of California.* Berkeley, CA: Heyday, 2006. A solid history of the Anza Expedition.

Websites

Juan Bautista de Anza Historical Trail. The National Park Service manages this 1200-mile trail from Nogales, Arizona to San Francisco, California. The website includes a guide that has maps, a historical background, and an audio library of trail sounds. http://www.nps.gov/juba/index.htm

Web de Anza. The University of Oregon provides primary sources and historical background relating to Anza's journey. http://anza.uoregon.edu/

2000

Patrick Flores, who became the first Mexican American Roman Catholic bishop in 1970, is held hostage by a man from El Salvador who feared deportation. Nelson Antonio Escolero held Flores, now archbishop of San Antonio, for nine hours before releasing him unharmed. Flores retired in 2004.

Books

McMurtrey, Martin. *Mariachi Bishop: The Life Story of Patrick Flores*. San Antonio, TX: Corona, 1987. The only biography of the priest.

Williams, Franklin C. Jr. *Lone Star Bishops: The Roman Catholic Hierarchy in Texas*. Waco, TX: Texian Press, 1997. A voluminous tome on the leaders of the Catholic Church in this heavily Catholic state.

June 28

2006

The U.S. Supreme Court rules, in *League of United Latin American Citizens v. Perry*, that the redistricting plan passed by the Texas State Legislature did not violate the U.S. Constitution but did violate parts of the Voting Rights Act of 1965. The case began when a federal judge created a redistricting plan following the 2000 census. Legislators did not like the plan and created one that critics argued diluted racial minority voting strength and was designed to maximize partisan advantage. A district court ruled in favor of Texas and the plaintiffs appealed to the Supreme Court. Justice Anthony Kennedy, writing for a majority of the justices, stated that District 23 had been redrawn in such a way as to deny Latino voters as a group the opportunity to elect a candidate of their choosing, thereby violating the Voting Rights Act. However, the court found that Texas had a right to redraw its district boundaries.

From *League of United Latin American Citizens v. Perry*:

. . . After the 2002 election, it became apparent that District 23 as then drawn had an increasingly powerful Latino population that threatened to oust the incumbent Republican, Henry Bonilla. Before the 2003 redistricting, the Latino share of the citizen voting-age population was 57.5%, and Bonilla's support among Latinos had dropped with each successive election since 1996. . . . In the newly drawn district, the Latino share of the citizen voting-age population dropped to 46%, though the Latino share of the total voting-age population remained just over 50%. . . . The District Court summed up the purposes underlying the redistricting in south and west Texas: "The change to Congressional District 23 served the dual goal of increasing Republican seats in general and protecting Bonilla's incumbency in particular, with the additional political nuance that Bonilla would be re-elected in a district that had a majority of Latino voting age population—although clearly not a majority of citizen voting age population and certainly not an effective voting majority."

(*Source: League of United Latin American Citizens v. Perry* [2006]. http://www.law.cornell.edu/supct/html/05–204.ZS.html)

Books

Bullock, Charles S. *Redistricting: The Most Political Act in America.* New York: Rowman & Littlefield, 2010. A balanced analysis of redistricting by a political scientist.

Monmonier, Mark. *Bushmanders and Bullwinkles: How Politicians Manipulate Electronic Maps and Census Data to Win Elections.* Chicago: University of Chicago Press, 2001. Unusual and interesting study of redistricting from the perspective of a mapmaker.

Websites

League of United Latin American Citizens v. Perry (2006)—Oyez, U.S. Supreme Court Media, Chicago-Kent School of Law. Provides a summary of the Supreme Court decision as well as audio links to the oral arguments and the opinion announcement. http://www.oyez.org/cases/2000–2009/2005/2005_05_204

League of United Latin American Citizens v. Perry (2006). This Cornell University Law School site provides the full text of the decision. http://www.law.cornell.edu/supct/html/05–204.ZS.html

1973

New Mexico senator Joseph M. Montoya, who traced his ancestry back to 18th-century Spanish immigrants, called on President Richard Nixon to testify before the Senate Watergate committee to refute charges by former presidential aide John Dean. Montoya, one of the most prominent Latinos to hold a Congressional seat, served on the committee investigating the Watergate scandal. The scandal dominated headlines in 1973 and 1974 until Nixon resigned from office, the only president to leave the White House in such a disgraceful manner. Montoya, a highly respected senator who represented the San Antonio areas as a Democrat, held office from 1964 until he was defeated in a re-election bid in 1977.

Books

Gould, Lewis L. *The Most Exclusive Club: A History of the Modern United States Senate.* New York: Basic Books, 2005. Excellent general history of this American institution.

Liebovitch, Louis. *Richard Nixon, Watergate, and the Press: A Historical Retrospective.* Westport, CT: Praeger, 2003. One of the best general histories of the Watergate scandal.

Website

Watergate. Provides a chronological account of Watergate as well as an archive that includes several speeches in audio and video formats by Richard Nixon. http://watergate.info/

June 29

1884

The Dominican scholar, Pedro Henríquez Ureña, is born. Ureña is known for creating a global history of Latin American literature. With *El nacimiento de Dionisos* (The Birth of Dionysus) in 1916, he wrote the first book to be published by a Dominican author in the United States. He developed an interest in American arts and literature while living in New York from 1901 to 1904. He earned a PhD from the University of Minnesota and taught at the school for a few years in the 1920s.

Books

Febres, Laura. *Pedro Henríquez Ureña: Crítico de América.* Caracas, Venezuela: Ediciones La Casa de Bello, 1989. Addresses Ureña's criticisms of the United States.

Lara, Juan Jacobo de. *Pedro Henríquez Ureña: Su Vida y Su Obra.* Santo Domingo: Universidad Nacional Pedro Henríquez Ureña, 1975. The life and works of Ureña in Spanish.

1957

Actress, singer, and model Maria Conchita Alonso is born in Cuba. She is raised in Venezuela and becomes Miss Venezuela in 1975. Alonso acted in Venezuelan telenovelas while becoming a bestselling Latin American recording artist. She came to Hollywood in 1982 and has acted in a number of movies. She won a Grammy Award in 1985 for Best Latin Artist.

Website

Maria Conchita Alonso. The Internet Movie Database provides a biography, a list of acting credits, and photographs of the actor. http://www.imdb.com/name/nm0000744/

1968

The Crusade for Justice, a Chicano group, joins with other concerned citizens to march in Denver, Colorado, to protest the shooting and killing of 15-year-old Joseph Archuleta. Patrolman Theodore Zavashlak shot the youth while he was running away and before the officer could determine if Archuleta had committed any crime. Zavashlak contended that his pistol had accidentally discharged as he stumbled and fell. Witnesses claim that the patrolman had shot twice at Archuleta and did not fall. The marches are met at police headquarters by a police contingent armed with rifles and tear gas. No violence occurs.

Books

Acuña, Rodolfo. *Occupied America: A History of Chicanos*. New York: Harper Collins, 1988. The standard history of the Chicano movement.

Vigil, Ernesto B. *The Crusade for Justice: Chicano Militancy and the Government's War on Dissent.* Madison: University of Wisconsin Press, 1999. Vigil was a member of Crusade for Justice.

June 30

2012

Yomo Toro, a salsa musician, born Victor Guillermo Toro Vega Ramos Rodríguez Acosta in Ensenada, dies in the Bronx in New York City. Toro was a virtuoso on the cuatro, a mandolin-like Puerto Rican instrument that has 10 strings in five groupings of two each, either octaves or unisons. Through the 1950s in New York, Toro played traditional Puerto Rican and Mexican music on standard and requinto guitar as well as the cuatro. In the 1960s and 1970s, salsa bands began moving their best instrumental soloists to the foreground. Toro's cuatro sound became instantly recognizable on records by Willie Colón, Hector Lavoe, Larry Harlow, and the Fania All-Stars. He also worked on David Byrne's 1989 album *Rei Momo* and Linda Ronstadt's 1992 album *Frenesi* as well as the soundtracks for the television show *Dora the Explorer*.

Website

Yomo Toro, King of the Cuatro. Nelson O. Figueroa writes this short tribute to the musician. http://www.beinglatino.us/entertainment/music/yomo-toro-king-of-the-cuatro/

Yomo Toro. YouTube provides this video clip of Toro playing the cuatro. http://www.youtube.com/watch?v=yd74ACZkTQw

July

July 1

1998

Northwest Regional Education Laboratory offers a guide to making schools friendly for immigrants. Children pose a unique immigration problem. While they are under the control of parents, they are also subject to the demands of educational officials. When the period of mass immigration began in the mid-19th century, many Americans began to think of the expanding public school system as a place in which devotion to America could be taught along with reading, writing, and arithmetic. In the late 20th century, educational leaders became more supportive of multiculturalism. Instead of forcing Americanization upon children, they looked for ways to welcome immigrant students and celebrate other ethnicities. The Northwest Regional Education Laboratory, now Education Northwest, is one of 10 regional Equity Centers created by the U.S. Department of Education in the 1960s to assist with desegregation.

From "Self-Report Card—Teacher, Checklist for Measuring the Immigrant-Friendliness of Your Classroom":

Am I familiar with the values, traditions, and customs of students in my classroom?

Am I knowledgeable about the immigrant experience of my students' families?

Do I visit at home with the families of immigrant students in my classroom to gain insight into the students' lives and support systems?

Do I learn some vocabulary in the native language of my students to better communicate with them?

Do I encourage immigrant parents to help their children maintain their native language at home while learning English at school?

Do I base my academic expectations on the individual ability of each student rather than on broad or stereotypical assumptions?

(*Source:* Northwest Regional Education Laboratory Equity Center, *Improving Education for Immigrant Students: A Guide for K-12 Educators in the Northwest.* Portland, OR: Northwest Regional Education Laboratory, 1998, p. 55.)

Books

Clevedon, England: Multilingual Matters, 2000. Examines the debate over multiculturalism.

Crawford, James. *At War with Diversity: U.S. Language Policy in an Age of Anxiety.*

Dinnerstein, Leonard, Roger L. Nichols, and David M. Reimers. *Natives and Strangers: A Multicultural History of Americans.* New York: Oxford University Press, 1996. One of the most respected books on immigration history.

Websites

Education Northwest. Offers material designed to strengthen K-12 teaching and administration. http://educationnorthwest.org/

Multicultural Pavilion, EdChange. Provides the pros and cons of multicultural education as well as a wealth of material supporting multicultural education. http://www.edchange.org/multicultural/index.html

July 2

1969

Jenni Rivera, a banda and norteña singer, is born in Long Beach, California, to Mexican immigrant parents. She released her first album, *Chacalosa,* in 1996 on the Capitol/EMI label. Rivera has since been nominated for multiple Latin Grammys and has sold about 20 million albums worldwide.

Website

Jenni Rivera: Official Web Site. Provides a biography and discography, in English and Spanish, for the singer.

July 3

1832

María Amparo Ruíz de Burton, the first Hispanic author to publish a novel in English, is born in Baja California. She moved with her family to Alta California in 1847 and became a U.S. citizen with the end of the Mexican-American War a year later. In 1872, she published *Who Would Have Thought It?*. The book, set in the antebellum and Civil War North, criticizes northern racism and U.S. imperialism. Ruiz de Burton, a widow with children to support, likely took up the pen as it was one of the few avenues open to women who needed to earn a living.

Books

Goldman, Anne, and Amelia María de la Luz Montes, eds. *María Amparo Ruiz de Burton: Critical and Pedagogical Perspectives*. Lincoln: University of Nebraska Press, 2004. A guide to teaching about the writer and her works.

Ruiz de Burton, María Amparo. *Who Would Have Thought It?* Ed. Amelia María de la Luz Montes. New York: Penguin Books, 2009. The writer's most famous work holds up well over the decades.

Sánchez, Rosaura, and Beatrice Pita, eds. *Conflicts of Interest: The Letters of María Amparo Ruiz de Burton*. Houston, TX: Arte Público Press, 2001. Provides insight into the thoughts of an observant and witty woman.

Website

Gazing East: María Amparo Ruiz de Burton's Who Would Have Thought It. A short, engaging biographical sketch of the writer and her most famous work. http://www. aztlanreads.com/2011/08/24/gazing-east-maria-amparo-ruiz-de-burtons-who-would-have-thought-it/

1907

Folk healer Pedrito Jaramillo dies in Falfurrias, Texas. Celebrated as one of the great faith healers, Jaramillo was born in Guadalajara, Mexico. He moved to Texas in 1881. With doctors rare in southern Texas, he may have been the only medical provider that many poor Mexican Americans ever saw. His grave has become a shrine.

Books

Paredes, Américo. *A Texas-Mexican Cancionero: Folksongs of the Lower Border*. Urbana: University of Illinois Press, 1976. Includes a folk song about Jaramillo.

Torres, Eliseo. *Healing with Herbs and Rituals: A Mexican tradition*. Albuquerque: University of New Mexico Press, 2006. A history of green medicine that includes a discussion of Jaramillo.

Trotter, Robert T., and Juan Antonio Chavira. *Curanderismo: Mexican American Folk Healing*. Atlanta: University of Georgia Press, 1997. Argues that this type of folk healing is derived from Catholic traditions.

Website

Don Pedrito Jaramillo. Eliseo Torres supplies this short biography of Jaramillo. http://www.unm.edu/~cheo/DonPedrito.htm

July 4

1851

Josefa Loaiza (maybe Segovia) is executed for stabbing a drunken Anglo gold miner who knocked down her door in Downieville, California, and called her obscene names. There may have been more to the incident as Josefa was known to keep a knife by her bed for safety. A bloodthirsty Anglo mob gathered after the miner's death to accuse Josefa of murder. She was immediately put on trial and executed two hours after her conviction.

Accounts at the time did not provide Josefa's last name, typical of the way Mexican women who resisted Anglo abuse were treated—as being of questionable morality. An independent California scholar discovered Josefa's married name in 2003.

Books

Rojas, Maythee. *Women of Color and Feminism: Seal Studies.* New York: Seal Press, 2009. Includes a profile of Loaiza.

Torrez, Robert J. *Myth of the Hanging Tree: Stories of Crime and Punishment in Territorial New Mexico.* Albuquerque: University of New Mexico Press, 2008. Argues that violence was relatively rare in the Old West.

July 5

2002

Katy Jurado, a Mexican actress who enjoyed success both in her native land and in Hollywood, dies. Jurado, born María Cristina Jurado García into a wealthy family on January 16, 1924, in Guadalajara, Mexico, regularly appeared in Westerns in the 1940s and 1950s, including such classics as *High Noon* and *One-Eyed Jacks.* One of the few Mexican actors able to succeed in Hollywood, she was typically cast as a Native American and lamented that she rarely got to play her Mexican self. Jurado became the first Latin American actress to be nominated for an Academy Award, as Best Supporting Actress for her work in 1954's *Broken Lance.*

Book

Rodriguez, Clara E. *Heroes, Lovers, and Others: The Story of Latinos in Hollywood.* New York: Oxford University Press, 2008. Discusses the career of Jurado, who was cast as the sultry Mexican woman when she was not playing an Indian.

Website

Katy Jurado. The Internet Movie Database provides a biography and a list of acting credits for Jurado. http://www.imdb.com/name/nm0432827/

July 6

1907

The painter Frida Kahlo is born in Coyoacán, Mexico. Kahlo blended Hispanic and Native American themes in her art while living a life known for its drama. Although Kahlo spent her life in Mexico, she has become one of the most admired Hispanic women in the United States in the decades since her 1954 death. On June 21, 2001, Kahlo became the first Latina to be honored with a U.S. postage stamp.

Books

Grimberg, Salomon. *Frida Kahlo: Song of Herself.* New York: Merrell, 2008. A collection of interviews with Kahlo.

Monasterio, Pablo Ortiz, ed. *Frida Kahlo: Her Photos.* Mexico: Editorial RM, 2010. A collection of biographical essays about aspects of Kahlo's life combined with some of her photographs.

Websites

The Life and Times of Frida Kahlo. Introduces the 2005 PBS film of the same name by providing an introduction to Kahlo's life and art.

A Tribute to Frida Kahlo. Provides an essay about Kahlo's art as well as a chronology, a bibliography, and images of selected artworks. http://www.fridakahlo.com/

July 7

1990

Brazilian rock musician Cazuza, born Agenor Miranda Araújo Neto, dies of complications from AIDS. Born in 1958 in Rio de Janeiro, Cazuza spent a few years in San Francisco and would later cite Beat literature as one of his major influences. His lyrics were known for their poetics. A star by 1985, the bisexual Cazuza was infected with AIDS about the same time. His openness about the illness helped to change the perception of AIDS in Brazil.

Website

Cazuza. A Portuguese-language website devoted to the singer. http://www.cazuza.com.br/

Living Life in Art. Supplies a biography with photographs of the singer. http://www.cazuza.com.br/sec_biografia.php?language=en

July 8

1999

Puerto Rican nationalist José Solís Jordan is sentenced to 51 months in federal prison for planting pipe bombs outside an army recruiting station in Chicago. One bomb was defused while another caught fire instead of exploding and destroyed a Marine Corps car. A University of Puerto Rico professor who favors independence for the island, Solís was teaching at DePaul University in Chicago at the time of the bombing.

Books

Duany, Jorge. *The Puerto Rican Nation on the Move: Identities on the Island and in the United States.* Discusses cultural nationalism among Puerto Ricans.

Negrón-Muntaner, Frances, and Ramón Grosfoguel, eds. *Puerto Rican Jam: Rethinking Colonialism and Nationalism.* Minneapolis: University of Minnesota Press, 1997. Offers essays that examine the debate over the political status of Puerto Rico.

Website

Puerto Rican Nationalism and the Drift toward Statehood. The Council on Hemispheric Affairs provides this excellent summary of the history of nationalism on the island. http://www.coha.org/puerto-rican-nationalism-and-the-drift-towards-statehood/

July 9

1971

El Museo del Barrio opens in its new quarters in a 19th-century building in Spanish Harlem in New York City. The Puerto Rican museum began in 1969 but it had a vagabond existence, existing in schools and homes. With its new space, it accommodated an initial exhibit by 19 artists, including a painting by Puerto Rican New Yorker Lillian Almodóvar. By 2012, it had become New York's leading cultural institution for Latinos with a focus on the Caribbean and Latin America. The museum offers poetry readings, film showings, art exhibitions, and a book club focusing on Latino writers.

From "Barrio Museum: Hope Sí, Home No":

> The museum, whose name is intended not only to reflect El Barrio, the Puerto Rican ghetto in East Harlem but all mainland Puerto Rican communities, is very much in business . . . it is bravely girding itself to meet, in the words of its director, Ralph Ortiz, "the needs of Puerto Ricans for a cultural identity." "As a people, Puerto Ricans have been disenfranchised economically, politically, and culturally," he says. "As a group like the Young Lords was born to deal with the political and economic disfranchisement, so Museo is an attempt to begin to come to terms with our cultural disfranchisement. But I want it to be more than a stuffy museum—I want it to be a working thing that will give folk culture as much value as fine culture. . . . " Museo was born in June 1969, the brainchild of Martin W. Frey, superintendent of School District 4 . . . "There were a number of black cultural facilities but nothing for Puerto Ricans," says Mr. Frey . . . "We need El Museo," says Mr. Ortiz, "to help Puerto Ricans in New York develop a sense of pride in their community."

(*Source:* Glueck, Grace. "Barrio Museum: Hope Sí, Home No." *New York Times,* July 30, 1970, p. 32.)

Books

Cuevas, Celina Noqueros, ed. *Frescoes: 50 Puerto Rican Artists under 35*. Barcelona, Spain: Actar, 2011. Eight essays offer context on the artists, who were chosen by 10 internationally recognized curators.

Davila, Arlene. *Barrio Dreams: Puerto Ricans, Latinos, and the Neoliberal City*. Berkeley: University of California Press, 2004. An ethnographer, Davila focuses on conflicts over space and cultural representation in East Harlem.

Websites

El Museo del Barrio New York. The official website for the museum. http://www.el museo.org/

Puerto Rican Painter. Offers biographies, artist statements, and a gallery of works of all types of Puerto Rican visual artists. http://puertori canpainter.com

July 10

1951

Venezuelan shortstop Alfonso (Chico) Carrasquel of the Chicago White Sox becomes the first Latino player selected for major league baseball's All-Star Game. An excellent defensive player who could hit the baseball, Carrasquel had a 10-year career. He led the American League in fielding for three years and appeared in a total of four All-Star Games.

Books

Freedman, Lew H. *Latino Baseball Legends: An Encyclopedia*. Santa Barbara, CA: Greenwood, 2010. Contains biographical essays.

Wendel, Tim. *Far From Home: Latino Baseball Players in America*. Washington, D.C.: National Geographic Society, 2008. A long photographic essay about the challenges of playing so far from home.

Website

Chico Carrasquel Baseball Stats. Offers a short biography and career statistics. http://www. baseball-almanac.com/players/player.php?p= carrach01

1985

Coca-Cola brings back the old formulation of its classic beverage. Roberto C. Goizueta, a Cuban American, made one of the worst blunders in business history when, as CEO of Coca-Cola, he introduced New Coke on April 23, 1985. The new beverage had a changed formula that people in taste tests preferred over old Coke. However, Goizueta did not realize the attachment of the public to Coca-Cola. After a tremendous public outcry, he reintroduced the old formula as Classic Coke. The episode is now a standard study in business schools and is memorialized in the Coca-Cola Museum in Atlanta.

Books

Hays, Constance L. *The Real Thing: Truth and Power at the Coca-Cola Company*. New York: Random House, 2005. A biography of the iconic American company.

Kline, Daniel B., and Jason Tomaszewski. *Worst Ideas Ever: A Celebration of Embarrassment*. New York: Skyhorse, 2011. Includes the New Coke debacle.

Website

Coke Lore: The Real Story of New Coke. The Coca-Cola Company offers a background to its disastrous recipe change. http://www. thecoca-colacompany.com/heritage/cokelore_ newcoke.html

July 11

1928

Pedro Juan Soto, one of the major members of the "Generation of 1940," is born in Cataño, Puerto Rico. His 1954 short story, "Los inocentes," about a developmentally challenged 30-year-old Puerto Rican in New York City, won the prestigious Best

Prize from the Ateneo de Puerto Rico. Soto's 1956 collection of short stories, *Spiks,* is acclaimed as one of the best depictions of the Puerto Rican exodus to New York City.

Books

Simpson, Victor C. *Colonialism and Narrative in Puerto Rico: A Study of Characterization in the Novels of Pedro Juan Soto.* New York: P. Lang, 2004. One of the few English-language critical analyses of the novelist's work.

Soto, Pedro Juan. *Spiks.* Río Piedras, PR: Editorial Cultural, 1980. A Spanish-language edition of his well-known work.

July 12

1970

In the keynote speech at the Texas state convention of the La Raza Unida Party, María L. de Hernández said, "Our ancestors were here long before the Anglo-Americans. It is they who are the newcomers." She then called on Mexican Americans to recover their indigenous and mestizo (Spanish/Mexican/Indian/African) heritages. La Raza Unida was begun in Crystal City, Texas, in January 1970 to promote Chicano nationalism.

Book

Navarro, Armando. *La Raza Unida Party: A Chicano Challenge to the U.S. Two-Party Dictatorship.* Philadelphia: Temple University Press, 2000. A history of the Chicano nationalist group.

Website

La Raza Unida Party. Provides a short summary of the party along with its poster urging Latinos to vote and information on "liking" the group on Facebook and MySpace. http://www.pnlru.org/

July 13

1926

Microbiologist Eugene Cota-Robles is born in Nogales, Arizona, to parents who had been active in the Mexican Revolution and had twice fled its violence. Cota-Robles discovered the mechanism by which enzymes in bacterial cells convert nitrogen and thereby help plants grow. He died in 2012.

Website

Dr. Eugene Cota-Robles, Microbiologist. The SACNAS Biography Project supplies an autobiographical essay by the microbiologist for the use of educators. http://bio.sacnas.org/beta/pdf/cota_robles_eugene_H.pdf

1946

Comedian and actor Richard "Cheech" Marin is born in Los Angeles to Mexican American parents. Marin rose to fame in the 1970s as half of the comedy duo, Cheech & Chong, notorious for their references to marijuana. The expression, "cheeched," meaning under the influence of marijuana, has been derived from Marin's nickname. The two comedians went their separate ways in 1985 with Marin focusing on an acting career. He has enjoyed considerable success in movies such as *Born in East L.A.* and on television shows like *Nash Bridges.* Marin may be the foremost collector of Chicano art. Paintings from his collection have been exhibited throughout the United States and featured in his 2002 book, *Chicano Visions: American Painters on the Verge.*

Books

Marin, Cheech. *Chicano Visions: American Painters on the Verge.* Boston: Little, Brown and Co., 2002. Focuses on Marin's collection of paintings.

Sharon, Adam. *The Cheech and Chong Bible.* Harrison, NY: Brown Stone Books, 2002. A guide to the popular Stoner movies made by the comedy pair.

July 14

1959

Susana Martinez, the first Latina governor in the United States, is born in El Paso, Texas. Martinez, a Republican, became governor of New Mexico in 2011. Her paternal grandparents emigrated from Mexico and she is the great-granddaughter of Toribio Ortega, the man who fired the first shots of the Mexican Revolution. As governor, Martinez has reduced state spending, cut the state workforce, and increased local control of schools by opting out of No Child Left Behind. She differs from many Republicans on spending for the poor and sick largely as a result of having an older sister, Leticia, with cerebral palsy.

From "She Knows How to Beat Obama: Why the Country's First Latina Governor Might Be Mitt's Best Veep Pick":

> Martinez had always attended Democratic meetings and supported Democratic candidates. . . . A couple of GOP leaders invited her and her husband, ChuckFranco, to lunch. Martinez was wary. But soon she found that she agreed with them on issue after issue. She was pro–welfare reform (having witnessed the "cycle of dependency" as a prosecutor). She was pro–Second Amendment (having carried a gun since she started "securing bingos in parking lots" for the family's security firm as a teen). She was against higher taxes (having seen her father struggle to hire new employees). And she was anti-abortion (being Catholic). Afterward, Martinez turned

to Franco. "I'll be damned," she said. "We're Republicans. Now what?". . .

> Martinez insists that she won't leave New Mexico any time soon. "Partly it's my responsibility to my sister," she says. "But also, I have to deliver the results I promised, because as the first Hispanic female governor, I'm going to pave a path of some kind. I want it to be one that little Hispanic girls will want to follow."

> I nod, but I'm reminded of a story Martinez told me earlier. When she was 14, a group of teachers gathered some female students to talk about their hopes and dreams: where do you want to be in five years? Where do you want to be in 10 years? When they got to 20 years, Martinez confessed that she was considering a career in politics. "I didn't know at what level," she recalled. "I didn't have a whole lot of role models. So I finally said, 'I think I'd like to be a mayor.' And they said, 'Why stop there?'"

(*Source:* Andrew Romano, *Newsweek,* May 21, 2012, pp. 13–15.)

Books

Dolan, Julie Anne, et al. *Women and Politics: Paths to Power and Political Influence.* New York: Longman, 2010. Examines the strategies that women have used to gain political power.

Whitaker, Lois Duke. *Women in Politics: Outsiders or Insiders.* New York: Longman, 2010. This collection of readings examines gender differences in political attitudes and examines the effect of gender on voting patterns.

Websites

Office of the Governor Susana Martinez. Provides information on the governor's legislative actions and her official activities as well as biographical information. http://www.governor.state.nm.us/

On the Issues: Susana Martinez. Provides the governor's position on a long list of political topics. http://www.ontheissues.org/Susana_Martinez.htm

1973

Senator Joseph M. Montoya (D–New Mexico) asks the General Services Administration to make surplus silver available to Native American tribes whose jewelry projects are suffering because of a silver shortage caused by a price freeze. Montoya, who traces his roots back to 18th-century Spanish immigrants, entered the U.S. Senate in 1964. He worked especially hard on behalf of Native Americans and the elderly but also advocated for Hispanic culture and heritage. As the only Spanish-speaking U.S. senator, Montoya also frequently went on international missions as the president's representative. He left office in 1977.

Book

Gould, Lewis L. *The Most Exclusive Club: A History of the Modern United States Senate*. New York: Basic Books, 2005. Excellent general history of this American institution.

Website

Joseph Manuel Montoya. A profile of the senator from the Biographical Dictionary of the United States Congress. http://bioguide.congress.gov/scripts/biodisplay.pl?index=M000876

July 15

2007

Ricardo Favela, a poster artist and cofounder in 1972 of the Royal Chicano Air Force (RCAF), dies. The RCAF art collective, which began as the Rebel Chicano Art Front, furthered the goal of civil rights for Mexican Americans through art making and creative organizing. The members, who also initially included José Montoya, Esteban Villa, Rudy Cuellar, Juanishi V. Orozco, and Louie González, adopted the air force name after repeatedly getting confused with the Royal Canadian Air Force. When the Royal Chicanos made an appearance, they dressed in flight jackets, aviator glasses, vintage helmets and other military garb, traveling together by jeep. Chiefly active in the Sacramento Valley, the group used humor in a political way to further Chicano goals. They also supported community service projects such as Chicano bookstores and art programs for underprivileged children.

Ricardo Favela speaks about his activism:

> Everyone contributed to the myth of the RCAF. . . . It was very easy to do because it was all in fun. It is what we call in the barrio *cábula,* which means you play with humor and you use it as a means of resistance or defiance. As a means of doing something to your oppressor so that they don't know what you are doing to them. With that cultural awareness on our part, we had a field day.

(*Source:* Jackson, Carlos Francisco. *Chicana and Chicano Art: ProtestArte.* Tucson: University of Arizona Press, 2009, p. 148.)

Books

Cockcroft, Eva Sperling, and Holly Barnet-Sánchez, eds. *Signs from the Heart: California Chicano Murals.* Venice, CA: Social Public Art Center, 1990. Excellent study of Chicano murals, part of a distinguished history of Mexican murals.

Jackson, Carlos Francisco. *Chicana and Chicano Art: ProtestArte.* Tucson: University of Arizona Press, 2009. The only study of Chicano art that focuses on the use of art as a tool of protest.

Websites

Chicanoart.org. A website dedicated to exploring the Mesoamerican roots and current directions of Chicano art. http://www.chicanoart.org/

Royal Chicano Air Force. Official webpage of the organization. http://www.chilipie.com/rcaf/

July 16

1769

Fray Junípero Serra, one of the best known Catholic priests from the Franciscan order in the Spanish colonial era, establishes a mission in present-day San Diego while being accompanied by Spanish troops. It is Alta California's first mission and presidio. A museum about Serra stands on the site of the mission, San Diego de Alcalá, today. The Spanish mission is the first of 10 missions Serra will found throughout California. Father Serra is believed to have been responsible for converting nearly 7,000 Native Americans

Books

Beebe, Rose Marie, and Robert M. Senkewicz, eds. *"To Toil in that Vineyard of the Lord": Contempory Scholarship on Junipero Serra.* Berkeley, CA: Academy of American Franciscan History, 2010. A collection of essays on Serra's historical impact.

Sandos, James A. *Converting California: Indians and Franciscans in the Missions.* New Haven: Yale University Press, 2004. Discusses the complicated process of bringing religion into colonization.

Websites

Junípero Serra. PBS offers a short biography of the priest as part of its series on the American West. http://www.pbs.org/weta/thewest/people/s_z/serra.htm

The Junípero Serra Museum. An introduction to the museum, a San Diego landmark. http://www.sandiegohistory.org/serra_museum.html

1918

José de Diego, one of the leaders of the Puerto Rican independence movement, dies. Born in Aguadilla, Puerto Rico, de Diego studied law in Spain. He also wrote satirical articles and poems that were critical of the royal family, the nobility, and the church and wound up in jail four times as a result. Released in 1885, he sailed for Puerto Rico. He practiced law in Mayagüez and joined the rebellion against Spain. Upon the American takeover and passage of the Foraker Act, de Diego joined the new Puerto Rican cabinet in 1900. He thus became one of the men running Puerto Rico. De Diego, a fierce proponent of independence, objected to using English as the main language in schools and founded the Antillean Academy of the Language to preserve the purity of written and spoken Spanish. He died of filariasis, a disease spread by mosquitoes in the tropics.

Books

Duany, Jorge. *The Puerto Rican Nation on the Move: Identities on the Island and in the United States.* Discusses cultural nationalism among Puerto Ricans.

Negrón-Muntaner, Frances, and Ramón Grosfoguel, eds. *Puerto Rican Jam: Rethinking Colonialism and Nationalism.* Minneapolis: University of Minnesota Press, 1997. Offers essays that examine the debate over the political status of Puerto Rico.

July 17

1859

Luis Muñoz Rivera is born in Barranquitas, Puerto Rico. Educated and prosperous, Muñoz aimed to improve life for other Puerto Ricans. He joined the newly-formed Autonomist Party in 1887 to promote self-governance. He also pursued a career as a newspaper editor, publishing the first issue of *La Democracia* in 1890. He later published *El Diario*. Muñoz helped push the Jones Act, giving Puerto Rico its own legislature, through the U.S. Congress. He died in

Barranquitas in 1916, a few months before the Jones Act became law.

Books

Reynolds, Mack. *Puerto Rican Patriot: The Life of Luis Muñoz Rivera*. New York: Crowell-Collier Press, 1969. The only full-length biography of the man in English.

Sterling, Philip. *The Quiet Rebels, Four Puerto Rican Leaders: José Celso Barbosa, Luis Muñoz Rivera, José de Diego, Luiz Muñoz Marín*. Garden City, NY: Doubleday, 1968. Sets the Puerto Rican patriot in the context of his peers.

Website

Jones Act. The Foraker Act (Organic Act) of 1900. The Library of Congress, as part of its "The World of 1898: The Spanish-American War," provides this short summary of the legislation. http://www.loc.gov/rr/hispanic/1898/foraker.html, http://www.loc.gov/rr/hispanic/1898/jonesact.html

July 18

1995

José Feliciano, a Puerto Rican singer-guitarist, begins a week-long run at the famed Blue Note club in New York City. He was born blind to poor parents in Lares, Puerto Rico. Feliciano's family moved to New York when he was six. He taught himself to play concertina from records. Three years later, he performed at the Puerto Rican Theater. Soon he picked up the guitar, quit school at 17 to help support his family, and broke into the coffee-house circuit, playing for tips. Most people learned of Feliciano's existence in 1968 when he controversially improvised on the "Star-Spangled Banner" during the fifth game of the World Series. Over the next decades, Feliciano performed in 30 countries and earned 40 gold and platinum records despite having only two hit singles in the United States.

Website

José Feliciano. The musician's official web page contains his biography, photos, and video clips. http://josefeliciano.com/

July 19

1941

Singer Vicki Carr is born as Florencia Bisenta de Casillas Martínez Cardona in El Paso, Texas. Carr first tasted success with "He's a Rebel" in 1962. In subsequent years, she sang in most musical genres but found greatest popularity with Latin pop. She won a Grammy Award in 1986 for Best Mexican American Performance with her album *Simplemente Mujer*.

Website

Vicki Carr Official Fan Club Website. Provides information about Carr's biography, timeline, and appearances. http://www.vikkicarr.net/

July 20

1938

Baseball player Tony Pedro Oliva is born in Pinar del Río, Cuba. Oliva, the 1964 American League Rookie of the Year, spent his entire baseball career with the Minnesota Twins. He played in the right field and served as a designated hitter before retiring in 1976 and embarking on a coaching career. The Twins retired Oliva's uniform number—six—as a tribute to the eight-time All-Star.

Books

Freedman, Lew H. *Latino Baseball Legends: An Encyclopedia*. Santa Barbara, CA: Greenwood, 2010. Contains biographical essays.

Wendel, Tim. *Far From Home: Latino Baseball Players in America*. Washington, D.C.:

National Geographic Society, 2008. A long photographic essay about the challenges of playing so far from home.

Website

Tony Oliva Statistics and History. Supplies a profile of the famed baseball player. http://www.baseball-reference.com/players/o/olivato01.shtml

July 21

1981

Romeo Santos, the "king of bachata," is born in the Bronx as Anthony Santos. Half Dominican and half Puerto Rican, he specializes in a romantic form of Dominican music and has popularized it among a younger audience as the lead singer in the boy band Aventura. He grew up listening to bachata, developing a passion for the chords and melodies. He collaborated with Usher on the Latin hit, "Promise," a song that made No.1 on the charts in February 2012.

From "The Sensual Bachata King Is Making Them Swoon":

> You can't turn on Latin radio without hearing the Spanglish crooning of Romeo Santos, the "Bachata King" to his fans. The 30-year-old artist's smooth vocals tell stories of love and yearning in his modernized version of bachata, a sensual Dominican style that fuses R&B, hip-hop and merengue. Though Santos is well-known as the frontman of the boy band Aventura, he's attracting a broader audience solo. . . . Promise is the only song Santos has recorded in English and Spanish. He hopes to be a crossover success without making English versions of his other songs. In his collaborator's opinion, Santos has what it takes to win over English speakers. "If you

only understand English," it's harder to enjoy a Spanish-language song, Usher acknowledges, "but when you listen to (Romeo), you're not put off by it."

Sensual, sexy bachata appealed to Santos, even though "the youth was not really up on this type of music." In 1994, the church singer, his cousin and two friends changed all that by starting Aventura on the streets of the Bronx, N.Y., before being signed to BMG five years later. In 2010, Aventura had the top Latin tour, according to Billboard, including four sold-out Madison Square Garden performances. Solo, he has just sold out two February shows at the Garden, which will kick off his national tour. . . . Since the early days of Aventura, Santos has been accustomed to girlish screams. Perhaps that's why one male fan is particularly memorable. He showed the singer the "Romeo" tattoo on his wrist and told Santos he had been an inspiration. "I want to touch people's lives," Santos says. "(That fan) made me feel like, 'Mission accomplished.'"

(*Source:* Biano, Robert. "The Sensual Bachata King Is Making Them Swoon." *USA Today,* p. 10D.)

Books

Hernandez, Debra Pacini. *Bachata: A Social History of a Dominican Popular Music.* Philadelphia: Temple University Press, 1995. Bachata began in the 1960s as a music of the poor and dispossessed, gradually gaining legitimacy.

Pons, Frank Moya. *The Dominican Republic: A National History.* New York: Markus Weiner, 2010. Arguably the best history of the country by one of its most respected historians.

Websites

History of Bachata: The Guitar Music of the Dominican Republic. Provides a short history of the music as well as a listing of traditional singers, modern singers, and lyrics from some bachata songs. http://www.iasorecords.com/music/history-of-bachata-the-guitar-music-of-the-dominican-republic

Romeo Santos. The official webpage of the singer. http://www.romeosantosofficial.com/us/home

1956

Mónica Lozano, heir to a Spanish-language newspaper empire, is born in Los Angeles to Mexican American parents. In 1989, she became the first Latina to be named publisher of a Spanish-language daily newspaper in the United States when she took over the helm of *La Opinión,* which had been founded by her grandfather Ignacio E. Lozano Sr. in 1926. In 1992, she became the first Hispanic woman to receive the Legal Defense and Education Fund award from the National Organization for Women (NOW) for her political journalism.

Websites

La Opinión. The official website for the Los Angeles-based newspaper. http://www.laopinion.com/

Mónica Lozano. A *Forbes* magazine profile of the publisher. http://www.forbes.com/profile/monica-lozano/

July 22

1884

Puerto Rican essayist and novelist Miguel Meléndez Muñoz is born in Cayey. After completing primary school, Meléndez Muñoz worked in grocery stores before becoming the administrator of an agricultural concern. He finally became a landowning farmer but lost his farm because of a tobacco slump. Meléndez Muñoz had more contact with the people of the countryside than most Puerto Rican intellectuals and he is particularly known for his sympathetic portrayal of farmworkers. He began to publish in newspapers in 1904, focusing on spiritual values and social problems. Meléndez Muñoz died in 1966.

Books

Colberg, Juan Enrique. *Cuatro Autores Clásicos Contemporáneos de Puerto Rico: Concha Meléndez, Miguel Meléndez Muñoz, José A. Balseiro, Cesáreo Rosa-Nieves.* San Juan, PR: Editoral Cordillera, 1966. Sets the essayist in the context of his contemporary writers.

Meléndez Muñoz, Miguel. *Fuga de Ideas.* San Juan, PR: Imprenta Venezuela, 1942. A collection of his writings.

1932

Fashion designer Oscar de la Renta is born in Santo Domingo, Dominican Republic. He came to the United States in 1963 to work on Elizabeth Arden's custom-made clothing line for women. He opened his own fashion house in 1965 and it subsequently gained international renown. Firmly established as one of the stars of fashion, he headed the Council of Fashion Designers of America in the mid-1970s.

Books

Druesedow, Jean L. *Oscar de la Renta: American Elegance.* Kent, Ohio: Kent State University Museum, 2006. A short biography of the designer with photographs for a museum exhibit.

Mower, Sarah. *Oscar: The Style, Inspiration and Life of Oscar de la Renta.* New York: Assouline, 2002. A full-length biography of the designer.

July 23

1746

Bernardo de Gálvez y Madrid, Count of Gálvez, is born in Malaga, Spain. A military leader, he fought the Apaches in Northern Mexico as commandant in 1770. The Spanish government sent Gálvez to Louisiana in

1777 as colonel and interim governor. Unlike his predecessor, Gálvez gave arms to Native Americans but with a dark aim—hoping they would slaughter each other. He supported the American Revolution by shipping supplies to the revolutionaries and, after Spain declared war against Great Britain, defeated the British at Pensacola in 1781.

Books

LaFarelle, Lorenzo G. *Bernardo de Gálvez: Hero of the American Revolution.* Austin, TX: Eakin Press, 1992. The title is misleading as the Spanish backed the Revolution as a means of gaining power at British expense and not because of any interest in the revolutionary goals.

Raab, James W. *Spain, Britain, and the American Revolution in Florida, 1763–1783.* Jefferson, NC: McFarland , 2008. Covers the Battle of Pensacola.

1933

Famed Mariachi musician Natividad "Nati" Cano is born in Ahuisculco, Jalisco, a small rural town outside of Guadalajara, Mexico, to a family of musicians. After learning about mariachi music in an ethnomusicology class in college, he formed a mariachi band with several other students. He immigrated to Los Angeles in 1957 as a member of Mariachi Chapala. In 1961, he founded the Grammy Award–winning Los Camperos and is widely credited with advancing mariachi music in the United States. Cano was drawn to mariachi music by its sound—expressive, rhythmic, and with trumpets front and center. Mariachi music, played across Mexico, is symbolic of Mexican culture but it was only in the second half of the 20th century that the music emerged in the United States. Los Angeles, largely because of the work of Cano and other musicians, is the center of Mexican American mariachi.

Natividad "Nati" Cano speaking of the status of the mariachi:

[We mariachis] were ignored and insulted. The musicians of the symphony, the philharmonic, saw us as musicians and music that were worthless. . . . It hurt me greatly because I adored and I still adore mariachi music a great deal.

(*Source:* Sheehy, Daniel. *Mariachi Music in America: Experiencing Music, Expressing Culture.* New York: Oxford University Press, 2006, p. 9.)

Books

Fogelquist, Mark, and Patricia W. Harpole. *Los Mariachis! An Introduction to Mexican Mariachi Music.* Danbury, CT: World Music Press, 1989. Basic introduction to mariachi music.

Sheehy, Daniel. *Mariachi Music in America: Experiencing Music, Expressing Culture.* New York: Oxford University Press, 2006. Superb scholarly introduction to the musical form with a CD included.

Websites

Puro Mariachi. Provides an introduction to mariachi as well as the history of the musical form and many links to mariachi music. http://www.mariachi.org/

Smithsonian Folkways—Artist Spotlight—Nati Cano. Profiles Cano and his band, Mariachi Los Camperos. http://www.folkways.si.edu/explore_folkways/nati_cano.aspx

1928

Aerospace engineer Orlando A. Gutiérrez is born in Havana, Cuba. In the 1960s, Gutiérrez worked for the National Aeronautics and Space Administration (NASA) on heat transfer problems. He subsequently became one of the world's experts on sound problems related to the use of jet engines.

Book

Stone, James R., Vernon H. Gray, and Orlando A. Gutiérrez. *Forced-Flow Once-Through*

Boilers: NASA Research. Washington, D.C.: Scientific and Technical Information Office, National Aeronautics and Space Administration, 1975. Contains some of Gutiérrez's work.

July 24

1969

Singer, dancer, and actress Jennifer Lopez is born in New York City to Puerto Rican parents. Nominated for several Grammy awards, she received her big acting break when chosen to play the lead in *Selena,* a 1997 biography of the late Tejano pop singer. She continued to act in films in subsequent years but also branched out into fashion design and appearances on television shows.

Websites

Jennifer Lopez. The Internet Movie Database Site provides a short biography, photographs, and performing credits on film and television for the star. http://www.imdb.com/name/nm0000182/

Jennifer Lopez. The official website of the performer and designer. http://jenniferlopez.com/

July 25

1832

The fiesta of Saint James the Apostle begins in Loíza Aldea, Puerto Rico. The town, a former slave community, continues a religious tradition brought to the New World by the Spaniards. According to Iberian tradition, Saint James the Apostle is portrayed in his historic role as defender and protector of Spain. Originally a pilgrim who traveled to Spain preaching the Gospel, Saint James became a heavenly soldier on horseback, the slayer of Spain's greatest enemy in the Middle Ages, the Moors. The people of Loíza Aldea celebrate their patron saint as a divine military hero and as a friend of all Loiceños.

In the fiesta, four masked figures reenact Saint James's exploits.

Books

Kendrick, T.D. *St. James in Spain.* London: Methuen, 1960. The standard biography of the saint.

Zaragoza, Edward C. *St. James in the Streets: The Religious Processions of Loíza Aldea, Puerto Rico.* Lanham, MD: Scarecrow Press, 1995.

1853

Bandit Joaquín Murrieta is reportedly killed in California by State Rangers and his body decapitated. Murrieta was a Mexican miner who immigrated to California about 1850. Accounts of his life vary. He may have turned to crime to avenge the rape of his wife. Many Mexicans living in California saw him as a sort of Robin Hood who avenged the wrongs being committed against them by the newly arrived Anglo-Americans by stealing from the rich and giving to the poor. Both Mexican Americans and Anglo-Americans agree that Murrieta and his band were skilled cattle and horse thieves, prolific robbers, and ruthless killers.

From "Corrido de Joaquin Murrieta":

> I came from Hermosillo
> In search of gold and riches
> The good and simple Indian
> I defended fiercely;
> The sheriffs had put
> A good price on my head.

> I have been in every café
> Fighting with the Americans;
> "You then are the captain
> Who killed my brother;
> You caught him unarmed,
> Proud American."

> I was traveling in California
> In the year [Eighteen hundred and] fifty
> With my pistol in my belt

And the cartridge belt was full;
I'm that Mexican
Whose name is Joaquin Murrieta. . .

(*Source:* Silber, Irwin, and Earl Robinson, eds. *Songs of the Great American West.* New York: Macmillan, 1967, p. 137.)

Books

Burns, Walter Noble. *The Robin Hood of El Dorado: The Saga of Joaquin Murrieta, Famous Outlaw of California's Age of Gold.* Albuquerque: University of New Mexico Press, 2011. First published in 1932, this book romanticizes Murrieta.

Silber, Irwin, and Earl Robinson, eds. *Songs of the Great American West.* New York: Macmillan, 1967, p.137. A good introduction to the place of Murrieta in folklore.

Websites

Joaquín Murrieta: Literary Fiction or Historical Fact? This essay by William Mero provides an excellent biography of the folk hero along with illustrations. http://www.cocohistory. org/essays-murrieta.html

Zorro: The Legend through the Years. Murrieta is the basis for the Zorro legend. http:// zorrolegend.com/

1898

The United States invades Puerto Rico as part of the Spanish-American War. Famously described as a "splendid little war," the conflict lasted only a few months, ending in July 1898. Americans, already angered by Spanish conduct in Cuba, declared war when the battleship USS *Maine* sank in February in Havana Harbor, presumably from a Spanish bomb. As a Spanish colony, Puerto Rico came under attack and the U.S. Navy blockaded it. The U.S. Army soon followed. In the peace agreement, the United States obtained Puerto Rico along with several other former Spanish possessions. Puerto Rico, at the apex of the Greater and Lesser Antilles, became the cornerstone of the U.S. strategic military structure in the Caribbean. Imperialists saw the formation of a U.S. empire as part of America's Manifest Destiny. However, anti-imperialists argued that a democracy could not rule over territories and still remain democratic.

From Albert J. Beveridge's "The March of the Flag":

The Opposition tells us that we ought not to govern a people without their consent. I answer, the rule of liberty that all just government derives its authority from the consent of the governed, applies only to those who are capable of self-government. We govern the Indians without their consent, we govern our territories without their consent, we govern our children without their consent. . . . And, regardless of this formula of words made only for enlightened, self-governing people, do we owe no duty to the world? Shall we turn these people back to the reeking hands from which we have taken them? Shall we abandon them, with Germany, England, Japan, hungering for them? . . .

(*Source:* Fernlund, Kevin J. *Documents to Accompany America's History, Volume 2: Since 1865.* Boston: Bedford/St. Martin's, p. 155.)

Books

O'Toole, G.J.A. *The Spanish War: An American Epic, 1898.* New York: W. W. Norton, 1986. An exhaustive yet very readable study of the war that gave the United States an empire.

Paterson, Thomas G., and Stephen G. Rabe, eds. *Imperial Surge: The United States Abroad, The 1890s–Early 1900s.* Lexington, MA: D.C. Heath, 1992. Sets the American conquest of Puerto Rico in historical context.

Websites

Spanish American War. Contains a wealth of information about the war, including the Spanish and American units that served in Puerto Rico as well as firsthand accounts of the invasion of Puerto Rico. http://www.spanamwar.com/

The World of 1898: The Spanish American War. This Library of Congress site, part of the Hispanic Reading Room, offers resources and documents about the war with a section devoted to Puerto Rico. http://www.loc.gov/rr/hispanic/1898/

1946

Jesús T. Piñero, head of the Popular Democratic Party, is appointed by President Harry S. Truman to become the first native governor of Puerto Rico. Piñero succeeds Rexford Guy Tugwell. The appointment gives fuel to the argument that Puerto Ricans are capable of self-government.

Website

Jesús T. Piñero. The Library of Congress, as part of its Hispanic Americans in Congress series, provides a photograph and short biography of the political leader. http://www.loc.gov/rr/hispanic/congress/pinero.html

1957

Círculo de Puerto Rico forms in Washington, D.C., to facilitate the settlement of Puerto Rican immigrants and encourage Puerto Rican participation in the social and civic activities of the city. Still in existence in the 21st century, it continues to aim to unite the Puerto Rican community.

Website

Círculo de Puerto Rico. The official website for the organization. http://circulodepr.com/

July 26

1969

The Young Lords of New York receive a charter from the Young Lords Organization, a street gang that turned into a political organization in Chicago. The New York Lords began as a group of Puerto Rican college students who wanted to better understand the situation of less-privileged Puerto Ricans in East Harlem. At first the Young Lords engaged in community service, such as cleaning up garbage and providing social services. With branch offices throughout New York City and a headquarters in East Harlem, the group eventually explicitly rejected sexism and machismo. In 1970, women began to occupy leadership positions. The Young Lords also began recognizing and tackling heterosexism, a rare decision among organizations of this era. As the group became more political, it aggressively turned inward and began attacking members who were not pure enough. In 1976, the Young Lords went defunct.

From "Position on Women's Liberation" from the Central Committee of the Young Lords Party, May 1971:

Puerto Rican, Black, Asian, Native American and other Third World Women are becoming more aware of how we have been especially oppressed. Women have historically been at the bottom of the ladder; under capitalism, this has been intensified so that we are oppressed three ways. First, we are oppressed as Puerto Ricans, Blacks, Chicanas, Native Americans or Asians. Second we are oppressed as women. Third, we are oppressed by our own men who have been brainwashed by this capitalist system into believing a whole set of false, empty standards of what manhood is supposed to be—machismo. The Third World Woman thus becomes the most oppressed person in the world today. . . .

In the Young Lords Party we disagree with the analysis made by the right wing. We feel that the greatest conflict in the world today lies between capitalism (and capitalism's invasion of other countries, imperialism) and socialism, and people's drives to bring socialism to their countries, to their lives. We believe that the new society we are talking about will not come about by women separating themselves from men, but through sisters and brothers struggling with one another, working together, to deal with the negative things inside all of us. For sisters, this feeling that we are supposed to be passive towards brothers, you know, let them run things; with brothers, this feeling that we are supposed to be superior or better than sisters, you know, acting out those macho roles. The Party knows that Puerto Rican, Black, and other Third World Women make up over half of the Revolutionary Army; in the struggle for the liberation of Puerto Ricans, sisters and brothers must press for the equality of women—the women's struggle is part of the Revolution within the Revolution. . . .

The right wing in the women's movement says men are evil and can't be changed. Babies are not born oppressors. Therefore, our major enemy is capitalism rather than men.

But there ain't no doubt about it, there are a few rich men who control this planet. They are our enemies. Not because they are men, but because they are capitalists. Some of the rulers are women (and some of them are in the right-wing women's movement). They are also our enemy, not because they are women, but because they are capitalists. . . .

The progressive, must see that most of the right wing in the women's movement are white, and their racism is being reinforced heavily against Third World People, brothers and sisters.

We reject those women's groups that turn their backs on socialism because they say it was created by men, or they reject the groups like the YLP who have discipline because they say discipline and structure is a man's thing. We support those groups that are anti-capitalist, anti-imperialist, and see the fight for women's liberation as part of the fight for socialism.

All oppressed people together will make the Revolution within the Revolution and end all kinds of oppression.

(*Source:* Enck-Wanzer, Darrel, ed. *The Young Lords: A Reader.* New York: New York University Press, 2010, pp. 180–81.)

Books

Enck-Wanzer, Darrel, ed. *The Young Lords: A Reader.* New York: New York University Press, 2010. A short history of the Young Lords combined with primary documents from the organization.

Melendez, Miguel. *We Took the Streets: Fighting for Latino Rights with the Young Lords.* New York: St. Martin's, 2003.

1995

Classical guitarist Laurindo Almeida dies in California. Born in Brazil, he helped spread bossa-jazz, the fusion of bossa nova and American jazz, through the use of an Afro-Brazilian rhythm called the baiao in the 1950s. He died in 1995.

Books

Buenosaires, Oscar de. *Bossa Nova and Samba: History, People, Scores, Books, Lyrics, Recordings.* Albuquerque, NM: FOG Publications, 1999. A superb introduction to these musical forms.

McGowan, Chris, and Ricardo Pessanha. *The Brazilian Sound: Samba, Bossa Nova, and the Popular Music of Brazil.* Philadelphia: Temple University Press, 2009. A history of the music of Brazil.

Website

Laurindo Almeida. A webpage dedicated to the late guitarist that offers photographs, sheet

music, and links. http://www.laurindoal
meida.com/

July 27

1857

Physician José Celso Barbosa is born in Bayamón, Puerto Rico. Of African heritage,
Barbosa earned a medical degree from the
University of Michigan in 1880 and returned to Puerto Rico. A proponent of
self-governance but not independence, Barbosa became a leader of the Autonomist
Party. After the United States took control
of Puerto Rico, Barbosa became a member
of the Executive Council, the highest level
of power available to Puerto Ricans, serving
from 1900 to 1917. He supported a bill of
rights and backed a law giving scholarships to
Puerto Rican students enrolled in U.S. colleges. He also wrote a number of newspaper
articles that advocated giving opportunities
to black men like himself. Barbosa died on
September 21, 1921, of cancer.

Website

José Celso Barbosa. The Library of Congress,
through its "The World of 1898: Spanish-
American War" series, provides a short biography of Barbosa. http://www.loc.gov/rr/his
panic/1898/barbosa.html

2011

Saxophonist Gil Bernal dies in Los Angeles
at the age of 80. Raised in the Watts section
of South Central Los Angeles by his Mexican
mother, Bernal was strongly influenced by
the African American music that he heard in
his majority-black neighborhood. He began
playing jazz in 1948, right out of high school.
In the early 1950s he began playing R&B,
joining with the Robins (later known as the
Coasters) on "Riot in Cell Block No. 9" and
"Smokey Joe's Café." After pioneering as
one of the earliest Chicano R&B musicians,

Bernal spent the rest of his career playing
jazz.

Website

Gil Bernal (1931–2011). Find a Grave provides
a photograph, a short biography, and burial information for the musician. http://www.find
agrave.com/cgi-bin/fg.cgi?page=gr&GRid=
74025588

July 28

1982

Cain Velasquez, a Mexican American mar-
tial artist who won the Ultimate Fighting
Championship in the heavyweight division
in 2010, is born in Salinas, California. Velasquez, a former All-American wrestler for Arizona State University, holds a brown belt in
Guerilla Jiu Jitsu. A number of mixed mar-
tial arts organizations named Velasquez as the
fighter of the year in 2010.

Website

Cain Velasquez, Official UFC Fighter Profile.
The Ultimate Fighting Championship offers
videos of the fighter in action, an interview
with him, and his career statistics. http://
www.ufc.com/fighter/Cain-Velasquez

July 29

1983

Film director Luis Buñuel dies in Mexico
City. Born in Spain, Buñuel is regarded as
one of the greatest directors of the 20th century and a founder of the Surrealist movement. He began his career in silent films,
adding a surrealist dimension to his avant-
garde works. Buñuel came to Hollywood
in 1934 at the request of Metro-Goldwyn-
Mayer (MGM) after his anti-Catholic film,
L'Age d'Or, caused a major scandal in Europe. Buñuel soon insulted studio boss Irving

Thalberg and wound up back in Spain. Buñuel returned to the United States in the late 1930s to advise Hollywood on films being made about the Spanish Civil War. However, the war ended about the time that Buñuel landed in America. With the Fascists in power in Spain, Buñuel could not return because he had worked for the Republican government. He remained in the United States to work for the Museum of Modern Art and the Office of the Coordinator of Inter-American Affairs to produce antifascist propaganda for distribution in Latin America. Buñuel applied for U.S. citizenship in 1942 but did not get it because of his communist beliefs. He acquired Mexican citizenship in 1949.

Books

Baxter, John. *Buñuel*. London: Fourth Estate, 1995. A full biography of the father of surrealist realism.

Kyrou, Adonis. *Luis Buñuel*. New York: Simon and Schuster, 1963. A good popular biography of the director.

Websites

Luis Buñuel. The Internet Movie Database provides a biography, photographs, and a list of film credits. http://www.imdb.com/name/nm0000320/

Luis Buñuel. Provides a film list and biography of the director. http://www.luisbunuel.com/

July 30

2003

The last old-style Volkswagen Beetle rolls off an assembly line in Puebla, Mexico. The iconic vehicle, first built in the 1930s by its German manufacturer, became the model for compact cars built by General Motors and Ford, among others. The Beetle featured a four-speed manual transmission, two doors, a rear engine, and a trunk in the front of the car. By the end of its run, over 21 million Type 1 Beetles had been built.

Books

Hiott, Andrea. *Thinking Small: The Long, Strange Trip of the Volkswagen Beetle*. New York: Ballantine, 2012. A substantial history of the car that began in Adolf Hitler's Germany and wound up as an iconic vehicle made in Mexico.

McLeod, Kate. *Beetlemania: The Story of the Car that Captured the Hearts of Millions*. New York: Smithmark, 1999. A short book that shows the popularity of the Bug.

July 31

2012

A protest is held by Latinos outside a Back-to-School meeting of the Tucson (Arizona) United School District to protest the elimination of Mexican American studies. UNIDOS, Tucson Freedom Summer and allies asserted the right of Latinos to culture, history, identity, language, and education. They called on the school board and Superintendent John Pedicone to rethink their position on banning books relating to Mexican Americans.

Book

Biggers, Jeff. *State Out of the Union: Arizona and the Final Showdown over the American Dream*. New York: Nation, 2012. Discusses the battle over immigration and civil rights in Arizona.

August

August 1

1846

Mexican legislators consider declaring war against the United States. They cite American instigation of an insurrection by Texan colonists, the incorporation of Texas into the United States, and an invasion by an army onto the right bank of the Rio Bravo. After provoking the Mexicans, the United States declares war on Mexico. The war is one of the more controversial ones that the United States has fought because it appeared to many, including essayist Henry David Thoreau, to be a land grab. Thoreau wrote "Civil Disobedience" in 1849, with the Mexican War on his mind, to argue that citizens had the right to refuse to support an immoral government.

From Henry David Thoreau's "Civil Disobedience," 1849:

I heartily accept the motto—"That government is best which governs least" and I should like to see it acted up to more rapidly and systematically. Carried out, it finally amounts to this, which also I believe—"That government is best which governs not at all;" and when men are prepared for it, that will be the kind of government which they will have. Government is at best but an expedient; but most governments are usually, and all governments are sometimes, inexpedient. The objections which have been brought against a standing army, and they are many and weighty, and deserve to prevail, may also at last be brought against a stand govern. The stand army is only an arm of the standing government. The government itself, which is only the mode which the people have chosen to execute their will, is equally liable to be abused and perverted before the people can act through it. Witness the present Mexican war, the work of comparatively a few individuals using the standing government as their tool; for, in the outset, the people would not have consented to this measure.

This American government—what is it but a tradition, though a recent one, endeavoring to transmit itself unimpaired to posterity, but each instant losing some of its integrity? It has not the vitality and force of a single living man; for a single man can bend it to his will. It is a sort of wooden gun to the people themselves; and, if ever they should use it in earnest as a real one against each other, it will surely split. But it is not the less necessary for this; for the people must have some complicated machinery or other, and hear its din, to satisfy that idea of government which they have. Governments show thus how successfully men can be imposed upon, even impose on themselves, for their own advantage. It is excellent, we must all allow; yet this government never of itself furthered any enterprise, but by the alacrity with which it got out of its way. *It* does not keep the country free. *It* does not settle the West. It does not educate. The character inherent in the American people has done all that has been accomplished; and *it* would have done somewhat more, if the government had not sometimes got in its way. For government is an expedient by which men would fain succeed in letting one another alone; and, as has been said, when it is most expedient, the governed are most let alone by it. Trade and commerce, if they were not made of India rubber, would never manage to bounce over obstacles which legislators are continually putting in their way; and, if one were to judge these men wholly by the effects of their actions, and not partly by their intentions, they would deserve to be classed and punished with those mischievous persons who put obstructions on the railroads.

(*Source:* Thoreau, Henry David. "Civil Disobedience." 1849. http://sniggle.net/Experiment/index5.php?entry=rtcg#p18)

Books

Henderson, Timothy J. *A Glorious Defeat: Mexico and Its War with the United States.* New York: Hill and Wang, 2007. Discusses the causes of the war.

Martinez, Orlando. *The Great Landgrab: The Mexican-American War, 1846–1848.* London: Quartet Books, 1975. As the title indicates, the author views the war as an effort to expand the boundaries of the United States and spread slavery.

August 2

1942

The murder of José Díaz in the early hours starts the Sleepy Lagoon Case in Los Angeles. Díaz attended a party because he wanted to see his friends and neighbors one last time before reporting to the U.S. Army recruitment center for his induction. Just after Díaz began to walk home, a gang of young men and women crashed the party and assaulted the partygoers. Díaz also came under attack. Beaten with fists, struck over the head with a club, and stabbed twice in the stomach with an ice pick, he died later that morning without ever having regained consciousness. Díaz's death initially attracted very little media attention. However, the governor's office sent a memo to the law enforcement agencies of Los Angeles County ordering them to crack down on street violence and youth gangs. The Los Angeles Police Department launched a much publicized war on juvenile delinquency and turned the investigation into a major media event. In the weeks that followed the murder, the LAPD conducted mass dragnets throughout the neighborhoods of Los Angeles, targeting those areas heavily populated by Mexican Americans. More than 600 young men and women were taken into custody as a result. Believing that a group of friends from 38th Street constituted a criminal gang, the LAPD thought that the group had also attacked Díaz. Using beatings and other forms of coercion, the police forced confessions out of some of the youths. During the subsequent trial, the Citizens' Committee for the Defense of Mexican American Youth sought money to appeal the expected conviction of the young men. Better known as the Sleepy Lagoon Defense Committee (SLDC), this group changed the public perception of the case. On October 28, 1944, Judge Clement Nye dismissed the case and ordered the boys to be released and their records cleared.

From "News Release: Support for the Sleepy Lagoon Defendants . . . ":

When on January 13, 1943, the defendants in the Sleepy Lagoon case were convicted, Radio Berlin and Radio Tokio [Radio Berlin and Tokyo provided anti-American propaganda to hurt the American war effort] short-waved the news of the conviction to Latin America and implied that nowhere in the USA was there to be found a friend of the Mexican or Mexican American . . .

From the Transport Workers Union in New Orleans, from a college professor, from a group of men in Naval training, from soldiers convalescing in a midwestern hospital, from a group of Negro youth, from Japanese-Americans at Manzanar—come signatures to the petition which reads in part:

"We, the undersigned, interested in the maintenance of our democratic institutions and the eradication of race prejudice hereby petition you, the Attorney General . . . personally to take charge of and thoroughly investigate this case in order that your office shall not be used as an instrumentality for the support of convictions based upon race prejudice."

(*Source:* Sleepy Lagoon Defense Committee Records, 1944, Department of Special Collections, UCLA Library, Online Archive of California, http://www.oac.cdlib.org/view?docId=hb096nb3tm&brand=oac4&chunk.id=meta)

Books

Escobar, Edward J. *Race, Police, and the Making of a Political Identity: Mexican Americans and the Los Angeles Police Department, 1900–1945*. Berkeley: University of California Press, 1999. Focuses on the problematic relationship between Mexican Americans and the police.

Págan, Eduardo Obregón. *Murder at the Sleepy Lagoon: Zoot Suits, Race, and Riot in Wartime L.A.* Chapel Hill: University of North Carolina Press, 2003. A balanced, well-written history of the case.

Websites

Finding Aid for the Sleepy Lagoon Defense Committee Records, Online Archive of California. Many of the publications and other written materials relating to the defense of the young Mexican Americans are available online. http://www.oac.cdlib.org/findaid/ark:/13030/tf3b69n8z8

People and Events: The Sleepy Lagoon Murder. Excellent history of the case by PBS, on a site devoted to the Zoot Suit Riots. http://www.pbs.org/wgbh/amex/zoot/eng_peopleevents/e_murder.html

1935

The Federal Theatre Project, part of President Franklin D. Roosevelt's New Deal, is announced. The Tampa Federal Theatre Project in Florida was the only Latino company in the program. Under the direction of Manuel Aparicio, it performed some of the stock *zarzuelas* and melodramas from the Hispanic repertoire as well as works translated into Spanish. The "Cuban Company," as it was known in the Federal Theatre Project, also opened Sinclair Lewis's *It Can Happen Here* at the same time that Federal Theatre companies around the country did. The Federal Theatre program ended in 1939.

Book

Bentley, Joanne. *Hallie Flanagan: A Life in the American Theatre*. New York: Alfred A. Knopf, 1988. Flanagan headed the Federal Theatre Project.

Website

The New Deal Stage: Selections from the Federal Theater Project. This online presentation includes over 13,000 images of items selected from the Federal Theatre Project Collection at the Library of Congress. http://memory.loc.gov/ammem/fedtp/fthome.html

August 3

1965

Author María Cristina Mena dies. Born in Mexico City in 1893, Mena emigrated to New York City at the age of 14. She is best known for the English language stories that she published in magazines although Mena also penned five children's books. Mena's short stories were written for early-20th-century editors who expected an appealing version of life in Mexico. Accordingly, critics have often condemned her as a "local color" writer who tended to create obsequious Mexican characters who fit the expectations of American readers. More recent readings of Mena's work by Chicana scholars have credited her with artfully responding to contemporary political and social issues particularly with respect to the changing roles of women. In "The Birth of the God of War," originally published in *Century* in May 1914, Mena offers Coatlicue as an alternative to feminine role models such as the Virgin of Guadalupe.

From "The Birth of the God of War":

Such was the conception of the Mexican god of war, and it brought strife into the home of Coatlicue. All ignorant of the miracle that had been wrought, the children of Camatzin presumed to be scandalized at the ineffable happiness that had descended upon their mother, and to conspire against her life. Her own daughter was the malignant ringleader, taunting her two brothers with cowardice, and invoking vengeance in the name of the dead father's honor . . .

In sharp whispers, with narrowed eyes, my grandmother would go on to describe how the two conspirators followed their mother furtively into the gloom of the temple. Armed with a knife, the son fell upon her as she prayed. A terrible cry filled the space.

"Son of mine, stop thy hand! Wait! Give heed!"

"Adulteress!"

She feared not death, but wished to pray for the assassin, whose fate, she knew, would be more dreadful than his crime. But now sounded a new voice, a stentorian voice which made the temple quake: Mother, fear not! I will save thee!

The hills repeat the echo of those words. All space shines with a beautiful light, which bathes directly the face of Coatlicue. The assassin remains immobile, and the sister mute with terror, as from the bosom of Coatlicue springs forth a being gigantic, strange. His head is covered with the plumage of hummingbirds; in his right hand he carries the destructive *macana,* on his left arm the shining shield. Irate the face, fierce the frown. With one blow of the *macana* he strikes his brother lifeless, and with another his sister, the instigator of the crime. Thus was born the potent Huitzilopochtli, protector-genius of the Aztecs.

And Coatlicue, the gentle Coatlicue of my childish love? Throned in clouds of miraculously beautiful coloring, she was forthwith transported to heaven. Once I voiced the infantile view that the fate of Coatlicue was much more charming than that of the Virgin Mary, who had remained on this sad earth as the wife of a carpenter; but *mamagrande* was so distressed, and signed my forehead and her own so often, and made me repeat so many credos, and disquieted me so with a vision of a feathered Apache coming to carry me off to the mountains, that I was brought to a speedy realization of my sin, and never repeated it.

(*Source:* Amy Doherty, ed. *The Collected Stories of María Cristina Mena.* Houston: Arte Público Press, 1997, pp. 68–69.)

Books

Chambers, María Cristina Mena. *The Boy Heroes of Chapultepec: A Story of the Mexican War.* New York: Winston, 1953. Possibly the most popular of Mena's children's stories.

Doherty, Amy, ed. *The Collected Stories of María Cristina Mena.* Houston: Arte Público Press, 1997. Reprints all of Mena's short stories and provides a good introduction to the writer.

Websites

Bibliography on María Cristina Mena. Donna M. Campbell, a Washington State University literature professor, provides a listing of all of Mena's works. http://public.wsu.edu/~campbelld/amlit/menabib.htm

María Cristina Mena Biography. This Book Rags site contains a 10-page biography of the author. http://www.bookrags.com/biography/maria-cristina-mena-dlb2/

1905

Actress Dolores del Río is born in Durango, Mexico. Working during the era of silent films and in the Golden Age of Hollywood, del Río became the first Latin American international movie star, an extraordinary accomplishment for a Latina of her era. She made her first film *Joanna* in Hollywood in 1925. She has a star on the Hollywood Walk of Fame for her contributions to movies.

Books

Hershfield, Joanne. *The Invention of Dolores del Rio*. Minneapolis: University of Minnesota Press, 2000. Discusses how del Rio transformed herself into a star acceptable to white audiences.

Rodriguez, Clara E. *Heroes, Lovers, and Others: The Story of Latinos in Hollywood*. New York: Oxford University Press, 2008. Discusses the career of del Río.

Website

Dolores del Rio. The Internet Movie Database provides a biography of the actress along with her film credits and photographs. http://www.imdb.com/name/nm0003123/

1933

Mexicans provided much of the labor for the low-paying cigar-making industry in San Antonio, Texas. On this date, women workers walked out of the Finck Cigar Company to protest unfair wages, poor working conditions, and ill treatment. They organized a union and engaged in a struggle with the company for two years.

Books

Cooper, Patricia A. *Once a Cigar Maker: Men, Women, and Work Culture in American Cigar Factories, 1900–1919*. Urbana: University of Illinois Press, 1992. Covers the working conditions that prompted the Mexicans to strike.

Ingalls, Robert P., and Louis A. Pérez Jr. *Tampa Cigar Workers: A Pictorial History*. Gainesville: University Press of Florida, 2003. The photographs would also apply to the labor performed by the Mexican workers in San Antonio.

August 4

1942

The United States and Mexico sign a *bracero* (laborer) agreement that would lead to the employment of tens of thousands of Mexicans in the United States in the controversial Bracero Program. The advent of World War II created a labor shortage in the United States while Mexico needed to find jobs for its people. With the agreement, *braceros*, desperate for work, ultimately took jobs at wages that American workers would not accept. Discriminatory treatment and acts of violence against Mexicans were common. Growers often ignored the protections guaranteed in the treaty. In response, Mexico prohibited *braceros* from working in Texas from 1943 to 1947 although abuses had also occurred in other states. The Bracero Program continued in various forms until 1964, supplying a considerable number of poorly-paid migrant agricultural workers to American farms and also providing them with few protections against abusive treatment.

From U.S. Department of State. *Treaties and Other International Agreements of the United States of America 1776–1949*, vol. 9:

In order to effect a satisfactory arrangement whereby Mexican agricultural labor may be made available for use in the United States and at the same time provide means whereby this labor will be adequately protected while out of Mexico, the following general provisions are suggested:

1) It is understood that Mexicans contracting to work in the United States shall not be engaged in any military service.

2) Mexicans entering the United States as result of this understanding shall not suffer discriminatory acts of any kind in accordance with the Executive Order No. 8802 issued at the White House June 25, 1941.

3) Mexicans entering the United States under this understanding shall enjoy the guarantees of transportation, living expenses, and repatriation established in Article 29 of the Mexican Labor Law.

4) Mexicans entering the United States under this understanding shall not be employed to displace other workers, or the purpose of reducing rates of pay previously established.

(*Source:* U.S. Department of State. *Treaties and Other International Agreements of the United States of America 1776–1949,* vol. 9. Compiled by Charles I. Bevans. Washington, D.C.: GPO, 1972, pp. 1069–75.)

Books

Calavita, Kitty. *Inside the State: The Bracero Program, Immigration, and the I.N.S.* New York: Routledge, 1992. Arguably the most accessible and best source on the *braceros* and the immigration concerns surrounding the program.

Daniel, Cletus E. *Bitter Harvest: A History of Californian Farmworkers, 1879–1994.* Ithaca: Cornell University Press, 1981. A good general history of farmworkers that also includes *braceros*.

Websites

Bracero History Archive. Images, personal accounts and other resources make this one of the best educational websites on Latino history. http://braceroarchive.org

The Bracero Program—The Farmworkers Website. Features a solid history of the *braceros* with excerpts of primary sources. http://www.farmworkers.org/bracerop.html

August 5

2002

Richard H. Carmona is sworn in as the 17th Surgeon General of the United States, the second Latino to hold the post. Born in Spanish Harlem in New York City on November 22, 1949, Carmona came from a poor Puerto Rican family. He joined the Army in 1966 and earned his high school equivalency degree through an Army program. After winning a Bronze Star and two Purple Hearts in Vietnam, Carmona earned a MD in 1979 from the University of California at San Francisco. He specializes in trauma care.

Books

Buckingham, Jane, and Tiffany Ward. *What's Next: The Experts' Guide: Predictions from 50 of America's Most Compelling People.* New York: Harper, 2008. Carmona makes predictions about the future of medicine.

Parascandola, John. *Sex, Sin, and Science: A History of Syphilis in America.* Westport, CT: Praeger, 2008. Carmona provides the foreword to the book.

August 6

2009

The U.S. Senate confirms the nomination of Sonia Sotomayor to the U.S. Supreme Court. Nominated on May 26 by President Barack Obama, Sotomayor is sworn in on August 8 as the first Hispanic and the third woman to serve on the Court. Born on June 25, 1954, in New York City to parents from Puerto Rico, Sotomayor graduated summa cum laude from Princeton University and edited the *Yale Law Journal* while attending Yale Law School. She worked as a prosecutor in the Manhattan District Attorney's office and in private practice before becoming a federal judge in 1992. She replaced retiring justice David Souter.

Quote from Sonia Sotomayor:

> I've noticed that if you're a woman you have to work twice as hard, be twice as good. The doors do eventually open, but sometimes it's just so daunting to get them to open. I've had to face that fact that I could probably never be president—not because I'm Puerto Rican, but because I'm a woman. I've come to seriously doubt whether I'll ever see a woman president in my lifetime, and that's very, very disappointing.

(*Source:* Felix, Antonia. *Sonia Sotomayor: The True American Dream.* New York: Penguin, 2010, p. 182.)

Books

Felix, Antonia. *Sonia Sotomayor: The True American Dream.* New York: Penguin, 2010. Popular biography on Sotomayor and one of the few aimed at the adult market.
Greene, Meg. *Sonia Sotomayor: A Biography.* Westport, CT: Greenwood Press, 2012. Solid overview of Sotomayor's life.

Websites

Background on Judge Sonia Sotomayor. This White House press release, an inspiring biography, came out when President Obama nominated Sotomayor to the Supreme Court. http://www.whitehouse.gov/the_press_office/Background-on-Judge-Sonia-Sotomayor
Supreme Court of the United States. This is the official website, with a listing of decisions and general information about the Court. http://www.supremecourt.gov/

1980

Cuban-born Roberto C. Goizueta is named as the next chairman and chief executive officer of Coca-Cola. He is the first Latino to lead one of the largest corporations in the world. A Yale-educated chemical engineer, Goizueta began to work for Coca-Cola in 1954 in his native Havana. He fled Cuba in 1960 with his wife, $40, and 100 shares of Coca-Cola. As head of the company, he introduced Diet Coke, one of the best-selling sugar-free products in the United States. He was also responsible for one of the worst decisions in business history—briefly changing the formula of 99-year-old Coca-Cola to the sweeter New Coke in 1985. He died in 1997.

Books

Greising, David. *I'd Like the World to Buy a Coke: The Life and Leadership of Roberto Goizueta.* New York: John Wiley and Sons, 1998. The only biography of one of the most significant leaders in Coca-Cola history.
Krass, Peter, ed. *The Book of Leadership Wisdom: Classic Writings by Legendary Business Leaders.* New York: Wiley, 1998. Includes an essay by Goizueta on the real essence of business.
Pendergrast, Mark. *For God, Country, and Coca-Cola: The Definitive History of the Great American Soft Drink and the Company that Makes It.* New York: Basic Books, 2000. A substantial history of a company strongly associated with the United States.

Website

Roberto C. Goizueta. The *New Georgia Encyclopedia* supplies this biography of the business leader with a guide to further reading. http://www.georgiaencyclopedia.org/nge/Article.jsp?id=h-1916

August 7

1958

Marathon runner Alberto Salazar is born in Havana, Cuba. He moved with his family to the United States as a child and ultimately settled in Wayland, Massachusetts. Salazar is best known for his running exploits in the 1980s. He made the 1980 track and field team that did not compete in the Moscow Olympics as well as the 1984 Olympic team. From 1980 to 1982, Salazar won three consecutive New York City Marathons. He won the Boston Marathon in 1982. In retirement, Salazar works as a coach for Nike in Oregon.

From Alberto Salazar and John Brant, *14 Minutes*:

I was clinically dead for 14 minutes . . .

In October 1981, I set a world record (or WR, in runners' parlance) at the New York City Marathon, covering the 26.2-mile distance in 2 hours, 8 minutes, and 13 seconds. That performance sealed my standing as the greatest distance runner of my era. I lived a life of extreme athletic excess, as far gone, in my way, as a drug addict or alcoholic. I was famous—or many would say, notorious—for my obsession to outwork any rival and for my absolute refusal to lose. I would later pay a harrowing, decade-long penance for that excess, but at the time, in the late '70s and early '80s, the height of the first running boom, my obsessiveness put me on top of the world. My photo appeared on the cover of national magazines, I shook hands with President Ronald Reagan at a ceremony at the White House, and Nike named an apparel line after me.

Now, 25 years later, here I was racking up a second, albeit unofficial, WR: 14 minutes . . .

We were headed for the central green to do the plyometric drills, and we were talking about where to go for lunch. I was 48 years old, on top of my profession, and blessed with a happy,

healthy family. I was cutting across the gleaming campus of a mighty multinational corporation whose resources lay at my disposal. Nike had even named one of the office buildings after me; you could see the roof of the Alberto Salazar Building from where we were walking. I was with people I cared about, doing the work that I loved. Everything seemed about perfect, and yet I was moments away from dying.

The perfection of that morning was marred by a barely conscious worry about my health. During the previous week in Indianapolis, I had suffered transient stabs of pain in my back and neck and a general feeling of exhaustion. But I was too busy to worry much about these symptoms. I attributed the pain to sleeping in an awkward position on the long flight from Oregon and the weariness to the accumulated stress of preparing my athletes for this meet. Although I'd retired from competition 13 years earlier, I kept myself in excellent condition. I ran 5 miles a day at 7-minute-a-mile pace, lifted weights, never smoked, drank alcohol moderately, followed a healthy diet, and controlled hereditary high blood pressure and elevated cholesterol with medication. Like most fit people my age, I felt invincible.

Still, when I returned home to Portland after the nationals, I reported the symptoms to my family physician. She gave me a thorough exam and couldn't find anything wrong. She then referred me to a cardiologist, who ordered a treadmill stress test, which I was scheduled to undergo the following week. So, healthwise, I had all my bases covered. According to statistics cited by the American Heart Association, 50 percent of fatal heart attacks in men, and 64 percent in women, occur without warning. I had plenty of warning.

(*Source:* Salazar, Alberto, and John Brant. *14 Minutes: A Running Legend's Life and Death and Life.* New York: Rodale, 2012. http://hereandnow.wbur.org/2012/04/16/alberto-salazar-minutes)

Books

Brant, John. *Duel in the Sun: The Story of Alberto Salazar, Dick Beardsley, and America's Greatest Marathon.* New York: Rodale, 2007. Tells the story of Salazar's 1982 Boston Marathon victory over Beardsley.

Connelly, Michael. *26 Miles to Boston: The Boston Marathon Experience from Hopkinton to Copley Square.* Guilford, CT: Lyons Press, 2003. Gives the experience of running a marathon as well as the history of the Boston Marathon.

Websites

Alberto Salazar, National Distance Running Hall of Fame. Provides a brief biography of Salazar. http://www.distancerunning.com/inductees/2000/salazar.html

"Five Lessons Learned from Alberto Salazar." This essay by Mario Fraioli in *The Competitor* magazine focuses on Salazar's advice to runners competing in the 2012 Olympic Games. http://running.competitor.com/2012/08/training/five-lessons-learned-from-alberto-salazar_57069

1943

Victor E. Marquez, inventor of a compound that inhibits allergic reactions, is born in Caracas, Venezuela. He has chiefly been employed at the National Cancer Institute of the National Institutes of Health.

Book

Martin, John C., ed. *Nucleotide Analogues as Antiviral Agents.* Washington, D.C.: American Chemical Society, 1989. Includes an essay by Marquez on nucleotide dimers as anti human immunodeficiency virus agents.

1944

Miguel Antonio Otero II dies, after serving as governor of New Mexico Territory from 1897 to 1906. Otero, a member of a prominent New Mexico family, published a three-volume autobiography, *My Life on the Frontier,* in 1935. He was acquainted with several of the iconic figures of the Old West and became one of the first to write positively of Billy the Kid, whom he met while the Kid was a prisoner.

Books

Otero, Miguel Antonio. *Otero: An Autobiographical Trilogy.* New York: Arno Press, 1974. This is the three-volume autobiography that Otero originally published.

Otero, Miguel Antonio. *The Real Billy the Kid: With New Light on the Lincoln County War.* Houston, TX: Arte Público Press, 1998. Otero's recollections of the Old West.

August 8

1947

Chicano poet Alurista is born as Alberto B. Urista in Mexico City. His first book, *Floricanto en Aztlán* (Flower and Song in Aztlán) promoted the concept of Aztlán, the ancient homeland of the Aztecs, as a unifying metaphor for Mexican Americans.

Books

Alurista. *Floricanto en Aztlán: Poetry.* Los Angeles: UCLA Chicano Studies Research Center Press, 2011. A collection of works that focus on the Aztecs.

González, Rigoberto, ed. *Xicano Duende: A Select Anthology: Poetry by Alurista.* Tempe, AZ: Bilingual Press/Editorial Bilingüe, 2011. A selection of the poet's works.

1971

During a three-day fiesta held in Denver to raise funds to build a swimming pool, an Anglo youth trades angry words with a Mexican American girl. The young man subsequently gets into a fight and is stabbed. A crowd forms while Brown Berets call for an ambulance and try to break up the crowd to prevent further problems. The police arrive and begin shoving the largely Mexican American crowd. A riot breaks out and 90 people are arrested. The Denver police chief alleges that the Brown Berets planned the riot. Mexican Americans blame the police and no longer want them in their community.

Books

Acuña, Rodolfo F. *Occupied America: A History of Chicanos.* New York: Pearson Longman, 2007. The standard history of Chicanos.

Haney-López, Ian. *Racism on Trial: The Chicano Fight for Justice.* Cambridge, MA: Belknap Press of Harvard University Press, 2003. Includes a chapter on the Brown Berets.

1992

Boxer Oscar de la Hoya wins a gold medal in the 1992 Olympics. A native of East Los Angeles, California, de la Hoya came from a family that enjoyed boxing success in Mexico. He would pick up the nickname "Golden Boy" for his good looks, charm, and professional success both in and out of the ring. He won titles at several levels but fought his best known bouts as a welterweight.

Books

Kawakami, Tim. *Golden Boy: The Fame, Money, and Mystery of Oscar de la Hoya.* Kansas City, MO: Andrews McMeel, 2000. A biography of the boxer for an adult audience.

Quinn, Rob. *Oscar de la Hoya.* Broomall, PA: Chelsea House, 2001. A short biography of the boxer for a juvenile audience.

Website

Oscar de la Hoya. The A&E television network provides this profile of the boxer. http://www.biography.com/people/oscar-de-la-hoya-9542428

August 9

2012

The U.S. women's water polo team wins its first gold medal at the London Olympics with Latina players including Brenda Villa. The Americans defeated the Spanish team by a score of 8 to 5. At the 2008 Beijing Games, the United States lost to the Netherlands in the final. A sport that developed in the 19th century, men's water polo has been an Olympic feature since the 1900 Olympics in Paris. Women's water polo was introduced at the Sydney Games in 2000. It remains one of the less popular sports probably because of the difficulties involved in getting access to a large pool.

From "Everybody into the Pool":

> The most improbable American water polo pipeline began here one generation and four trash cans ago when a coach wanted to give her youth swim team a rest. To break the monotony of training, the coach, Sandy Nitta, plopped four trash cans into the pool to serve as makeshift water polo goals.
>
> Fast forward 30 years. Commerce, a working-class industrial city of 12,500 southeast of Los Angeles, has developed one of the most prolific and sophisticated youth water polo programs in the United States. The city employs two full-time and three part-time youth water polo coaches and spends more than $250,000 a year on its programs. "It's not a rich community, but what the city has done for water polo there has opened so many doors," said Nitta, a former Olympic swimmer who now

coaches youth water polo teams in Las Vegas.

Villa and Cardenas are first-generation Mexican-Americans. Cardenas's parents and Villa's mother have roots in the Mexican town of Tecalitlan. In Commerce, their mothers worked as cleaners, and Villa and Cardenas stumbled into water polo by tagging along with their older brothers. Before long, their weekends were crammed with as many as 10 games. The pool became their social hub. "It was the thing to do," Villa said. Villa competed with and against boys at Bell Gardens High School, enduring plenty of snide comments. But the competition only improved her game, helping her develop the smarts and instincts that have contributed to her becoming one of the best players in the world despite being just 5 feet 4 inches. "She's small," United States Coach Guy Baker said. "But she makes up for it with intelligence and being deceptively strong for her size." Villa, who played at Stanford, is a celebrity in Commerce, and is called upon to appear for Cinco de Mayo, Fourth of July and Mexican independence day celebrations. Villa is so revered that when Cardenas spoke recently to a fifth-grade class in Commerce, the first question was, "Do you know Brenda Villa?" When Cardenas laughed and answered yes, the students, in unison, said, "Wow!"

Like Villa, Cardenas spent her childhood playing with boys and being toughened up by her older brothers. One brother, Ivan, would kneel on her arms to execute something he called the Happy Slapper, which involved him slapping her face until she screamed for help. Cardenas became so tough that after the webbing between her toes was ripped open during a youth game, she insisted on being taped up so she could continue playing. . . . Water polo may be a fixture in Commerce, but it is not nearly as popular in the rest of the United States. None of the members of the women's national team have the individual sponsorships that are common in swimming, soccer and gymnastics . . . "Obviously, we're not in this sport to make money," said Villa, who has played professionally in Sicily. "I'm grateful. It paid for school and I've traveled the world playing this sport. I think if more people knew how cool and special and unique the sport is, more people would play . . . "

(*Source:* Thamel, Pete. "Everybody into the Pool." *New York Times,* June 18, 2008, p. D2.)

Books

Egan, Tracie. *Water Polo: Rules, Tips, Strategy, and Safety.* New York: Rosen, 2011. Aimed at young athletes, this is a general introduction to the sport.

Mullen, P. H. *Gold in the Water: The True Story of Ordinary Men and Their Extraordinary Dream of Olympic Glory.* New York: St. Martin's Griffin, 2003. Details the struggles involved for a group of Californians in just getting to the 2000 Sydney Olympic Games.

Websites

Brenda Villa. This U.S. Water Polo site profiles the most decorated athlete in women's water polo. http://www.usawaterpolo.org/NationalTeams/PlayerBio.aspx?ID=33

Women's Water Polo—United States. This official London Olympics site includes a team roster and match results. http://www.london2012.com/water-polo/event/women/teams/team=united-states-wpw400usa01/

1988

President Ronald Reagan nominates Lauro F. Cavazos to become secretary of education, the first Latino to hold this or any other cabinet post. Cavazos, a physiologist, served as the first Latino president of Texas Tech University at the time of his nomination. He spent two years in office, also serving under President George H. W. Bush until 1990.

Books

Cavazos, Lauro. *A Kineño Remembers: From the King Ranch to the White House*. College Station: Texas A&M University Press, 2006. The autobiography of the education leader.

Wallison, Peter J. *Ronald Reagan: The Power of Conviction and the Success of His Presidency*. Boulder, CO: Westview Press, 2003. Covers the history of the man who put Cavazos in the West Wing.

August 10

1680

Popé, a San Juan Pueblo Indian medicine man, leads a provincewide revolt against the Spanish in New Mexico. Working from Taos Pueblo, he sent messengers throughout the kingdom to announce that if people respected the katsina and called them properly, then they would return to usher in a new age. The katsina showed Popé how to defeat the Spaniards, who were hated for their brutality toward the Native Americans. The revolt began when Indians stole or killed the mules and horses of the Spanish to remove their principal means of warfare. All roads were then blocked as the Spanish settlements were pillaged and razed by the Indians, who scavenged whatever armaments they could. By August 13, all of the villages in the Rio Arriba area except Santa Fe had been leveled. After a siege, the Spanish fled from Santa Fe south to El Paso. The Spanish were genuinely confused by what had happened and put all of the blame on the Indians, who had matched the massive destruction by the Spanish of katsina masks, kivas, and other Indian sacraments during the Spanish conquest. Pedro Nanboa, a Pueblo Indian,

told the Spanish that for more than 70 years, the Indians had resented Spanish rule because the Christians had destroyed their religious objects and prohibited their religious ceremonies.

Edited excerpts from the declarations of Josephe, a Spanish-speaking Indian; Juan Lorenzo, a Queres Indian; Pedro Naranjo, a Queres Indian; and Pedro García, a Tano Indian:

> The Queres Indians objected to the "ill treatment and injuries" they had received from the Spanish constables who "would not leave them alone, [had] burned their estufas [kivas]," and constantly beat them. They had wanted to be "free from the labor they had performed for the religious and the Spaniards." They had grown "weary of putting in order, sweeping, heating, and adorning the church." The Tano Indians agreed. They too had "tired of the work they had to do for the Spaniards and the religious, because they did not allow them to plant or do other things for their own needs." Had the Christians shown them respect there might not have been a rebellion, explained Josephe. Instead, "they beat [us], took away what [we] had, and made us work without pay."

(*Source:* Gutiérrez, Ramón. *When Jesus Came, the Corn Mothers Went Away: Marriage, Sexuality, and Power in New Mexico, 1500–1846*. Stanford, CA: Stanford University Press, p. 132.)

Books

Gutiérrez, Ramón. *When Jesus Came, the Corn Mothers Went Away: Marriage, Sexuality, and Power in New Mexico, 1500–1846*. Stanford, CA: Stanford University Press. A multi–award winning account of the clash between the Spanish and the Native Americans in New Mexico.

Knaut, Andrew L. *The Pueblo Revolt of 1680: Conquest and Resistance in Seventeenth-Century New Mexico.* Norman: University of Oklahoma Press, 1995.

Websites

Background on the Revolt of the Pueblo Indians. American Journeys provides an essay on the event along with a guide to further reading and web links. http://www.americanjourneys.org/aj-009b/summary/index.asp

The Indian Pueblo Cultural Center. This New Mexico museum offers information about Pueblo Indian culture and history. http://www.indianpueblo.org/intro/index.cfm

2012

Researchers urge Mexican Americans to return to a traditional Mexican eating pattern in a study made public on this day in the *Journal of Immigrant and Minority Health.* Mexicans who adopt an American diet tend to gain weight. Nangel Lindberg at the Kaiser Permanente Center for Health Research reported that Mexican American women who ate less sugar, more fruits and vegetables, and a better balanced diet lost weight.

Books

Drago, Lorena, and Cynthia M. Goody, eds. *Cultural Food Practices.* Chicago, IL: American Dietetic Association, 2010. Looks at the effects of the Mexican American diet on diabetes care.

Long-Solis, Janet, and Luis Alberto Vargas. *Food Culture in Mexico.* Westport, CT: Greenwood Press, 2005. Focuses on the basics in the Mexican diet: corn, beans, squash, tomatillos, and chili peppers.

August 11

1979

Leonel Castillo resigns after serving as the first Latino to head the U.S. Immigration and Naturalization Service (INS). A native Texan and the grandson of a Mexican immigrant, he was appointed by President Jimmy Carter to head the INS in 1977.

Books

Golash-Boza, Tanya Maria. *Due Process Denied: Detentions and Deportations in the United States.* New York: Routledge, 2012. Examines the difficulties of managing immigration policy.

Kretsedemas, Philip. *The Immigration Crucible: Transforming Race, Nation, and the Limits of the Law.* New York: Columbia University Press, 2012. Looks at immigration policy and enforcement in the United States.

August 12

1895

María Ruiz de Burton, the first Hispanic novelist to write in English for an American audience, dies penniless in Chicago. Born to an aristocratic family in Mexico-owned California, Ruiz de Burton lost most of her lands to Anglo-American squatters attempting to homestead her property in the years after the Mexican-American War. She turned to writing to generate income. Her first book, *Who Would Have Thought It?,* published in 1872, attacked the New England establishment that had supported the Civil War to liberate a race of people and yet remained steeped in its own prejudices about that race. Ruiz de Burton's second book, 1885's *The Squatter and the Don,* condemned underhanded government policies that favored business interests over moral right. Her works faded into obscurity but were discovered and republished by Arte Público Press.

Books

Goldman, Anne, and Amelia María de la Luz Montes, eds. *María Amparo Ruiz de Burton: Critical and Pedagogical Perspectives.* Lincoln: University of Nebraska Press, 2004. A guide to teaching about the writer and her works.

Ruiz de Burton, María Amparo. *Who Would Have Thought It?* Ed. Amelia María de la Luz Montes. New York: Penguin Books, 2009. The writer's most famous work holds up well over the decades.

Sánchez, Rosaura, and Beatrice Pita, eds. *Conflicts of Interest: The Letters of María Amparo Ruiz de Burton*. Houston, TX: Arte Público Press, 2001. Provides insight into the thoughts of an observant and witty woman.

Website

Gazing East: María Amparo Ruiz de Burton's Who Would Have Thought It. A short, engaging biographical sketch of the writer and her most famous work. http://www.aztlanreads.com/2011/08/24/gazing-east-maria-amparo-ruiz-de-burtons-who-would-have-thought-it/

2012

Mexico's Movement for Peace with Justice and Dignity begins its march against drug violence in San Diego. Poet Javier Sicilia and 70 other members of the group plan to trek through more than 20 cities in the United States. Family members of those killed in Mexico's drug war will discuss their experiences and help develop a new network with U.S. nonprofit organizations to work against what they argue are the devastating effects of the fight against drug trafficking.

Books

Kenny, Paul, and Monica Serrano. *Mexico's Security Failure: Collapse into Criminal Violence*. New York: Routledge, 2012. Provides essays that explore the collapse of the Mexican government's ability to protect the well-being of its people.

Langton, Jerry. *Gangland: The Rise of the Mexican Drug Cartels from El Paso to Vancouver*. Mississauga, Ontario: John Wiley & Sons Canada, 2012. Examines the rise of organized crime and the inability of governments to halt these violent gangs.

Website

Caravan for Peace and Justice. The official website for the event includes photographs. http://www.caravanforpeace.org/caravan/

August 13

1994

Fidel Castro announces that Cubans wishing to emigrate will not be prevented from doing so. In response, nearly 30,000 depart the island in small boats and rafts. The U.S. government responds by intercepting refugees heading to Florida. Ending a 30-year policy of granting admittance to Cuban refugees, the government sends captured would-be immigrants to Guantanamo Naval Base in Cuba. The crisis ends in September with the New York Agreement in which the Cuban government agrees to limit emigration and the U.S. government agrees to accept at least 20,000 Cuban immigrants annually. The Cuban government subsequently agrees that Cubans returned to Cuba will not suffer any reprisals for attempting to leave. Repatriation occurs if Cubans are intercepted in the water by the Coast Guard while those on land are permitted to stay. The policy is known as "Wet feet, dry feet."

Books

Bourne, Peter G. *Fidel: A Biography of Fidel Castro*. New York: Dodd, Mead, 1986. A portrait of the communist dictator who has bedeviled the U.S. government since 1959.

Erikson, Daniel P. *The Cuba Wars: Fidel Castro, the United States, and the Next Revolution*. New York: Bloomsbury Press, 2008. Examines Castro's influence across the Caribbean and South America.

August 14

2009

Javier Suarez Medina, a Mexican immigrant to the United States, is executed in Huntsville, Texas, for the December 1988 shooting death by an Uzi of undercover Dallas police officer Lawrence Rudy Cadena. The execution draws protests from around the world and damages relations between the United States and Mexico. Medina, born in 1969, shot the officer to steal money that he was holding for a proposed cocaine buy. Medina stated that he was delivered a $4,000 bag of cocaine and had a gun in case anything went wrong. He denied deliberately shooting Cadena. He was sentenced to die on June 5, 1989, for committing a murder in the course of a robbery.

From "An Execution in Texas Strains Ties with Mexico and Others":

> The decision by President Vicente Fox of Mexico to cancel a meeting with President Bush . . . after the execution of a Mexican citizen is the latest confrontation over the death penalty between the United States and some of its closest allies. Mr. Fox moved swiftly to protest the execution of Javier Suarez Medina in Huntsville, Texas announcing the cancellation of his trip a few hours after Mr. Suarez was declared dead by lethal injection. Mexican officials say that he was denied his right to help from his government when he was arrested in 1988. Some 16 other nations filed court briefs or wrote letters pleading for clemency for Mr. Suarez, including Poland, Switzerland, Brazil and Argentina . . .
>
> The Mexican government said Mr. Fox canceled his trip, scheduled for Aug. 26, as an "unequivocal sign of repudiation" of Mr. Suarez's execution. Mexico has the death penalty but does not apply it. The government's statement added, "Mexico is confident that the cancellation of this important presidential visit contributes to strengthening respect among all nations for the norms of international law, as well as the conventions that regulate the relations between nations."
>
> White House officials said that Mr. Bush had spoken by phone with Mr. Fox on Tuesday, but would not discuss details of the conversation. Nonetheless, they portrayed the White House as well aware of Mr. Fox's political problems with the execution, and said they had not been surprised by his decision. White House officials also refused to portray it as a crisis or even an embarrassment, saying that there was nothing the president legally could have done to stop the execution.
>
> Mr. Fox has recently reinforced government help to Mexican citizens on death row in the United States. Of some 120 foreigners on death row, almost half are from Mexico. Earlier this year, pressure on the part of Mr. Fox helped to prevent the execution of Gerardo Valdez for murder in Oklahoma. An Oklahoma appeals court vacated the execution order and set a new sentencing hearing. It was a rare triumph, however. Mr. Suarez was executed despite letters from around the world to Gov. Rick Perry of Texas and the State Department, and a phone call by Mr. Fox to Mr. Bush.

(*Source:* Thompson, Ginger. "An Execution in Texas Strains Ties with Mexico and Others." *New York Times,* August 16, 2002, p. A6.)

Books

Bedau, Hugo Adam, and Paul G. Cassell, eds. *Debating the Death Penalty: Should America Have Capital Punishment? The Experts from Both Sides Make Their Case.* New York: Oxford University, 2005. Provides seven different points of view on the death penalty, showing that the decision is not as simple as being for or against capital punishment.

Hood, Roger. *The Death Penalty: A Worldwide Perspective.* New York: Oxford University Press, 2003. A comprehensive look at the death penalty around the world by a well-regarded English scholar.

Websites

"Foreign Nationals: Javier Suarez Medina." This International Justice Project website provides information about the Medina case from the perspective of an anti–death penalty organization. http://www.internationaljusticeproject. org/nationalsJMedina.cfm

"Javier Suarez Medina." An extremely comprehensive account of the Medina case from the perspective of the prosecutor's office, including the prisoner's experiences in prison and his last words. http://www.clarkprosecutor.org/ html/death/US/medina790.htm

1949

The Asociación Nacional México Americana (Mexican American National Association) is founded in Albuquerque, New Mexico. It advocated for human rights and encouraged Mexican Americans to join unions. Rumors of communist ties dogged the organization, however, with the Catholic hierarchy challenging it and the U.S. government placing it on its subversive list in 1954. The intense harassment triggered the collapse of the group.

Books

Gómez-Quiñones, Juan. *Mexican American Labor, 1790–1990*. Albuquerque: University of New Mexico Press, 1994. A general history of Mexican American workers.

Vargas, Zaragosa. *Labor Rights are Civil Rights: Mexican American Workers in Twentieth-Century America*. Princeton, NJ: Princeton University Press, 2005. Concludes with a chapter on the rise of the Mexican American civil rights movement out of the labor struggles of the 1930s and 1940s.

August 15

1905

Ernesto Galarza, an educator and a harsh critic of the Bracero Program, is born in Jolocotan,

Mexico. During the Mexican Revolution, his family moved to Sacramento, California where Galarza picked crops. As one of the few people in the farmworkers' camp who could speak English well, he was asked to protest poor living conditions. Galarza subsequently earned a doctorate from Columbia University in 1947. He spent most of his life working to improve living conditions for laborers and the quality of bilingual education.

Books

Galarza, Ernesto. *Farm Workers and Agri-Business in California, 1947–1960*. Notre Dame, IN: University of Notre Dame Press, 1977. Big business demanded cheap workers, thereby influencing U.S. immigration policy.

Galarza, Ernesto. *Merchants of Labor: The Mexican Bracero Story: An Account of the Managed Migration of Mexican Farm Workers in California, 1942–1960*. Santa Barbara: McNally & Loftin, 1964. Galarza criticized the program because it permitted the abuse of Mexican workers.

August 17

1981

The United Nations Committee on Decolonization began hearings that could force the United States to submit to a yearly examination of its treatment of Puerto Rico. The committee's chair, Frank O. Abdulah of Trinidad and Tobago, reported that most of those testifying wanted Puerto Rico to be restored to the roster of non-self-governing territories from which it was removed in 1953. If this happened, the yearly report from the United States would be debated by the committee and, perhaps, the General Assembly of the UN, providing a forum to critics of the United States. The American government categorized the hearings as "inappropriate."

Books

Conforti, Benedetto, and Carlo Focarelli. *The Law and Practice of the United Nations*. Boston:

Martinus Nijhoff Publishers, 2010. Explains the effect of UN decisions.

Mezerik, A. G., ed. *Colonialism and the United Nations*. New York International Review Service, 1964. Somewhat dated but still the only book that addresses the issue of decolonization and the UN.

1988

President Ronald Reagan signs legislation establishing Hispanic Heritage Month, running from September 15 to October 15. This expands the week of celebration that Congress had approved in 1968.

Websites

Alexander, Linda B., and Nahyun Kwon, eds. *Multicultural Programs for Tweens and Teens*. Chicago: American Library Association, 2010. Aimed at librarians, this book suggests programs for Hispanic Heritage Month.

Ryder, Willet. *Celebrating Diversity with Art: Thematic Projects for Every Month of the Year*. Glenview, IL: GoodYear Books, 1995. Includes material for Hispanic Heritage Month.

August 18

1846

General Stephen Kearny and the U.S. Army of the West enter Santa Fe during the Mexican-American War and bring Mexican rule over New Mexico to an end without firing a shot. New Mexican governor Manuel Armijo had decided not to defend New Mexico for reasons that are unclear. He retreated to Mexico.

Books

Francaviglia, Richard V., and Douglas W. Richmond, eds. *Dueling Eagles: Reinterpreting the U.S.-Mexican War, 1846–1848*. Fort Worth: Texas Christian University Press, 2000. Offers essays that challenge the Anglo-centric view of this war.

Reilly, Tom. *War with Mexico!: America's Reporters Cover the Battlefront*. Lawrence: University Press of Kansas, 2010. Examines the information given to Americans about the war.

Websites

The Mexican-American War. Northern Illinois University Libraries offers a history of the war along with primary documents. http://dig.lib.niu.edu/mexicanwar/about.html

The U.S.-Mexican War. PBS provides a graphic-heavy history of the war with a timeline, biographies of key figures, and a link to additional resources. http://www.pbs.org/kera/usmexicanwar/

August 19

1967

Graphic artist Rafael Navarro is born. His comic book, *Sonámbulo,* features a *luchador* superhero or an ordinary person who becomes larger than life when he puts on a mask.

Book

Aldama, Frederick Luis. *Your Brain on Latino Comics: From Gus Arriola to Los Bros Hernández*. Austin: University of Texas Press, 2009. Provides an overview of Latino comics.

August 20

1775

The city of Tucson, Arizona, is founded as a Spanish presidio by Hugo O'Conor, Commandant Inspector of the Frontier Provinces of New Spain. O'Conor orders the garrison at Tubac to relocate to the new presidio, San Agustin del Tucson, as part of a plan to protect the northernmost outpost of Spain in Arizona. Francisco Garcés, a Franciscan missionary, led O'Conor to the presidio site and, with Pima Indians, helped build the presidio. Garcés is one of the few men to have a footbridge named in his honor; it is a historic site in Tucson. He died in the Yuma Indian uprising in 1781.

Books

Kessell, John L. *Spain in the Southwest: A Narrative History of Colonial New Mexico, Arizona, Texas, and California.* Norman: University of Oklahoma Press, 2002. Includes the conflicts with Native Americans.

Schroeder, Susan, ed. *Native Resistance and the Pax Colonial in New Spain.* Lincoln: University of Nebraska Press, 1998. As indicated by several Native American revolts, the Spanish struggled to control the northern part of their empire in the Americas.

1903

Comedian Beatriz Escalona Pérez, known as Noloesca, is born in San Antonio, Texas. A versatile vaudeville performer, she created the comic persona of La Chata (button-nose) and operated her own variety troupe, Atracciones Noloesca. In 1975, she was honored by the Mexican National Association of Actors.

Book

Arrizón, Alicia. *Latina Performance: Traversing the Stage.* Bloomington, IN: Indiana University Press, 1999. Contains a chapter on Noloesca's work.

1915

Cuban-born medical researcher Carlos Juan Finlay dies. In 1954, the International Congress of Medical History formally and officially acknowledged Finlay's contribution to the linking of yellow fever with a mosquito. Finlay, who received his medical education in Philadelphia, was the first to suggest, about 1881, the mosquito as a vector for the transmission of the disease to humans. Walter Reed of the U.S. Army proved the link years later.

Books

Crosby, Molly Caldwell. *The American Plague: The Untold Story of Yellow Fever, the Epidemic That Shaped Our History.* New York: Berkley Books, 2006. Interesting history of the impact of the disease.

Pierce, John R., and Jim Writer. *Yellow Jack: How Yellow Fever Ravaged America and Walter Reed Discovered Its Deadly Secrets.* Hoboken, NJ: John Wiley, 2005. Finlay actually discovered yellow fever's deadly secret but Reed gets most of the attention.

August 21

1946

George Foyo is born in Havana, Cuba. He immigrated with his family to the United States at 16. Foyo, a telecommunications executive, is largely responsible for making DIRECTV the leading provider of pay-TV operations in Latin America.

Book

Comor, Edward A. *Communication, Commerce, and Power: The Political Economy of America and the Direct Broadcast Satellite, 1960–2000.* New York: St. Martin's Press, 1998. Explores the importance of direct broadcasting.

1989

Mexican American attorney and democrat Patricia Díaz Dennis resigns from her seat on the Federal Communications Commission. Appointed by President Ronald Reagan in 1986, she was the first Hispanic woman and only the second female to serve on the commission.

Book

Paglin, Max D., ed. *The Communications Act: A Legislative History of the Major Amendments, 1934–1996.* Silver Spring, MD: Pike & Fischer, 1999. In the absence of a good history of the Federal Communications Commission, the history of its enabling legislation is a helpful means of understanding its charge.

August 22

1966

The United Farm Workers of America is formed under its initial name, the United Farm Workers Organizing Committee. The group joins together the National Farm Workers Association and the Agricultural Workers Organizing Committee, both of which are in the midst of strikes against California grape growers. César Chávez leads the new organization.

Books

Del Castillo, Richard Griswold, and Richard A. Garcia. *Cesar Chavez: A Triumph of Spirit*. Norman: University of Oklahoma Press, 1995. The best account of Chávez and his links to the Chicano Movement.

Levy, Jacques E. *Cesar Chavez: Autobiography of La Causa*. New York: W. W. Norton, 1975. Provides an account of Chávez's early years, his initial efforts as an organizer, and his rise to the leadership of Mexican American farmworkers.

Websites

César Chávez: Labor Leader. Enchanted Learning offers a biography of Chávez as well as numerous activities for children that teach about the union leader. http://www.enchantedlearning.com/history/us/hispanicamerican/chavez/

The Story of César Chávez. The United Farm Workers provides a biography of its famed leader. http://www.ufw.org/_page.php?inc=history/07.html&menu=research

August 23

1843

Mexico warns the U.S. government that the proposed American annexation of Texas would be the equivalent of a declaration of war. The United States annexed Texas in 1845 as the 28th state.

Books

Pace, Robert F., and Donald S. Frazier. *Frontier Texas: History of a Borderland to 1880*. Abilene, TX: State House Press, 2004. Explores the relationship between Mexico and Texas.

Winders, Richard Bruce. *Crisis in the Southwest: The United States, Mexico, and the Struggle over Texas*. Wilmington, DE: SR Books, 2002. Covers the annexation of Texas by the United States.

August 24

2011

Anna Maria Chávez is appointed to serve as CEO of Girl Scouts of the USA. She officially takes her new post in November. Chávez grew up in Eloy, Arizona, in a Mexican American family. She held a number of federal and Arizona government posts before accepting the position of CEO of Girl Scouts of Southwest Texas in 2009. She holds a law degree from the University of Arizona and a bachelor's degree in American History from Yale University. Chávez has one child, a son. Girl Scouts of the USA has 3.2 million members worldwide.

From Allen, Paula. "Anna Maria Chávez—New Ways to Be a Girl Scout":

As a former Girl Scout herself, Chávez knows how much the program has changed. Growing up in Eloy, Ariz., during the 1970s, she went to Girl Scout camp at ages 10 to 12 and did all the traditional activities there. "What had the biggest impact was that it was the first opportunity I had to go away by myself, without my family," says Chávez. "That and being among other girls my own age from all over the state. I got the sense that it was cool to be a girl, that it was a bigger world than I'd thought and that I could do anything I wanted."

When Yale offered her admission with a full scholarship, Chávez accepted, encouraged by her family and teachers. She set off on the 3,000-mile trip to New Haven, Conn., by herself, staying in a hotel her first night there and waking up to see what looked like every other student moving in with the help of their parents. "At that time, there weren't a lot of Mexican-American students at Yale," says Chávez. "I was one of 16 out of 1,000 in my class. Most of us were from Arizona, Texas and California, and we all missed Mexican food."

To cover her personal expenses, Chávez, a history major, worked two jobs, one as a home health aide well off campus. At the end of her work hours, she says, "I had to run down the hill to make it to the dining hall before they stopped serving. If I didn't make it in time, I didn't eat dinner." One December, just before final exams, she was down to one dollar, which she taped up above her desk, knowing that if she spent it, she would have nothing. "Yale taught me perseverance," Chávez says. "I learned that regardless of my background, I could compete at that level . . . "

When Chávez first heard about the opening with the Girl Scouts of Southwest Texas, she says, "I didn't even know they had professional CEOs." As with most people, she says, "For me, the face of the Girl Scouts was the volunteer troop leader." Recruited once again to helm the 21-county Girl Scout council headquartered in San Antonio, she was intrigued by what she was learning about the organization, which now addresses a variety of issues girls experience, providing programs with positive messages about female leadership, self-esteem, career possibilities and health and wellness.

(*Source:* Allen, Paula. "Anna Maria Chávez—New Ways to Be a Girl Scout." *San Antonio Woman,* http://www.sawoman.com/categories/mayjune-2011/girlscout)

Books

Christiansen, Betty. *Girl Scouts: A Celebration of 100 Trailblazing Years.* New York: Stewart, Tabori, and Chang, 2011. This is the official biography of the group, written with the cooperation of Girl Scouts USA.
Cloninger, Kathy. *Tough Cookies: Leadership Lessons from 100 Years of Girl Scouts.* New York: Wiley, 2011. Written by a retired Girl Scouts CEO, this book addresses the lessons learned from the massive reorganization that the group undertook to become relevant in the 21st century.

Websites

Girl Scout Cookies. Offers information about the iconic Girl Scouts program including a cookie app. http://www.girlscoutcookies.org/
"Girl Scouts of the USA: Official Website." Provides news, research updates, and volunteer opportunities. http://www.girlscouts.org/

1951

Oscar Hijuelos, a Cuban-American novelist who became the first Latino to win the Pulitzer Prize, is born in Manhattan. He won in 1989 for his novel, *The Mambo Kings Play Songs of Love.*

Book

Hijuelos, Oscar. *Thoughts without Cigarettes.* New York: Gotham Books, 2011. Looks at the people and places that inspired the novelist.

August 25

2001

Muralist and University of California at Los Angeles art professor Judy Baca is honored by the Hispanic Heritage Awards Foundation as Educator of the Year. Baca is best known for starting the Great Wall of Los Angeles mural in 1976. Influenced by the social ferment of the 1970s as well as the great Mexican muralists of the past, Baca joined with the Social and Public Art Resource Center (SPARC), a group that she helped found, to continue where the old muralists had stopped. The Great Wall, painted by Latino artists, is thought to be the longest mural in the wall. It is more than 13 feet high and almost a half mile in length. Commissioned by the Army Corps of Engineers and situated in the Tujunga Flood Control Channel in North Hollywood, it has served as the flagship for a movement that has since spread out to become the greatest creation of public art since the New Deal of the 1930s. The art has earned Los Angeles the accolade of being the mural capital of the world. Murals are a very delicate art form, however, and the Los Angeles murals have suffered damage from age, graffiti, and those who clean up graffiti.

From "Where Miles of Murals Preach a People's Gospel":

"To the extent that people outside of Southern California know about the mural tradition here, they have to know about Judith Baca's 'Great Wall of Los Angeles,'" said Howard Fox, the curator of modern and contemporary art at the Los Angeles County Museum of Art. "It is the largest, most ambitious and articulated of all the projects. It was conceived and produced in the spirit of public service and community celebration. It has an exalted status, and it has earned it." "I believe people are going to look back at Los Angeles in the period from the 1970's through the 1990's as having the equivalent importance for the Latino community as the Harlem Renaissance held for the African American community," said Raymond Paredes, a former vice chancellor at UCLA and the current director of arts and culture at the Rockefeller Foundation. "Those murals were one of the most significant creations of that historical phenomenon. Coming to terms with the mural will be test of whether Los Angeles has come to terms with itself; whether it can become a world-class city with a great sense of pride in itself and its heritage."

(*Source:* Tannenbaum, Barbara. "Where Miles of Murals Preach a People's Gospel." *New York Times,* May 26, 2002, p. B29.)

Books

Dunitz, Robin J. *Street Gallery: Guide to Over 1000 Los Angeles Murals*. Los Angeles: RJD Enterprises, 1998. Many, if not most, of these murals were created by Latinos.

Olmstead, Mary. *Judy Baca: Hispanic-American Biographies*. New York: Heinemann-Raintree, 2004. A children's book about the muralist.

Websites

Judy Baca. Judith F. Baca's official webpage. http://www.judybaca.com

Social and Public Art Resource Center. Provides a wealth of material about SPARC's history, the Great Wall of Los Angeles, the Save LA Murals Campaign, and Judy Baca. http://www.sparcmurals.org

August 26

2011

Mexico's President Felipe Calderón declares that the United States bears partial responsibility for the attack on a casino in

Monterrey on August 25 that killed at least 52 people. Gunmen set fire to the casino as part of a battle between rival drug cartels. Calderón urged the U.S. Congress to stamp out drug consumption and stop illegal trafficking of weapons across the border into Mexico.

Books

Kenny, Paul, and Monica Serrano. *Mexico's Security Failure: Collapse into Criminal Violence.* New York: Routledge, 2012. Provides essays that explore the collapse of the Mexican government's ability to protect the well-being of its people.

Langton, Jerry. *Gangland: The Rise of the Mexican Drug Cartels from El Paso to Vancouver.* Mississauga, Ontario: John Wiley & Sons Canada, 2012. Examines the rise of organized crime and the inability of governments to halt these violent gangs.

August 27

1918

The Battle of Ambos Nogales, the last major engagement of the Border War between the United States and Mexico, begins. A Mexican suspected of gun smuggling crossed the border into Nogales, Mexico, followed by U.S. army soldiers and a customs agent. A Mexican soldier fired on the group, striking a soldier and prompting the Americans to return fire and kill the Mexican soldier. Reinforcements from both sides then converged on the location and the battle began. Between 30 to 129 Mexicans, 2 German military advisors to the Mexicans, and 7 Americans died in the fighting.

Books

Hall, Linda B., and Don M. Coerver. *Revolution on the Border: The United States and Mexico, 1910–1920.* Albuquerque: University of New Mexico Press, 1988. Covers the fighting between Mexican and U.S. forces.

St. John, Rachel. *Line in the Sand: A History of the Western U.S.-Mexico Border.* Princeton, NJ: Princeton University Press, 2011. Addresses violence across the border.

August 28

1565

Pedro Menéndez de Avilés, leading a Spanish army, founds the city of St. Augustine in northern Florida. Menéndez aimed to eliminate the French presence in Spanish territory. In 1564, France had established a colony, Fort Caroline, on the south bank of present-day St. John's River. Menéndez arrived at St. Augustine with a 600-ton ship as well as 10 sloops and 1500 men. In October 1565, Menéndez and 500 of his men attacked the French, slaughtering nearly all of the soldiers and hanging their bodies from trees, as the Catholic leader believed befitted Lutherans. The French women and children were unharmed. The French and Spanish would continue to wrestle for control of Florida until the 18th century. Menéndez died in Spain in 1574.

Books

Lyon, Eugene. *The Enterprise of Florida: Pedro Menéndez de Avilés and the Spanish Conquest of 1565–1568.* Gainesville: University Presses of Florida, 1976. Provides a good discussion of Spain's involvement in Florida.

Roberts, Russell. *Pedro Menéndez de Avilés.* Bear, DE: Mitchell Lane, 2003.

Websites

Pedro Menéndez de Avilés Claims Florida for Spain. Exploring Florida offers a biography of the conquistador. http://fcit.usf.edu/florida/lessons/menendz/menendz1.htm

Pedro Menéndez de Avilés. Provides a detailed biography of Avilés, albeit with a somewhat shaky command of the language. http://www.nndb.com/people/654/000097363/

1953

Puerto Rico formally asks the United Nations to recognize its new status as a self-governing commonwealth by dropping the island from its list of dependent territories. Antonio Fernod-Isern, a U.S. delegate and resident commissioner of Puerto Rico, made the request because, as he argued, any semblance of a colonial relationship between the United States and Puerto Rico no longer exists.

Book

Cardona, Luis Antonio. *A History of the Puerto Ricans in the United States of America*. Bethesda, MD: Carreta Press, 1998. Covers the colonial status of Puerto Ricans and the meaning of self-government.

1972

The United Nations Colonialism Committee approves a resolution recognizing the right of the Puerto Rican people to self-determination and independence. The committee declined to support Cuba's call for Puerto Rico to be designated a colony of the United States.

Book

Pérez-Stable, Marifeli. *The United States and Cuba: Intimate Enemies*. New York: Routledge, 2011. Covers the enmity between the two countries since Fidel Castro came to power in 1959.

1975

A California law takes effect that provides for a vote within seven days after workers on a farm have petitioned for union representation. The United Farm Workers (UFW) and César Chávez had pushed for the legislation. The UFW won the right to represent workers at 17 farms within a month.

Books

Del Castillo, Richard Griswold, and Richard A. Garcia. *Cesar Chavez: A Triumph of Spirit.*

Norman: University of Oklahoma Press, 1995. The best account of Chávez and his links to the Chicano Movement.

Levy, Jacques E. *Cesar Chavez: Autobiography of La Causa*. New York: W. W. Norton, 1975. Provides an account of Chávez's early years, his initial efforts as an organizer, and his rise to the leadership of Mexican American farmworkers.

Websites

César Chávez: Labor Leader. Enchanted Learning offers a biography of Chávez as well as numerous activities for children that teach about the union leader. http://www.enchantedlearning.com/history/us/hispanicamerican/chavez/

The Story of César Chávez. The United Farm Workers provides a biography of its famed leader. http://www.ufw.org/_page.php?inc=history/07.html&menu=research

August 29

1970

The National Chicano Moratorium Committee sponsors a march against the Vietnam War that draws about 20,000 to 30,000 people into the streets of Los Angeles. The marchers accused the U.S. government of internal racism for drafting Chicanos out of proportion to their percentage of the overall population. Chicano activist Corky Gonzales is scheduled to speak but does not have the opportunity to do so before violence erupts. The Los Angeles police use "non-lethal projectiles" and tear gas to subdue the peaceful protesters on the grounds that liquor store thieves had blended into the crowd. *Los Angeles Times* columnist Rubén Salazar is struck in the head and killed by a tear gas canister while 40 people are injured. Gonzales, who had been stopped for riding in a crowded truck, is arrested along with 28 other people who were also on the same flatbed truck on suspicion of robbery because it is police practice to do so when a person is found with a gun and a substantial amount of money. Gonzales challenges the notion that 29 people jump a flatbed truck to make a getaway.

Clarita Trujillo, a nun from Our Lady of Victoryknoll, recalls the day:

> The sisters present had on modified habits and we walked on the edges of the march as a sign of peace. There were priests, sisters, people with their children, old women, it was a community affair. At the rally, I remember sitting on the grass. I heard a yell and saw the police coming from behind. A tear gas canister fell at my feet. A boy helped me jump a fence and we walked all the way home. I knew it was a terrible betrayal by the police.

(*Source:* Medina, Lara. *Las Hermanas: Chicana/Latina Religious-Political Activism in the U.S. Catholic Church*. Philadelphia: Temple University Press, 2004, p. 38.)

Books

Acuña, Rodolfo. *Occupied America: A History of Chicanos*. New York: HarperCollins, 1988. First published in 1972, this is the classic work on the history of Mexican Americans.

Rosales, F. Arturo. *Chicano: The History of the Mexican American Civil Rights Movement*. Houston: Arte Público, 1997. An award-winning history filled with photographs and primary documents.

Websites

Chicano Moratorium. YouTube clip of a part of the event showing the Brown Berets. www.youtube.com/watch?v=famNeiosTVk

40th Anniversary Committee of the Chicano Moratoriums. Archival site with photographs and quotes from participants that has not been updated. http://chicanomoratorium.org/

1953

Speedy Gonzales, a Warner Brothers cartoon star, first appears in *Cat-Tails for Two,* a Merrie Melodies cartoon. Mel Blanc, a famous voice star, spoke for Speedy, "the fastest mouse in Mexico." The 46 Speedy Gonzales cartoons have been problematic due to their depiction of Latinos. Until the 1970s, there were few rounded Latino characters on television or in the movies. Early televisual and film depictions of Latinos showed them as criminals, clowns, or hot-blooded lovers. While Speedy is not a thug or a buffoon, he does speak with an exaggerated Mexican accent and wears an oversized sombrero. It is his associates who match the offensive stereotype of Mexicans. The other male Mexican mice are depicted as lazy, hard-drinking womanizers.

From "Adios Speedy, Not So Fast":

> AY caramba The Cartoon Network just can't seem to stay out of the line of fire in the culture wars. Last year it angered Bugs Bunny purists by omitting racially insensitive cartoons from what would have been a complete marathon broadcast of the Wascally Wabbit's oeuvre. Now it's Speedy Gonzales fans who are hot as jalapenos—over the plucky Mexican mouse's virtual absence from the cable network's broadcasts. In an interesting twist, Hispanics are among those leading the criticism. The Web site HispanicOnline.com, specializing in Latino news and entertainment, has posted articles taking the network to task for what many see as a cave-in to political correctness; the site also offers a link to a bring-back-the-mouse petition drive. But the Cartoon Network says P.C. isn't the overarching reason the Looney Tunes star is scarce on the channel (not banned, it insists); rather, Speedy shorts don't

make the rotation because they simply aren't a ratings winner among the channel's vast archive of more than 8,500 cartoons.

Laurie Goldberg, a network spokeswoman, conceded, however, that part of the audience appeal problem is the toons' negative stereotypes—like Speedy's lazy cousin, Slowpoke Rodriguez—and their depictions of drinking and smoking, clear parent turnoffs. Yet many Hispanics view Speedy as a positive ethnic reflection because he always outsmarts the "greengo" cat Sylvester, says Virginia Cueto, associate editor of the Florida-based HispanicOnline, who has been covering the issue for the English-language site. Noting that Cartoon Network International still shows Speedy regularly in Latin American nations, Ms. Cueto said the network's main concern in the United States "seems to be what non-Latinos would get from watching these cartoons," as if Hispanic preferences here don't matter. And so people are peeved. Here are excerpts from the overwhelmingly pro-Speedy (and mostly anonymous) postings on HispanicOnline:

THIS is an Outrage!!! Viva la Mouse! Viva Speedy Gonzales!

Demeaning? Pleeeease, we need to get over the stupid P.C. expletive. I am of Mexican parents and I have much better things to do than worry about Speedy G, unless of course he was in my house—then I would get Senor Sylvester to take care of him.

That little mouse is a hero. . . . How about banning Pepe LePew, for stinking and being French, or Boris and Natasha, for being Russian, or . . . Rocky the Flying Squirrel for not being P.C. to squirrels . . .

If you ask me, the cartoons depict "gringo" society (those crafty American cats . . .) as a not-too-bright, conniving species that exploits anyone who happens to be handy. The Mexican mice are always content in their own pueblos, doing their own thing, and here come the gringos into Mexican turf, interfering and looking out for their own interests. And Speedy always wins! So who is being depicted negatively here?

(*Source:* Kuntz, Tom. "Adiós Speedy, Not So Fast." *New York Times,* April 7, 2002, p. D4.)

Books

Bruns, Roger A. *Icons of Latino America.* Westport, CT: Greenwood Press, 2008. Speedy Gonzales is one of the icons central to popular culture that are covered in this book.

Maltin, Leonard. *Of Mice and Magic: A History of American Animated Cartoons.* New York: Plume, 1987. Exhaustive history of animated film.

Websites

Speedy Gonzales—IMDb. The Internet Movie Database provides a cast list and a history of the cartoon.

Speedy Gonzales—YouTube. A number of Speedy Gonzales cartoons can be found on YouTube. http://www.youtube.com/watch?v=DDZBzvTDhGU

1963

The Chamizal Treaty is signed between the United States and Mexico to set an international boundary line. The treaty is named after land between El Paso, Texas and Juárez, Mexico owned by Pedro Ignacio García. Upon the signing of the treaty, 5,000 residents of El Paso had to leave land that would be transferred to Mexico.

Book

St. John, Rachel. *Line in the Sand: A History of the Western U.S.-Mexico Border.* Princeton, NJ:

Princeton University Press, 2011. Includes coverage of the Chamizal Treaty.

1989

Ileana Ros-Lehtinen of Miami becomes the first Cuban American to be elected to the U.S. Congress. A Republican state legislator, she fills the seat left vacant by the death of Claude Pepper. She is also the first Latino woman to sit in the House of Representatives.

Books

Fernandez, Mayra. *Ileana Ros-Lehtinen, Lawmaker*. Cleveland: Modern Curriculum Press, 1994. Short biography aimed at a juvenile audience.

Meier, Matt S. *Notable Latino Americans: A Biographical Dictionary*. Westport, CT: Greenwood Press, 1997. Includes a biographical essay on Ros-Lehtinen.

2001

Puerto Ricans hold a nonbinding referendum. Sixty-eight percent vote to ask the U.S. Navy to stop the Vieques bombing immediately and leave the island while 30 percent support the Navy.

Books

Barreto, Amicar Antonio. *Vieques, the Navy, and Puerto Rican Politics*. Gainesville: University Press of Florida, 2002. Analyzes the political response by Puerto Ricans and U.S. officials to the Vieques controversy.

McCaffrey, Katherine T. *Military Power and Popular Protest: The U.S. Navy in Vieques, Puerto Rico*. New Brunswick, NJ: Rutgers University Press, 2002. Focuses on the grassroots mobilization in opposition to the U.S. Navy.

Websites

History of the Navy in Vieques. Good, anti-training practice site filled with a timeline, news articles, and other sources about the U.S. Navy on Vieques. http://www.vieques-island.com/navy/

Vieques, Puerto Rico Naval Training Range: Background and Issues for Congress. Provides the U.S. Navy's view of the Vieques dispute with a focus on the post-2001 period. http://www.history.navy.mil/library/online/vieques.htm

August 30

1894

Félix Rigau Carrera, also known as El Águila de Sabana Grande (The Eagle from Sabana Grande), is born in Sabana Grande, Puerto Rico. Rigau Carrera became the first Puerto Rican pilot. After obtaining his pilot license, Rigau Carrera joined the 1st Marine Aviation Force which went to France in July 1918 to serve in World War I. He was the first Latino fighter pilot in the U.S. Marine Corps. Somewhat surprisingly—considering the risks involved with early aviation—Rigau Carrera lived to age 60 and died having amassed a fortune in the concrete business.

Books

Grattan, Robert F. *The Origins of Air War: The Development of Military Air Strategy in World War I*. New York: Tauris Academic Studies, 2009. It took some time for military strategists to realize that airplanes could be used for more than surveillance of enemy troop movements.

Kaufman, Roxanne M. *100 Years of Marine Corps Aviation: An Illustrated History*. Washington, D.C.: U.S. Government Printing Office, 2011. Addresses the rise of military aviation, a form of warfare that would make battleships obsolete.

August 31

1923

Musician Arsenio Rodríguez is born in Cuba. Blinded as a young boy when a horse kicked him in the head, Rodríguez became a famed bandleader known as *El Ciego*

Maravilloso (The Marvellous Blind Man). He came to New York in the 1950s in a futile attempt to find a cure for his blindness. Remaining in the United States, he gained fame as a mambo musician.

Book

Starr, Larry. *American Popular Music: From Minstrelsy to MP3*. New York: Oxford University Press, 2010. Introduces mambo.

September

September 1

1972

La Raza Unida Party holds its first national convention in El Paso, Texas. Over 3,000 Mexican Americans from 18 states attend the four-day meeting to plan a political strategy for the 1972 elections and to adopt a national platform. Texan José Ángel Gutiérrez, founder of La Raza Unida, chairs the meeting and is chosen to be responsible for organizing the party's national political platform. Corky Gonzales is Gutiérrez's main rival for leadership of the meeting. La Raza Unida reaffirms that it is independent from the Democratic and Republican parties though many delegates want to show support for César Chávez and the United Farm Workers, who are backed by the Democrats. There is also a dispute over whether La Raza Unida should focus on local and state elections until it gains in strength or immediately become involved in presidential-level politics.

From the Partido de la Raza Unida, 1972, Colorado State Platform:

> We believe that it is man's right—inherent with his existence—to control and influence those factors that affect his life and his community. Only through control of his life and community can any person, or group of people, combat and overcome poverty, injustice, inequality and racism.
>
> FURTHERMORE: It is the duty and responsibility of all people, and groups of people, to seek control of their lives and their communities in a manner beneficial to those living in that community.
>
> THEREFORE: It is the right, responsibility and obligation of Chicanos, urban and rural, to seek and gain control of their lives and communities—politically, economically, educationally and socially.
>
> In accordance with this belief, it is our immediate declaration that all institutions, organizations, and agencies existing in, or purporting to exist for, Chicano communities become accountable to the people that are the basis of their existence.

(*Source:* Marín, Christine. *A Spokesman of the Mexican American Movement: Rodolfo "Corky" Gonzales and the Fight for Chicano Liberation, 1966–1972.* San Francisco: R & E Research Associates, 1977, p. 41.)

Books

Marín, Christine. *A Spokesman of the Mexican American Movement: Rodolfo "Corky" Gonzales and the Fight for Chicano Liberation, 1966–1972.* San Francisco: R & E Research Associates, 1977. The only biography of the Chicano leader contains a wealth of primary sources.

Rosales, F. Arturo. *Chicano!: The History of the Mexican American Civil Rights Movement.* Houston: Arte Público, 1996. Winner of the Gustavus Myers Outstanding Book Award for its coverage of the movement.

Websites

The Chicano Civil Rights Movement. A timeline of the movement from the Experience Music Project at the Science Fiction Museum and Hall of Fame. http://www.empmuseum. org/documents/education/onlineCourse/Ci vil_Rights_Timeline.pdf

The Chicano Movement: Brown and Proud. A brief history of the movement by Nadra Kareem Nittle. http://racerelations.about.com/ od/historyofracerelations/a/BrownandProud TheChicanoMovement.htm

September 2

1966

Actress Salma Hayek is born in Veracruz, Mexico. After experiencing considerable success in Mexico, Hayek came to Hollywood in 1991. She received a Best Actress Academy Award nomination for her portrayal of Frida Kahlo in 2002's *Frida,* a film that she also coproduced.

Book

Valdivia, Angharad N. *Latina/os and the Media.* Cambridge: Polity, 2010. Hayek is covered as the executive producer of the television show, *Ugly Betty.*

Website

Salma Hayek. The Internet Movie Database provides a short biography, photographs, and a listing of professional credits for the performer and producer. http://www.imdb.com/name/nm0000161/

September 3

1915

Mexican American author Americo Paredes is born in Brownsville, Texas. A folklorist and professor at the University of Texas, Paredes received the Orden del Águila Azteca, Mexico's highest honor for foreigners, in 1991. By collecting folktales, he preserved an essential part of Mexican and Mexican American culture. Folktales, especially ones by ethnic minorities, were often not recorded because they were not valued.

Books

Paredes, Américo, ed. *Folklore and Culture on the Texas-Mexican Border.* Austin, TX: CMAS Books, Center for Mexican American Studies, University of Texas at Austin, 1993. Provides a depiction of life on the border lands.

Paredes, Américo, ed. *Folktales of Mexico.* Chicago: University of Chicago Press, 1970. Paredes collected many tales that had not been recorded before.

September 4

1781

A Spanish expedition under the command of Lt. Col. Gaspar de Portolá founds the present city of Los Angeles as the El Pueblo de la Reina de los Angeles. The original European settlers consisted of 22 adults and 22 children. A farming community, the town grew with the addition of soldiers and settlers.

Book

Acuña, Rodolfo F. *Occupied America: A History of Chicanos.* New York: Pearson Longman, 2007. Covers the early history of the Spanish in California.

1965

Restaurateur and philanthropist Félix Tijerina dies. A Mexican immigrant, he began one of the first restaurant chains in Texas. His Felix Mexican Restaurants, serving Tex-Mex food, remained in operation from 1937 to 2008. Tijerina also served as president of United Latin American Citizens (LULAC) from 1956 to 1960. He created the Little School of the 400 program, the inspiration for Head Start.

Book

Kreneck, Thomas H. *Mexican American Odyssey: Felix Tijerina, Entrepreneur and Civic Leader, 1905–1965.* College Station: Texas A&M University Press, 2001. The only biography of the community leader.

2011

The first retrospective on the Chicano performance and conceptual art group, Asco, opens at the Los Angeles County Museum of

Art. *Asco: Elite of the Obscure, A Retrospective, 1972–1987* covers the group started by four artists from East Los Angeles: Harry Gamboa Jr., Gronk, Willie Herrón, and Patssi Valdez. Taking their name from the forceful Spanish word for disgust and nausea, Asco used performance, public art, and multimedia to respond to social and political turbulence. Asco remained active until the mid-1980s, contracting and expanding to include Diane Gamboa, Sean Carrillo, Daniel J. Martinez, and Teddy Sandoval, among others.

Book

Chavoya, C. Ondine, and Rita Gonzalez, eds. *Asco: Elite of the Obscure: A Retrospective, 1972–1987.* Los Angeles: Los Angeles County Museum of Art, 2011. An exhibition catalogue.

September 5

1940

Actress Raquel Welch is born as Jo Raquel Tejada in Chicago to a Bolivian father and an American mother. She grew up in Southern California and embarked upon a film career after winning beauty contests. On the strength of her appearance in a fur bikini in *One Million Years B.C.* in 1966, Welch became one of the iconic sex symbols of the era. *Playboy* magazine named her as the "Most Desired Woman" of the 1970s. Welch had made an attempt to gain recognition for her acting skills by playing a transsexual in *Myra Breckinridge* but the movie bombed. Welch won a Golden Globe in 1974 for *The Three Musketeers* but the award did not lead to more nuanced roles. In the 1980s and 1990s, she finally began to be recognized for something other than her breasts with well-received television appearances and a second Golden Globe in 1987 for playing a woman stricken with Lou Gehrig's disease in *The Right to Die.* As she moved into her 60s, Welch continued to act and model. She has also succeeded in business with a wig collection.

From "Raquel Welch is Reinvented as a Latina":

On "American Family," the PBS television series about a Mexican-American family in East Los Angeles, now in its first season, Aunt Dora is the drama queen of the family, a passionate, romantic woman who might have become a Hollywood star had she vigorously pursued her acting career. The actress playing Aunt Dora is Raquel Welch, who infuses the role with her familiar sultriness and smoky voice.

Nevertheless the sight of Ms. Welch in that role might bewilder some fans. . . . Dora, you see, is a Latina, a title Ms. Welch herself is claiming for the first time after nearly 40 years in show business. "I'm happy to acknowledge it and it's long overdue and it's very welcome," she said in a recent interview at the Watergate Hotel in Washington. "There's been kind of an empty place here in my heart and also in my work for a long, long time. . . . Latinos are here to stay," she told her audience at a National Press Club luncheon last month. "As citizen Raquel, I'm proud to be Latina."

As both citizen Raquel and Raquel Welch, sex symbol and pinup girl, Ms. Welch has bridged two eras. She has worked in the Hollywood that made her a blonde and tried to take away her first name as well as in the Hollywood that now considers Latinos hip and pays Jennifer Lopez up to $12 million a picture. Ms. Welch grew up with a father who tried to assimilate at all costs, even banning Spanish at home. But now, at 61, she is riding the wave of new Latino generations that flaunt their ethnic pride and behave with the confidence of a major demographic force. These days Ms. Welch is learning Spanish from tapes, planning her first trip to Bolivia in August to meet relatives and working on her own Latino film project. After fifty-some movies and worldwide celebrity, she is embracing the identity she said she had to reject to break into film. "It was told to me that if I wanted to be typecast, I would play into that," she said, by emphasizing her Hispanic background. "You just couldn't be too different . . ."

Ms. Welch said she never hid her ethnic background, but it never became common knowledge. . . . Then again, for Ms. Welch, who grew up in La Jolla and San Diego, playing a Latina would have been more of a departure than playing a glamorous bombshell. She said her father was dead set on raising his three children as American as apple pie. An ambitious immigrant who came to the United States from Bolivia to study engineering, Armando Carlos Tejada never looked back. Ms. Welch said her family never visited Bolivia. And it was not until her 30's, when her grandmother came for a visit, that Ms. Welch finally met her namesake.

(*Source:* Navarro, Mireya. "Raquel Welch Is Reinvented as a Latina: A Familiar Actress Now Boasts Her Heritage." *New York Times,* June 11, 2002, p. E1.)

Books

Pfeiffer, Lee, and Dave Worrall. *Cinema Sex Sirens.* New York: Omnibus, 2012. Contains a chapter on Welch.
Welch, Raquel. *Raquel Welch: Beyond the Cleavage.* New York: Weinstein Books, 2011. More of a guide to living than a film memoir, Welch writes about the challenges she has faced in life while providing beauty advice.

Websites

Hairuwear. This is the website for Welch's collection of wigs. http://www.hairuwear.com/raquel-welch

"Raquel Welch." The Internet Movie Database lists all of Welch's roles, offers a solid biography, and provides photos of the actress. http://www.imdb.com/name/nm0000079/

1915

Raymond Telles Jr., the first Mexican American mayor of a major city, is born in El Paso. After serving in the U.S. Army Air Force during World War II and in the U.S. Air Force during the Korean War, Telles became mayor of El Paso in 1957.

Book

García, Mario T. *The Making of a Mexican American Mayor: Raymond L. Telles of El Paso.* El Paso: Texas Western Press, 1998. The only biography of the mayor.

September 6

1944

Entomologist Pedro Barbosa is born in Guayama, Puerto Rico. His research focuses on the ways in which plants protect themselves from predators. Besides winning the Science Award of the Institute of Puerto Rico of New York, he has been made a fellow of the Entomological Society of America.

Book

Barbosa, Pedro, and Ignacio Castellanos, eds. *Ecology of Predator-Prey Interactions.* New York: Oxford University Press, 2005. Prey evolve in response to the creatures that attack them, thereby causing the predators to change in order to hunt effectively.

September 7

1959

Space physicist Ramón E. López is born in Aberdeen, Maryland, to Puerto Rican parents. He is a world authority on storms that occur in the magnetosphere, the section of space that is influenced by Earth's magnetic field.

Book

López, Ramón E. *Getting Scientists Involved in Science Education*. Washington, D.C.: National Academy Press, 1993. Scientists have been reluctant to communicate with the public with the result that scientific illiteracy is relatively high.

1996

Radio pioneer Nathan Safir dies in San Antonio, Texas. Raised in Mexico by parents who had immigrated from Russia, Safir was inducted in 1989 into the Broadcasting Hall of Fame for managing the first full-time Spanish-language station in the United States and for playing a key role in the acceptance and expansion of Spanish-language broadcasting. In 1940, Safir began a weekly Spanish program on KTSA, in San Antonio, which is said to have been the city's first Spanish broadcasting. While serving in the infantry and stationed in London during World War II, he produced and announced Spanish programs for Armed Forces Radio. Safir worked for KCOR in San Antonio from 1953 until his retirement in 1990.

Book

N.A. *History of Armed Forces Radio and Television Service, the First 50 Years*. Alexandria, VA: American Forces Information Service and Armed Forces Radio and Television Service, 1993. A history of the broadcasting service that employed Safir during World War II.

September 8

1965

The grape boycott begins, as a protest by the United Farm Workers (UFW) for a wage equal to the federal minimum wage and to force the growers to negotiate a union contract. In the course of a strike that lasts five years and draws international attention, César Chávez becomes the public face of the farm workers movement. By utilizing consumer boycotts, marches, community organizing, and nonviolent resistance, the boycott succeeds in drawing attention to the plight of the people who pick food for American tables. The boycott ends with the UFW reaching collective bargaining agreements with table grape growers, affecting about 10,000 farm workers.

From "Grape Boycott: Struggle Poses a Moral Issue":

> The frigid, steel-gray dawn was still hesitating about making an appearance one morning recently when several hundred demonstrators set out on a slow march through the cobblestone streets of Pittsburgh's wholesale produce market. It was a motley group. There were housewives in well-tailored slacks and students in faded jeans, priests in Roman collars, and blacks with Afro hair-do's, a few businessmen in conservative suits and a barrel-chested union leader. But they all had the same message—don't eat grapes. . . . Cesar Chavez, the slight, sad-eyed leader of the United Farm Workers Organizing Committee mounted the steps and began to speak: "I'm proud that we were able to have a peaceful march. Anyone will respond to our cause if we do it in that spirit. We've worked hard in California but that is not enough. Our last hope for success lies with you." This scene has been repeated dozens of times this fall as Mr. Chavez has toured the country soliciting support for a boycott of California table grapes. . . . It is very difficult to measure the effectiveness of the boycott. Officials assert that 27 percent fewer grapes have been shipped from California this year than last. Moreover, reports indicate that many big chain stores, such as A&P, no longer carry grapes in their city stores.

(*Source:* Roberts, Steven V. "Grape Boycott: Struggle Poses a Moral Question." *New York Times,* November 12, 1969.)

Books

Friedman, Monroe. *Consumer Boycotts: Effecting Change through the Marketplace and Media.* New York: Routledge, 1999. Examines how successful boycotts, including the grape boycott, have been organized.

Levy, Jacques E. *Cesar Chavez: Autobiography of La Causa.* Minneapolis: University of Minnesota Press, 2007. The definitive biography of Chávez, written with the cooperation of the labor leader and his closest associates.

Websites

Exploring the United Farm Workers' History by Claire Peterson and Susana Diaz. Good history of the grape boycott, Chávez, and the union. http://l3d.cs.colorado.edu/systems/ag entsheets/New-Vista/grape-boycott/Histo ry.html

United Farm Workers. The official webpage of the union, with considerable information on Chávez. http://www.ufw.org/

1985

Artist Ana Mendieta dies in a mysterious fall from her New York City apartment. Her husband is accused in her death but never convicted. A painter, sculptor, performance artist, and celebrated member of the feminist art movement, the Cuban-born Mendieta's works reflect the influence of the Santería faith.

Books

Moure, Gloria. *Ana Mendieta.* Galicia, Spain: Centro Galego de Arte Contemporánea, 1996. An exhibition catalogue with essays about the artist's work and impact.

Redfern, Christine, and Caro Caron. *Who Is Ana Mendieta?* New York: Feminist Press, 2011. Mendieta practiced feminist art and pushed museums to show more works by female artists.

Viso, Olga. *Unseen Mendieta: The Unpublished Works of Ana Mendieta.* New York: Prestel, 2008. Mendieta worked with a range of media and this includes some of those works.

September 9

1955

Orlando Figueroa, director of the Mars Exploration Program of the National Aeronautics and Space Administration (NASA), is born in San Juan, Puerto Rico. He has led the program since 2001 and has sent out several spacecraft to study Mars.

Books

Doeden, Matt. *Human Travel to the Moon and Mars: Waste of Money or Next Frontier?* Minneapolis: Twenty-First Century Books, 2012. Debates the merits of space travel.

Haerens, Margaret. *NASA.* Detroit: Greenhaven Press, 2012. A popular history of the space agency.

September 10

2010

The U.S. government issues a warning to U.S. citizens traveling to and from Mexico because of the risk of kidnappings and the high rate of violence in the northern Mexico border cities. U.S. government personnel in Monterrey, in particular, are advised to send their children back to the United States. The violence seriously slows the movement of people between Mexico and the United States and badly damages the Mexican tourism industry.

Books

Kenny, Paul, and Monica Serrano. *Mexico's Security Failure: Collapse into Criminal Violence.* New York: Routledge, 2012. Provides essays that explore the collapse of the Mexican government's ability to protect the well-being of its people.

Langton, Jerry. *Gangland: The Rise of the Mexican Drug Cartels from El Paso to Vancouver.* Mississauga, Ontario: John Wiley & Sons Canada, 2012. Examines the rise of organized crime and the inability of governments to halt these violent gangs.

Website

Caravan for Peace and Justice. The official website for the Movement for Peace and Justice's trip through the United States to protest American involvement in Mexico's drug violence.

September 11

1911

Liga Femenil Mexicanista (Mexican Women's League) is founded in Laredo, Texas. With a membership consisting chiefly of teachers, the short-lived Liga focused on a project to provide free instruction to poor Mexican children who could not afford to attend school.

Book

Vargas, Zaragosa. *Crucible of Struggle: A History of Mexican Americans from Colonial Times to the Present Era.* New York: Oxford University Press, 2011. A classroom text about the challenges that have faced Mexican Americans.

1941

Nuyorican poet and playwright Miguel Algarín is born in Santurce, Puerto Rico. His family came to the United States in the 1950s in search of a better life after the industrialization of Puerto Rico. Algarín began writing seriously in 1967 and subsequently opened the Nuyorican Poets Café, in which writers read their work for an audience.

Books

Algarín, Miguel, and Lois Griffith. *Action: The Nuyorican Poets Café Theater Festival.* New York: Simon & Schuster, 1997. A hefty anthology of writings.

Algarín, Miguel, and Bob Holman, eds. *Aloud: Voices from the Nuyorican Poets Café.* New York: Henry Holt, 1994. An anthology of writings.

1946

Antonio Fernós-Isern, a Popular Democrat from Puerto Rico, is appointed to the 79th Congress as resident commissioner. Subsequently elected to the post, he served until 1965. Fernós-Isern was assigned to committees, on agriculture, armed services, and public lands, but was not allowed to accrue seniority since Puerto Rico lacks statehood. Accordingly, he was always ranked below all elected representatives.

Book

N.A. *Resident Commissioner to the United States from Puerto Rico: The Evolution of the Office.* Library of Congress: Congressional Research Service, 1972. Changes in the office affected Fernós-Isern.

Websites

Antonio Fernós-Isern. The Biographical Dictionary of the United States Congress profiles the resident commissioner. http://bioguide.congress.gov/scripts/biodisplay.pl?index=F000087

Antonio Fernós-Isern. The Library of Congress supplies a biography of the Puerto Rican political leader as part of its Hispanics in Congress series. http://www.loc.gov/rr/hispanic/congress/fernos.html

2001

The terrorist attacks by Al Qaeda upon the Pentagon and New York's World Trade Center prompts the United States to tighten security along its borders. Within the next 10 years, the surge more than doubles the number of Border Patrol agents to 20,000 while adding 700 miles of fencing, lights, sensors, cameras, and unmanned surveillance drones.

Book

St. John, Rachel. *Line in the Sand: A History of the Western U.S.-Mexico Border*. Princeton, NJ: Princeton University Press, 2011. Covers the changes in the way the border has been guarded since 9/11.

September 12

1847

The Battle of Chapultepec begins between Mexican and U.S. forces. When the U.S. Army is victorious on September 13, Mexico City falls and the Mexican-American War effectively ends. Some shooting between forces continues after the city falls, with the last resistance ending on September 15.

Journalist James Freaner witnesses the Battle of Chapultepec:

> Our [U.S.] guns proved to be very destructive as we found after the work was taken 500 dead men unburied by thrown in ditches. The [castle] was completely riddled. The Engineers throughout all operations, have performed a most dangerous and laborious duty. They have proved themselves to be men of sterling worth—of masterly ability, and bright ornaments of their profession.
>
> [General John A. Quitman handed an American flag to the officers leading the first assault on Chapultepec and explained that it had been used:] to conquer Seminoles, Black Hawks, and Mexicans. Those colors were the first that waves over the Castle on Chapultepec. . . .
>
> A thousand heroic deed were acted at all points, to refer to which I have no space, nor could words have power to describe them. . . .

> General Scott and Staff, in full feather, escorted by the Cavalry, entered the city, amidst the huzzas of the soldiery on all sides. Throughout the 14th and on the morning of the 15th, the Mexicans continued to fire from the corners and tops of the houses, killing some and wounding many.

> (*Source:* Reilly, Tom. *War with Mexico!: America's Reporters Cover the Battlefield*. Lawrence: University Press of Kansas, 2010, pp. 180–81.)

Books

Francaviglia, Richard V., and Douglas W. Richmond, eds. *Dueling Eagles: Reinterpreting the U.S.-Mexican War, 1846–1848*. Fort Worth: Texas Christian University Press, 2000. Offers essays that challenge the Anglo-centric view of this war.

Reilly, Tom. *War with Mexico!: America's Reporters Cover the Battlefront*. Lawrence: University Press of Kansas, 2010. Examines the information given to Americans about the war.

Websites

The Mexican-American War. Northern Illinois University Libraries offers a history of the war along with primary documents. http://dig.lib.niu.edu/mexicanwar/about.html

The U.S.-Mexican War. PBS provides a graphic-heavy history of the war with a timeline, biographies of key figures, and a link to additional resources. http://www.pbs.org/kera/usmexicanwar/

September 13

1984

Mexican boxer Julio César Chávez defeats Mario Martinez with a knockout in the eighth round to win the super featherweight title of the World Boxing Council. Chávez is considered by many to be the greatest boxer of the 1980s and 1990s. Idolized among boxing fans in the United States and Mexico, Chávez had a career record of 107–6–2 with 86 knockouts and six world titles in three weight divisions (super featherweight, super lightweight, junior welterweight). He retired in 2005.

Book

Boddy, Kasia. *Boxing: A Cultural History*. London: Reaktion, 2009. A history of the "sweet science" that has also attracted working class men looking to get ahead.

Websites

Julio César Chávez . The Cyber Boxing Zone provides career statistics for the retired boxer. http://www.cyberboxingzone.com/boxing/chavrec.htm

Julio César Chávez. The official site of the boxer contains a biography and promotes his business interests with energy drinks and a car dealership. http://www.juliocesarchavez.net/

September 14

1923

Puerto Rican writer and lawyer Nemesio R. Canales dies. Born in Jayuya in 1878, he obtained a law degree in the United States in 1903. He then returned home to open a law office. He founded the weekly newspaper, *Juan Bobo,* in 1915 and wrote for a number of other periodicals including *El Día,* which published his column "Paliques." The essays were gathered into a popular book in 1913. The Nemesio Canales Award in Literature every year is presented to promising young Puerto Rican writers. In 1909, as a member of the Puerto Rican legislature, Canales introduces legislation to give civil rights to women and is credited with ultimately helping Puerto Rican women win the right to vote. Canales died in New York City while traveling.

From Nemesio R. Canales, "Wealth and Poverty," *Paliques* (1915):

Someone will tell me, too, that without the poor—without laboring machines—neither rich nor poor will be able to survive. And I reply: how nice that our own pockets contain the guarantee of the life of the poor. A gilt-edged guarantee, the pocket!

But seeing that the poor must continue existing, how to perform the miracle of ridding ourselves of poverty without finishing off the poor? How do we cure the pip without killing the fowl? How save ourselves from rabies without killing the dog?

I don't think it's quite as hard as it looks. What has prevented it till now has been man's ignorance, that accursed source of all the prejudices afflicting us. Furthermore, it has always kept us far from the root of the question, our mania for obfuscating the simplest problems, wrapping them in the fog of doctrinaire philosophy which poisons and putrefies everything. . .

Let us make money as cheap as water from the faucet. Why are we at such pains to supply everyone, even the wretchedest hovel, with water? Because the voice of our own interest tells us that the absence of water exposes us to the horror of an epidemic.

So, let's do likewise with money. Not let anyone go without it, but make it flow—spread it all around like a jubilant, kindly rain. Then we'll save ourselves from poverty, the evil of evils, mother of all epidemics.

(*Source:* Zavala, Iris M., and Rafael Rodriguez, eds. *The Intellectual Roots of Independence: An Anthology of Puerto Rican Political Essays.* New York: Monthly Review Press, 1980, p. 145.)

Books

Canales, Nemesio R. *Paliques*. San Juan: Ediciones Isla, 1967. Reprints the famous 1913 collection of essays.

Montaña Peláez, Servando. *Nemesio Canales: Lenguaje y situación*. Rio Piedras: University of Puerto Rico Press, 1973.

Websites

Biografía de Nemesio Canales. Biografías y Vidas provides a short biography of Canales. http://www.biografiasyvidas.com/biografia/c/canales.htm

Biografía de Nemesio Canales. Puerto Rico en breve provides a short biography of Canales and the full text of the legislation that he introduced to emancipate women. http://www.preb.com/qs/qsoy90.htm

1843

Poet and political activist Lola Rodríguez de Tió is born in San German, Puerto Rico. In 1868, she wrote the lyrics to what would become the Puerto Rican national song, "La Borinqueña." In 1877, the Spanish government exiled Rodríguez de Tió and her family for their activities on behalf of Puerto Rican independence. In 1899, following the Spanish-American War, Rodríguez de Tió returned to a hero's welcome in Puerto Rico. A romantic poet and an advocate for women's rights, she died on November 10, 1924, in Cuba.

Book

Mendoza Tió, Carlos F. *Lola Rodríguez de Tió*. San Juan, PR: Mendoza Tió, 1978. A biography of the Puerto Rican author.

1920

Mathematician Alberto P. Calderón is born in Mendoza, Argentina. By focusing on the practical applications of mathematics, he developed a different approach to mathematics from the one common in the 1950s and 1960s. A professor at MIT and the University of Chicago, Calderón won the National Medal of Science in 1991.

Books

Calderón, Alberto P. *Singular Integrals*. New York: American Mathematical Society, 1965. Shows his approach to the study of mathematics from a practical angle.

Christ, Michael, Carlos E. Kenig, and Cora Sadosky, eds. *Harmonic Analysis and Partial Differential Equations: Essays in Honor of Alberto P. Calderón*. Chicago: University of Chicago Press, 1999. A collection of essays by mathematicians influenced by Calderón.

1988

Dolores Huerta, one of the founders of the United Farm Workers and a Latino icon, is badly beaten by San Francisco police during a peaceful protest in the course of a campaign appearance by Vice President George H. W. Bush. Huerta, 58 years old at the time, standing 5 feet 2 inches tall, and weighing 110 pounds, was speared and stabbed in the abdomen using a club to the point that her spleen shattered and six ribs were broken. She required emergency surgery to save her life.

From Scott Forter, "UFW Official Operated on after S.F. Beating," *The Daily Californian*, September 16, 1988:

> San Francisco officials Thursday launched two investigations into an alleged police beating that left United Farm Workers union co-founder Dolores Huerta with broken ribs and forced doctors to remove her spleen. . .
>
> San Francisco Mayor Art Agnos, a Democrat who has known Huerta for 20 years, visited her at her sickbed Thursday. "I am deeply concerned and disturbed about this incident," Agnos said. . . .
>
> Earlier in the day [Wednesday], at a rally in the Fresno County farming community of Kingsburg, [George H.W.] Bush had said he opposed the UFW boycott against California table grapes. Huerta planned to hand out copies of a news release she prepared Wednesday rebutting Bush's opposition to the boycott.

The 1,000 demonstrators crossed police barricades and began heading across Powell Street, said San Francisco Police Officer David Ambrose. . . . "We do not hit them over the head, but we do strike in the midsection, on the arms," he said. "And that's an accepted police practice."

A Roman Catholic, Huerta was resting Thursday on a Catholic feast day that has special significance for her—the Feast Day of Dolores, Our Lady of Sorrows. Father Ken Irrgang, a Catholic priest who works at the UFW headquarters, said that Huerta has suffered a great deal during the 30 years she has worked on behalf of farm workers. "It's a nice little reminder to us," he said of the coincidence. . .

(*Source:* García, Mario T., ed. *A Dolores Huerta Reader.* Albuquerque: University of New Mexico Press, 2008, pp. 119–21.)

Books

García, Mario T., ed. *A Dolores Huerta Reader.* Albuquerque: University of New Mexico Press, 2008. Comprises a collection of essays about Huerta and several interviews with her.

Levy, Jacques E. *Cesar Chavez: Autobiography of La Causa.* New York: W. W. Norton, 1975. Chávez received the bulk of media attention for the work of the United Farm Workers but Huerta also played a significant role and she is mentioned here.

Website

The United Farm Workers provides information on the activities of the organization and its leaders. http://www.ufw.org

September 15

1988

The first Hispanic Heritage Month is celebrated, with the celebrations lasting until October 15. This September date is chosen in order to coincide with the Independence Day celebrations of five Latin American countries: Costa Rica, El Salvador, Guatemala, Honduras, and Nicaragua.

Books

Alexander, Linda B., and Nahyun Kwon, eds. *Multicultural Programs for Tweens and Teens.* Chicago: American Library Association, 2010. Suggests programming for libraries for Hispanic Heritage Month.

N.A. *Español!: Hispanic Heritage Month Information Booklet: September 15 to October 15, 1992.* Washington, D.C.: U.S. Dept. of Labor, Bureau of Labor Statistics, 1992. One of several booklets produced over the years by the U.S. government to promote the Latino celebration.

1997

The U.S. Postal Service issues a 32-cent commemorative stamp in honor of Padre Félix Varela. Born in Cuba, Varela went into exile in the United States in 1823 as a result of his political beliefs and writings. He established *El Habenero,* an early Spanish-language newspaper, but may be better known for promoting tolerance of all immigrants.

Books

McCadden, Joseph, and Helen M. McCadden. *Félix Varela: Torch Bearer from Cuba.* San Juan, PR: Félix Varela Foundation, 1998. The only biography of the Puerto Rican political activist.

Varela, Félix. *El Habanero: Papel Político, Científico y Literario.* Miami, FL: Ediciones Universal, 1997. Reprints the newspaper.

September 16

1874

Mexican revolutionary journalist Ricardo Flores Magón is born on September 16, 1874, in San Antonio Eloxochitlán. Jailed four times in Mexico for his radical journalism, Flores Magón finally went into exile in the United States. In 1904, he began publishing his newspaper, *Regeneración,* in San Antonio before moving it to St. Louis and then Canada. In 1907, now in Los Angeles, he founded *Revolución* and revived *Regeneración* the next year. Flores Magón and his brothers, Enrique and Jesús, smuggled the newspapers into Mexico in cans or wrapped inside other newspapers. The newspapers also proved popular among Mexican American workers engaged in unionizing efforts. Flores Magón openly embraced anarchism by the time of World War I and fell under the U.S. government crackdown on radicals. Federal authorities arrested Flores Magón in 1918 for breaking neutrality laws. He died in Leavenworth prison in 1922 under mysterious circumstances, possibly succumbing to lack of medical care for heart disease and diabetes.

Books

Bufe, Chaz, and Mitchell Cowen Verter, eds. *Dreams of Freedom: A Ricardo Flores Magón Reader.* Oakland, CA: AK Press, 2005. An anthology of his writings.

Day, Douglas. *The Prison Notebooks of Ricardo Flores Magón.* New York: Harcourt Brace Jovanovich, 1991. Contains his thoughts on American prisons.

MacLachlan, Colin M. *Anarchism and the Mexican Revolution: The Political Trials of Ricardo Flores Magón in the United States.* Berkeley: University of California Press, 1991. Examines the U.S. government's crackdown on this political radical, one of many who suffered repression in the era.

1948

Tennis player Rosemary Casals, the daughter of Salvadoran immigrants, is born in San Francisco. She became the first Latino to become a top-rated professional tennis player. In 1966, she teamed with Ian Crookenden to become the first Latino to win the U.S. mixed doubles tennis championship. A year later, she joined with Billie Jean King to win the doubles tennis championship at Wimbledon. The Casals–King team dominated women's doubles for years, winning 59 tournaments on every possible surface. Casals also had success individually, ranked No. 3 in the world at one point. Casals bucked against several traditional tennis practices. Besides disdaining white uniforms in favor of brightly colored outfits, she strongly objected to the practice of paying male players more than female players. In 1970, she joined other women in threatening a boycott. Pay increased as a result of her actions. Having won 112 professional doubles championships during her career, Casals joined the International Tennis Hall of Fame in 1996.

Book

Telgen, Diane, and Jim Kamp, eds. *Latinas!: Women of Achievement.* Detroit: Visible Ink Press, 1996. Contains a short biographical essay on Casals.

1969

The first Chicano Liberation Day is celebrated, on Mexican Independence Day. Chicano activist Corky Gonzales picked the date to protest against the lack of bilingual and bicultural education for Mexican Americans throughout the Southwest. Thousands of students in Denver and California walk out of classes in acknowledgement of the day.

Book

Macdonald, Victoria-María, ed. *Latino Education in the United States: A Narrated History from 1513–2000.* New York: Palgrave Macmillan, 2004. A solid history of education with documents.

September 17

1907

Luis Leal, the founder of Chicano Studies and the most prominent Mexican American literary critic of the 20th century, is born in Linares, Nuevo León, Mexico to a prosperous ranching family. He left Mexico to study at Northwestern University, just outside of Chicago. Leal subsequently interrupted his pursuit of a doctoral degree at the University of Chicago, at a time when very few Mexican Americans attended graduate school, to serve in the U.S. Army in the Pacific during World War II. He taught at the University of Mississippi, Emory University, the University of Illinois at Urbana, and the University of California at Santa Barbara. While at Illinois in the 1960s, Leal developed an interest in Chicano literature. As he would often emphasize, Mexican Americans could trace a literary genealogy within the borders of the United States as far back as the Spanish colonial period. However, it was not until the 1960s with the rise of the Chicano civil rights movement that specific attention came to be focused on Chicano cultural and artistic contributions. Leal took the lead in championing Chicano literature. His stature as an academic in the early days of Chicano literary criticism made it difficult for others to dismiss this research area as nothing more than political rhetoric. Leal stressed a binational identity, seeing Mexico and the United States as a single self. He died, aged 102, on January 25, 2010.

From "In Search of Aztlán":

> One of the functions of the critic is to discover and analyze literary symbols with the object of broadening the perception that one has of a certain social or ethnic group. . . . In the case of Chicano literature, a literature that has emerged as a consequence of the fight for social and human rights, most of the symbols have been taken from the surrounding social environment. For that reason, Chicano literary symbolism cannot be separated from Chicano cultural background. . . . The social and literary symbols are the same. Their origin is found in the sociopolitical struggle, from where they have passed on to literature.

(*Source:* Stavans, Ilan, ed. *A Luis Leal Reader.* Evanston, IL: Northwestern University Press, 2007, p. 5.)

Books

García, Mario T. *Luis Leal: An Auto/Biography*. Austin: University of Texas Press, 2000. Examines Leal's life and provides a selected bibliography of his works.

Stavans, Ilan, ed. *A Luis Leal Reader*. Evanston, IL: Northwestern University Press, 2007. Reprints Leal's major writings.

Websites

Luis Leal: A Journey of 100 Years Trailer. Introduces Janette Garcia's 56-minute documentary on Leal that came out in 2009. http://www.youtube.com/watch?v=ACsdKK6LpJc

Luis Leal: 1907. Provides a short biography of Leal but has not been updated since 2009. http://biography.jrank.org/pages/3916/Leal-Luis-1907-Scholar-Literary-Critic.html

1794

A letter with this date is the first recorded evidence of the Brothers of Our Father Jesus of Nazareth, commonly known as the Penitentes. The group consists of men of Hispanic descent who form a lay and religious mutual aid society in New Mexico. It is one of the first, perhaps the very first, Hispanic voluntary associations in the Southwest. In 1910, the Penitentes were influential in officially making New Mexico a bilingual state. They helped place Article 7 into the New Mexico State Constitution that stated no citizen shall be restricted from holding office or sitting on juries due to religion, race, language, color, or ability to speak, read, or write English or Spanish.

Book

Szasz, Ferenc Morton. *Larger than Life: New Mexico in the Twentieth Century*. Albuquerque:

University of New Mexico Press, 2006. Designed for classroom use, this is an extensive look at the state's history.

1968

The U.S. Congress passes legislation to celebrate Hispanic Heritage Week. The week becomes a month in 1988, in an era when other minority groups are getting months in which to recognize and celebrate their heritage.

Books

Alexander, Linda B., and Nahyun Kwon, eds. *Multicultural Programs for Tweens and Teens.* Chicago: American Library Association, 2010. Suggests programming for libraries for Hispanic Heritage Month.

N.A. *Español!: Hispanic Heritage Month Information Booklet: September 15 to October 15, 1992.* Washington, D.C.: U.S. Dept. of Labor, Bureau of Labor Statistics, 1992. One of several booklets produced over the years by the U.S. government to promote the Latino celebration.

September 18

1889

The doors of Hull-House open in Chicago. Founded by Jane Addams and Ellen Gates Starr, the settlement house helped generations of poor immigrants adjust to life in the United States and carve a bright future for themselves. About 1917, a Mexican barrio or *colonia* began to emerge on the Near West Side of Chicago. By the late 1920s, more than 7,000 Mexican men, women, and children lived around Hull-House, in Chicago's largest Mexican settlement. Meanwhile, Hull-House opened kilns for potters in 1927. A number of Mexicans participated in the Hull-House pottery program. At first, pottery classes were viewed by Addams as a means of providing recreation and fostering an appreciation of Mexican traditions.

By the 1930s, the Hull-House kilns represented a cottage industry, emphasizing self-help, artistry, and sales.

From *Pottery from Hull-House:*

The Mexicans at Hull House have a method of their own in building animals. The body is made first. The head and neck are added next. This part is then supported upon a temporary fork of clay and the legs are added. The whole animal is now shaped, finished, and smoothed. When the legs have dried off sufficiently to support the weight of the body the support is taken off. . . .

The Mexicans at Hull House often decorate with colored slips such things as plates and bowls in a manner reminiscent of Indian designs. They are apt at fitting their designs to the piece. These designs usually have meaning and are based on personal experience. They value highly this means of self-expression. In this connection an interesting story is told by a traveler in Mexico. He asked the cost of a decorated piece of pottery and was told the price. He then asked about an undecorated piece of the same size and shape and was told a much higher price—the reason being that if the undecorated piece were sold the potter would be deprived of the privilege of making the decoration upon it.

At Christmas time there is often on display a Mexican nativity scene with angels, Mary and Joseph, shepherds, kings, and devils. The devils have animal heads and they face away from the manger, because they cannot bear the sight of the Christ Child. Though the artist has made many of these there are never two exactly alike. . .

The organization of the Hull House Kilns was a natural outgrowth of the Pottery Department of the Hull House

Art School. It was established because there was a demand for the repetition of the type of thing being done in the school. The method of allowing each clayworker of the school to make his pottery according to his own ideas naturally resulted in a product especially well suited to vigorous surrounding such as gardens, porches, sun parlors, fire places, country homes, tea rooms, studios, etc.

When workers are needed in the shop they are chosen from the best available students trained in the school. Thus the Kilns are supplied with trained workers and those of the school most interested in clay work often find it possible to earn a livelihood doing a thing which gives them pleasure. . . .

Besides the ware which is duplicated and sold from samples, individual pieces are made—some to order and others to keep alive the free creative impulses of the individual. These pieces are sold thru exhibitions and to interested visitors.

(*Source:* N.A. *Pottery from Hull-House.* Chicago: Hull-House, 1933, pp. 3–5)

Books

Elshtain, Jean Bethke. *Jane Addams and the Dream of American Democracy.* New York: Basic Books, 2002. A well-regarded biography of Addams, once the most admired woman in the United States.

Ganz, Cheryl R., and Margaret Strobel. *Pots of Promise: Mexicans and Pottery at Hull-House, 1920–40.* Urbana: University of Illinois Press, 2004. Provides four essays relating to Hull-House, its pottery program, and Mexican immigration to Chicago along with many photographs of Hull-House pottery.

Websites

Hull House Kilns. The Wisconsin Pottery Association offers a short history of Hull-House pottery along with images of the claywork. http://www.wisconsinpottery.org/Hull%20House/index.htm

The Nobel Peace Prize 1931: Jane Addams. Provides a biography of Addams, who won a Nobel, as well as recommended readings about her life and work. http://www.nobelprize.org/nobel_prizes/peace/laureates/1931/addams-bio.html

1936

One of the most famous transgendered persons, Babe Bean, dies. Born in San Francisco, Elvira Mugarrieta may have married a man named Bean. During the summer of 1897, the police in Stockton, California, received reports of a young woman posing as a man. After two weeks of searching, they finally apprehended Bean in August but soon released him. Bean remained in Stockton but never hid, never stopped wearing male clothing, and never again experienced arrest. Bean became a local celebrity and then became a newspaper correspondent in the Philippines during the Spanish-American War.

Books

Rupp, Leila J. *A Desired Past: A Short History of Same-Sex Love in America.* Chicago: University of Chicago Press, 1999. Sets Bean in context.

Sullivan, Louis. *From Female to Male: The Life of Jack Bee Garland.* Boston: Alyson, 1990. The only full biography of the person also known as Babe Bean.

1936

Puerto Rican boxer Félix Trinidad Jr. defeats Óscar de la Hoya to become both International Boxing Federation and the World Boxing Council welterweight champion. Trinidad was introduced to boxing by his father, who held the featherweight championship in 1979. He left the ring in 2008 with 42 wins (35 by knockout) and three losses (one by knockout).

Book

Boddy, Kasia. *Boxing: A Cultural History*. London: Reaktion, 2009. A history of the "sweet science" that has also attracted working class men looking to get ahead.

September 19

1952

Carlos Alberto Torres, a Puerto Rican nationalist, is born. The U.S. government linked Torres to bombers associated with Fuerzas Armadas de Liberación Nacional (FALN). Torres went underground in 1976 and made the FBI's Most Wanted List. Torres denied participating in any bombings but, upon capture, received a 78-year prison sentence for seditious conspiracy. After 30 years, he was released in 2010. Supporters of Torres view him as a political prisoner.

Books

Duany, Jorge. *The Puerto Rican Nation on the Move: Identities on the Island and in the United States*. Discusses cultural nationalism among Puerto Ricans.

Negrón-Muntaner, Frances, and Ramón Grosfoguel, eds. *Puerto Rican Jam: Rethinking Colonialism and Nationalism*. Minneapolis: University of Minnesota Press, 1997. Offers essays that examine the debate over the political status of Puerto Rico.

Website

Puerto Rican Nationalism and the Drift toward Statehood. The Council on Hemispheric Affairs provides this excellent summary of the history of nationalism on the island. http://www.coha.org/puerto-rican-nationalism-and-the-drift-towards-statehood/

September 20

1946

Artist and activist Judy Baca is born in Los Angeles to a Mexican American family. A muralist, she is probably best known as the director of the Great Wall of Los Angeles. Murals are a traditional Mexican art form.

Books

Dunitz, Robin J. *Street Gallery: Guide to Over 1000 Los Angeles Murals*. Los Angeles: RJD Enterprises, 1998. Many, if not most, of these murals were created by Latinos.

Olmstead, Mary. *Judy Baca: Hispanic-American Biographies*. New York: Heinemann-Raintree, 2004. A children's book about the muralist.

Websites

Judy Baca. Judith F. Baca's official webpage. http://www.judybaca.com

Social and Public Art Resource Center. Provides a wealth of material about SPARC's history, the Great Wall of Los Angeles, the Save LA Murals Campaign, and Judy Baca. http://www.sparcmurals.org

1949

Tennis player Richard "Pancho" Gonzales, the national singles amateur champion, announces that he is turning professional and signs a $60,000 contract with promoter Bobby Riggs. Born in Los Angeles in 1928, Gonzales captured back to back U.S. championships in 1948 and 1949 with one of the most beautiful serves in tennis. A moody and ferocious player, he dominated men's professional tennis throughout the 1950s and 1960s. Gonzales joined the International Tennis Hall of Fame in 1968 as one of the legends of the court.

Books

Gonzales, Pancho, and Cy Rice. *Man with a Racket: The Autobiography of Pancho Gonzales*. New York: Barnes, 1959. The autobiography of the tennis star.

Heldman, Gladys, ed. *Tennis by Pancho Gonzales and Dick Hawk*. New York: Cornerstone, 1967. Gonzales offers tips on how to play the game that he dominated.

Websites

Ricardo "Pancho" Gonzales. Latin Sports Legends provides this biography of the tennis player. http://www.latinosportslegends.com/pancho_gonzales_bio.htm

Richard Pancho Gonzales. Journalist Bud Collins provides this superb short biography of Gonzales for the ATP World Tour. http://www.atpworldtour.com/Tennis/Players/Go/R/Richard-Pancho-A-Gonzales.aspx

1952

Mechanical engineer Juan Fernández de la Mora is born in Madrid, Spain. He earns a PhD from Yale in physics in 1981. Mora focuses on electrosprays, liquids dispersed into very fine particles, which is a subfield of nanoscience.

Book

Kulkarni, Pramod, Paul A. Baron, and Klaus Willeke, eds. *Aerosol Measurement: Principles, Techniques, and Applications.* Hoboken, NJ: Wiley, 2011. Includes de la Mora's work on high pressure aerosols.

September 21

1976

Orlando Letelier, former Ambassador to the United States from the Chilean government of socialist Salvador Allende, is killed along with his assistant, Ronni Moffitt, when a bomb attached to their car explodes on Massachusetts Avenue in Washington, D.C. Michael V. Townley, an American, subsequently admits to planting the bomb at the direction of the Chilean secret police. Letelier went into exile in the United States after Allende's government was overthrown in 1973 by a right-wing group led by Gen. Augusto Pinochet. Employed as a senior fellow by the Institute of Policy Studies and as a professor at American University, Letelier became the leading voice of Chilean exiles and a powerful lobbyist against the Pinochet government.

Book

Freed, Donald. *Death in Washington: The Murder of Orlando Letelier.* Westport, CT: Lawrence Hill, 1980. An account of one of the most shocking episodes in diplomatic history.

2010

The U.S. Senate declines to support a procedural measure that would have permitted a vote on the DREAM (Development, Relief, and Education for Alien Minors) Act. The legislation has had bipartisan appeal, as indicated by its sponsors Senator Orrin Hatch (R-Utah) and Senator Richard Durbin (D-Illinois), but it is controversial because of its connection to illegal immigration. The DREAM Act provides a conditional path to citizenship for undocumented youth who came to the United States because adults, typically their parents, brought them here. It covers about 65,000 youth who have spent the majority of their lives in the United States, who identify as American, and who have been educated at the expense of the U.S. taxpayer. To become a citizen, these individuals would need to complete two years of military service or earn an honorable discharge or complete a college degree or have completed two years in good standing toward a bachelor's degree or more advanced degree. It is estimated that 2.4 million young adults under the age of 24 are undocumented.

From "Basic Information about the DREAM Act":

> The following is a list of specific requirements one would need in order to qualify for the current version of the DREAM Act.
>
> • Must have entered the United States before the age of 16 (i.e. 15 and younger)

- Must have been present in the United States for at least five (5) consecutive years prior to enactment of the bill
- Must have graduated from a United States high school, or have obtained a GED, or have been accepted into an institution of higher education (i.e. college/university)
- Must be between the ages of 12 and 35 at the time of application
- Must have good moral character

(*Source:* DREAM Act Portal. "Basic Information about the DREAM Act." http://dreamact.info/students)

Books

Perez, William. *We Are Americans: Undocumented Students Pursuing the American Dream.* New York: Stylus, 2009. Argues that the United States will benefit economically if undocumented students are allowed to give back to the communities that raised them.

Spickard, Paul. *Almost All Aliens: Immigration, Race, and Colonialism in American History and Identity.* New York: Routledge, 2007. Good general history of U.S. immigration.

Websites

Dream Activist—Undocumented Students Action and Resource Network. Provides stories of undocumented students and promotes political activism. http://www.dreamactivist.org/

DREAM Act Portal. Provides information about legislative and protest activities over the DREAM Act. http://dreamact.info/

September 22

1554

Spanish conquistador Francisco Vásquez de Coronado dies in Mexico City after leading an expedition through present-day New Mexico, Arizona, and the Great Plains. Coronado set off from Mexico City in 1540 with about 1000 men in search of gold and silver. Coronado tried to claim the territory for the Spanish king but the Native Americans were unimpressed and strongly resisted. Coronado was subsequently tried for dereliction of duty in connection with abuses of the Indians but cleared.

Books

Flint, Richard. *No Settlement, No Conquest: A History of the Coronado Entrada.* Albuquerque: University of New Mexico Press, 2008. A good history of a monumental failure.

Flint, Richard, and Shirley Cushing Flint, eds. *The Latest Word from 1540: People, Places, and Portrayals of the Coronado Expedition.* Albuquerque: University of New Mexico Press, 2011. Essentially recreates the world of the expedition.

1911

The Primer Congreso Mexicanista in Laredo concludes, having begun on September 14. The Idar newspaper family called the conference to combat racism against Latinos in Texas, especially the many lynchings of Mexicans by ranchers and Texas Rangers. The male-dominated Congress also focused on school discrimination, the need to teach Spanish, the education of women, and the need for Mexican American unity, especially among the working class.

Book

Vargas, Zaragosa. *Crucible of Struggle: A History of Mexican Americans from Colonial Times to the Present Era.* New York: Oxford University Press, 2011. A general history of the challenges that have faced Mexican Americans.

September 23

1868

El Grito de Lares, the first major call for Puerto Rican independence, takes place in the town of Lares when several hundred

Puerto Ricans demand freedom from Spanish rule. The demand essentially goes nowhere with Puerto Rico only freed from Spanish governance when the United States took over the nation with the conclusion of the Spanish-American War in 1898.

Book

Wagenheim, Olga Jiménez de. *Puerto Rico: An Interpretive History from Pre-Columbian Times to 1900*. Princeton, NJ: Markus Wiener Publishers, 1998. One of the few histories of Puerto Rico in this era that is in English.

September 24

2000

Horacio "Rivets" Rivero Jr., the first Puerto Rican four-star admiral, dies. Rivero, a native of Ponce, Puerto Rico, also served as the first Latino U.S. ambassador to Spain from 1972 to 1974. Born in 1910, Rivero picked up his nickname at the U.S. Naval Academy when an officer had trouble reading the name on his uniform. Rivero graduated from the academy in 1931 and served on several ships before the outbreak of World War II. He served in the Pacific onboard the USS *San Juan,* earning a Bronze Star by providing gunnery cover for Marines landing at Guadalcanal and the Gilbert Islands. He concluded the war as executive officer on the USS *Pittsburgh*. During the Korean War, Rivero commanded the USS *Noble* during the assault on Inchon. He became a rear admiral in 1955. As vice chief of naval operations, Rivero directed the ships that blockaded Cuba during the 1962 Cuban Missile Crisis. He ascended to four-star admiral in 1964. In Vietnam, he oversaw the daily activities of the Navy. In 1968, he became the commander of North Atlantic Treaty Organization (NATO) forces in Southern Europe. Rivero retired in 1972.

Books

Fernandez, Virgil. *Hispanic Military Heroes*. Austin, TX: VFJ Publications, 2006. Provides a brief profile of Rivero and many other Latinos who achieved military renown.

Fursenko, Aleksandr, and Timothy Naftali. *"One Hell of a Gamble": Khrushchev, Castro, and Kennedy 1958–1964: The Secret History of the Cuban Missile Crisis*. New York: W. W. Norton, 1997. An account of the crisis based partly on documents from the Soviet archives.

Munton, Don, and David A. Welch. *The Cuban Missile Crisis: A Concise History*. New York: Oxford University Press, 2007. A brief but highly readable account of one of the most dramatic episodes in U.S. history.

Rivero, Horatio. *Reminiscences of Admiral Horatio Rivero, Jr., U.S. Navy (Retired)*. Annapolis, MD: U.S. Naval Institute, 1978. Rivero's autobiography.

Websites

Naval History and Heritage Command, Biographies in Naval History—Admiral Horacio Rivero http://www.history.navy.mil/bios/rivero_horacio.htm. This is the official U.S. Navy biography of Rivero.

Puerto Rico Herald: Puerto Rico Profile—Admiral Horacio Rivero. http://www.puertorico-herald.org/issues/vol4n08/ProfileRivero-en.html. This biography sets Rivero in the context of Puerto Rican pride.

September 25

1998

Dominican Sammy Sosa, a Chicago Cub, hits his 66th and last home run of the baseball season in a thrilling battle for the all-time season record with St. Louis Cardinal Mark McGwire. The contest rejuvenated a sport that had lost fans in the wake of a destructive labor strike. McGwire would ultimately win with 70 home runs. In 1998, Sosa won the National League's Most Valuable Player award (MVP), the All-Star MVP award, and the Roberto Clemente Award, major league's highest honor for outstanding service to the community. By 2003, however, rumors of steroid use were swirling around all of baseball's sluggers, including Sosa. There is no concrete evidence that Sosa used illegal substances. Major League Baseball did not test for performance-enhancing drugs when he hit most of his homeruns. He concluded his career in 2007 with 609 homeruns and a .273 batting average, marking him as one of the greatest sluggers to ever play the game. Sosa is one of only five major leaguers to hit over 600 home runs.

From "The Year of the Hitter":

The Yankee manager, Joe Torre, called it "the best year I've been involved with, and it was at the proper time"—by which he meant that this summer's heroics may finally have restored the game of baseball to its rightful place at or near the top of the American sporting pyramid, and laid to rest the sullen memories of the strike-ridden seasons of 1994 and 1995. . . . This has been the year of the booming bat, with balls soaring to left, right, center and plain out of sight. Mark McGwire and Sammy Sosa, both of whom broke Roger Maris's 37-year-old record of 61 home runs, battled for the home-run prize until the very last weekend, when McGwire seemed to settle the issue by belting four homers in two days for a mind-boggling total of 70. Theirs was a splendid rivalry that excited interest even among casual observers of the game.

(*Source:* Editorial, *New York Times,* September 28, 1998, http://www.nytimes.com/1998/09/28/opinion/the-year-of-the-hitter.html?ref=sammysosa)

Books

Bryant, Howard. *Juicing the Game: Drugs, Power and the Fight for the Soul of Major League Baseball.* New York: Viking, 2005. Addresses the steroid debate that may cost Sosa a chance to be elected to the Baseball Hall of Fame.

Noden, Merrell. *Home Run Heroes: Mark McGwire, Sammy Sosa, and a Season for the Ages.* New York: Simon & Schuster, 1998. Focuses on the highlight of Sosa's career.

Websites

Major League Baseball. The official site for the sport allows a search for material about Sosa. http://mlb.mlb.com

Sammy Sosa. This *New York Times* website provides links to newspaper articles about Sosa as well as a listing of his baseball statistics. http://topics.nytimes.com/topics/reference/timestopics/people/s/sammy_sosa/index.html

September 26

1957

West Side Story opens on Broadway. An adaptation of Shakespeare's *Romeo and Juliet* set in the streets of New York, Leonard Bernstein's musical focused on the clash between a Puerto Rican gang and an American gang. Bernstein wrote it to take advantage of a Latin music craze sweeping through the United States at the time. While audiences loved it and it went on to become a classic musical, many Puerto Ricans were offended about being depicted as vengeful, aggressive adolescents. The depiction of Puerto Rico in the song "America," the most overtly Latino number in the musical, also drew heavy criticism. Written chiefly by Bernstein to provide music for a dance, "America" combined the indigenous Mexican form, the *huapango,* with the Puerto Rican genre of the *seis.* Rosalia's nostalgic reminiscences about her homeland are countered with Anita's *bombas,* verbal blows aimed at one of the singer's audience members. Stephen Sondheim wrote the lyrics.

From the lyrics of "America":

Rosalia

Puerto Rico,
You lovely island . . .
Island of tropical breezes.
Always the pineapples growing,
Always the coffee blossoms blowing . . .

Anita

Puerto Rico . . .
You ugly island . . .
Island of tropic diseases.
Always the hurricanes blowing,
Always the population growing . . .
And the money owing,
And the babies crying,
And the bullets flying.
I like the island Manhattan.
Smoke on your pipe and put that in!

Others

I like to be in America!
O.K. by me in America!
Ev'rything free in America
For a small fee in America!

Rosalia

I like the city of San Juan.

Anita

I know a boat you can get on.

Rosalia

Hundreds of flowers in full bloom.

Anita

Hundreds of people in each room!

All

Automobile in America,
Chromium steel in America,
Wire-spoke wheel in America,
Very big deal in America!

Rosalia

I'll drive a Buick through San Juan.

Anita

If there's a road you can drive on.

Rosalia

I'll give my cousins a free ride.

Anita

How you get all of them inside?

All

Immigrant goes to America,
Many hellos in America;
Nobody knows in America
Puerto Rico's in America!

(*Source:* The Official West Side Story Site, http://www.westsidestory.com/site/level2/lyrics/america.html. Music by Leonard Bernstein, lyrics by Stephen Sondheim.)

Books

Garebian, Keith. *The Making of West Side Story*. Toronto: ECW Press, 1995. Focuses on the creation of the musical, not its reception by Latinos.

Wells, Elizabeth A. *West Side Story: Cultural Perspectives on an American Musical*. Lanham, MD: Scarecrow Press, 2011. This collection of essays reflects on the musical's genesis, women, gangs, and Latino elements. It also includes lyrics to selected songs and cast lists from various productions.

Websites

The Official West Side Story Site. Includes archival material, lyrics, merchandise, and licensing information. http://www.westsidestory.com/

West Side Story—IMDb. Internet Movie Database provides a cast list, photographs, and details about the play's movie version, which earned Latina Rita Moreno a Best Supporting Actress Oscar.

1918

Writer Fernando Alegría is born in the Maruri barrio section of Santiago, Chile. He came to the United States in 1938 to participate in a Youth for Peace meeting. He settled in California in 1947 to teach at the University of California at Berkeley. Alegría traveled frequently to Chile to engage with Chilean writers. In 1973, he was scheduled to meet President Salvador Allende but was warned at 5:00 in the morning of September 11, by a journalist, of a possible coup. Allende died in fighting a few hours later. Alegría has continued to promote Chilean literary works in the United States.

Book

Ruiz, René. *Fernando Alegría: Vida y Obra.* Madrid: Playor, D.L., 1979. Covers the life and writings of Alegría.

1942

Author and editor Rafael Catalá is born in Cuba. He settles in New York City in 1961. Catalá focuses on searching for new Latin American man in his writings, one that is linked to the liberation of all oppressed people. As the editor of the *Index of American Periodical Verse,* Catalá included Hispanic poets in the United States, a group that had till then been excluded.

1942

Chicana feminist writer and poet Gloria Anzaldúa is born near Edinburg in South Texas to a family that traced it roots to Basque and Spanish families who settled the area in the 16th and 17th centuries. Like many Tejanos with deep roots, however, Anzaldúa felt marginalized in the Anglo world. Many of her writings deal with various forms of marginalization. One of her best known works is the co-edited collection with Cherríe Moraga, *This Bridge Called My Back: Writings by Radical Women of Color* (1981). Besides writing, Anzaldúa taught at a number of universities. She suffered poor health her entire life and died of complications from diabetes in 2004.

From "Puddles":

The gay man always left a puddle on his chair, along with the tip on the table. It got so Prieta ceased being surprised. With one hand she'd wipe it up with a towel (the puddle wasn't very big) and with the other, pocket the quarter. . . . After half a dozen times of wanting to, Prieta finally dipped her finger in. . . .

The next morning, as she washed her face she noticed that the tip of her tongue had turned green. She scrubbed it with her toothbrush. She rinsed it with mouthwash. No changes. She was running late for work. Never mind the green tongue. She planned to confront the man whose puddle had turned her tongue green. Was he carrying some weird disease? . . .

Amy looked at her funny . . . "Your face is all lighted up. You wearing some kind of fluorescent makeup? The color's all wrong, got sort of a greenish tinge. Oh, your knees look sort of wrinkled," she said bending down to get a closer look. Prieta craned her head to look at her knees. . . . The green had begun to creep from her finger to the back of her hand. . . .

All day as she bustled from table to counter to kitchen she kept an eye on the door. But the man who made puddles did not come in that day, or the next. She noticed the customers kept eyeing her knees.

By the fourth day, she knew what each customer was going to order before they opened their mouths. She also knew that the "green man" was never coming back—he didn't have to, he'd done his deed. . . . By then she had only to cast her eyes over some man hunched over lunch or dinner and she'd know if he was sticking it to his daughter. She would slap the check, along with a napkin, face down on the table. The bold green letters on the napkin would read, "I know what you are doing to your daughter. If you do it again your thing will turn green and fall off." By the end of the week she did not need this particular waitressing job. A few days later her green skin began to flake off. Underneath it she could see her original brown skin emerge. She began to get glimpses of other "afflicted" people—something in their eyes marked their difference.

She decided to drop by Les Amis to see if Amy was ready. If she was, Prieta would leave her the gift and say goodbye. Prieta had found out what her real work was—to move from town to town, work in restaurants, keep her knees covered, and when no one was looking touch an exposed knee to a chair and let slide a puddle of tears.

(*Source*: Gonzalez, Ray, ed. *Currents from the Dancing River: Contemporary Latino Fiction, Nonfiction, and Poetry.* New York: Harcourt Brace, 1994, pp. 118–20.)

Books

Anzaldúa, Gloria. *The Gloria Anzaldúa Reader.* Durham: Duke University Press, 2009. A collection of the writer's short stories.
Keating, AnaLouise, and Gloria González-López, eds. *Bridging: How Gloria Anzaldúa's Life and Work Transformed Our Own.* Austin: University of Texas Press, 2011. A biography of and a memorial to the writer.

1983

Katherine D. Ortega takes office as treasurer of the United States. Ortega, born in Tularosa, New Mexico, is descended from a family that settled in New Mexico before the United States took control of the territory. The first female president of a California bank, she founded Alamogordo Bank. Although holding a largely ceremonial post, she became the most prominent Hispanic member of the Reagan administration and remained in office until 1989.

Book

Boyko, Carrie, and Kimberly Colen, comp. *Hold Fast Your Dreams: Twenty Commencement Speeches.* New York: Scholastic, 1996. Contains a speech by Ortega.

September 27

1936

Pharmacologist Pedro Cuatrecasas is born in Madrid, Spain. He immigrated to the United States to attend college. Cuatrecasas has participated in the development of more than 40 commercial drugs for the treatment of such ailments as diabetes, depression, asthma, and hypertension.

Book

Spilker, Bert, and Pedro Cuatrecasas. *Inside the Drug Industry.* Barcelona: Prous Science Publishers, 1990. Explains the research, testing, and marketing needed to get a drug to a patient.

1990

Carlos Saldaña creates his comic book, *Burrito: Jack-of-All-Trades.* Saldaña is also a founder of the short-lived organization PACAS (Professional Amigos of Comic Art Society).

Book

Aldama, Frederick Luis. *Your Brain on Latino Comics: From Gus Arriola to Los Bros Hernández.* Austin: University of Texas Press, 2009. Provides an overview of Latino comics.

September 28

1960

Ted Williams, the son of a Mexican mother and the first Latino to be elected to the Hall of Fame, plays his final game of a 19-year career. Williams achieved his boyhood dream of becoming one of the best hitters ever in Major League Baseball. Batting left-handed, the "Splendid Splinter" won six American League batting championships despite losing five years during his prime to service as a U.S. Marine fighter pilot in World War II and the Korean War. His accomplishments include a .406 season in 1941, two Triple Crowns, two MVPs, 521 home runs, a lifetime average of .344, and 17 All-Star game selections. Notoriously press shy, Williams sought no acclaim for his personal generosity. He raised millions of dollars for the Jimmy Fund, a charity established at Boston's Dana Farber Cancer Institute. (The Farber Institute has a Williams exhibit to thank him.) Upon being inducted into the Baseball Hall of Fame, Williams made a point of recognizing great African American players who were, at the time, not eligible for induction because they had been prevented from playing alongside whites during the days of segregation. He died in 2002.

From Ted Williams's speech upon being inducted into the Baseball Hall of Fame:

> [Ball] players are not born great. They're not born hitters or pitchers or managers and luck isn't the key factor. No one has come up for a substitute for hard work. I've never met a great baseball player who didn't have to work harder at learning to play baseball than anything else he ever did. To me it was the greatest fun I ever had which probably explains why today I feel both humility and pride because God let me play the game and to learn to be good at it, proud because I spent most of my life in the company of so many wonderful people. . . . Baseball gives every American boy a chance to excel, not just to be as good as someone else but to be better than someone else. This is the nature of man and the name of the game and I've always been a lucky guy to have worn a baseball uniform, to have struck out or to have hit a tape measure home run. And I hope that someday the names of Satchel Paige and Josh Gibson in some way can be added as a symbol of the great Negro players that are not here only because they were not given a chance.

(*Source*: Baseball Hall of Fame, http://baseballhall.org/node/11160)

Books

Montville, Leigh. *Ted Williams: The Biography of an American Hero*. New York: Anchor, 2005. The definitive biography of the baseball player.

Williams, Ted, and John Underwood. *The Science of Hitting*. New York: Simon and Schuster, 1986. Since its original publication in 1971, this has become the classic treatise on how to hit a baseball.

Websites

Baseball Hall of Fame. Includes Williams's baseball statistics and the speech he gave upon being inducted into the Hall of Fame in 1966. http://baseballhall.org/node/11160

The Official Ted Williams Website. Rich in information about the slugger's life, this site includes stories about his military career, his baseball statistics, and hitting tips from the master.

1897

Mycologist Carlos E. Chardón is born in Ponce, Puerto Rico. Known as the "father of mycology in Puerto Rico," he discovered the aphid *Aphis maidis* that spread a virus among sugarcane. The discovery significantly helped the sugarcane industry, a major business.

Book

Chardón, Carlos E, and Rafael A. Toro. *Mycological Explorations of Colombia*. San Juan, PR: Bureau of Supplies, Printing, and Transportation, 1930. Examinations of fungi in Colombia.

September 29

1898

Puerto Rico is officially ceded to the United States as part of the peace agreement with Spain. No Puerto Rican participated in the peace negotiations that ended the Spanish-American War and resulted in the awarding of the island nation to the United States. The Puerto Ricans, who had sought independence from Spain, now found themselves as dependents of a country that was far more powerful and quite determined to keep its new possession.

From Simeon Baldwin, "The Constitutional Questions Incident to the Acquisition and Government by the United States of Island Territory," *Harvard Law Review, 1899,* from "The Year of the Hitter":

> Our Constitution was made by a *civilized and educated people.* It provides guarantees of personal security which seem ill adapted to the conditions of society that prevail in many parts of our new possessions. To give the *half-civilized Moros of the Philippines or even the ignorant and lawless brigands that infest Puerto Rico, or even the ordinary Filipino of Manila, the benefit of such immunity* from the sharp and sudden justice—or injustice—which they have been hitherto accustomed to expect, would, of course, be a serious obstacle to the maintenance there of an efficient government.

(*Source:* Soltero, Carlos R. *Latino and American Law: Landmark Supreme Court Cases.* Austin: University of Texas Press, 2006, p. 22.)

Books

Nugent, Walter. *Habits of Empire: A History of American Expansion.* New York: Vintage, 2009. An account of imperial expansion that covers the Louisiana Purchase to the U.S. acquisitions of protectorates, such as Puerto Rico, in the Caribbean and Pacific.

Soltero, Carlos R. *Latino and American Law: Landmark Supreme Court Cases.* Austin: University of Texas Press, 2006. Examines court cases relating to Puerto Rico's status in the legal system.

September 30

1822

Joseph Marion Hernández begins serving as the first Latino representative to the U.S. Congress. A Whig, he represented Florida until March 3, 1823, when he served in Florida's Territorial House of Representatives. Hernández, born in St. Augustine, fought in the Seminole War in 1835 as a brigadier general of volunteers and led the group that captured Seminole chief Osceola.

Website

Joseph Marion Hernández. The Library of Congress supplies a short biography and an image of Hernández as part of its Hispanic Americans in Congress series. http://www.loc.gov/rr/hispanic/congress/hernandezj.html

1946

Héctor Lavoe, a Puerto Rican salsa singer, is born. He played with Willie Colón's band in the 1960s before striking out on his own. His hits include "El Cantante" and "Bandolera." He died in 1993 after a period of poor health.

Book

Padura, Leonardo. *Faces of Salsa: A Spoken History of the Music.* Washington: Smithsonian Books, 2003. Salsa musicians, not including Lavoe, explain their musical form.

October

October 1

1942

Meteorologist Eugenia Kalnay is born in Buenos Aires, Argentina. In the 1980s, as a National Weather Service director, Kalnay improved environmental modeling to the point that three-day weather forecasts became as reliable as one-day forecasts.

Book

Kalnay, Eugenia. *Atmospheric Modeling, Data Assimilation, and Predictability*. New York: Cambridge University Press, 2003. Discusses how to predict the weather accurately.

October 2

1672

Construction of Castillo de San Marcos in St. Augustine, Florida, begins. The oldest surviving fort in North America, Castillo de San Marcos formed a wall around the city of St. Augustine. Though it was located in a relative backwater of the Spanish empire, the fort nevertheless came under attack by the English and the French in the constant wars for empire of the 17th and 18th centuries.

Book

National Park Service. *Castillo de San Marcos: A Guide to the Castillo de San Marcos National Monument, Florida*. Washington, D.C.: U.S. Dept. of the Interior, 1993.

Website

Castillo de San Marcos. The National Park Service supplies a brief history of the fort as well as information about visiting the site. http://www.nps.gov/casa/historyculture/index.htm

1996

The Puerto Rican Traveling Theater (PRTT) is honored with a New York State Governor's Arts Award. The awards were initiated in 1966. PRTT aims to inform the general public about works written by playwrights of Latino ancestry, to help develop emerging and established artists, and, generally, to contribute to the diversity of American theater.

Book

De La Roche, Elisa. *Teatro Hispano! Three Major New York Companies*. New York: Garland, 1995. Provides a history of the Puerto Rican Travelling Theater.

October 3

1916

Marine biologist Angeles Alvariño is born in Spain. After coming to the United States in 1956, she contributed to knowledge about the nature and distribution of marine zooplankton, tiny one-celled organisms that form the base of the marine food web.

Book

Newton, David E. *Encyclopedia of Water*. Westport, CT: Greenwood Press, 2003. Contains a biographical essay on Alvariño.

1942

Raymond S. "Jerry" Apodaca, Democratic governor of New Mexico from 1975 to 1979, is born in Las Cruces, New Mexico. Apodaca, who ran his own insurance agency, had served in the New Mexico Senate since 1966. He became the first Mexican American governor of New Mexico in 60 years. Once in the governor's office, he reorganized the cabinet to more effectively provide services to the public. In 1978, President Jimmy Carter named Apodaca, a former football player who ran the Boston Marathon that same year, to the President's Council on Physical Fitness. After leaving office, Apodaca focused on magazine publishing for the Latino audience.

From an interview with Jerry Apodaca, 1978:

Born to bilingual parents in the dusty poverty of Las Cruces, young Jerry was held back in first grade to improve his English—an experience friends believe may have fired his furious drive to excel. (As governor, Apodaca has made kindergartens mandatory throughout the state, so Chicano children can become bilingual earlier.) All-state football in high school, he won a scholarship to the University of New Mexico, where he majored in education. After graduating in 1957, he married his high school sweetheart, Clara Melendres, then taught history and coached football at an Albuquerque high school. But ambition and his growing family caught up with him. Moving back to Las Cruces, he opened a storefront insurance agency. "I've never been a hard-sell kind of guy," he says. "But I had to try something." When the agency prospered, he branched out into shoe stores and real estate.

In 1964, after working on a friend's unsuccessful campaign for mayor, [Apodaca] decided to try politics himself. Against all advice, he ran for state senator as a Democrat—and lost, partly because his nervousness as a public speaker left an impression of quaking timidity. Undaunted, Apodaca took speech lessons and two years later won the seat. Today the governor speaks immaculate newscaster's English in public, though a slight Spanish inflection creeps through after hours. Then following eight years in the senate, he decided to run for governor, though most New Mexicans had no idea who he was. To make a virtue of Apodaca's anonymity, his campaign manager posed him in a borrowed, bone-white running suit for a series of billboards, labeling him tersely, THE MAN NO-BODY OWNS. "I used to be out campaigning," recalls Apodaca with a grin, "and people would light up and say, 'Hey, I know you—you're the man nobody owns.'" He defeated his Republican opponent by a squeaky 3,700 votes.

As governor Apodaca has streamlined the state's bureaucracy (which he once called a "700-pound marshmallow") and fired many state employees—a step that made him cringe "because you know how it affects their families." He issued an order cutting back on long lunches and another forbidding government employees from drinking during the workday. "I think I've got the marshmallow down to about 500 pounds now," he says. Setting an example for his fellow public servants, he arrives at the office by 8:30 a.m. but slips away from the state-house whenever he can to watch his children carry on the family athletic tradition. "I've never pressured any of my children to go into sports," says Apodaca proudly. "The only thing I've told them is that if they make up their minds to do something, they can't ever, ever quit. That goes for everything else too."

(*Source:* Demaret, Kent. "New Mexico Gov. Jerry Apodaca Survives Agony of the Boston Marathon—But Barely." *People,* May 1, 1978, http://www.people.com/people/archive/article/0,,20070732,00.html)

Book

Szasz, Ferenc Morton. *Larger Than Life: New Mexico in the Twentieth Century*. Albuquerque: University of New Mexico Press, 2006. A good general history of the Land of Enchantment.

October 4

1919

Playwright and essayist René Marqués is born in Arecibo, Puerto Rico. In the mid-20th century, he was Puerto Rico's foremost writer. He founded the Teatro Experimental del Ateneo in 1951. Many of Marques's writings focus on the theme of political independence. Although he was not a Nationalist, he was the first writer in Puerto Rico to make use of their activities as thematic material.

Book

Pilditch, Charles R. *René Marqués: A Study of His Fiction*. New York: Plus Ultra, 1976. One of the few critical examinations of this writer's works.

October 5

1939

Louis Anthony Fernandez, a geologist, is born in New York City to Puerto Rican parents. For his work in establishing the American Geological Institute's Minority Participation Program, he was honored by the Hispanic Caucus of the American Association for Higher Education in 2004.

Book

Burke, Ronald J., and Mary C. Mattis, eds. *Women and Minorities in Science, Technology, Engineering and Mathematics: Upping the Numbers*. Northampton, MA: Edward Elgar, 2007. Examines the same state of the profession that Fernandez has tried to address.

October 6

2004

Raul Yzaguirre retires as president and chief executive of the National Council of La Raza. He turned the organization from one that in 1974 lived off a $500,000 grant and a focus on urban Hispanics to one with an annual budget of $28 million, 125 staffers, and status as the nation's most prominent Latino advocacy group. He is credited with helping to change the perception of Latinos in the United States.

Book

Cisneros, Henry G., and John Rosales. *Latinos and the Nation's Future*. Houston, TX: Arte Publico, 2009. Yzaguirre contributes an essay on the future of civil rights for Latinos.

October 7

1975

President Gerald Ford signs legislation allowing women to attend U.S. military academies. Linda Garcia (later Cubero) becomes the first Latina to graduate from a service academy when she earns a B.S. in political science from the U.S. Air Force Academy in 1980. Cubero serves seven years in the air force, reaching the rank of captain.

Book

Stiehm, Judith. *Bring Me Men and Women: Mandated Change at the U.S. Air Force Academy*. Berkeley: University of California Press, 1981. Looks at the controversy over the admission of women to the U.S. Air Force Academy.

1979

The United Neighborhoods Organization (UNO) holds its first convention with about 4,500 participants. The group, founded in East Los Angeles in 1975 under the leadership of Bishop Juan Arzube and Father

Pedro Villarroya, aimed to address community problems such as education, housing, financial reinvestment in Latino communities, and Immigration and Naturalization Service raids on undocumented Mexican workers. UNO provided Spanish speakers to the Sheriff's Department and registered voters.

Book

McKnight, John. *The Abundant Community: Awakening the Power of Families and Neighborhoods.* San Francisco: Berrett-Koehler Publishers, 2010. Discusses the same sort of power that UNO sought to develop.

October 8

1998

Salsa superstar and actor Marc Anthony announces that he is going to Puerto Rico to donate prefabricated homes to victims of Hurricane Georges. Born in New York City to Puerto Rican parents, Anthony has donated $100,000 for the project and hopes to house 100 families. The storm, a Category 4 hurricane, swept through the Caribbean in September and killed 604 people, mostly on the island of Hispaniola. Puerto Rico also suffered extensive damage.

Book

Barnes, Jay. *Florida's Hurricane History.* Chapel Hill: University of North Carolina Press, 2007. Covers the creation of hurricanes and the path of many that also struck Puerto Rico, including Georges, in 1998.

October 9

1969

PADRES (*Padres Asociados para Derechos Religiosos, Educativos y Socialiales* or Priests Associated for Religious, Educational, and Social Rights) is formed in San Antonio, Texas. The group formed to resist a long history of institutional racism, discrimination, and neglect of Mexican Americans by the U.S. Catholic Church. More than 90 percent of Mexican Americans are Catholic and they form a significant part of the Catholic population in the United States. Accordingly, Catholic priests played a major role in the Chicano movement. The activist priests aimed to focus the church on a Latino-specific agenda. Largely as a result of their efforts, thousands of Latino laypersons became involved at the local level in parish councils; the Spanish language became more common in formal church practices; the first Chicano and Latino bishops were appointed; and the dominance of white priests and nuns in Latino Catholic ministry was greatly diminished. PADRES disbanded in 1989. A similar organization for Latina nuns, Las Hermanas, remains in existence.

Father Patrick Flores, a PADRES member, spoke to a group of Catholic bishops in 1971 about the need for a Mexican American bishop:

> [I told them] we really felt that Hispanics were being overlooked in two ways, that they are not getting the services that they need . . . and that they're not being allowed to serve. . . . And then I said, for example, don't you find it embarrassing that if somebody were to ask you of the three hundred bishops in the United States, how many are Hispanic and Mexicans and so on? And you'll have to say none. And we've been here over two hundred years but not one Hispanic bishop . . . [One bishop said], "But you know why we don't have Hispanic bishops? Because none of them qualify. They're not good enough to be bishops." I said, "Do you think you qualify to be a bishop here in this diocese? You don't speak Spanish. And the diocese is predominantly Hispanic."

(*Source:* Martínez, Richard Edward. *PA-DRES: The National Chicano Priest Movement.* Austin: University of Texas Press, 2005, p. 92.)

Books

Hinojosa, Gilberto M., and Jay P. Dolan, eds. *Mexican Americans and the Catholic Church, 1900–1965.* Notre Dame, IN: Notre Dame University Press, 1994. A collection of essays that highlights the concerns that led to the founding of PADRES.

Martínez, Richard Edward. *PADRES: The National Chicano Priest Movement.* Austin: University of Texas Press, 2005. This is the only full-length study of this major Chicano organization.

Websites

Mexican Americans and Religion, The Handbook of Texas. This Texas State Historical Association webpage provides a solid history of Catholicism in the state. http://www.tshaonline.org/handbook/online/articles/pqmcf

Mexican American Catholic College. This Texas school was founded in 1972 by PADRES and Las Hermanas with the aid of the Archdiocese of San Antonio. http://www.maccsa.org/history.php

October 10

1849

The United States and Mexico Boundary Commission agree on the precise beginning of the international border south of the Port of San Diego in California. By the 21st century, the San Diego border crossing with Tijuana was one of the busiest in the world with nearly 60 million crossings each year and the place of greatest interaction between the United States and Mexico. As is typical with the border cities of the U.S.-Mexico boundary, the U.S. twin is the richer while the Mexican twin is the bigger.

Book

Montezemolo, Fiamma, René Peralta, and Heriberto Yepez. *Here Is Tijuana.* London: Black Dog, 2006. Uses photographs and text to explore the world on the Mexican side of the San Diego–Tijuana border.

1922

Luisa Capetillo, the first Puerto Rican woman to be a labor movement leader, dies in Arecibo. Known for an independent streak, Capetillo worked as reader in a tobacco factory. At work, she became familiar with labor unions and began to write in support of workers. During a 1905 strike of farmworkers, she became a leader in the American Federation of Labor. She is credited with helping to pass the first minimum wage law in Puerto Rico. An advocate of the right of women to vote and a feminist, she also founded a newspaper, *La Mujer.*

Book

Valle Ferrer, Norma. *Luisa Capetillo, Pioneer Puerto Rican Feminist.* New York: Peter Lang, 2006. The only English-language biography of the feminist.

October 11

1995

Mario Molina, a Mexican American, is awarded a share of the Nobel Prize in chemistry for his role in discovering how the Earth's ozone layer is formed and how it decomposes. He linked chlorofluorocarbons in the atmosphere to damage on the ozone layer.

Book

Guidici, Cynthia. *Mario Molina.* Chicago: Raintree, 2006. A biography of the chemist for a juvenile audience but also the only book-length biography available.

October 12

1926

Architect César Pelli is born in San Miguel de Tucumán, Argentina. He began his career in the United States with Eero Saarinen. A naturalized U.S. citizen, Pelli is best known for designing the Petronas Towers in Malaysia and the Pacific Design Center in Los Angeles. He became the first Latino to receive the gold medal from the American Institute of Architects in 1995.

Book

Pelli, Cesar. *Cesar Pelli: Selected and Current Works.* Mulgrave, Victoria: Images Publishing Group, 1993. Includes a conversation with the architect.

1946

The Puerto Rican Independence Party is founded by attorney Gilberto Concepción de Gracia. It aimed to win independence through legal and peaceful means and soon became one of the major political parties in Puerto Rico.

Books

Duany, Jorge. *The Puerto Rican Nation on the Move: Identities on the Island and in the United States.* Discusses cultural nationalism among Puerto Ricans.

Negrón-Muntaner, Frances, and Ramón Grosfoguel, eds. *Puerto Rican Jam: Rethinking Colonialism and Nationalism.* Minneapolis: University of Minnesota Press, 1997. Offers essays that examine the debate over the political status of Puerto Rico.

Website

Puerto Rican Nationalism and the Drift toward Statehood. The Council on Hemispheric Affairs provides this excellent summary of the history of nationalism on the island. http://www.coha.org/puerto-rican-nationalism-and-the-drift-towards-statehood/

1977

Hundreds of people line up at the U.S. Supreme Court building, waiting to hear the start of oral arguments in the case of *Regents of the University of California v. Allan Bakke,* which centered on the legality of affirmative action. The decision, announced on June 28, 1978, declared that admission quotas preferential to minority students violated the Fourth Amendment's Equal Protection Clause. Bakke, a white Vietnam veteran, had challenged the University of California at Davis Medical School's attempt to admit minorities to a professional school that had not admitted them in the past because of their poor performance on the standardized tests needed for admission. Other universities removed quotas as a result of the decision but preferential racial classification remained legal in some circumstances though inherently suspect.

Book

Dreyfuss, Joel, and Charles Lawrence III. *The Bakke Case: The Politics of Inequality.* New York: Harcourt Brace Jovanovich, 1979. Discusses the impact of the case upon affirmative action.

October 13

2011

Margarita "Mago" Orona Gándara's exhibition "Peregrinas Inmigrantes" opens at the University of Texas El Paso (UTEP). Born in El Paso in 1929 to a Mexican mother and Basque Mexican father, Gándara is famed as a muralist and sculptor as well as a border artist. She earned a degree in fine arts and education from UTEP and also studied at the Art Institute of Chicago. In 1973, Gándara completed a series of massive public art works in El Paso and, right across the border, in Juarez, Mexico. Gándara built a studio-house in Juarez, working alongside

Mexican laborers as they made adobe bricks on the site. She also retained a studio in El Paso. Famed as a monumental mosaic muralist, Gándara fled Juarez in 2010 upon being threatened by thugs. She has described this exhibition as her revenge.

From "When *Sicarios* Threatened to Kill Her, the Muralist Brought Her Art to El Paso":

Her art name means magician and just like a magician pulls a rabbit out of a hat, muralist Margarita "Mago" Gandara pulls creativity and rebellion from deep within her soul to produce intricate murals, sculptures and bronze pieces that mirror the Mexican-American culture that she fell in love with as a young child.

After living in Juárez for nearly 40 years, Gandara was threatened by "sicarios" or assassins, who targeted her after seeing her truck with Texas license plates outside of her adobe home studio in a southern Juárez colonia.

Immediately after being threatened, Gandara, with the help of her son, fled from her home taking as many pieces of art as she could, while still leaving some behind. Many of the pieces, along with additional new works will be displayed at an exhibit she calls, "Peregrinas Immigrantes" at UTEP on October 13th.

"The purpose of the exhibit is that since I was in Juárez for 35 to 40 years with my studio, I had a beautiful life. Then the sicarios threatened me to give them money, or else. So I had to flee and this exhibit is my response to that," says Gandara.

"I didn't want my peregrinas to look miserable and to be chopped in pieces and hacked. The evil gets enough publicity," says Gandara. "All that culture, all that energy, that was positive. I resent that they have so much publicity on the violence, they don't talk about these other things."

Her bright artwork is deeply submerged in the historic culture of the Mexican-American people, a culture she was born into with two Mexican-Americans as her parents. Her voice fills the room and her face lights up with excitement when she speaks about her father whom she closely relates to in many ways.

According to Gandara, her father faced ex-communication from the Catholic church, exile and corrupt governments in the time of Pancho Villa, a moment in history that she believes is repeating itself today.

"He was kicked out of Mexico, and I've been kicked out," says Gandara. "It is history all over again except this is worse – if that can possibly be. The Mexican is killing the Mexican."

(*Source:* Treviño, Marisa. "When *Sicarios* Threatened to Kill Her, the Muralist Brought Her Art to El Paso." *Borderzine,* October 4, 2011, http://latinalista.com/2011/10/when-sicarios-threatened-to-kill-her-the-muralist-brought-her-art-to-el-paso)

Books

Cockroft, Eva Sperling, and John Weber. *Toward a People's Art: The Contemporary Mural Movement.* Albuquerque: University of New Mexico Press, 1998. Provides a contemporary history of a traditional Mexican art form.

Vargas, George. *Contemporary Chicano Art: Color and Culture for a New America.* Austin: University of Texas Press, 2010. Contains an extensive biography of Gándara and sets her in the context of contemporary Chicano art.

Websites

Biografia Margarita "Mago" Gandara, Youtube. A short but excellent biography of the artist in Spanish that contains archival photos and an interview with Gándara. http://www.youtube.com/watch?v = nWhtXGk_zm0

"Chicano Mural Movement." The Handbook of Texas, Texas State Historical Association. Provides a short history of the movement. http://www.tshaonline.org/handbook/on line/articles/kjc03

October 14

1962

The Cuban Missile Crisis begins when American intelligence experts discover Soviet missile sites under construction in Cuba. The episode brings the United States and the Soviet Union to the brink of nuclear war. President John F. Kennedy, instead of attacking Cuba, attempts to defuse the situation by blocking the island and preventing Soviet ships from resupplying it. The Soviet ships turn around instead of attacking the U.S. Navy ships. On October 28, Nikita Khrushchev agrees to remove the missiles. Both countries then take steps to reduce Cold War tensions.

Books

Fursenko, Aleksandr, and Timothy Naftali. *"One Hell of a Gamble": Khrushchev, Castro, and Kennedy 1958–1964: The Secret History of the Cuban Missile Crisis.* New York: W. W. Norton, 1997. An account of the crisis based partly on documents from the Soviet archives.

Munton, Don, and David A. Welch. *The Cuban Missile Crisis: A Concise History.* New York: Oxford University Press, 2007. A brief but highly readable account of one of the most dramatic episodes in U.S. history.

2003

Mexican American Grace Flores-Hughes reveals the federal government's history of "Hispanic" and "Latino" in an interview with Darrell Fears of the Washington Post. Flores-Hughes sat on the highly contentious Ad Hoc Committee on Racial and Ethnic Definitions while working for the Department of Health, Education and Welfare. She reports that the committee chose the word "Hispanic." Members of the ad hoc committee said it was hastily formed early in 1975, after educators of Puerto Rican, Cuban, Mexican, and Native American descent stormed out of a meeting called to discuss a report at the Federal Interagency Committee on Education. The group never got around to discussing the report, on the education of Chicanos, Puerto Ricans and Indians. They were livid over how it wrongly identified certain groups. Caspar W. Weinberger, secretary of Health, Education and Welfare ordered that a committee be convened to solve the identity matter for good. Flores-Hughes commented that "Hispanic" was better than anything she had been called as a child in Texas and noted that she did not care for Latino because it also included Italians.

Book

Shorris, Earl. *Latinos: A Biography of the People.* New York: W. W. Norton, 1992. Shorris does not include Italians in his narrative history.

October 15

1951

I Love Lucy premieres on CBS television. Starring Lucille Ball as zany Lucy and Desi Arnaz as her frustrated Cuban bandleader husband, the series becomes one of the most beloved situation comedies. Arnaz, married to Ball in real life, was born in Santiago, Cuba in 1917. He established a career in U.S. music, theater, and film in the 1940s, at a time when few Latinos appeared in performance spaces. When he and Ball decided to work together on a television series, they had to convince network executives that the United States would accept a bicultural couple that included a Cuban husband. Network executives balked until the two stars did a successful nightclub act on the road. Along with starring in *I Love*

Lucy, Arnaz proved a talented impresario and worked as an executive with Desilu Productions.

From "Why Millions Love Lucy: In the Comical Trials of Lucy and Ricky Ricardo TV Audiences Recognize the Exasperation and Warmth of Their Own Lives":

> Last week's signing of record $8,000,000 contract to keep "I Love Lucy" on television another two years was economic confirmation of the obvious. . . . By every reasonable criterion they are something very special. . . . "I Love Lucy" is marriage projected in larger-than-life size but never so distorted that it loses its communion with the viewer at home. . . . Mr. Arnaz, alias Ricky, is a success story in himself. Before TV he was known primarily as an orchestra conductor. The very qualities which presumably hampered his advance at that pursuit were turned to advantage on "I Love Lucy." His rather marked accent and his unprofessional style of performing were wisely left alone. The result was a leading man far removed from the usual stereotyped stage husband.

(*Source:* Jack Gould. "Why Millions Love Lucy: In the Comical Trials of Lucy and Ricky Ricardo TV Audiences Recognize the Exasperation and Warmth of Their Own Lives." *New York Times,* March 1, 1953, p. SM16.)

Books

Arnaz, Desi. *A Book.* New York: Warner Books, 1977. Arnaz's autobiography covers the *I Love Lucy* years.

Beltrán, Mary C. *Latina/o Stars in U.S. Eyes: The Making and Meanings of Film and TV Stardom.* Urbana: University of Illinois Press, 2009. Argues that Arnaz succeeded because he was marketed as a white Latino star instead of a man with a strong Cuban identity.

Websites

I Love Lucy. This site, operated by the Museum of Broadcast Communications, sets the show in the context of 1950s television and provides a cast list. http://www.museum.tv/eot vsection.php?entrycode = ilovelucy

LucyLibrary. Provides everything that a fan would want from an episode guide to video and audio clips from the show. http://www. lucylibrary.com/index.html

1992

Congress passes the Cuban Democracy Act. Also known as the Torricelli Bill, the legislation prohibits family remittances to Cuba, travel to Cuba by U.S. citizens, and trade with Cuba by foreign-based subsidiaries of U.S. companies.

Book

Simons, Geoff. *Cuba: From Conquistador to Castro.* New York: St. Martin's Press, 1996. Includes discussion of the Cuban Democracy Act.

October 16

1990

Cuban American classical pianist Jorge Bolet dies. Born in Havana in 1914, he studied at the Curtis Institute for Music in Philadelphia. He provided the piano soundtrack for the 1960 biography of Franz Liszt, *Song without End.* The film won an Oscar for Best Music Score. Bolet is best known for his playing of Romantic music.

Book

Bechstein, C., ed. *The World of Pianos: Fascination with an Instrument.* Berlin: Nicolai, 2003. Includes an essay on Bolet.

October 17

1950

The Salt of the Earth strike begins in Silver City, New Mexico, when zinc miners go on strike. The largely Mexican Mine-Mill Workers Union struck against the Empire Zinc Corporation to protest racial discrimination, lack of equal pay, and poor job safety. The Mexican American families, as one example of discrimination, lacked running water or restrooms in their company-provided homes while Anglo families had these necessities. When a local judge issued a Taft-Hartley injunction on June 12, 1951 prohibiting the mine workers from picketing the mines, the women's auxiliary continued to picket. Since the women often had their children by their side, this became the first major strike conducted by women and children. The strike ended on January 24, 1952, when the union obtained minor concessions. The incident is the subject of the famous 1954 film, *Salt of the Earth,* which features a number of miners and their families instead of professional actors. The film, directed by Herbert J. Biberman, was selected for the National Film Registry in 1992 by the Library of Congress.

From "History Makers Reflect on *Salt of the Earth:* Even More Relevant Now," by Libero Della Piana:

Anita and Lorenzo Torrez were a young married couple thrown into the midst of the Empire Zinc strike in Hanover, N.M., in 1950. They were radicalized in the course of the strike and became members of the Communist Party USA. They went on to become involved in the historic film, Salt of the Earth, with both having small parts. Lorenzo speaks a few lines in one of the union hall scenes. This year marks the 50th anniversary of that classic labor film.

Lorenzo worked as a miner for 25 years. The couple later left New Mexico and became active in labor and people's struggles in California. They eventually settled in Arizona, where, among other things, they helped to found the Salt of the Earth Labor College in Tucson in 1992. We had an opportunity to interview them during their recent visit to New York [in 2003].

World: What was the political environment of the strike at Empire Zinc?

Lorenzo: The conditions were harsh. Zinc mining is underground mining. The miners were Mexican Americans. We came back from World War II with the idea of democracy in our heads, and we found the same discrimination we faced before. We rebelled against it. We used the union to break the discrimination that had existed all along. We were determined to break through and be treated equally.

Even the pay lines were segregated, one for the Anglos, the other for the Mexicanos. Housing was segregated. The movie theaters were segregated, with Mexicanos on one side and Anglos on the other. We couldn't sit together. The swimming pool was segregated. There was one day a week that the Mexicanos could go swimming, and then they would drain the pool and refill it.

The Mexicanos were fed up. The Anglos were in the skilled jobs. The underground work was for the Mexicanos or African Americans—the dirtiest, the roughest jobs. Native American Indians, who had been brought in by the company to work the mines during the labor shortage of World War II, had been forced to move back to the reservations. The company pushed them out and tore down their housing after the war.

(*Source:* Della Piana, Libero. "History Makers Reflect on *Salt of the Earth*: Even More Relevant Now." *People's World,* October 31, 2003, http://peoplesworld.org/history-makers-reflect-on-salt-of-the-earth-even-more-relevant-now/)

Books

Baker, Ellen R. *On Strike and On Film: Mexican American Families and Blacklisted Filmmakers in Cold War America*. Chapel Hill: University of North Carolina Press, 2007. Examines the impact of women's picketing on Mexican American families with a particular focus on the Salt of the Earth strike.

Wilson, Michael, and Deborah Silverton Rosenfelt. *Salt of the Earth*. New York: The Feminist Press at CUNY, 1993. This is a screenplay, by Wilson, of the movie with added commentary, by Rosenfelt, that analyzes the significance of the strike and film.

Websites

Salt of the Earth: The Movie Hollywood Could Not Stop. A good history of the production of the film and its reception in Cold War America that was originally published in *American History* magazine in February 2002. http://www.historynet.com/salt-of-the-earth-the-movie-hollywood-could-not-stop.htm

Salt of the Earth. This Internet Movie Database site provides details about the film and its production, including a cast list. http://www.imdb.com/title/tt0047443/

1859

Miguel A. Otero II, the first Latino governor of New Mexico, is born to a prominent New Mexican family that had significant interests in mining, ranching, real estate, and banking. His father and namesake was also a New Mexican politician. The younger Otero served as governor of the territory from 1897 to 1907. He subsequently received an appointment in 1917 as U.S. marshal of the Panama Canal Zone.

Website

Miguel A. Otero II. The New Mexico Office of the State Historian provides this biography of the famed governor. http://www.newmexicohistory.org/filedetails.php?fileID = 23589

1959

Severo Ochoa joins his former colleague, Arthur Kornberg, in winning the Nobel Prize in physiology or medicine for his research on the synthesis of RNA and DNA, the two families of chemical compounds that carry and transmit genetic code. A Spaniard, he is a professor at New York University.

Books

Garretson, Gregory. *Severo Ochoa*. Chicago: Raintree, 2006. A biography of the biochemist for a juvenile audience but also the only biography in the English language.

Gómez-Santos, Marino. *Severo Ochoa : la Emoción de Descubrir*. Madrid: Pirámide, 1993. A full-length biography of the chemist.

October 18

1947

Catalina Esperanza Garcia, one of the founders in the early 1970s of the Mexican American Business and Professional Women, is born in El Paso, Texas, to parents of Mexican ancestry. An anesthesiologist, she also helped found the Hispanic Women's Network of Texas in 1987. The organizations promote the career development of Latinas as well as civic involvement and cultural awareness.

Book

Peña, Milagros. *Latina Activists across Borders: Women's Grassroots Organizing in Mexico and Texas*. Durham: Duke University Press, 2007. Covers women's activism in El Paso.

October 19

1922

Aurelio Pompa, a Mexican immigrant from Sonora, shoots and kills his foreman, William McCue, at the site of the new Los Angeles post office. Pompa had apparently used tools without McCue's permission and was beaten by McCue as a result. Pompa went home, retrieved a revolver, returned to the worksite, and shot McCue without warning. Mexican witnesses, however, reported that a second argument ensued before Pompa shot McCue. The police arrived just before white workers could lynch Pompa. The Mexican community saw the case as one of self-defense, with President Alvaro Obregón of Mexico sending an appeal for mercy to the governor of California. Nearly13,000 people signed a petition for clemency. A *corrido* was composed about the incident and a play depicting the event was performed to raise money for Pompa's defense. Convicted of first-degree murder in April 1923, Pompa went to the gallows on March 3, 1924.

Book

Stavans, Ilan, ed. *Wáchale!: Poetry and Prose about Growing Up Latino in America.* Chicago: Cricket Books, 2001. Contains an essay by Manuel Gamio on the life, trial, and death of Aurelio Pompa.

October 20

1969

Baseball player Juan González is born in Vega Baja, Puerto Rico. A right fielder who mostly played for the Texas Rangers, González received acclaim for his ability to knock in runs. One of the most feared batters of the 1990s, González averaged 37 homeruns and 117 runs batted in per season between 1991 and 1999. A three-time All Star, he won the Silver Slugger award six times and won the Home Run Derby in 1993. He retired in 2005 with the Cleveland Indians.

From "Gonzalez Giving of Time, Money":

> Jose Canseco and Juan Gonzalez love to cruise to Texas Rangers' spring-training games in Canseco's red Lam-

borghini Diablo. As you would expect, these sluggers talk power.

> Not home-run power, but political power. "We don't talk about baseball," Canseco says. "We talk about world problems, economics, Japanese art, Korean art. There are a lot of things you don't know about us."

> That's more true of Gonzalez, who led the American League with 43 home runs last season, than Canseco, who has one homer title and shared another.... Gonzalez speaks Spanish but little English. He took English courses in the offseason in Puerto Rico. Gonzalez was the second Puerto Rican native to hit 40 or more homers in a season. The other: Orlando Cepeda (46 in 1961). Gonzalez knows the importance of heroes such as Cepeda and Roberto Clemente in Puerto Rico, so he spent his offseason speaking to kids at 52 schools, says Luis Mayoral, who works for the Rangers in public relations.

> The son of a math teacher, Gonzalez, who signed when he was 16, has a solid social conscience. He still pays utility and medical-prescription bills for people stuck in a depressed, drug-infested area of his hometown, Vega Baja. "He doesn't forget his roots," Mayoral says. When he's not speaking to kids or lifting weights, Gonzalez is reading up on political history.... Gonzalez would rather hit fewer home runs and improve his average and RBI. "His thing is to help the team win," Mayoral says. "He's not into the ego trip of being the home-run king."

(*Source:* Antonen, Mel. "Gonzalez Giving of Time, Money." *USA Today,* March 30, 1993, p. 4C.)

Books

Wendel, Tim. *The New Face of Baseball: The One Hundred Year Rise and Triumph of Latinos in America's Favorite Sport.* New York: HarperCollins, 2004. One of the most prolific baseball writers gives the story of Latino players on the field.

Wendel, Tim, and Jose Luis Villegas. *Far From Home: Latino Baseball Players in America.* Washington, D.C.: National Geographic, 2008. Tells of the challenges of playing baseball in the United States through essays and photographs.

Websites

Juan Gonzalez Player Page. Provides statistics for the outfielder's career. http://www.baseball-reference.com/players/g/gonzaju03.shtml

Juan Gonzalez Stats. Offers numbers for each year of the player's career as well as a brief biography. http://www.baseball-almanac.com/players/player.php?p = gonzaju03

1937

Playwright José Corrales is born near Havana. He left Cuba in December 1964 and eventually moved to New York City. He collaborated with the Dumé Spanish Theater as a literary adviser and actor. This group also premiered his 1978 comedy, *Juana Machete, la muerte en bicicleta* (Juana Machete, death on a bicycle).

Book

Bulman, Gail A. *Staging Words, Performing Worlds: Intertextuality and Nation in Contemporary Latin American Theater.* Lewisburg: Bucknell University Press, 2007. Includes coverage of the playwright's work.

1977

Raúl Hector Castro, the first Latino governor of Arizona, officially leaves office as he is sworn in as ambassador to Argentina. Born in Cananea, Mexico, in 1916, Castro moved as a child to Pertleville, Arizona. In 1964, he was appointed ambassador to El Salvador. In 1968, he became ambassador to Bolivia.

October 21

1934

Botanist Arturo Gómez-Pompa is born in Mexico City. He moved to the United States in 1985. Gómez-Pompa is one of the world's foremost authorities on the ecology of tropical rain forests and one of the first people to warn about the threat to the planet posed by the destruction of these forests.

Book

Gómez-Pompa, Arturo. *The Lowland Maya Area: Three Millenia at the Human-Wildland Interface.* New York: Food Products Press, 2003. Examines the ecological impact of humans in Mexico.

October 22

1982

Robinson Canó, a second baseman with the New York Yankees, is born in San Pedro de Macorís, Dominican Republic. Canó made his major league debut in 2005. He has since won the Silver Slugger Award four times, been named to the All-Star Game on four occasions, and earned a Gold Glove Award in 2010. Canó won the Home Run Derby in 2011. He collected a World Series ring with the Yankees in 2009. Canó's father, José, pitched briefly for the Houston Astros in 1989 and named his son after baseball legend Jackie Robinson.

Book

Bretón, Marcos. *Home is Everything: The Latino Baseball Story.* El Paso, TX: Cinco Puntos Press, 2002. Looks at the challenges that Latino baseball players face while living in the United States.

October 23

1936

Sociologist Rodolfo Alvarez is born. He becomes the third Mexican American to earn a doctorate in sociology in the United States when he completes his degree in 1966. His work addresses the ways in which institutional discrimination based on class, race, and gender affects an institution's workers, employee recruitment, and relationship with the general public.

Book

Alvarez, Rodolfo, et al. *Discrimination in Organizations*. San Francisco: Jossey-Bass, 1979. A look at why and how people discriminate within organizations.

October 24

1894

Cirilo Villaverde, a seminal figure in Cuban literature, dies in exile in New York City. Villaverde is best known today for his 1824 novel, *Cecilia Valdés,* arguably the most important novel written in 19th-century Cuba. Villaverde, imprisoned for his political activities, escaped and fled the island in 1849. He remained in the United States, devoting himself almost exclusively to writing in support of a Cuban revolution in various exile newspapers including *La Verdad* and *El Espejo.* In the 1850s, he argued for the U.S. annexation of Cuba but later supported Cuban independence.

Book

Villaverde, Cirilo. *Cecilia Valdés or El Angel Hill.* Ed. Sibylle Fischer. Oxford; New York: Oxford University Press, 2005. One of the few editions of Villaverde's work in English with an introduction and note by Fischer.

1935

During a dispute over the Americanization of Puerto Rico, the governor places armed police on the grounds of the University of Puerto Rico at Río Piedras. On this date, the police arrested several Nationalist Party members near campus, allegedly for possessing bombs, and took them to jail. Enroute, four Nationalists and a bystander were shot to death by the police. The incident, known as the Rio Piedras massacre, further inflames tensions over American control of Puerto Rico.

Books

Duany, Jorge. *The Puerto Rican Nation on the Move: Identities on the Island and in the United States.* Discusses cultural nationalism among Puerto Ricans.

Negrón-Muntaner, Frances, and Ramón Grosfoguel, eds. *Puerto Rican Jam: Rethinking Colonialism and Nationalism.* Minneapolis: University of Minnesota Press, 1997. Offers essays that examine the debate over the political status of Puerto Rico.

Website

Puerto Rican Nationalism and the Drift toward Statehood. The Council on Hemispheric Affairs provides this excellent summary of the history of nationalism on the island. http://www.coha.org/puerto-rican-nationalism-and-the-drift-towards-statehood/

October 25

1932

Environmentalist Sister Paula Gonzalez is born in Albuquerque, New Mexico, to Mexican American parents. She is best known for moving into an energy efficient building, La Casa del Sol, that she had built out of an old chicken coop in Cincinnati in the mid-1970s. Gonzalez created the structure to prove that a living space could be constructed along sound environmental principles.

Book

Bingham, Sally G. *Love God, Heal Earth.* Pittsburgh, PA: St. Lynns Press, 2009. Contains an essay by Gonzalez on global warming.

1996

Last Round, a string orchestra composition from Argentine American Osvaldo Golijov premieres. Golijov created the composition to honor the memory of Astor Piazzolla, the last great Tango composer. The title reflects an imaginary chance for Piazolla's spirit to fight one more time and the piece is an idealized bandoneón (a type of button-accordion and the instrument played by Piazolla).

Books

Golijov, Osvaldo. *Rose of the Winds.* Brooklyn: Ytalianna Music Publications, 2009. A musical score by Golijov.

Keller, James M. *Chamber Music: A Listener's Guide.* New York: Oxford University Press, 2011. Includes information on listening to Golijov's works.

October 26

2001

Ernesto Pedregón Martínez is inducted into the El Paso Artists' Hall of Fame. A self-taught artist who worked as a graphic artist on federal government weapons manuals, Martínez began his painting career when MEChA (Movimiento Estudiantil Chicano de Aztlán) sponsored an exhibit of his works in 1974. In 1997, The Texas House of Representatives honored him with a resolution while the state of Texas named him 1997–1998 Artist of the Year. A heavily-decorated U.S. Army veteran who served in World War II and helped liberate the Mittelbau-Dora Concentration Camp, Martínez has also given lectures about the Holocaust.

October 27

2004

A survey of Latino voters released on this day by the *Washington Post,* Univision, and the Tomas Rivera Policy Institute shows that an overwhelming majority do not believe that the Iraq War was worth fighting and that Hispanics have suffered a disproportionate amount of casualties. By a 2 to 1 margin, Hispanic voters believe the war was a mistake. The survey found that nearly 3 in 10 Latinos believe that Hispanics are disproportionately represented among the dead and wounded in Iraq compared with other racial or ethnic groups, while 6 in 10 disagree.

October 28

1950

Microbiologist John F. Alderete is born in Las Vegas, New Mexico, to Mexican parents. Besides developing diagnostic tools for sexually-transmitted diseases, Alderete has organized a number of programs to encourage minority students to take an interest in science.

Book

Wright, David, and Leonard Archard, eds. *Molecular and Cell Biology of Sexually Transmitted Diseases.* New York: Chapman & Hall, 1992. Contains an essay by Alderete.

2000

The Victims of Trafficking and Violence Protection Act (VTVPA) becomes law. The legislation allows victims to remain in the United States. In 2002, the government estimated that 45,000 to 50,000 women and children were trafficked into the United States and forced into slavery-like conditions, many in prostitution.

Book

Neumann, Caryn E. *Sexual Crime.* Santa Barbara, CA: ABC-CLIO, 2010. Traces the history of various sex crimes, including human trafficking.

October 29

1920

Immunologist Baruj Benacerraf is born in Caracas, Venezuela. A resident of the United States since 1940, he was a corecipient of the 1980 Nobel Prize in medicine for his discovery of the genetic mechanism that regulates a body's response to attack by foreign materials. When applying to medical school in 1942, Benacerraf was denied admission by 25 schools. He attributed the rejection to his Jewish background and Venezuelan heritage.

Book

Benacerraf, Baruj. *From Caracas to Stockholm: A Life in Medical Science.* Amherst, NY: Prometheus Books, 1998. An entertaining autobiography of the Venezuelan American immunologist.

October 30

1937

Writer Rudolfo Anaya is born in New Mexico. Since the release of his first novel, *Bless Me, Última,* in 1972, Anaya has become one of the leading Chicano writers. However, he struggled to find a publisher for *Bless Me, Última* because the publishing industry has historically neglected Latino/a writers. It took 22 years before Warner Books, a major publisher, accepted the work that had first been printed by Quinto Sol, a small independent press. Several of Anaya's other books have met similar fates. Yet he has achieved critical recognition for his novels, short stories, plays, and poems. Acclaimed as one of the founding fathers of Chicano literature, Anaya sets many of his works in New Mexico where he feels inextricably bound to the land.

From "Walt Whitman Strides the Llano of New Mexico":

Save our children now! I shout. Put
Leaves of Grass in their
lunch boxes! In the tacos and tamales!
Let them call him Abuelo! As I call him
    Abuelo!

(*Source:* Anaya, Rudolfo. *The Anaya Reader.* New York: Warner Books, 1995, pp. 559–60.)

Books

Anaya, Rudolfo. *The Anaya Reader.* New York: Warner Books, 1995, pp. 559–60. The collected works of the writer as of 1994.

Dick, Bruce, and Silvio Sirias, eds. *Conversations with Rudolfo Anaya.* Jackson: University Press of Mississippi, 1998. A collection of 15 interviews spanning the years from 1976 to 1998.

Websites

Bless Me, Última Reader's Guide. This National Endowment for the Humanities site provides a reader's, teacher's, and audio guide to Anaya's famous novel as well as an interview with the author. http://www.neabigread.org/books/blessmeultima/anaya04_about.php

Hispanic Heritage: Rudolfo Anaya. A brief biography of the writer with selected readings and a listing of awards that he has won. http://www.gale.cengage.com/free_resources/chh/bio/anaya_r.htm

1950

A violent rebellion breaks out in Puerto Rico in opposition to U.S. control over the country. The armed revolt, supported by the National Party of Puerto Rico, extended to various towns (Arecibo, Jayuya, Utuado, Adjuntas, Ponce, Naranjito, and Mayagüez). The nationalists argued that armed revolution was the only way to achieve Puerto Rican independence.

Books

Duany, Jorge. *The Puerto Rican Nation on the Move: Identities on the Island and in the United*

States. Discusses cultural nationalism among Puerto Ricans.

Negrón-Muntaner, Frances, and Ramón Grosfoguel, eds. *Puerto Rican Jam: Rethinking Colonialism and Nationalism*. Minneapolis: University of Minnesota Press, 1997. Offers essays that examine the debate over the political status of Puerto Rico.

Website

Puerto Rican Nationalism and the Drift toward Statehood. The Council on Hemispheric Affairs provides this excellent summary of the history of nationalism on the island. http://www.coha.org/puerto-rican-nationalism-and-the-drift-towards-statehood/

1968

Actor Ramón Novarro, born José Ramón Gil Samaniego in Mexico, dies in Los Angeles. A major sex symbol during the silent film era, he specialized in action films. His brutal murder by two young thugs served as the subject of the Peggy Lee song, "Tango," and a short story by Charles Bukowski, "The Murder of Ramon Vasquez."

Books

Berumen, Frank Javier Garcia. *Ramon Novarro: The Life and Films of the First Latino Hollywood Superstar*. New York: Vantage Press, 2001. A popular narrative of Novarro's life and death.

Ellenberger, Allan R. *Ramon Novarro: A Biography of the Silent Film Idol, 1899–1968: With a Filmography*. Jefferson, NC: McFarland, 1999. A good guide to the actor and his work.

Soares, André. *Beyond Paradise: The Life of Ramon Novarro*. New York: St. Martin's Press, 2002.

A good biography that shows the challenges that faced the gay actor who was the heartthrob of many women.

October 31

1919

The Tejana laundresses of El Paso, Texas, go on strike. They had established a local of the Laundry Workers International Union on October 23, 1919, with the support of other trade unionists. A week later, Acme Laundry fired two union members for recruiting other members. When management rejected demands that the women be reinstated, 200 workers went on strike. Women at other laundries walked off their jobs in solidarity. The workers averaged $5.50 a week and the *Labor Advocate* newspaper asked, "What chance has a girl or woman to live a decent, respectable life at the wages of this kind?" Ultimately, the strike brought the laundresses neither improved wages nor any other benefits. The strikers were replaced with other workers.

1921

Celso-Ramón García, the leader of the team that conducted the first large-scale tests in Puerto Rico in the 1950s of the first oral contraceptive (the Pill), is born in New York City to Spanish immigrants. García was nominated for the Nobel Prize for this work. He speculated that he did not win because the Nobel committee was reluctant to offend the Catholic Church by awarding the prize for this achievement.

November

November 1

1950

Puerto Rican nationalists attempt to assassinate U.S. president Harry S. Truman at his temporary residence in Blair House in Washington, D.C. Both Oscar Collazo and Griselio Torresola were active in the Puerto Rican Nationalist Party. They thought that killing Truman would draw attention to their cause. Truman had been taking a nap when the shooting began and he rushed to a window with a view of the shooting. A White House guard saw the president and ordered him to take cover. Truman suffered no injuries but White House police officer Leslie Coffelt and Torresola died. The surviving would-be assassin, Collazo, severely wounded in the shoot-out, received a death sentence but Truman commuted it to life shortly before his execution date. Only one shot fired by Collazo struck anyone, a police officer named Donald Birdzell. President Jimmy Carter commuted the life sentence in 1979, releasing Collazo from prison and allowing him to die in Puerto Rico in 1994 at the age of 80.

Books

Duany, Jorge. *The Puerto Rican Nation on the Move: Identities on the Island and in the United States.* Discusses cultural nationalism among Puerto Ricans.

Negrón-Muntaner, Frances, and Ramón Grosfoguel, eds. *Puerto Rican Jam: Rethinking Colonialism and Nationalism.* Minneapolis: University of Minnesota Press, 1997. Offers essays that examine the debate over the political status of Puerto Rico.

Websites

Puerto Rican Nationalism and the Drift toward Statehood. The Council on Hemispheric Affairs provides this excellent summary of the history of nationalism on the island. http://www.coha.org/puerto-rican-nationalism-and-the-drift-towards-statehood/

Truman Library: Assassination Attempt. The Harry S. Truman Presidential Library provides an account of the attempted murder of the president. http://www.trumanlibrary.org/trivia/assassin.htm

November 2

1966

The Cuban Adjustment Act is approved, providing a special procedure to enable Cuban immigrants to obtain green cards and become permanent residents. Eligible Cubans must have been in the United States for one year and must meet other immigration criteria. The legislation was passed in an effort to aid the tens of thousands of Cubans who fled Cuba in the wake of Fidel Castro's rise to power.

From the Cuban Adjustment Act, 1966:

> That, notwithstanding the provisions of section 245(c) of the Immigration and Nationality Act the status of any alien who is a native or citizen of Cuba and who has been inspected and admitted or paroled into the United States subsequent to January 1, 1959 and has been physically present in the United States for at least one year, may be adjusted by the Attorney General, in his discretion and under such regulations as he may prescribe, to that of an alien lawfully admitted for permanent residence if the alien makes an application for such adjustment, and the alien is eligible to receive an immigrant visa and is admissible to the United States for permanent residence. Upon approval of such an application for adjustment of

status, the Attorney General shall create a record of the alien's admission for permanent residence as of a date thirty months prior to the filing of such an application or the date of his last arrival into the United States, whichever date is later. The provisions of this Act shall be applicable to the spouse and child of any alien described in this subsection, regardless of their citizenship and place of birth, who are residing with such alien in the United States.

In the case of any alien described in section 1 of this Act who, prior to the effective date thereof, has been lawfully admitted into the United States for permanent residence, the Attorney General shall, upon application, record his admission for permanent residence as of the date the alien originally arrived in the United States as a nonimmigrant or as a parolee, or a date thirty months prior to the date of enactment of this Act, whichever date is later. . . .

Except as otherwise specifically provided in this Act, the definitions contained in section 101 (a) and (b) of the Immigration and Nationality Act shall apply in the administration of this Act. Nothing contained in this Act shall be held to repeal, amend, alter, modify, affect, or restrict the powers, duties, functions, or authority of the Attorney General in the administration and enforcement of the Immigration and Nationality Act or any other law relating to immigration nationality, or naturalization.

The approval of an application for adjustment of status to that of lawful permanent resident of the United States pursuant to the provisions of section 1 or this Act shall not require the Secretary of State to reduce the number of visas authorized to be issued in any class in any alien who is physically present in the United States on or before the effective date of the Immigration and Nationality Act Amendments of 1976.

(*Source:* Cuban Adjustment, Public Law 89–732, November 2, 1966, http://www.state.gov/www/regions/wha/cuba/publicl aw_89–732.html)

Books

Davies, Philip, and Iwan Morgan, eds. *America's Americans: Population Issues in U.S. Society and Politics*. London: Institute for the Study of the Americas, University of London, School of Advanced Study, 2007. Includes a chapter on the Cuban Adjustment Act by Jessica Gibbs.

Lopez, Juan J. *Democracy Delayed: The Case of Castro's Cuba*. Baltimore: Johns Hopkins University Press, 2002. Includes a discussion of U.S. relations with Cuba.

Website

Cuban Adjustment Act. Full text of the legislation. http://www.state.gov/www/regions/wha/cuba/publiclaw_89–732.html

1999

Pablo Raúl Alarcón Sr. retires from the company that he founded in 1983, Spanish Broadcasting Systems. The firm is the largest Hispanic-owned media company in the United States. Alarcón's involvement with the media dates to the 1950s when he began a radio station in Camagüey, Cuba. Upon arriving in the United States, Alarcón became an on-air personality for a New York City radio station. He bought his first American radio station, WSKQ-AM, in New York in 1983, starting Spanish Broadcasting. Alarcón died in 2008 in Miami.

Books

Matsaganis, Matthew D., Vikki S. Katz, and Sandra J. Ball-Rokeach. *Understanding Ethnic*

Media: Producers, Consumers, and Societies. Los Angeles: SAGE, 2011. An exhaustive history of ethnic newspapers, radio, and television.

Nuñez, Luis V., ed. *Spanish Language Media after the Univision-Hispanic Broadcasting.* New York: Novinka, 2006. Provides a history of Spanish-language television in the United States.

Websites

Spanish Broadcasting System. The official web-page of Alarcón's company. http://www.spanishbroadcasting.com/

Pablo Raúl Alarcón, Sr. Find a Grave provides a biography of the broadcaster along with information about his burial site. http://www.findagrave.com/cgi-bin/fg.cgi?page=gr&GRid=27518853

2005

Héctor Ibarra of West Branch Middle School in West Branch, Iowa, is named as the Wal-Mart National Teacher of the Year. Born in Mexico near the one-room schoolhouse where his mother taught, Ibarra taught science to sixth and seventh graders.

From "Hector Ibarra: He'll Do Just About Anything to Motivate Kids":

A native of Clear Lake [Iowa], he said he developed his work ethic working 40 to 55 hours a week in the fields.

"I grew up working very hard," he said. "I know what a summer's hard work is. If people know what work is, they'll have a different work ethic."

Ibarra said helping create a competitive drive in his students has helped them achieve.

"Teachers like myself have a competitive drive," he said. "Having a competitive drive means never being satisfied."

This means revising his curriculum every year and using real-life objects such as dirty oil filters to teach environmental science.

"(It's) taking a unit that's applicable to their lives," Ibarra said. "Instead of using the book, you bring your own material."

(*Source:* Daniel, Rob. "Hector Ibarra: He'll Do Just About Anything to Motivate Kids." *Iowa City Press-Citizen,* [2005?], http://www.goiowacity.com/heartand-soul/ibarra.html)

Books

Altenbaugh, Richard J. *The American People and Their Education: A Social History.* Upper Saddle River, NJ: Pearson, 2003. A study of the American educational system that includes a focus on Latinos.

Macdonald, Victoria-Maria. *Latino Education in the United States: A Narrated History from 1513–2000.* This study, a mix of narrative and primary documents, is the only history of Latino education to cover such a broad span of time.

Website

Héctor Ibarra. Provides a short biography of Ibarra as well as an audio clip of Ibarra discussing the most important qualities of a teacher. http://www2.ed.gov/programs/teacherfellowship/fellows/ibarra.html

November 3

2005

U.S. representative Duncan Hunter, a Republican who represents the San Diego area, introduces an amendment to the Border Protection, Anti-Terrorism, and Illegal Immigration Control Act of 2005 to construct a reinforced fence up to 700 miles in length along the entire U.S.–Mexico border. The bill, with the amendment, passes the House in December.

From Border Protection, Antiterrorism, and Illegal Immigration Control Act of 2005, H.R. 4437:

Title X—Fencing and Other Border Security Improvements

Sec. 1001. Findings

The Congress finds the following:

(1) Hundreds of people die crossing our international border with Mexico every year.

(2) Illegal narcotic smuggling along the Southwest border of the United States is both dangerous and prolific.

(3) Over 155,000 non-Mexican individuals were apprehended trying to enter the United States along the Southwest border in fiscal year 2005.

(4) The number of illegal entrants into the United States through the Southwest border is estimated to exceed one million people a year.

Sec. 1002. Construction of Fencing and Security Improvements in Border Area from Pacific Ocean to Gulf of Mexico

Section 102(b) of the Illegal Immigration Reform and Immigrant Responsibility Act of 1996 (Public Law 104–208; 8 U.S.C. 1103 note) is amended—

(1) in the subsection heading by striking 'Near San Diego, California'; and

(2) by amending paragraph (1) to read as follows:

(1) SECURITY FEATURES-

(A) REINFORCED FENCING- In carrying out subsection (a), the Secretary of Homeland Security shall provide for at least 2 layers of reinforced fencing, the installation of additional physical barriers, roads, lighting, cameras, and sensors—

(i) extending from 10 miles west of the Tecate, California, port of entry to 10 miles east of the Tecate, California, port of entry;

(ii) extending from 10 miles west of the Calexico, California, port of entry to 5 miles east of the Douglas, Arizona, port of entry;

(iii) extending from 5 miles west of the Columbus, New Mexico, port of entry to 10 miles east of El Paso, Texas;

(iv) extending from 5 miles northwest of the Del Rio, Texas, port of entry to 5 miles southeast of the Eagle Pass, Texas, port of entry; and

(v) extending 15 miles northwest of the Laredo, Texas, port of entry to the Brownsville, Texas, port of entry.

(B) PRIORITY AREAS- With respect to the border described—

(i) in subparagraph (A) (ii), the Secretary shall ensure that an interlocking surveillance camera system is installed along such area by May 30, 2006 and that fence construction is completed by May 30, 2007; and

(ii) in subparagraph (A) (v), the Secretary shall ensure that fence construction from 15 miles northwest of the Laredo, Texas port of entry to 15 southeast of the Laredo, Texas port of entry is completed by December 31, 2006.

(C) EXCEPTION- If the topography of a specific area has an elevation grade that exceeds 10%, the Secretary may use other means to secure such area, including the use of surveillance and barrier tools.'

Sec. 1003. Northern Border Study

(a) In General- The Secretary of Homeland Security shall conduct a study on the construction of a state-of-the-art barrier system along the northern international land and maritime border of the United States and shall include in the study—

(1) the necessity of constructing such a system; and

(2) the feasibility of constructing the system.

(b) Report- Not later than one year after the date of the enactment of this Act, the Secretary of Homeland Security shall report to the Congress on the study described in subsection (a).

(*Source:* Border Protection, Antiterrorism, and Illegal Immigration Control Act of 2005, H.R. 4437, http://thomas. loc.gov/cgi-bin/query/F?c109:1:./ temp/~c109YyfYvk:e286872)

Books

Gutiérrez, David. *Walls and Mirrors: Mexican Americans, Mexican Immigrants, and the Politics of Ethnicity.* Berkeley: University of California Press, 1995. Discusses the politics behind determining who belongs and who does not.

Hernández, Kelly Lytle. *Migra! A History of the U.S. Border Patrol.* Berkeley: University of California Press, 2010. A heavily-documented history of this controversial federal agency.

Websites

Border Fence Pros and Cons. Jennifer McFadyen examines the issue. http://immigration.about. com/od/bordersportsandcustoms/i/Fence_ Issue.htm

U.S. Customs and Border Patrol. The official webpage for the federal agency. http://www.cbp. gov/

November 4

1961

Henry B. González becomes the first person of Mexican ancestry to be elected to the U.S. House of Representatives when he wins a special election for the Twentieth Congressional District in Texas. González angered his Republican opponent when he brought Cantiflas, a Mexican film star, and a Mexican senator across the border to campaign for him. The large number of Latinos in San Antonio likely helped González to victory. He remained in the House for the next 37 years and is known particularly for his civil rights leadership. A member of the powerful House Banking Committee, he attacked the banking excesses of the 1980s and Alan Greenspan's control of the Federal Reserve. A rather combustible man, González also shoved a congressman who called him a "pinko" and, famously, slugged a man in a San Antonio restaurant who had disparaged him as a communist. He was 70 at the time that he threw that punch. González died in 2002.

Books

Auerbach, Robert D. *Deception and Abuse at the Fed: Henry B. González Battles Alan Greenspan's Bank.* Austin: University of Texas Press, 2008. Discusses González's efforts to support the little people by reigning in the power of the Federal Reserve.

Rodriguez Jr., Eugene. *Henry B. Gonzalez: A Political Profile.* New York: Arno Press, 1976. The only book-length biography of the political leader.

Websites

González, Henry Barbosa. The Handbook of Texas Online provides an excellent short biography of the politician. http://www.tsha online.org/handbook/online/articles/fgo76

González, Henry Barbosa. The official Congressional synopsis of González's political career. http://bioguide.congress.gov/scripts/biodis play.pl?index=g000272

1969

Jesús Colon loses an election bid for comptroller of New York City, running on the Communist ticket. Colon, who arrived in Brooklyn in 1918 as a stowaway on the SS *Carolina* from Puerto Rico, wrote a daily column for the communist newspaper, *The Daily Worker,* as well as poems, stories, and other literary pieces. His writings, which focused on social justice, anticolonialism, democracy, and racism, had a major impact on how Puerto Ricans were perceived in the United States. Colon died in 1974.

From Miguel Barnet's *La Vida Real:*

That's what they talked about in the barbershop. That and the presence of nationalist leaders and their benefactors and their opportunistic yes-men. . . .

There's still plenty of discussion of these political matters. The nationalists go off one way, the socialists another— a regular "mess" or "revolta" as they themselves call it. The oldtimers very much remember Jesús Colon and Bernardo Vega, the founder of the newspaper, Gráfico, from the 1920s—those they think of as the spokesmen of justice for the Boricuas.

(*Source:* Barnet, Miguel. *La Vida Real: Novela.* La Habana: Editorial Letras Cubanas, 1983, pp. 264–65.)

Books

Colon, Jesús. *A Puerto Rican in New York and Other Sketches.* New York: Mainstream, 1961. Colon's memoir of living in the Big Apple written for *The Daily Worker.*

Zimmerman, Marc. *Defending Their Own in the Cold: The Cultural Turns of U.S. Puerto Ricans.* Urbana: University of Illinois Press, 2011. Examines the impact of Puerto Ricans on culture in the United States with coverage of Colon's influence.

Websites

Jesús Colon. A short but good biography of the writer and political activist. http://www.ccc. commnet.edu/latinoguide/secondary/Jesus Colon.htm

Jesús Colon's Biography. Encapsulates Colon's life with links to an essay about his writings and brief synopses of his books. http://www.angel fire.com/pa5/jessemoli/JesusColon.bio.html

1970

Denver police raid the headquarters of the Crusade for Justice ostensibly to look for weapons. Crusade offices are destroyed, windows are smashed, doors are ripped off their hinges, taped recordings and equipment are seized, and files are removed. Property damage is estimated at $5,000. Corky Gonzales, head of the Crusade, publicly voices suspicions that the raid is connected with efforts to organize the Raza Unida Party. Police do not make a statement about their reasons for the raid. The incident further inflames Mexican American suspicion of the police.

Books

Acuña, Rodolfo. *Occupied America: A History of Chicanos.* New York: Harper Collins, 1988. The standard history of the Chicano movement.

Vigil, Ernesto B. *The Crusade for Justice: Chicano Militancy and the Government's War on Dissent.* Madison: University of Wisconsin Press, 1999. Vigil, a member of Crusade for Justice, was at the Downing Street apartment when the situation with the police began.

Website

Chicano Leader Rodolfo "Corky" Gonzales, 1929–2005. Democracy Now provides an obituary for the civil rights leader. http://www.democracynow.org/2005/4/15/chicano_leader_rodolfo_corky_gonzales_1929

2008

Barack Obama becomes the first African American to win the White House when he defeats Republican John McCain. Obama wins with considerable Latino support. The growth in the number of Latinos who registered and voted contributed to Obama's wins in key states, including Nevada, Colorado, Florida, New Mexico, and California. Obama took the White House with 67 percent of the Latino vote.

Books

Barreto, Matt A. *Ethnic Cues: The Role of Shared Ethnicity in Latino Political Participation.* Ann Arbor: University of Michigan Press, 2010. Discusses whether ethnic affiliation will trump political affiliation.

DeSipio, Louis. *Counting on the Latino Vote: Latinos as a New Electorate.* Charlottesville: University Press of Virginia, 1996. Covers the potential voting power of Latinos and barriers keeping them from the polls.

Website

President Barack H. Obama. An official biography of the president from the White House. http://www.whitehouse.gov/administration/president-obama

November 6

1964

The Puerto Rico Forum announces plans for a massive assault on poverty among Puerto Ricans in New York City. The group is requesting antipoverty funds from the city and the federal government to improve job skills and family income; to raise educational levels; and to strengthen family life and Puerto Rican cultural influences. The Puerto Rican Forum argues that the Puerto Rican, rather than the African American, occupies the lowest step on the ladder.

Books

Baker, Susan S. *Understanding Mainland Puerto Rico Poverty.* Philadelphia: Temple University Press, 2002. Examines Puerto Ricans within the U.S. economic structure.

Lewis, Oscar. *La Vida: A Puerto Rican Family in the Culture of Poverty – San Juan and New York.* New York: Vintage, 1968. An interesting study of how one Latino family copes with poverty.

Website

Poverty 2009 and 2010: American Community Briefs. The U.S. Census provides this report on the rate of poverty in all 50 states plus Puerto Rico. http://www.census.gov/prod/2011pubs/acsbr10–01.pdf

November 7

1958

Punk rocker and archivist Alice Bag is born as Alicia Armendariz in Los Angeles. With childhood friend, Patricia Morrison, Armendariz cofounded one of the first bands on the Los

Angeles punk scene in the 1970s, the Bags. Each member of the group took Bag as her last name. With a menacing stage appearance and booming voice, Bag is shown in the landmark 1981 Penelope Spheeris documentary, *Decline of Western Civilization,* which traced the roots of L.A. punk. As a Chicana, Bag became a role model for many women of color in the punk scene. After leaving the Bags, she played with several other L.A. bands including Las Tres, Stay at Home Bomb and Cholita!. Now also known as Alicia Vasquez, Bag maintains an archive that contains photos and interviews of women involved with punk rock while also writing the blog, "Diary of a Bad Housewife."

From Elona Jones, "Go Ask Alice: A Q + A with Author and Punk Veteran Alice Bag":

Q. How has punk rock contributed to your identity as a feminist?

A. Punk, overall, made me feel I could take that power of being onstage and translate it into power I could use in my community. If I could have a punk show where people were on the same wavelength as me, then that could be a community that works together to achieve common goals. We could be a force that changes the world. And you could be a leader. You can be the person making the change happen, not just someone who is along for the ride. Punk rock really taught me that I had much more power than I realized.

Q. In your book, you express that you originally wanted the Bags to be an all-female group. Why? And how do you think the band would have been different had it been all women?

A. I think women are just more supportive of each other in different ways. I was writing a lot when we first started the band. Then, as soon as our guitar player, Craig Lee joined, I kind of stopped writing. So did Patricia, my bass player. When we first started the band, we had written about 75 percent of the songs, and near the end we each had maybe one or two songs in the set. It's not that the guys in the band treated us any differently. It was

just easy, for me, to hand over the reins and stop challenging myself because the guys had more experience, which was bad for me in the long term. The same thing happened to me in high school. When the guys are being asked to answer more than girls, you know you can just sit there and smile and nod. There's not a lot of pressure to produce or excel.

Q. In your book, you discuss how the early L.A. punk scene was very egalitarian. What do you think fostered this inclusion?

A. None of us really fit in within our own neighborhoods. Even though I claim my Chicana identity, when I first tried to join MEChA, which is the student movement in school for Chicanos, they kind of snickered at the way I was dressed. I felt like I wasn't welcome. You had to project a certain image to be considered a serious Chicano activist. Being a freaky Hollywood glam fan wasn't going to be taken seriously.

Hollywood was place [punks] could go that was accepting. We all had the same attitude. If anything was innovative you would give it a chance, and if anything was wrong you were going to write or create something to show how you felt about it. It was more than a music scene, it was a community.

Q. The future waves of punk in L.A., like 80s hardcore, weren't as inclusive. What happened?

A. There were a lot of drug-use problems in our scene, and there was another scene, hardcore, that was coming up really strong and was picking up fans. That scene became the one that was better documented. For a while, I think people thought that was punk. You know, it's a bunch of white guys slamming into each other. There's no room for people of color, women, or people who identify as queer in the mosh pit. It was really homogenous and it was really the opposite of what punk had started as.

(*Source: Bitch,* Summer 2012, issue no. 55, pp. 39–41.)

Books

Bag, Alice. *Violence Girl: East L.A. Rage to Hollywood Stage, a Chicana Punk Story*. Port Townsend, WA: Feral House, 2001. Bag's well-written and fascinating autobiography of growing up in an abusive home as the child of Mexican-born parents, learning English as a second language, and pioneering on the punk scene of 1970s Los Angeles.

MacLeod, Dewar. *Kids of the Black Hole: Punk Rock in Postsuburban California*. Norman: University of Oklahoma Press, 2010. Sets Bag's story in historical context by providing a history of punk rock.

Websites

Alice Bag. The official website of Alice Bag focuses on her punk rock career. http://alicebag.com/

Diary of a Bad Housewife. Bag's blog documents her life as a mother, a musician, and an artist specializing in prints. It also contains interviews with Bag. http://alicebag.blogspot.com/

2006

Arizonan voters make English the official language of the state with 74 percent of ballots cast. Advocates for the measure state that record levels of immigration into the United States threaten to overwhelm assimilation. They argue that a common language brings political unity and stability. Opponents view the measure as an attack on illegal immigrants out of frustration for the nation's failed immigration policy. While the legislation prohibits the use of all languages other than English, it is commonly believed to target Spanish-speakers, a substantial proportion of the state's population. The law contains an exemption for "areas where foreign language use is protected," including emergency medical services. A 1988 Arizona law designating English as the official language was thrown out by the courts because it violated the Fourteenth Amendment. At that time, the judges found that the law unconstitutionally inhibited the free discussion of governmental affairs by depriving limited- and non-English-speaking persons from access to government information, and by depriving elected officials and public employees of their ability to communicate with their constituents and with the public.

From Arizona's Proposition 103:

> Whereas, the United States is comprised of individuals from diverse ethnic, cultural and linguistic backgrounds, and continues to benefit from this rich diversity; and
>
> Whereas, throughout the history of the United States, the common thread binding individuals of differing backgrounds has been the English language, which has permitted diverse individuals to discuss, debate and come to agreement on contentious issues; and
>
> Whereas, in recent years, the role of the English language as a common language has been threatened by governmental actions that either ignore or harm the role of English or that promote the use of languages other than English in official governmental actions, and these governmental actions promote division, confusion, error and inappropriate use of resources . . .
>
> THE OFFICIAL LANGUAGE OF THE STATE OF ARIZONA IS ENGLISH.

(*Source:* Arizona Department of State, 2006 Ballot Propositions, http://www.azsos.gov/election/2006/info/pubpamphlet/english/Prop103.htm)

Books

Gonzalez, Roseann Duenas, and Ildiko Melis, eds. *Language Ideologies: Critical Perspectives on the Official English Movement*. New York: Routledge, 2000. Focuses on the impact of the English Only movement on education.

Tse, Lucy. *Why Don't They Learn English: Separating Fact from Fallacy in the U.S. Language Debate*. New York: Teachers College Press, 2001. Shows how incorrect assumptions about language influence policy debate in the United States.

Websites

English Only. This PBS site explores the history of English only initiatives, tracing the debate back to anti-German language efforts in the late 18th century. http://www.pbs.org/speak/seatosea/officialamerican/englishonly/

U.S. English. The official site of the U.S. English Foundation, which is dedicated to promoting English as a common language. The foundation is separate from English Only, which promotes legislation making English the only language of the United States. http://www.us-english.org/

November 8

1994

California voters approve a ballot initiative, Proposition 187, that ends access to health, education, and social services for the state's illegal aliens, the majority of whom are Latin Americans. Fifty-nine percent of voters supported 187 as did Gov. Pete Wilson. The law also required state employees to identify suspected illegal aliens to law enforcement officials for arrest and deportation. Statewide exit polls showed that Latinos opposed the proposition by 77 percent to 23 percent. Opponents of Proposition 187 immediately challenged the law in federal court. In 1998, a U.S. District Court ruled 187 to be unconstitutional and the state of California declined to appeal, essentially killing the law.

From Proposition 187:

1994—California

This initiative measure is submitted to the people in accordance with the provisions of Article II, Section 8 of the Constitution.

This initiative measure adds sections to various codes; therefore, new provisions proposed to be added are printed in {+ italic type+} to indicate that they are new.

PROPOSED LAW

SECTION 1. Findings and Declaration.

The People of California find and declare as follows:

That they have suffered and are suffering economic hardship caused by the presence of illegal aliens in this state.

That they have suffered and are suffering personal injury and damage caused by the criminal conduct of illegal aliens in this state.

That they have a right to the protection of their government from any person or persons entering the country unlawfully.

Therefore, the People of California declare their intention to provide for cooperation between their agencies of state and local government with the federal government, and to establish a system of required notification by and between such agencies to prevent illegal aliens in the United States from receiving benefits or public services in the State of California.

(*Source:* Holden, Robert H., and Eric Zolov, eds. *Latin America and the United States: A Documentary History*. New York: Oxford University Press, 2011, p. 348.)

Books

Jacobson, Robin Dale. *The New Nativism: Proposition 187 and the Debate over Immigration*. Minneapolis: University of Minnesota Press, 2008. Examines the fight over Proposition 187 with a particular focus on the role that race played in the debate.

Ono, Kent A., and John M. Sloop. *Shifting Borders: Rhetoric, Immigration, and California's Proposition 187*. Philadelphia: Temple

University Press, 2002. A scholarly look at the racial rhetoric surrounding immigration

Websites

Deborah Escobedo. "Propositions 187 and 227: Latino Immigrant Rights to Education." Section of Individual Rights and Responsibilities, American Bar Association. Essay that sets 187 in historical context. http://www.americanbar.org/publications/human_rights_magazine_home/irr_hr_summer99_escobedo.html

Proposition 187 Approved in California, Migration News. This University of California at Davis site provides an objective history of the legislation. http://migration.ucdavis.edu/mn/more.php?id=492_0_2_0

November 9

1973

César Chávez of the United Farm Workers announces that the grape and lettuce boycott is being expanded from 32 cities to 65 cities as 1,000 more union workers are preparing to work on the boycott. The boycott will be timed to coincide with the harvest. The schedule is to strike the lettuce fields of California's Imperial Valley this winter, the Salinas lettuce fields next spring, then the grape fields of Delano and Fresno next July and August.

Allan Grant, California Farm Bureau president, recalls the effects of the boycott, 1975:

> We were trying for twelve years to get farm labor legislation. I started working on this before Governor Ronald Reagan was elected. Therefore, we were very pleased that Governor [Jerry] Brown saw fit to work so hard on it. He could do some things that the former governor couldn't do, because he is a Democrat, and he had a Democratic legislature.
>
> All the farm organizations supported the governor's bill, with the exception of one or two. The boycott was only a minor reason. It did affect us. It put a lot of small grape growers out of business, and it had some effect in lettuce. But more important was the violence that took place, the property destruction, and the very strong antipathy between the two unions.
>
> The growers had gotten along with unions for several years, and they're just the same as any other employer. They could adjust to whatever situation comes along, and costs would have to be passed along to the consumer.

(*Source*: Levy, Jacques. *César Chávez: Autobiography of La Causa.* New York: W. W. Norton, 1975, pp. 533–34.)

Books

Del Castillo, Richard Griswold, and Richard A. Garcia. *Cesar Chavez: A Triumph of Spirit.* Norman: University of Oklahoma Press, 1995. The best account of Chávez and his links to the Chicano Movement.

Levy, Jacques E. *Cesar Chavez: Autobiography of La Causa.* New York: W. W. Norton, 1975. Provides an account of Chávez's early years, his initial efforts as an organizer, and his rise to the leadership of Mexican American farmworkers.

Websites

César Chávez: Labor Leader. Enchanted Learning offers a biography of Chávez as well as numerous activities for children that teach about the union leader. http://www.enchantedlearning.com/history/us/hispanicamerican/chavez/

The Story of César Chávez. The United Farm Workers provides a biography of its famed leader. http://www.ufw.org/_page.php?inc=history/07.html&menu=research

November 10

1972

Southern Airways Flight 49 is hijacked to Cuba. The plane, with 31 passengers and three crew members, also carried Melvin Cale, Louis Moore and Henry D. Jackson Jr. All three men were facing various criminal charges and decided to escape from prosecution. The flight, which took off from Birmingham, flew 4,000 miles over 30 hours. The hijackers brandished handguns and grenades while demanding $10 million and threatening to crash the plane into the Oak Ridge, Tennessee nuclear reactor. Eventually, the hijackers flew to Havana where Fidel Castro declined to welcome them, much to their surprise. Jackson and Moore were each sentenced to 20 years in a Cuban prison while Cale received 15 years. Cuba returned the airplane, hostages, and ransom money to the United States. After serving their sentences in Cuba, the hijackers were extradited to the United States to face further charges. The incident led to a brief thaw in relations between the United States and Cuba as well as a short-lived treaty to extradite hijackers. The hijacking, the 170th of the year, led to the first federally-mandated security screenings at airports.

Books

Brent, William Lee. *Long Time Gone: A Black Panther's True-Life Story of His Skyjacking and Twenty-five Years in Cuba*. New York: Times Books, 1996. Brent hijacked a passenger jet to Cuba in 1969.

Joyner, Nancy Douglas. *Aerial Hijacking as an International Crime*. Dobbs Ferry, NY: Oceana, 1974. A look at hijacking at a time when it was somewhat in vogue.

Website

This Day in Aviation History: November 10. Provides a short summary of the hijacking. http://www.nycaviation.com/2011/11/on-this-day-in-aviation-history-november-10th/

November 11

2009

Longtime anchorman Lou Dobbs resigns from CNN under pressure from Presente.

org, a Latino advocacy group. Dobbs, who had won many, many journalism awards as well as high television ratings, had also made a number of offensive statements about immigrants and Latinos. The Presente.org campaign, "Basta Dobbs" won the Campaign of the Year award from the New Organizing Institute, a leading progressive organization.

Books

Dávila, Arlene. *Latino Spin: Public Image and the Whitewashing of Race*. New York: New York University Press, 2008. Examines attitudes that celebrate the Latino middle class while denigrating Latino immigrants.

Dobbs, Lou. *Independents Day: Awakening the American Spirit*. New York: Viking Adult, 2007. Argues that the American political strategies of the 1980s, 1990s, and 2000s, including immigration policy, have left the United States in a mess.

Website

Basta Dobbs. The Presente.org account of its campaign against Lou Dobbs. http://www.presente.org/campaign/basta-dobbs/

November 13

1863

Chipita Rodríguez is ordered to be executed for first degree murder by Judge Benjamin Neal in San Patricio County, Texas. Rodríguez, a woman in her sixties who ran an inn on the Aransas River, was convicted of the murder of traveler John Savage. His body was found near her house in San Patricio. Possibly a Confederate gunrunner or horse trader, Savage had spent the night at Rodríguez's inn. A few days later his body, wrapped in burlap bags, was discovered floating down the river, and the $600 in gold he had been known to be carrying lay nearby. He had been murdered with an ax. The jury recommended leniency and most townspeople, Anglo and

Mexican, believed Rodríguez to be innocent. The case, viewed as an example of a society demanding revenge for the murder of a white man, has been the subject of two operas and many books. On June 13, 1985, Texas governor Mark White signed legislation absolving Rodríguez of murder.

From Minutes of the District Court of San Patricio County:

The State of Texas vs. Juan Silvera [possibly Rodriguez's son] and Chepita Rodriguez Indictment for Murder.

In this cause now comes the State by J. S. Givens and T. H. O'Callaghan assistant counsel for the State and the said defendants in their proper persons and by their counsel and the parties having announced themselves ready for trial and the said defendants Juan Silvera and Chepita Rodriguez were arraigned and the indictment having been read to them they pleaded not guilty to the same whereupon came a jury of good and lawful men to wit: Owen Gaffney, foreman, Thomas Haley, E.S. Nash, John Henderson, James H. Toomey, James Gallagher, Cornelius McTiernan, George McCown, George Williams, J. E. Hendrickson, and Pat Hart, who were duly empaneled and sworn according to law to try the said cause and having heard the evidence the argument of a sworn Bailiff to consider of the verdict and returned the following verdict to wit,

We the jury find the defendant Chepita Rodriguez Guilty of murder in the first degree but on account of her old age and the circumstantial evidence against her do recommend her to the mercy of the court. (Signed) Owen Gaffney

We the jury find the defendant Juan Silvera guilty of murder in the second degree and assess the penalty of five years in confinement in the penitentiary.(Signed) Owen Gaffney, Foreman

And the jury having poled each juror severally declared this to be his verdict. The court was now adjourned until tomorrow morning at half past ten o'clock. Saturday the sixth day of court met pursuant to adjournment. . . .

In this cause the motion for new trial having been withdrawn by the defendant counsel and the said defendant Chepita Rodriguez being now before the court in her own person and having been asked if she had anything to say why judgment should not be rendered and sentence pronounced against her said nothing but that what she had heretofore said. It is therefore ordered, and adjudged and decreed by the court that the said Chepita Rodriguez be taken hence to the jail of San Patricio County or to some other secure place and there closely and securely confined until Friday the thirteenth day of November A.D. one thousand eight hundred and sixty-three when she will be taken to the place of execution and there between the hour of eleven o'clock and sunset of said day she be executed according to the law by hanging by the neck until she be dead and the clerk of the court is required to issue to the sheriff a warrant for the execution of the judgment.

(*Source:* Minutes of the District Court of San Patricio County, p. 111, http://www.tamu.edu/faculty/ccbn/dewitt/irishchipita.htm)

Books

Cole, Stephanie, and Alison M. Parker. *Beyond Black and White: Race, Ethnicity, and Gender in the U.S. South and Southwest*. College Station, TX: Texas A&M University Press, 2004. Essays address violence against Mexicans in Texas.

Untiedt, Kenneth L. *Death Lore: Texas Rituals, Superstitions, and Legends of the Hereafter*. Denton,

TX: University of North Texas Press, 2008. Includes an essay on Rodriguez, the only woman hanged in Texas during the Civil War.

Websites

The Legend of Chipita Rodriguez. A good history of Rodriguez's case that includes an epic poem and the few remaining official records of her trial. http://www.tamu.edu/faculty/ccbn/dewitt/irishchipita.htm

Mystery Still Surrounds Last Woman Executed in Texas. This article, by Michael Holmes of the Associated Press, looks at Rodriguez's case. http://www.texnews.com/1998/texas/last0126.html

November 15

1945

Poet Isaac Goldemberg is born in Chepén, Peru, to a Russian Jewish father and a Peruvian mother. He came to New York City in 1965. Besides organizing Hispanic American book fairs, he writes poems that blend South American social activism with Jewish literary tradition.

Books

Dolan, Maureen, ed. *Isaac Goldemberg: A Bibliography and Six Critical Studies*. Hanover, NH: Ediciones del Norte, 2003. One of the few collections of Goldemberg's poems in the English language.

Goldemberg, Isaac. *La Vida Son Los Ríos: Collage*. Lima: Fondo Editorial del Congreso del Perú, 2005. A 393-page collection of Goldemberg's poems.

Websites

Isaac Goldemberg. The poet's official City University of New York webpage includes biographical data. http://www.hostos.cuny.edu/oaa/igoldemberg.htm

Isaac Goldemberg. Reprints several of Goldemberg's poems that have been translated into English. http://www.zeek.net/709poetry/

November 16

1857

Miguel Teurbe Tolón, one of the very few exiled Cuban intellectuals to work for the English-language press in the United States, dies. Born in Matanzas in 1820, Tolón came to the United States in 1848 because of his opposition to Spanish rule over Cuba. He worked as an editor for Latin American affairs in the 1850s on the *New York Herald*. He had been an editor of Cuba's *La Guirnalda,* where he also launched his career as a poet. In exile, he translated Thomas Paine's *Common Sense* into Spanish, possibly as a dig at the Spanish monarchy. He is one of the founders of Latino exile literature, both because of the topic of his poems and his status as the leader of the literary exile community.

Books

Tolón, Miguel Teurbe. *The Elementary Spanish Reader and Translator*. New York: D. Appleton, 1882. A collection of essays for people with weak Spanish reading skills.

Tolón, Miguel Teurbe. *A Spanish Reader*. New York: D. Appleton, 1901. Reflects Tolón's interest in promoting Spanish language education.

Websites

Miguel Teurbe Tolón. A biography of the writer in Spanish that includes illustrations of the man and one of his poems. http://www.latinamericanstudies.org/filibusters/teurbe-tolon.htm

Symbols of the Cuban Nation: Miguel Teurbe Tolón y de la Guardia. A short biography of the Cuban exile. http://www.nacion.cult.cu/en/mtt.htm

November 17

1936

Playwright Luis Rafael Sánchez is born in Humacao, Puerto Rico. His works, which deal with the theme of Puerto Rican national identity, have brought him fame. *La pasión según Antígona Pérez* is his most acclaimed play.

Books

Barradas, Efraín. *Para Leer en Puertorriqueño: Acercamiento a la Obra de Luis Rafael Sánchez*. Río Piedras, PR: Editorial Cultural, 1981. A critical examination of Sánchez's works.

Sánchez, Luis Rafael. *Macho Camacho's Beat*. Trans. Gregory Rabassa. Normal, IL: Dalkey Archive Press, 2001. A humorous novel with a musical focus.

Website

Biografia de Luis Rafael Sánchez. A Spanish-language profile of the playwright. http://www.biografiasyvidas.com/biografia/s/sanchez_luis.htm

November 18

1973

Festival de Flor y Canto, the first national Chicano literature festival, ends in Los Angeles. The three-day event, the festival of flower and song, brings together dozens of Chicano novelists, short-story writers, and poets. It inspires similar festivals around the country over the next few years.

Books

McNally, John. *The Creative Writer's Survival Guide: Advice from an Unrepentant Novelist*. Iowa City: University of Iowa Press, 2010. Addresses book festivals.

Menard, Valerie. *The Latino Holiday Book: From Cinco de Mayo to Dia de los Muertos – the Celebrations and Traditions of Hispanic-Americans*. New York: Marlowe, 2000. Explains the importance of celebrating that which we value.

November 19

1997

President Bill Clinton signs the Nicaraguan Adjustment and Central American Relief Act (NACARA). The law gives immigration preference to Nicaraguan, Cuban, Salvadoran, and Guatemalan nationals, who receive a blanket amnesty and the right to apply for permanent residency because they are presumably anti-Communist.

From the Nicaraguan Adjustment and Central American Relief Act:

IN GENERAL.—Notwithstanding section 245(c) of the Immigration and Nationality Act, the status of any alien described in subsection (b) shall be adjusted by the Attorney General to that of an alien lawfully admitted for permanent residence, if the alien—

(A) applies for such adjustment before April 1, 2000; and

(B) is otherwise eligible to receive an immigrant visa and is otherwise admissible to the United States for permanent residence, except in determining such admissibility the grounds for inadmissibility specified in paragraphs (4), (5), (6)(A), and (7)(A) of section 212(a) of the Immigration and Nationality Act shall not apply. . . .

RELATIONSHIP OF APPLICATION TO CERTAIN ORDERS.—An alien present in the United States who has been ordered excluded, deported, removed, or ordered to depart voluntarily from the United States under any provision of the Immigration and Nationality Act may, notwithstanding such order, apply for adjustment of status under paragraph (1). Such an alien may not be required, as a condition of submitting or granting such application, to file a separate motion to reopen, reconsider, or vacate such order. If the Attorney General grants the application, the Attorney General shall cancel the order. If the Attorney General renders a final administrative decision to deny the application, the order shall be effective and enforceable to the same extent as if the application had not been made.

The benefits provided by subsection (a) shall apply to any alien who is a national of Nicaragua or Cuba and who has been physically present in the United States for a continuous period, beginning not later than December 1, 1995, and ending not earlier than the date the application for adjustment under such subsection is filed, except an alien shall not be considered to have failed to maintain continuous physical presence by reason of an absence, or absences, from the United States for any periods in the aggregate not exceeding 180 days.

PROOF OF COMMENCEMENT OF CONTINUOUS PRESENCE.—For purposes of establishing that the period of continuous physical presence . . . commenced not later than December 1, 1995, an alien—

(A) shall demonstrate that the alien, prior to December 1, 1995—

    (i) applied to the Attorney General for asylum;

    (ii) was issued an order to show cause under section 242 or 242B of the Immigration and Nationality Act (as in effect prior to April 1, 1997);

    (iii) was placed in exclusion proceedings under section 236 of such Act (as so in effect);

    (iv) applied for adjustment of status under section 245 of such Act;

    (v) applied to the Attorney General for employment authorization;

    (vi) performed service, or engaged in a trade or business, within the United States which is evidenced by records maintained by the Commissioner of Social Security; or

    (vii) applied for any other benefit under the Immigration and Nationality Act by means of an application establishing the alien's presence in the United States prior to December 1, 1995; or

(B) shall make such other demonstration of physical presence as the Attorney General may provide for by regulation.

DURING CERTAIN PROCEEDINGS.—Notwithstanding any provision of the Immigration and Nationality Act, the Attorney General shall not order any alien to be removed from the United States, if the alien is in exclusion, deportation, or removal proceedings under any provision of such Act and has applied for adjustment of status under subsection (a), except where the Attorney General has rendered a final administrative determination to deny the application. . . .

IN GENERAL.—Notwithstanding section 245(c) of the Immigration and Nationality Act, the status of an alien shall be adjusted by the Attorney General to that of an alien lawfully admitted for permanent residence, if—

(A) the alien is a national of Nicaragua or Cuba;

(B) the alien is the spouse, child, or unmarried son or daughter, of an alien whose status is adjusted to that of an alien lawfully admitted for permanent residence under subsection (a), except that in the case of such an unmarried son or daughter, the son or daughter shall be required to establish that they have been physically present in the United States for a continuous period, beginning not later than December 1, 1995, and ending not earlier than the date the application for adjustment under this subsection is filed;

(C) the alien applies for such adjustment and is physically present in the United States on the date the application is filed;

(D) the alien is otherwise eligible to receive an immigrant visa and is otherwise admissible to the United States for permanent residence, except in determining such admissibility the grounds for exclusion specified in paragraphs (4), (5), (6)(A), and (7)(A) of section 212(a) of the Immigration and Nationality Act shall not apply; and

(E) applies for such adjustment before April 1, 2000.

PROOF OF CONTINUOUS PRESENCE.—For purposes of establishing the period of continuous physical presence referred to in paragraph (1)(B), an alien—

(A) shall demonstrate that such period commenced not later than December 1, 1995, in a manner consistent with subsection (b)(2); and

(B) shall not be considered to have failed to maintain continuous physical presence by reason of an absence, or absences, from the United States for any period in the aggregate not exceeding 180 days. . . .

N GENERAL.—For purposes of calculating the period of continuous physical presence under section 244(a) of the Immigration and Nationality Act (as in effect before the title III-A effective date) or section 240A of such Act (as in effect after the title III-A effective date), subparagraph (A) and paragraphs (1) and (2) of section 240A(d) of the Immigration

and Nationality Act shall not apply in the case of an alien, regardless of whether the alien is in exclusion or deportation proceedings before the title III-A effective date, who has not been convicted at any time of an aggravated felony (as defined in section 101(a) of the Immigration and Nationality Act) and—

(I) was not apprehended after December 19, 1990, at the time of entry, and is—

(aa) a Salvadoran national who first entered the United States on or before September 19, 1990, and who registered for benefits pursuant to the settlement agreement in American Baptist Churches, et al. v. Thornburgh (ABC), 760 F.Supp. 796 (N.D.Cal.1991) on or before October 31, 1991, or applied for temporary protected status on or before October 31, 1991; or

(bb) a Guatemalan national who first entered the United States on or before October 1, 1990, and who registered for benefits pursuant to such settlement agreement on or before December 31, 1991;

(II) is a Guatemalan or Salvadoran national who filed an application for asylum with the Immigration and Naturalization Service on or before April 1, 1990;

(III) is the spouse or child (as defined in section 101(b)(1) of the Immigration and Nationality Act) of an individual, at the time a decision is rendered to suspend the deportation, or cancel the removal, of such individual, if the individual has been determined to be described in this clause (excluding this subclause and subclause (IV));

(IV) is the unmarried son or daughter of an alien parent, at the time a decision is rendered to suspend the deportation, or cancel the removal, of such alien parent, if—

   (aa) the alien parent has been determined to be described in this clause (excluding this subclause and subclause (III)); and

   (bb) in the case of a son or daughter who is 21 years of age or older at the time such decision is rendered, the son or daughter entered the United States on or before October 1, 1990; or

(V) is an alien who entered the United States on or before December 31, 1990, who filed an application for asylum on or before December 31, 1991, and who, at the time of filing such application, was a national of the Soviet Union, Russia, any republic of the former Soviet Union, Latvia, Estonia, Lithuania, Poland, Czechoslovakia, Romania, Hungary, Bulgaria, Albania, East Germany, Yugoslavia, or any state of the former Yugoslavia. . . .

(*Source:* From Nicaraguan Adjustment and Central American Relief Act, Public Law 105–100, http://www.uscis.gov/ilink/docView/PUBLAW/HTML/PUBLAW/0-0-0-15244.html)

Books

Coutin, Susan Bibler. *Nations of Emigrants: Shifting Boundaries of Citizenship in El Salvador and the United States*. Ithaca: Cornell University Press, 2007. This Spanish language book includes a chapter on the Nicaraguan Adjustment and Central American Relief Act.

Generazio, Marc R. *Immigration Law: A Guide to Laws and Regulations*. Chicago: American Bar Association, 2011. A definitive guide to

using the Nicaraguan Adjustment and Central American Relief Act.

Website

Nicaraguan Adjustment and Central American Relief Act. Reprints the entire law. http://www.uscis.gov/ilink/docView/PUBLAW/HTML/PUBLAW/0-0-0-15244.html

November 21

1983

Professional wrestlers and identical twins Brie Garcia-Colace and Nikki Garcia-Colace are born in Scottsdale, Arizona, to Mexican American parents. While wrestling has a history of attracting an enthusiastic fan base in Mexico, the sport has not generally attracted Latinas as participants. The Garcia-Colace twins upend gender norms by playing as a wrestling tag team known as the Bella Twins; they have performed since 2008. Both women won World Wrestling Entertainment Divas Championships in 2011. The style of wrestling in which the Bella Twins compete requires both physical skill and acting prowess.

Books

Madigan, Dan. *Mondo Lucha a Go-Go: The Bizarre and Honorable World of Wild Mexican Wrestling*. New York: Rayo/HarperCollins, 2007. A photographic history of Mexican wrestling.

Morton, Gerald W., and George M. O'Brien. *Wrestling to Rasslin: Ancient Sport to American Spectacle*. Bowling Green: Bowling Green State University Popular Press, 1985. The best available history of the sport in the United States.

Websites

Bella Twins. This website for the wrestlers includes photographs and interviews. http://www.bella-twins.net/

The Bella Twins—Nicole and Brianna. This more subdued website includes photographs, interviews, and a place to purchase videos starring the twins. http://nicoleandbrianna.com/

November 22

1999

Elián González is rescued after a boat bearing the boy and 14 other people from Cuba to Miami capsizes in the Florida Straits. González's mother is among the dead. Knowing that the boy will be returned to Cuba, Elián's great uncle, Lázaro González, applies for legal custody. The Cuban government begins steps to have Elián returned to his father, Juan Miguel González, in Cuba as soon as possible. Cuba argues that the father has custody rights to the child. The Cuban community in Miami strongly backs Elián's Miami family, however, and the case quickly becomes a cause célèbre. It ends at dawn on April 23, 2000, when police and Immigration and Naturalization Service (INS) agents forcibly remove Elián from Lázaro's home. He is returned to Cuba.

From comments by Richard Nuccio, former adviser to President Bill Clinton on Cuban Affairs:

> [It] might be the first time in the country's history that such a small child has been involved in a web of international politics of such magnitude. In a way, Elián is an instrument for both sides, who are using the case for their arguments, since, on the one hand, the Cuban accords are treasonous and against the best interests of the Cuban people. On the other, those who want an end to the embargo and a change in U.S. policy toward Cuba see the matter as an opportunity to cooperate and reduce tensions.

(*Source:* Fernández, Alfredo A. *Adrift: The Cuban Raft People.* Houston: Arte Publico, 2000, p. 245.)

Books

Bardach, Ann Louise. *Cuba Confidential: Love and Vengeance in Miami and Havana.* New York: Random House, 2002. An excellent history of the Elián González case based on a great number of interviews and other sources.

Fernández, Alfredo A. *Adrift: The Cuban Raft People.* Houston: Arte Publico, 2000. Provides the context for Elián González's exit from Cuba but focuses on the 1994 refugees.

Websites

Elián Gonzalez—The Real Cuba. This site, heavily biased against Fidel Castro, shows the strong opinions generated by the child custody case. http://www.therealcuba.com/elian_gonzalez.htm

The Elian Gonzalez Case: An Online Newshour Focus. This PBS site is an archive of articles and photographs related to the case. http://www.pbs.org/newshour/bb/law/elian/

November 23

1883

José Clemente Orozco is born in Ciudad Guzmán, Mexico. A social realist painter, Orozco formed part of the Mexican Mural Renaissance along with Diego Rivera and David Alfaro Siqueiros. Known as the most complex of the muralists, Orozco employed symbolism and themes of suffering in his work. Between 1922 and 1948, Orozco painted murals throughout Mexico and the United States, including one of his most famous ones at Dartmouth University. He died in 1949 in Mexico City.

José Clemente Orozco explains his work in the *Museum of Modern Art Bulletin,* August 1940:

> The public wants explanations about a painting. What the artist had in mind when he did it. What he was thinking of. What is the exact name of the picture, and what the artist means by that. If he is glorifying or cursing. If he believes in Democracy.
>
> Going to the Italian Opera, you get a booklet with a full account of why Rigoletto kills Aida at the end of a wild party with La Boheme. . . . And now

the public insists on knowing the plot of modern painted opera, though not Italian, of course. They take for granted that every picture must be the illustration of a short story or of a thesis and want to be told the entertaining biography and bright sayings of the leaders in the stage-picture, the ups and downs of hero, villain, and chorus. . . .

It seems incredible that science and industry have not yet provided the artist with better materials to work with. Not a single improvement through the centuries. The range of colors available is still extremely limited. Pigments are not permanent at all in spite of manufacturers' claims. Canvas, wood, paper, walls are exposed to continuous destruction from moisture, changes in temperature, chemical reactions, insects, and germs. Oils, varnishes, wax, gums, and tempera media are dirty substances darkening, changing, cracking, and disintegrating all the time.

Fresco painting is free from the inconveniences of oils and varnishes, but the wall upon which the painting is done is subjected to many causes of destruction, such as the use of the wrong kind of building materials, poor planning, moisture from the ground or from the air, earthquakes, dive bombing, tanking or battleshipping, excess of magnesia in the lime or the marble dust, lack of care resulting in scratches or peeling off, et cetera. So, fresco must be done only on walls that are as free as possible from all these inconveniences.

There is no rule for painting *al fresco*. Every artist may do as he pleases provided he paints as thinly as possible and only while the plaster is wet, six to eight hours from the moment it is applied. No retouching of any kind afterwards. Every artist develops his own way of planning his conception and transferring it onto the wet plaster.

Every method is as good as the other. Or the artist may improvise without any previous sketches.

(*Source:* Frank, Patrick, ed. *Readings in Latin American Modern Art*. New Haven: Yale University Press, 2004, pp. 48–49.)

Books

Orozco, José Clemente. *The Artist in New York: Letters to Jean Charlot and Unpublished Writings, 1925–1929*. Trans. Ruth L. C. Sims. Austin: University of Texas Press, 1974. The Mexican muralist lived in the United States between 1927 and 1934, painting murals.

Orozco, José Clemente. *Autobiografía*. Mexico: Ediciones Era, 1970. The author's view of his life.

Websites

José Clemente Orozco: The Epic of American Civilization. The Hood Museum of Art at Dartmouth University contains one of Orozco's most famous works, "The Epic of Civilization." This site offers a brochure about the mural, an audio guide, and a tour. http://hoodmuseum.dartmouth.edu/collections/overview/americas/mesoamerica/murals/

José Clemente Orozco: Orozco, Man of Fire. PBS offers a good biography of the artist, the subject of one of its episodes of *American Masters*. http://www.pbs.org/wnet/americanmasters/episodes/jose-clemente-orozco/orozco-man-of-fire/82/

1970

The Association for the Advancement of Mexican Americans is incorporated in Houston, Texas. It aims to create future community leaders in Texas by promoting a positive self-image in youth and encouraging educational achievements. Among Mexican American youth in Texas, school dropout rates and the incidence of drug abuse are particularly high. The organization offers educational, employment, and rehabilitative programs for youths.

Books

Gonzalez, Juan. *Harvest of Empire: A History of Latinos in America*. New York: Penguin, 2000. An excellent popular history of Mexican Americans and other Latinos in the United States.

Rosales, F. Arturo. *The History of the Mexican American Civil Rights Movement*. Houston: Arte Público, 1997. The association is part of the Chicano movement.

Website

The Association for the Advancement of Mexican Americans. The official website for the organization contains financial audits of the group, upcoming events, and news. http://www.aama.org/

1974

Nicaraguan boxer Alexis Arguello, "El Flaco Explosivo (the Explosive Thin Man)," wins his first title when he knocks out Mexican Ruben Olivares to become the World Boxing Association Featherweight Champion. In 1976, Arguello immigrated to the United States. He is remembered as a boxer who won 80 out of 88 professional bouts with an amazing 65 knockouts and as a winner of three world championships. He was inducted into the International Boxing Hall of Fame in 1992. Arguello died in 2009.

Books

Lang, Arne K. *Prizefighting: An American History*. Jefferson, NC: McFarland, 2008. Includes Latinos in the history of the sport.

Liebling, A.J. *The Sweet Science*. New York: North Point Press, 2004. A classic work on the history of boxing by a famed sportswriter.

Websites

Alexis Arguello. BoxRec provides the career statistics of Arguello. http://boxrec.com/list_bouts.php?human_id=2179&cat=boxer

The Best of Alexis Arguello. This is one of the better video clips of Arguello in his boxing heyday that can be found on YouTube. http://www.youtube.com/watch?v=HiAu4J06lJw

1997

Jorge Mas Canosa, a spokesperson for the anti-Castro Cuban American community, dies. Mas Canosa fled for Miami in 1960 after his student activism against the new Castro government landed him in hot water. He formed the Cuban American National Foundation, a lobbying group, in the 1980s. The group kept the Cuban embargo alive. A hard liner, Mas Canosa worked for the defeat of any political candidate who called for normalization of relations with Cuba. He is also credited with getting the U.S. taxpayer–funded Radio Martí on the air, filling the airwaves with anti-Castro editorializing.

Books

Bonachea, Rolando, comp. *Jorge Mas Canosa: En Busca de una Cuba Libre: Edición Completa de sus Discursos Entrevistas y Declaraciones, 1962–1997*. Coral Gables, FL: North-South Center Press, University of Miami, 2003. A complete collection of Mas Canosa's speeches relating to Cuba.

Sweig, Julia E. *Cuba: What Everyone Needs to Know*. New York: Oxford University Press, 2009. Includes a general history of Mas Canosa and the Cuban American National Foundation.

Websites

The Cuban American National Foundation. The official website of the organization includes a media center and the group's position on various issues. http://www.canf.org/

The Jorge Mas Canosa Freedom Foundation. The official website for the organization dedicated to the promotion of freedom and democracy. http://www.jorgemascanosa.org/

November 24

1946

Nuyorican poet José Angel Figueroa is born in Mayagüez, Puerto Rico, to migrant workers who traveled between the island and the United States. A community organizer who became involved in radical politics in the 1960s, his first book of poetry, *East 100th Street,* came out in 1970. Figueroa's work often links Anglo society and its power structure with sterility and chemical products that carry ideological, brainwashing connotations.

From José Angel Figueroa's "Noo Jork: From an Island to an Inner City":

As the months faded into years, I was less the newcomer than a prisoner of the New York City Board of Education, fighting to maintain my own integrity. I felt English was some gigantic nuisance or adversary on a mission to sabotage my Puerto Rican essence, blasting me with the Who, What, Where, When, Why and How! I was entangled in a web of assimilation and acculturation. It left a lasting impression on me. I was not allowed to speak my own language. I was instead, pulled back, red-penciled in, or pushed aside and railroaded into classes where learning was some dead-end dream. Frankly, the kind of education I received, I would never give to a rock. When I wasn't making colorful pot-holders in home economics classes, I was drawing perfectly beautiful square houses with sunshine gushing out the skies as the romantic palm trees stood paralyzed near the seashore. And if you were magnificent at mumbling, picking your nose, or losing your soul during some English exam, you were the class genius or clown. . . .

I simply refused to give up my romantic accent. I was not going to be deprived of my freedom of Self. While many fought back by joining street gangs like the Purple Knights or Young Savages with switchblade tempers flashing out of their back-pockets, I was reading the dictionary like bible study. Grandma Felipa and Mama had taught me well. And what happened when I stood defiant and spoke my native tongue? My teacher, Mrs. Schaefer, who I first experienced puppy-love, held my hand down as she scratched it with her outrageous fingernails, waiting for me to stop speaking Spanish when I did not understand her words. I was sent to the dean, a mild-mannered hypocrite who rolled his newspaper tightly and with his reliable night-stick on my head, he screamed "Speak English only! Spanish is bad for you! Repeat: Speak English only! Again! Spanish is bad for you!"

I knew then that the United States had declared war on my cultural heritage. But I was no longer resentful of the English language. I knew then it was a deliberate conspiracy to fear In-glish and as a result, succumb to invisibility. Instead I chose to befriend English and to master the possibilities, but kept my Spanish close to the heart. Still, it was a damn pity that one could not be accepted nor admired for having the best of two worlds, two great languages and cultures. I was determined to survive the American Dream machine with its pressure to conform while you turned your back on your own identity.

(*Source:* Figueroa, José Angel. "Noo Jork: From an Island to an Inner City." *Journal of Educational Facilitation* 2, No. 1, January 1996, pp. 9–13. http://centropr.hunter.cuny.edu/voices/letras/jose-angel-figueroas-testimonial)

Books

Bernard-Carreño, Regina. *Nuyorganics: Organic Intellectualism, the Search for Racial Identity, and Nuyorican Thought.* New York: Peter Lang, 2010. Examines the links between ethnic identity and intellectual thought.

Mohr, Eugene V. *The Nuyorican Experience: Literature of the Puerto Rican Minority.* Westport, CT: Greenwood Press, 1982. Provides criticism of and samples of Nuyorican literature.

Websites

José Angel Figueroa. Includes a biography of the poet, several of his poems, and a passage from his memoir. http://centropr.hunter.cuny.edu/voices/letras/jos%C3%A9-angel-figueroas-bio

José Angel Figueroa. Supplies a biography of the poet. http://phatitude.org/online/programs/phatitude-tv/the-writers/jose-angel-figueroa/

November 25

1982

The Thanksgiving holiday is celebrated. The origins of Thanksgiving are a bit murky with both Massachusetts and Virginia claiming credit for holding the first celebration of this American holiday. Traditionally viewed as a celebration of the end of the harvest, Thanksgiving became an official holiday in 1863. The traditional meal of turkey became standardized in the 20th century as modern holiday traditions, such as football games, shopping, and parades, developed.

From "Grateful for Hope, Newcomers Join in Thanksgiving Tradition":

They have never heard of the Pilgrims. Plymouth Rock might as well be a new kind of dance or a type of car. They have only eaten cranberry sauce as a jam on bread, and the only place they have ever expressed their thanks before is inside a cathedral. But no matter that they are not especially fond of turkey or that it makes no sense to them to stage a celebration on a Thursday instead of a weekend night, members of the Niquio family—who arrived in the United States several months ago from Argentina—will be sitting down today to their first Thanksgiving dinner.

Like so many other newcomers to this country, Mr. and Mrs. Rodolfo Niquio do not always understand American customs. Thanksgiving appeared one day out of nowhere, with its explosion of crepe paper turkeys and cardboard leaves, and suddenly their building in Elmhurst, Queens, was aflutter with talk of what to put in the stuffing. . . . In the case of the Niquios, the news also came from their 9-year-old daughter, Karina, who came home one day from dance class imitating a turkey, and their 5-year-old son, Mauricio, who came home from school sporting a paper Indian headress. "The Indians helped the Americans," Mauricio announced to his mother in what was just another detail about this holiday she still did not understand. But Mr. and Mrs. Niquio, who have thrown themselves into American life the way one does into a swimming pool off the high board, rushed out and bought a turkey, too. "You can't live in a country and not try to belong," said Mrs. Niquio. "Now that we're in America, we have to do as the Americans."

(*Source:* Kleiman, Dana. "Grateful for Hope, Newcomers Join in Thanksgiving Tradition." *New York Times,* November 25, 1982, p. B1.)

Books

Baker, James W. *Thanksgiving: The Biography of an American Holiday.* NP: New Hampshire, 2009. This is a scholarly, in-depth study of a very

American holiday by the former director of research at Plimoth Plantation.

Hillstrom, Laurie Collier. *Thanksgiving: The American Holiday*. NP: KWS Publishers, 2011. Focuses on the customs, foods, and symbols of the holiday.

Websites

"Thanksgiving." Provides a New England–centered history of the holiday. http://www.history.com/topics/thanksgiving

"The Thanksgiving Story." Offers a history of the holiday plus copies of George Washington's and Abraham Lincoln's Thanksgiving proclamations. http://wilstar.com/holidays/thankstr.htm

1920

Ricardo Montalbán, a television and movie actor, is born in Mexico City, Mexico. In August 1970, he joined with Gilbert Avila, Val de Vargas, Rudolfo Hoyos Jr., Tony de Marco, Robert Apodaca, Luis De Cordoba and others to found Nosotros to strategically change the stereotypical image portrayed by Latino actors. The men had tired of playing degrading roles as Latin lovers, rogues, thugs, and servants. In 1999, Nosotros bought the historic Doolittle Theater in Hollywood and renamed it in Montalbán's honor. It became the first major arts facility to carry the name of a Latino performing artist. Montalbán died in 2009.

Books

Montalbán, Ricardo, and Bob Thomas. *Reflections: A Life in Two Worlds*. Garden City, NY: Doubleday, 1980. The actor's autobiography.

Rodríguez, Clara E. *Heroes, Lovers, and Others: The Story of Latinos in Hollywood*. Washington, D.C.: Smithsonian Books, 2004. Excellent history of the difficulties that Latinos, including Montalbán, have faced in the movies.

Websites

Ricardo Montalbán. The Internet Movie Database provides credits for all of the Mexican actor's film and television work. http://www.imdb.com/name/nm0001544/

Ricardo Montalbán. Provides a detail-heavy short biography of the actor along with a listing of his acting credits. http://www.nndb.com/people/748/000022682/

1999

Elián González, a six-year-old Cuban boy, is rescued off the coast of Florida as one of only three survivors on a boat that came from Cuba. His mother, Elisabeth Brotons González and her boyfriend had drowned in the attempt to flee the communist island. The boy had left Cuba without the permission of his father, Juan Miguel González, who wanted his son returned. However, González had a great uncle and cousins on his maternal side in Miami who did not want the child sent back to communism. The cousins gained support from activists, chiefly Republicans, opposed to Fidel Castro's rule over Cuba. The father gained support from international law which gave him, rather than distant relatives, custody of his child. The controversy turned into one of the nastiest custody battles in the history of the United States over the course of the next six months. The U.S. government tried to maintain a neutral stance. Eventually, Janet Reno, as attorney general, ordered federal agents on April 22, 2000 to storm the Miami home of the cousins in the early morning hours and return Elián to his father. Hundreds of angry protesters then rioted in Little Havana in Miami. On June 28, 2000, Elián returned to Cuba with his father. The entire affair may have cost Vice President Al Gore votes in the presidential election of 2000 in Florida since many Cuban Americans blamed the Clinton administration for allowing the boy to return to Castro's Cuba.

From "Online Focus: Asylum Arguments":

Margaret Warner: For more, we turn to two experts on asylum law and policy. Wend Young is Washington liaison and staff attorney for the Women's Commission for Refugee Women and Children, a nonprofit education and advocacy group. The commission filed an amicus brief with the court, arguing that the INS should grant the boy an asylum hearing. And Philip Schrag is a law professor at Georgetown University and director of the school's asylum law clinic . . .

Professor, in a nutshell, what's the nub of this case?

Philip Schrag, **Georgetown University:**

Well, the important threshold question to understand is that to win asylum, a person who arrives in the United States must show a well-founded fear if that individual would be persecuted if returned to the country from which they came. It's not enough to show that there are many human rights violations in the country. It's not enough to show that the country treats its own citizens shabbily. . . .

Normally in the United States, we allow a father or mother, the surviving parent, if there is only one, to speak for

Margaret Warner:

Wendy Young, **Women's Commission for Refugee Women and Children:**

a child. And so normally we have a very strong presumption that the parent here would ask the government to give the boy an asylum hearing, which means a thorough evaluation of his asylum claim. Because the parent here, Juan Miguel, said he didn't want an asylum hearing for the boy, but the boy's Uncle Lazaro said he did, the government looked at Lazaro's papers, his application and gave the boy some . . . gave the claim some consideration, but not a full asylum hearing, and determined that there wasn't enough there to make a judgment that there should be a full asylum hearing, which is a very long, drawn-out proceeding, and rightfully so.

So would you agree, that's the nub of it: Whether the INS had to consider Elian Gonzalez's claim despite the fatherWW's wishes?

Yeah, I believe also, though, that an issue that is very fundamental and very critical is before the court as well, which is, does a child have the right to seek asylum? The statute is very plain in its language: Any alien may apply for asylum. If you look at international law and if you look at the INS's own internal guidelines, they acknowledge that that includes children, that regardless of age, an individual does have the right to seek asylum. This is an issue that I hope the 11th Circuit will state very clearly, and affirm that the child does have the right to do so.

(*Source:* "Online Focus: Asylum Arguments." May 11, 2000, http://www. pbs.org/newshour/bb/law/jan-june00/ elian_5–11.html)

Books

Bardach, Ann Louise. *Cuba Confidential: Love and Vengeance in Miami and Havana.* New York: Vintage, 2003. Captures the soap opera-ish elements of the fight over the future of Gonzalez.

Dubinsky, Karen. *Babies without Borders: Adoption and Migration across the Americas.* New York: New York University Press, 2010. Identifies Gonzalez as the national baby of Cuba.

Websites

The Elián González Case. The PBS show "Online Newshour" provides media coverage of the incident. http://www.pbs.org/ newshour/bb/law/elian/

"Thanks to Janet Reno, Eric Holder, and Bill Clinton, Elián González Is Now a Full Slave of the Castro Regime." Captures the anger that

many Cuban Americans still hold about the saga. http://www.therealcuba.com/elian_ gonzalez.htm

2002

Lalo Alcaraz, the American-born son of Mexican immigrants, debuts his satiric comic strip, *La Cucaracha,* in *L.A. Weekly.* He uses a cockroach as his title character because the insect is a traditional literary figure in Mexican pop culture. Alcaraz, nationally syndicated by Universal Press Syndicate, has won a number of awards for his cartoons including the Latino Spirit Award from the California Latino Legislative Caucus.

Books

Alcaraz, Lalo. *La Cucaracha.* Kansas City, MO: Andrews McMeel, 2004. The cartoonist's most famous strips in a book form.

Rall, Ted. *Attitude: The New Subversive Political Cartoonists.* New York: Nantier, Beall, Minoustchine, 2002. Part of the new view toward comics that views them as much more than a low art form.

Websites

Lalo Alcaraz: Artist, Cartoonist, Writer. The official website of the cartoonist contains his biography and portfolio. http://laloalcaraz. com/

Lalo Alcaraz: Pocho. Contains news and satire chosen and written by the artist. http:// pocho.com/author/lalo/

November 26

1722

Alejandro Wauchope, a Scottish lieutenant colonel in Spain's Irish Brigade and the newly appointed governor of Pensacola, arrives at Pensacola Bay to reclaim the colony from the French at the end of the War of the Quadruple Alliance. Little of the old Spanish settlement of Presidio Santa María de Galve remained—only an old oven, a cistern, and a hut. Wauchope abandoned the old presidio site in favor of new fort locations on Santa Rosa Island, a barrier island that separates the Gulf of Mexico from Pensacola Bay, and present-day downtown Pensacola. The Spanish built Presidio Isla de Santa Rosa and Presidio San Miguel de Panzacola, holding on to the forts until 1821 when the United States took over Florida.

Books

Bense, Judith A. *Presidio Santa María de Galve: A Struggle for Survival in Colonial Spanish Pensacola.* Gainesville: University Press of Florida, 2003. Examines the impact of the war on Spanish control of Florida.

Grady, Timothy Paul. *Anglo-Spanish Rivalry in Colonial South-East America, 1650–1725.* Brookfield, VT: Pickering & Chatto, 2010. Looks at the waning of Spanish influence in Southeast North America.

Websites

Pensacola History. A history of the county seat of Escambia County that includes its Spanish past. http://www.travelgrove.com/travel-guides/United-States/Florida-Pensacola-History-c2127618.html

Presidio de Isla Santa Rosa (1722–1752). The Department of Anthropology and Archaeology at the University of West Florida provides a map and description of the old Spanish fort. http://uwf.edu/anthropology/research/colonial/santarosa/

1968

Corky Gonzales, head of the Crusade for Justice, joins with other members of the Chicano organization to present a list of demands to the Board of Education in Denver, Colorado. Gonzales, who had picked beets in the fields alongside his migrant-worker father, founded the Crusade for Justice in Denver. He began working in politics when he coordinated the Viva Kennedy campaign during the presidential election of 1960. In 1965, he became the chairman of the board of the War on Poverty in Denver, another political assignment by the Democratic Party. However, Gonzales became increasingly disillusioned by traditional politics, especially after he was forced to resign his post because of allegations that he had discriminated against Anglos and blacks. He targeted the Anglo system as the enemy of Mexican Americans. He founded Crusade for Justice to create a civil rights organization that was completely independent of any economic or political ties with the white power structure. In 1967, Gonzales wrote the famous poem, "Yo Soy Joaquin."

From Corky Gonzales's protest speech to the Denver Board of Education:

A. That the school board through its office of education enforce the inclusion in all schools of this city the history of our people, our culture, i.e. language, etc., and our contributions to this country.

B. That all federal, state and city support funds be withheld from any school that does not comply with the above statement.

C. That payment for the psychological destruction of our people, i.e. inferiority complexes, anglo superiority myth, rejection of our own identity, and self worth, will be settled by a free education for all Mexican American youth . . . from Headstart through College. All books, dues, materials, lunch, tuition, expenses, etc., will be free. Recompensation for the ethnic educational genocide perpetuated by this educational system can never repay in total the damage already inflicted on our people.

D. That bi-lingual education from elementary school through college become a reality and that the protection of our cultural rights as cited in the Treaty of Hildago, 1848, be recognized and abided by.

E. That each neighborhood complex have its own school board with no at large membership.

F. That teachers live in the community in which they teach and that they are bi-lingual and well versed in the history, culture and contributions of our people.

(*Source:* Marín, Christine. *A Spokesman of the Mexican American Movement: Rodolfo "Corky" Gonzales and the Fight for Chicano Liberation, 1966–1972.* San Francisco: R&E Research Associates, 1977.)

Books

Marín, Christine. *A Spokesman of the Mexican American Movement: Rodolfo "Corky" Gonzales and the Fight for Chicano Liberation, 1966–1972.* San Francisco: R&E Research Associates, 1977. The only biography of the Chicano leader contains a wealth of primary sources.

Rosales, F. Arturo. *Chicano!: The History of the Mexican American Civil Rights Movement.* Houston: Arte Publico, 1996. Winner of the Gustavus Myers Outstanding Book Award for its coverage of the movement.

Websites

The Chicano Civil Rights Movement. A timeline of the movement from the Experience Music Project at the Science Fiction Museum and Hall of Fame. http://www.empmuseum.org/documents/education/onlineCourse/Civil_Rights_Timeline.pdf

The Chicano Movement: Brown and Proud. A brief history of the movement by Nadra Kareem Nittle. http://racerelations.about.com/od/historyofracerelations/a/BrownandProudTheChicanoMovement.htm

2008

Cecilia Muñoz, a former vice president of the National Council of La Raza and a MacArthur Fellow for her work with civil rights and immigration, is named as director of intergovernmental affairs for the administration of president-elect Barack Obama.

Born in Detroit in 1962, Muñoz is the daughter of Bolivian immigrants. She learned the art of politics from her father, who would press friends to write letters in support of various bills. Muñoz's support of Obama's deportation policies proved controversial among Latino activists. She later headed the White House Domestic Policy Council.

From "Cecilia Muñoz: White House Director of Intergovernmental Affairs":

After graduate school at the University of California at Berkeley, Munoz moved to Chicago to help the Diocese of Chicago legalize undocumented immigrants. "I was working 14-, 16-hour days. It was intense," she told the Detroit News in 1997. "I had a real sense of obligation not to mess up." But Munoz also said she faced sexism from some priests, discrimination that ultimately led her to reconsider her role with the Catholic Church.

In 1988, Munoz moved to the National Council of La Raza, a Hispanic-rights organization. "I decided I wanted to be part of a Latino institution," she told the News. "I can go to a meeting on the Hill where I'm the only Latino, have someone say something awful to me, and when I come back to the office, I don't have to explain why it was offensive." As senior vice president, Munoz ran the organization's advocacy and legislative agenda. . . .

Munoz has centered her advocacy work on fighting for the rights of Hispanic Americans. "The line between anti-immigrant and anti-Latino is pretty thin," Munoz told The Washington Post in 2000. "The day when my kids can walk down the street and be called American, that's the goal."

(*Source:* Cecilia Muñoz: White House Director of Intergovernmental Affairs. http://www.washingtonpost.com/politics/cecilia-munoz/gIQAaNcv9O_topic.html)

Books

Alaniz, Yolanda, and Megan Cornish. *Viva La Raza: A History of Chicano Identity and Resistance.* Seattle: Red Letter Press, 2008. A history of liberation efforts.

Allison, Jay et al., ed. *This I Believe: The Personal Philosophies of Remarkable Men and Women.* New York: Picador/Henry Holt, 2007. Muñoz discusses how getting angry can be a good thing.

Websites

Cecilia Muñoz: White House Director of Intergovernmental Affairs. Provides a short biographical essay on Muñoz as well as sections on her background, path to power, and prioritized issues. http://www.washingtonpost. com/politics/cecilia-munoz/gIQAaNcv9O_ topic.html

White House Profile: Cecilia Muñoz. A short biography of the political leader. http://www. whitehouse.gov/blog/author/Cecilia%20Mu% C3%B1oz

November 27

1891

Cuban independence leader José Martí gives a speech that outlines the goals of the United Cuban Revolutionary Party to Cuban cigar workers in Ybor City, Florida. The Latino section of Tampa, Ybor City, was also known as the cigar capital of the world and likely had the largest contingent of Cuban immigrants in the United States in the late 19th century. Martí's speech was reproduced in newspapers and journals throughout the United States and Cuba, adding further fuel to the Cuban fight for independence from Spain.

Books

Font, Mauricio A., and Alfonso W. Quiroz, eds. *The Cuban Republic and José Martí: Reception and Use of a National Symbol.* Lanham, MD: Lexington Books, 2006. Discusses the importance of Martí in the Cuban imagination.

Pérez, Louis A., Jr. *José Martí in the United States: The Florida Experience.* Tempe: Center for Latin American Studies, Arizona State University, 1995. The only examination of Martí's life among fellow Cubans in the Sunshine State by one of the foremost historians of Cuba.

Websites

Jose Marti. A biographical essay by Carlos Ripoll that also contains some of the Cuban leader's poetry. http://www2.fiu.edu/~fcf/ jmarti.html

La Página de José Martí. This Spanish-language site contains a wealth of information on Martí for students and educators. http://www.jose-marti.org/

November 28

1861

Teacher, historian, and pioneer Adina de Zavala is born on November 28 in Harris County, Texas. Zavala is one of the individuals who played a role in the contested history of the Alamo. She is also a founder of the Daughters of the Republic of Texas (DRT), the group that for long took responsibility for managing the Alamo site. The DRT saved the Alamo from destruction in 1905 but divided over the preservation of the site. The petite Zavala staged a sit-in that attracted considerable media attention but she ultimately lost the battle to preserve the upper-storey of the long barracks. As a Tejana, Zavala for long did not get the recognition that she had earned for preserving a critical part of American history.

Books

Flores, Richard R., ed. *History and Legends of the Alamo and Other Missions in and around San Antonio.* Houston, TX: Arte Público, 1965. Zavala wrote this book before her 1955 death.

Lord, Clifford L., ed. *Keepers of the Past.* Chapel Hill: University of North Carolina Press, 1965. Includes a chapter on Zavala.

Websites

Adina Emilia de Zavala. The Texas State Historical Association provides a brief biography of this Texas historian. http://www.tshaonline.org/handbook/online/articles/fzafg

Adina de Zavala: Alamo Crusader. A good biography of the determined preservationist. http://www.tamu.edu/faculty/ccbn/dewitt/adp/history/bios/zavala/zavala.html

1942

Shoe designer Manolo Blahnik is born in Santa Cruz de la Palma, Spain. A maker of high-end shoes that generally sell for $300 to $400, Blahnik gained considerable public recognition for creating the favorite pumps of the Carrie Bradshaw character on the 1998–2004 HBO television show, *Sex and the City.* He began designing shoes in 1971 at the urging of famed fashion writer, Diana Vreeland. He has since won a number of awards from the Council of Fashion Designers of America, including the Stiletto.

From "Blahnik Puts His Foot Down":

> Remember those blue Manolo Blahnik pumps with the sparkly pilgrim buckles in the "Sex and the City" movie? The ones that Carrie said cost a whopping $525? Well, the real ones cost $945, and they go on sale Friday at Bergdorf Goodman, where Mr. Blahnik is expected to greet customers for an hour and autograph their shoes. In the film, Carrie wears the shoes in a climactic scene, but many critics (including this one) thought that particular Blahnik style was a letdown. Nevertheless, the power of Carrie speaks. Teril Turner, a spokeswoman for Bergdorf Goodman, said the store has since been besieged with more than 100 requests from customers to buy the shoes. "Oh, good lord," Mr. Blahnik said in a telephone interview from London, where he was apparently unaware of the demand for the shoes in New York. "I think that's quite obscene."

(*Source:* Wilson, Eric. "Front Row: Blahnik Puts His Foot Down." *New York Times,* September 11, 2008, p. G4.)

Books

McDowell, Colin. *Manolo Blahnik.* London: Orion, 2003. A biography of the designer that also includes a look into his shoe factory.

Roberts, Michael, and Anna Wintour, eds. *Manolo Blahnik Drawings.* A collection of sketches that Blahnik makes at the outset of his design process with introductions to each of the drawings by Wintour and Roberts.

Websites

Manolo Blahnik. The designer's official webpage. http://www.manoloblahnik.com/

Manolo Blahnik—Design Museum. Provides a biography of the designer and a timeline of major events in his career. http://designmuseum.org/design/manolo-blahnik

November 29

1990

The collapse of a Ponzi scheme, the Latin Investment Bank, wipes out the savings of about 2,500 Salvadorans in the Washington, D.C., area. The depositors, mostly illiterate or unsophisticated Spanish-speaking-only immigrants, lost nearly $6 million. They were easy targets in part because they did not know to check if the bank was FDIC-insured. The Securities and Exchange Commission alleged that the five principals of the company, including President Fernando Leonzo, illegally sold securities in the form of passbook savings accounts. In addition, millions of dollars in company funds were diverted to the personal use of the owners in the form of house and business loans. A U.S. District Court judge later ordered the men to pay damages of $6.5 million to depositors but much of the money could not be recovered.

From "One Depositor's Fading Dream":

Alibal Bonilla is one of the guys you might see at a bus stop about 5 a.m., headed for a construction site, hauling hammers and saws and wearing an asbestos mask and steel-toe shoes. You might see him in a car pool at the end of the day, with five or six others, caked with mud, splattered with concrete and hoping to find a cold brew before passing out from fatigue. Bonilla, 29, was born in Usuluta'n, El Salvador. He lived there until 1980, when he acted on his dream of coming to America. He got a job as a welder, which paid enough for him to send money to his parents back home. Later, he decided to save some for himself.

He did not know that the bank he would choose for a savings account, Latin Investment Corp. in Northwest Washington, was about as secure as a shoe box. But he does now that 5,000 of his hard-earned dollars have disappeared. "I feel real bad," Bonilla said yesterday, as he sought financial advice from a friar at Sacred Heart Church. "It's not like I got robbed," he said, slapping his forehead. "I walked into this so-called bank and gave my money away."

Bonilla was one of about 2,000 customers who together appear to have lost $6 million to $13 million when the unchartered Latin Investment Corp. suddenly closed Nov. 29 amid rumors of financial difficulties. His friend Julio Caesar Batista, 30, said he had saved $10,000 working as a construction site concrete spreader. He also kept his cash with Latin Investment. "I had this idea for a small piece of land and a nice little house so I could live with my family," Batista said. "The dream is still in my head, but there is no money in the bank." Their mood was melancholy. "I told my family in Salvador that I'd be home for Christmas," Bonilla said. "I told them I would bring gifts."

Bank customers have hired a lawyer who said he has met with the Salvadoran ambassador to the United States in an effort to freeze the foreign assets of Latin Investment's president, Fernando Leonzo, who is a native of El Salvador. . . . The ordeal has brought the already close Salvadoran community even closer. As in the aftermath of an earthquake that damaged their country four years ago, they are once again sharing food, clothes, shelter and toys—seemingly as determined as ever to realize the American dream. "We know how to come together in time of big problems," said Boris Canjura, coordinator of the Latin Investors Food emergency campaign, which distributes food to those affected by the bank closure. "But that doesn't mean we like to suffer."

(*Source:* Milloy, Courtland. "One Depositor's Fading Dream." *The Washington Post,* December 16, 1990, p. C3.)

Books

Mahler, Sarah J. *Salvadorans in Suburbia: Symbiosis and Conflict.* New York: Allyn and Bacon, 1996. Sociological study of the issues facing Salvadoran immigrants.

Menjívar, Cecilia. *Fragmented Ties: Salvadoran Immigrant Networks in America.* Berkeley: University of California Press, 2000. A comprehensive study of Salvadoran immigration.

Websites

Salvadoran Americans—Countries and Their Cultures. A good essay on the history of Salvadoran immigration to the United States. http://www.everyculture.com/multi/Pa-Sp/Salvadoran-Americans.html

Salvadoran Immigrants in the U.S.—Migration Information Source. Provides details about these immigrants including places of migration and numbers. http://www.migrationinformation.org/USFocus/display.cfm?id=765

1995

The notorious Puerto Rican criminal and folk hero, Antonio García López, dies after being shot by a police officer. Nicknamed "Toño Bicicleta" (Tony Bicycle) because he never owned a car, García was born in Lares in 1943. In 1968, he beheaded his lover with a machete in front of her four-year-old son when the woman announced her intent to return to her husband. Sentenced to life in prison, he escaped two years later. Captured while farming in 1974, García returned to prison only to escape again. His escapes, seven in all, made him famous despite his penchant for violent crime. García left prison without permission for the last time in 1983. Four years later, he murdered his uncle and stepfather as well as another man. In 1995, he was working at a coffee plantation in Castañer, Puerto Rico, when police arrived and Officer Luis Rosa Merced shot him. Three thousand people attended García's burial.

Websites

Personajes Notorios. Includes a short profile of Toño Bicicleta among other notorious Puerto Rican criminals. http://www.proyectosa lonhogar.com/link%20p.r/www.linktopr.com/ notorios.html

Toño Bicicleta. A synopsis of a 2007 film about the famed criminal. *http://terpconnect.umd. edu/~dwilt/Tono2.htm?pagewanted=all*

November 30

1982

Sandra Cisneros submits the manuscript for *The House on Mango Street* to her publisher. The book, eventually published in 1984 after several revisions, immediately received rave reviews. It tells the story, in poetry and prose, of Esperanza Cordero, a Mexican American girl. Frequently used in classrooms, the book is translated into 12 different languages and

has sold more than 2 million copies. Like her protagonist, Cisneros is the daughter of Mexican Americans. She was born in Chicago on December 20, 1954. After graduating from Loyola University in 1976, she joined the famed Iowa Writers Workshop. She earned a Master of Fine Arts degree in creative writing in 1978 from the University of Iowa and then returned to Chicago. She taught at the Latino Youth Alternative High School. *The House on Mango Street* was her first novel. She is adapting the book into a screenplay.

From *The House on Mango Street:*

> In English my name means hope. In Spanish it means too many letters. It means sadness, it means waiting. It is like the number nine. A muddy color. It is the Mexican records my father plays on Sunday mornings when he is shaving, songs like sobbing.
>
> It was my great-grandmother's name and now it is mine. She was a horse woman too, born like me in the Chinese year of the horse—which is supposed to be bad luck if you're born female—but I think this is a Chinese lie because the Chinese, like the Mexicans, don't like their women strong . . .
>
> At school they say my name funny as if the syllables were made out of tin and hurt the roof of your mouth. But in Spanish my name is made out of a softer something, like silver, not quite as thick as sister's name—Magdalena—which is uglier than mine. Magdalena who at least can change and become Nenny. But I am always Esperanza . . .

(*Source:* Cisneros, Sandra. New York: Vintage Contemporaries, 1989, pp. 10–11.)

Books

Brackett, Virginia. *A Home in the Heart: The Story of Sandra Cisneros.* Greensboro, NC: Morgan Reynolds, 2005. Biography of the writer.

Rivera, Carmen Haydée. *Border Crossings and Beyond: The Life and Works of Sandra Cisneros.* Santa Barbara, CA: Praeger, 2009. Scholarly yet readable biography and critical examination of the author.

Websites

Sandra Cisneros. Official and frequently updated website of the author that contains information about publications and appearances as well as book recommendations and writing tips. http://www.sandracisneros.com/

Sandra Cisneros—Modern American Poetry. This site provides biographical information and a critical essay on the author's career. http://www.english.illinois.edu/maps/poets/a_f/cisneros/cisneros.htm

1994

The Committee to Protect Journalists reports that journalists working for ethnic news organizations in the United States are routinely subjected to intimidation, death threats, beatings, and arson that are part of organized terror campaigns by military or criminal organizations or foreign governments. The group cites the 1992 New York City murder of Manuel de Dios Unanue, a Cuban American journalist killed by a teenager hired by a leader of the Cali, a Colombia drug cartel that sought to stop de Dios's exposes.

Books

Committee to Protect Journalists. *Attacks on the Press in 2011: A Worldwide Survey.* New York: Committee to Protect Journalists, 2012. The CPJ annually releases a report on the state of press freedom.

Gonzalez, Juan. *Roll Down Your Window: Stories of a Forgotten America.* New York: Verson, 1995. Contains a chapter on the murder of Manuel de Dios Unanue.

Website

Press Freedom Online—Committee to Protect Journalists. The official page of the organization contains news about reporters who are under attack and lists those who have been killed in the line of duty. http://cpj.org/

December

December 1

1939

Professional golfer Lee Trevino is born in Dallas to a family of Mexican ancestry. He began to play on the Professional Golfers of America (PGA) tour in 1967. Trevino won six major tournaments during his career, including the U.S. Open and the Masters. In 1981, he entered the World Golf Hall of Fame.

From a 2012 interview with Lee Trevino:

Mike Bailey: What is the state of the game right now?

Lee Trevino: I think it's in trouble. I know that it's very exciting on tour, but it's not exciting for a lot of people to have to play these courses that they're building for the tour players. They build these hard golf courses, and now they're talking about playing the forward tees (Tee it Forward). They should have never built those back tees in the first place. Why do you want a golf course that's 7,400 yards long? I mean the majority of your members are elderly, and they can't hit it anywhere.

Bailey: So you're not a big fan of the Tee it Forward program?

Trevino: Guys feel like they're going to the ladies tees when you push them up forward. They don't like that. Golfers want to be macho, play it from the tips. Why they're building these golf courses longer than 6,900 yards is beyond me.

Bailey: But don't they have to build the courses longer to accommodate the modern game?

Trevino: We build these courses that are supposedly going to challenge the pros. Well, wait a minute; we build hundreds and hundreds of golf courses in this country that most people can't play. They take too long to play because they're too difficult. And also it costs too much for maintenance. And that, in return, sends the dues (and green fees) up and people are dropping out. We're in a lot of trouble right now.

(*Source:* Bailey, Mike. "Lee Trevino: Golf Is Too Long and Difficult." *Travel Insider,* April 26, 2012, http://www.golfchannel.com/news/travel-insider/lee-trevino-state-of-golf-courses/)

Books

Trevino, Lee, and Sam Blair. *The Snake in the Sandtrap (and Other Misadventures on the Golf Tour).* New York: H. Holt, 1987. Trevino, one of the more outspoken golfers, recalls his career as a professional golfer.

Trevino, Lee, and Sam Blair. *They Call Me Super Mex.* New York: Random House, 1982. The golfer's autobiography.

Website

Lee Trevino. The PGA Golf Tour supplies an official profile of the famed golfer. http://www.pgatour.com/golfers/002213/lee-trevino/

December 2

1989

Ruth Mary Reynolds, a founder in the 1940s of the American League for Puerto Rico's Independence, dies. In 1951, Reynolds received a six-year prison sentence for sedition for plotting to overthrow the U.S.-backed government in Puerto Rico. She had pledged loyalty to the Nationalist Party and allegedly ridden in a car that carried guns. Reynolds gained her freedom with an appeal to Puerto Rico's Supreme Court and spent the remainder of her life working with Puerto Rican political prisoners and lobbying for independence.

Books

Bosque-Pérez, Ramón, and José Javier Colón Morera. *Puerto Rico under Colonial Rule: Political Persecution and the Quest for Human Rights.* Albany: State University of New York Press, 2006. Examines various responses to continued political domination of Puerto Rico by the United States.

Meléndez, Edgardo, and Edwin Meléndez, ed. *Colonial Dilemma: Critical Perspectives on Contemporary Puerto Rico.* Boston, MA: South End Press, 1993. A collection of essays examining calls for independence for the island.

December 3

1998

Initiative 200 takes effect in Washington State banning all preferential treatment given on account of race, sex, color, ethnicity, or national origin, in state contracting, hiring, and admissions to public colleges and universities. A ballot initiative promoted by anti-affirmative action activist Ward Conerly of California, the legislation passed with 58.22 percent of the vote in the November election.

Book

Nelson, Patricia M. *Affirmative Action Revisited.* Huntington, NY: Nova Science, 2001. Includes an essay by Andorra Bruno on Initiative 200.

December 4

1998

Joseph F. Unanue dies of cancer at 41. As an executive for Goya Foods, Unanue helped lead the nation's largest family-owned Hispanic foods business. Unanue broadened Goya's reach beyond ethnic markets and throughout the Midwest and South. His grandfather founded Goya in 1936 in New York.

Book

Dávila, Arlene. *Latino Spin: Public Image and the Whitewashing of Race.* New York: University Press, 2008. Includes Goya Foods as an example of whitewashing.

Website

Joseph F. Unanue. Find a Grave provides a short biography of Unanue as well as burial information. http://www.findagrave.com/cgi-bin/fg.cgi?page=gr&Grid=8273523

December 5

2010

The Partido del Pueblo Trabajador (Working People's Party), a Puerto Rican political party, is founded. The party is a response to the fiscal crisis of the mid-2000s. It calls for development that does not damage the environment as well as greater productivity and efficiency that does not come at the expense of working people. The organization achieved official party status in Puerto Rico in 2012 after gaining enough supporters.

Website

Partido del Pueblo Trabajador. The official website of the organization provides information on its political plank and current events. http://www.pueblotrabajador.com/

December 6

1955

Country singer–songwriter Tish Hinojosa is born in San Antonio, Texas, to Mexican immigrant parents. Her first album, *Homeland,* came out on the A&M label in 1988. She won the NAIRD Indie Folk Album of the Year in 1992 for *Culture Swing,* a blend of country, folk, and Latino elements.

Book

Gilb, Dagoberto, ed. *Hecho en Tejas: An Anthology of Texas-Mexican Literature.* Albuquerque: University of New Mexico Press, 2006. Includes Hinojosa's writing.

Website

Tish Hinojosa. The musician's official page, on MySpace, includes a short biography and information about upcoming concerts. http://www.myspace.com/tishhinojosa

1982

Fourteen students at James A. Garfield High School, in East Los Angeles, retake the Advanced Placement calculus examination after they had been accused of cheating. The story, involving poor Latino teenagers with enough background in mathematics to even attempt a calculus exam, captured the attention of journalists as did their teacher, Jaime Escalante. At the time, 45 percent of Mexican American and Puerto Rican children did not finish high school. Escalante, born in Bolivia and only teaching in the United States since 1974, managed to inspire these students and teach them a difficult subject.

His story and that of the students became the subject of the 1988 movie, *Stand and Deliver.* He also won the Presidential Medal for Excellence in Education in 1988. Escalante died in 2010.

From *Escalante: The Best Teacher in America*:

> Although all of Escalante's 1982 calculus students traced at least part of their ancestry to Mexico, Maria Jiménex was one of the few actually born there. When she was two, her parents left Aguascalientes for California. They sneaked across the border with Maria and her two older brothers. . . . Escalante treated his calculus students like a well-drilled team looking forward to the big game. . . . He liked to mix the routine—drills and jokes and a quiz and lecture and more jokes and drills and card tricks and a bit of volleyball and more drills. He became the coach, also a big brother, an uncle, in some cases a father, and used that relationship to lay heavy guilt on all who did not do their homework.

(*Source:* Mathews, Jay. *Escalante: The Best Teacher in America.* New York: Henry Holt, 1988, p. 141.)

Books

Gradillas, Henry, and Jerry Jesness. *Standing and Delivering: What the Movie Didn't Tell.* Los Angeles: R & L, 2010. Escalante provides the foreword to this book, a guide for teachers and administrators who want to replicate his achievements.

Mathews, Jay. *Escalante: The Best Teacher in America.* New York: Henry Holt, 1988. Biography of Escalante written with the assistance of the teacher and many of his students.

Websites

Jaime Escalante. Contains a clip from the PBS television show in the early 1990s that featured

Escalante teaching his students about how math is used in a variety of fields, a video of Escalante discussing his teaching, and other biographical material. http://www.thefuture schannel.com/jaime_escalante.php

Jaime Escalante. A short biography of the teacher. http://www.biography.com/people/jaime-escalante-189368

December 7

1941

Japan attacks Pearl Harbor and the United States enters World War II. The Japanese leaders, who viewed the United States as a weak, mongrel nation, thought that a big blow would help it win control of Asia. Pearl Harbor was undoubtedly a Japanese victory but the entry of the United States into World War II brought substantial men and materiel into the conflict. Japan woke up a sleeping giant. There is no tabulation of the number of Latinos in uniform but it is estimated that between 500,000 and 750,000 served; the majority of them were Mexican Americans. With the end of the war, thousands of Latino veterans returned to the United States having been immersed in the ideals of freedom and equality, ideas that they sought to realize at home.

Frank J. Galván Jr., a lawyer in El Paso who also served as president of LULAC from 1936 to 1937 recalls:

> I volunteered into the service. I was not drafted. I didn't wait to be drafted. I was anxious to get into the struggle, precisely because I have a love and affection for my country, my adopted country. I volunteered into the service on March the 3rd, I think, 1942. Right after Pearl Harbor, I made arrangements to close the law office, and volunteered. . . . I was impatient and the draft wasn't doing anything, so I closed the office.

(*Source:* Márquez, Benjamin. *LULAC: The Evolution of a Mexican American Political Organization.* Austin: University of Texas Press, 1993, p. 19.)

Books

Rivas-Rodríguez, Maggie, ed. *Mexican Americans and World War II.* Austin: University of Texas Press, 2005. A collection of essays that explore the range of experiences of Mexican Americans in the war years.

Rivas-Rodríguez, Maggie, and Emilio Zamora, eds. *Beyond the Latino World War II Hero: The Social and Political Legacy of a Generation.* Austin: University of Texas Press, 2010. A scholarly look at home front issues and government relations during the war.

Websites

VOCES Oral History Project. This University of Texas at Austin project collects oral histories from Latino veterans of World War II, the Korean War, and the Vietnam War. http://www.lib.utexas.edu/voces/

World War II Records. The National Archives holds a wealth of documents relating to World War II, including service records. http://www.archives.gov/research/military/ww2/index.html

1928

Octaviano Larrazolo becomes the first Latino to serve as a U.S. senator. He is elected to complete the term of A. A. Jones, who died in office. Born in Allende, Chihuahua, Mexico in 1859, Larrazolo came to the United States in 1870 to further his education. A strong advocate of Mexican American civil rights, Larrazolo is notable for switching from being Democrat to Republican in 1911 because the State Convention of the Democratic Party had denied his request that half of statewide nominees be Latino to represent the 60 percent of the population of New Mexico that was Latino at the time.

He is also credited with helping to get provisions protecting Spanish speakers into the 1912 New Mexico constitution. He left office in 1929 and died a year later.

Books

Gross, Norman, ed. *Noble Purposes: Nine Champions of the Rule of Law*. Athens, OH: Ohio University Press, 2007. Includes Larrazolo among the champions.

Zannos, Susan. *Octaviano Larrazolo*. Hockessin, DE: Mitchell Lane, 2004. A short biography aimed at a juvenile audience but also the only biography of the politician available in a book.

Website

Octaviano Larrazolo. The Library of Congress provides a photograph and a good biography of the New Mexican senator. http://www.loc.gov/rr/hispanic/congress/larrazolo.html

1955

Behavioral neuroscientist Francisco Gonzalez-Lima is born in Puerto Rico. He produced some of the earliest research on metabolic changes that take place in the brain as a result of learning.

Book

Davidson, Cathy N. *Now You See It: How Technology and Brain Science Will Transform Schools and Business for the 21st Century*. New York: Penguin, 2012. Discusses the practical implications of Gonzalez-Lima's work.

December 8

1976

Representative Edward R. Roybal of California announces the formation of the Congressional Hispanic Caucus. He gathered forces with E. Kika de la Garza of Texas and Baltasar Corrado of Puerto Rico to work toward the creation of a national policy that prioritizes the needs and concerns of Latinos. Members of the caucus are expected to vote with their conscience on all congressional issues but consult each other and vote as one on Hispanic issues.

Book

Vigil, Maurilio E. *Hispanics in Congress: A Historical and Political Survey*. Lanham, MD: University Press of America, 1996. Coverage includes the 19th and 20th centuries but the emphasis is on the post-1960 decades.

Website

Edward R. Roybal. The Library of Congress provides a short biography and photograph of the Democrat from California. http://www.loc.gov/rr/hispanic/congress/roybal.html

December 9

1961

A series of four woodcuts is displayed at Princeton University, in the first exhibition of post-1898 Cuban art in the United States. The prints address the relationship between Cuba and the United States.

December 10

1996

Mexico allows Mexicans to preserve their nationality, regardless of whether they acquire another nationality or citizenship. The reform allows Mexicans who are citizens of other countries to regain Mexican nationality. Prior to the passage of this legislation, Mexicans living abroad lost all of their Mexican rights if they became naturalized in their host countries to improve their migratory and legal status. If they did not obtain another nationality, they were unable to fully exercise their rights in their host country.

Book

Hansen, Randall, and Patrick Weil. *Dual Nationality, Social Rights and Federal Citizenship in the U.S. and Europe: The Reinvention of Citizenship.* New York: Berghahn Books, 2002. Includes a discussion of the conflict between citizenship laws.

December 11

1931

Rita Moreno, one of the very few performers to ever win an Oscar, a Grammy, a Tony, and an Emmy, is born in Puerto Rico as Rosita Dolores Alverío. She moved to New York City at the age of five and soon began taking dance lessons. At 13, Moreno made her first appearance on Broadway. At 18, she appeared in her first film. Moreno's major break came when she won the role of Anita in the film version of "West Side Story." She won a Best Supporting Actress Oscar for her performance but then had trouble finding work in anything but stereotyped Latina "spitfire" parts. While she had accepted these roles in the past, she refused to do them any longer. Moreno has stated that she believes she was blocked from roles that would challenge her acting abilities and potentially make her a star because movie executives could not perceive Latinas as people of note. She ultimately sidelined her film career to play more challenging parts on stage and television.

Quote by Rita Moreno:

> I played the role [of the Latin spitfire] to the hilt, but at least it got me attention. It amused and charmed people. "Isn't she something! What a firecracker!" If that's all I could get then that's what I settled for. There was never a possibility of being anything else in my head, in my perception. The people around didn't help; the society didn't help.

(*Source:* Suntree, Susan. *Rita Moreno.* New York: Chelsea House, 1993, p. 49.)

Books

Beltrán, Mary C. *Latina/o Stars in U.S. Eyes: The Making and Meaning of Film and TV Stardom.* Urbana: University of Illinois Press, 2009. Examines Moreno's career through a critical lens that highlights her fight for dignity and integrity.

Suntree, Susan. *Rita Moreno.* New York: Chelsea House, 1993. An excellent biography of the star.

Websites

IMDb-Rita Moreno. This Internet Movie Database site provides photos, film and television credits, and a biography of the star along with tidbits such as quotes. http://www.imdb.com/name/nm0001549/

"Rita Moreno Acts Out Own Career in 'A Life without Makeup.' " Provides a transcript of an interview that Moreno gave to KQED San Francisco about the trajectory of her career from ethnic performer to major star. http://www.pbs.org/newshour/bb/entertainment/july-dec11/ritamoreno_09-30.html

December 12

1963

The New York City Board of Education announces plans to recruit more blacks and Puerto Ricans to supervisory positions in an effort to speed integration of public schools. Civil rights groups had been criticizing the city for its progress on integration and threatening to boycott schools in protest. Antonia Pantoja, founder of ASPIRA, is chosen to help train prospective supervisors.

December 13

1913

Puerto Rican political activist, lawyer, and journalist Rosendo Matienzo Cintrón dies in his hometown of Luquillo. Born in 1855, Cintrón supported Puerto Rican autonomy when the island remained under the control of Spain. After the United States took charge in 1898, Cintrón backed annexation as a member of the Puerto Rican Republican Party. He later changed his political orientation and argued for independence. Throughout his life, Cintrón contributed essays to Puerto Rican newspapers on political matters. He also served as president of the Puerto Rico House of Representatives.

From Rosendo Matienzo Cintrón, "The Guachafita Fá" (1911):

> La guachafita fá is American citizenship for Puerto Ricans. If you ask for it in good faith, they won't give it to you, on the ground that you already have Puerto Rican citizenship in a union of Americans; that American citizenship is a very bad thing that would ruin Puerto Rico, since there are already too many niggers in the United States to be adding a million more.
>
> If you don't want it, if you want independence for your country, they'll tell you: ask for citizenship and you'll get it. Why not? Ask Congress for it again and if Congress won't give it the people will, the noble American people. Don't be downhearted. Within a century or two you'll be able to form a state. Meanwhile we Puerto Rican Americans will enjoy here the pure and honest delights of a colony—not just any old colony but a charming colony. . . . The Americans say among themselves: boy, we oughta help those espiquitis [possible version of the English insult "spic"] get American citizenship, it would fit them like a pair of slippers on a church Christ . . .
>
> But it won't work out quite like that because an American citizen is a sovereign citizen, and this the Puerto Rican will never be albeit clad in the citizenly toga. There would in fact be three American citizenships, the two

continental ones and the Puerto Rican: that is to say, the citizenship of North American whites, of North American blacks, and of Puerto Ricans. That of the masters, that of the freed slaves, and that of the poor idiots in non-contiguous countries who don't speak English.

(*Source:* Zavala, Iris M., and Rafael Rodriguez, eds. *The Intellectual Roots of Independence: An Anthology of Puerto Rican Political Essays.* New York: Monthly Review Press, 1980, pp. 115–16.)

Books

Díaz Soler, Luis M. *Rosendo Matienzo Cintrón: Orientador y guardian de una cultura.* San Juan: University of Puerto Rico Press, 1960. A two-volume study of the political leader.

Trias Monge, José. *Puerto Rico: The Trials of the Oldest Colony in the World.* New Haven: Yale University Press, 1999. Surveys Puerto Rico's 500-year history and argues that no one has the right to rule over another.

Websites

Biografia de Rosendo Matienzo Cintrón. The Biographies of Illustrious Persons site offers a short summary of Cintrón in Spanish. http://biografiasdepuertorico.blogspot.com/2011/08/biografia-de-rosendo-matienzo-cintron.html

Matienzo Cintrón, Rosendo. This Encyclopedia of Puerto Rico site provides a brief biography of the politician. http://www.enciclopediapr.org/esp/article.cfm?ref=09091703

1968

Mexican American militant leader Reies López Tijerina, also known as "King Tiger," is acquitted by a New Mexico jury on charges of kidnapping after joining an armed group in attacking the Rio Arriba County Courthouse in Tierra Amarilla. The group planned to make a citizen's arrest of the district attorney but was unable to find him. In the resulting tumult, two police officers were shot. Tijerina saw himself as upholding rights guaranteed to him by the Treaty of Guadalupe Hidalgo, which was supposed to protect the property rights of Mexicans living in territory ceded to the United States. Tijerina is the leader of the Alianza Federal de Mercedes Reales, an organization seeking the return of millions of acres of Southwest land to the heirs of Spanish land grant holders.

From "60s Latino Militant Now Pursues a Personal Quest":

> The man once called King Tiger, a description fitting for one of the most militant of radical Latino leaders of the 1960s, now walks with a cane. Almost forgotten by a new generation of Latinos clamoring for immigrant rights, the man, Reies López Tijerina, faces his own immigration dilemma. Hobbled by diabetes and years of self-exile in Mexico, Mr. Tijerina, born 79 years ago to a family of cotton pickers in South Texas spends his days at a community center [in El Paso], or in a modest two-room house in Cuidad Juárez, searching for a way for his wife to return legally with him to the United States. Immigration authorities have refused to grant residency to his Mexican-born wife, Esperanza García, whom Mr. Tijerina married more than a decade ago in Mexico. "It's as if I'm being pursued because of my past acts," Mr. Tijerina said in a rare interview. . . . His existence is far removed from the days when he was a leader in the land-rights struggle in New Mexico. . . . That violence led to a manhunt for Mr. Tijerina and more than two years in prison; his exploits were celebrated in folk songs like "The Ballad of Rio Arriba." That event injected radicalism into the Chicano rights movement and was the crowning moment for a man with an unconventional personal trajectory. Largely self-educated,

Mr. Tijerina traveled throughout the United States as a Pentecostal evangelist before founding a utopian religious community in the Arizona desert with 17 families in 1956. It was as leader of that group, Valle de Paz, where Mr. Tijerina says he had a vision involving three angels, an event advancing him into advocacy over the land grants the Spanish crown had given settlers centuries ago in what is today's Southwest.

(*Source:* Romero, Simon. "60s Latino Militant Now Pursues a Personal Quest." *New York Times,* May 5, 2006, p. A16.)

Books

Rosales, F. Arturo. *Chicano!: The History of the Mexican American Civil Rights Movement.* Houston: Arte Público Press, 1997. A superb history of the movement with quite a bit of coverage of Tijerina.

Tijerina, Reies López. *They Called Me King Tiger: My Struggle for the Land and Our Rights.* Houston: Arte Publico Press, 2000. Originally printed in Spanish, this is Tijerina's biography.

Websites

Reies López Tijerina: A Chicano Leader's Lifetime of Achievement is Honored. Article from *Borderzine* that covers the Mexican government's 2009 decision to honor Tijerina for sacrificing to protect Mexican Americans. http://borderzine.com/2009/07/reies-lopez-tijerina-a-chicano-leader%E2%80%99s-lifetime-of-achievement-is-honored/

Reies Tijerina and the Mexican Land Grants. Discusses the land grant dispute and provides a link to a video program by Richard Goodman. http://www.laits.utexas.edu/onda_latina/program?sernum=000510985&theme=Politics

December 14

1944

Actress Lupe Vélez, "The Mexican Spitfire," dies in Hollywood. Born in San Luis Potosí,

Mexico, in 1908, Vélez came to the United States to work in vaudeville. She made her first film appearance in 1924. With the advent of talking pictures, she worked chiefly in comedies as a volatile but beautiful foil to men. She is best known for the *Mexican Spitfire* series of films in which she spoke broken English and displayed a talent for physical comedy. She died by suicide, perhaps as a result of untreated mental illness.

December 15

1944

The Liberty Ship *SS Salvador Brau,* named after the Puerto Rican historian, is launched in Panama City, Florida. Liberty ships were quickly built cargo ships that attempted to replace shipping sunk by the Germans during World War II. More than 2,400 Liberty Ships survived the war, including the *Salvador Brau,* which went into mothballs in 1948.

December 16

2005

The U.S. House of Representatives passes a bill that would make illegal immigrants felons and wall off about a third of the U.S.-Mexico border. The senate had earlier passed a bill that would enhance border security while offering a guest worker program and the possibility of eventual citizenship for many undocumented workers already in the country. House Republicans opposed any sort of amnesty program, however, despite President George W. Bush's support of the legislation. The passage of the House bill helped to prompt a series of marches and other protests by illegal immigrants over the next few months. In October 2006, President Bush signed into law a bill providing for construction of 700 miles of fencing along the Mexico-U.S. border as part of immigration reform. The other parts of the House bill did not advance through the legislative process.

From Ian de Silva, "A Sheep in Wolf's Clothing: Bush Wrong on Illegals":

As an immigrant who is deeply grateful to America, I do not enjoy criticizing American presidents. And, as a naturalized American who is a committed conservative, it pains me to criticize a Republican president. However, as most conservatives would agree, this president's approach to immigration is anything but conservative.

Everyone has heard of the proverbial wolf in sheep's clothing. In contrast, the president's guest-worker proposal is a sheep in wolf's clothing. His new, ostensibly tough rhetoric about border security seeks to disguise what amounts to a surrender to illegal aliens. The president insists his proposal is not an amnesty, yet that is exactly what it is. The legalizing of people who came here illegally is an amnesty, plain and simple . . .

Once the illegal aliens are gone and are no longer undercutting wages, employers will find Americans and legal immigrants who are willing to do dirty jobs, for those jobs will then pay a reasonable wage. (Having pulled myself up by my own bootstraps, I can tell you there is no job that legal immigrants will not do for a reasonable wage.) After all, before the illegal aliens came and undercut wages, it was legal immigrants and Americans who did all the dirty jobs.

(*Source*: De Silva, Ian. "A Sheep in Wolf's Clothing: Bush Wrong on Illegals." *The Washington Times,* December 9, 2005, p. A23.)

Books

Haugen, David M. *Illegal Immigration: Opposing Viewpoints.* Farmington Hills, MI: Greenhaven,

2011. Part of the popular Opposing Viewpoints series, this book provides articles, speeches, and other materials that illustrate the immigration debate.

Marquardt, Marie Friedmann, et al. *Living "Illegal": The Human Face of Unauthorized Immigration*. New York: New Press, 2011. Examines the lives of ordinary people who reside in the United States without permission.

Websites

"Illegal Immigrants Rally in Chicago." This article, written by conservative pundit Michelle Malkin and placed on her website, includes quotes from bloggers and marchers. http://michellemalkin.com/2006/03/10/illegal-aliens-protest-in-chicago/

"Rallies across U.S. Call for Illegal Immigrant Rights." This CNN Politics site offers an article on the 2006 marches in support of better treatment of illegal immigrants. http://articles.cnn.com/2006-04-10/politics/immigration_1_jaime-contreras-national-capital-immigration-coalition-illegal-immigrant-rights?_s=PM:POLITICS

1846

During the Mexican-American War, the U.S. 101st Infantry ("Mormon") Battalion under the command of Col. Philip St. George Cooke peacefully occupies the presidio in Tucson. The battalion had marched from Council Bluff, Iowa, and badly needed provisions by the time it reached Arizona. Despite the fact that Tucson lay within Mexican territory, the townspeople and the Mexican military forces agreed to a peaceful trade of American buttons and clothing for Mexican grain and salt. The U.S. flag flew briefly over the presidio on this date. The battalion then continued on its march to San Diego. In 1996, Tucson erected a sculpture to commemorate the peaceful exchange and the blend of cultures in Tucson.

1863

Philosopher George Santayana is born in Madrid. He came to Boston as a child and faced relentless teasing because he knew virtually no English. He wound up studying at Harvard and becoming a Harvard professor. He is best known for writing "Those who cannot remember the past are condemned to repeat it."

December 17

1972

A clash between Teamsters and United Farm Workers (UFW) pickets leaves 2 dead, 300 injured, and 3,000 picketers jailed. The dispute began when the Teamsters, supporters of President Richard Nixon, warned the UFW to stay away from the lettuce fields. The UFW ignored the advice and picketed the American Farm Bureau Federation Los Angeles convention, where Teamster president Frank Fitzsimmons was scheduled to speak. The Teamsters reacted violently.

December 18

1920

Casimiro Barela, the only Latino to serve as a delegate to the Colorado state constitutional convention in 1875, dies. He secured a provision protecting the civil rights of Spanish-speaking citizens as well as a rule providing for the publication of laws in Spanish, English, and German. Born in New Mexico, Barela's family came to Colorado in 1867 and he eventually became one of the wealthiest men in the state. Elected as a state senator in 1876, he served until 1916.

1952

Psychologist Victor De La Cancela is born in New York City to Puerto Rican parents. His research focuses on the special psychological issues and problems faced by individuals from minority communities. A prolific writer, De La Cancela has won an award for exemplary leadership and service from the National Hispanic Psychological Association.

1980

Singer Christina Aguilera is born to a father from Ecuador and an Irish American mother. In 2000, she received the New Entertainer of the Year award at the American Latin Media Awards.

December 19

1946

Playwright Miguel Piñero is born in Gurabo, Puerto Rico, and then raised on the Lower East Side of New York City. Part of the Nuyorican literary movement, he began writing and acting while serving time in Sing Sing prison for armed robbery. His 1973 play, *Short Eyes,* about prison violence and the dynamics of power won an Obie and the New York Critics Circle Award for best American play of the 1973–1974 season.

December 20

1835

Tejanos and Anglo-Texans sign the first Texas declaration of independence in Goliad. At this time, Texas is controlled by Mexico. The signing contributes to the conflict that ultimately results in the Battle of the Alamo and Texas independence.

1861

Brigadier General Henry H. Sibley issues a proclamation claiming New Mexico for the Confederacy. Sibley then wins the Battle of Valverde but is unable to take Fort Craig at the capital of Santa Fe. When the Confederacy wins at Glorieta Pass, it loses so many men that Sibley has to retreat from New Mexico. The support of the Confederacy for slavery would not have boded well for race relations with Mexican Americans had the Confederacy succeeded. For this reason, a number of Mexican American men served with Union forces in New Mexico.

Books

Edrington, Thomas S., and John Taylor. *The Battle of Glorieta Pass: A Gettysburg in the West, March 26–28, 1862*. Albuquerque: University of New Mexico Press, 1998. Relates the story of a little known but significant battle for control of the American Southwest.

Wilson, John P., ed. *From Western Deserts to Carolina Swamps: A Civil War Soldier's Journals and Letters Home*. Albuquerque: University of New Mexico Press, 2012. Lewis R. Roe's accounts of serving in New Mexico are one of the very, very few surviving accounts from Civil War soldiers in the region.

December 21

1916

Emma Tenayuca joins with Homer Brooks to publish the first document analyzing the condition of Mexican workers in the United States from the point of view of the workers. "The Mexican Question in the Southwest" promoted the enlistment of Mexican workers in labor unions and the Communist Party. A lifelong labor organizer from San Antonio, Texas, Tenayuca helped organize the famous 1938 Pecan Shellers' Strike at the Southern Pecan Shelling Company. The South Texas Civil Rights Project has dedicated an annual award, The Emma Tenayuca Award, given to individuals working to protect civil rights.

December 22

1935

Writer and university chancellor Tomás Rivera is born in Crystal City, Texas, to migrant workers. Though he published only a few poems and two books, Rivera greatly influenced Chicano literature in the 1970s and 1980s. He worked for a few years as a college professor before he realized that he could have a greater impact on Chicanos as a university administrator at the University of Texas at El Paso and, in 1979, at the University of California at Riverside. He became the first Mexican American to serve as chancellor in the University of California system. Rivera began to publish his writings in the late 1960s when they appeared in Chicano publications.

Books

Lattin, Vernon E, Rolando Hinojosa, and Gary D. Keller, eds. *Tomás Rivera, 1935–1984: The Man and His Work*. Tempe, AZ: Bilingual Review/Press, 1988. Includes some works, letters in memoriam, photographs, his CV, and a bibliography of writings about him.

Olivares, Julián, ed. *Tomás Rivera: The Complete Works*. Houston: Arte Publico Press, 1991, p. 272. Essential guide to Rivera with critical essays included.

Websites

Guide to the Tomás Rivera Archive. Part of the Online Archive of California, this site contains a short biography and a guide to 198 document boxes but no online items. http://www.oac.cdlib.org/findaid/ark:/13030/tf6r29p0kq

Research Archive—The Tomás Rivera Policy Institute. The Institute, part of the University of Southern California School of Policy, Planning, and Development, uses this site to provide articles related to policy issues affecting Latino communities. http://www.trpi.org/archive/

1984

Los Angeles mayor Tom Bradley proclaims this day as Pedro J. González Day, in honor of the man who started the first Spanish-language radio program in the United States. A native of Chihuahua, Mexico, who worked as Pancho Villa's telegraph operator as a boy during the Mexican Revolution, González had shows on KMPC and KEWL in the 1920s and 1930s. He used his platform to protest the deportation of Mexican Americans during the Great Depression. Viewed

as a threat by white community leaders, González went to prison in 1934 on a rape charge by a woman who later admitted that authorities had induced her to lie. González spent six years in San Quentin until huge protests and appeals by two Mexican presidents secured his release. A mural celebrating his life is installed on Coronado Bridge at a spot known as Chicano Park. González died at age 99 in 1995.

December 23

1751

José Campeche, one of the first colonial artists to gain worldwide fame, is born in San Juan, Puerto Rico. In 1776, Campeche began to study under exiled Spanish painter Luis Paret y Alcázar. He moved from Paret's rigid style to a more humanistic style. By the 1780s, he had become a popular painter of portraits of the nobility and government officials. By the start of the 19th century, he was receiving commissions from all around the Spanish colonies to paint portraits and religious scenes. Campeche died on November 7, 1809, in San Juan.

December 24

1916

Chicano pop singer Lalo Guerrero is born in Tucson, Arizona. In 1938, he moved to Los Angeles and began recording with his quartet, Los Carlistas. His first solo effort, *Pecadora,* came out in 1948. His songs received substantial air play on Spanish-language radio stations. Typecast by the music industry as someone who performed Mexican music because he had Mexican ancestry, Guerrero actually preferred to sing American pop in the style of Bing Crosby, Rudy Vallee, and Al Jolson. In 1955, as Americans became obsessed with Davy Crockett following a television show, "The Ballad of

Davy Crockett" topped the national charts for five weeks. Crockett died in the Battle of the Alamo, an event that set the Mexican-American War in motion. Guerrero decided to mock Crockett's popularity by releasing "The Ballad of Pancho Lopez." It sold more than 500,000 copies. He released other parodies such as "Tacos for Two" and "I Left My Car in San Francisco." By 1975, Guerrero was viewed as a trailblazer, a Chicano musician who had persevered in the decades when Chicanos were all but invisible in American culture. In 1997, Guerrero received a National Medal of the Arts from President Bill Clinton.

December 25

1825

Joel Poinsett, U.S. ambassador to Mexico, spots a plant with beautiful red flowers, *flor de nochebuena,* as part of the nativity scene at the Taxco church of Santa Prisca. Poinsett ships several of the plants to friends in Charleston, South Carolina, and the plant soon becomes known as the Poinsettia. The plant, known to the Aztecs as *cuetlaxochitl,* is also the national flower of Argentina.

December 26

1981

Theoretical chemist Henry Eyring dies. Eyring, born in the Mormon settlement of Colonia Juàrez, Mexico, in 1901, developed the transition state theory of chemical reactions, one of the most important developments in 20th-century science. The theory explains the reaction rates of elementary chemical reactions. Eyring came to the United States at age 11 when thousands of Mormon immigrants were driven out of Mexico by the Mexican Revolution. He taught at Princeton University and the University of Utah.

December 27

1512

Ferdinand of Aragón, king of Spain, issues the Laws of Burgos to end the exploitation of Native Americans in the Americas. The legislation, which regulates work hours, pay, and hygiene while requiring Indians to be converted to Catholicism, is the first codified set of laws governing Spanish conduct in the New World. The regulations initially applied only to Hispaniola (present-day Dominican Republic and Haiti) but were later extended to Puerto Rico.

December 28

2011

Puerto Rican rappers Dyland and Lenny lead a protest march through Mayagüez against domestic violence and against shooting guns in the air. Many New Year's festivities in the Caribbean involve firing shots into the air and accidental injuries, sometimes fatal, result when the bullets come down. The musicians declare that they are alarmed by the rate of murders in Puerto Rico and feel an obligation, as role models for youngsters, to take a stand.

December 29

1896

The most politically active Mexican muralist, David Alfaro Siqueiros, is born. During his two stays in the United States, in 1932 and 1936, he painted murals that influenced later artists with respect to public political art and experimental techniques.

1969

The Young Lords Party, a New York–based group, begins its 11-day occupation of the First Methodist Church in order to establish a free breakfast-for-children program. The organization consists chiefly of the children of Puerto Rican immigrants.

December 30

1853

The southern border of the United States is established when James Gadsden, U.S. minister to Mexico, and Gen. Antonio López de Santa Anna, the president of Mexico, sign the Gadsden Purchase in Mexico City. As part of the agreement, the United States agrees to pay $15 million (later reduced to $10 million) for approximately 30,000 square miles of land in what is now southern New Mexico and Arizona. The United States wanted the land for a possible transcontinental railroad that never came to fruition. Santa Anna allegedly just wanted the money. The sale did not improve Santa Anna's reputation among Mexicans.

December 31

1972

Baseball player Roberto Clemente dies. A right fielder for the Pittsburgh Pirates, Clemente is arguably the most honored Latino player to ever play the game. Clemente led the National League in batting four times and won 12 consecutive Gold Gloves for his stellar defense during his career from 1955 to 1972. He helped win the 1971 World Series with the first fully integrated team in baseball history. The Puerto Rican native died in a plane crash while helping to ferry food and other relief supplies to earthquake victims in Nicaragua. He subsequently received many more honors, including a U.S. postage stamp adorned with his image. However, during his lifetime, Clemente never appreciated his treatment by American sportswriters. He felt underappreciated, resented being categorized as a hypochondriac, and hated being

quoted in broken English. Upon his death, Baseball Commissioner Bowie Kuhn waived the waiting period to get into the Hall of Fame. Clemente entered the hall in 1973, voted in by sportswriters, as the first Latin American Hall of Famer with 93 percent of the vote. (Many of the voters opposed Clemente on the grounds that they did not want to break the five-year wait requirement.)

From President Richard Nixon's talking points regarding Clemente's death, prepared by presidential aide Richard A. Moore:

> Apart from baseball, Clemente was known for his year-round service to good causes and his love of Puerto Rico, where he was virtually a folk hero. He was aboard the airplane because he had heard that a previous shipment [to Managua] had been diverted by profiteers and he wanted to make certain that the food and clothing reached the people in need. Clemente had been the chief engineer in raising $150,000 plus tons of clothing and foodstuffs. . . . Members of the [Pittsburgh Pirates] and other Pittsburgh friends will fly to Puerto Rico in a chartered plane tomorrow for a special memorial service.

(*Source:* Maraniss, David. *Clemente: The Passion and Grace of Baseball's Last Hero.* New York: Simon and Schuster, 2006, p. 346.)

Books

Maraniss, David. *Clemente: The Passion and Grace of Baseball's Last Hero.* New York: Simon and Schuster, 2006. A popular biography of the Pittsburgh Pirate.

Markasun, Bruce. *Roberto Clemente: The Great One.* Pittsburgh: Sports Publishing, 2001.

Websites

Beyond Baseball: The Life of Roberto Clemente. This superb bilingual Smithsonian Institution site includes a virtual museum exhibition about Clemente as well as classroom activities for middle school children and further links. http://www.robertoclemente.si.edu/

Latino Legends in Sports—Roberto Clemente. Provides a solid biography of the superstar baseball player as well as many of his statistics. http://www.latinosportslegends.com/clemente.htm

1968

Novelist Junot Díaz is born in Santo Domingo, Dominican Republic. In 1974, the family followed Díaz's father to New Jersey. Always in love with books, Diaz earned a BA from Rutgers in 1992 in English. Yet his life was far from privileged as he had to work his way through school by pumping gas and washing dishes. Díaz earned an MFA from Cornell in 1995 and published his first book, *Drown,* two years later. The book received enormous notice in the New York media with Díaz named as a rising literary star. In 2008, Díaz won the Pulitzer Prize for Fiction for *The Brief Wondrous Life of Oscar Wao.* All of his books have focused on life in the United States for Dominican Americans. Díaz teaches creative writing at the Massachusetts Institute of Technology in Boston.

From "In Praise of Geekdom":

His debut novel won one of the most coveted literary prizes awarded to American authors. But Junot Diaz didn't speak a word of English until he was six years old, and this deeply influences the way he writes.

"I think my whole relationship to writing has to do with learning English. I can remember learning almost each and every word when I was young," he says. "I can remember the process of it, how all you want to do is be able to speak it fluently, but that eludes you."

The Dominican-American author won the 2008 Pulitzer Prize for Fiction . . . for his book *The Brief Wondrous Life of Oscar Wao.* As in much of

his writing, Diaz admits there are elements of his upbringing and culture on the pages. But he says his influences are far broader than his own life.

"You spend a lot of time with various people, you come into contact . . . with histories . . . with incidents, and every now and then ideas that may not be visible to your conscious mind are triggered by something you encounter in the outside world," he says. "It's almost as if you've got this pile of kindling in your subconscious and as you're walking through your life, a spark will suddenly light it ablaze, and illuminate . . . what you're interested in, what you didn't even know you were interested in. I mean, I didn't know I was interested in writing about an overweight nerd 'til the inspiration struck me."

Born in the Dominican Republic, Diaz moved to New Jersey with his family when he was six [in 1974]. He "absolutely loved school—I had great teachers" and, while his parents wanted all their children to become doctors, architects or, if they really messed up, lawyers, Diaz says he was never in a position "where it was like, 'do well, or be a loser'".

He realized early on that he loved art of all kinds—*Oscar* is full of references to comic books, a passion the nerdy protagonist shares with the author—and loved what art does to people. And so the author decided to write. He realised the power of a story to connect with a reader, and how important that power was.

"Having been moved enough by various books," Diaz says, "I wanted to be able to create the kind of work that gave other people the opportunity to have that kind of experience."

He also emphasises the impact other writers have on him, saying he enjoys being inspired and influenced by their work. He describes himself as "somewhere between a glass of water and a plant", a plant being an organism that filters in certain influences, while the composition of liquid changes completely if something is thrown in.

Diaz is driven by the idea that everything he writes, whenever it's read, and by how many—or few—people, increases "by that increment, the possible range of reading for people".

But his biggest inspiration is his love of reading. He warns that being a writer is "a tough gig", and that compassion for yourself is essential. And for the many people who believe they have a story to tell, the author has some words of wisdom.

"In the end, if you don't love reading more than anything in the world, there's no reason to be a writer," Diaz says.

"And if you love reading more than anything in the world, the reading is what will get you through. . . . When you're stuck, find books that inspire you, and read them."

(*Source:* Cox, Karly. "In Praise of Geekdom: Pulitzer Prize-Winning Author Junot Díaz Talks to Karly Cox About His Calling and What Inspires Him to Write Literature." *South China Morning Post,* March 21, 2010, p. 1.)

Books

Díaz, Junot. *Drown.* New York: Riverhead Trade, 1997. The publication of this set of 10 short stories about Dominican American life instantly made Díaz into a literary figure of note.

Díaz, Junot. *The Brief Wondrous Life of Oscar Wao.* New York: Riverhead Trade, 2008. The Pulitzer Prize–winning novel about a Dominican American youth that addresses the impact of Dominican history upon a family.

Websites

Junot Díaz. The writer's official page includes a biography and contact information. http://www.junotdiaz.com/

"Junot Díaz on Becoming American." This NPR site includes a transcript of Díaz discussing how he adjusted to life in the United States and a September 2008 reading by the author of passages from *The Brief Wondrous Life of Oscar Wao.* http://www.npr.org/templates/story/story.php?storyId=97336132

1976

The Chicano Alliance of Drug Abuse Programs (CADAP) is formed to fight the high rate of substance abuse in Mexican American communities. The founders of the Texas-based group include Ramon "Manchi" Adame, an ex-convict and drug addict; Mario Obledo, former secretary of health and welfare for the state of California; and Henry Collins, head of a drug treatment center.

Bibliography

Abalos, David T. *Latinos in the United States: The Sacred and the Political.* Notre Dame, IN: University of Notre Dame Press, 2007.

Abel, Christopher, and Nissa Torrents, eds. *José Martí: Revolutionary Democrat.* Durham, NC: Duke University Press, 1986.

Aldama, Frederick Luis. *Spilling the Beans in Chicanolandia: Conversations with Writers and Artists.* Austin: University of Texas Press, 2006.

Alvarez, Luis. *The Power of the Zoot: Youth Culture and Resistance during World War II.* Berkeley: University of California Press, 2008.

American Institutes for Research and WestEd. *Effects of the Implementation of Proposition 227 on the Education of English Learners, K–12: Findings from a Five-Year Evaluation.* Sacramento: California Department of Education, 2006.

Andreas, Peter. *Border Games: Policing the U.S.-Mexico Divide.* 2nd ed. Ithaca, NY: Cornell University Press, 2009.

Anreus, Alejandro. *Orozco in Gringoland: The Years in New York.* Albuquerque: University of New Mexico Press, 2001.

Arriola, Christopher. *Knocking on the Schoolhouse Door: Méndez v. Westminster, Equal Protection, Public Education, and Mexican Americans in the 1940's.* Berkeley, CA: Boalt Hall School of Law, 1995.

Avila, Eric. "Turning Structure into Culture; Reclaiming the Freeway in San Diego's Chicano Park." In *The Cultural Turn in U.S. History: Past, Present, and Future,* edited by James W. Cook, Lawrence B. Glickman, and Michael O'Malley. Chicago: University of Chicago Press, 2009, pp. 267–83.

Ayala, César J., and Rafael Bernabe. *Puerto Rico in the American Century: A History since 1898.* Chapel Hill: University of North Carolina Press, 2007.

Baker, Colin. *Foundations of Bilingual Education and Bilingualism.* 4th ed. Bristol, UK: Multilingual Matter, 2006.

Beebe, Rose-Marie, and Robert M. Senkewicz. *Land of Promise: Chronicles of Early California, 1535–1846.* Berkeley, CA: Heyday Books, 2001.

Beebe, Rose Marie, and Robert M. Senkewicz, eds. *Testimonios: Early California through the Eyes of Women, 1815–1848.* Berkeley, CA: Heyday Books, 2006.

Berger, Joseph. "The Making of an American." *New York Times,* late edition, June 4, 2006: WC1.

Bielby, Denise D., and C. Lee Harington. *Global TV: Exporting Television and Culture in the World Market.* Albany: NYU Press, 2008.

Boyle, Susan Calafate. *Los Capitalistas: Hispano Merchants and the Santa Fe Trade.* Albuquerque: University of New Mexico Press, 1997.

Brack, Gene. *Mexico Views Manifest Destiny 1821–1846: An Essay on the Origins of the Mexican War.* Albuquerque: University of New Mexico, 1975.

Brands, H. W. *Lone Star Nation: The Epic Story of the Battle for Texas Independence*. New York: Anchor Books, 2005.

Brear, Holly Beachley. *Inherit the Alamo: Myth and Ritual at an American Shrine*. Austin: University of Texas Press, 1995.

Brotherton, David, and Luis Barrios. *The Almighty Latin King and Queen Nation: Street Politics and the Transformation of a New York Gang*. New York: Columbia University Press, 2004.

Broyles-González, Yolanda. *El Teatro Campesino: Theater in the Chicano Movement*. Austin: University of Texas Press, 1994.

Burgos, Adrian, Jr. *Cuban Star: How One Negro-League Owner Changed the Face of Baseball*. New York: Hill and Wang, 2011.

Cambridge, Vibert C. *Immigration, Diversity, and Broadcasting in the United States, 1990–2001*. Athens: Ohio University Press, 2004.

Campbell, Randolph B. *Gone to Texas: A History of the Lone Star State*. New York: Oxford University Press, 2003.

Cavazos, Sylvia. *The Disposable Mexican: Operation Wetback, 1954: The Deportation of Undocumented Workers in California and Texas*. Ann Arbor: University of Michigan Press, 1988.

Chávez, César. *The Words of César Chávez*. College Station: Texas Aamp;M Press, 2002.

Chávez, Ernesto. *¡Mi Raza Primero! (My People First!): Nationalism, Identity, and Insurgency in the Chicano Movement in Los Angeles, 1966–1978*. Berkeley: University of California Press, 2002.

Chávez, Ernesto. *The War with Mexico: A Brief History with Documents*. Boston: Bedford/St. Martin's, 2007.

Chicano Coordinating Council on Higher Education. *El Plan de Santa Barbara*. Oakland, CA: La Causa Publications, 1969. http://www.sscnet.ucla.edu/00W/chicano101-1/SBplan.pdf.

Christensen, Carol, and Thomas Christensen. *The U.S.-Mexican War*. San Francisco: Bay Books and Tapes, 1998.

Cohen, Deborah. *Braceros: Migrant Citizens and Transnational Subjects in the Postwar United States and Mexico*. Chapel Hill: University of North Carolina Press, 2011.

Coltman, Leychester. *The Real Fidel Castro*. New Haven, CT: Yale University Press, 2003.

Constantakis-Valdés, Patricia, and Horace Newcomb. "Telemundo." In *Encyclopedia of Television*, 2nd ed., edited by Horace Newcomb. Chicago: Museum of Broadcast Communications, 2004, pp. 2290–2292.

Contreras, Sheila Marie. *Blood Lines: Myth, Indigenism, and Chicana/o Literature*. Austin: University of Texas Press, 2008.

Costello, Julia G. *Documentary Evidence for the Spanish Missions of Alta California*. New York: Garland, 1991.

Couve de Murville, M.N.L. *The Man Who Founded California: The Life of Blessed Junípero Serra*. San Francisco: Ignatius Press, 2000.

Craig, Richard B. *The Bracero Program: Interest Groups and Foreign Policy*. Austin: University of Texas Press, 1971.

Crimm, Ana Carolina Castillo. *De Leon, a Tejano Family History*. Austin: University of Texas Press, 2004.

Crisp, James E. *Sleuthing the Alamo: Davy Crockett's Last Stand and Other Mysteries of the Texas Revolution*. New York: Oxford University Press, 2005.

Daniel, Cletus E. "Cesar Chavez and the Unionization of California Farm Workers." In *Labor Leaders in America*, edited by Melvyn Dubofsky and Warren R. Van Tine. Chicago: University of Illinois Press, 1987, pp. 350–82.

Dávalos Fernández, Rudolfo. *United States vs. the Cuban Five: A Judicial Coverup*. Havana, Cuba: Editorial Capitán San Luis, 2006.

Dávalos, Karen Mary. *Exhibiting Mestizaje: Mexican (American) Museums in the Diaspora*. Albuquerque: University of New Mexico Press, 2001.

Davidson, Linda Kay, and David Martin Gitlitz. *Pilgrimage: From the Ganges to Graceland: An Encyclopedia*. Santa Barbara, CA: ABC-CLIO, 2002.

Davis, Barbara J. *The National Grape Boycott: A Victory for Farmworkers*. Minneapolis, MN: Compass Point Books, 2008.

De Genova, Nicholas. *Racial Transformations: Latinos and Asians Remaking the United States*. Durham, NC: Duke University Press, 2006.

De la Pena, Jose Enrique. *With Santa Anna in Texas: A Personal Narrative of the Revolution*. Trans. Carmen Perry. College Station: Texas A&M University, 1997.

De la Roche, Elisa. *Teatro Hispano!: Three Major New York Companies*. New York: Taylor & Francis, 1995.

Del Valle, Sandra. *Language Rights and the Law in the United States: Finding Our Voices*. Bristol, UK: Multilingual Matters, 2003.

Denelo, David J. *The Border: Exploring the U.S.-Mexican Divide*. Mechanicsburg, PA: Stackpole Press, 2008.

Dent, David W. *The Legacy of the Monroe Doctrine: A Reference Guide to U.S. Involvement in Latin America and the Caribbean*. Westport, CT: Greenwood Press, 1999.

DiMaggio, Paul, and Patricia Fernández-Kelly, eds. *Art in the Lives of Immigrant Communities in the United States*. New Brunswick, NJ: Rutgers University Press, 2010.

Donato, Rubén. *The Other Struggle for Equal Schools: Mexican Americans during the Civil Rights Era*. New York: SUNY Press, 1997.

Driscoll, Barbara A. *The Tracks North: The Railroad Bracero Program of World War II*. Austin, TX: Center for Mexican American Studies Books, 1999.

Egendorf, Laura K. *Immigration*. Farmington Hills, MI: Greenhaven Press, 2006.

Eisenhower, John. *So Far from God: The U.S. War with Mexico, 1846–1848*. New York: Random House, 1989.

Epstein, David, et al. *The Future of the Voting Rights Act*. New York: Russell Sage Foundation, 2006.

Espinosa, Jack. *Cuban Bread Crumbs*. Philadelphia: Xlibris Corporation, 2008.

Ferriss, Susan, and Ricardo Sandoval. *The Fight in the Fields: César Chávez and the Farmworkers Movement*. New York: Mariner Books, 1998.

Flores, Richard R. *Remembering the Alamo: Memory, Modernity, and the Master Symbol*. Austin: University of Texas Press, 2002.

Folsom, Ralph H. *NAFTA and Free Trade in the Americas in a Nut Shell*. St. Paul, MN: Thomson/West, 2008.

Francaviglia, Richard V., and Douglas W. Richmond, eds. *Dueling Eagles: Reinterpreting the U.S.-Mexican War, 1846–1848*. Fort Worth: Texas Christian University Press, 2000.

Gándara, Patricia. "Learning English in California: Guideposts for the Nation." In *Latinos: Remaking America,* edited by Marcelo Suarez-Orozco and Mariela Páez. Berkeley: University of California Press, 2008, pp. 339–59.

García, Eugene E., Francisco A. Lomelí, and Isidor D. Ortiz, eds. *Chicano Studies: A Multidisciplinary Approach*. Amsterdam, NY: Teachers College Press, 1984.

Garcia, Ignacio M. *Viva Kennedy: Mexican Americans in Search of Camelot*. College Station: Texas A&M University Press, 2000.

Garcia, Juan Ramon. *Operation Wetback: The Mass Deportation of Mexican Undocumented Workers in 1954*. Westport, CT: Greenwood Press, 1980.

García, Mario, ed. *A Dolores Huerta Reader*. Albuquerque: University of New Mexico Press, 2008.

Gendzel, Glen. "It Didn't Start with Proposition 187: One Hundred and Fifty Years of Nativist Legislation in California." *Journal of the West* 48, no. 2 (Spring 2009): 76–85.

Geniesse, Peter A. *Illegal: NAFTA Refugees Forced to Flee*. Bloomington, IN: iUniverse, 2010.

Gómez-Quiñones, Juan. *Chicano Politics: Reality and Promise, 1940–1990*. Albuquerque: New Mexico University Press, 1990.

Gonzales, Manuel G. *Mexicanos: A History of Mexicans in the United States*. Bloomington: University of Indiana Press, 2009.

González, Deena J. *Refusing the Favor: The Spanish-Mexican Women of Santa Fe, 1820–1880*. New York: Oxford University Press, 1999.

Gonzalez-Pando, Miguel. *The Cuban Americans*. Westport, CT: Greenwood Press, 1998.

Graham, Hugh Davis. *Collision Course: The Strange Convergence of Affirmative Action and Immigration Policy in America*. New York: Oxford University Press, 2003.

Griswold Del Castillo, Richard. *Chicano San Diego: Cultural Space and the Struggle for Justice*. Tucson: University of Arizona Press, 2007.

Griswold Del Castillo, Richard. *The Treaty of Guadalupe Hidalgo: A Legacy of Conflict*. Norman: University of Oklahoma Press, 1990.

Grofman, Bernard, and Chandler Davidson, eds. *Controversies in Minority Voting: The Voting Rights Act in Perspective*. Washington, D.C.: Brookings Institution Press, 1992.

Gutiérrez, David G. *Walls and Mirrors: Mexican Americans, Mexican Immigrants, and the Politics of Ethnicity*. Berkeley: University of California press, 1995.

Gutiérrez, Ramón A., and Robert J. Orsi, eds. *Contested Eden: California Before the Gold Rush*. Berkeley: University of California, 1998.

Haney-López, Ian. *Racism on Trial: The Chicano Fight for Justice*. Cambridge, MA: Harvard University Press, 2004.

Hardin, Stephen L. *Texian Iliad: A Military History of the Texas Revolution*. Austin: University of Texas Press, 1994.

Hayden, Tom. *Street Wars: Gangs and the Future of Violence*. New York: New Press, 2006.

Henderson, Timothy J. *A Glorious Defeat: Mexico and Its War with the United States*. New York: Hill and Wang, 2007.

Hernández, José M. *Cuba and the United States: Intervention and Militarism, 1868–1933*. Austin: University of Texas Press, 1993.

Herrera, Andrea O'Reilly, ed. *Remembering Cuba: Legacy of a Diaspora*. Austin: University of Texas Press, 2001.

Hing, Bill Ong. *Ethical Borders: NAFTA, Globalization, and Mexican Migration*. Philadelphia: Temple University Press, 2010.

Hoffman, Abraham. *Unwanted Mexican Americans in the Great Depression: Repatriation Pressures, 1929–1939*. Tucson: University of Arizona Press, 1974.

Horsman, Reginald. *Race and Manifest Destiny: The Origins of American Racial Anglo-Saxonism*. Cambridge: Harvard University Press, 1981.

Hudson, David M. *Along Racial Lines: Consequences of the 1965 Voting Rights Act*. New York: Peter Lang, 1998.

Huerta, Jorge. *Chicano Drama: Performance, Society, and Myth*. New York: Cambridge University Press, 2000.

Huffines, Alan. *The Texas War of Independence 1835–1836: From Outbreak to the Alamo to San Jacinto*. New York: Osprey Publishing, 2005.

Hyslop, Stephan G. *Bound for Santa Fe: The Road to New Mexico and the American Conquest, 1806–1848*. Norman: University of Oklahoma Press, 2002.

Ingalls, Robert P., and Louis A. Perez. *Tampa Cigar Workers: A Pictorial History*. Gainesville: University Press of Florida, 2003.

Jackson, Robert H., and Edward Castillo. *Indians, Franciscans, and Spanish Colonization: The Impact of the Mission System on California Indians*. Albuquerque: University of New Mexico Press, 1995.

Jacobo, José Rodolfo. *Los Braceros: Memories of Bracero Workers 1942–1964*. San Diego, CA: Southern Border Press, 2004.

Jacobs, Elizabeth. *Mexican American Literature: The Politics of Identity*. New York: Routledge, 2006.

Jacobson, Robin Dale. *The New Nativism: Proposition 187 and the Debate over Immigration*. Minneapolis: University of Minnesota Press, 2008.

Johannsen, Robert W. *To the Halls of Monteczumas: The Mexican War in the American Imagination.* New York: Oxford University Press, 1985.

Johnson, Kevin R. "On the Appointment of a Latina/o to the Supreme Court." *Harvard Latino Law Review* 5 (Spring 2002): 1–16.

Johnson, Kevin, and George A. Martínez. "Discrimination by Proxy: The Case of Proposition 227 and the Ban on Bilingual Education." *UC Davis Law Review* (Summer 2001): 1227–1276.

Kanellos, Nicolás. *Hispanic Literature of the United States: A Comprehensive Reference.* Westport, CT: Greenwood Press, 2003.

Kaplowitz, Craig A. *LULAC, Mexican Americans and National Policy.* College Station: Texas A&M University Press, 2005.

Kells, Michelle Hall. *Héctor P. García: Everyday Rhetoric and Mexican American Civil Rights.* Carbondale: Southern Illinois University Press, 2006.

Kettenmann, Andrea. *Diego Rivera, 1886–1957: A Revolutionary Spirit in Modern Art.* Cologne, Germany: Taschen, 2001.

Kurnaz, Murat. *Five Years of My Life: An Innocent Man in Guantanamo.* New York: Palgrave Macmillan, 2008.

Laham, Nicolas. *Ronald Reagan and the Politics of Immigration Reform.* Westport, CT: Greenwood Press, 2000.

Laney, Garrine P. *The Voting Rights Act of 1965: Historical Background and Current Issues.* Hauppauge, NY: Nova Publishers, 2003.

Lastra, Frank Trebín. *Ybor City: The Making of a Landmark Town.* Tampa, FL: University of Tampa Press, 2006.

Latorre, Guisela. *Walls of Empowerment: Chicana/o Indigenist Murals of California.* Austin: University of Texas Press, 2003.

L'Hoeste, Héctor Fernández, and Juan Poblete, eds. *Redrawing the Nation: National Identity in Latin/o American Comics.* New York: Palgrave Macmillan, 2009.

Libura, Krystyna M., Luis Gerardo Morales Moreno, Jesús Velasco Márquez, eds. *Echoes of the Mexican-American War.* Trans. Mark Fried. Toronto, Canada: Groundwood Books, 2005.

Lipman, Jana K. *Guantánamo: A Working-Class History between Empire and Revolution.* Berkeley: University of California, Press, 2009.

Livingstone, Grace. *America's Backyard: The United States and Latin America from the Monroe Doctrine to the War on Terror.* London: Zed Books, 2009.

López, Ian F. Haney. "Race and Erasure: The Salience of Race to Latinos/as." *The Latino Condition: A Critical Reader.* Eds. Richard Delgado and Jean Stefancic. New York: NYU Press, 1998.

Lozano, Luis Martin, and Juan Coronel Rivera. *Diego Rivera, The Complete Murals.* Cologne, Germany: Taschen, 2008.

Maffi, Mario. *Gateway to the Promised Land: Ethnic Cultures on New York's Lower East Side.* Amsterdam: Editions Rodopi, 1994.

Maldanado, A. W. *Luis Muñoz Marín: Puerto Rico's Democratic Revolution.* San Juan, PR: Editorial Universidad de Puerto Rico, 2006.

Marciniak, Katarzyna. *Alienhood: Citizenship, Exile, and the Logic of Difference.* Minneapolis: University of Minnesota Press, 2006.

Marín, Guadalupe Rivera. *Diego Rivera the Red.* Trans. Dick Gerdes. Houston, TX: Arte Público Press, 2004.

Márquez, Benjamin. *LULAC: The Evolution of a Mexican American Political Organization.* Austin: University of Texas Press, 1993.

Marshall, James. *Santa Fe: The Railroad That Built an Empire.* New York: Random House, 1945.

Martinez, Deirdre. *Who Speaks for Hispanics?: Hispanic Interest Groups in Washington.* Albany: State University of New York Press, 2009.

Martínez, Oscar. *Mexican-Origin People in the United States: A Topical History.* Tucson: University of Arizona Press, 2001.

Martinez, Ruben. *Crossing Over: A Mexican Family on the Migrant Trail.* New York: Picador, 2002.

Mazón, Mauricio. *The Zoot Suit Riots: The Psychology of Symbolic Annihilation.* Austin: University of Texas Press, 1988.

McCaffrey, James M. *Army of Manifest Destiny: The American Soldier in the Mexican War, 1846–1848.* New York: New York University Press, 1992.

McCarthy, Jim, and Ron Sansoe. *Voices of Latin Rock: People and Events That Created This Sound.* Milwaukee: Hal Leonard Corporation, 2004.

Meier, Matt S., and Feliciano Ribera. *Mexican Americans/American Mexicans: From Conquistadors to Chicanos.* New York: Hill and Wang, 1993.

Melendez, Miguel. *We Took the Streets: Fighting for Latino Rights with the Young Lords.* New York: St. Martin's Press, 2003.

Mendheim, Beverly. *Ritchie Valens: The First Latino Rocker.* Austin: University of Texas Press, 1987.

Mendoza-Denton, Norma. *Homegirls: Language and Cultural Practice among Latina Youth Gangs.* Malden, MA: Blackwell, 2008.

Mintz, Steven. *Mexican American Voices: A Documentary Reader,* 2nd ed. Malden, MA: Blackwell Publishing, 2009.

Montejano, David. *Anglos and Mexicans in the Making of Texas, 1836–1936.* Austin: University of Texas Press, 1987.

Montejano, David. *Quixote's Soldiers: A Local History of the Chicano Movement, 1966–1981.* Austin: University of Texas Press, 2010.

Mora, Carlos. *Latinos in the West: The Student Movement and Academic Labor in Los Angeles.* Lanham, MD: Rowman & Littlefield, 2007.

Moraga, Cherríe, and Gloria Anzaldúa, eds. *This Bridge Called My Back: Writings by Radical Women of Color,* 3rd ed. Third Woman Press, 2002.

Morales, Ed. *The Latin Beat: The Rhythms and Roots of Latin Music from Bossa Nova to Salsa and Beyond.* Cambridge, MA: Da Capo Press, 2003.

Munguia, Ruben. *A Cotton Picker Finds Justice: The Saga of the Hernández Case.* Publisher unknown, 1954.

Muñoz Jr., Carlos. *Youth, Identity, Power: The Chicano Movement.* London: Verso, 2007.

Munton, Don, and David A. Welch. *The Cuban Missile Crisis: A Concise History.* New York: Oxford University Press, 2006.

Nava, Julian. *Julian Nava: My Mexican-American Journey.* Houston, TX: Arte Público Press, 2002.

Navarro, Armando. *Mexican Political Experience in Occupied Aztlán.* Walnut Creek, CA: Altamira Press, 2005.

Nevins, Joseph. *Operation Gatekeeper: The Rise of the "Illegal Alien" and the Remaking of the U.S.-Mexico Boundary.* New York: Routledge, 2001.

Normark, Don. *Chávez Ravine: 1949: A Los Angeles Story.* Vancouver, BC: Chronicle Books, 1999.

Notgrass, Ray. *American Voices: A Collection of Documents, Speeches, Essays, Hymns, Poems, and Short Stories from American History.* Cookeville, TN: Notgrass Company, 2007.

Offner, John L. *An Unwanted War: The Diplomacy of the United States and Spain over Cuba, 1895–1898.* Chapel Hill: University of North Carolina Press, 1992.

Ojeda, Martha A., and Rosemary Hennessy. *NAFTA from Below: Maquiladora Workers, Farmers, and Indigenous Communities Speak Out on the Impact of Free Trade in Mexico.* Missouri City, TX: Coalition for Justice in the Maquiladoras, 2006.

Oropeza, Lorena. *¡Raza Si! ¡Guerra No!: Chicano Protest and Patriotism during the Viet Nam War Era.* Berkeley: University of California Press, 2005.

Ouellette, Jeannine. *A Day without Immigrants: Rallying behind America's Newcomers.* Mankato, MN: Compass Point Books, 2008.

Pacheco, Alex, and Erich Krauss. *On the Line: Inside the U.S. Border Patrol.* New York: Citadel Press Books, 2004.

Pagán, Eduardo Obregón. *Murder at the Sleepy Lagoon: Zoot Suits, Race and Riots in Wartime L.A.* Chapel Hill: University of North Carolina Press, 2003.

Parker, Matthew. *Panama Fever: The Epic Story of the Building of the Panama Canal.* New York: Anchor Books, 2009.

Perrigo, Lynn Irwin. *Hispanos: Historic Leaders of New Mexico.* Santa Fe, NM: Sunstone Press, 1985.

Pessar, Patricia R. *A Visa for a Dream: Dominicans in the United States.* Boston: Allyn and Bacon, 1995.

Pike, Fredrick B. *FDR's Good Neighbor Policy: Sixty Years of Generally Gentle Chaos.* Austin: University of Texas Press, 1995.

Pitt, Leonard, and Ramón A. Gutiérrez. *Decline of the Californios: A Social History of the Spanish-Speaking Californians, 1846–1890.* Berkeley: University of California Press, 1998.

Portes, Alejandro, and Alex Stepick. *City on the Edge: The Transformation of Miami.* Berkeley: University of California Press, 1993.

Post, Charles Johnson. *The Little War of Private Post: The Spanish-American War Seen Up Close.* Lincoln, NE: Bison Books, 1999.

Pulido, Laura. *Black, Brown, Yellow, and Left: Radical Activism in Los Angeles.* Berkeley: University of California Press, 2006.

Pulido, Laura. "A Day without Immigrants: The Racial and Class Politics of Immigrant Exclusion." *Antipode* 39, no. 1 (Jan. 2007): 1–7.

Ramírez, Catherine Sue. *The Woman in the Zoot Suit: Gender, Nationalism, and the Culture Politics of Memory.* Durham, NC: Duke University, 2009.

Rangel, Javier. "The Educational Legacy of *El Plan de Santa Barbara:* An Interview with Reynaldo Macías." *Journal of Latinos and Education* 6, no. 2 (2007): 191–199.

Rivas-Rodriguez, Maggie. *A Legacy Greater Than Words: Stories of U.S. Latinos and Latinas of the World War II Generation.* Austin, TX: U.S. Latino and Latina WWII Oral History Project, 2006.

Rivera, Jose A. *The Political Thought of Luis Muñoz Marín.* Bloomington, IN: Xlibris Corporation, 2002.

Rivera Ramos, Efrén. *American Colonialism in Puerto Rico: The Judicial and Social Legacy.* Princeton, NJ: Markus Wiener, 2007.

Rochin, Refugio I., and Dennis N. Valdés, eds. *Voices of a New Chicana/o History.* East Lansing: Michigan State University Press, 2000.

Rodriguez, Luis J. *Always Running: La Vida Loca: Gang Days in LA.* New York: Touchstone, 1993.

Rosales, F. Arturo. *Chicano! The History of the Mexican American Civil Rights Movement.* Houston, TX: Arte Público Press, 1996.

Rosenus, Alan. *General Vallejo and the Advent of the Americans.* Berkeley, CA: Heyday Books/Urion Press, 1999.

Ruiz, Vicki. *From Out of the Shadows: Mexican Women in Twentieth Century America.* New York: Oxford University Press, 1998.

Saccetti, Maria. "Home in a Strange Land; Teen Starts New Life As Immigrant Parents Return to Colombia." *Boston Globe,* Oct. 15, 2007: A1.

San Miguel, Guadalupe. *Tejano Proud: Tex-Mex Music in the Twentieth Century.* Texas Station: Texas A&M University Press, 2002.

Santana, Maria. *Puerto Rican Newspaper Coverage of the Puerto Rican Independence Party: A Content Analysis of Three Elections.* New York: Routledge, 2000.

Schmal, John P. *The Journey to Latino Political Representation.* Westminster, MD: Heritage Books, 2007.

Schmidt Camacho, Alicia. *Migrant Imaginaries: Latino Cultural Politics in the U.S.-Mexico Borderlands.* New York: NYU Press, 2008.

Schulman, Ivan A., ed. *José Martí Reader: Writings on the Americas,* 2nd ed. New York: Ocean Press, 2006.

Segale, Sister Blandina. *At the End of the Santa Fe Trail.* Whitefish, MT: Kessinger Publishing, 2005.

Shanks, Cheryl. *Immigration and the Politics of American Sovereignty, 1890–1990.* Ann Arbor: University of Michigan Press, 2001.

Shapiro, Marc. *Carlos Santana: Back on Top.* New York: Macmillan, 2008.

Shaw, Randy. *Beyond the Fields: Cesar Chavez, the UFW, and the Struggle for Justice in the 21st Century.* Berkeley: University of California Press, 2008.

Soltero, Carlos R. *Latinos and American Law: Landmark Supreme Court Cases*. Austin: University of Texas Press, 2006.

Soto-Crespo, Ramón E. *Mainland Passage: The Cultural Anomaly of Puerto Rico*. Minneapolis: University of Minnesota Press, 2009.

Strauss, Michael J. *The Leasing of Guantanamo Bay*. Westport, CT: Praeger Security International, 2009.

Streeby, Shelley. *American Sensations: Class, Empire, and the Production of Popular Culture*. Berkeley: University of California Press, 2002.

Suchlicki, Jaime. *Cuba: From Columbus to Castro and Beyond*, 5th ed. Dulles, VA: Potomac Books, 2002.

Thernstrom, Abigail. *Voting Rights—and Wrongs: The Elusive Quest for Racial Fair Elections*. Washington, DC: American Enterprise Institute, 2009.

Torres-Saillant, Silvio, and Ramona Hernandez. *The Dominican Americans*. Westport, CT: Greenwood Press, 1998.

Tucker, James Thomas. "The Politics of Persuasion: Passage of the Voting Rights Act Reauthorization Act of 2006." *Journal of Legislation* 33, no. 2 (2007): 205–267.

United States Army. *Correspondence Relating to the War with Spain Including the Insurrection in the Philippine Islands and the China Relief Expedition: April 15, 1898, to July 30, 1902*.

United States House Committee on Naval Affairs. *Hearings on the Disposition of the Wreck of the U.S.S. Maine in Habana Harbor, Cuba*. Washington, DC: GPO, 1910.

U.S. Government Printing Office. *Acceptance of the Statue of Dennis Chavez Presented by the State of New Mexico: Proceedings in the Rotunda, United States Capitol, March 31, 1966*. Washington, D.C.: U.S. Government Printing Office, 1966.

Valdez, Luis. *Zoot Suit and Other Plays*. Houston, TX: Art Público Press, 1992.

Valencia, Reynaldo Anaya, et al. *Mexican Americans and the Law*. Tucson: University of Arizona Press, 2004.

Valencia, Richard. *Chicano Students and the Courts: The Mexican American Legal Struggle for Educational Equality*. New York: NYU Press, 2008.

Vargas, Zaragosa. *Labor Rights Are Civil Rights: Mexican American Workers in Twentieth-Century America*. Princeton, NJ: Princeton University Press, 2007.

Vásquez, Francisco H. *Latino/a Thought: Culture, Politics, and Society*, 2nd ed. Lanham, MD: Rowman & Littlefield, 2009.

Vazquez, Francisco H. *Latino/a Thought Culture, Politics, and Society*. Lanham, MD: Rowman & Littlefield, 2008.

Walker, Dale L. *Bear Flag Rising: The Conquest of California, 1846*. New York: Forge Books, 2000.

Weber, David J. *The Mexican Frontier, 1821–1846: The American Southwest under Mexico*. Albuquerque: University of New Mexico Press, 1982.

Yarsinske, Amy Waters. *All for One, and One for All: A Celebration of 75 Years of the League of United Latin American Citizens*. Virginia Beach, VA: Donning Company, 2004.

Young, Cynthia A. *Soul Power: Culture, Radicalism, and the Making of a U.S. Third World Left*. Durham, NC: Duke University Press, 2006.

Zamora, Herlinda. "Identity and Community: A Look at Four Latino Museums." *Museums and Their Communities*. Ed. Sheila Watson. London: Routledge, 2007, pp. 324–30.

Zelden, Charles L. *Voting Rights on Trial: A Handbook with Cases, Laws, and Documents*. Santa Barbara, CA: ABC-CLIO, 2002.

Index

About the Authors

CARYN E. NEUMANN is a Lecturer in Integrative Studies and an Affiliate in History at Miami University in Ohio. She earned a PhD from Ohio State University and an MA from Florida Atlantic University. Dr. Neumann has authored *Term Paper Resource Guide to African American History* and *Sexual Crime*.

TAMMY S. ALLEN is a Senior Lecturer in Spanish and Portuguese and the coordinator for humanities and fine arts at Miami University in Ohio. She earned an MA from Miami University. An award-winning teacher, Ms. Allen has been recognized for her service to the Latino community.